Practical
Industrial Cybersecurity

Industrial Cybersecurity

Practical
Industrial Cybersecurity
ICS, Industry 4.0, and IIoT

Charles J. Brooks

Philip A. Craig Jr.

WILEY

ISBN: 978-1-119-88302-9
ISBN: 978-1-119-88303-6 (ebk)
ISBN: 978-1-119-88304-3 (ebk)

For general information on our other products and services or for technical support, please contact our Customer Care Department within the United States at (800) 762-2974, outside the United States at (317) 572-3993 or fax (317) 572-4002.

Wiley also publishes its books in a variety of electronic formats. Some content that appears in print may not be available in electronic formats. For more information about Wiley products, visit our web site at www.wiley.com.

Library of Congress Control Number: 2022936106

Cover image: © Andrei Merkulov / Adobe Stock

Cover design: Wiley

SKY10034328_050522

About the Authors

Charles J. Brooks is currently co-owner and vice president of Educational Technologies Group Inc., as well as co-owner of eITPrep LLP, an online training company. He is in charge of research and product development at both organizations.

A former electronics instructor and technical writer with the National Education Corporation, Charles taught and wrote on post-secondary ETG curriculum, including introductory electronics, transistor theory, linear integrated circuits, basic digital theory, industrial electronics, microprocessors, and computer peripherals.

Charles has authored several books, including seven editions of *A+ Certification Training Guide*, *The Complete Introductory Computer Course*, and *PC Peripheral Troubleshooting and Repair*. He also writes about green technologies, networking, residential technology integration, and IT convergence.

For the past eight years Charles has been lecturing and providing instructor training for cybersecurity teachers throughout the United States and abroad. His latest projects have been associated with IT and OT cybersecurity courses and hands-on lab activities and include Cybersecurity Essentials – Concepts & Practices; Cybersecurity Essentials – Environments & Testing; and Industrial Network Cybersecurity.

Philip A. Craig Jr. is the founder of BlackByte Cyber Security, LLC, a consultancy formed to develop new cybersecurity tools and tactics for use in US critical infrastructure. He oversees research and product development for the US Department of Energy (DOE), the Defense Advanced Research Projects Agency (DARPA), and the National Rural Electric Cooperative Association (NRECA), as well as providing expert knowledge in next-generation signal isolation techniques to protect automated controls in energy generation, transmission, and distribution systems. Mr. Craig has authored regulation for both the Nuclear Regulatory Commission (NRC) and the National Energy Reliability Corporation (NERC) and is an active cyber responder in federal partnerships for incident response.

About the Technical Editor

James R. McQuiggan, CISSP, SACP, is a security awareness advocate for KnowBe4. Prior to joining KnowBe4, McQuiggan worked for Siemens for 18 years, where he was responsible for various roles, including his most recent as the product and solution security officer for Siemens Gamesa Renewable Energy. In this role, he consulted for and supported various corporate divisions on cybersecurity standards, information security awareness, and securing product networks. In addition to his work at Siemens, McQuiggan is a part-time faculty professor at Valencia College in the Engineering, Computer Programming & Technology Division.

Within the Central Florida community, he is the president of the Central Florida (ISC)² chapter, where he supports cybersecurity professionals with education and networking opportunities.

Acknowledgments

Charles J. Brooks

First, I would like to thank Greg Michael, formerly of Howard W. Sams, for getting me involved in writing about microcomputer systems back in the early days of the IBM PC.

As always, I want to thank the staff here at ETG/Marcraft for making it easy to turn out a good product. In particular, thanks to Cathy Boulay and Luke Johns from the Product Development department for their excellent work in getting the text and lab books ready to go and looking good.

In addition, I would like to say thanks to Brian Alley of Dell Computers and Philip Craig, formerly of Pacific Northwest National Laboratory (PNNL) and now the owner of Black-Byte Cyber Security, LLC, for their expertise and guidance in bringing this group of books and their accompanying Lab Guides to fruition.

As always, I want to thank my wife, Robbie, for all of her understanding, support, and help with these projects, as well as Robert, Jamaica, Michael, and Joshua.

Philip A. Craig Jr.

To the folks who commit their lives and careers to developing new approaches to cyber-security that protect the immense landscape of computing infrastructures from the malicious and sometimes deadly outcomes of cyberattacks, I dedicate this work to you. The next generation of cyber protectors will gain significant value from this book and hopefully will find its content sparking new dedication to the cyber challenges we will face in the years ahead.

I also dedicate this effort to my wife, Caralee, who has endured my long stays in our nation's capitol for many years, mostly for her understanding of the importance of my commitment to cybersecurity. As we celebrate her birthday on September 11 every year, we are reminded of what it means to our daily lives.

To the leadership at Marcraft, whose vision recognizes the value of teaching through hands-on experiences and not just text, thank you for recognizing and implementing your approach to our trade.

Contents at a Glance

Contents

Foreword

Imagine waking up in a house one day with no electricity. Or maybe your gas heater won't turn on, or you have no water flowing to your house. Simple everyday conveniences? No, these resources are critical dependencies that provide health, safety, nourishment, and general stability and security—not only in our homes and businesses but throughout society as a whole. These are exactly the outcomes of a coordinated cyberattack against critical infrastructure. Now imagine this type of cyber event on a national scale. We should all be concerned about this type of cyber event, not only regarding these basic necessities, but concerning stability if our financial or healthcare services are compromised. We are at an unbalanced period of cyberthreats versus our ability to identify and react to cyberattacks on this type of scale.

A few years ago, I had the pleasure of working with the coauthor of this book, Mr. Phil Craig Jr. Together we provided our skills to support a critical electric infrastructure security program sponsored by the Defense Advanced Research Projects Agency (DARPA). The project explored and developed cybersecurity tools to quickly recover the US electrical grid from a persistent and aggressive cyberattack that would severely impact the stability of a large-scale power grid. We learned that the threats were real, and the challenge could be overwhelming.

Understanding, operating, and defending the digital environments that provide stable controls and communications in a highly connected environment are paramount tasks when preventing the cyber events we fear will affect our daily lives. Mr. Craig and his colleagues have amassed years of experience in the evolution of operational technology systems and in creating technology to identify and mitigate cyberthreats in them, and Mr. Charles Brooks has been a significant contributor to exceptional "hands-on" training techniques and materials for many years. With their combined knowledge, the book provides a perspective of how immense the opportunity is for cyber intrusions and attacks and introduces impactful techniques to increase cyber defenses against them. Both Mr. Brooks's and Mr. Craig's technical acumen are surpassed only by their passion for educating new generations of cyber defenders to protect these essential systems and networks from those who try to alter our way of life.

This book is a useful resource for both newcomers and experienced individuals who are attempting to broaden their knowledge of industrial control systems and cybersecurity countermeasures as cyberthreats continue to grow. The book strongly supports and identifies critical skills that are desperately needed to provide protective measures to counter these threats. It is logically organized and provides references for technicians working in the OT trade and attempting certification as Global Industrial Cyber Security Professionals (GICSPs). Finally, this book provides a comprehensive resource for any cybersecurity professional who desires to expand their breadth of security knowledge on the latest cyber techniques used in the industry.

Mr. Joseph Minicucci
Lt. Col USMC

Introduction

Welcome to Wiley's *Practical Industrial Cybersecurity: ICS, Industry 4.0, and IIoT*. This book is designed to provide a solid theory and practical platform for cybersecurity personnel in the industrial process control and utility environments.

While this book does not stand on its own as a complete guide to becoming an industrial cybersecurity professional, it does prepare readers to prepare for the leading industry certification in this area—the Global Industrial Cyber Security Professional (GICSP) exam from Global Information Assurance Certification (GIAC), an affiliate of the SANS Institute. The GICSP exam is designed to bring industrial control skills to the cybersecurity forefront. While there are multitudes of IT-centric computer, network, and cybersecurity courses and certifications in the field, there are not many individuals who possess the skills and knowledge of cybersecurity as it relates to industrial control systems and operations technology. The search for people with these skills and knowledge has becoming a driving force in the cybersecurity world.

The published topic areas for each GICSP Exam Certification Objectives & Outcome Statements are as follows:

- Access Management—Knowledge of access control models, directory services, and user access management

- Configuration/Change Management—Knowledge of change management, baselines, equipment connections, and configuration auditing

- Configuration/Change Management-software updates—Knowledge of distribution and installation of patches, knowledge of software reloads and firmware management

- Cybersecurity Essentials for ICS—Knowledge of attacks and incidents (e.g., man in the middle, spoofing, social engineering, denial of service, denial of view, data manipulating, session hijacking, foreign software, unauthorized access)

- Cybersecurity Essentials for ICS—Knowledge of availability (e.g., health and safety, environmental, productivity)

- Cybersecurity Essentials for ICS—Knowledge of cryptographics (e.g., encryption, digital signatures, certificate management, PKI, public versus private key, hashing, key management, resource constraints)

- Cybersecurity Essentials for ICS—Knowledge of security tenets (e.g., CIA, non-repudiation, least privilege, separation of duties)

- Cybersecurity Essentials for ICS—Knowledge of threats (e.g., nation-states, general criminals, inside and outside malicious attackers, hacktivists, inside non-malicious)

- Disaster Recovery and Business Continuity—Knowledge of system backup and restoration

- ICS Architecture—Knowledge of communication medium and external network communications

- ICS Architecture—Knowledge of field device architecture (e.g., relays, PLC, switch, process unit)
- ICS Architecture—Knowledge of industrial protocols (e.g., Modbus, Modbus TCP, DNP3, Ethernet/IP, OPC)
- ICS Architecture—Knowledge of network protocols (e.g., DNS, DHCP, TCP/IP)
- ICS Architecture—Knowledge of network segmentation (e.g., partitioning, segregation, zones and conduits, reference architectures, network devices and services, data diodes, DMZs)
- ICS Architecture—Knowledge of wireless security (e.g., Wi-Fi, wireless sensors, wireless gateways, controllers)
- ICS Modules and Element Hardening—Knowledge of application security (e.g., database security)
- ICS Modules and Element Hardening—Knowledge of embedded devices (e.g., PLCs, controllers, RTUs, analyzers, meters, aggregators, security issues, default configurations)
- ICS Modules and Element Hardening—Knowledge of network security/hardening (e.g., switchport security)
- ICS Modules and Element Hardening—Knowledge of OS security (Unix/Linux, Windows, least privilege security, virtualization)
- ICS Modules and Element Hardening—Configuration and endpoint hardening—knowledge of anti-malware implementation, updating, monitoring, and sanitization. Knowledge of endpoint protection including user workstations and mobile devices
- ICS Security Assessments—Knowledge of security testing tools (e.g., packet sniffer, port scanner, vulnerability scanner)
- ICS Security Assessments—Assessments and testing—knowledge of device testing (e.g., communication robustness, fuzzing) (e.g., risk, criticality, vulnerability, attack surface analysis, supply chain), penetration testing and exploitation, security assessment
- ICS Security Governance and Risk Management—Knowledge of risk management (e.g., PHA/HAZOP usage, risk acceptance, risk/mitigation plan)
- ICS Security Governance and Risk Management—Knowledge of security policies and procedures development (e.g., exceptions, exemptions, requirements, standards)
- ICS Security Monitoring—Knowledge of event, network, and security logging, including knowledge of archiving logs
- ICS Security Monitoring—Knowledge of event, network, and security monitoring
- Incident Management—Knowledge of incident recognition and triage (e.g., log analysis/event correlation, anomalous behavior, intrusion detection, egress monitoring, IPS), knowledge of incident remediation/recovery, and knowledge of incident response (e.g., recording/reporting, forensic log analysis, containment, incident response team, root cause analysis, eradication/quarantine)

- Industrial Control Systems—Knowledge of basic process control systems (e.g., RTU, PLC, DCS, SCADA, metering/telemetry, Ethernet I/O, buses, Purdue [ISA 95])

- Industrial Control Systems—Knowledge of safety and protection systems (e.g., SIS, EMS, leak detection, FGS, BMS, vibration monitoring)

- Physical Security—Knowledge of physical security

Additional information about the GICSP exam is presented in Appendix A.

What Does This Book Cover?

This book prepares readers to prepare for the leading industry certification in this area— the Global Industrial Cyber Security Professional (GICSP) exam from Global Information Assurance Certification (GIAC), an affiliate of the SANS Institute.

The *Practical Industrial Cybersecurity: ICS, Industry 4.0, and IIoT* book is a basic training system designed to provide a solid understanding of industrial cybersecurity challenges, tools, and techniques, as well as to develop the foundations of a professional cybersecurity skill set. This is accomplished in a progressive process, as follows:

Chapter 1: Industrial Control Systems

Unless you've been working in an industrial process environment, the operations, devices, protocols, and standards involved in those types of environments are probably foreign to you. This initial chapter is designed to introduce the reader to the functions of components and systems involved in basic industrial process control operations. The latter sections of the chapter address common industrial safety and protection systems.

Chapter 2: ICS Architecture

For individuals acquainted with typical enterprise/IT networking, an industrial network is still an alien environment in many ways. Even the most basic components and tenets of operating an OT network are different from those found in a traditional IT network. This chapter presents the reader with an introduction to basic OT field device architecture and contrasts the basic functions of common industrial and enterprise network protocols.

Chapter 3: Secure ICS Architecture

This chapter builds on the basic information introduced in the preceding chapter to show how those components are organized to produce secure operational technology (OT) network architecture. This involves two major topic areas—network segmentation and security zoning as well as wireless network security.

Chapter 4: ICS Modules and Element Hardening

Industrial network security efforts begin with hardening hardware. However, it also extends to the local host's operating system, its file system, and its applications. This chapter covers techniques and practices involved in OT module and element hardening in six major areas—endpoint protection, embedded device security, OS security, application security, and use of anti-malware products in IT and OT networks as well as network security/hardening efforts.

Chapter 5: Cybersecurity Essentials for ICS

The opening sections of this chapter deal with the most fundamental cybersecurity tenets—CIA, AAA, nonrepudiation, the principle of least privilege, and separation of duties policies. Unlike in the typical IT network environment, data confidentiality is not usually the top security tenet associated with OT networks. Instead, the most important tenet is typically availability. ICS networks are real-time environments, and having data available in real time is usually more important than its confidentiality.

The middle sections of the chapter turn to address the knowledge of threats to industrial/utility environments. This includes descriptions of the different players involved in cybersecurity realms, as well as the nature of different types of attacks conducted against them.

The final sections of the chapter deal with employing cryptographic techniques to encrypt and protect data. Information covered in these sections includes digital signatures, certificate management, PKI, public/private keys, hashing, and key management.

Chapter 6: Physical Security

The beginning of all security is physical security. Even though it is often not mentioned in the same text as computer, network, or cybersecurity, those forms of security cannot exist without physical security. This chapter defines physical security and examines how infrastructure security fits into cybersecurity. The information in this chapter will enable readers to differentiate between authentication and authorization, identify typical physical access control devices, and identify strengths and weaknesses of different types of security and surveillance systems and devices.

Chapter 7: Access Management

Access control is basically a strategy for identifying people doing specific jobs, authenticating them through some type of identification system, and then giving only them keys to the assets they need access to. The previous chapter addressed this at the physical level. This chapter deals with logical access control models and practices associated with controlling access in enterprise and OT networks. Key topics here include coverage of typical directory services and user access management procedures and policies.

Chapter 8: ICS Security Governance and Risk Management

Policies, procedures, and guidelines are governance elements that work together to provide employees with adequate guidance to perform their tasks within an organization. This chapter examines these elements and how they are developed to meet the needs of the organization. Key ICS topics developed here include standards, requirements, exemptions, and exceptions.

The chapter also deals with how organizations manage risk in the development, deployment, and maintenance of their policies and procedures. This includes calculating and evaluating risk factors to determine risk mitigation and risk acceptance strategies. When an organization undertakes an OT security assessment, risk mitigation, and security policy generation plan, they must address certain areas of risk. You will be introduced to standard risk management tools used in the ICS network environment, such as risk mitigation plans and PHA Hazard and Operability (HAZOP) studies.

Chapter 9: ICS Security Assessments

A security assessment involves testing the network architecture and its policies, procedures, and guidelines in a realistic way to determine its effectiveness. This chapter discusses penetration testing and exploitation in the OT network environment. This includes becoming familiar with security testing tools and the ICS device testing strategies involved in security assessments. You will be introduced to security assessment exercises designed to locate vulnerabilities within an organization's network and computing environment.

Chapter 10: ICS Security Monitoring and Incident Response

After the research has been conducted, the network has been designed and implemented, and the security assessment has been conducted and validated, continued security must be provided by monitoring and auditing the network for activities that indicate it is being threatened or has already been compromised. This chapter addresses ongoing security in the form of event, network, and security monitoring and logging activities. Key topics related to these efforts include change management, distribution and installation of patches, software reloads, and firmware management.

The second half of the chapter examines the implementation of an effective incident response plan. In modern networks of all kinds, it is naive to think that any of them will not be attacked—it's not if, it's when. The key to successfully managing these events is having a well-developed and tested incident response plan and being knowledgeable of incident recognition, triage, and remediation/recovery steps and techniques.

Chapter 11: Disaster Recovery and Business Continuity

Organizations must be able to continue operations despite all types of small emergencies and large disasters to ensure the health and continuation of the organization. This involves looking ahead and creating a robust disaster recovery plan and business continuity plan. This chapter examines best practices associated with creating these two interrelated documents.

The book concludes with discussions of how to recover from a successful attack or natural disaster. The best solution for these types of events is having the ability to recover quickly and get back to partial and then full operations. This section discusses different system backup and restoration options and practices.

An abundance of assessment material is available with this book. At the end of each chapter are 15 open-ended/fill-in-the-blank questions and 10 multiple-choice questions. The 10 multiple-choice questions test your knowledge of the basic concepts presented in the chapter, while the 15 open-ended questions are designed to test comprehension and critical thinking.

Appendix A contains information specific to enrolling and taking the GICSP exam from GIAC. The scope and sequencing of this course was developed from the objectives list of the Global Industrial Cyber Security Professional (GICSP) exam.

Appendix B contains an extensive glossary of GICSP terms.

Appendix C contains key references used in the development of this book and are provided to give you a source of materials to round out the topics covered here.

Reader Support for This Book

We provide email addresses for reader support in the following sections.

How to Contact the Publisher

If you believe you've found a mistake in this book, please bring it to our attention. At John Wiley & Sons, we understand how important it is to provide our customers with accurate content, but even with our best efforts an error may occur.

To submit your possible errata, please email it to our Customer Service Team at wileysupport@wiley.com with the subject line "Possible Book Errata Submission."

How to Contact the Author

We appreciate your input and questions about this book! Email me at chuckb@marcraft.com.

Chapter 1

Industrial Control Systems

OBJECTIVES

Upon completion of this chapter, you should be able to:

1. Describe the functions of components and systems involved in basic industrial process control operations, including:

   - Closed loop
   - RTU
   - IED
   - PLC
   - DCS
   - SCADA
   - Metering/telemetry
   - Ethernet I/O
   - Bus (field)
   - Purdue (ISA 95)

2. Describe common industrial safety and protection systems, including:

   - SIS
   - EMS
   - Leak detection
   - FGS
   - BMS
   - Vibration monitoring

Introduction

In general, people everywhere are becoming more aware of how interactions involving inter-networked systems can affect their personal and financial security. However, we tend to be less aware of how security issues associated with the critical industrial processing and utility services infrastructure involve us. These critical infrastructure sectors include the following:

- Industrial processing
  - Manufacturing
  - Chemical processing
  - Agriculture
- Utility services
  - Water
  - Electricity
  - Wastewater
  - Oil and gas
  - Transportation

Consider the areas called out in these two sectors and think about how much of your life would be impacted if any of these critical infrastructure sectors became severely damaged or disabled by a security event. Then consider that most participants in both infrastructure sectors have increased their usage of cyber technologies to make their operations more automated, efficient, and productive. In doing so, they have exposed their operations to the same types of cybersecurity threats that are associated with personal and organizational networks.

While cybersecurity policies and practices for industrial and utility organizations seem similar to those associated with enterprise network security, they are quite different in application. Personnel trained in enterprise network security may see only a passing similarity to the networks they are familiar with if they were introduced to an industrial or utility network environment.

It's not as though there are no transferable skill and knowledge sets between IT networks and industrial/utility network environments. In fact, as you read this book, we will blend basic organizational IT networking information with new information you will need to understand to be successful in the industrial/utility network security environment.

Basic Process Control Systems

The basis of all industrial production and utility services operations is the implementation of automated process control systems. Let's begin by examining the basic elements associated with any industrial process control system. Figure 1.1 depicts a generic automated process in block diagram format.

FIGURE 1.1   Blocks of an automated process

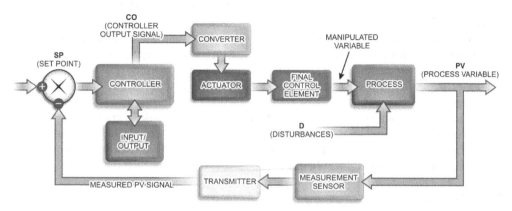

Within the block labeled "process" is some variable such as temperature, pressure, flow rate, level, rotational speed, or position that needs to be regulated. Any physical parameter that can change spontaneously or from external influences is a dynamic variable. A *dynamic variable* that is being controlled by the controller block is more specifically referred to as the *process variable (PV)*.

The overall objective of process control is to cause the PV to remain at some specific predetermined value referred to as the *set point (SP)*. The SP may be a fixed reference, such as a simple liquid level sensor mounted on a post, or it can be an adjustable reference like a common thermostat where the user can set a desired temperature to be maintained.

Because the PV is dynamic, the overall control system must constantly sample the state of the variable, compare it to the set point, and apply any corrective actions needed to maintain the PV at the desired SP. The devices that gather information about the system are collectively referred to as *input transducers* or *sensors*.

The output of the sensor may feed directly into the controller block, or this might be accomplished with an optional block titled "transmitter." If the sensor is located at some distance from the controller or its output is simply incompatible with the controller's input, an *interface* device must be used to convert the transducer's output signal to a signal that is better suited for transmission or that is compatible with the controlling device.

The heart of any process control system is the block marked "controller." The controller is responsible for taking the input information, comparing that information to a predetermined condition or a reference, making decisions about what action should be taken, and finally sending corrective *error signals* to the final element, which adjusts the *manipulated variable*. Industrial control units may consist of magnetic relays, a collection of digital integrated circuits, analog electronic circuitry, pneumatic devices, microprocessors, or some combination of these devices.

Operator settings and system status information are entered and obtained from the block titled "Input/Output" or "I/O." The I/O block may be an integral part of the controller or located at some remote location. A portion of the I/O block may be dedicated to displays and control mechanisms that enable a human operator to interact with the control system.

The correction signal issued from the controller may be applied directly to the *actuator* block or to an optional output signal converter that is used to make the controller's output signal compatible with the actuator. The task of the actuator is to apply the corrective action necessary to regulate the process variable to the established set point. Typical industrial control actuators are devices such as electric motor starters and pneumatic or solenoid-activated valves.

To understand how these elements work together to provide process control, consider the simple temperature control system depicted in Figure 1.2. This example depicts a control system that employs a liquid-filled sensing device, a simple set of electrical switch contacts, and an electrically operated solenoid gas valve.

FIGURE 1.2   A simple temperature control system

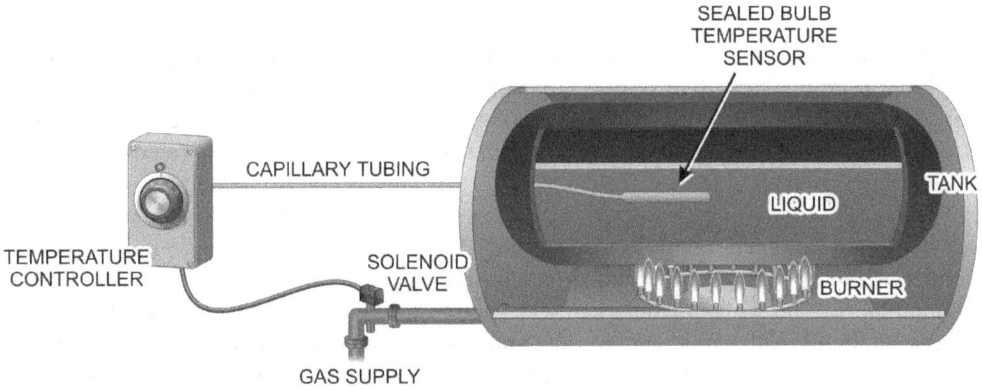

In the example in Figure 1.2, the PV (liquid temperature) is constantly monitored by the fluid in the sealed bulb and capillary tubing. As temperature increases in the enclosure, the fluid expands in the bulb and tubing, causing it to press against a diaphragm at the end of the tubing. The movement of the diaphragm in turn pushes against one of a pair of electrical switch contacts, causing it to move closer to the other contact.

When the temperature in the enclosure reaches a predetermined level established by the sensor fluid's coefficient of expansion and the distance between the switch contacts, the contacts will go closed, creating an electrical circuit that activates a solenoid control valve. The electromagnet in the valve creates an electromagnetic field that pulls the valve stem upward, sealing off the flow of gas (the manipulated variable) to the heating element inside the enclosure (the final element).

The removal of the heat source will cause the temperature inside the enclosure to decrease until the bulb contracts and pulls the diaphragm away from the switch contacts. When this occurs, the contacts will open, cutting off the flow of electricity to the solenoid. The valve will open, and gas will once again flow into the heating element, causing the temperature to increase again.

Closed-Loop Control Systems

This simple temperature control system is a type of process control referred to as *closed-loop* control. As the block diagram in Figure 1.3 shows, there is a *feedback* pathway from the output of the process (temperature of the enclosure) that feeds back to the controller (the diaphragm and switch contacts), which then applies appropriate corrective action to the process input (the pneumatic gas valve and burner).

FIGURE 1.3   Closed-loop process blocks

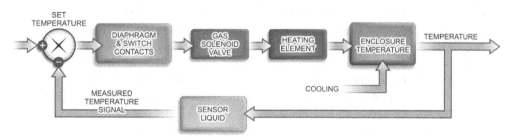

The feedback loop through the controller enables the closed-loop system to be self-adjusting. The controller examines the measured process variable and compares it to the set point reference (in the earlier example the reference point was the position of the fixed-switch contact). It then creates an error response based on the outcome of the comparison.

Typically, if the process variable value is higher than the reference's value, a positive action is created, such as applying more gas to the heating element. Conversely, if the process variable value is equal to or higher than the reference value, the controller will produce a negative corrective action, such as shutting off the gas flow to the heating element.

In the example in Figure 1.3, the process control mode is simply On/Off: the valve is either completely open or completely closed. However, if analog output devices and input sensors are employed and the controller is intelligent (it has advanced decision-making capabilities such as a microprocessor-based controller), the closed-loop system can be built and configured to provide smooth, accurate, and sensitive control responses. These systems are the basis for all automated process control systems.

Industrial Process Controllers

As already discussed, the center of any process control system is its controller. Historically, process controllers have been based on a number of different technologies, including mechanical devices, pneumatic devices, analog electronics, discrete digital electronics, or microprocessor-based computer electronics. However, currently most process controllers are built on some type of microprocessor-based computer control technology.

While *industrial process controllers (IPCs)* share many qualities with microprocessor-based computing devices designed for the *information technology (IT)* industry (personal computers and network servers), they are very different in many ways. Unlike IT computers, industrial process controllers are not designed to store data and process it later. Instead, they produce output conditions based on the current states of their inputs according to their internal configuration or programming.

 Industrial control systems are designed to control variables in the physical world, while IT systems are designed to manage data.

The following are key requirements for industrial process controllers:

- *Availability*: Many processes are continuous operations and require that the controller have high availability, reliability, and maintainability ratings. Availability is typically the highest objective in an industrial control system, along with data integrity. Confidentiality has traditionally been a secondary concern with process control systems; this is completely reversed from the general confidentiality, integrity, and availability (CIA) requirements associated with IT systems.

- *Timeliness*: Process control is a time-sensitive operation that requires quick response times. IT systems generally do not have timeliness constraints. For this reason, front-line intelligent process controllers operate on real-time operating systems.

- *Industrial interfacing*: Industrial controllers typically provide few if any user-friendly interface features, such as keyboards, pointing devices, or LCD displays. Instead, they provide industrial-style input and output ports for connecting sensors and actuators.

- *Physical hardening*: IPCs are designed to operate in harsh environments such as industrial factories and open air venues.

Field Devices

Industrial controllers that are designed to be deployed in close proximity to the process being controlled, as opposed to supervisory computing devices that are more routinely placed in an office or control room environment, are referred to as *field devices*. These are the most common field devices encountered in industrial and utility process control systems:

- Programmable logic controllers (PLCs)
- Remote telemetry units (RTUs)
- Intelligent electronic devices (IEDs)

In a dedicated control system, the field device or devices are placed between the sensors that gather information from the physical process and the actuators that supply corrective actions to the physical process. However, in a distributed control system, the field devices are logically located between the sensors and actuators and the supervisory control system with its human machine interfaces. Figure 1.4 shows how field devices are typically implemented in industrial control systems.

FIGURE 1.4   Field device implementations

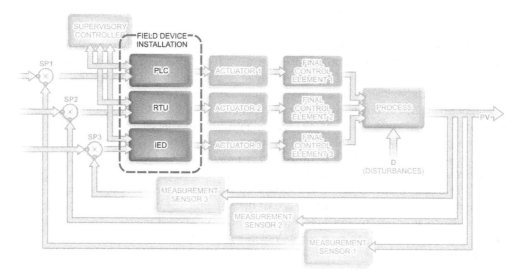

Programmable Logic Controllers

The preferred local control device in modern industrial processing and utility environments is the *programmable logic controller*, or *PLC*. PLCs are intelligent digital computing devices that are designed specifically to perform industrial control functions, such as opening and closing valves, switches, and relays to control processes.

Internally, PLCs like the one depicted in Figure 1.5 share most of their technology with IT computing devices. They contain a microprocessor, RAM memory, read-only firmware, and an operating system. However, this is where the similarities end.

FIGURE 1.5   A typical PLC

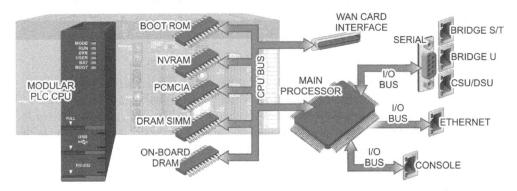

Because they are intelligent, PLC operation can be changed simply by reprogramming them with new instructions. PLCs use a programming method designed to resemble the *relay ladder logic* (because PLCs were originally designed to replace relay controllers that were widely used before digital processors were developed). These diagrams are discussed in Chapter 2, "ICS Architecture." Newer PLCs can be programmed in many different ways, including through popular computer programming languages.

Programming can be downloaded or entered directly into the PLC's programmable RAM area. PLC instruction sets can be used to implement specific control functions such as counting and timing loops; three-mode proportional, integral, derivative (PID) control; arithmetic operations; and I/O control. Programming can be accomplished through a programming interface installed on a local host computer.

PLC inputs are connected to sensors—temperature, pressure, or positional switches—that monitor process variables. On the other side of the equation, the PLC's output terminals are attached to actuators—relays, solenoid valves, or mechanical positioners—which are devices used to control process variables, as illustrated in Figure 1.6.

The figure depicts a *point-to-point wiring* scheme for a PLC and its sensors and actuators. It also indicates that individual connections between the PLC and its devices can be made through wiring racks and junction boxes located throughout the production plant. However, each device is connected to an input or output terminal by a dedicated run of cable.

PLCs are available in different form factors including compact devices and modular units connected via a *backplane* system and housed in a common *rack*. Figure 1.7 depicts a typical compact PLC. It is a self-contained processing unit that offers input terminals along its top edge, output terminals along its bottom edge, and a power supply connection at its lower-left corner. The figure also illustrates that this PLC model makes provisions for connecting it to other devices through its serial communications terminals, as well as through a traditional Ethernet network connection.

FIGURE 1.6   PLC controlling a process

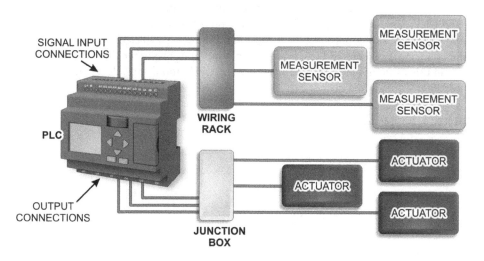

FIGURE 1.7   A typical compact PLC

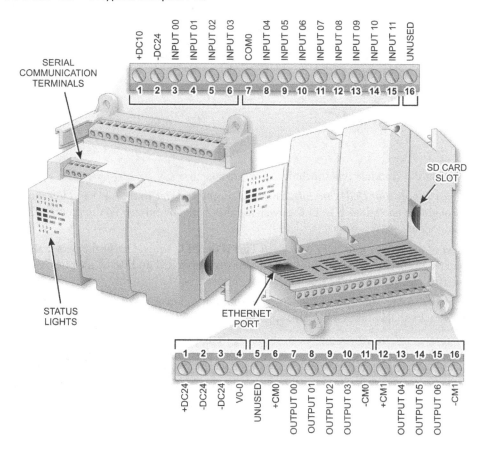

Modular form-factor PLCs offer flexible input and output configurations, as multiple input or output modules can be added to the backplane. Figure 1.8 shows a typical PLC rack and backplane. The backplane is a printed circuit board that provides a common data bus and a series of slot connectors for connecting different modules to the system. One of the slot connectors is reserved for a power supply module. The other slot connectors (eight of them in this example) are designed to accept the CPU module and different types of I/O modules.

FIGURE 1.8   Modular PLC rack and backplane

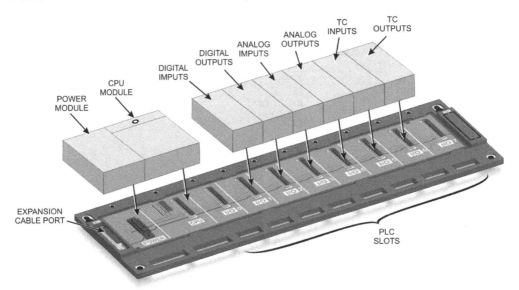

Common PLC module types include the following:

- *Power supply unit (PSU) module*: This unit supplies power to the CPU and I/O modules through the backplane bus. PLC power supplies typically furnish 24Vac power to its components.

- *Central processing unit (CPU) module*: This is the PLC equivalent of the personal computer's motherboard. It contains the microprocessor, RAM and ROM memory, I/O interfacing circuitry, and communications support.

- *Input modules*: There are two basic types of input modules that can be installed in the PLC rack: analog input modules and digital input modules.

  - *Analog inputs*: Analog input modules are designed to operate with sensing devices, such as thermocouples and pressure sensors, that produce a continuously variable range of output values between a minimum and maximum (such as 0–10V). Because microprocessor-based control devices do not understand analog signals, the modules must perform an A/D conversion process on the signal to achieve a digital equivalent of the measured analog value that the CPU can work with.

- *Digital inputs*: This type of module is used to handle discrete digital input devices such as limit switches, photo/optical switches, proximity switches, and any other device that provides a two-state output. These modules are available to handle from 8 up to 128 devices.

- *Output modules*: Like input modules, output modules come in two basic varieties, analog and digital.

  - *Analog outputs*: These outputs provide analog signals that can be used to drive analog actuators, such as valve positioners. To produce this type of output signal, the module must perform a D/A conversion process on the values received from the CPU before they can be applied to the output terminals.

  - *Digital outputs*: These modules provide On/Off output signals for controlling two position actuators. Like digital input modules, digital output modules are available that can supply from 8 to 128 different output connections.

- *Comm modules*: These are communication modules that allow the CPU to communicate with other intelligent devices across the backplane's I/O bus. This has historically been done through standard asynchronous serial communication protocols such as RS-232 and RS-485 channels. However, newer industrial communications options are being introduced to the PLC communications, including different IT and telephony-based protocols, such as TCP/IP communication over Ethernet, Bluetooth, and Zigbee.

Remote Telemetry Units

Another common industrial controller is the *remote telemetry unit*, commonly referred to simply as an *RTU*. RTUs are small intelligent control units deployed at selective locations within a process, or set of processes, to gather data from different sensors and deliver commands to control relay outputs. Figure 1.9 shows a typical RTU.

FIGURE 1.9 An RTU controller

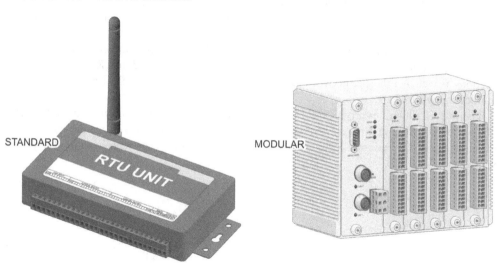

STANDARD

MODULAR

Telemetry is the process of using sensors to collect information in a remote location and transmitting it to another location for processing.

Like PLCs, RTUs can employ digital or analog input sensor devices designed to measure variables such as electrical currents and voltages, pressure, light levels, flow rates, fluid levels, turbidity, pH, rotary speed, etc. The analog inputs accept input signals from sensors within a given range. Common analog input signal ranges include 0 to 1mA or 4 to 20mA current ranges, or 0 to 10Vdc ranges, as well as +/-2.5V or +/-5.0V ranges. For sensor types that produce signal ranges outside of these parameters, some type of signal level translating interface device must be installed between the sensor and the input port. These industry-standard signaling methods and ranges are selected by different equipment manufacturers based on sensors used in different applications.

Voltage signaling is used in many sensor applications because it is relatively simple to implement. However, voltage signaling is susceptible to electrical noise interference and transmission distance limitations. Current signaling standards have historically been the accepted method of transporting sensor information because their response is more linear than voltage signaling methods as well as providing greater noise immunity.

While there have been different current loop standards presented, the 4 to 20 mA DC current standard has been the go-to standard for the industrial sensor market. This standard offers linear signal response, good noise immunity, longer transmission distances, and intrinsic safety for personnel and in hazardous environmental conditions.

RTUs can also provide analog and digital outputs to work with a wide array of different control devices. However, analog outputs are not commonly used with RTUs. The digital outputs provide On/Off control for actuators such as electrical circuits, solenoid valves, lights, and heaters, etc., as needed to manage the process. RTUs that do offer analog output channels can be used to provide continuously variable control of devices such as valve positioners and heating elements.

Unlike PLCs, RTUs are not designed to be stand-alone controllers. Instead, they are better suited for operations in widely distributed control systems. While they have internal memory and do control local activities, they are designed to work with a supervisory controller in distributed or SCADA-based control systems. However, they can also receive process data from local IED controllers.

Communications with supervisory controllers and IED controllers are conducted using standard communication media and protocols. These include RS-232 and RS-485 serial connections as well as Ethernet network connections. Modbus is the prevalent protocol for communicating with RTUs.

Figure 1.10 illustrates a typical RTU implementation. In this example, multiple RTUs are involved in controlling different sections of a distributed process. As with the earlier PLC example, the RTUs maintain local control under the direction of the remote supervisory controller.

FIGURE 1.10 A typical RTU implementation

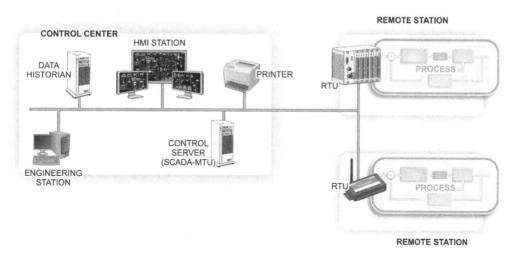

Intelligent Electronic Devices

In an electric power generation and distribution environment, a third type of intelligent process controller is becoming more popular—the *intelligent electronic device*, or *IED*. These controllers are a form of RTU designed to provide protection, control, monitoring, and communications directly with a supervisory controller. These devices provide a direct interface for monitoring and controlling the different sensors and actuators in the process, and they can communicate directly with the supervisory controller, a local RTU, or other IEDs.

Like RTUs, IEDs typically have small memory units that hold programming for controlling the local process so they can act without direct or constant instructions from the supervisory controller; however, they are not designed to take over full control of a process. Common IED applications include intelligent protective relays, digital fault recorders, power/current/voltage meters, and RTU functions.

Distributed Control Systems

When processes become too complex for a single controller or its components are geographically separated, it becomes necessary to distribute the control function over multiple controllers to form a *distributed control system (DCS)*.

Figure 1.11 shows a process that is segmented into three discrete subsections, or *process units*, each of which has its own local controller. A unit process is defined as a group of operations within a production system that can be defined and separated from the other unit processes of the system. Each process unit is defined by a specific set of inputs and outputs associated with the tasks the process unit was designed to perform. Even though the process control function has been distributed across multiple controllers, the control system is not complete. In this example, there are three different devices applying control functions to their segments of a continuous process without regard to activities occurring in the other segments.

FIGURE 1.11   Distributed controllers

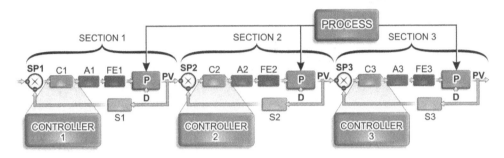

Field Buses

For efficient control of the entire process, some additional control method must be added to the control system to coordinate the activities of the three local controllers. The most fundamental method of doing this is to interconnect the controllers and then make one of them the *master controller*, as illustrated in Figure 1.12. The controllers are physically linked together through a *field bus* and logically linked through an industrial communications protocol. The protocols used over these buses include the Modbus and DNP3 protocols described in detail in the Industrial Network Protocols section of Chapter 2.

FIGURE 1.12   A master controller configuration

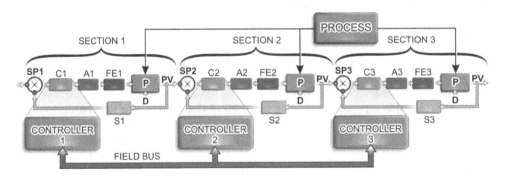

A field bus can be any one of several proprietary instrumentation buses designed by industrial control groups to provide communication and coordination between intelligent control devices. These buses can also be used to connect smart IED sensors and actuators to the controllers and eliminate the need to construct *point-to-point wiring* bundles from each process unit's controllers to their sensors and actuators.*

*Smart IED devices can be added to a field bus provided they can communicate through the same protocol as the other devices on the field bus. However, analog and non-microprocessor-based digital sensors and actuators still require independent wire runs between the devices and the controller's inputs and outputs.

Supervisory Controllers

The other method commonly used to efficiently control multiple process units in a distributed process operation is to add a *supervisory controller* to the ICS, as illustrated in Figure 1.13. In this configuration, the supervisory controller is programmed to monitor the operation of each local field control device and send coordinating instructions back to each controller as needed. In such systems, the supervisory controller does not directly control the different process units; it merely oversees and coordinates the operations of their local controllers.

FIGURE 1.13   Adding a supervisory controller

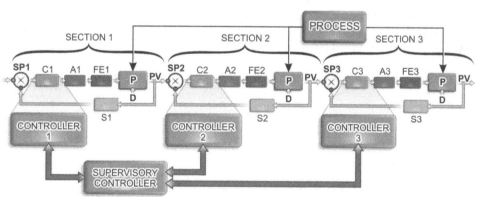

This arrangement represents a typical DCS that would be implemented to efficiently control a complex or widely distributed process. As with the previous example, the controllers in this distributed ICS could be interconnected through any one of several field bus types.

This distributed intelligence model optimizes the computing power of all the control devices to execute, control, manage, and protect the complete process. The local controllers are typically intelligent devices attached directly to the input and output devices used to monitor and control their portions of the overall process.

Most industrial process control scenarios require high-speed, real-time data acquisition and control functions to maintain proper control of the process. This is a very different requirement than those typically applied to enterprise computing devices that typically do not need to process data in real time.

> One of the key differences between intelligent devices designed for use in industrial control systems and those designed for enterprise computing and networking environments is the need for real-time processing. This means that ICS devices and programming must be geared to high-speed, low-overhead processing.

Because the supervisory controller is not directly involved in the details of controlling the process, it does not need to be optimized for speed. These controllers are often normal stand-alone computers or industrial servers running supervisory control and data acquisition software applications.

The presence of the local field controllers enables more task-specific intelligent processing to be performed local to the process, while the supervisory controller provides coordination and cooperation between these devices through some type of industry-standard communications channel.

In addition to interfacing with the field-level controllers, the supervisory computers often provide interactive visual control panels, such as the one depicted in Figure 1.14, for human operators involved with the process. This control panel is referred to as a *man-machine interface (MMI)* or a *human-machine interface (HMI)*. The interactive portion of the interface provides human operators with on-screen tools to adjust or override control actions that they see or feel are not occurring as they should.

FIGURE 1.14   Providing the HMI

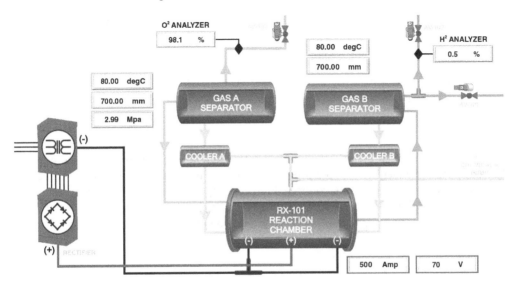

Other ICS Buses

As you saw in previous illustrations, in addition to being connected to the field bus, the controller can also be connected into a local area network that connects it to two standard OT network components.

- *The engineering workstation*: This computing device is used to program the field devices for the current operations.

- *The data historian*: This device contains a database that is used to collect and store process values for inspection and processing.

These units are interconnected to the controller through a separate local area network (LAN) referred to as the *local control loop*. Figure 1.15 depicts a typical ICS with a local control network loop. This type of network loop is typically implemented in the form of a TCP/IP-based Ethernet network segment. In an ICS environment, it has become common to refer to this network segment as the *operational technology (OT)* network to differentiate it from the organization's IT network.

FIGURE 1.15   Adding a supervisory network loop

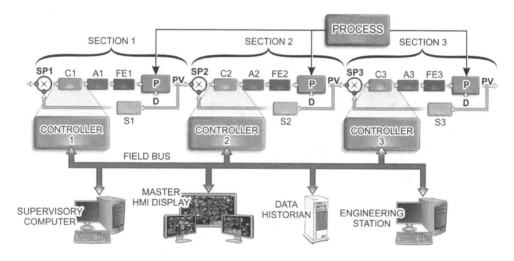

Depending on the complexity of the ICS, the network may be divided into multiple control segments or loops, as illustrated in Figure 1.16. In this example, the complete network structure consists of four distinct network segments and types, shown here:

- *A field bus loop*: This loop provides direct interaction between the local field devices and the sensors and actuators. The field bus is commonly used to connect PLCs to the various input sensors and output actuators. It can also connect to a separate human machine interface console used to display the activities of the process and its various sensors.

- *A local control/supervisory loop*: This loop provides direct interaction between the local field devices and the components of the distributed control system (data historian, engineer's station, HMI, and supervising computers).

- *The organization's local area network*: This loop provides connectivity between the organization's IT network and its ICS network. This connection represents a path outside of the organization's ICS, which opens the network to possible manipulation from non-ICS personnel within the organization.

- *The organization's IT network*: This loop provides connectivity between the organization's local IT network and its wide area network connections. It also provides a pathway between the ICS and a world of possible manipulation by nonorganization personnel.

FIGURE 1.16   Multiple ICS network loops

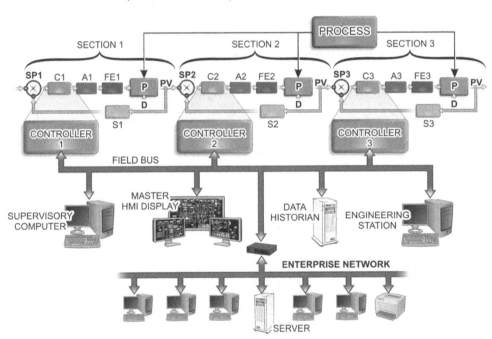

Network gateway devices are used to translate between different network types, such as a given field bus type and a TCP/IP-based Ethernet network. For example, the connection that brings the field bus and the local control LAN together in the previous example must translate between the physical and logical protocols each segment is based on.

Ethernet I/O Modules

The field bus and local control network portions of the ICS network have historically been implemented over asynchronous serial network topologies, such as standard RS-232 and RS-485 serial bus connections. However, the industrial controls community has slowly come around to the idea of adopting the *Ethernet /IP 802.x suite* of standards for their control and data communications. It has become increasingly popular in industrial control settings.

Ethernet has been the connectivity standard for IT networks since the 1990s. It employs a physical star topology (hub and spokes), even though it actually operates as a logical bus topology. The full suite of Ethernet standards runs across many different media types including twisted-pair copper cabling, fiber-optic cabling, and wireless Wi-Fi channels.

Figure 1.17 shows the physical connectivity of a standard hardwired Ethernet connection. This connection uses twisted-pair copper data cables that are terminated in 8P8C modular plugs and jacks (sometimes incorrectly referred to as RJ-45). In industrial settings, these connections are wired according to TIA/EIA-568-BC standards.

FIGURE 1.17   Ethernet connections

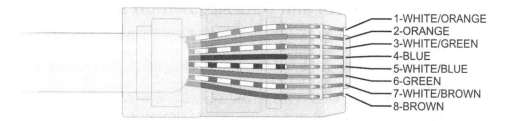

- 1-WHITE/ORANGE
- 2-ORANGE
- 3-WHITE/GREEN
- 4-BLUE
- 5-WHITE/BLUE
- 6-GREEN
- 7-WHITE/BROWN
- 8-BROWN

RJ-45 CONNECTOR - T568B STANDARD

The adoption of Ethernet/IP technologies and related techniques has led to a convergence of organizational enterprise networks with their industrial control network counterparts. With both portions of the network integrated into a cohesive data communications vehicle, the organization is enabled to apply real-time production data to its business decisions.

Modules for connecting PLCs to an Ethernet network have historically been separate network interface adapters that involved RS-485 connections between the PLC and the Ethernet adapter and an Ethernet connection with the rest of the network. However, newer PLC models include built-in Ethernet interfaces. Figure 1.18 illustrates the difference in these two approaches.

FIGURE 1.18   PLC Ethernet connections

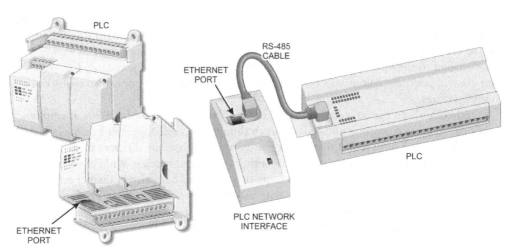

Supervisory Control and Data Acquisition Systems

In some processes, such as an oil pipeline control operation, the different control components of the process may be separated by large distances. In such cases the local controllers must be connected to the supervisory controller through long-distance communications technologies such as radios, telephony, satellites, or wide area networking.

As its name implies, a *supervisory control and data acquisition (SCADA)* system is a type of distributed control system that provides two distinct functions: data acquisition (input) and supervisory control functions (output). As you saw earlier in this chapter, PLCs, RTUs, or IEDs typically provide local control of the processes they are monitoring. However, they also package the *acquired data* and transmit it to the supervisory control system over some type of industrial communications link or network connection.

Because industrial processes operate in real time, the operation of the individual local controllers in a distributed control system must be synchronized with each other. The SCADA controller is responsible for providing a common clock signal to coordinate the actions of the different controllers.

The *supervisory control* portion of the SCADA system monitors the data received from its local control devices and stores the information for processing, analysis, and/or response. Responses from the SCADA system are typically reserved for performing supervisory interventions or responding to alarm conditions in the process (such as a motor overheating, a sensor reading out of range, or a cooling system failure). The SCADA system also provides the HMI interface that enables human operators to monitor and assume direct control of the process control system.

Physically, the SCADA system is an industrial software application running on some type of computer platform. These units are referred to as *SCADA servers* or *SCADA masters*. SCADA masters have traditionally communicated with their local control devices using industry-standard ICS protocols and field buses. This arrangement is depicted in Figure 1.19.

FIGURE 1.19   Adding the ICS segment to the network

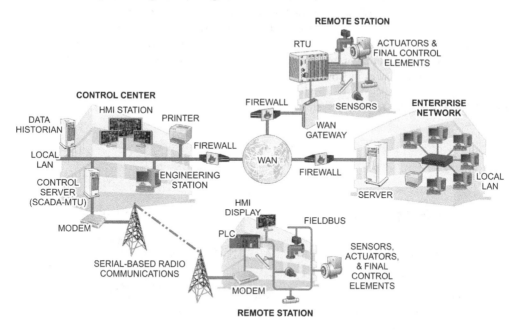

SCADA servers are also capable of operating within the organization's enterprise network. This is accomplished using standard IT network protocols running over standard IT networking infrastructure.

Part of that software application is a database management system that stores historical data in the form of control points referred to as *tags*. Tags basically consist of two elements: a data point and a timestamp. With these two pieces of information the SCADA system can generate tracking and trending data for graphical display or auditing purposes. This database is called the *historian*.

The SCADA software provides the supervisory role for all the PLCs operating in the process. It also provides the HMI that enables human operators to observe the operating parameters of the different processes and take charge of the processes to change parameters or make corrections.

Over time, SCADA systems have migrated from large mainframes (first generation) at the organization's offices, to individual task computers networked together through LANs (second generation), to networked wide area SCADA systems (third generation), and now to cloud-based, Industrial Internet of Things (IIoT) SCADA systems (fourth and current generation).

System Telemetry

As mentioned earlier, *telemetry* is the process of using sensors to collect information in a remote location and transmitting it to another location for processing. This is a prerequisite for widely distributed control systems. There are many industries (airlines, water, gas, oil,

and electrical transportation and distribution) that require operations in geographically separated locations to be coordinated through widely distributed control systems.

Figure 1.20 illustrates a widely distributed control system where controllers in three
remote field sites are monitoring and controlling three different portions of a distribution
process. Using modern data communication links, these controllers can be physically located
away from the process area in isolated environments.

FIGURE 1.20   ICS telemetry systems

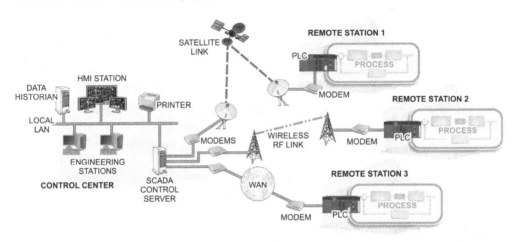

In this example, the remotely located SCADA controller is connected to each field site
using a different long-distance communication link. Station 1 connects to the Control Center
through a wireless RF communication link, while Station 2 employs a satellite link and
Station 3 uses a wide area network (WAN) connection.

Industrial and utility networks also employ different wireless communication protocols to
transmit data and telemetry throughout their processes. In particular, the WiMax and Zigbee
wireless protocols have made significant inroads into industrial control networks, particularly in electrical utility network settings.

The *Zigbee (IEEE 802.15.4)* standard is a wireless, mesh-networked personal area network (PAN) protocol that provides for a 10-meter communication range with data transfer
rates at 250 Kbps, as shown in Figure 1.21. The Zigbee standard has been embraced by the
smart home automation and industrial controls communities, as well as several areas of the
smart grid consortium.

The *IEEE 802.16 – WiMAX* specification was established to provide guidelines for wider
area wireless networking capabilities. WiMAX is a broadband wireless access standard
designed to provide Internet access across large geographic areas, such as cities, counties, and
in some cases countries, as shown in Figure 1.22. It is also designed to provide interoperability with the 802.11x Wi-Fi standard.

FIGURE 1.21   Zigbee PAN

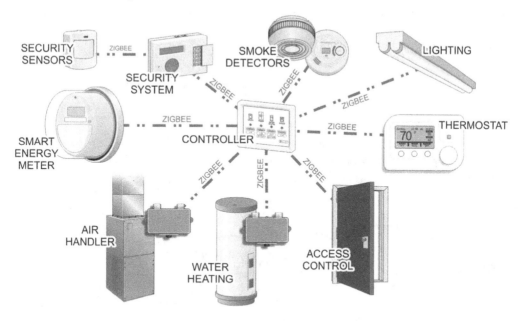

FIGURE 1.22   A WiMAX network

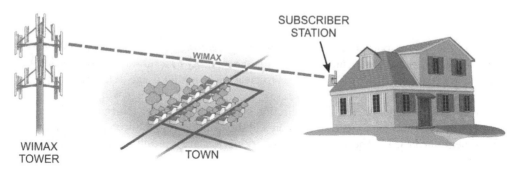

Utility Networks

Virtually all utility organizations rely on *wide area networks* to optimize the efficiency of their operations. This is illustrated in Figure 1.23, which depicts a typical electrical utility's *smart grid* network infrastructure that spreads across four different network types—two wide area networks and two local area networks:

- The power generation control network (a dedicated industrial control network)
- The power transmission/distribution control network (a widely distributed industrial control network)

- The customer (meter) data collection network (a wide area network)

- The host utility's data management network (part of the in-house enterprise network)

FIGURE 1.23   A utility network system

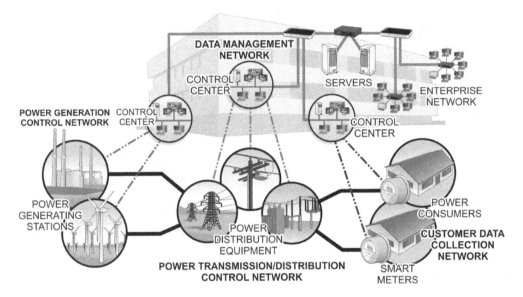

One of the most important aspects of telemetry is *metering*. A metering device, or meter, is an endpoint sensor that measures and records the quantity of a substance (collects data). The primary function of any utility meter is to measure customer usage—electricity, water, gas, oil, etc.

The utility's customer (meter) data collection system collects usage information about every customer connected to its transmission and distribution system through the smart meters mentioned earlier. These metering network devices are typically configured to do the following:

- Communicate with the other smart grid components in the user's *home area network (HAN)*

- Provide current cost information to the members of the HAN

- Provide current *time-of-use (TOU)* information to the members of the HAN

- Communicate with the host utility across the WAN

- Package customer data for transmission to the host utility

- Interact with the host utility's *meter data management (MDM)* system

Figure 1.24 shows a typical *advanced metering infrastructure (AMI)* wireless mesh network architecture used to provide communications throughout the metering network. These networks are designed to provide reliability, redundancy, and bandwidth while still meeting the budgetary requirements of the electrical utility. In addition, they must enable several different types of devices to communicate with each other.

FIGURE 1.24   AMI mesh architecture

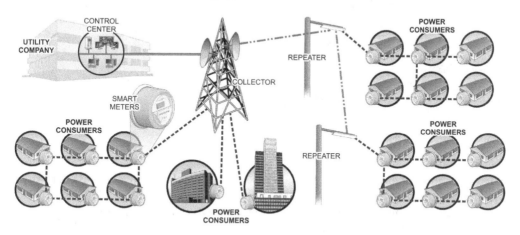

This example depicts three distinct zones networked together through two aggregators and a collector. In residential areas, the smart meters are connected in neighborhood area network (*NAN*) meshes and communicate with each other (meter-to-meter) and with aggregators (meter-to-aggregators) as well as directly with the collector (meter-to-collector).

The aggregators communicate directly with the collector (aggregator-to-collector). Notice also that industrial and larger commercial customers connect directly to the collector. The collector is responsible for communicating with all the meshes to handle all the functions listed earlier in this section. In addition, it must have the communication and computing capacity to do this for thousands or tens of thousands of meters. Security issues associated with these networks and their devices are presented in Chapter 4, "ICS Module and Element Hardening."

OT/IT Network Integration

Historically, industrial production organizations have operated their networks as two separate entities: the enterprise (IT) network and the process control (OT) network, as illustrated in Figure 1.25. The IT network is designed to process and store business data, while the OT network is designed to control processes that produce products and generate revenue. Normally, great effort is applied to minimizing the interactivity points between these two networks.

FIGURE 1.25   Industrial networks

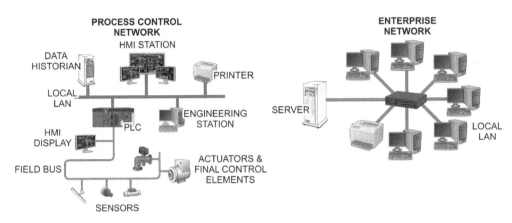

However, in many organizations, the supervisory controller has been added to their existing enterprise network structure as a separate network segment, as illustrated in Figure 1.26. This connection permits other business operations to interface with the production sector of the company. However, it also creates an access path between the two networks that exposes the ICS to new threats typically associated with IT networks. As you will see in greater detail in Chapter 3, "Secure ICS Architecture," the industrial control portion of such a network should be segregated or heavily segmented from the organization's enterprise network.

FIGURE 1.26   Adding the ICS segment to the IT network

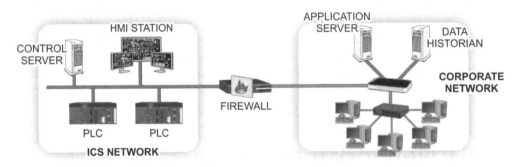

Because the movement to connect OT and IT networks together has grown to a significant level, the *International Society of Automation (ISA)* has developed a set of standards known as *ISA-95* to define automated information exchange interfacing between enterprise and industrial control system networks.

The original version of this standard was referred to as the Perdue Enterprise Reference Architecture for ICS cybersecurity and is used for grouping IT/OT network segments into security zones. This set of standards establishes a five-level integration process:

- Level 0: Physical Protection
- Level 1: Production Process Sensing and Manipulation

- Level 2: Automated Control of the Production Process
- Level 3: Workflow Control
- Level 4: Basic Plant Scheduling

Levels 0, 1, and 2 apply to the ICS functions of the organization provided by the SCADA or DCS systems, while level 4 maps in the business functions of the organization that track to the enterprise network's operation. Level 3 functions provide the information exchange interface between the OT and IT networks. Figure 1.27 illustrates the distribution of the different network devices described in the ISA-95 standard.

FIGURE 1.27   The ISA-95 standard

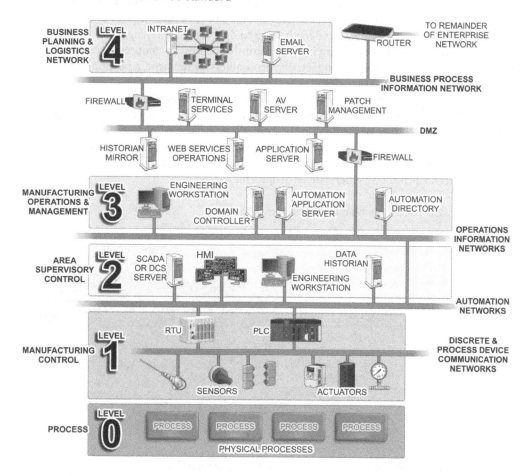

While the ISA-95 architecture model remains the standard for IT/OT integration, advances in IIoT and cloud technologies are beginning to redefine manufacturing integration. The question going forward is whether the ISA-95 model will be taken over by a radically different model or whether these new technologies (IIoT, cloud computing, and edge computing) will converge with the basic structure of the ISA-95 model. Currently, members of the ISA-95 committee are working on additions to the standard to accommodate such new industry requirements as IIoT and Industry 4.0 standards and practices.

Industrial Safety and Protection Systems

Industrial production and utility environments tend to be inherently more hazardous than enterprise network environments. Basically, if a word processor crashes or is compromised, the user might be upset and likely have to do a lot more typing to recover their lost information. However, if an industrial control process is compromised, the organization could suffer loss of productivity, profitability, equipment, a portion of the community, or worse.

As an example, re-examine the simple liquid heating process described in Figure 1.2 and represented in Figure 1.28. While this process already has a *process control system* in place to control the temperature of the fluid in the tank, there are several potentially hazardous conditions that could occur if any part of that system malfunctioned or failed. As such, these hazards become part of the risk analysis process that makes it different than a risk assessment performed for an enterprise environment.

FIGURE 1.28   A simple heating process revisited

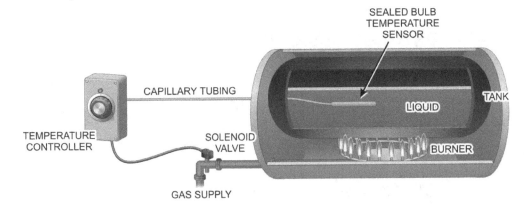

A quick examination of the process shows several potential hazards:

- The tank is heated with a gas-fed heating system.
- The tank contains a liquid that is being heated.
- The temperature sensor, controller, and solenoid valve all represent single points of failure.

The process control system depicted offers no provisions for monitoring or controlling the gas other than the single solenoid valve. As such, the gas heating system represents a number of potentially explosive conditions, as any leak in the system provides an opportunity for uncontrolled ignition.

For example, if the gas piping *outside the tank* developed a leak, the gas would exit the pipe and fill the space around the leak. If an ignition source is introduced within the area where the gas is accumulating, an explosion will occur. In addition, the unignited gas could become a hazard to humans working in the area as it mixes with the air they are breathing.

There is also no provision for monitoring the condition of the gas within the tank. If the fire at the burner went out, this system would still provide gas to the burner. This would allow the gas to build up inside the tank, posing possible uncontrolled combustion hazards if the burner is reignited or personnel open the tank to examine the burner system.

The liquid being heated inside the tank may also be a source of uncontrolled explosion. As the liquid is heated, its molecules gain energy, move more rapidly, and move farther apart (the liquid expands). At some point, it will change from a liquid state to a gaseous state. When this occurs, the pressure inside the tank increases. If left unvented, the pressure can eventually increase to the point that the tank ruptures—maybe violently. The process control system depicted has no provision for monitoring the amount or condition of the liquid inside the tank.

The fact that many of the process control system's devices are the only devices performing a given function makes them all potential sources of problems. For example, if the temperature sensor fails for any reason, the controller will not receive the feedback signal it needs to control the process properly. If the sensor fails so that the controller thinks the temperature is lower than its set point, it will continue to apply gas to the burner, causing the same hazard conditions described earlier.

If the controller fails, the actuator will not receive the error correction signal it requires to control the gas flow and heating process. Depending on the nature of the failure and the design of the final control element, the tank could be allowed to overheat and produce the potential explosion hazards described earlier. Ideally the design of the system is such that any failure would cause the final control element to *fail safe* (shut down the gas flow to the burner).

As you can see, even simple processes like the one presented here provide multiple potential threats to equipment, personnel, and productivity. As such, industrial safety systems must be added to the basic process control system to mitigate the risks pointed out by these concerns. This concept is discussed in detail in Chapter 10, "ICS Security Monitoring and Incident Response." The remainder of this chapter will be used to introduce safety instrument systems and discuss common safety and protection subsystems.

Safety Instrument Systems

Safety instrument systems (SISs) are basically automated process control systems specifically designed to monitor and control conditions in and around the process that have been defined as unsafe or potentially unsafe. The SIS is typically created as an integral part of the overall ICS package (but not the same components). The SIS must be able to successfully perform its functions when the process control system fails. Together these two systems are referred to as the *integrated control and safety system (ICSS)*.

Like the ICS, the SIS is composed of sensors, controllers, and actuators. What the SIS does and to what level is determined through a formal *hazard and operability (HAZOP)* study performed as part of the *process hazard analysis (PHA)* process required for every industrial process. This process is used to identify hazardous scenarios that require *safety instrumented functions (SIFs)* to mitigate. The IEC 61508, 61511, and ANSI/ISA 84 standards define a SIF as "a safety function with a specific *Safety Integrity Level (SIL)* which is necessary to achieve functional safety." This process will also be discussed in detail in Chapter 10.

The standards all address establishing specific requirements for SIS systems:

- IEC 61508, "Functional Safety of Electrical/Electronic/Programmable Electronic Safety-related Systems (E/E/PE, or E/E/PES)"; IEC 61511, "Functional safety – safety instrumented systems for the process industry sector"; IEC 61513 (nuclear); IEC 62016 (manufacturing/machineries)
- ANSI/ISA 84, "The Standard for Safety Instrumented Systems"

The various SIFs identified by the HAZOP are brought together to design and implement the complete SIS. The SIL for each SIF can be defined either as the amount of defined risk reduction to be provided by the safety instrumented function or as the level of dependability of the SIF. There are four discrete SIL ratings being used:

- *SIL 1*: The lowest associated safety level/highest probability that a system will fail to perform properly.
- *SIL 2*: Increased associated safety level/decreased probability of failure to perform properly. These systems are generally more complex than SIL 1–rated systems and tend to be more expensive to install and maintain.
- *SIL 3*: Highest usable rating for associated safety level/decreased probability of failure to perform properly. Because systems rated at this level tend to be expensive to acquire and maintain, many organizations will reengineer their processes to work with lower-rated systems when the results of a HAZOP specify this level of SIL.
- *SIL 4*: The highest associated safety level/lowest probability that a system will fail to perform properly. However, these systems are too complex and costly for most process industries to install and implement. Any process that requires an SIL 4 system should be considered as having fundamental design problems and be redesigned.

SIS Equipment

The safety sensors are designed to monitor different areas of the production environment to detect those conditions that have been defined as unsafe or hazardous through the risk assessment process.

The safety controller is responsible for acquiring the sensor's information and acting on it based on its design and programming. The safety controller may be programmed to provide several different responses, depending on the nature of the hazard detected and the level of protection deemed necessary to mitigate the safety condition:

- *Unit safety shutdown (USD)*: A USD is a shutdown of an individual process or utility system to prevent equipment from operating in an unsafe manner (outside of process limits). At this level, the safety control system shuts down the local process where the safety condition has been detected. However, it will not affect the operation of other processes running in the plant.

- *Process shutdown (PSD)*: This type of shutdown results from undesirable process conditions that may degrade the quality of the product if allowed to continue. This level of shutdown may shut down and isolate related processes or equipment to prevent the condition from affecting those processes, leading to an emergency shutdown condition.

- *Emergency shutdown (ESD)*: An ESD results from a more serious condition detected in the process that threatens the process equipment, personnel, environment, plant, or community. This type of shutdown typically results from conditions related to serious safety concerns, such as runaway process variables.

- *Emergency depressurization shutdown (EDP)*: This level of shutdown is actually an extension of an ESD in that shutdown of the process and its related equipment and processes may cause some undesirable conditions to exist due to the ESD (such as pressure built up in gas lines or inside vessels like the tank in Figure 1.28).

The SIS also employs actuators that operate to control or remove the unsafe conditions. These actuators must be designed and selected to perform specific actions that will limit or remove the threats caused by the unsafe condition(s). SIS system components and operations are designed and selected with special attention to their failure states (what they do or how they respond when something fails). There are two basic modes to consider:

- *Fail safe* is a device or system designed so that in the event of a power or component failure, the process being controlled will remain in its safe condition (on or off). For example, the gas control valve in the sample process should be selected so that it naturally fails safe (moves to a closed position) any time it loses signal from the controller. This would ensure that the gas flow into the tank would be cut off in the event of any failure.

- *Fail secure* is a device or system designed so that the process being controlled will assume its most secure condition in the event of a power or component failure.

Because the security controller is primarily a security device, one of its main responsibilities is to provide proper notification when a security event occurs. When the controller receives an active input signal from one of its security sensors, it evaluates the conditions presented according to its programming (and the type of emergency response required) and, if necessary, sends the appropriate alarm signals to annunciators (sirens or bells). It may also activate any number of visual indicators such as flashing lights, operator panel lights, or icons on a control panel.

The controller may also communicate with designated security and supervisory contacts (security supervisors, monitoring services, or emergency services) as directed by its programming. These systems are designed to react when no one is present. They may use any of several methods to accomplish this:

- *Dial-up telephone connections*: Use a telephone dialer to alert remote security contacts that a hazardous condition exists over a standard telephone line.

- *Cellular Channels*: Use a cellular channel to send prepared text messaging to designated security or supervisory contacts.

- *IP-based notification*: Use an IP network (such as the Internet) to notify designated security and supervisory personnel concerning a hazard condition.

Redundant Systems

Component and system *redundancy* is one of the most basic practices in industrial security. We've already identified several key components that represent *single points of failure* in the simple process example presented in this chapter. The reason the SIS is made up of different components than the process control system is that the SIS must step in and take control when a component in the process control system fails. If they are the same device in both systems, then both systems fail.

For example, to address the hazards associated with the process that were identified earlier in the chapter, we could look at adding several sensors to the system:

- Gas detection sensor outside the tank

- Flame detection sensor inside the tank

- Pressure sensor inside the tank

- Safety temperature sensor inside the tank

In each case, these sensors are redundant to the process control sensors in the original design.

Basic actuators that can be added to the process to mitigate potential hazards include the following:

- Manual shut-off valve upstream from the solenoid control valve

- Security shut-off valve between the manual and process control valves

- Pressure relief valve on the shell of the tank

As with the proposed security sensors, these additional actuators are redundant to the actuators in the original process control system design.

Emergency Shutdown Systems

Emergency shutdown systems (EMSs) are a specific type of SIS designed to minimize the consequences of certain emergency conditions. They operate at the prevention safety layer and act to prevent a hazardous event such as a fire, a chemical release, or an explosion from occurring. As systems, they consist of ESD sensors, ESD controller, and ESD actuators.

Returning to our process control example, we can build a simple block diagram of an ESD that could be implemented to perform the shutdown procedure. The foremost consideration for any emergency would be shutting the gas supply off. The redundancy list presented earlier provides two options for doing this—an automated solenoid valve connected to the SIS controller and a manual shutoff valve, as illustrated in Figure 1.29.

FIGURE 1.29   Adding an ESD system

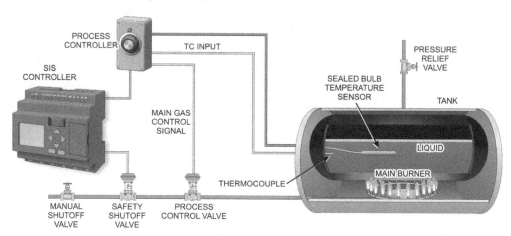

The other hazard mentioned in our quick analysis was that the pressure in the tank could increase to a dangerous level if the burner is allowed to continuously heat the liquid. This would eventually cause the tank to fail in an explosive manner. To mitigate this possibility, a pressure relief valve could be installed on the shell of the tank. When the controller detects a failure, it will cause the valve to fail open, relieving the pressure inside the tank by venting it into the outside atmosphere.

Figure 1.29 also shows the addition of redundant sensors and controller to the original process control system. These devices represent a few of the typical safety sensors found in industrial process Safety Instrumentation Systems. The following sections of the chapter deal with specific safety systems identified in the GICSP certification objectives.

Fire and Gas Systems

Fire and gas systems (FGSs) are part of the SIS that operate at the mitigation safety layer and act to limit the consequences of an ESD event. They are implemented in the SIS to continuously monitor plant activity and in case of hazardous conditions initiate appropriate actions. For example, if an FGS detects a combustible gas (such as the gas being used to heat the tank in Figure 1.29), a toxic gas, smoke, flame, or excessive heat, it may issue a visual and audible warning along with activating a fire suppression system and/or process shutdown.

In our simple process, the FGS would use gas leak detection devices located at intervals and joints along the length of the supply pipe. The controller may be as simple as a PLC programmed to perform the SIS functions or a proprietary FGS controller. Figure 1.30 illustrates the implementation of a simple FGS on our sample process.

FIGURE 1.30   Adding an FGS to the system

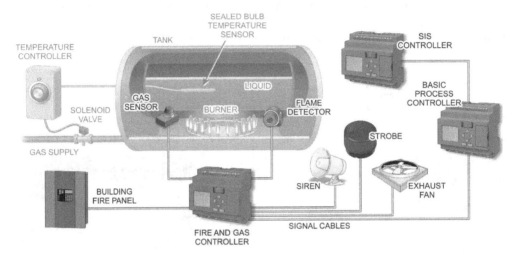

The controller decision is typically based on the size of the process. PLCs tend to be better suited for medium and large installations (where more than 25 sensors are involved), while dedicated controllers are more appropriate for small and medium installations. PLC controllers are relatively inexpensive and flexible to implement and change. In addition, PLCs are able to communicate with other controllers in distributed control environments. Proprietary controllers are relatively easy to install and maintain and generally do not require programming.

Unlike ESD systems, Fire and Gas Systems can be quite complex and highly distributed. However, they are critical to plant safety, and their efficiency and reliability are key concerns, not only for plant operators but for environmental and business insurance authorities as well.

Industrial Leak Detection

One of the major components of an FGS is the *leak detector*. These devices are added to the SIS to detect the leakage of hazardous gases, chemicals, and liquids. They are used across the spectrum of industrial processes in any type of equipment that holds liquids or gases that can potentially leak.

There are many types of leak detectors available for use in industrial settings. Each type employs a different type of physics to detect the leak and convert it into a signal:

- *Fluid accumulation detectors*: This type of detector uses two separate probes to detect the presence of excess fluids that build up between the probes and create a closed-circuit condition.

- *Resistive change detectors*: This class of leak detector uses electrochemical sensors to detect the presence or concentration level of fluids or gases around the device. When the chemical composition of the fluid or gas mixture changes (such as gas being added to air around the outside of the pipe), the resistance of the probe changes, and this change is sensed by the controller.

- *Differential flow detectors*: This type of detector measures the difference in pressure between two points in a conduit (such as a pipe). If the conduit is closed, there should be no difference in pressure between the two points. However, if the pressure changes between the measurement points, a leak is assumed.

Figure 1.31 depicts a simple differential pressure detection system. The gas pipe is tapped at two points along the pipe. In this illustration, there is a pipe joint present between the measurement points that is being monitored for leakage. The taps are connected to each side of a sealed container with a flexible diaphragm in the center. The diaphragm is mechanically connected to a movable switch contact.

FIGURE 1.31   A simple differential pressure detection system

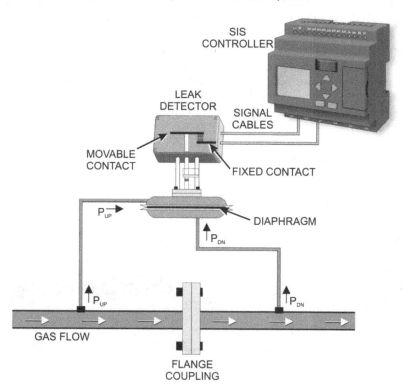

As long as the upstream and downstream pressures are the same, the diaphragm will remain in the middle of the container, and the movable contact will not touch the fixed switch contact. Therefore, the sensing circuit remains open. However, if the pressure decreases at the downstream tap, the greater pressure from the upstream tap will push the diaphragm to the right in the diagram. When the pressure differential is great enough, the movable contact will connect with the fixed contact, and the sensor circuit will be made.

At this point, the safety controller will perform its designated SIF, which could include sounding an audible alarm, initiating one or more visual cautions and closing the safety valve.

Burner Management Systems

As our process example illustrates, gas-fired burners are widely used to heat gases and liquids in industrial processes. To secure the gas delivery system outside of the tank, gas leak detectors were deployed to monitor the area along the pipe. However, gas leak detectors are less useful inside the tank of our process example.

There should be gas in the burner area, but it must be controlled in a precise manner to provide safe operation of the system. Suppose the flame on the burner was extinguished. The gas sensor would detect the presence of the gas pouring into the burner area, and the safety controller would act to shut off the gas flow.

So, how do you get the burner relit in a safe manner? There must be gas and flame present to accomplish this. However, the security sensor/controller would continue to hold the valve shut until the gas sensor indicated that there was no more gas in the area. For this reason, *burner management systems (BMSs)* are used to assure the safe startup, operation, and shutdown of burners in a process control system. Figure 1.32 depicts the components of a simple BMS.

FIGURE 1.32   A simple BMS

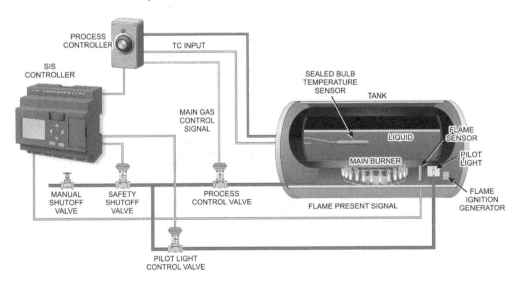

This simple system begins with a small unit called the *pilot light*. This is a device that maintains a small flame near the main burner at all times. The pilot light flame is directed toward the flame sensor—normally a thermocouple—that generates an electrical signal whenever the flame is being applied to the sensor.

The safety controller uses the electrical signal from the thermocouple to hold a fail-closed safety valve open. If the pilot light flame is not present, the *safety valve* will close. This valve is located downstream from the manual shut-off valve and upstream from the original process control valve.

This pilot light system is designed to maintain the small ignition source near the main burner so that when the process control valve is opened and gas is applied to the burner, the gas will ignite without building up around the burner unit. When the process controller closes the process control valve to limit the gas flowing to the burner, the pilot light will remain lit. When the process needs more heat, the controller can open the control valve to the burner so that it lights in a safe manner.

To ignite the pilot light, an operator must manually override the closed safety valve to introduce gas to the pilot light mechanism. In addition, they must administer a flame source to the pilot light assembly to get it started. After the flame sensor detects the pilot light flame, the safety controller should take over control of the system. The flame source is typically some type of electrical spark generator.

Of course, actual BMS deployments in industrial security settings tend to be much more complex than the simple design presented here. However, they all employ sensors, controller(s), and actuators designed and selected to perform the same functions as this example.

Vibration Monitoring

The last SIS subsystems listed in the GICSP certification objectives for this chapter are *vibration monitoring systems*. These systems are generally added to industrial equipment to monitor moving machines for signs of pending failures. Excessive vibration is one of the signs that point to a machine beginning to show signs of deterioration. By monitoring the amount of vibration, organizations can make informed decisions about when to repair or replace the machine.

All moving machines vibrate to some degree. However, as their moving parts age, they gradually vibrate more intensely. Devices called *accelerometers* are attached to rotating machines to monitor their vibration patterns over time. The recorded vibration patterns can be compared to previous points in time to determine the rate of machine wear.

Figure 1.33 shows the addition of an emergency exhaust fan unit to the FGS system. If the FGS system detects a gas leak, the fan unit is activated to vent the fumes out of the area. The motor that drives the fan is a vital piece of the safety system, but it is rarely or never used, other than during safety tests. Therefore, it is imperative that it be kept in good working order in case it is needed in an emergency. The figure also illustrates the addition of a vibration sensor system to the exhaust fan motor so that its condition can be tracked through regular testing.

FIGURE 1.33   Adding a vibration detection system

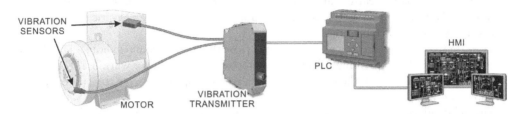

Vibration detection systems are also used to test or monitor human health and safety systems. In the United States, the OSHA Technical Manual (OTM) covers three areas of human-related vibration monitoring. For example, some pieces of equipment that require a human operator may be subjected to vibration monitoring. This is typically done to make sure the operation of the machine does not exceed recommended vibration limits that expose the operator to vibration levels that could damage the human body.

Review Questions

The following questions test your knowledge of the material presented in this chapter. You can check your answers against those listed in Appendix D.

1. The overall objective of process control is _____.

2. In an ICS environment, what small intelligent control units are commonly deployed at selective locations within a process, or set of processes, to gather data from different sensors and deliver commands to control relay outputs?

3. In any process control system, the _____ is responsible for taking the input information, comparing that information to a predetermined condition or a reference, making decisions about what action should be taken, and finally sending corrective error signals to the final element, which adjusts the manipulated variable.

4. The preferred local control device in modern industrial processing and utility environments is the _____.

5. PLCs and RTUs share much of their technology with computing devices found in IT networks. With this in mind, how do these technologies differ from each other?

6. When processes become too complex for a single controller, or its components are geographically separated, what type of control system is required to efficiently manage the operation of the process?

7. A distributed control system that provides data acquisition (input) and supervisory control functions (output) is referred to as a _____ system.

8. What process employs sensors to collect information in a remote location and transmits it to another location for processing?

9. In a SCADA-based process, the _____ enables human operators to observe the operating parameters of the different processes and take charge of the processes to change parameters or make corrections.

10. What type of automated process control systems are specifically designed to monitor and control conditions in and around the process that have been defined as unsafe or potentially unsafe?

11. What two major systems are brought together to form an integrated control and safety system (ICSS)?

12. _____ are a specific type of SIS designed to minimize the consequences of certain emergency conditions. They operate at the prevention safety layer and act to prevent a hazardous event such as a fire, a chemical release, or an explosion from occurring.

13. Why are devices called accelerometers commonly attached to rotating machines to monitor their vibration patterns over time?

14. What type of sensors are added to the SIS package to detect the presence of hazardous gases, chemicals, and liquids?

15. Burner management systems are used to _____.

Exam Questions

1. Key requirements for industrial process controllers include which of the following? (Select all that apply.)

   A. Availability

   B. Timeliness

   C. Industrial interfacing

   D. Confidentiality

2. The most common field devices encountered in industrial and utility process control systems include which of the following? (Select all that apply.)

   A. DSC devices

   B. Remote telemetry units

   C. SCADA devices

   D. Programmable logic controllers

3. From the following list, identify types of modules commonly available for modular PLC devices. (Select all that apply.)

   A. Power supply unit (PSU) modules

   B. Central processing unit (CPU) modules

   C. SCADA modules

   D. DCS modules

   E. Output modules

   F. Communication modules

4. When processes become too complex for a single controller, or its components are geographically separated, it becomes necessary to distribute the control function over multiple controllers to form a _____.

   A. Distributed control system (DCS)

   B. SCADA system

   C. Telemetry system

   D. Purdue system

5. Which of the following best describes a SCADA system?

   A. A data acquisition system that collects data from field devices such as PLCs, RTUs, and IEDs

   B. A supervisory control system that sends data to field devices such as PLCs, RTUs, and IEDs

   C. A human machine interface (HMI) application that enables human operators to observe the operating parameters of the different processes and take charge of the processes to change parameters or make corrections

   D. An industrial software application running on some type of computer platform that includes a database management system that stores historical data in the form of control points

6. A _____ device or system is one that is designed so that the process being controlled will assume its most secure condition in the event of a power or component failure.

    A. Fail soft

    B. Fail safe

    C. Fail secure

    D. Fail over

7. In a basic OT network, the _____ connects the PLCs, RTUs, and IEDs with the various input sensors and output actuators in the process.

    A. Ethernet network

    B. Field bus

    C. RS-485 serial bus

    D. SIS network

8. A _____ is a shutdown of an individual process or utility system to prevent equipment from operating in an unsafe manner (outside of process limits). At this level, the safety control system shuts down the local process where the safety condition has been detected. However, it will not affect the operation of other processes running in the plant.

    A. PSD

    B. ESD

    C. ESP

    D. USD

9. Using the Purdue Model as a guide, at which level of the standard do the production system's sensing and manipulation devices reside?

    A. Level 0

    B. Level 1

    C. Level 2

    D. Level 3

    E. Level 4

10. At which level of the Purdue Model standard do the production system's DSC or SCADA systems reside?

    A. Level 0

    B. Level 1

    C. Level 2

    D. Level 3

    E. Level 4

Chapter

2

ICS Architecture

OBJECTIVES

Upon completion of this chapter, you should be able to:

1. **Explain knowledge of communication medium and external network communications:**

   ▪ Copper

   ▪ Light

   ▪ Wireless

2. **Describe basic field device architecture including:**

   ▪ Relays

   ▪ PLC

   ▪ Switch

   ▪ Process unit

3. **Understand the functions of common Industrial Control System protocols:**

   ▪ Modbus

   ▪ Modbus TCP

   ▪ DNP3

   ▪ Ethernet/IP

   ▪ OPC

4. **Discuss the functions of common network protocols:**

   ▪ DNS

   ▪ DHCP

   ▪ TCP/IP

Introduction

In the previous chapter you were introduced to the basic components of a typical industrial/ utility control system. This chapter will build on those introductory topics to describe standard ICS architectures. In particular, it will bring together four major areas of knowledge associated with operational OT architectures:

- Communication media

- Field device architecture

- Industrial network protocols

- IT network protocols

The ICS Architecture objectives listed for the GICSP certification exam also list the subsections Network Segmentation and Security Zones, as well as Wireless Security. These topics will be addressed in Chapter 3, "Secure ICS Architecture."

In the introduction to the previous chapter, it was mentioned that OT networks tend to be very different than the IT networks found in enterprise and small business environments. For example, as you already know, many of the connectivity and computing devices employed in industrial manufacturing and utility networks are considerably different than those typically found in enterprise networks. In particular, the OT networks used in industrial/utility networks contain different types of process control equipment such as *programmable logic controllers (PLCs)* and *remote terminal units (RTUs)*.

These environments also differ greatly in the area of software. In the industrial network environment, business applications running on Windows and Linux operating systems in enterprise networks have been replaced by process control applications that provide *supervisory control and data acquisition (SCADA)* and *man-machine interface (MMI)* functions.

Even the network communications may be quite different than those encountered in the enterprise network. While CATx twisted-pair cabling, Ethernet protocols, and TCP/IP are widely used in that environment, other protocols and technologies (such as RS-485 serial communication links, Modbus networking, and SONET ring wide area networks) exist, as well as a multitude of wireless technologies.

Network Transmission Media

Digital data travels from one network device to another across the network *communication media*. There are basically three general types of transmission media used to move data between networked devices:

- Copper wire (twisted copper cabling and coaxial cabling)
- Light waves (fiber-optic cabling and infrared light)
- Wireless radio frequency (RF) signals (WiFi, WiMAX, Bluetooth, ZigBee, Z-Wave)

Each media type offers advantages that makes it useful for networking in certain conditions. The main media-related considerations include their cost to implement, maximum data transmission rates, and noise immunity characteristics. Likewise, each media type has some limitations on its ability to transfer information.

This factor is also wrapped up in two considerations—its *bandwidth* and its *attenuation*. *Bandwidth* is the media's total ability to carry data in a given instance. *Attenuation* is a measure of how much signal loss occurs as the information moves across the medium. As you will see in the following sections, some media types can literally carry a signal for miles and still deliver it as recognizable information.

The final media-related consideration is its noise immunity capabilities. Stray electrical energy (referred to as *noise*) moves through the atmosphere as a natural course. Electrical machines and devices can also generate electronic noise. These stray signals can interfere with organized data signals and make them unrecognizable. Therefore, cabling used to transmit data is expected to have some resistance to these stray signals.

Copper Cabling

Under the heading of *copper cabling*, there are basically two categories to consider: twisted-pair cabling and coaxial cabling. Twisted-pair cabling consists of two or more pairs of wires twisted together to provide noise reduction. The twist in the wires causes induced noise signals to cancel each other out. In this type of cabling, the number of twists in each foot of wire indicates its relative noise immunity level.

When discussing twisted-pair cabling with data networks, there are two basic types to consider: *unshielded twisted pair* (UTP) and *shielded twisted pair* (STP). UTP networking cable contains four pairs of individually insulated wires, as illustrated in Figure 2.1.

STP cable is similar with the exception that it contains an additional foil shield that surrounds the four-pair wire bundle. The shield provides extended protection from induced electrical noise and cross talk by supplying a grounded path to carry the induced electrical signals away from the conductors in the cable. This additional feature makes STP costlier, heavier, and more difficult to install than UTP cable. However, it also offers higher data speeds and greater noise immunity.

FIGURE 2.1   UTP and STP cabling

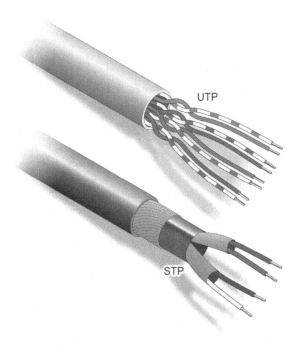

Coaxial cable (often referred to simply as coax) is familiar to most people as the conductor that carries cable TV into their homes. Coaxial cable is constructed with an insulated solid or stranded wire core surrounded by a dielectric insulating layer and a solid or braided metallic shield. Both the wire and shield are wrapped in an outer protective insulating jacket, as illustrated in Figure 2.2.

In the past, coaxial cable was widely used for Ethernet LAN media. However, because the thickness and rigidity of coaxial cable make it difficult and time-consuming to install, the networking industry and network standards development groups have abandoned coaxial cable in favor of unshielded twisted-pair cabling.

Fiber-Optic Cabling

Fiber-optic cable is plastic or glass cable designed to carry digital data in the form of light pulses. The signals are introduced into the cable by a laser diode and bounce along its interior until they reach the end of the cable, as illustrated in Figure 2.3. At the end, a light-detecting circuit receives the light signals and converts them back into usable information.

Light moving through a fiber-optic cable does not attenuate (lose energy) as quickly as electrical signals moving along a copper conductor. Therefore, segment lengths between transmitters and receivers can be much longer when using fiber-optic cabling. In some fiber-optic applications, the maximum cable length can range up to 2 kilometers.

FIGURE 2.2   Coaxial cable

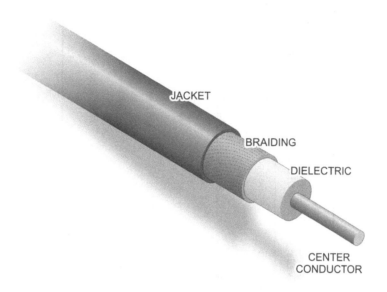

JACKET

BRAIDING

DIELECTRIC

CENTER
CONDUCTOR

FIGURE 2.3   Transmitting over fiber-optic cable

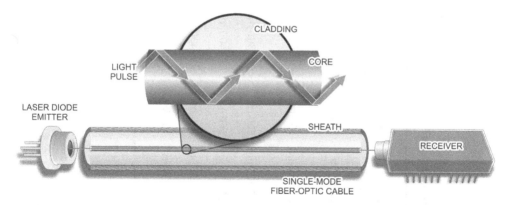

CLADDING

LIGHT
PULSE

CORE

LASER DIODE
EMITTER

SHEATH

RECEIVER

SINGLE-MODE
FIBER-OPTIC CABLE

Depending on the type of fiber-optic cabling used, fiber links offer potential signaling rates in excess of 200 Gbps. However, current access protocols provide fiber-optic LAN speeds up to 100 Gbps. Table 2.1 illustrates the relationship between transmission speed and distance for different grades of single-mode (OS2) and multimode (OM1, 2, 3, 4, and 5) fiber.

TABLE 2.1 Fiber-Optic Cable Speeds and Distances

Fiber Type	Core Diameter	1 Gb/s Ethernet Max Distance	10 Gb/s Ethernet Max Distance	40 Gb/s Ethernet Max Distance	100 Gb/s Ethernet Max Distance	40Gb/s SWDM4	100Gb/s SWDM4
OM1 Multimode	62.5/125 µm	275 m	33 m	Not Supported	Not Supported	Not Supported	Not Supported
OM2 Multimode	50/125 µm	550 m	82 m	Not Supported	Not Supported	Not Supported	Not Supported
OM3 Multimode	50/125 µm	550 m	300 m	100 m	70 m	240 m	75 m
OM4 Multimode	50/125 µm	550 m	400 m	150 m	150 m	350 m	100 m
OM5 Multimode	50/125 µm	550 m	400 m	150 m	150 m	440 m	150 m
OS1/OS2 Single-mode	9/125 µm	100 km	40 km	40 km	40 km	Not Supported	Not Supported

As you can see from the table, single-mode fiber-optic cable is optimized for long-distance signal transmission (up to 5 km), while multimode fiber provides higher transmission speeds for shorter distances.

Fiber-optic cable also provides a much more secure data transmission medium than copper cable, because it cannot be tapped without physically breaking the conductor. Basically, light introduced into the cable at one end does not leave the cable except through the other end. Electrical utilities have been using fiber-optic cabling to monitor and control their widely distributed transmission and distribution networks for more than 30 years.

Industrial Network Media Standards

Historically, industrial data communications were limited to fixed, point-to-point transmissions between devices through *direct cable connections*. The communication channels were manually configured to provide local and distant connections as necessary to serve each specific application.

This *point-to-point* method, illustrated in Figure 2.4, represents the simplest control topology option but also tends to be more expensive to implement and maintain. Each network implementation requires a great deal of engineering and planning before it can be implemented. Communication channels must be mapped from point to point for each device to ensure correct data movement.

FIGURE 2.4   Point-to-point connections

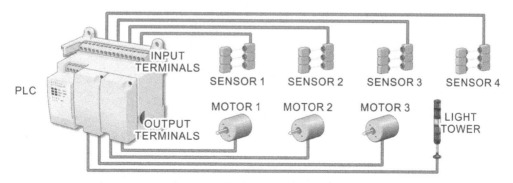

Asynchronous Serial Standards

Fixed point-to-point connectivity proved to be well suited for industrial process control systems with relatively low device counts and a need for determinacy. However, when multiple controllers were required to manage multiple process units, additional intelligence was also required. To operate cohesively in such environments, the controllers needed to be able to communicate with each other.

Initially, the *RS-232 asynchronous serial communication standard* became the industrial network device connectivity standard for communication paths up to 100 feet in length. This connection standard was adopted for communications in several other industries, including IT computer and peripheral connectivity.

The physical link for the RS-232 protocol employed a multiple conductor cable and specific hardware connectors. Separate Send (TX) and Receive (RX) lines were specified along with two sets of transmission control signals (Request-to-Send and Clear-to-Send/ Data Terminal Ready and Data Set Ready). The cable also included a number of ground lines. The physical connection was specified through paired 9-pin D-shell connectors (male and female).

RS-232 devices continue to be used in industrial control systems for programming some PLCs, variable frequency, and servo drive controllers, as well as CNC machining systems. This has led some computer accessory suppliers to create USB to serial cables featuring DB-9 male connectors, as illustrated in Figure 2.5.

FIGURE 2.5   USB to RS-232 serial connections

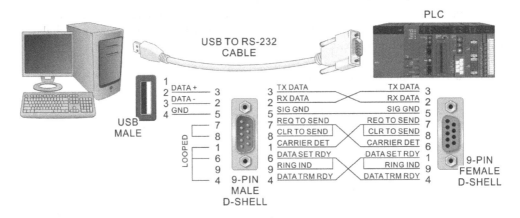

Eventually, improved line balanced versions of the RS-232 serial standard, referred to as the *RS-422* and *RS-485* standards, emerged that enabled industrial devices to use shared physical medium in a bus or ring topology while increasing the allowable distances between devices.

The *RS-422* (EIA 422) *Asynchronous Serial Communications* protocol standard was published in 1975. It is similar in many respects to RS-232. However, it is faster (up to 100 Kbps) than RS-232 and offers better *noise immunity*. The RS-422 protocol makes use of two pairs of twisted-pair conductors (one pair for transmit and one pair for receive) along with a differential amplifier/driver for each pair of lines. These two features combine to provide heightened *Common Mode Noise Rejection* across the physical link to attenuate electromagnetic interference (EMI) noise that is induced into both lines.

Under the RS-422 protocol, communication links can be established as directly connected, peer-to-peer channels, or as *main/secondary device networks*. In these connections, an RS-422 master transmitter device can be used to host up to 10 slave devices on a single media channel. For devices to share the same physical communication media, some type of Primary/Secondary or token-passing protocol must be employed to avoid device access contention problems.

The *RS-485 serial protocol standard*, first published in 1998, is faster and more flexible than either the RS-232 or RS-422 version. In addition, it supports transmissions using the TCP/IP protocol. Like the RS-422 standard, RS-485 can effectively carry communications over longer distances of up to 4,000 feet (over 1200 m). Figure 2.6 shows a serial RS-232/485 connection scheme for a modern PLC.

FIGURE 2.6   Serial connections

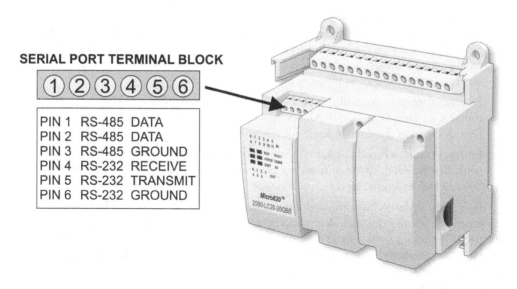

The RS-485 standard also supports main/secondary device configurations. As such, these asynchronous standards have proven to be well suited for centralized intelligence and device polling techniques required to implement DCS and SCADA systems in distributed industrial processes. This was particularly true when it came to providing wider geographical connectivity.

Ethernet Connectivity

Asynchronous communications, such as the RS-485 links described earlier, dominated industrial control system connectivity for more than 20 years because they are very efficient in transferring data in *real time*. However, the rise and expansion of IT networking technologies has caused organizations to look to these technologies for sharing control and data of their OT networks. While IT networks have launched several different types of network topologies (rings, trees, and buses), the *802.x Ethernet* technology has largely been accepted as both the local and wide area standard for networking.

However, the problem that OT networks have with Ethernet technology is that data delivery times can vary and are not deterministic due to the underlying design of the Ethernet standard. An Ethernet packet can be delayed for several basic reasons.

- Ethernet nodes get held up by other traffic on the network. Because Ethernet traffic is based on the premise that the node that gets to the network media first wins the right to the media, important data that is moved to the bus later than less important traffic has to wait.

- Data collisions occur. Network nodes "listen" to the network media to find an opening when they can transmit their data across the bus. If they see an opening and begin putting their data on the bus, but so does another node, a collision occurs, and the data on the media is scrambled. All nodes back off for specified times and try again. This process can be very time-consuming in network years.

- Ethernet data can take multiple paths to get to its final destination. This is due to the routable nature of the TCP/IP packet. It was designed to seek an alternative route to its final destination if the most direct route is slow or blocked.

- Ethernet traffic is broadcast across the network, so it goes to all the nodes on the network. Unabated, this type of signaling places a relatively heavy traffic load on the network, which can result in network bandwidth reductions and data loss.

These types of delays are almost unnoticeable in a typical IT network. However, in the OT network environment, such delays can be dangerous to personnel, equipment, and productivity. Operations in industrial plants typically require speed and determination due to the nature of the ability to deliver within a designated time frame. If not, molten metal gets poured onto the work floor, moving pieces do not stop where they are supposed to, and critical commands do not reach controllers in time to perform the required activity.

While these issues may make Ethernet sound like it could never be used in an OT network, the truth is that more than 30 different industrial protocols have been specifically developed for OT networking. There are several reasons for this: many organizations have designated their IT staff to implement and maintain both their IT and OT networks; Ethernet networking on the IT side has provided a wealth of inexpensive, off-the-shelf hardware and software tools; Ethernet is widely known, so there is a larger pool of technicians and administrators who are already familiar with it; and organizations want their IT and ICS networks to work together for improved productivity and profits.

Later in this chapter you will encounter several of the Ethernet-based ICS protocols mentioned. Of these, there are three protocols that dominate the ICS networking market: Ethernet/IP, Modbus TCP, and ProfiNet. In each case, the task is to get the messages and data of the overriding protocol into an Ethernet TCP/IP packet.

External Network Communications

In widely distributed processes such as those associated with public utilities, wide area communications technologies must be employed to obtain real-time input from the field sites and enable central operators to provide efficient supervisory control functions from their operation control center. Figure 2.7 shows typical long-distance/wide area communication technologies commonly employed for this purpose.

FIGURE 2.7   Remote access ICS communications

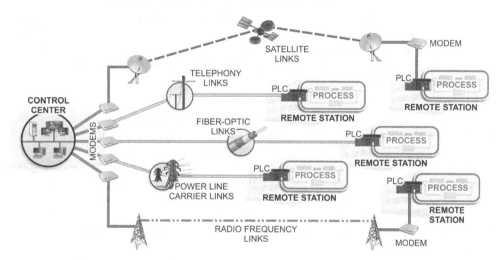

The different communication links depicted in the figure provide different features appropriate for particular scenarios.

- *Telephony technologies*: One of the most dependable point-to-point communications systems ever devised is still the *public switched telephone network* (*PSTN*) system. These systems use physical cabling to transmit voice grade signals between a sender and a receiver. These communications links can be provided through the public switched lines, through leased lines, or through private lines where the organization has become its own telephone company.

- *Radio frequency technologies*: Different over-the-air *radio technologies* have been employed to provide long-distance communication links between field sites and the control station. These include licensed and unlicensed *radio frequency* (*RF*) transmissions, cellular telephony links, and ultra-high frequency microwave transmissions.

- *Satellite communication technologies*: Many companies employ *very small aperture terminals (VSAT) satellite communications* between their headquarters and their field sites to carry supervisory control data. These systems are self-contained and do not involve third-party technologies such as the public telephone system. Unfortunately, many of these systems were very poorly secured, using nonsecure communication protocols, poor password strength requirements, and factory default settings.

- *Fiber-optic technologies*: Fiber-optic cabling offers an excellent high-speed, long-distance data transmission media. Data is encoded into light waves that are injected into the fiber-optic cable. Because light does not attenuate quickly, it can travel for great distances over the cable. Fiber-optic cable is also more difficult to install than other cable types, as the fibers and components within the cable are susceptible to damage or breakage from bending, stretching, twisting, splitting, or scratching. However, because the light does not radiate outside of the cable, an attacker must physically interrupt the cable to intercept signals moving across it.

- *Power line carrier (PLC) technologies*: These technologies encode serialized digital data directly onto the power distribution lines of the grid for transportation between different remote locations. PLC technologies have been more widely adopted for data transmission in European electricity grids than in the United States. US grids have tended to adopt wireless technologies over PLC options.

For each different communication technology and media type, a *modulator/demodulator (modem)* communication device is required at each end of the long-distance communication link to convert the information into a suitable signal format for transmission over the media and then convert it back to a format usable by the control/network device.

Modem communications are used to connect industrial devices at distances well beyond that, which is possible using asynchronous serial connections. The modulator portion of the modem serializes and modulates data into signals that can be transmitted across the particular media type being used. At the other end, the demodulator portion of the other modem demodulates the signal and then de-serializes the data so it can be used by the OT devices.

The field site may contain several local controllers or IEDs that need to communicate with the remote supervisory system. In those cases, there are several topology options available for organizing the controllers' communications.

- *Point-to-point topologies*: Each field site controller or IED is provided its own dedicated communications link with the control center. This is accomplished by attaching a modem to each controller in the field site and providing the communication link to a compatible modem in the remote control center. This topology is simple to implement and operate but also tends to be the most expensive option.

- *Series connection topologies*: Series connection topologies reduce the number of long-distance communication channels to one. Device contention protocols must be implemented at the field site to control when and how its different controllers can access the communication channel. Sharing the communication channel can have an adverse impact on the timeliness of the data acquisition and control transmissions.

- *Multiple-drop topologies*: Multi-drop configurations provide an individual communication channel to each controller. However, the link between the remote field sites and the control center is a single link.

- *Series-star topologies*: This is a combination of series and individual channels; however, it decreases the timeliness of the data acquisition process.

Figure 2.8 illustrates common device communication topologies used to coordinate communications in remote field sites.

FIGURE 2.8   Remote access ICS communications

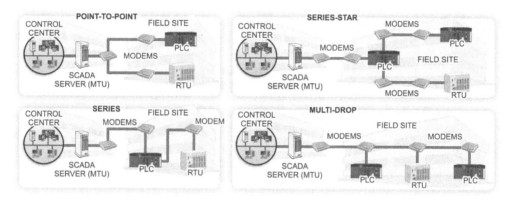

Transmission Media Vulnerabilities

Like other components of the network, transmission media security must be considered at two levels: physical security and logical security. Physical security involves securing the physical medium, along with the communication equipment and physical ports that interconnect the networked equipment. If an attacker can gain uninterrupted access to the transmission media, they can find a way to exploit it.

Securing physical media becomes challenging when it leaves the controllable area of the private facility (the network that is owned and maintained by the organization). Within the facility, optical and copper communication media are relatively safe, as a physical tapping of the media is required to extract information from it.

When the media leaves the confines of the facility, the information it carries becomes vulnerable to interception and capture along its route, or at the receiving port of the message. To secure data that must travel across third-party media and/or interact with second-party associates, it must be encrypted before transmission and preferably transferred using a network tunneling strategy.

The same cannot be said for wireless communications, as they may be extracted from the air through a simple antenna. Therefore, all wireless transmissions should be performed using encrypted communications links. Wireless transmissions and security are covered in Chapter 3.

Field Device Architecture

In Chapter 1, "Industrial Control Systems," you were introduced to typical field devices found in ICS systems. Recall that the preferred local control device in modern industrial processing and utility environments is the PLC. The Industrial Cyber Security specialist must be familiar with the structure and operation of PLCs to know what to expect from them and understand their vulnerabilities. PLCs, like the one depicted in Figure 2.9, share most of their technology with IT computing devices; they contain a microprocessor, RAM memory, read-only firmware, and an operating system.

FIGURE 2.9 PLC structure

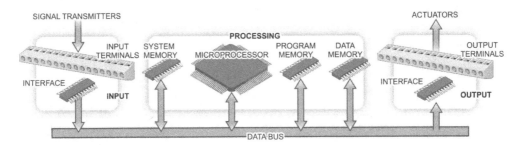

The heart of the PLC is its *microprocessor*. Like all other digital computing devices, it obtains instructions and data from its supporting memory areas and performs arithmetic and logic functions based on the program instructions it receives. Also, like other computing devices, the overall performance of the PLC is largely dependent on the capabilities of the processor.

While the speed, bus size, and processing power of the microprocessor are major contributors to the performance level of any computing device, the efficiency of the software and programming provided represents the other major factor involved in the performance of the PLC.

In a PLC, the processor's operation is relatively straightforward. It has three basic functions to perform:

- It scans the status of each input terminal in sequence.
- It processes the input status according to its programming.
- It passes the results to specified output terminals.

The organization of the PLC's memory units is also comparable with typical PCs. There is a permanent *system memory* area (similar to the BIOS/CMOS of a PC) where the operational capabilities of the PLC are encoded. These capabilities are programmed into the PLC by its manufacturer and are not directly available to the user. This memory area typically resides in integrated circuit EPROM or EEPROM storage devices on the controller's circuit board.

The second storage area is the *program memory* (or *user memory*) area that holds the programming supplied by the user. This programming is generated by the user and downloaded into this memory area for use by the PLC. The memory area is physically implemented in *random access memory (RAM)* modules on the PLC's circuit board. The size of the RAM modules determines the amount of programming that can be loaded into the PLC.

A third memory area in the PLC is the *data memory* area. This area is designed to temporarily store intermediate data values that are obtained during program execution. The program can reference this data when needed by other program sequences or to activate designated output terminals.

All three of these memory areas are mapped into the PLC's *address map*. This map, illustrated in Figure 2.10, represents the numerical locations of each available memory location in the physical memory devices on the PLC's circuit board.

FIGURE 2.10   PLC address map

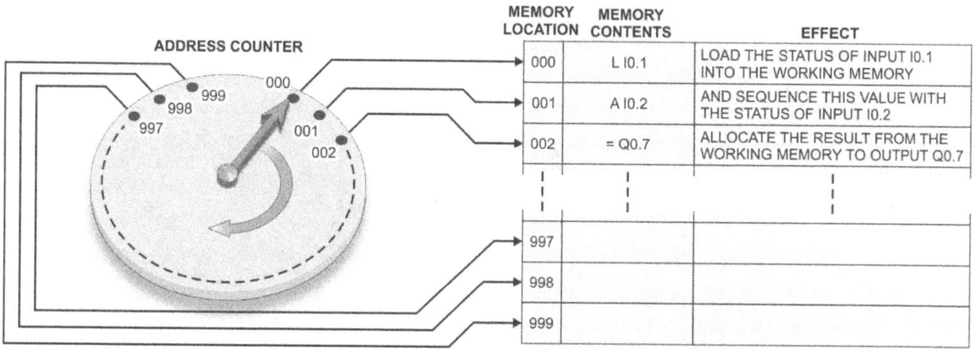

The microprocessor's address counter selects these locations in order to obtain each instruction in a step-by-step manner. As it obtains and reads each instruction, the PLC's processor determines the following:

- What activity should be performed (i.e., load the status of Input 1 into memory)?

- What data should be used for the activity, and where can it be found (i.e., if the Input 1 data = 1, turn on Output Terminal 4)?

After these two pieces of information have been obtained (referred to as the *instruction cycle*), the PLC's processor moves into its execution cycle, where it carries out the instruction. The processor then moves to the next instruction address in memory where its instruction cycle/execution cycle sequence repeats itself until the program provides some type of Stop instruction or until the processor runs out of memory locations to process.

The linear processing of the instructions can also be altered by Jump or Conditional Jump instructions that direct the microprocessor to reset its instruction counter to some new memory location and begin executing instructions from there. This type of operation is depicted in Figure 2.11.

FIGURE 2.11   Jump instructions

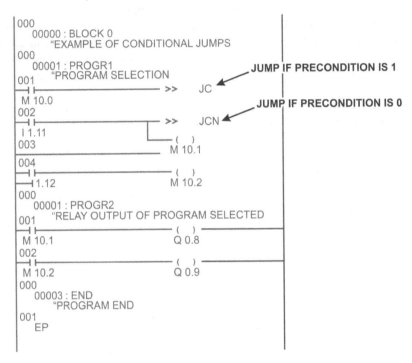

PLC I/O Sections

While the internal structure of the PLC is similar to a personal computer, its input and output are quite different than those associated with personal computers. In the ICS environment, I/O connectivity is typically made through individual, secure screw-down terminals, whereas in personal computers, it's done with Ethernet, USB, eSATA, PS2, HDMI, and VGA-specific connection ports.

The Input Section

The input section of the PLC converts electrical voltages from the individual input terminals to levels that can be processed by its digital devices (i.e., 24 Vdc or 120/240 Vac signals to digital 0/5 Vdc levels). This section also provides filter circuits to remove electrical noise from the input signals before they are introduced to the PLC's digital circuitry. The input section is galvanically isolated from the digital circuitry through opto-coupler circuits to prevent any residual electrical noise from entering the digital circuitry.

Some PLCs accept analog input signals that are converted into digital equivalents through analog-to-digital (A/D) conversion circuits before they are introduced to their digital circuitry. The input section may include *Input Voltage Source* connections, like those illustrated in Figure 2.12. These connections are used to supply compatible voltages for the PLC's input terminals and the field devices that provide its input signals. On this example, a 24 Vdc power source is supplying the same 24V potential for the PLC's input terminals and input switching devices.

FIGURE 2.12 PLC input power supply connections

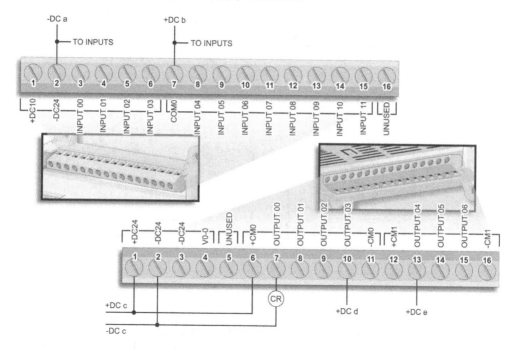

Input Sinking and Sourcing Configurations

There are two common conventions for wiring sensors to the DC input terminals of the PLC.

- *Sinking inputs*: A connection scheme where the inputs of the PLC accept conventional current flow from a sensing device
- *Sourcing inputs*: A connection scheme where the PLC's input terminals provide conventional current flow to the sensing device

Figure 2.13 provides descriptions of a typical sinking connection scheme, as well as a sourcing connection scheme. In the sinking scheme, the positive side of the power supply is attached to the away side of the sensing switches. The negative side of the power source is attached to the PLC's inputs' Common (COM) connection. When one of the switches is moved to its closed position, a conventional current flow path is established between the power source and the input's Common terminal.

FIGURE 2.13 Sinking and sourcing configurations

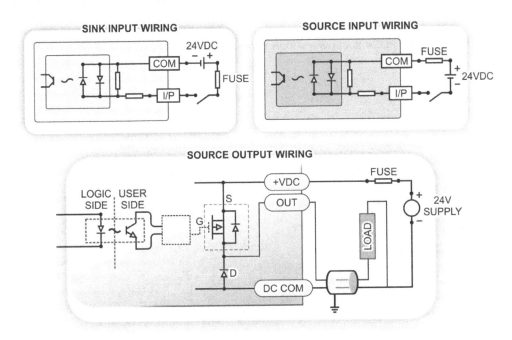

Likewise, when a sourcing scheme is in place and the signal switch moves to its closed condition, a path for conventional current flow between the PLC's input terminal and the external power supply is formed. To accomplish this, the power supply's positive side is attached to the PLC inputs' Common terminal, and its negative side is attached to the away side of the sensing devices.

The decision to wire a PLC's inputs in either a sinking or a sourcing configuration is based on the current flow requirement of the field input devices. If they are current sourcing devices, you must configure the sensor wiring for sourcing. Conversely, if the devices are sinking devices, the inputs must be configured for sinking operation. You cannot mix device types or configurations unless the PLC offers multiple common terminals associated with different input terminal groups. This information can be located in the PLC's User/Installation Guide.

The Output Section

The output unit is responsible for producing output voltages at each output terminal that reflect the real-time condition of the program's response to the PLC's input terminals. The voltages at the PLC's output terminals are then used to activate or deactivate field actuator devices. As with inputs, some PLCs provide analog output capabilities. In these cases, digital-to-analog (D/A) devices are used to convert internal digital values into representative analog output voltages. Like the input section, the output section is galvanically isolated from the PLC's digital processing circuitry.

When dealing with PLC outputs, there are two basic types of output terminals to be aware of.

- *Transistor outputs*: Outputs that are supplied by solid-state switching devices. Because these outputs are supplied through semiconductor devices, their output capabilities are limited to low-power DC signals. Such signals may be used to turn on lamps or activate external solenoids and relays, which in turn manipulate actuators.

- *Relay outputs*: Outputs that can directly interact with the relatively high load actuator devices. These outputs also provide built-in filter circuits that protect the output and the PLC from arching associated with switching high current loads, such as motors, on and off.

Figure 2.14 shows an industry-standard representation of both digital transistor outputs and relay outputs. Notice that in both cases the output sections include an output power supply connection. Some PLCs even provide multiple (separate) output power supply options for different output terminal groupings.

FIGURE 2.14   PLC output types

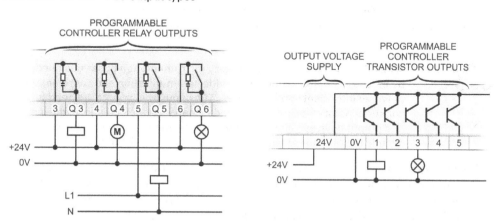

While the voltages and currents used with solid-state outputs is limited (typically = /< 24 Vdc and 0.5 Adc), the capabilities of relay outputs can be much higher (240 Vac/Vdc) and can control much higher current loads.

The input/output (I/O) capabilities of compact PLCs are limited to the number of terminals provided on the device.* However, modular PLCs make it possible to extend the numbers of input and output terminals through the addition of I/O modules to the backplane.

*Additional I/O capabilities for compact PLCs can be extended by
connecting multiple PLCs together using a field bus connection. Historically, this connection has been made through an asynchronous RS-
485 data interface.

As with PLC inputs, solid-state outputs must be physically connected correctly to make
each output circuit work. This involves establishing either sinking or sourcing paths for the
type of output drivers of the selected PLC. This can be achieved by carefully following the
PLC's installation guidelines.

PLC Implementations

As mentioned in Chapter 1, PLCs have been the preferred local controller for industrial
processing and utility operations for many years. Depending on the particular process control application, PLCs may be used in three general implementations:

- As a stand-alone controller working in a single process unit
- As a local field device operating in a DCS distributed control system
- As a local field device operating in a SCADA-based control system

Figure 2.15 depicts a PLC being used as the primary controller in a small batch
processing operation. The PLC is connected to the various input sensors and output actuators through a *field bus network*. The field bus also connects to a separate human machine
interface console to display the activities of the process and its various sensors.

A field bus is one of a few proprietary instrumentation buses designed
by industrial control groups to provide communication and coordination
between intelligent control devices. These buses eliminate the need to
construct point-to-point wiring bundles between the PLC and all the input
and output devices. The communication protocols used over these buses
include the Modbus and DNP3 protocols discussed later in the chapter.

The PLC also connects to a pair of IT computing devices through an OT local area network connection. The first is a local host computer designated as the *engineering workstation*. The second is a data storage server known as the *data historian*. This component is
responsible for recoding data obtained from field devices—PLCs, RTUs, and IECs. Because

the data historian is located on the local area network, it becomes more available to other computing devices that can connect to this type of network. This can become a major point of concern if the LAN serving the ICS network is connected to the organization's IT network.

FIGURE 2.15   Stand-alone PLC implementation

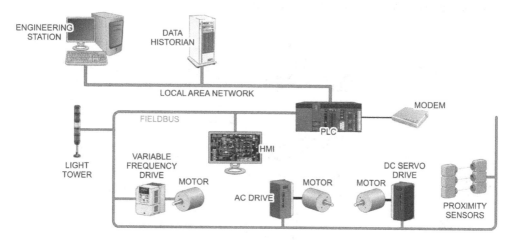

Figure 2.16 illustrates the PLC control loop from the previous example being integrated into a distributed control system, along with two other PLC-based control loops. Notice that with the control elements being added to the local area network in the previous example, the OT network has become the *local control network* in this example. The LCN is the equivalent of the local area network in an IT network. In addition, a master *DCS server* has been added to that portion of the network along with a master HMI display. These devices all reside at the supervisory level control loop of the topology.

Industrial Sensors

The starting point of all process control operations is the sensor. These devices convert the value of a measured physical quantity such as temperature, fluid flow rate, or pressure into a corresponding signal (pressure, electrical, differential pressure, etc.) that can be understood by a control system.

Some commonly used industrial sensing devices include the following:

- *Thermocouples* that convert temperature into corresponding millivolt signals
- *Turbine meters* that convert flow rates of liquids into corresponding pulse rates or voltages

- *Orifice plates* that convert flow rates into corresponding differential pressures
- *Flexible diaphragms* that convert pressure into mechanical energy
- *Photocells* that convert light energy into a corresponding electrical energy
- *Switches* that convert physical position into electrical signals

FIGURE 2.16   DCS-based PLC implementation

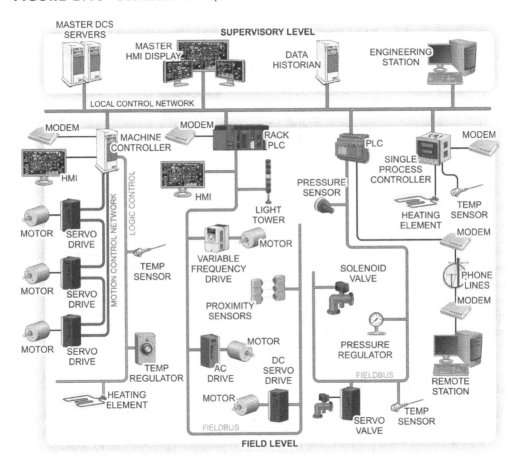

Industrial process control equipment manufacturers have adopted a number of standard signal ranges for the transmission and processing of process information. Information signals may be transmitted in digital formats, where the signal assumes one of two possible levels—high or low—to represent that state of the variable. The following are standard digital signal levels used in industrial processes:

- 0 and 5 Vdc for integrated circuits 0 and 24 Vdc for inter-device control circuits
- 0 and 120 Vac for switch/relay control circuitry

NOTE

Digital On/Off signals can be referred to as *bit signals*, as opposed to analog signals, which can be referred to as *value signals*.

Information and control signals may also be produced and transmitted in analog formats where the signal level can vary through an infinite number of values between a high limit and a low limit. These signals may be transmitted in the form of voltages/currents or as pneumatic/hydraulic pressures. Some sample standard ranges for these types of signals include the following:

- 0 to 5 Vdc
- 4 to 20 mA
- 3 to 15 lbs of pressure

NOTE

Notice that nearly all of these ranges have a lower limit somewhere above 0 because of the difficulty of precisely measuring and verifying a zero quantity.

In an industrial process setting, this sampling process must occur in real time (without delay or jitter). This dependence on real-time sensor data is a fundamental difference between OT and information-based IT systems. Without real-time sampling, the process controller may not be able to respond in a timely fashion to variations in the PV. This leads to poor regulation of the PV.

In some cases, the measurement process must be performed in two steps: *measurement* and *translation*. In cases when there is no direct correlation between the output signals of the sensor measuring the PV and an input value that the controller can understand and work with, a *transducer* must be placed between the two components to translate the sensor's output signal into one the controller can accept, as described in Figure 2.17.

FIGURE 2.17 Input signal processing blocks

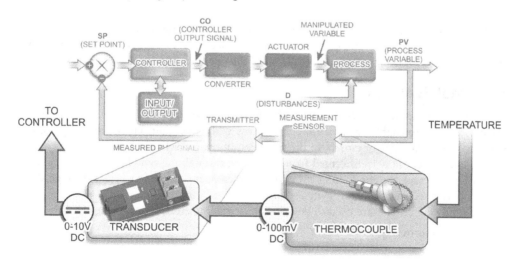

As the figure illustrates, the transducer must be capable of receiving the output of the given sensor and converting it into a corresponding signal that is compatible with the particular controller. In many applications, the transducer must be *calibrated* so that the zero point and signal range of the sensor's output (span) is faithfully converted into a corresponding signal that matches the controller's zero point and operates within its signal range.

In this case, a thermocouple is measuring the temperature inside a furnace. Thermocouples are bimetallic devices that generate a range of millivoltages over a range of temperatures. The usable range of the thermocouple depends on the two types of metal used to create it. The level of these voltages is very small when compared to standard controller input ranges, such as a 0–5 Vdc analog input range.

A transducer is needed to convert the thermocouple's range of millivoltages into a 0–5 Vdc signal. This conversion could be accomplished with a simple amplifier. However, mapping the output of this thermocouple to the inputs of a digital controller would require an *analog-to-digital (A/D) conversion* process. Some *intelligent sensors* package the sensing device with an A/D circuit and an embedded microprocessor, as depicted in Figure 2.18, so that they can communicate directly with the controller, a master controller, or other types of control systems.

FIGURE 2.18   Smart sensors

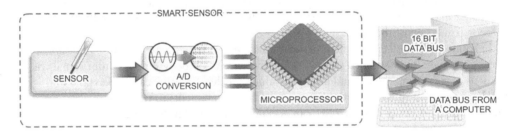

Because sensors are the fundamental elements in any industrial control system, they represent a significant target to attackers. If they can gain access to the sensor or its communication path to the controller, they can compromise the operation of the entire process.

Industrial Switches

The most widely used industrial sensor is the electromechanical *switch*. Electrical switches are devices used to enable or interrupt current flow within a circuit. There are two possible states for a switch: *open* or *closed*. In the *open* condition, a mechanical gap is created in the circuit, and current flow is prevented from occurring through the switch. When the contacts are pushed together, the conducting circuit is completed, and current can flow through the switch. This is referred to as the switch's *closed* state.

The following criteria are used to describe electrical and electronic switches:

- Poles and throws

- Actuation method
- Passive/active state configuration

Poles and Throws

Switches contain two key mechanisms—movable internal circuit contacts and fixed external circuit connection points. These elements are referred to as *poles* (the number of internal contacts) and throws (the number of possible connection points or external circuits the switch can connect to).

- *Single pole, single throw (SPST)*: SPST switches are simple On/Off switches. Figure 2.19 shows the schematic symbol for an SPST switch. As the figure illustrates, there is a single internal contact point represented by a small circle and a movable contact. These two pieces of the figure represent the "pole." In this figure there is a gap between the end of the movable contact and the fixed contact of the circuit connection point (the throw).

  When the switch is in its normal state (as drawn), the gap represents a physical break in the circuit that prevents current from flowing through the switch. However, when the switch is activated, you can envision the circle and movable contact representing the pole as rotating downward, so the movable contact makes physical connection with the fixed contact, allowing current to flow through the completed circuit path.

  When the switch is deactivated, you can imagine that the pole components rotate counterclockwise, away from the fixed contact, breaking the circuit and cutting off the path for current flow.

FIGURE 2.19   An SPST switch

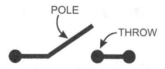

- *Single pole, double throw (SPDT)*: SPDT switches, like the one depicted in Figure 2.20, offer a single movable pole contact and two fixed external circuit contacts. When the switch is in its normal position (as drawn), the movable contact is against fixed contact A (throw 1). This shows a complete path for current through the pole to circuit 1.

  However, there is no connection to the other throw and circuit. When the switch is activated, the pole rotates so that the movable contact makes a connection with fixed contact B (throw 2). This breaks the circuit with contact 1 and creates a circuit path through throw 2 and circuit 2.

  When discussing double throw switches, you may encounter two different varieties: true double throw switches that can also be described as changeover switches. This definition refers to the switch only being able to change from one throw to another. However, there are other DT switches that offer a stable, unconnected center or off position. You may see these switches designated as XXCO (such as SP Change Over) or XXTT (for triple throw, even though the center position is never an active circuit).

FIGURE 2.20   An SPDT switch

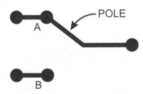

- *Double pole, single throw (DPST)*: DPST switches, like the one shown in Figure 2.21, have two movable contacts and two fixed contacts. Notice that the movable contacts are connected in the diagram via a dotted line. This dotted line represents a mechanical connection between the movable contacts that forces them move as a single entity.

   Because the electrical circuits are completely insulated from each other, this DPST switch functions like two separate SPST switches that are mechanically linked together. Because there is a single movement to make or break the external circuits, this type of switch is considered to have a single throw.

FIGURE 2.21   A DPST switch

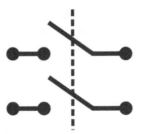

- *Double pole, double throw (DPDT)*: DPDT switches, as depicted in Figure 2.22, act like two separate SPDT switches that are mechanically linked together like the DPST switch earlier. The mechanical linkage forces both poles to rotate away from fixed contacts 1A and 1B and into contact with fixed contacts 2A and 2B when the switch is activated.

   While other complex switch contact arrangements do exist in the market, the fundamental switch types just discussed cover the majority of all switches you are likely to encounter in the ICS field.

FIGURE 2.22   A DPDT switch

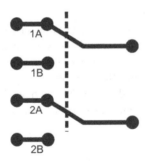

Actuation Methods

Switches are also characterized by the way they are activated. The *switch actuator* is typically a mechanical device that moves the switch's contacts apart (or together) through some type of mechanical linkage. Common switch activation methods include the following:

- *Toggle switches*: A *toggle switch* employs a mechanical lever to move the switch contacts from one condition to the other. Typically, human interaction is used to manually position the switch lever. This action is illustrated in Figure 2.23.

FIGURE 2.23   A typical toggle switch

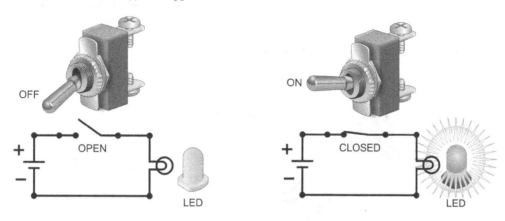

- *Rocker switches*: *Rocker switches* are closely related to toggle switches. The mechanical activation portion of the switch is a rocking mechanism that activates and deactivates the switching mechanism, as shown in Figure 2.24.

FIGURE 2.24   Rocker switches

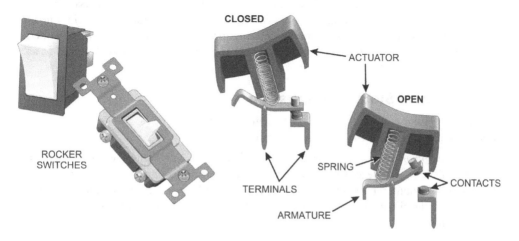

- *Push button switches*: *Push button switches* possess an actuator mechanism that is operated by pushing in on the actuator button. This type of switch can be designed so that the action is a "Push to make" or a "Push to break" configuration. In a push-to-make configuration, the switch contacts are pushed together when the actuator button is pressed. This action completes the circuit, and current can flow through the switch.

  Of course, in a *push-to-break switch*, pressing on the actuator causes the switch's contacts to come apart, so the circuit is broken, and no current will flow. The symbols used to designate these types of actions are shown in Figure 2.25. *Emergency stop switches* for gas pumps and heavy equipment are prime examples of push-to-break switches. When the switch is pressed, the circuit is broken, and the pump or equipment stops working.

FIGURE 2.25   Push-to-make/break switches

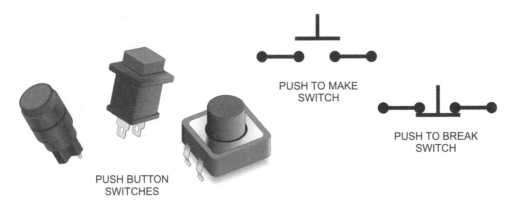

- *Momentary contact switches*: Up to this point, the descriptions for switching actions have indicated that when a switch is set to its active or inactive state, it stays there until it is changed through additional human interaction. However, there is a class of switches designed so that the switching action occurs only while the interaction is maintained or for a predetermined time. When the interacting force is removed or the activation period expires, the switch action reverts to its original state. These switches are referred to as *momentary contact switches*.

Passive/Active State Configuration

Another terminology commonly used with switches is their resting or nonactuated condition—also known as their "normal" condition.

- *Normally open*: With a *normally open* (also denoted as *NO*) switch, when the activation mechanism is in its deactivated (normal) state, the circuit is open, and no current will flow through the switch contacts, as depicted in Figure 2.26. When the switch is activated, the circuit shifts into the other state—closed—and current can flow through the switch.

FIGURE 2.26   NO and NC switches

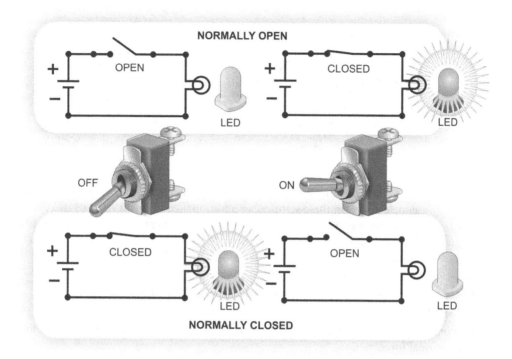

- *Normally closed*: Conversely, a switch that is designated as *normally closed (NC)* will have its contacts made when the switch activator is in its deactivated position and current can flow through the switch. When the actuator is moved into the active state, the contacts are moved away from each other, and the circuit is opened. No current will flow through the switch in this state.

There are switches, such as the double-throw switches described earlier, that possess both an NO and an NC set of contacts in the same switch. When the switch is activated, each contact pair will switch to its active designation.

Final Control Elements/Actuators

On the other end of the process control system, the *final control element* accepts a correction signal from the controller and responds accordingly to manipulate the process variable. In some cases, this can be accomplished through a direct connection between the controller and the final element, as illustrated in Figure 2.27. This example shows an electric controller with an analog output supplying varying levels of electrical current to an electrical heating element inside a warming oven. The capabilities and output type of this controller are sufficient to directly drive the heating element. Therefore, no transducer or interfacing mechanism is required for this portion of the control loop.

FIGURE 2.27   Direct final element control

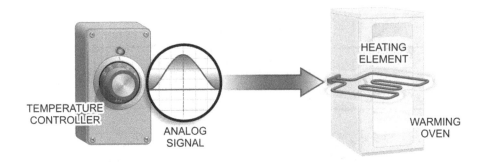

However, most industrial controllers are digital electrical devices, and many final elements are analog and nonelectrical. In these settings, an additional component referred to as an *actuator* is required. The actuator is the part of the control element that supplies and transmits a measured amount of energy for the operation of another mechanism or system. In other words, it controls the actions of the actual *control mechanism*.

Typical industrial actuators include the following:

- *Electric motors*: Devices that convert electrical energy into rotational mechanical energy (motion)

- *Pneumatic actuators*: Devices that convert pneumatic energy (compressed air) into linear or rotational force/motion

- *Hydraulic actuators*: Devices such as pistons that convert hydraulic pressure (compressed liquids) into linear force/motion

- *Electric solenoids/relays*: Electrical switching devices that convert On/Off electrical signals into other levels of On/Off electrical signals

As this list shows, typical industrial actuators have very different input requirements than are available directly from a typical industrial controller. In many cases there are at least two steps involved in getting the corrective information from the controller into a format needed to provide efficient control of a process.

In the first step, the digital output of the controller needs to be converted into an analog signal that is compatible with the final control element. This requires a *digital-to-analog (D/A) conversion* process, which is the opposite of the A/D process required for many sensors.

Depending on the type of actuator involved, the second step of the signal conditioning process may be to amplify the analog electrical signal to make it powerful enough to work with the final element, or it may have to be converted into a corresponding nonelectrical signal, such as a pneumatic pressure, as illustrated in Figure 2.28.

FIGURE 2.28   Actuator signal conversion

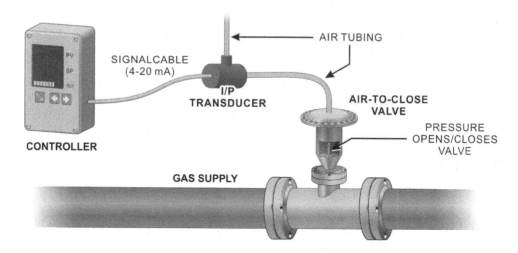

Relays

A *relay* is an electromechanical switching device used to control the operation of electrical circuits. It consists of two major components, as illustrated in Figure 2.29. The main component is an *electromagnetic coil* with a movable electromechanical armature. The *coil* and its connections represent the controlling circuit in the relay. The other major component is one or more sets of *electrical contacts* with external connection points. The contacts and connection points are the basis of the controlled circuit (or circuits).

FIGURE 2.29   A typical industrial relay structure

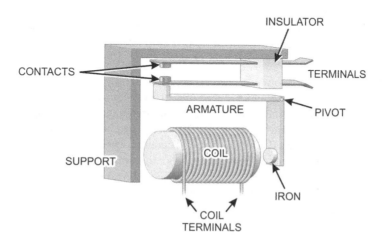

When current flows through the relay coil, the magnetic armature is forced to move because of its reaction with the electromagnetic field generated by the coil. When the armature moves, the mechanical linkage will also move the movable portion of the contact set. Depending on the design of the contact set, the motion of the armature may cause the two halves of the contact set to come together (also referred to as *making*) or to move apart (referred to as *breaking*).

Because the two parts of the contact set are attached to an external circuit, as illustrated in Figure 2.30, when the contacts make, a circuit path is created and the external circuit is energized. Conversely, when the contacts break, an open is created and the path is broken. This of course prevents current from flowing through the circuit controlled by the relay.

FIGURE 2.30 The controlled circuit

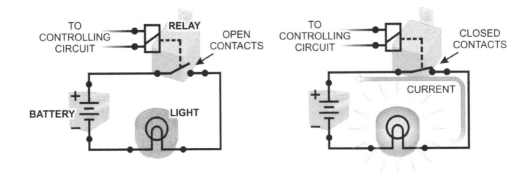

When there is no current flowing in the relay coil, both the relay and the circuits connected to its contacts are said to be in their "normal" states.

Passing a current through the coil sends the relay, its contacts, and their attached circuits into their "active" states. While this state exists, it is not typically used to describe the operation of the relay or its circuits—only the normal state is referred to.

Relay Logic

Before intelligent controllers were introduced into process control, the relay was the most widely used electronic final element. Relays were also used to create very sophisticated digital control systems. It was common for multiple relays to be interconnected in different configurations to provide digital control of complicated processes.

These formats and interconnection techniques became so standardized in the process control industry that they have continued into the design and operation of microprocessor-based intelligent controllers. Even in these environments both logical and physical outputs are still commonly referred to as coils.

Of course, the coils control the states of one or more contacts associated with the coil.

Figure 2.31 shows a type of electrical diagram called a *ladder logic diagram*, commonly used with relays in industry. By convention, the vertical line on the left side of the diagram represents the voltage side of the power source, and the vertical line on the right side represents the ground connection.

FIGURE 2.31   Relay ladder logic diagram

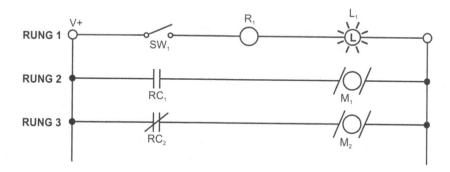

The relay is shown in the drawing in its two basic parts—its coil and its contact sets. The coil (R1) is shown on the top horizontal line (rung #1) as being in series with a switch and a light. The relay's contact sets (RC1 and RC2) are shown on the middle and bottom horizontal lines (rungs 2 and 3) as being in series with two different motors, the forward motor (M1) and the reverse motor (M2). RC1 is shown as a normally open contact (an open space between the two contacts), while RC2 is shown as a normally closed contact (the slash mark indicates a path of current between the two contacts).

When switch SW1 is open, as shown in the diagram, there is no path of current through rung 1, so the coil of the relay is not energized. Therefore, contact RC1 will be in its normal (open) state, and RC2 will be in its normal (closed) state. Because RC1 is open, no path exists for current to pass through motor M1. Therefore, the motor will not run. On the other hand, the closed state of RC2 does provide a path for current to flow through motor M2. Therefore, the reverse motor will run.

When SW1 is closed, a current path is created through the relay coil, and it becomes energized. This, in turn, causes the armature to move inside the coil, and contacts RC1 and RC2 move to their active states. In the case of RC1, the contact goes closed and provides a current path through M1, causing it to run. The RC2 contact moves to the open state and breaks the current path through M2, causing it to stop.

The coil will remain energized, and the contacts will remain in their active states as long as SW1 remains closed. If the switch is opened again, the coil will de-energize, and the contacts will revert to their normal states—the reverse motor will run, and the forward motor will stop.

Programming the PLC

One of the biggest features of using PLCs in control systems is the ability to redefine their operation whenever the process changes. Today the production line may be set up to produce plastic forks, and tomorrow it will be creating plastic spoons and the day after plastic knives. After that, the line may be used to bring together small packages of salt and pepper to be shipped in a package with the items made the first three days. With the PLC, different prewritten programs can be uploaded into the device as needed to control all of these operations.

There are three common methods of programming PLCs:

- Using graphical software tools that create *ladder diagrams* (LDs) like those described earlier

- Software tools that build *function charts* (FCs), which can be converted into PLC code

- Programming tools that can be used to build strategies directly from the PLC's *instruction set* (IS)

In each case, the software package selected to generate the PLC control program provides the programming interface, as well as the tools required to translate the instructions created into *machine code* (1s and 0s) that the PLC's microprocessor can run.

For modern PLCs, the programming software is located and runs on the engineer's station, which is typically a personal computer. When the program is needed, it can be transferred to the PLC via field bus link, to the network connection, or directly from the PC. Some newer PLCs even provide micro-SD card slots that allow existing programs to be uploaded directly into the device.

Process Units

In Chapter 1 you were introduced to process units. Recall that process units were described as groups of operations within a production system that could be defined and separated from the other unit processes of the system. Figure 2.32 depicts a portion of a simple production line that consists of three separate operations. However, the ICS solution for this portion of the production line divides the overall process into two process units:

- *Process unit 1*: A conveyor belt/product-sorting system (consisting of two distinct operations)

- *Process unit 2*: A product transfer system (consisting of two distinct operations)

When an item is placed in the Entry zone of the conveyor, a proximity switch detects it and alerts PLC-1 that it is present. The PLC will energize the conveyor's drive motor to move the product down the belt. As it moves, the product's size is sensed through a set of light emitters/sensor combinations that sense the height (short or tall) of the item as it passes by. This information is also read by the PLC.

FIGURE 2.32 A multiprocess unit production system

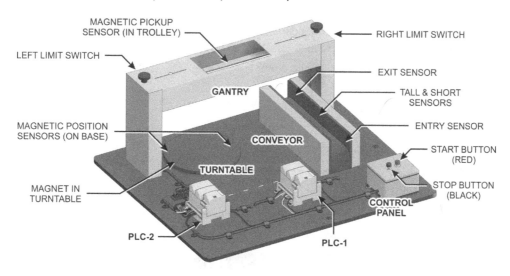

If the size of the item is determined to be correct, the PLC will stop the conveyor belt when the item is detected in the Exit zone of the conveyor belt. If the item is not the correct height, the PLC's programming will cause the belt to continue moving, dumping the defective part off the end of the belt.

The second process unit consists of an overhead gantry used to move the production item across the plant, and a turntable assembly that receives the product from the gantry and positions it for pickup by a robotic arm. Because these two machines require relatively few physical I/O connections, a single controller (PLC-2) has been tasked with managing both operations. In addition, there is no procedural reason for the operations of the two devices to be performed separately.

When PLC-1 stops the product item on the end of its conveyor, it notifies PLC-2 that it is available for pickup. This can be done through a field bus link established between the PLCs or through an Ethernet network connection, as illustrated in Figure 2.33.

PLC-2 checks the current position of the gantry's trolley module (left, right, or somewhere in between) and causes the trolley to move left until it reaches the pickup area. The PLC detects that the trolley is in position through a magnet and magnetic reed switch sensor and energizes the magnetic pickup on the bottom of the trolley's lift. This causes the metal top of the product to be attracted to the lift.

With the pickup magnet energized, the PLC causes the trolley to move to the left until it senses another magnet positioned at the drop zone location. At this point the PLC stops the trolley motor and de-energizes the lift's pickup magnet. The product drops onto the turntable's landing zone.

Next, PLC-2 energizes the turntable's drive motor, which causes it to turn until the PLC detects a magnet positioned at the stop zone. It then de-energizes the turntable motor, and the product is available for the robot to pick up.

FIGURE 2.33   PLC communication connections

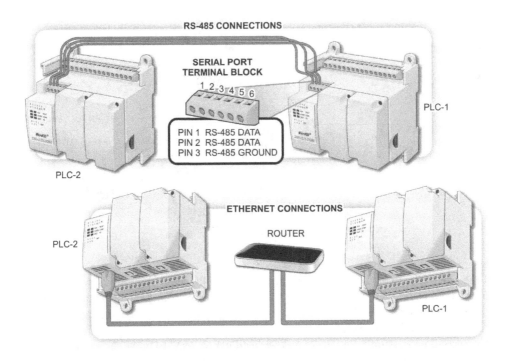

While the entire process depicted here could be controlled by a single PLC that possesses enough I/O capacity to handle all the physical input and output connections required, the designer chose to implement the ICS based on two smaller, compact PLCs. Conversely, the designer could also have chosen to allocate an individual PLC to each piece of equipment in the system and connect them together through one of the communication arrangements described earlier.

In this example, the PLC selected possesses only 12 digital inputs. Therefore, it can interface only with a process that has 12 or fewer variables that must be monitored. Likewise, if the PLC provides only seven digital or relay output channels and the process requires more than that number of variables to be controlled, then another controller must be found with sufficient output channels to handle the process. In other words, a given PLC can handle only the number of inputs and outputs as provided by its physical connection terminals.

Another factor that could prevent a single controller from effectively controlling a given process is its computational or decision-making power. If the device is too slow or does not possess enough computational resources to keep up with the decisions that have to be made to maintain control of the process, then a different controller must be found.

For microprocessor-based controllers, this is dependent on several factors—their processor bus sizes, processor clock speeds, and memory capacities. The controller's performance is also a function of the programming code written for the particular process. Overly complex or bloated programming code may not execute efficiently and prevent the controller from keeping up with the process control requirements.

Industrial Network Protocols

As with IT networks, the operation of OT networks must be governed by *protocols*. While IT networks have evolved over time to embrace the Ethernet and TCP/IP protocols for their primary networking standards, the industrial controls industry has generated a number of proprietary ICS protocols aimed at meeting the specific challenges associated with process control. However, many of these protocols have been further developed to work with Ethernet. In the end, the main concern of any protocol discussion is this: *Are there field and control devices available that do what needs to be done and that are compatible with the protocol in question?* A major consideration when designing or upgrading an ICS solution is to select field and control devices that perform the necessary functions for the process and that are compatible in terms of the protocol selected for the network. Remember, everything in the OT network must be using the same language.

Common Industrial Protocols

The *Open DeviceNet Vendors Association (ODVA)* created the *Common Industrial Protocol (CIP)* standard for their members to use in developing industrial networked products. CIP is a media-independent, object-oriented protocol that spans a suite of services for OT networks. CIP provides a vehicle for integrating several ICS-specific applications—such as configuration, control, synchronization, safety, and data—into a communication architecture that can work with the Ethernet networks used in the enterprise side of production organizations.

CIP is the basis of several other OT standard protocols including *EtherNet/IP*, *DeviceNet*, *CompoNet*, and *ControlNet*. These protocols compete, along with the *ProfiNet/ProfiBus* protocols, for market share in the industrial control network space. However, two protocols command 60 percent of that market: *EtherNet/IP* and *ProfiNet*. The following sections discuss these two protocols in greater detail.

EtherNet/IP Protocol

The adoption of Ethernet-based technologies and related techniques has led to a convergence of organizational IT networks with their industrial control network counterparts. With both portions of the network integrated into a cohesive data communications vehicle, the organization is able to apply real-time production data to its business-making decisions.

One of the keys to the OT/IT network integration process is the development of protocols that combine traditional OT functions with IT networks. Just as IT networks have expanded the TCP/IP protocol to carry audio and video signals across Ethernet networks, the ICS industry has developed similar techniques to transfer industrial signals and data across those networks. In all cases, the key became how to load ICS information into an Ethernet data frame.

The *EtherNet/IP protocol* was originally developed by Rockwell Automation for its Allen Bradley line of PLCs. Built on the CIP protocol, EtherNet/IP began in the early 1990s and has developed into one of the most widely accepted industrial protocols in the United States. Basically, it consists of CIP information being transferred between OT devices across Ethernet connections. It employs the TCP/IP suite of protocols and IEEE 802.x as its base and then integrates the CIP functions described earlier to provide ICS services for real-time control capabilities that extend to a wide variety of industrial products. The industrial Ethernet/IP protocol provides significantly better performance than similar standard Ethernet and TCP/IP networks.

For example, the EtherNet/IP protocol uses UDP packets for transferring basic data between nodes, as well as using TCP packets to upload and download device programs, set points, and data sets between network devices.

When referencing the industrial network protocol, the IP in EtherNet/IP stands for Industrial Protocol, not Internet Protocol.

The EtherNet/IP network is organized into two types of devices according to their communication roles:

- *Scanner devices*: Devices that open connections and initiate transfers
- *Adapter devices*: Devices that supply data to the scanner devices

These communicating devices include industrial robots, PLCs, smart sensors, smart actuators, and industrial machines, such as *Computer Numerical Control* (CNC) machines (routers, mills, and lathes). Like all other network devices, these devices must be equipped with physical connectivity to work with the network media, as well as protocol-specific device drivers, services, and applications.

Because EtherNet/IP is built on the TCP/IP stack, it is relatively easy to integrate ICS devices with enterprise servers and the Internet.

Modbus

The de facto standard communication protocol for interconnecting intelligent industrial control devices is known as *Modbus*. Modbus is a serial communication protocol that was developed specifically to provide networking capabilities for industrial control applications. Because it was designed specifically for these applications, Modbus was optimized to provide quick, low-overhead communications that do not include a great deal of data security features.

Modbus is derived from Modicon Bus, the company that originated the PLC.

It can be used to connect up to 254 devices together in an industrial control network. In particular, it is widely used to provide DCS or SCADA service between RTUs and the DCS or SCADA Main/Secondary. The devices can transmit a wide variety of different data types, such as temperature or pressure readings, across the network to the Main controller.

As with all other network communication schemes, the devices connected to the bus are assigned a unique address. One of the node addresses will be specified as the server that is responsible for initiating all network commands. Common Modbus frame formats include RTU-specific frames, ASCII character frames, and TCP frames. These different frame types are not interoperable between devices.

Physical implementation for serial communication Modbus versions occurs over RS-232 or RS-485 serial communication links. However, there is also a Modbus version that is used with Ethernet networks. The Modbus specification that works with TCP frames is referred to as *Modbus TCP/IP* and is designed to control and supervise OT equipment in intranet or Internet environments. Because the different Modbus protocol variants are not interchangeable, Modbus TCP devices must be used with this format. TCP port 502 is used to support the TCP/IP connection between a Modbus client and server.

The RS-232 connection and communication scheme was an integral part of the computer and personal computer market for many years—until it was replaced by the smarter, faster, more flexible Universal Serial Bus (USB) and FireWire (IEEE-1394) high-speed serial connection protocols.

ProfiNet/ProfiBus

ProfiNet, also known as *Process Field Net*, is an Ethernet-based industrial networking protocol developed in Germany to be a real-time Ethernet. This protocol suite incorporates three protocol levels to provide the very high-speed data transfers required for efficient control of some industrial processes.

- A basic TCP/IP protocol component (ProfiNet Component Based Automation [CBA] for production plants).

- A relatively quick *Real Time* (RT) protocol (ProfiNet CBA for IO applications). Profi-Net RT can provide sampling rates up to 4,000 per second.

- A very high-speed *Isochronous Real Time* (IRT) transfer protocol (ProfiNet IO). Newer versions of IRT can provide sampling rates up to 32,000 per second.

The *isochronous protocol* uses transmission techniques similar to the protocols built into high-speed USB ports to carry out streaming audio and video transfers. Devices attached to the ProfiNet network negotiate with each other to determine compatible packet sizes. After both sides have determined the packet size, the transmission between the devices can occur in a burst mode operation (unlike frame-by-frame transfers that occur in asynchronous and synchronous communications).

Each device attached to the ProfiNet network is identified by three types of addresses:

- *Its MAC address*: As with other network devices, this address is imprinted in the hardware piece and changes if the device is exchanged.

- *An IP address*: The IP address enables dynamic addressing techniques to be used to identify the device. The allocation of these addresses can be performed through Profi-Net's Discovery and Basic Configuration Protocol (DCP) process or through the DHCP process used in IT networks. DCP is mainly used in network environments that do not possess a DHCP server.

- *A device name*: This name provides a fixed identification for the device.

ProfiNet provides a flexible high-speed, highly deterministic industrial network system running over Ethernet cabling terminated in 8P8C or Euro-style M12 locking connectors. It has been widely adopted in several industry areas, such as manufacturing automation, building automation, process automation, and the power generation/distribution industry, as well as industrial safety control systems, high reliability systems, and redundancy systems.

The ProfiNet protocol is built on the *ProfiBus* field bus protocol originally created by Siemans in Germany to replace the aging 0–20mA standards of the time. It was designed to provide a bidirectional field bus standard for industrial control manufacturers to develop products against. Over time, it has been extended and refined into two distinct varieties of ProfiBus:

- *ProfiBus for "decentralized" peripherals (ProfiBus DP)*: The main version of ProfiBus that is used with ProfiBus sensors and actuators. Communications are conducted over a two-wire RS-485 twisted-pair cable that carries both power and data.

- *ProfiBus for Process Automation (ProfiBus PA)*: This ProfiBus variant is designed specifically to work in hazardous areas where explosive conditions might exist. This is primarily based on specialized cabling that delivers power directly to the field devices through the bus at current levels low enough to prevent ignition from occurring in the case of an event.

DNP3

The *Distributed Network Protocol (DNP3)* is actually a suite of open, public industrial communication protocols that was developed by the Harris Distributed Automation Products company to provide networking between central SCADA masters and different types of remotes (controllers such as IEDs, PLCs, and RTUs) in electrical grid systems. It is a newer standard than Modbus that functions as a layer 2 protocol with layer 4 and layer 7 components. While it was originally developed for use in electrical power grids, DNP3 has found its way into water utility SCADA systems. The maintenance, development, and ownership of the protocol standard continues under the DNP3 Users Group.

The protocol is fairly simple to work with. It specifies 27 basic function codes that can be used to exchange data between the main and secondary devices. Some are for obtaining data from the remotes, while the others are for configuring the remote's settings. One code is reserved to be used by the remote to notify the master when an alarm condition occurs in its operations. TCP port 2000 is used to facilitate communications between the DNP3 devices in the network.

DNP3 is commonly used to provide serial connectivity within utility substations as well as between substations and the SCADA master located in the remote control center. Within the substation, DNP3 runs on RS-232/485 serial connections or over TCP/IP Ethernet networking. Long-distance links are accomplished by using modems and phone lines or by using one of the other long-distance communication technologies described earlier.

DNP3 was designed to optimize the movement of OT data and commands from one device to another. This made DNP3 susceptible to all types of traditional network attacks including man-in-the-middle and spoofing attacks. Later developments have added authentication features to the protocol to enhance SCADA security. These include enclosing the DNP3 protocol in an SSL/TLS and IPSec protocol wrapper.

ICCP

The *Inter-Control Center Communications Protocol (ICCP)* has been adopted by utilities throughout the world and is used for real-time data communication between SCADA Master servers, utility control centers, and utilities across wide areas networks. In the United States this protocol is used to interconnect groups of utilities to improve the coordination of production and distribution across regional grid participants.

ICCP is a client-server networking system primarily running on TCP/IP Ethernet. However, it does not provide innate authentication or encryption protection, so these features must be supplied through an alternative means.

OPC

The *Open Platform Connectivity (OPC)* protocol standard is a widely accepted industrial client-server specification designed to facilitate the exchange of data between industrial control applications and intelligent control devices. OPC was originally designed to bring Microsoft/Windows products into the industrial control world. However, over time the OPC standard has evolved so that it can also be used with non-Microsoft platforms.

The purpose of developing the protocol was to create a common structure that SCADA hardware and software manufacturers could design to. This increases the interoperability of hardware servers and SCADA software packages (servers and clients).

BACnet

The *Building Automation and Control network (BACnet)* protocol was developed by the American Society of Heating, Refrigerating and Air Conditioning Engineers for networking building automation equipment together. Some BACnet networks are IP-based (BACnet/IP), while others are RS-485, Main/Secondary token passing (BACnet MS/TP) systems.

BACnet-compliant devices communicate with each other over these networks. Typical BACnet devices include those used in HVAC control systems, fire detection systems, lighting systems, and access control systems. BACnet also employs a number of BACnet-compliant network connectivity devices such as BAS routers, gateways, and controllers. TCP port 47808 is used to support TCP/IP connections between BACnet /IP devices.

BACnet has been shown to suffer from design vulnerabilities that leave it open to many different types of cybersecurity attacks—as is the case with most OT network protocols. One assessment lists 19 different BACnet services and 5 BACnet features that are vulnerable to different types of cybersecurity attacks.

Enterprise Network Protocols

Because organizations have based their IT networks on Ethernet technology and the *Transmission Control Protocol/Internet Protocol (TCP/IP)* protocol suite, it is only natural that the OT network engineers and administrators will have to deal with these technologies as well. The remaining sections of this chapter will discuss these technologies in detail.

TCP/IP

The US Department of Defense originally developed the TCP/IP protocol as a protocol for transmitting data across a network. It is considered to be one of the most secure of the network protocols. Because the US government developed TCP/IP, no one actually owns it, so it was adopted as the transmission standard for the Internet. Because of its capability to connect with many types of computers and servers, TCP/IP is used in the majority of all networks and is the preferred network protocol for all current systems.

No matter what type of computing device or software is being used, information must move across the network in the form of TCP/IP packets. This protocol calls for data to be grouped together in bundles called *network packets*. The TCP/IP packet is designed primarily to allow for message fragmentation and reassembly. It exists through two header fields, the IP header and the TCP header, followed by the data field, as illustrated in Figure 2.34.

The TCP/IP protocol was so widely accepted by the Internet community that virtually every computer operating system supports it, including Apple, Android, Windows, UNIX, Linux, and even networked printers. It can also be used on any topology. Therefore, all of these computer types can exchange data across a network using the TCP/IP protocol.

Over time, the TCP/IP protocol has expanded to include many options that network technicians and administrators must understand to ensure proper configuration and operation of TCP/IP systems. First, the TCP/IP protocol is not a single protocol; it is actually a suite of protocols that were originally developed by the Department of Defense in 1969. TCP/IP consists of two main parts: Transmission Control Protocol (TCP) and Internet Protocol (IP). These protocols work together with a number of other protocols in a structure referred to as a *protocol stack*.

FIGURE 2.34   TCP/IP packet

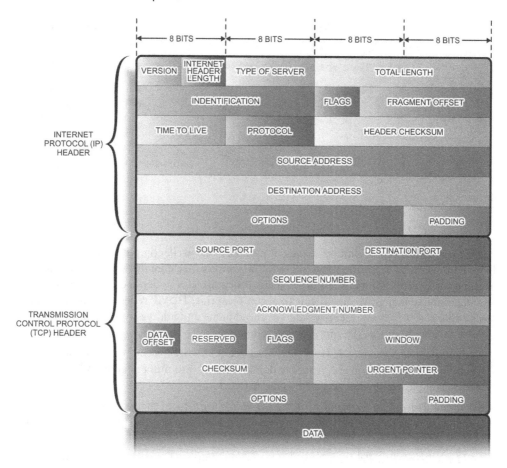

As mentioned earlier, the most important function of the network protocol is to make sure that information gets to the network location it is intended for. Ultimately this is the real function of the TCP/IP protocol. It accomplishes this by routing packets of information to locations specified by IP addresses. In the previous figure, you should have noticed that the TCP/IP header contained two addresses: the source address that the message comes from and the destination address that it is being sent to, as depicted in Figure 2.35.

FIGURE 2.35   TCP/IP routing

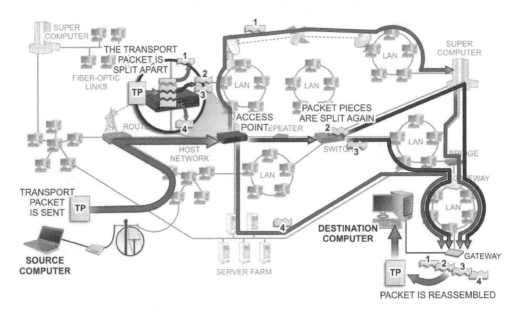

Because humans don't relate to strings of numbers very well, computers are typically identified by name. For information to get to the address that humans want it to go, there has to be some resolution between the numerical IP addresses understood by computers and the alphanumeric names we give them. To accomplish this, TCP/IP relies on a group of protocols and services that represent special advanced name and address resolution functions.

These protocols and services include the following:

- *Domain Name System (DNS) service*: A service that works with the hierarchical DNS naming system that converts readable domain names into numerical IP addresses used to locate computing devices attached to the network

- *Dynamic Host Configuration Protocol (DHCP)*: A protocol that is used by ISPs and other networks to automatically assign users IP addresses from a rotating pool of available addresses

- *Address Resolution Protocol (ARP)*: This protocol/utility is used to translate IP addresses to MAC addresses. Network devices use tables referred to as ARP caches to store ARP information (IP and MAC addresses) from other network devices they have communicated with.

Because the Internet is basically a huge TCP/IP network in which no two computers connected to it can have the same address, networks connected to the Internet must follow a specific IP addressing scheme assigned by an *Internet service provider* (ISP). However, any IP addressing scheme can be used as long as your network is not connected to the Internet. This is referred to as a *private network*.

When configuring a private network, you must design an IP addressing scheme to use across the network. Although, technically, you could use any IP addressing scheme you want in a private network without consulting an ISP, special ranges of network addresses in each IP class have been reserved for use with private networks. These are reserved addresses that are not registered to anyone on the Internet.

If you are configuring a private network, you should use one of these address options rather than create a random addressing scheme. The total number of clients on the network typically dictates which IP addressing class you should use. The following list of private network IP addresses can be used:

- *An IP address of 10.0.0.0, with the subnet mask of 255.0.0.0*: This Class A range provides more than 16 million private IP addresses.

- *An IP address of 169.254.0.0, with the subnet mask of 255.255.255.0 (the Microsoft AIPA default)*: This Class C range provides 254 private IP addresses.

- *An IP address of 172.(16-32).0.0, with the subnet mask of 255.240.0.0*: This Class B range provides 65,000 private IP addresses.

- *An IP address of 192.168.0.0, with the subnet mask of 255.255.0.0*: This Class C range provides 254 private IP addresses.

In addition, remember that all hosts must have the same network ID and subnet mask and that no two computers on your network can have the same IP address when you are establishing a private IP addressing scheme.

Domain Name System

To communicate with another computer in a TCP/IP network, your computer must have the IP address of the destination host. As users, we generally specify the name of a computer when establishing connections, such as Marcraft, not the IP address. These names need to be converted into the IP address of the destination computer. The process of matching a computer name to an IP address is called *name resolution*. The *Domain Name System* (*DNS*) can be used to perform name resolution for any TCP/IP client.

DNS is a service that runs on one or more servers in the network. These servers have databases that are used to perform the DNS name to IP address resolution function for the network. If your network employs DNS for name resolution, you must configure all the clients with the IP address of one or more DNS servers. DNS is also the name resolution service used for the Internet.

DNS Name Resolution

Each domain must have a *DNS name server* that is responsible for registering its clients with the next higher level of the network. Any computer that provides domain name services is technically referred to as a *DNS server*. In larger IT networks, the DNS server is typically located in the company's data center. For smaller businesses and residential networks, the DNS server is provided by their Internet service provider as part of their services package.

All *DNS servers* maintain a *DNS database* listing of name to IP address mappings that they are responsible for. When a *DNS client* submits a name resolution request to a local DNS server, the server will search through its DNS database and, if necessary, through the hierarchical DNS system, until it locates the host name or *fully qualified domain name (FQDN)* that was submitted to it. At this point, it resolves the IP address of the requested host name and returns it back to the client.

As illustrated in Figure 2.36, the simplified DNS process is as follows:

1. When you enter a web page address in a web browser, the client makes a query (a request for access) to a particular computer name, such as www.marcraft.com.

2. The local DNS server (the DNS server that the client computer is assigned to) checks to determine whether it has that domain name in its memory cache.

3. If the local DNS server cannot answer a query, it will normally forward the query to a root DNS server looking for a match (all functional DNS servers, including the local DNS server, contain a static list of the IP addresses of all root DNS servers).

4. The root server will refer the local DNS server to a list of primary .com (domain) servers. In turn, the local DNS server will select one of the .com servers from the list and query it for the address of marcraft.com. In response, the .com domain DNS server will refer you to a list of subdomain servers (if any exist—Example1.com and Example2.com). The local DNS server will then query the marcraft.com subdomain DNS server (or one of them) for the address of marcraft.com.

5. Depending on the structure of the marcraft.com subdomain, the selected marcraft.com server may refer you to a list of marcraft.com subdomain DNS servers for the marcraft.com address, or, if there are no additional subdomains, it will return the IP address for marcraft.com.

FIGURE 2.36   DNS process

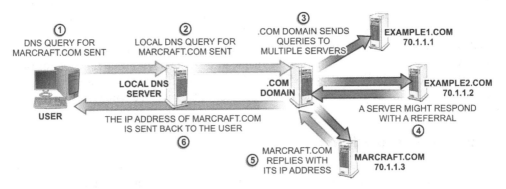

In addition to its domain name tracking function, the DNS system resolves (links names to addresses) individual domain names of computers to their current IP address listings. Some IP addresses are permanently assigned to a particular domain name so that whenever the domain name is issued on the Internet, it always accesses the same IP address. This is referred to as *static IP addressing*. However, most ISPs use a dynamic IP addressing scheme for allocating IP addresses.

Dynamic Host Configuration Protocol

The Dynamic Host Configuration Protocol (DHCP) is an Internet protocol that can be used to automatically assign IP addresses to devices on a network using TCP/IP. Using DHCP simplifies network administration, because software, rather than an administrator, assigns and keeps track of IP addresses. For this reason, many ISPs use the dynamic IP addressing function of DHCP to provide access to their dial-up users. The protocol automatically delivers IP addresses, subnet mask and default router configuration parameters, and other configuration information to the devices on the network.

The dynamic addressing portion of the protocol also means that computers can be added to a network without manually assigning them unique IP addresses. As a matter of fact, the devices can be issued a different IP address each time they connect to the network. In some networks, the device's IP address can even change while it is still connected. DHCP also supports a mix of static and dynamic IP addresses.

DHCP is an open standard, developed by the *Internet Engineering Task Force (IETF)*. It is a client-server arrangement in which a DHCP client contacts a DHCP server to obtain its configuration parameters. The DHCP server dynamically configures the clients with parameters appropriate to the current network structure.

The most important configuration parameter carried by DHCP is the IP address. A computer must be initially assigned a specific IP address that is appropriate to the network to which the computer is attached and that is not assigned to any other computer on that network.

If a computer moves to a new network, it must be assigned a new IP address for that new network. DHCP can be used to manage these assignments automatically. The DHCP client support is built into all computer operating systems. All computer server operating system versions include both client and server support for DHCP.

While DHCP is a highly regarded, time-saving tool in IT network environments, it is not as widely accepted in OT networks. The first major drawback to DHCP in these networks is that under DHCP a device can potentially obtain a different IP address each time it starts up. While this is common and acceptable practice in IT networks, industrial control systems typically need the control devices, such as PLCs, to be at the same IP address each time communications are required.

Not only does a control device typically need to maintain the same IP address at all times, but if that device fails, its replacement will also need to assume that IP address for proper interaction with the other components of the control system. The most straightforward method of accomplishing this is to connect to the device before installing it in the network and directly configure it with a static IP address using a software utility. The second alternative is to connect to the device from a network that includes a common DHCP server that has been configured to reserve a leased static IP address for that device. In this type of configuration, the IP address lease reservation is attached to the MAC address of the device.

Review Questions

The following questions test your knowledge of the material presented in this chapter. You can check your answers against those listed in Appendix D.

1. Why was asynchronous communication the dominant method for industrial control systems for so long?

2. Describe the three general types of communication media available to transmit data between devices and provide examples of each.

3. List the two major advantages associated with using fiber-optic communication links.

4. What type of control function is provided by a relay?

5. In the OT network structure, where are programs intended for use in the local PLCs created and stored?

6. What is the most widely used sensor in industrial process control environments?

7. Define the term *process unit*.

8. _____ is the de facto standard communication protocol for interconnecting intelligent industrial control devices.

9. What is the major consideration that must be taken into account when deploying an OT network based on the Modbus TCP protocol?

10. Which industrial networking protocol makes it relatively easy to integrate ICS devices with enterprise IT networks and the Internet?

11. _____ is a suite of industrial communication protocols that was developed to provide networking between central SCADA masters and different types of remote controllers (such as IEDs, PLCs, and RTUs) in electrical grid systems.

12. _____ is a widely accepted, industrial client-server specification designed to facilitate the exchange of data between industrial control applications and intelligent control devices. It was originally designed to bring Microsoft/Windows products into the industrial control world.

13. What is the networking service designed to convert readable domain FQDNs into numerical IP addresses used to locate computing devices across a network?

14. Which TCP/IP protocol is used to automatically assign users IP addresses from a rotating pool of available addresses?

15. Why has the industrial process control industry migrated toward using the TCP/IP protocol suite for OT networks?

Exam Questions

1. Refer to the relay logic ladder diagram in Figure 2.37 and determine what actions occur if the Start button is moved to its active state (depressed). Select the answer that expresses these actions correctly.

    A. The warning light illuminates, motor 1 turns off, and motor 2 turns on.

    B. The warning light illuminates, motor 1 turns on, and motor 2 turns on.

    C. The warning light illuminates, motor 1 turns off, and motor 2 turns off.

    D. The warning light illuminates, motor 1 turns on, and motor 2 turns off.

FIGURE 2.37   Relay ladder logic diagram

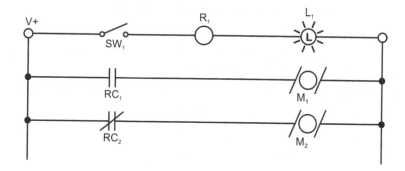

2. What type of mechanical switch has its contacts made when its activation mechanism is in its deactivated position and current can flow through it?

    A. Normally open

    B. Normally closed

    C. Push to close

    D. Momentary contact

3. A connection scheme where the inputs of the PLC accept conventional current flow from a sensing device refers to using _____.

    A. Analog inputs

    B. Digital inputs

    C. Sourcing inputs

    D. Sinking inputs

4. Which type of PLC output provides extended voltage and current handling capabilities over the others?

   A. Analog outputs

   B. Relay outputs

   C. Sinking outputs

   D. Solid-state outputs

5. From the following list, select common methods that can be used to program PLCs for operation. (Select all that apply.)

   A. Use commercial programming tools such as C or C+ to generate code that PLCs can run.

   B. Use graphical software tools that create ladder diagrams.

   C. Use off-the-shelf scripting tools to build PLC scripts to run.

   D. Use software tools to build function charts that can be converted into PLC code.

6. What is a major concern with using Ethernet technology for ICS networking?

   A. Ethernet is too slow to keep pace with most industrial process network operations.

   B. Ethernet technology is too susceptible to cyber attacks.

   C. Ethernet packets can be delayed for several basic reasons, causing delivery times to vary.

   D. Ethernet transmission has distance limitations.

7. _____ is the ICS network component responsible for recoding data obtained from field devices, PLCs, RTUs, and IECs.

   A. Engineer's station

   B. Data historian

   C. DCS server

   D. SCADA server

8. From the following list, identify the option that is not an available ProfiNet level.

   A. ProfiNet CBA for I/O applications (a basic real-time protocol version)

   B. ProfiNet CBA for production plants (basic TCP/IP protocol components)

   C. ProfiNet RT (basic real-time components)

   D. ProfiNet IO (high-speed isochronous real-time protocol)

9. Which of the following descriptions identifies how a PLC processes information?

   A. 1. It scans the status of each input terminal in sequence, 2. It checks its operating system to determine its next operation, 3. It processes the input status according to its programming, and 4. It passes the results to specified output terminals.

   B. 1. It scans the status of each input terminal in sequence, 2. It checks its operating system to obtain its first instruction, 3. It jumps to the indicated input register, 4. It performs the computational function it finds at the register, and 5. It passes the results to specified output terminals.

C. 1. It checks its operating system to obtain its first instruction, 2. It scans the status of each input terminal in sequence, 3. It jumps to the indicated input register, 4. It performs the computational function it finds at the register, and 5. It passes the results to specified output terminals.

D. 1. It scans the status of each input terminal in sequence, 2. It processes the input status according to its programming, and 3. It passes the results to specified output terminals.

10. Which industrial process control protocol was designed specifically to provide networking capabilities for industrial control applications?

A. Modbus

B. BACnet

C. DNP3

D. ICCP

Chapter 3

Secure ICS Architecture

OBJECTIVES

Upon completion of this chapter, you should be able to:

1. **Define and describe network segmentation and security zones:**
   - Segmentation
   - Partitioning
   - Segregation
   - Zones and conduits
   - Reference architectures
   - Network devices and services
   - Data diodes
   - DMZs

2. **Define and describe wireless security topics**
   - Wi-Fi
   - Wireless sensors
   - Wireless gateways
   - Controllers

Introduction

In the previous chapter you were introduced to the components used to build basic *operational technology (OT)* network structures. This chapter will build on that basic information to explain how those components are organized to produce secure OT network architecture. This will involve two major topic areas:

- Network segmentation and security zoning
- Wireless security

As indicated previously, the best *cybersecurity design* for a production plant is to keep the OT and IT networks separated from each other, both logically and physically, and to not provide a path to the OT network from the Internet. This will reduce the risk to the OT network associated with remote attackers gaining access to it through the IT network.

An isolated industrial process control network is normally a relatively safe and secure network environment. Threats are typically limited to natural and human accidents, physical access attacks, and malicious activities associated with disgruntled employees. These networks often have no connection to the Internet, where so many potential threats arise. In addition, they are based on devices and software that fewer individuals are aware of (and highly competent with) than their counterparts in the enterprise world.

When a connection is created between the ICS operational technology and corporate IT networks, the risk level to the OT network increases significantly. This is due to the additional attack vectors presented to the OT network through the IT network and its Internet connections. So, the best security option for interconnected OT and IT networks that is often practiced is to limit the network connections between the corporate IT network and the OT network to a single point of contact, as illustrated in Figure 3.1.

Prior to the early 2000s, the prevailing view in industrial processing was to keep IT and OT networks air-gapped (completely separated from each other). Above all, a pathway between the OT network and the Internet should never be provided, not even indirectly. However, the roles of computers and networks in process control systems have changed rapidly. Today, OT/IT network integration/interoperability has escalated from virtually nonexistent to being a requirement instead of a convenience.

FIGURE 3.1   Connecting the OT and IT networks

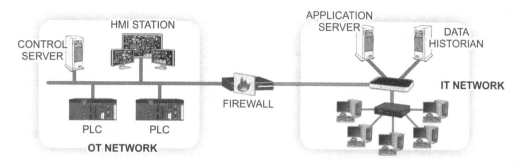

IT functions have become an integral part of the OT network to provide critical interfaces and interactions. IT/OT network interoperability is increasingly being used to maximize process productivity through monitoring, record keeping, maintenance, planning, and work scheduling. Of course, the cyber threats associated with these expanded/integrated networks are increasing concurrently.

Boundary Protection

With the industry continuing to press toward IT/OT connectivity, the goal becomes to establish *boundary protection* between the two networks that will permit the desired information to move between the networks while protecting the OT network from the threats associated with the IT network, non-ICS personnel, and the Internet.

Boundary protection refers to installing boundary protection devices to control the flow of information between security zones that have differing security requirements or policies. These devices include such items as gateways and routers, firewalls, IDS systems, antivirus/antimalware software, encrypted tunnels, VLANs, and data diodes.

Fortunately, the enterprise networking environment has already created a number of boundary protection devices and techniques that can be used for this purpose. These devices and techniques include the following:

- Access control strategies
- Gateways
- Routers
- Firewalls

- Intrusion detection systems (IDSs)
- VLANs
- Encryption and tunnels
- Antivirus and anti-malware products
- Network segregation and segmentation techniques
- DMZs
- Proxies

All the items mentioned in this list can and should be applied to guarding the ICS from the rest of the world.

Firewalls

The most common first line of defense between internetwork segments is a *firewall*. These devices consist of a combination of hardware and software used to control network traffic between untrusted or less secure networks and a protected network. This is accomplished by monitoring the network traffic and applying access rules to it to allow authorized traffic to pass through.

Firewalls can be implemented in various ways in different network arrangements. A firewall might be a mission-specific *hardware firewall device*, or it may be a function that is built into a router or switch, or it may be implemented in a computer that has multiple Ethernet interfaces. It can even be a pure *software firewall* installed on a host computer like any other application. Many network appliances are available that offer firewall and security capabilities along with other network features.

In a corporate or industrial network environment, an IT administrator controls firewall installations and configurations. The advantage of the network firewall is that it enables the administrator to control the flow of information to all the devices attached to their network, as illustrated in Figure 3.2.

FIGURE 3.2   Network firewall

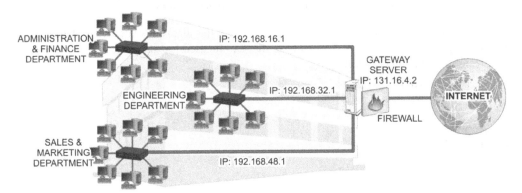

Firewalls used in OT environments are typically purpose-built to specifically monitor OT traffic and allow or reject traffic entering the OT or one of its subnets. Many IT firewall suppliers provide OT-specific capabilities with their products. The major challenges with using firewalls for OT security is implementing proper firewall rules to provide the protection needed in a given environment.

Firewalls generally act as gateway devices, authenticating and granting access to both network applications and protocols. They can also be configured to act as a proxy server, provide network address translation, and also act as a DHCP server. Firewalls will typically also filter not only incoming traffic but outgoing traffic as well.

A configured firewall will provide *packet filtering* using defined rules to reject or accept both incoming and outgoing packets. This can be more challenging to configure, but effective *firewall rules* are critical to security on most networks.

A *packet filtering firewall* can be established through routers by configuring them with packet filtering rules to allow or deny client access based upon factors such as a source address, destination address, or port number. There are two types of packet filtering firewalls to consider: *static packet filtering* and *stateful packet filtering*.

Static or *stateless packet filtering firewalls* do not keep track of the state of a connection between two devices. They operate in much the same manner as any *access control list (ACL)* does. This makes this variety of firewalls somewhat faster than other firewall options. They also tend to be relatively inexpensive and easy to maintain. Conversely, static packet filtering firewalls offer fewer security features than other firewall options.

Stateful packet filtering firewalls do keep track of the connection state between entities. These firewalls collect network connection information and maintain *dynamic state tables* that are used for subsequent connections. As illustrated in Figure 3.3, this enables ports to be opened and closed as needed. Once a client has completed a communication session, the stateful packet filtering firewall closes the specific port used until it is requested again.

Newer firewalls will also provide *quality of service (QoS)* functionality, which allows for the prioritization and differential treatment of network traffic based on special rules or policies. A common use for QoS is to ensure that a VoIP phone system will always have enough bandwidth for phone service, regardless of how busy the network is.

Some applications are more sensitive to latency, and using QoS can make sure those applications always have enough priority to keep packets flowing to them so that connections do not drop. QoS can also be a way to fairly share or allocate bandwidth on a busy network. Some firewalls will separate this sort of traffic management from QoS, but they are similar concepts.

Newer firewalls, known as *next-generation firewalls (NGFWs)*, are network appliances that combine the features of traditional firewalls (packet filtering, stateful inspection, and VPN awareness with additional capabilities) with *deep packet inspection (DPI)*, built-in intrusion prevention systems, threat intelligence from external sources, and application awareness/control.

FIGURE 3.3   Stateful firewall operations

FIREWALL NOTES REQUEST
② FOR FTP SERVICE AND OPENS
PORT 20 FOR FTP SERVICE

PORT 20
(CLOSED)

PORT 20
(OPEN)

20 | 192.168.0.4
DATA

TCP/IP
PACKETS

①
REQUEST FOR FTP
SERVICE SENT TO
REMOTE SERVER

INTERNET

ROUTER   FIREWALL

LOCAL HOST

PORT 20
(CLOSED)

④
FIREWALL NOTES CLOSED
FTP CONNECTION AND
CLOSES PORT 20

③ FTP CONNECTION
CLOSED

INTERNET

LOCAL HOST

⑤
FURTHER TRAFFIC TO
PORT 20 IS NOW BLOCKED

Using Firewalls

The recommendations of the NIST 800-82 r2 standard, "Guide to Industrial Control Systems (ICS) Security," rely heavily on the use of firewalls to control access and flow between and throughout the organization's different networks. While IT networks typically implement antivirus and local software firewalls to provide defense-in-depth segmentation, it is more common for OT networks to employ industrial firewalls for this function.

> **NOTE**   More information on NIST 800-82 r2 can be found at https://csrc .nist.gov/publications/detail/sp/800-82/rev-2/final.

Figure 3.4 shows a firewall deployed between an IT corporate network and its OT network. Notice that in this example there are no Internet connections. Even so, the firewall is implemented to restrict connectivity between the networks and prevent unauthorized access to their resources.

If greater internetwork security is required, a network router can be installed between the IT and OT networks along with the firewall from the previous example. This topology, depicted in Figure 3.5, provides a two-tiered opposition to attackers trying to access the OT network. The router is located on the IT side of the firewall to provide packet filtering services.

FIGURE 3.4   Internetwork firewall

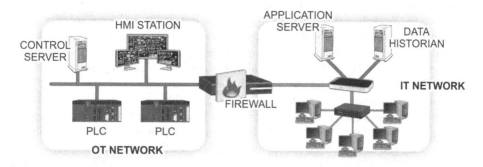

FIGURE 3.5   Internetwork router

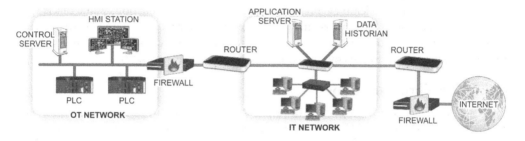

Also notice that this example includes a connection between the enterprise network and the Internet. This connection should also be protected with a router and firewall configuration at a minimum.

Figure 3.6 depicts a fully firewalled OT/IT network configuration. As you can see from the figure, in OT/IT network configurations, firewalls are used to filter traffic not only between the enterprise network and the Internet but between different security zones within the combined networks.

FIGURE 3.6   Implementing firewalls

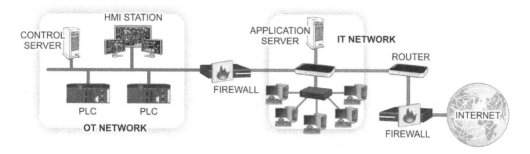

Firewalls are typically deployed between the OT and IT networks to restrict traffic between the process control devices and the organization's enterprise network computing systems. Placing the firewall at this location provides two important functions: security and increased performance. The firewall can be configured to provide a high level of control over the movement of packets coming into and leaving the OT network. This in turn reduces the level of nonessential traffic on the network, allowing for higher throughput of desired traffic. Local firewalls can be installed on (or in front of) individual control devices.

When installing boundary protection devices, they should always be configured to deny all traffic by default and then implement a *whitelisting* policy to only *allow* the required connections and traffic by exception. Typically, this involves preventing communications between authorized and unauthorized source and destination address pairs.

Firewalls used for boundary protection services should always be configured to block all unauthorized communications based on source/destination address, port, and service.

You should also be aware that poorly configured firewalls can inject delays into OT network communications, which may adversely impact their control function. While this is typically unnoticeable in an IT network, it can be potentially catastrophic in an OT network. Care must be taken to configure firewalls associated with OT networks so they do not add any more traffic burden to the communications than absolutely necessary.

Using Demilitarized Zones

Some organizations dedicate a portion of their network to a security structure called a *demilitarized zone*, or *DMZ*. The DMZ is a separate perimeter network that isolates one network from another yet enables access to outward-facing dedicated resources. Figure 3.7 shows a typical DMZ implementation.

FIGURE 3.7   A DMZ

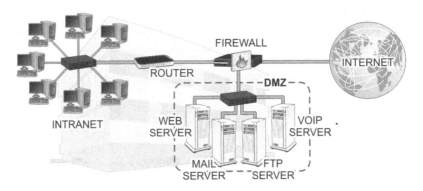

As the figure illustrates, select servers and other resources are positioned in the DMZ. These resources are referred to as *bastion hosts*. A bastion host may be a firewall, a router, a server, or a group of computers that are not protected behind another firewall.

DMZs are commonly used to provide isolation between enterprise and OT networks. The DMZ creates a neutral zone between the two network types to limit external information exchange with the enterprise based on the organization's security policy specifications.

Any ICS servers that the corporate network requires access to should be placed in the OT/IT DMZ, and only those servers should be accessible from the enterprise network, as shown in Figure 3.8. The only ports opened in the firewall should be those absolutely required for the specific communications required by the enterprise network.

FIGURE 3.8   Minimum ICS/IT network connectivity

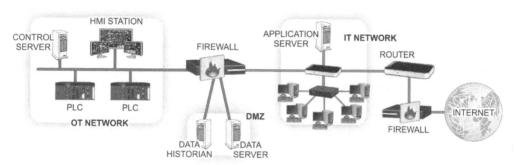

Access to the DMZ is controlled by one or more firewalls. In a *single-firewall DMZ*, like the one depicted in the figure, the firewall must be a *multihomed* device that can provide three separate network interfaces:

- One interface for the enterprise network

- One interface for the ICS network

- One interface for the DMZ network

Multihomed, single-firewall DMZs are typically selected over other security structures because they are relatively inexpensive to implement. However, in this configuration the firewall becomes a single point of failure for the entire network. If the firewall is breached, the attacker has gained access to the entire network. All that's required is a poorly configured firewall that leaves a port open to attack.

In a *dual-firewall DMZ*, such as the one shown in Figure 3.9, firewalls are positioned on each side of the DMZ to filter traffic moving between the intranet and the DMZ as well as between the DMZ and the Internet. These firewalls are used to route public traffic to the DMZ and internal network traffic to the Intranet.

Dual-firewalled DMZ configurations offer a much higher level of security in that an attacker would have to hack multiple devices to compromise the intranet. If they are successful at compromising the first firewall, they only gain access to the public-facing resources in the DMZ.

FIGURE 3.9   A dual firewall DMZ

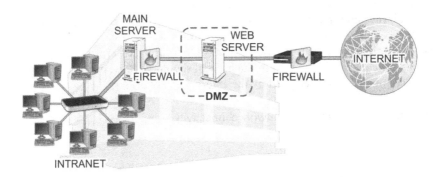

All inbound traffic to the ICS should be routed through a DMZ. The ICS firewall should also be configured to provide outbound filtering to prevent spoofed IP packets from leaving the DMZ. Recall that spoofed communications are often used in DoS attacks. The firewall must be configured to check outbound packets to make sure that their *source IP addresses* are correct for the DMZ. If not, the packet gets dropped.

Proxies

A *proxy* is a barrier that prevents outsiders from entering a local area network and prevents insiders from directly connecting to outside resources, as illustrated in Figure 3.10. Instead, it allows clients to make indirect network connections that are routed through it. The client connects to the proxy server, with or without any conscious authentication, and makes a request for a resource from a different server. The proxy server will handle the request either by returning the requested resource from its own cached copy or by forwarding the request to the other server (after potentially modifying the request).

FIGURE 3.10   Operation of a proxy server

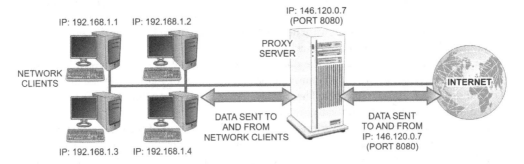

All addressing information sent to the Internet will use the IP address of the proxy server. Because the IP address of the client that's requesting the resource isn't used, an outside intruder has no way of accessing the local host.

Proxy filtering is a much more complex process than packet filtering. During this filtering process, each packet is disassembled, evaluated, and reassembled, making this type of connection significantly slower than other firewall types. Proxy filtering firewalls are configured to view entire packets for consistency, type of application, and appropriate ports. The data that is attempting to travel through these ports to a client must match what the proxy filtering firewall expects, or the unknown packet will be dropped, and the connection will be lost.

As shown in Figure 3.11, proxy servers can be installed to provide boundary protection by acting as the go-between insulating the OT network from external requests generated by the enterprise network. The proxy prevents direct connection to the OT network and handles the task of determining which resources being requested should be processed.

FIGURE 3.11   Boundary protection with a proxy server

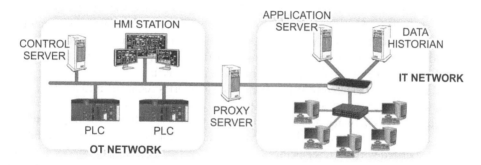

A *defense-in-depth strategy* is one that includes a number of different overlapping security mechanisms that will minimize the effects of a single mechanism being overcome by an attacker. In the following sections of this chapter, you will be introduced to security zoning concepts in both IT and OT environments. These concepts will eventually build into the *Purdue ISA-95 Reference Architecture*. These concepts will be expanded to include *IIoT* and *Cloud Services* variations.

In addition to the DMZs, routers, and firewalls described in these examples, both the IT and the OT networks should employ one of the security topology strategies discussed in the following section to maximize the overall defense-in-depth strategy.

Security Topologies

As mentioned earlier, the intent and operation of OT and IT networks are very different. OT systems require *real-time data*, while IT networks do not. OT networks are all about availability, integrity, and then confidentiality (AIC), while IT networks are designed to provide confidentiality first, followed by integrity and then availability (CIA).

Likewise, the types of activities carried out over the two networks are fundamentally opposed to each other. The IT network is designed to create, store, and manipulate data, while the OT network is designed to provide real-time measurement and control functions.

When delays occur in an IT environment (such as the Windows hourglass spinning on the display), user productivity is decreased. However, if similar delays occur in an OT environment, bad things happen:

- Production is disrupted.

- Products do not meet quality standards and must be scrapped.

- Production equipment is damaged or destroyed.

- Personnel are injured or killed.

IT corporate networks typically represent a significantly larger security risk than their OT counterparts. OT networks tend to run on devices, operating systems, applications, and networks that are more obscure than those used in IT networks. In addition, OT networks have historically not been connected to the public Internet in any way.

Because of the AIC nature of the OT network, care must be taken not to introduce security features into that portion of the network that will delay the movement of and access to data when needed. This includes such typical enterprise steps as adding antivirus/anti-malware products, slow firewall/proxy services, or intrusion detection/prevention (IDS/IPS) devices and services. However, there are many ways to make the IT side of the joined networks more secure, thereby making the OT network more secure.

Secure IT network designs routinely organize the network's segments into multiple layers of security structures. Each of the network security structures just covered could be part of a given organization's network design. For that matter, some portions of the organization's network, such as its intranet, could be subdivided into multiple segments, based on the security needs associated with each segment.

All the intelligent devices attached to the network must have a *network interface adapter* capable of connecting the device to the network's transmission media. This includes providing physical connection schemes such as plugs and jacks, as well as providing electrical compatibility between the device and the signals traveling across the transmission media (cables or airwaves).

In addition, the network typically contains other *connectivity devices* that connect different portions of the network together and perform different network management functions. These connectivity devices are usually switches or routers. In large or complex networks, you may also find devices called *bridges* used to interconnect sections of the network.

While each device provides physical connectivity, they also each have specific methods of operation that make them suitable for use in specific network applications. In some cases, a device with more features may be used to perform the functions of a lower-featured device.

Network Switches

Network switches are connectivity devices that function at layer 2 of the OSI model.* They are designed to connect *network devices* together to form a local area network. *Enterprise networks* typically employ combinations of switches to segment the network and establish efficient data traffic flows. They may be used in combination with other network connectivity devices, or they may be connected directly to the server room through a backbone cabling arrangement.

For example, a company whose organization spans several floors of an office building might employ a separate switch on each floor to provide connectivity for all the devices on that floor. The switches on individual floors would also be connected to each other through a switch or router. Figure 3.12 shows a typical network switch connection scheme.

 *Primarily, switches are layer 2 devices that function at the OSI Data Link layer. However, there are also layer 3 switches that act similar to routers (devices that have the functional capabilities of both routers and bridges, covered in the upcoming sections), layer 4 switches that include Network Address Translation (NAT) capabilities, and layer 7 (content) switches that distribute content based on server loading factors.

FIGURE 3.12   A network switch connection

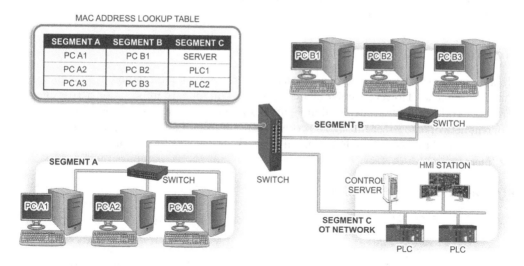

Switches collect MAC address information to keep track of the devices attached to them. As they interact with those devices, they record their MAC information in an onboard memory structure called a *MAC address table*.

When a switch receives a packet of network information at one of its *ports*, it can direct the information to its intended receiver provided the address of the receiver is known. If the address is not known, the switch will *broadcast* the information to all of its ports. Because information traveling through the switch is generally only sent to the port where it is intended, the performance of the entire network is improved greatly.

Switches can also be used to create logically secured *virtual local area networks (VLANs)*. A VLAN is a security topology that restricts visibility of network traffic by limiting the movement of network packets so that they pass only between designated ports.

Network switches are typically grouped into one of two categories by their configuration options. *Unmanaged switches* are *plug and play (PnP)* devices that do not include any options for user configuration. These tend to be low-price units intended for use in residential and small office settings, so they are rarely found in corporate IT networks.

The other category of switches is referred to as *managed switches*. These devices have programmable management functions built into them that enable administrators to configure them for the specific network environment they will be used in. As such, they provide some type of management console that the administrator can use to set parameters. Common management interfaces include the following:

- *Command-line programming*: This format provides a direct text-based method of programming the switch's settings. Command-line programming requires the administrator to be aware of the *instruction set* and parameter variables available for setting the different parameters.

- *Browser-based interfaces*: These interfaces provide a graphical, menu-driven tool for setting key switch parameters. A *Simple Network Management Protocol (SNMP)* tool is used to permit the administrator to access the switch's parameters through a remote client using its web browser.

Routers

Routers are network connectivity devices that forward network information in a manner similar to switches. However, unlike switches, routers can forward information across different network segments, as depicted in Figure 3.13. This gives routers the ability to join different networks together through a process known as routing. For example, a router is commonly used to connect small residential networks to the biggest network in the world—the Internet.

FIGURE 3.13   A network router

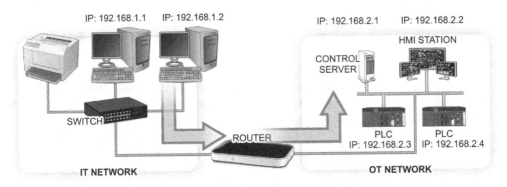

Routers are microprocessor-based intelligent devices that control the flow of data between networks. The microprocessor is a specialized device optimized to operate as a *route processor*. Like other microprocessor-based equipment, routers contain a ROM BIOS for bootup, an NVRAM CMOS configuration area to hold operational configuration parameters, and an onboard operating system stored in a flash memory unit.

Routers also contain different sections of DRAM memory to hold message routing information and to buffer data flow between its ports. The routing information is stored and updated in a logical memory table referred to as a *routing table*.

Each network segment is connected to the router through one of its physical port interfaces. These interfaces can be implemented as different types of physical/logical interface specifications, such as an RJ45/8P8C Ethernet connection port.

Almost all routers possess a physical interface that can be used to attach an external console cable for configuration purposes. They may also contain an asynchronous RS-232 serial hardware port that can be used by administrators to perform remote router management functions.

 The most widely recognized router/switch operating system is Cisco System's Internetwork Operating System (IOS). However, there are many other Linux/Unix-based router OS distributions available for use.

In large networks, routers communicate with other routers using a *routing protocol* to build and maintain their routing tables. These tables are used to record the best route between different network locations. Unlike the MAC table used in switches, routing tables store address and hop information about the path between devices.

Security Zoning Models

A *security zone* is a network segment created to provide specific levels of security for specific network assets (resources and data) based on their security vulnerability or criticality. The idea is to place more valuable or critical network assets into segments or security structures that offer more protection. *Network segmentation* is also referred to as *zoning*, and the individual layers of the security plan are referred to as *security zones*, as shown in Figure 3.14.

A *security topology* consists of the organization's various network security zones interconnected together. Security topologies go beyond simple network topologies in that they are designed specifically to protect key assets within each unique segment of the network. A complementary network strategy and security topology must be fully mapped out and implemented to provide effective operation and security for the organization's assets.

FIGURE 3.14   Network zoning

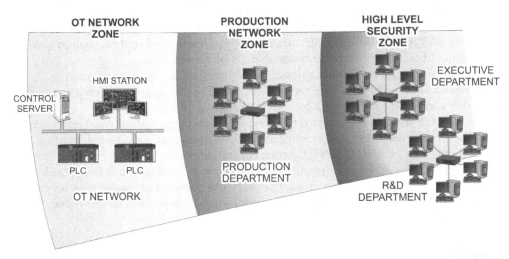

Good security topologies are designed to position and connect organizational assets, such as servers, firewalls, routers, switches, and client workstations, within shielded network segments to protect them from unauthorized access or attack.

An organization's security topology must be based on the general intent of its security goals. These goals are typically determined by a product security officer or a system information security officer CISO). They are responsible for balancing the network's security risks against its budgetary constraints to mitigate or minimize those risks to an acceptable level. This requires careful planning, departmental coordination, employee buy-in, and managerial support.

For example, a given organization may need liberal remote access and Internet connectivity to conduct its business effectively. So, severely limiting remote access and Internet access throughout the organization would not be an acceptable option for this organization.

However, sections of the organization that logically require restricted access, such as product development, accounting, human resources, and executive departments, may be made more secure by implementing network segmentation to create special security zones that offer network isolation for these sections of the organization.

A visual topology map should be created to show critical assets such as servers, firewalls, routers, switches, and VLANs, along with the subnets, security zones, or departments that they support. The map should clearly identify segmented networks and devices that employ static IP address configurations. With all these elements displayed in a graphical format, design flaws should become apparent, allowing critical resources to be relocated to more appropriate zones or departments.

Most logical models for IT network zoning can be thought of in terms of multilayered *trust zone* arrangements similar to the one depicted in Figure 3.15. In this example, there are four security zones arranged in rings of escalating security requirements. The innermost zone, which houses the most secure assets, is protected by the security layers around it. Likewise, each successive layer provides security for the rings adjacent to it.

FIGURE 3.15   Layered zones

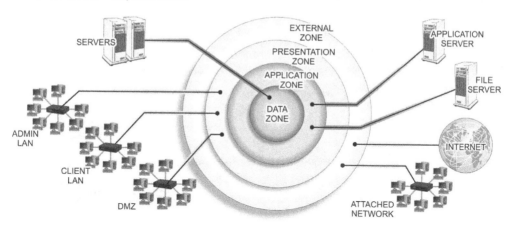

Typically, a given security zone will consist of similar network assets that share common security characteristics. These characteristics include shared data confidentiality and integrity requirements, access controls, and audit, logging, and monitoring requirements. However, each zone can consist of any number of subnets and cover any number of physical locations. The technologies typically used to create the *partitions* between the zones include devices such as switched VLANs, firewalls, or routers, as shown in Figure 3.16.

FIGURE 3.16   Zone partitioning technologies

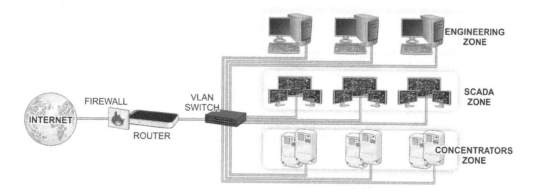

In very high security applications, network devices called *unidirectional security gateways* or *data diodes* may be used to create a one-way connection between networks or network segments that possess differing security classifications, as depicted in Figure 3.17.

FIGURE 3.17   A data diode

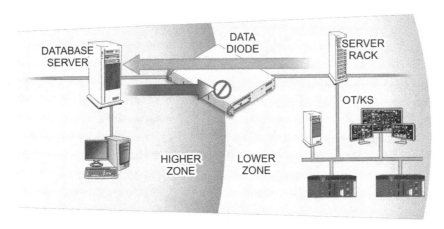

Data is usually considered the most valuable asset for enterprise organizations. This can include different types of data ranging from employee information to financial information, customer information, or health information. As such, information can range in classification from confidential to internal to public. Of course, confidential information is stored in the innermost zone of the topology, which is referred to as the *data zone*. This typically involves databases with confidential customer data, highly secure devices, infrastructures, strategies, and policies.

Access to the resources in this zone must be both authorized and authenticated. Data storage encryption is also employed in this zone. *Application-level encryption* is preferred, but *file system encryption* should be employed if application-level encryption options are not available.

Subsets of the organization's confidential data are typically and routinely moved into other security zones for processing and distribution. The security strategies for these internal layers differ depending on the confidentiality and availability requirements assigned to the asset.

For example, the *Application zone* just outside the Data zone contains applications for processing data. This zone is typically populated with file servers. Information in this zone is still considered to be the organization's internal data and is subject to greater security measures than "public" data.

Like the Data zone, access to the Application zone requires user authorization and authentication, as well as service authentication. An intrusion detection system is typically employed at this level to notify administrators of intrusion events.

The *Presentation zone* that separates the Application zone from the outermost security layer (typically the Internet) is where the organization's user network segments are housed. This can include segments dedicated to administrative LANs. The Presentation zone is also used to house public interfaces, such as web servers delivering "public" information, as well as the organization's transfer security tools and structures.

Access to resources in this zone still requires authentication even though the contents may be designated as public. Common security measures implemented at the Presentation level include the following:

- *Firewalls*: Firewalls are used to control the flow of information between the Presentation zone and the Application/Internet zones, as well as between subnets within the zone. Only access requests from within the zone or from adjacent zones are accepted.

- *Virus and malware scanners*: All assets in this zone should be required to possess antivirus and anti-malware protection.

- *Audit tools*: These tools are implemented at this level to log important application and security events for accountability and forensics purposes. Logged data should never include information that is classified as confidential.

- *Hardening techniques*: All assets in this zone should be protected by applying hardened techniques to them and their applications. These techniques are covered in detail later in this chapter.

- *Transfer security structures*: These are DMZs, VPNs, or reverse proxies to provide authentication for external users (these structures are discussed later in this chapter).

- *Data transfer encryption*: All data that is classified as confidential must be encrypted when it moves through the network. Secure protocols, such as HTTPS and SSL, must be used to replace less secure protocols such as HTTP and SFTP.

The outermost *Internet zone* in this security topology example represents uncontrolled (Internet) or externally controlled (third-party partners) networks. This zone includes all networks that are not controlled by the organization. As such, the content can be public, or it can be confidential data that belongs to trusted partners or customers. Access requirements in this zone can be either authenticated or anonymous in nature.

 In each case, the zone may be microsegmented (subdivided) into subnets referred to as *zone instances*. This permits different users within a given zone to be configured for different levels of availability and accessibility. It also limits the risk and impact of attacks within the zone.

Flat Network Topologies

Not every business network is designed with a layered, segmented security topology. Figure 3.18 illustrates a generic *flat network topology* that is used in many business networks, even some very large ones. Flat network strategies are also widely used in OT networks.

This model basically minimizes the use of connectivity devices (routers and switches) throughout the network. Instead, centralized switches are used to connect the nodes of the network together. In most cases, these networks are typically isolated from the Internet by a single router.

FIGURE 3.18   A flat network configuration

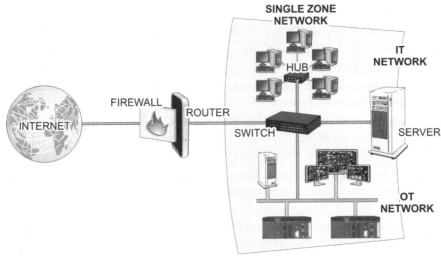

This strategy does reduce the cost of implementing and maintaining the network, as well as decreasing the complexity of administering its operation. However, it also produces a very low level of security for the network. In a flat network, traffic can move freely between all the network nodes, providing access to all the users connected to it.

It is in effect one large broadcast domain. Any device that sends an ARP broadcast looking for a valid network IP address will receive a reply. This means that if an attacker gains access to the network, they could see every asset in the network, including servers, endpoint devices, and data. With the right skill set and enough time, they can exploit all these devices.

If malicious software or malware like a worm, such as the famous Stuxnet virus, gains access to the network, then there is nothing to stop it from spreading to the entire network. Also, there is very little protection from any malicious activities that originate within the network.

Unfortunately, most OT networks are built on large, flat network topologies. This allows network attacks or disturbances to propagate through the network quickly after the initial penetration occurs. Flat topologies also make OT networks vulnerable to threats that do not appear on the network map, but pose a significant threat when the process control system is networked together. These threats include wireless devices that may enter the plant and communicate with the ICS network, as well as the ability for USB-based devices to be introduced to ICS systems.

OT Security Zoning

Inside the OT network, the process should be analyzed to determine whether the process control network can be organized into security segments as described previously in this chapter. If possible, the OT network should be segmented into *security zones* based on management authority, uniform trust levels, or network traffic. Like an IT network, a well-segmented OT network can make it significantly more difficult for attackers to successfully breach the system and minimize the effects of nonmalicious errors.

Consider the multilayered, defense-in-depth network security topologies presented earlier in the chapter. In the case of an OT network, there is generally no need for a highly protected database layer. Instead, the ICS security topology is more likely to segment the network into Operational, Control, DMZ, and non-ICS zones, as illustrated in Figure 3.19.

FIGURE 3.19   ICS security zones

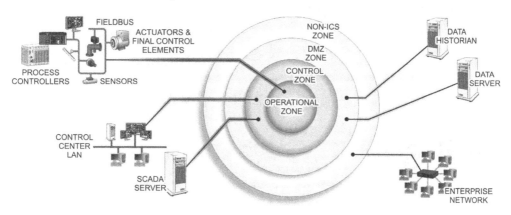

In this example, the DMZ is not positioned between the outer security level of the corporate network and the uncontrolled Internet. Instead, it is placed between the more secure OT network and the less trusted corporate IT network. Another DMZ should be created between the corporate network and the Internet.

ICS Reference Architecture

After examining all the network models presented in this chapter for both IT and OT networks, you might still be wondering: How would you actually implement these concepts to create a secure IT/OT network environment?

In Chapter 1, "Industrial Control Systems," you were briefly introduced to the *Purdue ANSI/ISA 95 Reference Model Architecture*. It has become the international standard for interconnecting IT and OT networks.

Recall that this model defines the generic IT/OT network as five layers ranging from the Processes and Sensors/Actuators level up to the Business, Planning, and Logistics network level. In doing so, it also presents the types of equipment, network connectivity, and business operations occurring at each level.

The area of most interest for this security zoning conversation is the zone depicted between Level 4 and Level 3, as depicted in Figure 3.20. This is where the DMZ is placed to separate the Business Planning and Logistics portion of the network from the Manufacturing Operations and Management portion. The DMZ places a firewall at each end of the zone programmed with different rule sets to provide the desired security functions for each interface.

FIGURE 3.20   Where OT meets IT

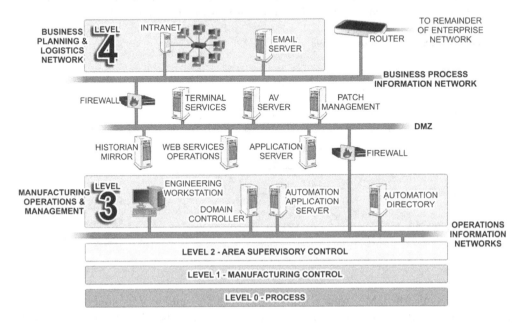

This configuration also makes it more difficult for intruders to hack their way through both devices to reach the inside of the network. In some organizations, the two firewalls may be managed by two separate administrators: the IT network admin might be responsible for managing the enterprise firewall while the process control admin controls the ICS firewall.

Expanded ISA-95 Structures

The basic ISA-95 structure is often expanded to meet security demands presented by a specific organization's needs. For example, if the organization presents a robust Internet presence, such as a corporate website that provides B2C and/or B2B services, the network model should be extended to provide an additional enterprise DMZ to separate the organization's enterprise network from the Internet, as illustrated in Figure 3.21.

FIGURE 3.21   Securing the enterprise zone

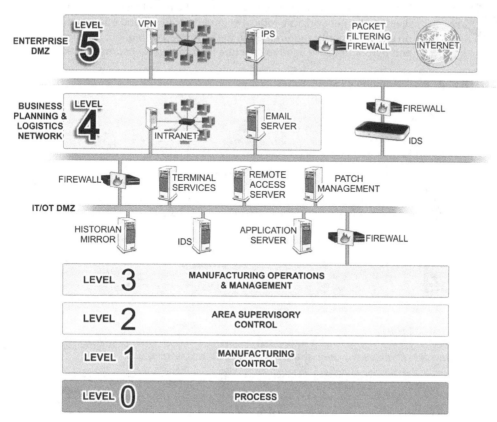

It has also been expanded with additional zones to provide specific services, as depicted in Figure 3.22:

- *Database zones*: As described earlier, the enterprise network should be layered to provide defense-in-depth strategies such as segregating the databases that hold the most sensitive data into the innermost zone of the network.

- *Monitoring zones*: These zones are created to monitor zones that process and store production information. In this case, a monitoring zone has been added at both level 3 and level 4. Both zones consist of a firewall and an intrusion detection system (IDS).

- *Security zones*: As described in Chapter 1, production systems typically include a separate instrumentation and control system (SIS) dedicated specifically to the operational safety of the processes. When included in the ISA-95 architecture model, this system is shown as its own level, located at the bottom of the structure where the processes and OT sensors, actuators, and controllers reside. It is shown at this level because the SIS must be its own redundant system that is disconnected (air gapped) from the OT network.

While the term *zoning* is used to describe the high-level process of dividing the network into logical segments of users and equipment based on shared security requirements, the terms *segmentation*, *segregation*, and *partitioning* are used to describe how zoning is accomplished.

FIGURE 3.22   Additional ISA-95 zones

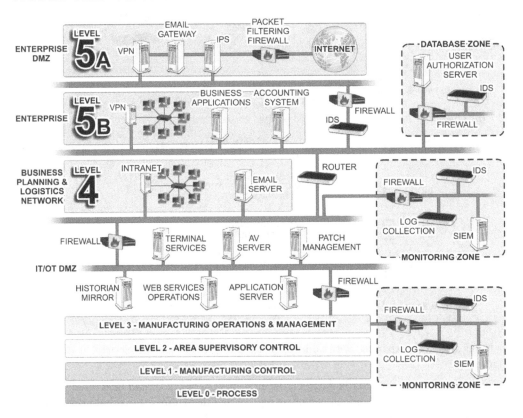

Evolving Architecture Models

An industry movement referred to as *Industry 4.0* has pushed ICS environments to begin integrating newer technologies into their IT/OT network topologies. These technologies include cloud services, edge computing, and advanced 5G wireless networks along with other smart device technologies. This movement has produced many variations of the Standard Security Architecture, including a three-part *Industrial Internet of Things (IIoT)* reference architecture, depicted in Figure 3.23.

FIGURE 3.23   IIoT Purdue Architecture Model

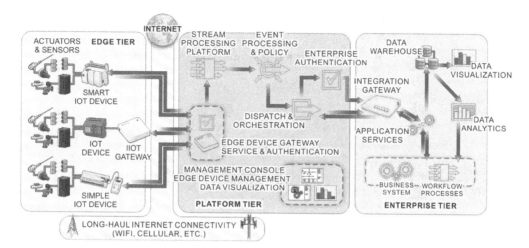

This IIoT version of the model regroups the five levels of the hierarchical Purdue model into three distinct horizontal tiers:

- *An edge tier*: This tier contains the level 0, 1, and 2 functions of the Purdue Model.

- *A (cloud) platform tier*: This tier is typically a platform-as-a-service (PaaS) cloud that contains data storage, analytic systems, and network communications facilities. This tier replaces level 3.

- *An enterprise tier*: This tier represents the organization's IT network, including its servers, user devices, and Internet connection(s). This tier corresponds to levels 4 and 5 of the Purdue Model.

In addition to the traditional sensors and actuators located in the edge tier, smart IIoT sensors and actuators can communicate with the platform tier directly or through an IIoT gateway. The enterprise tier, which may also be a cloud environment, communicates directly with the platform tier as well.

An IIoT/Purdue integration version proposed by the European Union Agency for Cybersecurity (ENISA) revises the hierarchical model to accommodate the operation of IIoT devices by combining an IIoT control platform with the traditional ISA-95 Level 3 functions. Figure 3.24 depicts the ENISA model.

At this point, there is no widely accepted standard for ISA-95/IIoT integration. However, ICS standards organizations around the world are working on both wholesale replacements for the ISA-95 model and hybrid solutions that integrate IIoT technologies into the model and maintain segmentation and traditional IT/OT data movement control.

FIGURE 3.24   IIoT Purdue Architecture Model

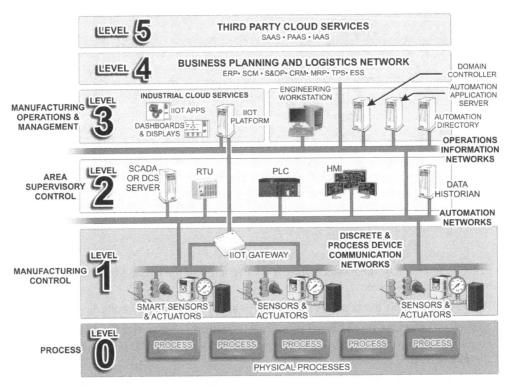

The SANS ICS410 Reference Model

The SANS (SysAdmin, Audit, Network and Security) organization has created and released an expanded version of the Purdue model that they have titled the ICS410 Reference Model. This expanded reference architecture, depicted in Figure 3-25a, makes provisions for the addition of Cloud Technologies and other technical advances to the OT environment, as well as the ever-increasing desire to push OT data up the organizational ladder through the IT networks.

Like the original ISA-95 Purdue model, the ICS410 model divides the IT/OT devices and networks into functional layers with appropriate cybersecurity devices and systems situated at the division points. However, it goes further than the Purdue model by dividing the Level-0 through Level-2 layers into distinct but separate silos (cells/lines/processes). The ICS410 also includes safety systems as part of the local Level 0-2 silos.

This model includes controls for integrating cloud services and other WAN communication channels to accommodate larger or widely distributed sites. The division between the traditional Level 0-2 and Level 3 is enforced by boundary protection set up on each side of the Cloud/WAN system. Minor enforcement boundaries are established on the Level 0-2 side while major boundary enforcement solutions are applied on the Level 3 side. The organization's management servers, HMIs, engineering stations, testing and staging systems, remote access, and cybersecurity operations are segmented into sub-layers at the Level 3 layer.

FIGURE 3.25a   The SANS ICS410 Reference Architecture

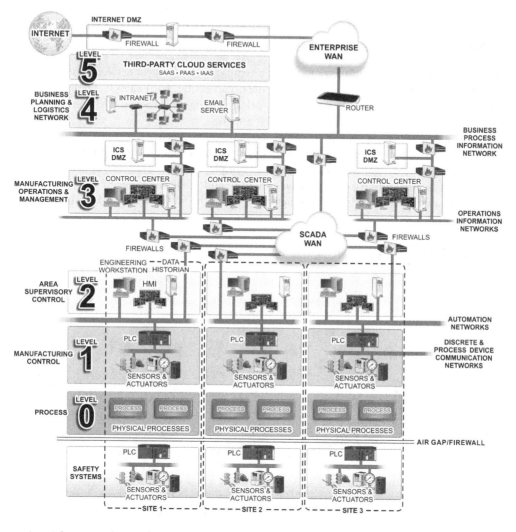

As with more advanced versions of the Purdue model, DMZs are strategically placed throughout the ICS410 model to provide the A-to-B push and the B-to-C pull, but not A-to-C or C-to-A communications paths between all IT and OT layers. Firewalls are the control device of choice between Layers 3 and 4 of this model. These firewalls should be configured to block all traffic in and out of the OT network with explicit permit rules implemented for the minimum required traffic. Firewalls are also called for between Levels 3 and 4, as well as between Levels 4 and 5.

Additional authentication methods, including multifactor authentication, should be employed for all access paths to the OT network. Malware-checking should be performed on all files entering or leaving the OT network. Likewise, all traffic entering or leaving the OT network should be logged. Finally, no Internet access should be allowed below Level 4.

Network Segmentation

Network segmentation is a subnetting technique employed to divide a network into layered segments based on the functional divisions of the organization. For example, there is generally no good reason for a department that is working on highly classified information to be directly networked with other departments that are not.

Typically, physical firewalls and routers are used to create network segmentation to control the movement of traffic between network tiers (segments). Figure 3.25 depicts a generically segmented business network. In this example, the router is configured to interface with the Internet and pass all packets with an IP address in the range of 134.141.x.x to the designated subnet inside the local network. When the packet reaches the subnet, it is accepted by the host with the designated fourth octet in the address (0–254).

FIGURE 3.25   A segmented network

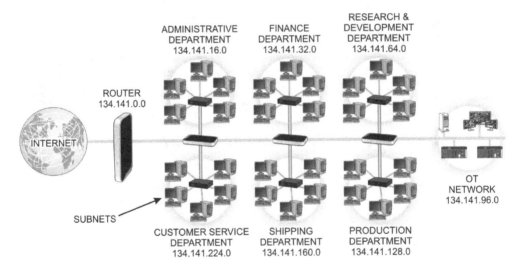

For our purposes, the main advantage of network segmentation is the added security created by making the segment's internal structure invisible to the other network segments and the outside world. A segmented network will act to limit the depth of any intrusions into the enterprise and to minimize the propagation of any attacks.

However, heightened security is not the only advantage of network segmentation. There are also increased performance levels within the local segment due to limiting the traffic flow from other segments. Another advantage is that segmentation isolates local failures to the segment, making them easier to detect, troubleshoot, and repair. However, segmentation also impacts the overall performance of the network and requires additional management.

In the following sections we investigate two methods that can also be used to create network segmentation with NAT segmenting and network virtualization using layer 2/3 switches.

Network Address Translation Segmenting

Network address translation (NAT) is a feature of most routers, servers, and firewalls. While the primary purpose of NAT is to shield the IP addresses of the internal network from those outside the network, it also provides a straightforward method of segmenting the internal physical structure of the organization's Intranet. Figure 3.26 illustrates a NAT-segmented network.

FIGURE 3.26   A NAT-segmented network

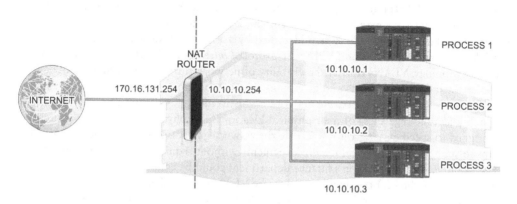

For example, in a network that is segmented by function, a NAT firewall could be installed to provide segmentation for a department that requires both minimal security and Internet access, while not using other security protocols.

However, NAT is not a security cure-all. It requires careful configuration and offers limited security. In fact, NAT is a hindrance to many other security protocols that you may want to use on your LAN. Primarily, NAT does not work well with any protocol that encrypts IP information. This makes tunneling protocols such as *Point-to-Point Tunneling Protocol (PPTP)* incompatible with a NAT firewall.

One of the most popular protocols, *IPSec* employs *Authentication Header (AH)* protocol to prevent packet changes in transport. Because NAT is designed to change the source IP address, IPSec authentication will fail if used on the same network segment. In addition, IPSec employs *Encapsulating Security Payload (ESP)* to check IP addresses in *Transport mode*, which will also fail if NAT translates the source IP address.

Any protocol that binds the source IP address with an authentication key will fail to authenticate or negotiate a session because NAT changes the source IP address. This would be true for *Internet Key Exchange (IKE)* as well as *Certificate Authorities (CAs)*. Likewise, because *File Transfer Protocol (FTP)* changes the source IP address into ASCII text, it is also not compatible with NAT on the same network segment.

It is possible, however, to establish IPSec connections across NAT gateways using a UDP encapsulation technique referred to as *Network Address Translation traversal (NAT-T)*. As described, the NAT device alters the authenticity of the packet that caused it to be dropped. NAT-T adds an unencrypted UDP header to encapsulate the IPSec ESP header. This causes the packet to be treated like a normal UDP packet so that it passes through the gateway. NAT-T operations require three ports to be open: UDP port 4500 (NAT-T), UDP port 500 (IKE), and IP protocol 50 (ESP).

Network Virtualization

Not all network structures are what they appear to be. A *virtual local area network (VLAN)* is a logical local area network that overlays one or more physical LANs. Virtualization software can be employed to partition a physical LAN into multiple logical LANs or to organize multiple physical LANs into a single logical LAN. In both cases, the organization and operation of the virtual LAN may bear little resemblance to the actual hardware the VLAN is operating on. Each virtual LAN is then identified by a *VLAN ID*, such as VLAN10.

VLANs (along with VPNs and VPLS) are *protocol-based virtual network structures*. As a security topology, VLANs restrict the visibility of network traffic by limiting the flow of traffic between designated ports and groupings. These structures are typically created using layer 2 managed switches to separate network segments along logical or functional chains of communication, regardless of their physical locations. The physical ports on the switches are assigned to specific user groups to create their own segments. This enables logical VLAN groups to span multiple physical network segments without requiring the use of a firewall.

For example, an organization's finance department could be connected to a VLAN that is uniquely established for the finance group. The VLAN is created as a set of specific switch ports, as illustrated in Figure 3.27. In this example, the switch ports are configured to create three separate VLANs: the executive network (VLAN10, ports 1 and 2), the finance department (VLAN20, ports 3, 4, and 5), and the sales department (VLAN30, ports 6, 7, and 8).

FIGURE 3.27   Sample VLAN organization

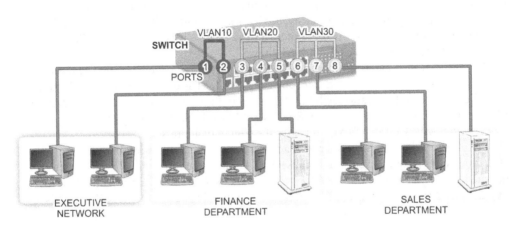

In a virtual area network, packets belong to the VLAN, not to the network devices. In this example, the finance department assets are connected to physical switch ports that are configured as VLAN20. As such, the switch will distribute finance data packets only to the designated VLAN20 ports, even if group members are located in geographically different areas of the organization's network.

Devices connected to a given *VLAN port* cannot communicate with devices in the network's other VLANs. If a device in one of the other VLANs requests a MAC address that is within the finance VLAN, the request is filtered out in the switch and never reaches the network. Therefore, no connection can be established.

Network Segregation

Simply dividing the network into segments does not actually improve the network's security, as traffic can still move from one subnet to another. However, when segmentation is combined with network segregation strategies, the two strategies combine to minimize the attack surfaces of different areas of the network.

Network segregation involves developing and enforcing communication *rule-sets* that control access between network segments (i.e., controlling which computing devices are permitted to communicate with other devices across the segment boundaries). They also control what types of information can move between security zones. These rules are normally based on data source and destination information, data type, or data content.

After the various segments of the network have been identified, the next step is to determine the control technologies to be employed in each zone. These technologies include *active controls* that can block or filter traffic as well as *passive controls*, which monitor activity and audit or report it. This is also the point at which to determine what rules to implement for each segment. This can be done by analyzing the communications paths dictated by the organization's business requirements.

In general, there are a few basic suggestions to keep in mind when designing a segmented/segregated network environment:

- *Segment the network based on common information security requirements.* The overall goal here is to create the most secure segments for the most sensitive data. Less secure data can be stored or manipulated in less secure segments, while public data can be placed in segments that have minimal security provisions. Map the network based on this approach and see if access to any segments is too open or too restrictive.

- *Implement security control segments as needed.* While it might appear as though the more security layers you can create the better, from the preceding discussion you should be able to see that this is not always true. Create the proper number of security segments to adequately protect the different classifications of the organization's data. Creating too few segments may leave some data more vulnerable than it should be, while creating excessive segments can weigh the organization's business processes down.

- *Establish access controls based on the rule of least privileged.* As mentioned in earlier discussions in this chapter, you may need to provide third-party access to your corporate IT network for a trusted vendor. However, you should limit their access to those areas of the network that are absolutely needed to efficiently conduct the business associated with the organization's relationship.

- *Determine the acceptable level of security for each segment.* It is never practical to attempt to completely block every kind of threat in a network environment. Instead, determine what activities are important and implement a strategy with acceptable communication paths for those activities and then block everything else. This can be accomplished by creating *allowlists* that specify what network traffic can access different segments, as opposed to *denylists* that specify what network traffic cannot have access. In addition, the rules of "least privilege" and "need-to-know" should be applied when granting segment access to users or groups.

Whitelisting is the practice of assigning access to the known good and denying all others, while blacklisting involves allowing everyone except those on the known bad list. A whitelist is a registry of users (usernames, IP addresses, URLs, MAC addresses, etc.) that are trusted to have specific privileges, services, or access to an asset. Blacklists, on the other hand, are lists of users who are untrusted (either known and untrusted or unrecognized). Users on a blacklist are configured to be blocked or denied access to the specified asset.

Segmentation and segregation can be accomplished through a variety of technologies and techniques, including VLANs, VPNs using encryption protocols, and data diodes. These technologies should be applied to the network at multiple layers, from the Data Link layer to the Application layer.

Partitioning

Partitioning is a form of network segregation that involves dividing the network into multiple smaller-scale networks (broadcast domains) and creating filters between those domains that permit only specified services to move across each domain's boundaries. Network administrators use partitioning tools and techniques to create intranets within the organization's network and provide complex boundary protection structures, as well as to create extranets and branch networks.

Partitioning provides administrators with centralized control and management capabilities that can be used to implement unified security policies throughout the organization, as defined by the organization's security policies.* It also enables single sign-on capabilities, remote procedure calls, and efficient intrusion detection operations.

*Policies are enforced between domains but not within domains.

Because this description is a natural extension of traditional firewall operations, physical firewalls and *access control lists (ACLs)* have been the mainstays of network partitioning. These tools deliver proven segmentation functions that are trusted by network security specialists. However, the processes for defining and configuring segmentation in this way are time-consuming and prone to human error that can result in security breaches. In addition, this type of implementation requires thorough knowledge of specific device configuration syntax, network addressing, application ports, and protocols.

The main drawback of network partitioning centers around the performance issues associated with current IP filtering devices. However, with new connectivity devices coming into the market, such as layer 4 filtering on switches and routers, it is expected that IP filtering performance will be less of an issue going forward.

Enterprise networks can also be segmented effectively and securely by organizing the network into multiple VLANs. Segmentation and segregation are both basic products of network virtualization. Each VLAN becomes a separate broadcast domain that only reveals related assets to the authorized members of that domain. Packets can only pass from one VLAN to another via a router (a layer 3 segmentation device).

In addition, each VLAN segment can be configured with unique security measures depending on the requirements of the segment's assets. In VLANs this multitier network security environment is established through the use of *distributed firewall rules*, as illustrated in Figure 3.28.

FIGURE 3.28 VLAN partitioning

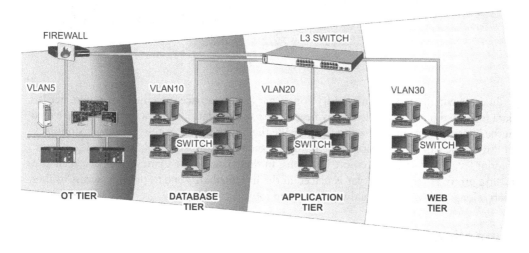

In this example, the physical network is segmented into four L2 VLAN segments with L3 segmentation between zones. The individual L2 segments can be virtualized into micro-segments to improve the overall performance of the L2 segment and provide additional security options within the segment. The result of this combination of segmentation and segregation efforts creates an innermost database tier, the mid-level application tier, and an outward-facing customer web tier.

Controlling Intersegment Data Movement

Ideally, users in a given security zone can only communicate with other users in their own segment or in the adjacent zone. The organization's security topology's policies must be implemented on the zoning hardware (firewalls, switches, and routers) to control the flow of information between its zones, as illustrated in Figure 3.29.

FIGURE 3.29   Intersegment DATA movement

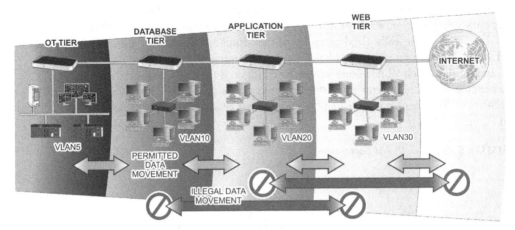

In cases where users are in security zones that are not adjacent to the zone where needed data is located (and they legitimately need access to that data), a gateway must be provided in the intermediary zone (or zones) to provide them with secure access. A prime example of this is when an organization has employees, such as sales personnel, who need to access interior levels of data from remote locations. In these situations, a gateway device such as a reverse proxy or terminal server is placed in the intermediate zone to provide access to these users, along with virus and malware scanning tools.

Tunneling

When data considered confidential is transferred between zones, it must be protected. This is accomplished by securing the data in motion using *data transfer encryption*.

Tunneling technology and techniques can be used to securely control data movement between security zones, as shown in Figure 3.30. As such, it is a viable security topology to consider when communicating privately between two zones such as with an extranet security zone. The tunneling protocol offers encapsulation of data and works hand in hand with specific encrypting protocols to produce a VPN that functions.

FIGURE 3.30   Secure tunneling

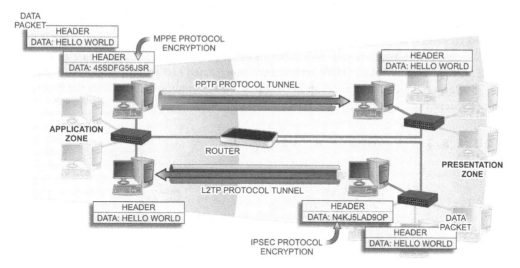

A tunneling protocol, such as PPTP, creates a VPN when used along with Microsoft's Point-to-Point Encryption (MPPE) protocol. Likewise, the Layer 2 Tunneling Protocol (L2TP) creates a VPN when it is used in conjunction with IPSec. Although IPSec is a component of a VPN, it is not a tunneling protocol like L2F, L2TP,* or PPTP.

The security benefit of using tunneling to transmit private data between security zones is that the connectivity devices that separate the zones are unaware that the communication is part of a private network. By encapsulating the private data and protocol information within a public transmission packet, the private data is hidden to the system. Anyone scanning the tunneled transmission across the network would not be aware of the message contents.

*L2TP has a limitation in that it works only on IP networks.

Wireless Networking

There is another technology beginning to impact the traditional structure of OT networks: *industrial wireless technology*. *Wireless networks* are already used to connect intelligent devices together using high-frequency radio waves in the enterprise side of the organizational network. The idea of using wireless sensors, controllers, and actuators to eliminate long cable runs between ICS devices in the process control network has been discussed and pursued for many years. However, movement toward actually implementing wireless OT networks has been slow.

Wireless network technologies have some well-known challenges that make them less interesting as ICS components. These drawbacks include decreased security, robustness, delays, reliability, and safety. Even so, the push to overcome these challenges and produce wireless ICS technologies continues.

A wireless IT/OT network reference model is depicted in Figure 3.31. Compare this model to the hardwired, networked OT/IT architecture constructed earlier in the chapter. Like the ISA-95 reference model, this model shows various sensors communicating with the controllers via wireless links. This section is referred to as the *wireless sensor network (WSN)*.

FIGURE 3.31   A wireless ICS reference network

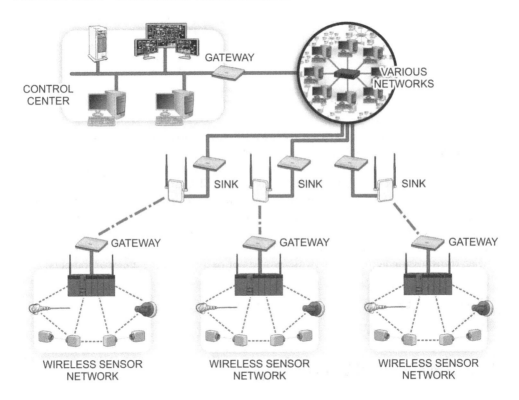

Notice that the other layers of this reference model are also using wireless network technologies to communicate with each other. While these network segments can be implemented using commercial wireless technologies, in some models it is seen as being just as easy to do so with traditional IT network devices and protocols.

Wireless Sensors

Wireless sensors offer the largest pool of devices being discussed and developed for wireless application to OT networks. These sensors include devices such as pressure transmitters, differential pressure transmitters, temperature transmitters, analog input transmitters, and universal I/O transmitters. Most are designed to replace the sensor, as well as the old *4-20mA current loop* signaling standard that industrial process control has relied on for so long.

The sensor devices are actually packaged versions of a physical sensor and a wireless transmitter or transceiver. The sensor does the work of converting the process variable into a meaningful electronic signal that can be applied to its wireless radio transmitter. On the other end, the controller either receives the radio signal directly using its own radio or uses a separate receiver to acquire the signal and then converts it into a signal that can be applied to the controller. These options are illustrated in Figure 3.32.

FIGURE 3.32   Wireless sensor communications

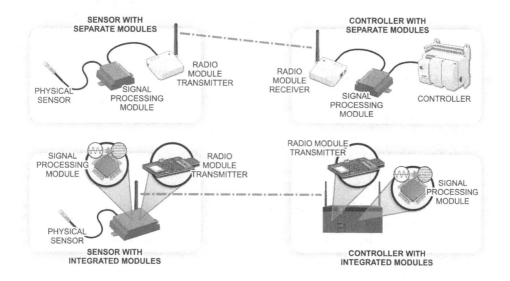

On the other end of the process control loop, wireless technologies can be implemented to receive control commands and data and deliver them to the remote actuator's final device. In either event, the radios at each end of the link must use the same transmission and signaling protocols to communicate. Common radio technologies used for this purpose include the following:

- Wi-Fi
- Bluetooth
- ZigBee

- WiMax
- Proprietary communication protocols/links

As seen multiple times, OT networks require real-time, dependable data to operate correctly and safely. One of the major drawbacks of using wireless technologies in OT networks is their vulnerability to *electrical interference* and the potential consequences if their data is interfered with.

Industrial production environments inherently tend to be electrically noisy. Electrical motors and switching devices radiate electrical noise into the air during their normal operations. This noise travels through the air in waves that can interfere with the radio signals also moving through the air. This interference can interrupt or mangle data encoded on those radio signals, causing delays and data loss. This is extremely problematic for real-time process control systems.

Another potential problem associated with wireless sensor networks is the need for local power supply or a battery. Adding local AC power connections to the plant in each sensor location can be quite costly. In addition, safe operation of the process may require backup power sources (batteries) for each sensor location. This too can be costly to install and maintain. If battery power is required for either reason, the task of tracking and changing out the batteries can become a maintenance issue.

Wireless Communication Protocols

Industrial and utility networks employ different wireless communication protocols to transmit data and telemetry throughout their processes. The IEEE organization oversees a group of wireless networking specifications under the IEEE-802.xx banner:

- *Wi-Fi*: The IEEE 802.11x (also known as *Wireless Fidelity*) wireless standards have gained wide acceptance as the preferred wireless networking technology for both business and residential network applications.

- *Bluetooth (IEEE 802.15.1)*: This is a wireless networking specification for personal area networks (PANs) that has gained widespread acceptance in some areas, such as meshing personal devices including speakers, cell phones, and digital cameras, as well as PCs, notebooks, and printers. This bringing together of different types of digital devices in a common forum is referred to as *convergence*.

    Bluetooth devices use low-power consumption, short-range radio frequency signals to provide a low-cost, secure communication link. The specification provides three power level/range options: 100mW/100meters, 2.5mW/10meters, and 1mW/1meter.

    The Bluetooth specification implements *Adaptive Frequency Hopping Spread Spectrum (AFHSS)* in the license-free 2.4 GHz range to provide security and avoid crowded frequency ranges. The Bluetooth protocol divides the 2.4 GHz frequency range into 79 different 1MHz communication channels. The frequency-hopping mechanism changes channels up to 1,600 times per second. The data transfer rate for Bluetooth 1.1 and 1.2 devices is 723.1 Kbps, and 2.1 Mbps for Bluetooth 2.0 devices.

Bluetooth devices can be connected to only one device at a time. Once a Bluetooth device has connected to another Bluetooth device, it will be prevented from connecting to other devices and showing up in inquiries until it is disconnected from the original Bluetooth device.

However, the standard also provides for constructing multipoint wireless networks using Bluetooth technologies. Under the Bluetooth specification, up to eight devices can be grouped together to form a *piconet*. Any device can become the master device and assume control of the network by issuing a request broadcast. The other seven devices become slave devices until the master device releases its position.

The master device uses time division multiplexing to rapidly switch from one slave device to another around the network. In this manner, the Bluetooth network operates like a wireless USB network. Any device in the network can assume the master device role when it is available.

In the computer networking environment, the Bluetooth specification enables several Bluetooth peripheral devices to simultaneously communicate with a host device. In particular, Bluetooth is used with local host computers to communicate with wireless input and output devices such as mice, keyboards, and printers.

- *Zigbee (IEEE 802.15.4)*: Like Bluetooth, the Zigbee standard is a wireless, mesh-networked PAN protocol that provides for a 10-meter communication range with data transfer rates at 250 kbps. The Zigbee standard has been embraced by the smart home automation and industrial controls communities, as well as several areas of the smart grid consortium. It is also being considered for use with *personal biomedical sensors* to provide secure, remote medical data acquisition.

- *WiMAX (IEEE 802.16)*: This specification was established to provide guidelines for wider area wireless networking capabilities. WiMAX is a broadband wireless access standard designed to provide Internet access across large geographic areas, such as cities, counties, and in some cases countries. It is also designed to provide interoperability with the 802.11 Wi-Fi standard.

Wireless Connectivity Devices

Depending on the distance between wireless controllers, sensors, and actuators, there may be several different types of wireless network connectivity devices included in the network. For example, the previous illustration suggested direct radio links between the various sensors and the controller. However, just as in residential or corporate IT networks, digital wireless devices could be communicating with the industrial process controller through a *wireless access point (WAP)* or a *wireless router/gateway* device.

The WAP acts as a bridging device that connects the wireless network devices with each other and a wired network. These devices employ antennas and a radio receiver/transmitter to communicate with other network devices using radio frequency signals in the unlicensed 2.4 GHz radio band. Conversely, it communicates with the wired network through a physical interface, such as an Ethernet connection on a switch or router, as shown in Figure 3.33.

FIGURE 3.33   A WAP

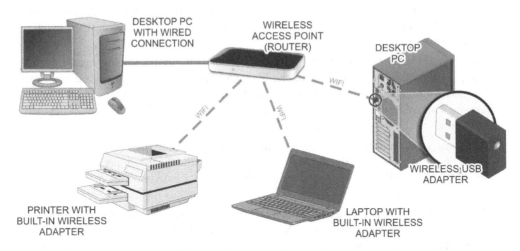

Wireless network client devices must possess a wireless network interface consisting of a radio transmitter, receiver, and antenna to communicate with the WAP. Each intelligent device that has a wireless network interface can communicate directly with other wireless-equipped devices or with the access point. Wireless network devices are also able to communicate with wired network devices on the Ethernet network through the access point.

Wireless Gateways

In communications and digital networking, a *gateway* is defined as a device that interfaces a network with another network that employs a different protocol. Recall that a protocol is a defined set of rules for carrying out communication between different devices or systems.

The protocol may be designed to match differences in physical connections (hardware protocols) or to match different signal logic levels, message formats, or information exchange speeds (software protocols). Some gateway devices are designed to perform both functions, as illustrated in Figure 3.34. The gateway in the figure translates a wired Ethernet/TCP/IP protocol format into a wireless/ZigBee protocol format.

FIGURE 3.34   Gateway operations

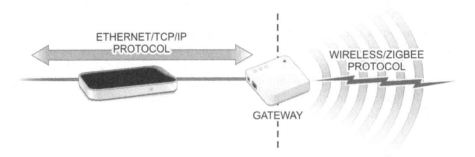

For communications to be successful, both parties must agree to use the same protocol. For example, for two people to communicate verbally, they must both be able to use a common language, for example, English and English or Spanish and Spanish. If not, you have an example of the old Chinese proverb about the chicken talking to the duck.

When a router is used to connect networks to always-on broadband Internet connections, they are referred to as *Internet gateways.* In addition to performing the routing functions, Internet gateway routers typically supply a number of other Internet-related services, such as DHCP and firewall services. These services are described in detail later in this chapter. You may also encounter routing switches, called *LAN switches,* that have built-in routing capabilities.

Modems

In Chapter 1 you were introduced to telemetry and metering systems associated with distributed OT networks. In these extended network segments, modems are employed to convert digital data into signal formats that can be transmitted over longer distances.

In addition to the radio module, each different long distance wireless communication technology requires a *modulator/demodulator (modem)* device at each end of the communication link. These devices are used to connect industrial field devices and controllers at distances well beyond those that are possible using digital or asynchronous serial connections.

The modulator portion of the modem serializes and modulates data into signals that can be transmitted across the particular media type being used. At the other end, the demodulator portion of the other modem demodulates the signal and then deserializes the data so it can be used by the OT devices.

There are industrial modems available that use a couple of different communication technologies: cellular radio and long-haul wireless Ethernet radios.

Industrial cellular modems rely on cellular telephone technology to provide wireless wide area network communications for industrial control and utility applications. These modems connect to the wired network (or device) through a standard wired-Ethernet or serial RS-485 connection and then provide wireless point to multipoint communications with the intelligent field devices using *General Packet Radio Service (GPRS)* modules, as illustrated in Figure 3.35.

FIGURE 3.35   Cellular modem implementation

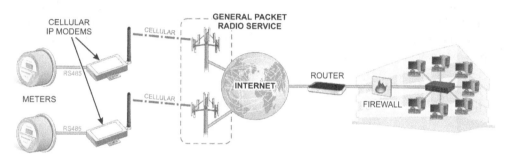

The GPRS modules can be integrated directly into the electronics of the field device as an embedded piece of hardware. The radios employ *frequency division duplexing (FDD)* and *time division multiple access (TDMA)* techniques to transfer IP packet data through existing cellular channels.

Long-haul wireless Ethernet modems typically operate in the 2.5 GHz, 5 GHz, and 900 MHz frequency ranges. Some models provide high-throughput, line-of-sight communications at distances from 5 to 20 kilometers. These models may also include built-in networking features such as internal routing and access control lists for deny-listing/allow-listing configurations. Additional features include functions such as wireless I/O mapping for networking multiple I/O devices together and user-selectable digital, analog, or combinational input and output types.

Other industrial modem models can be configured for mesh networking topologies that provide redundancy for industrial Ethernet devices. These modems may also provide built-in conversion from serial Modbus RTU to Modbus TCP.

Wireless Network Security

While wireless networks are common in residential and business networks due to their ease of installation, there are a number of security issues concerning using them to communicate confidential information. Transmissions from wireless network devices cannot simply be confined to the local environment of a residence or business.

Although the range of most wireless network devices is typically limited to a few hundred feet, RF signals can easily be intercepted even outside the vicinity of the stated security perimeter. Any unauthorized mobile terminal can accomplish this using an 802.11 receiver.

To minimize the risk of security compromise on a wireless LAN, the IEEE-802.11 wireless standard provides a security feature called the *Wi-Fi Protected Access (WPA) standard* that provides data encryption, using *Temporary Key Integrity Protocol (TKIP)* and IEEE 802.1X *Extensible Authentication Protocol (EAP)* user authentication protocol to provide security. This combination requires users to employ usernames and passwords to access the network. After the user logs in, the AP generates a temporary key that is used to encrypt data transfers between the AP and the client computer.

If possible, you should set up the router to use WPA-PSK along with a strong password. The PSK option enables WPA to use *Pre-Shared Keys* instead of a separate *Certificate Authority (CA)* computer to provide user authentication. The PSK permits a password to be set on the router and shared with the rest of the users.

In addition, after you've installed and authenticated all the wireless clients, you should set the SSID Broadcast option to Disable so that outsiders do not use SSID to acquire your address and data. It's highly recommended to change the SSID name from the default value to prevent unauthorized access.

Review Questions

The following questions test your knowledge of the material presented in this chapter.

1. One of the first lines of defense for interboundary communications is the _____.

2. A _____ is a plan that includes a number of different overlapping security mechanisms that will minimize the effects of a single mechanism being overcome by an attacker.

3. What mechanism is used with firewalls to cause it to reject or accept certain types of incoming and outgoing packets?

4. What is the purpose of segmenting a network into various security zones?

5. The term _____ involves developing and enforcing communication rule-sets that control access between different network segments (i.e., controlling which computing devices are permitted to communicate with other devices across the boundary). They also control what types of information can move between security zones. These rules are normally based on data source and destination information, data type, or data content.

6. Referring to the small business zoning configuration depicted in Figure 3.36, what types of devices would typically be expected to be in the Application Zone (Database) segment?

FIGURE 3.36   Small business network zoning

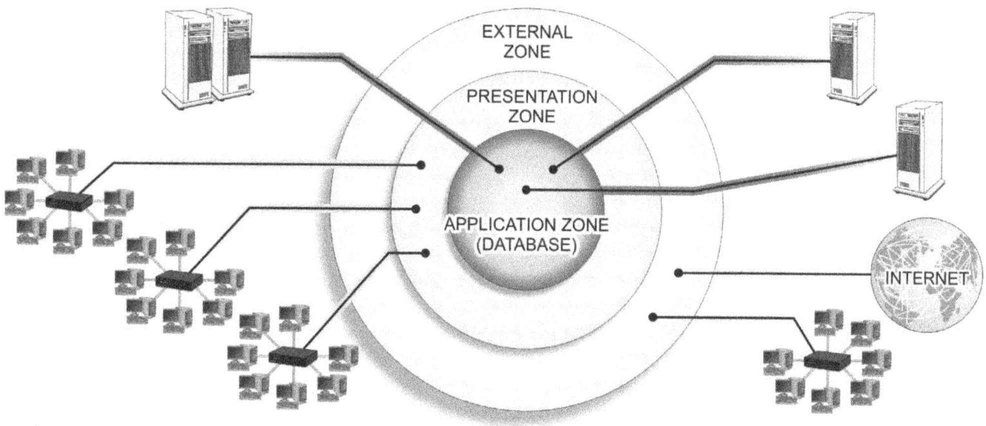

7. While flat network security topologies are the least expensive method of organizing a network, what are their major drawbacks?

8. What steps must be taken when network users are in security zones that are not adjacent to the zone where needed data is located (and they legitimately need access to that data)?

9. Describe the purpose that the Purdue ANSI/ISA 95 Reference Model Architecture was designed to accomplish.

10. Which type of network connectivity device is used to create VLANs?

11. What is the security benefit of using tunneling to transmit data between security zones?

12. What function does a data diode perform in a layered multizone network security topology?

13. In an enterprise network environment, it is common to see a DMZ implemented between the organization's internal trusted network and the external less-trusted Internet. Where is a DMZ more likely to be located in an ICS/IT network?

14. What do ICS network engineers see as the greatest benefit to having a secure wireless network technology?

15. What type of network device is required to connect a wireless ZigBee device network to a wired Ethernet network such as the organization's LAN?

Exam Questions

1. Managed network switches can be used to create a logically secured security structure that restricts visibility of network traffic by limiting the movement of network packets so that they only pass between designated ports. These structures are called _____.

    A. Security zones

    B. Security segments

    C. VPNs

    D. VLANs

2. The _____ collect network connection information and maintain dynamic state tables that are used for subsequent connections. This enables ports to be opened and closed as needed. Once a client has completed a communication session, the firewall closes the specific port used until it is requested again.

    A. Static packet-filtering firewalls

    B. Stateless packet-filtering firewalls

    C. Stateful packet-filtering

    D. Software firewalls

3. Referring to Figure 3.37, what type of edge protection structure is being displayed?

    A. A multihomed DMZ

    B. A dual-homed DMZ

    C. A honeypot

    D. A VPN

FIGURE 3.37

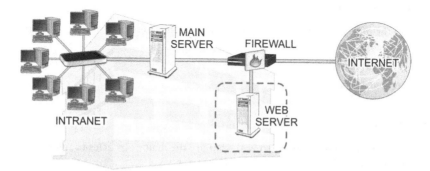

4. According to the Purdue ANSI/ISA 95 Reference Model Architecture, at what level should a DMZ be established to separate the Business Planning and Logistics portion of the network from the Manufacturing Operations and Management portion?

    A. At level 3

    B. At level 4

    C. Between level 4 and level 3

    D. Between level 4 and level 5

5. From the following list, identify network devices that are commonly used to create the partitions between different security zones in a network. (Select all that apply.)

    A. Servers

    B. Firewalls

    C. Routers

    D. IDS

    E. VLANs

6. A _____ is a barrier that prevents outsiders from entering a local area network and prevents insiders from directly connecting to outside resources.

    A. Firewall

    B. Proxy

    C. DMZ

    D. Extranet

7. What type of network devices are used to create DMZs?

    A. Routers

    B. Firewalls

    C. Managed switches

    D. Network appliances

8. What are the major drawbacks to implementing wireless networks in ICS environments? (Select all that apply.)

    A. Decreased reliability

    B. Increased connectivity ranges

    C. Decreased security

    D. Data delays

9. In an industrial processing environment, what are the major obstacles to implementing wireless sensors in OT networks? (Select all that apply.)

    A. Their vulnerability to electrical interference

    B. Their interference with other communication channels

    C. Their need for local power supply or battery

    D. Wireless sensors tend to be fragile and do not hold up well in industrial environments.

10. Which wireless protocol standard has been the most widely embraced by the industrial controls community?

   A. Bluetooth

   B. ZigBee

   C. WiMax

   D. Wi-Fi

Chapter

4

ICS Module and Element Hardening

OBJECTIVES

Upon completion of this chapter, you should be able to:

1. **Knowledge of endpoint protection:**
   - User workstations
   - Mobile devices

2. **Knowledge of OS security:**
   - Unix/Linux
   - Microsoft Windows
   - Least Privilege security
   - Virtualization

3. **Knowledge of application security:**
   - Application security
   - Database security

4. **Knowledge of anti-malware:**
   - Implementation
   - Updating
   - Monitoring
   - Sanitization

5. **Knowledge of embedded device security:**
   - PLCs
   - Controllers
   - RTU

- Analyzers
- Meters
- Aggregators
- Security issues
- Default configurations

6. Knowledge of network security/hardening:

- Server security
- Switch port security

Introduction

In computer and networking environments, the term *hardening* refers to the process of making a component or system more secure. As you can see from the test objectives listed, this occurs in several different areas of the OT/IT network and at several different levels. In this chapter, we will explore tools and techniques associated with hardening various areas of the ICS.

- Endpoints
- Operating systems
- Applications
- Embedded ICS devices
- Networks
- Servers
- Network connectivity devices

Endpoint Security and Hardening

An *endpoint* is defined as a user computing device connected to a TCP/IP network that enables the user to access information across the network. This designation typically includes desktop and notebook computers, in addition to mobile computing devices such as tablets and smart phones.

User Workstation Hardening

Computer hardening efforts begin with hardware. However, they also extend to the local host's operating system, its file system, and its applications. You can think of protecting individual IT or OT devices in terms of three layers of security.

- The *outer perimeter* is the space around the outside of the physical device and its housing (hardware).

- The *inner perimeter* should be viewed as the device's operating system and application programs (software).
- The *interior* of the device consists of the intangible data assets, such as the information created, obtained, and stored electronically in the device (data).

Figure 4.1 graphically illustrates these layers.

FIGURE 4.1   The three perimeters

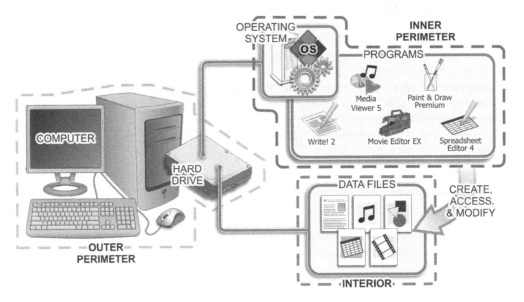

You should realize that what cybercriminals really want from such devices is the programs and data located inside. To secure these assets, you must consider how and where such people can get access to them in order to damage, destroy, or steal them. For both computing and intelligent control devices, there are three general locations where attackers can gain access to these items:

- While they're in memory (in use)
- While they're in storage devices such as hard drives and flash drives (at rest)
- When they're being transferred from one place to another (in transit)

In the case of the personal computer depicted in Figure 4.1, consider how you would penetrate its case to get to the intangible valuables inside.

The first level of securing endpoint devices is to control access to them. You can't damage, destroy, or steal what you can't get to. This applies to intelligent computing and control devices as well. So, the first step is to control physical access to the devices to the extent that is practical.

As with PCs and servers in IT environments, autonomous or semi-autonomous OT control devices, such as PLCs or stand-alone microcontrollers, can normally be placed in secure, lockable enclosures where access is limited to those people possessing the key.

The most obvious point of access through the outer perimeter of most computing devices is through their basic input devices such as keyboards, mice, or touch-sensitive displays. If someone can simply sit down in front of the device and freely use its input devices, they have an avenue for accessing the information inside. All they have to do is power cycle the device and wait for it to boot up.

BIOS Security Subsystems

There is one basic security tool built into the hardware of most personal computers that offers them some protection before the operating system bootup occurs. The *Basic Input/ Output System (BIOS)* offers basic hardware security options that can be configured through its CMOS setup utility. Figure 4.2 displays a typical Security Configuration screen. Normally, these options include setting user passwords to control access to the system and supervisory passwords to control access to the CMOS setup utility.

FIGURE 4.2 CMOS security configuration

```
                              BIOS Setup Utility
     Main        Advanced     Security     Boot      Exit

                                                    Item Specific Help
     Set User Password:          [Enter]
     Set Supervisor Password     [Enter]
                                                    Supervisor password
     Virus Check Reminder:       [Disabled]         controls access to Setup
     System Backup Reminder:     [Disabled]         utility.

     Password on boot:           [Disabled]
     Diskette Access:            [Disabled]
     Fixed disk boot sector:     [Normal]




     F1   Help  ↑↓  Select Item  -/+          Change Values    F9   Setup Defaults
     Esc  Exit  ←→  Select Menu  Press Enter  Select ► Sub-Menu F10  Save and Exit
```

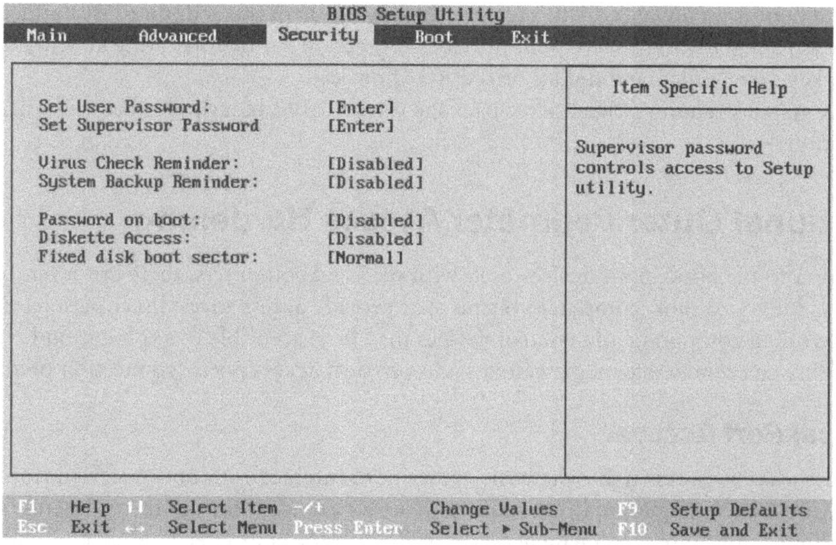

The Set User Password option enables administrators to establish passwords that users must enter during the startup process to complete the boot process and gain access to the operating system. Without this password the system never reaches an operational level that an intruder could use to access its internal perimeter and interior information.

However, this password does not provide access to the CMOS setup utility where the user and supervisory password options are configured. The Set Supervisory Password option must be used to establish a password that can be employed to access the CMOS setup utility.

The Security Configuration screen may also include options for setting virus check and backup reminders that pop up periodically when the system is booted. In addition to enabling these settings, administrators can specify the time interval between notices.

One of the main sets of security options in the CMOS setup utility consists of those that can be used to control access to the system's inner perimeter and interior assets. For the most part, these options cover such things as limiting access permitted through the asset's physical ports and removable media systems, as well as access to the boot sector of the system's disk drive.

Because the CMOS password controls access to all parts of the system (even before the bootup process occurs), there will be some inconvenience in the event that the user forgets a password. When this happens, it will be impossible to gain access to the system without completely resetting the content of the CMOS RAM.

Newer endpoints operate from an advanced firmware base referred to as the *Unified Extensible Firmware Interface (UEFI)*, which is an advanced, more powerful addition to the traditional BIOS. Systems that support UEFI boot up to the Windows operating system. This addition provides faster bootup, support for disc drives larger than 2 TB, and additional security features.

Secure boot is an advanced UEFI feature designed to help the endpoint resist attacks and infections from malware. Secure boot provides protection for the operating system's boot loaders, key system files, and unauthorized ROM devices.

Linux systems require a third-party package to sign UEFI binaries for use with their distributions.

Additional Outer Perimeter Access Hardening

In addition to the basic input devices used with personal computers, there are several other pathways built into most computer systems that provide access to the inner perimeter. Even non-networked computing and control devices may be susceptible to exploitation by outside sources through removable media systems and physical access ports (connection points).

Physical Port Access

Physical *hardware ports* enable the basic endpoint to interact with optional, removable devices, as shown in Figure 4.3. They also provide a potential security threat because individuals with malicious intent can gain access directly into the computer internal communication and processing system through these ports.

Be aware that the term *port* is also used to refer to logical UTP/TCP software ports used in computer network communications. You will encounter this version of the term shortly when you are introduced to firewalls.

FIGURE 4.3   Physical PC ports

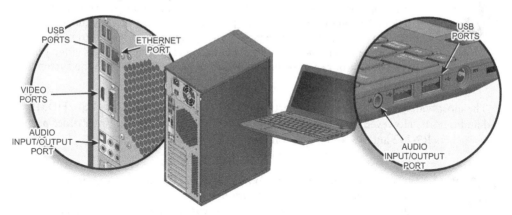

Hardware ports provide access to the computer's internal communications buses that link all its internal components together, including its data bus, memory, and internal storage devices (the three areas listed for gaining access to programs and data). Figure 4.4 depicts the layout of a typical PC's internal bus structure. The only component standing between someone with physical access to the port connection and the system's internal structure is the bus controller interface that is part of the computer's internal *chipset*. The operation of this circuitry is controlled by the system's BIOS and operating system.

FIGURE 4.4   PC chipset

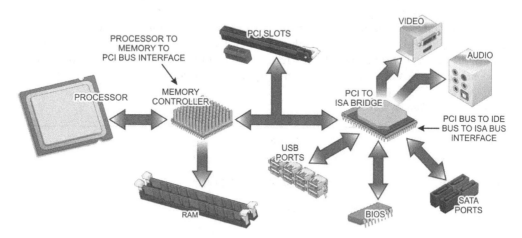

Data can be downloaded into removable media devices through these ports and quickly carried away. Likewise, malicious programs, such as viruses and worms that you will be introduced to later in this chapter, can be uploaded into the machine from the removable media source. Once these programs have been introduced to the host system, they infect it and can damage or destroy data and programs stored on it.

An endpoint device may possess several different hardware connection points. Not all these connections pose a security threat. Only those connection ports that provide access directly to the system's internal bus structure need to be considered. For example, a standard VGA video port is an output-only connection that does not provide access to the system's internal operation.

The most widely used hardware connection ports in newer endpoints are USB, HDMI, and audio ports. However, with OT computing devices you may still encounter older port types such as RS-232 and RS-485 serial communication ports.

It is also possible and common for people to penetrate the endpoint's outer perimeter and access its internal buses, memory, and storage devices through network and wireless connections. These access routes and how to secure them are discussed later in this chapter.

The most popular hardware port in modern computing devices is the *Universal Serial Bus (USB)* port. USB devices can be quite small and are easy to conceal and transport. Therefore, they provide an excellent vehicle for injecting malicious software into local host computers and intelligent control devices that might be very well protected from network access. For this reason, it is important to control access to USB ports on the computing device, as well as to control what individual users can use the ports for.

In the case of USB ports, the operation of the port connections is controlled by settings in the motherboard's CMOS setup utility. For the security reasons cited previously, it may be necessary to access the CMOS setup utility to disable its USB function.

There are some older legacy hardware ports you might not encounter too often. Table 4.1 summarizes physical port types used with endpoints. They are most often located on the back of the device, but some models may feature some of these ports on the front panel for convenience. Figure 4.5 describes the physical appearance of these ports.

TABLE 4.1   Legacy Ports

PORT	CONNECTOR
Keyboard	PS/2 6-pin mini-DIN
Mouse	PS/2 6-pin mini-DIN
COM1	DB-9M
LPT	DB-25F
VGA	DE-15F (3 row)

PORT	CONNECTOR
Game	DE-15F (2 row)
Modem	RJ-11
LAN	BNC/8P8C (RJ-45)
Sound	RCA 1/8″ minijacks or 3/32″ sub minijacks
SCSI	Centronic 50-pin

FIGURE 4.5   Typical I/O port connectors

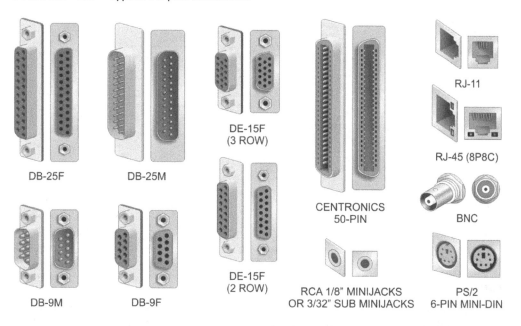

If you do encounter these ports, the ones that potentially can pose security risks include the RS-232/422/485 serial COM ports, Small Computer System Interface (SCSI), and the LPT parallel printer ports. These ports are all capable of handling two-way communications with the system's internal devices.

BIOS Port Enabling Functions

It is common for a system's BIOS to offer device control options that provide control over the computer's external hardware connection ports. By disabling these ports, users and administrators can help to ensure that unauthorized users cannot use the ports to gain unauthorized access to the system, transfer information out of the system, or download malware programs into the system.

In addition to controlling access through the USB ports, the BIOS may also offer control over serial ports, parallel ports, flash media readers, smart card slots, card bus slots and eSATA ports, if the system possesses them, as shown in Figure 4.6.

FIGURE 4.6   Port enabling options

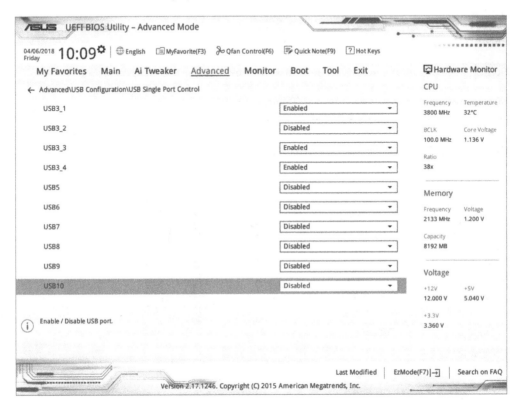

Removable Media Access

Removable computer media present multiple security risks. These risks include potential loss of data through theft due to the portable nature of the media, as well as the potential to introduce destructive malware into the host system.

Figure 4.7 shows different types of removable media associated with PC systems. These typically include the following:

- Magnetic storage media such as external hard drives and backup tapes

- Optical storage media such as CD and DVD discs

- Solid-state electronic storage devices such as external (SSD) solid-state drives, USB flash or thumb drives, MMC memory sticks, and SD cards

FIGURE 4.7   Removable media systems

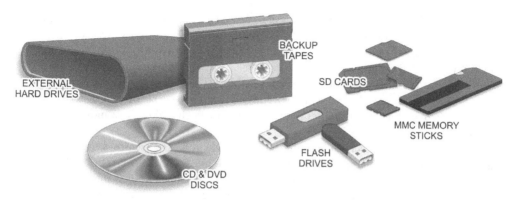

All three of these media device types provide access to the computer's internal system through its drives and hardware connection ports.

BIOS Boot Device/Sequence Controls

Most BIOS provide boot device enabling, disabling, and sequencing functions that should be used to control how the computer can be booted up for operation. Typically, the BIOS offers users and administrators the option to enable or disable the following types of devices:

- Optical disc drive(s)
- Hard disk drive(s)
- USB devices
- SD cards
- eSATA devices

Unless it is necessary to routinely boot the system from other devices, all boot options except the primary hard disk drive option should be disabled to provide the best security.

Microsoft Autorun Feature

Some versions of Microsoft's operating systems include a featured called *Autorun* that automatically runs executable programs found on removable media devices as soon as it detects the presence of the media in the drive or reader. This feature provides a very serious security threat, as malware programs located on the media can be designed to run automatically and infect the host device.

This feature has been blamed for up to 50 percent of all malware infections in older Windows systems. The threat can be removed simply by disabling the Autorun feature in Windows by downloading an app to turn it off. The other alternative is to modify the Windows registry to turn off Autorun.

Mobile Device Protection

The preceding chapter pointed out that wireless sensor and control networks have made some inroads into the OT environment. These sensors and control devices use conventional wireless technologies found in other mobile devices such as Bluetooth, Wi-Fi, Near Field Communication (NFC), and cellular.

Both Wi-Fi and Bluetooth have limited ranges, but within those ranges it is possible for a hacker to intercept, or at least disrupt, wireless connectivity. Of course, these networks bring with them all the vulnerabilities described earlier, which makes them more attractive to hackers.

In addition to wireless technologies migrating into the industrial sensor and control environment, there is a growing movement in businesses to allow employees to bring their own endpoint computing devices such as notebooks, tablets, and smart phones into the workplace. In many cases, they also supply Wi-Fi access to accommodate this *bring your own device (BYOD)* environment. Just as joining the OT network to the enterprise network opens new avenues for outsiders to exploit the previously more secure OT environment, BYOD devices connected to the OT network open even more vulnerabilities.

Network administrators and security personnel must determine whether such a BYOD environment creates security gaps for their networks. For example, vulnerabilities associated with a particular BYOD endpoint (or its particular configuration) could enable unauthorized users to access the network through the device and exploit the connection to hack proprietary or sensitive data. In these cases, the organization must include the additional vulnerabilities in their risk assessments to determine their level of risk acceptance for such policies and practices.

Near Field Communications

Near field communication (NFC) is a short-range wireless connectivity protocol standard that can be used to initiate communication between devices when they are in close proximity to each other. After the communication has been initiated, another wireless technology, such as Bluetooth or Wi-Fi, might take over to perform data exchanges. This high-frequency technology is very appropriate for some security applications because it requires close proximity between a tag (such as an RFID identification badge) and a reader device. The close proximity requirement is important, as this can minimize unauthorized access attempts. Many low-frequency (typically 125 KHz) systems have been used for security badge systems.

While not trivial, these systems are vulnerable to being exploited by those who possess some specialized hardware and a few skills. By getting close to a user with an RFID badge, a hacker can read the target's badge information using their own reader. Once they have captured the badge data, they can then make their own badge to circumvent access controls. This could occur while the user is in the cafeteria, at a local coffee shop, or even through a small *IIoT device* hidden in the office or production facility.

It isn't difficult to find the plans on the Internet for building an attack tool that can be inserted into a commercial RFID reader (which is also easy to acquire). Before supporting any NFC system, it is critical that network administrative and security personnel examine its security mechanisms, as some systems are more vulnerable than others.

Securing Mobile Devices

While *mobile device* security concerns are certainly greater with non-ICS applications, all mobile users should exercise caution when using mobile networks and when using their mobile devices in the workplace.

- Turn off Bluetooth autodiscovery unless you are pairing with a device and need this capability. Look for other security options on your Bluetooth devices as well.

- Avoid the use of public hotspots. However, if you do use them, be aware of the potential mischief and use TLS/SSL connections and only enter credentials into secured systems.

- Turn off automatic connection (reconnection) to Wi-Fi access points.

- Cellular networks are less likely to be compromised; use cellular when high security is needed.

- All wireless technologies are more secure if encryption is implemented from end to end.

OS Security/Hardening

Operating systems are programs designed to control and coordinate the operation of the computer system. As a group, they are easily some of the most complex programs ever devised. In all microprocessor-based environments, the operating system accepts commands from a program or an input source (such as a computer user) and carries them out to perform some desired operation. Likewise, the operating system acts as an intermediary between nearly as complex software applications and the computer hardware they run on.

> The most widely used operating systems in the world have nothing to do with personal computers. These operating systems are found in automobiles and consumer electronics products. They receive input from sensing devices such as airflow sensors (instead of keyboards and mice), process a control program according to a set of instructions and input data, and provide output to electro/mechanical devices such as fuel injector pumps (not video displays and printers). They also don't have much to do with storing data on disk drives.

The operating system acts as a bridge between application programs and the computer hardware, as described in Figure 4.8. These application programs enable the user to create files of data pertaining to certain applications such as word processing, multimedia delivery, remote data communications, business processing, and user programming languages.

Because the operating system is a major part of the electronic gateway to the computer's applications and data, you must be aware of the different general types of OS and what tools and techniques are available to protect them.

FIGURE 4.8   The position of the DOS in the computer system

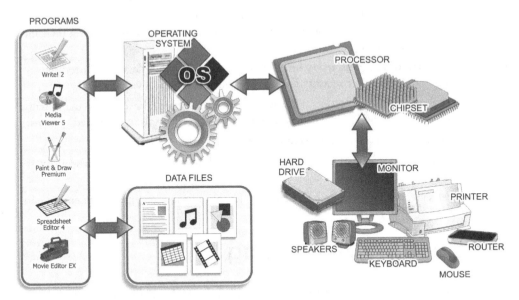

File System Security

The *file management system* is extremely important in protecting the existence and integrity of data stored on a disk, disc, or removable storage device. If the file system is destroyed or becomes corrupted, the data becomes inaccessible and is lost. In addition, if unauthorized users are given access to the file system and its stored data, they have been given the opportunity to damage, destroy, or steal it.

One of the main tools for protecting the file system and its data is the use of *access control lists (ACLs)*. The file system uses ACLs to grant or deny specific users access to its different files, as well as to control what types of activities the individual can perform once access has been granted. For example, you may be given the capability to run a file, read it, write it, or perform other actions on it under the control of the file management system.

The operating system's ACLs are also used to control access to other objects such as TCP/UDP ports as well as I/O devices. Their ACL tables maintain records that identify which access rights each user has to a particular system object.

Depending on the operating system, resource access control can be implemented in the form of *Mandatory Access Control (MAC)* or *Role-Based Access Control (RBAC)*. UNIX and Linux systems typically offer MAC approaches, while Microsoft Windows platforms provide RBAC control.

In MAC versions, the operating system determines who can do what and to what extent they can do it. Under RBAC the system restricts or permits access to objects based on the user's authorizations. The RBAC structure is typically the access control method employed in large enterprises.

In UNIX and UNIX-like operating systems, a set of interoperability standards called *Portable Operating System Interface (POSIX)* was developed to standardize variations of UNIX versions. POSIX-compliant systems (UNIX, Linux, and macOS systems) support some type of ACL for managing traditional UNIX file access permissions.

In Microsoft Windows environments, these capabilities are assigned to folders and files in the form of *permissions*. Permissions can also be defined as privileges to perform an action. In UNIX and Linux-based systems, users are assigned *access rights* to files.

Another tool for protecting data is to *encrypt* it so that becomes unusable without a key to decrypt it. The encryption/decryption process can be performed on data when it's stored and retrieved from a device or when it is being moved from one location to another.

Encrypting data involves taking the data and processing it with a key code (or *encryption key*) that defines how the original (*plaintext*) version of the data has been manipulated. This concept is illustrated in Figure 4.9.

FIGURE 4.9   Data encryption

Anyone who is given the encryption key can use it to decode the message through a decryption process using a decryption algorithm or *decryption key*. Anyone without the decryption key cannot determine what the original data was.

A particularly effective key system is *Public Key Encryption (PKE)*. This technique employs two keys to ensure the security of the encrypted data—a *public key* and a *private key*. The public key (known to everyone) is used to encrypt the data, and the private or secret key (known only to the specified recipient) is used to decrypt it. The public and private keys are related in such a way that the private key cannot be decoded simply by possessing the public key.

Data encryption in a digital device or network can occur at many levels:

- As file-system-level (file and folder level) encryption
- As disk-level encryption
- As transport-level encryptions

 The NIST Primary Cyber Security Guidelines specify protection strategies for protecting data at rest (PR.DS-1) and protecting data in motion (PR.DS-2).

Most of the major disk operating systems available offer some type of data encryption capabilities through their file management systems. Depending on the design of the operating system, encryption may be applied at the device level, the disk (or volume) level, or the file and folder levels. Third-party encryption applications are available for use with many of these operating systems as well.

The data encryption services available with different operating systems are discussed in the following section of this chapter. Data encryption techniques are covered in detail in Chapter 5, "Cybersecurity Essentials for ICS."

Operating systems that are enabled to employ *No-Execute (NX)* technology, available in some microprocessors, mark certain areas of memory as nonexecutable so that any code in those areas cannot be executed. This feature is used to prevent certain types of malware from injecting their code into these memory areas and executing it to take over the system. These attacks are referred to as *buffer overflow attacks* and are described in greater detail in the following section.

Operating systems also include *isolation mechanisms* to create containers on the host machine's memory that isolate different processes from each other. This enables the OS to run the process file system in isolation from other processes and protect it from unwanted changes. In UNIX/Linux systems, the change root (chroot) operation changes the apparent root directory. In Windows OS, the WIN32 API is responsible for password authentication, discretionary protection for sharable objects, access control, and rights management in the OS file system.

File System Attacks

Typical attacks mounted against OS file systems include the following:

- *Race condition attacks*: A race condition exists when an attacker exploits the timing of consecutive events in a multiuser/multitasking environment to insert malicious code into the system between the events.

  For example, a *time of check, time of use (TOCTOU)* condition exists when an operating system creates a temporary file. During the time between when the OS checks to see if a file by that filename exists and when it actually writes the file, the attacker executes a program to save a malicious code package using the filename of the temp file.

  The malicious code could contain higher access permissions so the attacker can read or manipulate the file, or it could contain a link to script file that grants access to the password file where the administrative password is stored.

- *Using Alternate Data Streams (ADS) to hide files*: Advanced hackers use this NTFS OS compatibility feature to hide rootkits or other hacker tools to establish an anonymous base from which to launch attacks on the system.

  The ADS feature was originally built into NTFS to provide support for Apple's HFS file system, which sometimes "forks" data into different files. However, this technique has been adopted for storing file metadata and to provide temporary storage.

As mentioned earlier, hackers use the ADS feature to hide their tools from the system, as it is virtually impossible to detect with native user interfaces. After the hidden ADS files have been embedded in some standard OS file, they can be executed without being detected as an illegitimate operation. The only sign of an ADS operation is an illegitimate timestamp on the file where the hidden tools have been injected.

- *Performing directory traversals*: These attacks exploit poorly secured software applications to access files that should not be accessible to "traverse" to a higher-level folder or directory, as illustrated in Figure 4.10. Such attacks are also referred to as *backtracking*, *directory climbing attacks*, or *canonicalization attacks*.

FIGURE 4.10   Directory traversal

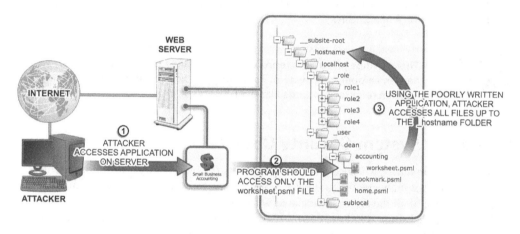

Hackers use this form of *HTTP exploitation* to access a web server's directory tree. After the hacker has gained access, they can navigate the tree to view restricted files or execute commands on the server. Such attacks are launched using common web browsers against poorly configured web servers. These attacks can be minimized through careful web server configuration, filtering web browser input, and use of *vulnerability scanner* software.

File System Hardening

Although the file system is part of the operating system, there are a few file system–specific techniques that can be used to improve or harden file system security.

- The first step is to employ a standardized file system across the organization if possible.
- Consider separating boot/system files from shared directories and data by placing them in different partitions on each server and user computing device.
  - For Windows systems, place the boot and system files in drive C:\ and shares in other drives such as D:\ or E:\.

- For Linux systems, change the mount options in /etc/fstab to limit user access. Also, user-writable directories such as /home, /temp, /var, and /temp should be mounted in other partitions.

- Remove any hidden sharing features from the boot/system partition as well as any other partition that has information that should not be shared.

- For key folder and file permissions, use individually assigned permissions instead of role-based access control options. Only use RBAC options for information that truly needs to be shared across groups. RBAC and other logical access control strategies are discussed later in this chapter.

- Employ file and folder encryption options where available.

- Establish periodic auditing and reporting for folders and files that are most critical to the organization's operations.

 The activities given here represent general steps that can be used to harden an operating system. For more specific procedures for hardening, you can refer to standards like NIST SP 800 or ISO 2700x.

Operating System Security Choices

Because of its popularity, Microsoft Windows presents the biggest target for both mischievous and malicious malware and grayware writers. Therefore, Windows receives an unrivaled percentage of all the attacks associated with viruses and spyware.

This fact has led some Windows customers to adopt other operating system platforms such as Linux or macOS, which are much less of a malware target. Table 4.2 summarizes common security features associated with various operating systems.

Linux SystemV vs Systemd

Modern Linux distributions are based on one of two basic designs—*SystemV* and *Systemd*. **SystemV** is an older platform that traces back to the original Linux, while **Systemd** is a newer platform that many Linux distributions have moved to. The Systemd design offers much faster booting and better dependency management.

Systemd employs a modern system service manager that is responsible for the **daemons** that run in the background and provide functionality for other programs. Some of these daemons are used to monitor security events and provide alerts. They also provide security features for isolating services and applications from the underlying operating system, as well as from each other.

Organizations such as Red Hat, CentOS, Fedora, Amazon, Debian, Ubuntu, and Mint have built their Linux Distributions on the Systemd platform. Distributions based on SystemV architecture include Alpine, Slackware, and Linux from Scratch.

TABLE 4.2 Operating System Security Comparisons

Name	Resource Access Control	Subsystem Isolation Mechanisms	Integrated Firewall	Encrypted File Systems	No Execute (NX)
Linux	POSIX, ACLs, MAC	Chroot, capability-based security, secomp, SELinux, AppAmor	Netfilter, varied by distribution	Yes	Hardware/emulation
macOS	POSIX, ACLs	Chroot, BSD file flags set using chflags	Ipfw	Yes	Hardware/emulation
Windows Server	ACLs, privileges, RBAC	Win32 WindowsStation, desktop, job objects	Windows Firewall	Yes	Hardware/emulation
Windows Client OS	ACLs, privileges, RBAC	Win32 WindowsStation, desktop, job objects	Windows Firewall	Yes	Hardware/emulation

Hardening Operating Systems

As noted earlier, the second level of hardening local computer systems against attacks is to secure their operating systems. This involves updating vulnerable code segments of the OS as they become known to the developers. OS hardening occurs through the application of new programming in the form of service packs, patches, and updates.

- *Service packs*: After an operating system has been in the field for some time, vendors may combine several product improvements and distribute a numbered *service pack* for the specific operating system being upgraded. Critical files should always be backed up in the event that the service pack or OS fails to work after installing the service pack.

- *Patches*: *Patches* (also referred to as *hotfixes* by Microsoft) are general improvements to a given operating system that has been released for distribution. Many patches and updates are purely cosmetic and convenient add-on features, while others are critical security upgrades designed to respond to a particular virus, discovered threat, or weakness found in the operating system.

- *Updates*: An *update* is a service pack or patch that improves the reliability, security, or attractiveness of an operating system. Some updates may make the OS more convenient but not necessarily more secure. Therefore, they should be tested before implementing. Consider backing up critical files in the event that the patch or OS fails to work after installation.

Common Operating System Security Tools

After the system has reached bootup, there are a few steps that can be taken to prevent unauthorized personnel from accessing the operating system and its applications. In particular, if the operating system does not take control over the system, it becomes difficult to access the information stored in the system (this is the real target of most malicious computer endeavors). These steps include the following:

- Implementing local login requirements
  - Establishing user and group accounts
  - Setting up password policies
  - Establishing lockout policies
- Implementing additional authentication options
  - Using biometric authentication devices
  - Using physical authentication devices
  - Using multifactor authentication devices
- Using local administrative tools

- Enabling system auditing and event logging
- Installing Microsoft sysmon
- Implementing data encryption tools
- Overseeing application software security

- Providing remote access protection

- Establishing firewall settings
- Configuring browser security options
- Establishing and implementing malicious software protection
- Applying security updates and patches

Figure 4.11 shows the Local Security Policy/Security Settings options available in the Microsoft Windows Control Panel. The first set of options includes password and account lockout policy choices to locally control access to the system. You can also implement local admin policies for system auditing, users' rights, and security policies.

FIGURE 4.11   Local Security Policy/Security Settings

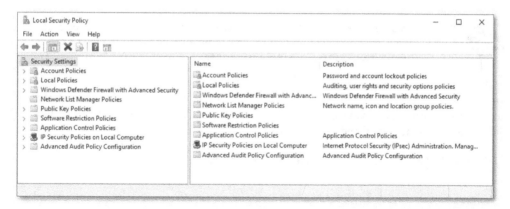

The Windows Firewall and Advanced Security tools enable the local administrator (or owner) to establish and configure a local firewall. The remaining tools in the figure are security tools that enable local policies to be established to control the local computer's interactions with an external network. In the following sections, we will examine these tools to determine how to implement them for best local host security practices.

Bastille Linux is a suite of Linux hardening tools used to lock down the OS and configure the system for optimum security. It is shipped as part of the distribution by the vendors of SuSE, Debian, Gentoo, and HP-UX Linux and UNIX products.

It should be apparent from a quick look that the tools in the figure are designed to control the interaction of the local computer with an external network. While the tools are local, they are also used in networked environments. There are cases where there are both local and network administrative policies that cover the same security elements. In these cases, the network policy will override the local policy if they are configured in conflict with each other.

Implementing Local Login Requirements

The main user authentication tool used with personal computing devices is the *username* and *password* login. In general, there are three types of user-related login to contend with: a logon to the local machine, a logon to a specific software application, and a network logon.

At the local computer level, the local logon is typically required.* This level of login validates the user for using the local computer's resources, files, and devices. However, in a shared computer environment where multiple users may be enabled to use the same computer, *local user and group credentials* are created and configured through a *user accounts database* that is stored on the local computer.

*In a network environment, the network login typically supersedes and replaces the local login option. This login level confirms the user's credentials for accessing remote resources.

These credentials are used to gain initial access to the computer, control access to its local resources, and control access to network resources. In a Windows environment, these accounts are created and managed through the Local Users and Groups utility under Computer Management, as depicted in Figure 4.12.

FIGURE 4.12   Microsoft Local User and Groups accounts

The first time a stand-alone system is started, an *administrator's account* is automatically created in the operating system's local accounts database. The administrator has rights and permissions to all the system's hardware and software resources. The administrator, in turn, creates other users and then grants them rights and permissions to system resources as necessary.

The administrator can deal with *users* on an individual basis or may gather users into *groups* that can be administered uniformly. In doing so, the administrator can assign permissions or restrictions on an individual or an entire group. The value of using groups is that it saves time to apply common rights to several users instead of applying them one by one.

The other default group created when the operating system first starts is a type of account known as a *Guests* group. This default group typically has minimized access to the system, and all of its members share the same user profile. The Guest user account is automatically a member of this group.

Each user and group in the local environment has a profile that describes the resources and desktop configurations created for them. Settings in the profile can be used to limit the actions users can perform, such as installing, removing, configuring, adjusting, or copying resources.

When users log into the system, it checks their profiles and adjusts the system according to their information. These credentials are used to gain initial access to the computer and control what access each user has to its local resources. In addition, access to certain software applications and other resources may be controlled by additional application-level passwords.

Passwords

For a password to be effective, it must possess a certain amount of *complexity*. Its *entropy* (measurement of its unpredictability) must be enough to thwart the efforts of the previously mentioned password-cracking techniques.

The length of a password directly affects the ease with which it can be cracked. The longer the password is, the more difficult it will be to crack. It is generally recommended that passwords should consist of between six and nine characters. Passwords of five characters or less must be avoided. If permitted by the OS, longer passwords can be used, provided the employees or clients can remember them.

The width of a password relates to the number of different types of characters that can be incorporated, including those not belonging to the alphabet. Combinations of numbers, special characters, and uppercase and lowercase letters make passwords stronger, especially when an operating system considers uppercase and lowercase letters as completely different characters.

Passwords can contain control characters, alternate characters, and even spaces in some operating systems. Ideally, all the following character sets should be drawn from when the administrator selects passwords for the server room or cloud access.

- Uppercase letters such as *A, B, C*
- Lowercase letters such as *a, b, c*
- Numerals such as 1, 2, 3
- Special characters such as $, ?, &
- Alternate characters such as μ, ∞, and √

The depth of a password involves how difficult it is to guess its meaning. Although a good password should be easy to remember, it should nevertheless be difficult to guess. The meaning of a password should not be something that could be easily guessed or deducted through simple reasoning.

One approach that seems to work well is to think in terms of phrases rather than simply words. Mnemonic phrases are often incorporated, allowing the creation of passwords that cannot be easily guessed yet do not need to be written down to be remembered. Then, the initials of some words in the phrase can be converted into alternate characters. For example, the number 4 could be substituted wherever the letter *f* is used.

In the United States, the National Institute for Standards and Technology has produced guidelines for secure password creation. For example, according to NIST, user-generated passwords should be at least eight characters in length, while machine-generated passwords must be a minimum of six characters long. The maximum length should be 64 characters.

Passwords should be hashed and salted during verification processing. NIST also suggests that the use of password "hints" be scrapped and replaced with knowledge-based authentication techniques to prove identity.

Additional Password Security

The need for additional password security has become more recognized with the increased ease with which scam artists continue to steal them. Passwords have ultimately been gathered as easily as simply asking for them. Personnel should simply never talk about passwords with anyone, no matter how harmless or legitimate such conversation might seem.

Although standard password protection practices are often adequate to keep would-be intruders at bay, certain situations require a more sophisticated approach. In these cases, extra protection can be afforded through the use of encryption techniques and *one-time passwords (OTPs)*.

Password encryption (hashing) is the process of taking a standard password and garbling it in such a way as to make it meaningless to sniffers, crackers, or other eavesdroppers. NIST recommends the use of hashing algorithms when passwords are stored or retrieved.

One-time passwords are good for only one transaction. Although this security method is very reliable, it requires the administrator to carry a secure password manager that stores the passwords or to use a third-party service to provide *privileged identity management (PIM)* for the organization's superuser accounts.

 True password security involves the user safeguarding their password from others. Administrators should be aware of situations where the user might realistically need to share their passwords.

Best password practices include the following:

- Using a consistent naming convention
- Always supplying a password to an account and making the user change it upon first login
- Protecting passwords (don't write them down in open spaces)
- Using a password manager for the organization

- Not using the default passwords
- Educating users to create strong passwords
- Enforcing password policies at all levels of an organization

Account Lockout Policies

Operating systems provide password *lockout policy settings* that enable administrators to enact password policies that prevent attackers from repeatedly trying to access the system. This prevents the attackers from using *brute-force attacks* to guess the account password so they can break into the system.

Brute-force attacks involve the repeated use of login attempts to try to guess the password. As shown in Figure 4.13, typical lockout policy settings include the following:

- *Account lockout duration/Failure Reset Interval*: How long the account will be locked out after a preconfigured number of failed login attempts. Setting this value to 0 will prevent the account from unlocking until the administrator manually resets it.

- *Account lockout threshold/Max Failures*: How many times account access can be attempted before the account is locked out. The default value for this setting is 0, which disables the account lockout function. NIST specifications call for 10 unsuccessful attempts before the user is locked out.

- *Reset account lockout counter after/Lockout Duration*: The amount of time that can pass before the account lockout value is returned to 0.

FIGURE 4.13   Windows/Linux lockout options

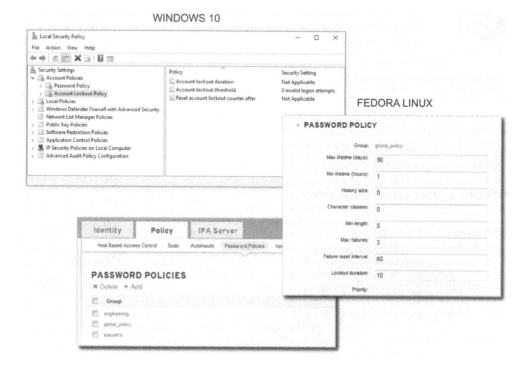

Computer Locking

Users should never leave their computer unattended after they have logged on. Doing so opens the door for others to access and manipulate their computer, data, and network. All users should be trained to either *log off* or *lock* their computers when they are away from them, even if only for a few minutes. Administratively, a system can be configured with policies that will log the user out after a given period of inactivity—such as between 7 and 15 minutes—and require them to log in again to use the system.

Locking the computer protects it from intruders and preserves the current system state. When the computer is unlocked, the applications and data that were active in the system are still open, making it much easier for the user to pick up where they left off. Users should also be instructed to make sure they log off at the end of the day. This closes all applications and ensures that data files are saved.

Physical Authentication Devices

When it's not feasible to physically lock up hardware as described earlier, there are hardware devices that can be used to make personal computer systems unusable by people other than authorized users. These devices include items such as smart cards and biometric devices.

The programmability of smart cards enables them to work with changing password strategies and to pass tokens and certificates back and forth with the host computer. The smart card system combines the users' secret *PINs*, which is something the users alone know. *Tokens* are generated by the network's *certificate authority* authentication system to generate a unique pass code. The pass code validates the user and their access to different resources.

Some organizations that use smart cards issue their employees smart cards that they can use to get into their buildings, log on to their PCs, and access appropriate applications with a single security device.

Using Biometric Scanners for Authentication

Biometric scanners are becoming significantly more sophisticated and now include improved devices of different kinds with searchable databases and supporting application programs. In addition to serving as authentication devices for physical facilities access, many biometric scanning devices have evolved for use with personal computers. Figure 4.14 shows different fingerprint scanner devices designed for use with PCs.

FIGURE 4.14 Fingerprint scanners

The biometric authentication device most widely used with personal computers is the fingerprint scanner. Some fingerprint scanner manufacturers offer miniature touchpad versions that sit on the desk and connect to the system through a cable and USB connector. Other fingerprint scanners are built into key fobs that simply plug directly into the USB port. Some manufacturers even build these devices into the top of the mouse.

After the fingerprint scanner software has been installed and configured, the password manager will prompt you to scan in your fingerprint rather than type a password on future login attempts. Some models actually store the scanned images and account access information on the device. This allows the identification file to travel with the user if they work with different computers at different locations.

Virtualization

Modern computing platforms have evolved to the point that it is possible to simulate multiple hardware platforms—such as servers, endpoints, switches, and most any other network resource—in a single hardware environment. This is due to *virtualization software* that enables computing hardware with multiple microprocessors, or *multicore processors*, to support multiple *virtual instances* of devices, each of which has the ability to function like the original host hardware.

For example, a single-server operating system could be used to host multiple Windows and Linux OS instances operating at specific IP addresses. These virtual instances, also known as *virtual machines (VMs)*, can be enabled as needed to handle demand and scalability or to provide tremendous amounts of portability.

Server and endpoint virtualization involves connecting different types of virtual devices together inside a hypervisor. The *hypervisor* is a *virtual operating platform* that hosts instances of other guest operating systems, as illustrated in Figure 4.15. As the figure illustrates, there are two general variations of hypervisors: native and hosted. Native hypervisors are built into the host operating system as a service, while hosted hypervisors are third-party products that are added onto an underlying host operating system.

It is also possible to create virtualized networks within the host using *white-box switches* (generic virtual routing and switching instances) created in the hypervisor. Each VM is assigned a virtual network adapter that is responsible for handling network traffic for the VM. These virtual adapters can be connected to any of the virtual switches created to form network connections within the hypervisor (inter-VM communications through the hypervisor's virtual switching components).

External virtual switches are used to connect the hypervisor to the underlying OS and one or more of its physical network adapter(s). This switch enables the virtual adapters connected to it to communicate with other physical networks. Router functions within the virtual environment are performed by VMs whose operating systems have been configured to perform that function.

FIGURE 4.15   Hypervisors

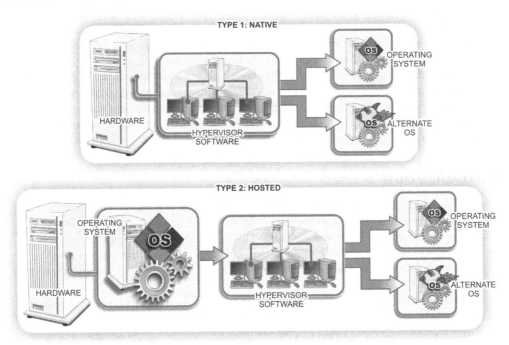

Creating virtual networks within a host provides several several security benefits:

- *Isolation*: Unless the host is configured for interconnection between its external physical network and its internal virtual network, virtual networks are by default isolated from the physical network. Communications within the virtual network never leave the virtual environment.

- *Segmentation*: Unless the host is configured otherwise, communications within the virtual network don't leave the virtual environment, so there is no need for network segmentation to be configured and maintained with the physical network or firewall.

- *Firewalling*: Installing a host-based firewall on a VM configured to be the head of the virtual network provides protection between the virtual network and the host's physical network connection.

- *Least privilege usage configuration*: Least privilege is a principle in information security that sets limits on what a given user or group can access, based on their need to do so in order to fulfill their job roles.

VM Security

Virtualization platforms, hypervisors, and VMs are all software products. As such, they all have flaws and vulnerabilities. Therefore, the basic security recommendations for these products are the same as those associated with operating systems and applications:

- Practice good patch/service pack/update management procedures for both the host and the users.

- Remove applications that have known vulnerabilities or histories of vulnerabilities.

- Test and apply virtual platform security patches.

In addition to these basic virtualization security precautions, there are a number of other steps that can be taken to harden a virtualized computing environment:

- Harden the host device. Implement file and folder permissions, control users and groups, and configure logging and time synchronization.

- Secure the communication links between the host and the network users. Most VM platforms support SSH, SSL, and IPSec for communications.

- Secure endpoint devices connected within the hypervisor. Most VM platforms feature L2 switching controls for their virtual switches. This allows for monitoring traffic within the virtual platform in the same manner as traditionally performed in external network environments.

- Create security between the VMs and the underlying host (VM escape vulnerabilities). This involves turning off any services not needed to carry out normal operations. If you don't need a particular service, turn it off.

Container Configuration Integrity

Containers are a form of application virtualization similar to virtual machines. However, unlike VMs, containers do not rely on a hypervisor to operate on the physical hardware. They do not require a packaged OS to operate. Instead, they virtualize the host operating system so that the container application, with its libraries and dependencies is the only component of the container. This structure makes them fast and portable compared to VMs. It also enables them to run independently in any environment, including desktop PCs, laptops, and cloud environments.

The advantages of containers have made them useful tools in hybrid and multi-cloud environments. Their portability enables them to operate across a mix of public cloud environments, as well as the organization's data centers.

Although containers make cloud deployments easier to implement, they also present a range of cybersecurity concerns. The shear number of containers most organizations typically employ in their cloud environments, and the frequency with which they are replaced or updated, brings opportunity for vulnerabilities on a wide scale. The more containers you are running, the larger your potential attack surface becomes. In addition, containers are often built on third-party code, which brings third-party vulnerabilities with it.

The first step in securing containers is to carefully implement **Identity and Access Management (IAM)** to control the roles and access privileges container users are assigned, as well as the conditions for granting or denying them permissions. As always, it is a good idea to follow the *Principle of Least Privilege* when assigning permission to containers. The next step in securing containers is to run vulnerability scans on them before they are deployed. You should also create and use a list of trusted sources for all images you use in your environment. There are open-source tools such as Notary that can be used for this purpose. See www.docker.com/blog/notary-v2-project-update. Finally, harden the entire environment, including the host and all daemons.

Application Software Security

Software *application packages* operate as extensions of the operating system. Depending on the type of operating system being used, an application program may directly control some system resources, such as printers and network interfaces, while the operating system lends fundamental support in the background. In more advanced systems, the operating system supplies common input, output, and disk management functions for all applications in the system.

Some applications include built-in security tools that control access to the application beyond the levels presented by the operating system. However, many applications are written with very little concern for security issues. The focus of such programs is functionality and sharing, leaving security issues to the operating system and security utilities.

Software Exploitation

The term *software exploitation* is used to describe cyberattacks designed to take advantage of vulnerabilities or weaknesses in software products, operating systems, and applications. These vulnerabilities may be the result of software that is created with little or no thought for security issues, or they may be the product of software that has been inadequately tested before being released for use.

There are two very conflicting objectives in the computer software industry:

- Make the product as open and easy to use as possible so that otherwise nontechnical users will be able to work with it.

- Make the application bullet-proof so that nothing bad can happen to it, ever. Software programmers are asked to meet both of these objectives in the same product.

In some cases, the programmers may be trying to create a truly open product without concerns about how it might be exploited by malicious people. In other cases, they may not be experienced enough to envision how their product might be exploited. With the worldwide pool of programmers continuously growing, there are many individuals with a significant knowledge base of how to test, manipulate, and modify programming. This includes *black-hat hackers.**

*A black-hat hacker is an individual who possesses extensive program-ming skills and uses them for the purpose of breeching or bypassing net-work security structures for malicious or criminal purposes. People in this category of hacker are also known as *crackers* or *dark-side hackers.*

> There are also white-hat and gray-hat hackers who seek to exploit Internet security vulnerabilities and weaknesses but for nonmalicious reasons, such as performing security system analysis checks.

Modern operating system and application programming is very complex. When programmers initially develop a product, they may make coding mistakes or create portions of a product that do not work well with elements created by other programmers in the development team. They may also download flawed code segments and libraries from open-source software repositories, such as GitHub. Attackers will often use software vulnerabilities to insert and hide malicious code that can be used to disrupt services or operations.

In particular, the attacker may alter the existing code to create a condition in the computer's memory known as a *buffer overflow*, which results in erratic behavior, memory access errors, and/or system crashes. The system is effectively disabled to the point where the user cannot use it. This type of attack is referred to as a *denial of service* or *DoS attack*.*

Denial-of-service (DoS) attacks are covered in greater detail in Chapter 5.

Information Leakage

One of the Top 10 OWASP cybersecurity vulnerabilities is specified as **information leakage**. Information leakage is a condition that exists when sensitive data is left exposed. The most common reasons for this exposed data are found in HTML or script comments, error messages, or source code that has not been scrubbed before being deployed, as well as through misconfigured servers or applications. These attack vectors provide attackers with access to systems to enter or extract data from them.

Software development teams are prime targets for malicious attackers. As software development increasingly occurs in widely distributed, full-time and contracted/outsourced teams, the number of potential attack surfaces in software packages has increased significantly.

Cloud-based computing and storage operations are another source of information leakage. Misconfigured cloud buckets (data storage areas in a cloud environment) offer attackers access to sensitive cloud data. Improperly configured cloud permissions on sites such as Azure, GCP, and Amazon S3 can make large amounts of data exposed to the Internet.

In addition, sites such as GitHub often house poorly configured, leaked, or shared code that can provide malicious actors with source code, API keys, and data that was never intended to be open to the public.

To prevent information leaks, organizations should employ the following activities:

- Standardize coding practices for all software development teams.

- Centralize encryption key and secret storage practices.

- Employ the Principle of Least Privilege with account access—particularly accounts associated with cloud-based computing or storage.

- Encrypt stored data (data at rest).
- Employ an external leak monitoring system to check attack surfaces such as exposed GitHub repositories, misconfigured permissions, and exposed cloud buckets.

Applying Software Updates and Patches

From the previous section you can see that due to the nature of product development and the pressures on software producers to bring new products to the market, new software releases never seem to be complete or perfect. As security issues with software products are revealed, their producers are forced to issue *security patches* for their products that correct the weakness.

Security patches are updates issued for the specific purpose of correcting an observed weakness to prevent exploitation of the vulnerability. Microsoft issues security patches for its products once a month and releases them on the second Tuesday of that month. Other software developers use dedicated security teams to develop and issue security patches as soon as possible after a vulnerability has been discovered.

For security and stability reasons you should always patch operating systems on computing devices that are connected to the Internet. In most organizations, the risk management team has a subset called the *patch review team* that is responsible for making decisions about patches being applied to OT devices. This team is discussed in greater detail in the "Controlling Patch Distribution and Installation" section of Chapter 10, "ICS Security Monitoring and Incident Response."

Ideally, organizations would implement procedures to schedule software upgrades and patch management procedures at routine intervals. In addition, these procedures would specify that security patches are applied promptly and that software suppliers' recommendations are implemented on a regular basis. These steps can substantially limit opportunities for hostile parties to target newly discovered vulnerabilities, which are widely publicized immediately.

However, in OT environments, software modifications may be contractually controlled by the ICS vendor. Changes to their OS and application software must adhere to their schedule, which involves extensive performance testing to guarantee real-time performance requirements are met. In many OT environments, controllers are often so processor-constrained that running any unproven software components (such as OS patches or security software) creates unacceptably high response delays that threaten process control stability. Therefore, their systems cannot be patched in a timely fashion. This often result is outdated software levels and little or no malware protection.

Database Hardening

The most valuable asset for most enterprise organizations is their information (data). This can include different types of data ranging from employee information to customer financial or health information. As such, information can range in classification from confidential to internal to public. This typically involves *databases* with confidential customer data and highly secure devices, structures, strategies, and policies.

Typically, databases represent the most valuable assets for most organizations and, of course, inviting targets for attackers. Recall from Chapter 3, "Secure ICS Architecture," that access to the resources in these devices must be both authorized and authenticated. Data storage encryption should also be employed on these devices. Also recall that application-level encryption is preferred, but file system encryption should be employed in the event that application-level encryption options are not available.

Databases are typically located on servers within the organization's network. In the case of OT networks, the most notable databases are those stored on the data historian machines. As with servers associated with enterprise networks, the most important question concerning database security is where in the network the database should be located.

As you learned in previous chapters, the most common method of securing the data historian is to place it in a secure network structure, such as a DMZ, between the IT and OT networks, as illustrated in Figure 4.16. The general server hardening tools and techniques described in detail later in this chapter should also be applied to data historians.

FIGURE 4.16 Data historian security

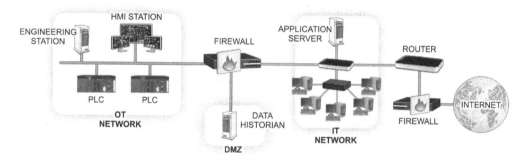

SQL Injection

Perhaps the most common and also most preventable software exploit is known as *SQL injection*. As shown in Figure 4.17, hackers may attempt to inject SQL commands into a public-facing form, such as a login form, in hopes that it will lead to their being granted access to the data stored in an underlying database.

Much of the power of the modern web is related to the use of online databases, and many web designers use SQL (or SQL-like) database engines to power them. Websites are often powerful web applications that may store enormous amounts of information. With SQL you can easily chain queries and commands, often as easily as just adding a semicolon (;) and then an SQL command.

Imagine a web form that might look up resources based upon a ZIP code. It would use a single query such as this:

```
SELECT * FROM Locations WHERE Zip='$zipcode';
```

FIGURE 4.17   SQL injection

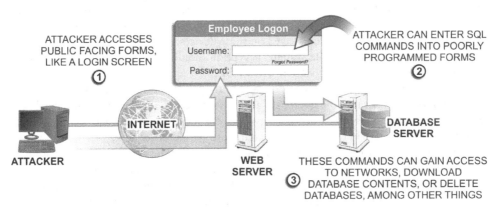

where $zipcode actually comes from an input field supplied by the user. If the hacker were to enter 99336; DROP TABLE Locations instead of just 99336, then the database might chain those commands and delete (drop) the Locations table entirely.

A common way that hackers determine whether the application is subject to SQL injection is to look for a single quote exploit on login forms. An authentication query might be something like this:

```
SELECT ID FROM Users WHERE Username = '$username'
AND Password = '$password';
```

If a hacker knows or can guess that you have a user named Steve, he can try the simple trick of entering the following password:

```
something' OR 'a'='a
```

Note that there is no beginning or ending single quote as the application query will provide that. Now the query that might be executed looks like this:

```
SELECT ID FROM Users WHERE Username = 'Steve'
AND Password = 'something OR 'a'='a';
```

Even though the password is not "something", 'a' will always equal 'a', and by using the logical OR only one of the comparisons needs to match to be true. The hacker might not even need to guess a username by trying the same trick in the username field.

```
SELECT ID FROM Users where Username = 'Steve' OR 'x'='x'
AND Password = 'something OR 'a'='a';
```

Here the hacker has guessed both a username and a password, but those won't matter because 'x'='x' and 'a'='a' will always be true. In addition, the OR clause ensures a match for each, and the hacker would be granted access. You might already be thinking that we just don't allow the entry of single quotes. With both username and password fields that option might work. However, if you are requesting numerical data as follows:

```
SELECT ID FROM Users where UserID=$inputValue;
```

and numeric fields do not require quoting, by simply entering the following information, the query should match because 5 does indeed equal 5 even if there is no UserID equal to 8686 in the database.

```
8686 OR 5=5
```

The good news is that such a condition is easy to prevent. Web application programmers simply need to filter or sanitize each input field before including it in a query. This can be done in various ways, but consider these approaches:

- Only allow input characters from a whitelist to be entered. Clearly, single quotes would not be on that whitelist.

- Escape input field data.

- Parse input field data and disallow OR and || (and certainly DROP).

- Always quote numeric input fields.

These methods will have some impact and with many forms might be enough. However, there always seems to be some injection string that can circumvent input validation. Escaping is problematic and may be a problem with some fields (consider a name field where a user might enter an apostrophe as a part of their name). If a hacker enters a backslash (\) character to escape their input or uses Unicode or other encodings, they may end up defeating your sanitization routines.

The best way to prevent SQL injection is to employ *SQL parameters*. Modern SQL systems support parameterized queries where the parameters are evaluated strictly as data and do not allow any command execution. Here's an example:

```
SELECT ID From Users where Username='@user' AND Password='@pass';
```

Somewhere in the code, the server will have stored procedures that handle these parameters and enforce strict data typing and validation to ensure that no code but the author's is executed. Programmers still need to be careful when crafting queries and also understand that tables and columns can't be parameters. However, this is considered the best practice when using SQL systems.

Anti-Malware

Increased connectivity through networks and the Internet have made personal computers vulnerable to an array of different types of *malware* and *grayware*. *Malware* is the term used to describe programs designed to be malicious in nature. The term *grayware* describes programs that have behavior that is undisclosed or that is undesirable.

It is common to install a number of different defensive products to protect endpoints and their data from unauthorized access and malicious interference. The products most widely used for these purposes are

- Antivirus programs

- Anti-spyware programs

Antivirus

For the most part, every computing device should have some means of protecting itself against computer viruses. The most common means of virus protection involves installing a virus-scanning (*antivirus*) program that checks disks and files before using them in the computer. Several companies offer third-party virus-protection software that can be configured to operate in various ways.

If the computer is a non-networked stand-alone unit, it might be nonproductive to have the antivirus software run each time the system is booted up. It would be much more practical to have the program check any removable media attached to the system, because this is the only possible non-network entryway into the computer.

All computers with connections to the Internet should be protected by an antivirus solution before they are ever attached to the Internet. In these cases, setting the software to run at each bootup is more desirable. In addition, most antivirus software includes utilities to check email and files downloaded to the computer through network or Internet connections.

When an antivirus application is installed on the system, it can be configured to provide different levels of virus protection. You will need to configure when and under what circumstances you want the virus software to run.

For OT control devices, there are no antivirus remedies. Because of the real-time operating requirement for these devices, the overhead of running these applications disqualifies them from use. Virus protection must be supplied through other options.

Anti-spyware

There are basically two types of *antispyware* products available—those that find and remove spyware after it has been installed and those that block spyware when it is trying to install itself. Both of these methods stand a better chance of keeping computers free from spyware when they are combined with user information about how to avoid spyware.

The *detect-and-remove method* is by far the simpler type of antispyware product to write. Therefore, there are several commercially available products that use this method. Like antivirus software packages, this type of antispyware product relies on databases of existing definitions to recognize spyware threats. These databases must be updated frequently to recognize new spyware versions that have been identified.

The real-time prevention type of antispyware product does not rely on historical data to identify spyware. Instead, they monitor certain configuration parameters and notify the user when suspicious installation activity occurs. The user then has the option to allow or block the installation effort. Some antispyware products incorporate both methods of dealing with spyware.

In addition to installing antispyware applications, users can fight spyware in a number of other ways:

- Install a secure web browser.

- Keep your browser up to date with the latest security patches, or download the newest browser version that offers the best security features.

- Work with ISPs who use their firewalls and proxies to block sites that are known to distribute spyware.
- Download software only from reputable sites to prevent spyware that comes attached to other programs.

Anti-Malware Implementation

In almost every environment, organizational policy will call for all servers to have a real-time scanning antivirus application installed, along with a real-time antispyware program. In particular, these applications are required if the server is a file server or has nonadministrative users who have remote access capabilities.

As mentioned earlier, any computing device running HTTP/FTP protocols that has access to the Internet should have anti-malware applications installed. However, there are two notable exceptions to this requirement: SQL servers and dedicated mail servers.

In the case of other endpoints on the network, all such machines should have an organization-standard antivirus and antispyware program installed and scheduled to run at regular intervals. Antivirus and malware scans should be run at least once per week on all user-controlled computing devices. No one except network or domain administrators should be permitted to stop malware definition updates or scans.

However, most OT networks consist of multiple *soft targets*, which are sensor and control devices that are vulnerable to disruption because they have few or no built-in security features and few options for adding them. These components typically feature little or no built-in security capabilities, and many may not possess enough resources (memory and processing capability) to support additional features, such as third-party security add-ons. If they can be accessed directly or virtually, they can easily be manipulated.

This makes antivirus and other anti-malware programs inappropriate for use with OT computing and control devices. These types of scanning applications are performance hogs when they are running. As mentioned, because of the real-time computing requirements of OT controllers, the presence of these types of security applications could introduce communication and computing delays that would be unacceptable and potentially dangerous to equipment and personnel.*

*If the little hourglass appears on the display of an IT computer, maybe due to an application such as an antivirus program using computing resources, it is only an inconvenience. However, if this were to occur in an OT network, bad things could happen. For that reason, anti-malware programs have not historically been used in OT environments; however, anti-malware programs are increasingly being introduced to endpoint devices in the OT environment. This typically requires extensive sandbox testing of the application before being introduced to the actual OT environment.

Instead of applying antivirus and other anti-malware products to OT networks, defense-in-depth strategies (firewalls and DMZs) must be employed before reaching these devices on the OT side of the network.

Updating Anti-Malware

Anti-malware applications and their definition files must be kept up to date to cope with the flood of new malware appearing daily. Some organizations require that antivirus definitions be updated at least once per day. Unlike server and application software products, antivirus and other anti-malware product updates should not require sandbox testing before installation.

 The global anti-malware protection system refers to the complete system of installed antivirus and other anti-malware products on both servers and endpoint devices.

Monitoring

The organization's global anti-malware protection system must be continually *monitored* by network administrators to detect events that may indicate suspicious or malicious activities. When a significant event occurs, the system should be configured to log the event and to notify the administrator (or administrators).

When an event is communicated, the administrator should consult the antivirus or anti-malware application's log files for information about the nature and parameters of the event. However, administrators should routinely and periodically review these log files for indications of impending problems. In addition to the standard operational data these logs contain, administrators can use the logs to do the following:

- Identify endpoints (and users) that encounter a higher than usual numbers of viruses. This could indicate that the user of this endpoint is a high-risk operator and may require additional training.

- Link network endpoints to specific users.

- Identify inside threats associated with users who possess high-risk hacking tools at their disposal. While this software may have legitimate uses in some settings, the ability to identify such users makes it easier to identify potential insider threats.

- Identify insider threats associated with users who possess software with file and folder names that are identified with different types of hidden monitoring tools, such as key loggers.

- Track endpoints that failed to obtain updates.

- Track endpoints and their OS and engine versions.

It is becoming more common to implement *endpoint detection and response (EDR)* applications to IT networks. EDRs place endpoint data collection agents on all of a network's endpoints to monitor them and collect data about their operation. That data is applied to a centralized *Security Operations Center (SOC)* where it is analyzed in real time.

The analysis typically examines the amount of activity occurring on each endpoint, the connections to it, and the data transferred through it. This permits the EDR to *diagnose* threats and automatically trigger responses based on the nature of the threat and its configuration parameters.

When a threat has been detected, the EDR acts to *contain* the attack. Once the containment action has been taken and the threat has been *sandboxed*, the EDR then investigates the nature of the threat and takes action to *eliminate it*.

Anti-Malware: Sanitization

Most malware is distributed in the form of active content embedded in standard file formats such as DOC, XLS, PDF, PPT, etc. The attacker simply hides the malicious code (macros, scripts, web links, or binary objects) inside the content and delivers it to the target through email, web links, or removable media. The malware payload is usually designed to hide from antivirus and other anti-malware scans.

You may recall that the famous *Stuxnet attack*[*] used these same elements to severely damage Iranian efforts to advance their nuclear capabilities. More recently a similar operation referred to as the *Dragonfly Campaign* was launched against OT networks. In this attack, the organizations' websites were compromised, and files from trusted providers were infected. When administrative end users executed these files as trusted software, the exploit bypassed all firewall, whitelisting, and antivirus security controls.

[*]The Stuxnet virus is a famous example of an attack that repurposed a specific application and used its authorized access to the PLC to disrupt the controller.

Anti-malware producers have developed new file *sanitization tools* to search files attached to emails or introduced through web links, thumb drives, and other removable media for these types of objects. When they are found inside a file that should not have them, the tools *sanitize* (strip out) the exploitable objects from the overall content and deliver a clean version of the file to the user.

Sanitization is a different technique than those used in traditional detect/quarantine/delete methods that anti-malware products use to compare files to databases of virus/malware definitions in order to determine what to flag or pass to the user. In most cases, sanitization is combined with traditional anti-malware efforts to deliver truly trusted, sanitized files, as illustrated in Figure 4.18.

In this three-part process, the file is processed through the traditional antivirus/anti-malware solution to eliminate those obviously infected files. Files that clear the first inspection are introduced to the file sanitizer, where algorithms specifically designed for the indicated file type are applied to them to locate any malicious objects hiding within the file structure. If malicious code is detected, it is stripped out of the file without disturbing the integrity of its content. Finally, the sanitized file is delivered to the end user.

To protect an OT network without affecting availability, the sanitizer is typically deployed between the enterprise network and the OT network in the same fashion as the traditional DMZ, as described in Figure 4.19. The sanitizer function can be provided by a server working within a DMZ or in the form of a network appliance within (or instead of) the DMZ.

FIGURE 4.18   Sanitizing files

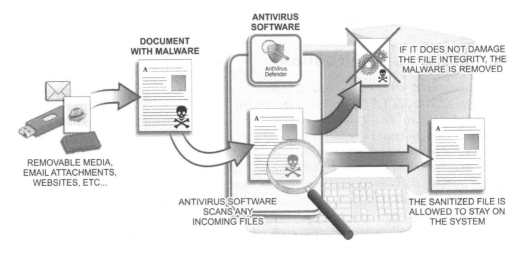

FIGURE 4.19   Sanitizer deployment

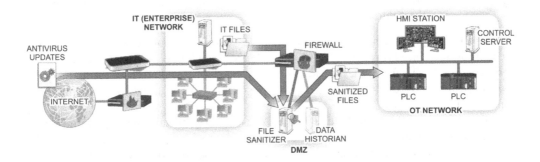

Embedded Device Security

Embedded devices are defined as computing devices that provide a designated function within a larger system. In the ICS environment, this includes devices such as controllers, PLCs, RTUs, and IEDs, to which you were introduced in preceding chapters. However, depending on the exact type of OT network being discussed, there may be other types of embedded devices to consider, such as analyzers, meters, and aggregators (consolidators).

Computing and control devices in industrial networks require the same types of local security as their IT counterparts. Physical access to an industrial control device (or an ICS control room) can provide an attacker with a means of destroying or damaging the process, system, or device. Gaining physical access to the control room also places the attacker in an improved position to gain logical control of the system or its devices. If this level of penetration is achieved, the attacker has the opportunity to exercise control over the physical process. If they gain access to the servers or ICS primary systems, they can potentially control the entire OT system.

 Embedded devices outside of the OT environment—such as smart thermostats, garage door openers, vehicle antitheft devices, and control systems—have generated a considerable amount of attention based on security breaches and cyberattacks associated with them.

One advantage OT systems have over enterprise networks is that their computing and control devices typically operate on proprietary operating systems and network infrastructure that fewer individuals are familiar with. Therefore, there are fewer potential attackers with sufficient knowledge of these software and network types than you find in enterprise environments. This is referred to as *security through obscurity*.

However, this also creates an environment where individuals responsible for these systems must have an advanced knowledge of the components and software to keep the system running correctly. While enterprise and publicly distributed operating systems and applications feature relatively easy installation, setup, and maintenance, management of OT versions can be much more involved. ICS software changes must be done carefully.

While the ICS industry has been producing devices with native security tools and security devices that can be added to existing OT networks for more than 10 years, there are still many OT networks and devices running with few or no security capabilities. In many cases, ICS systems contain components that are designed specifically for performing a given task or were developed before cybersecurity became an issue in the industrial control environment.

Because PLCs and RTUs have so few resources to protect themselves, it becomes important to provide protection for these devices by hardening the perimeter around them. As with the enterprise network devices, the main emphasis at this perimeter is to prevent logical access to OT assets by doing the following:

- Physically securing IT and OT computing devices to the infrastructure (docking stations, locking cables, chains, lockable cabinetry).

- Requiring strong access controls (complex passwords).

- Employing strong authentication methods (smart cards, biometric scanners, etc.).

- Disabling or uninstalling removable media drives and ports (CD/DVD drives, USB/FireWire ports, SD Card slots) on all computing and control devices in the ICS portion of the organization. The ICS security policy should prohibit the use of any unauthorized removable media on any computing/control device in the OT (or connected to it) to prevent the introduction of malware or the inadvertent loss or theft of data.

- Controlling printed output (disposal and destruction policies, shredding, burning).

- Controlling access to backup data and media (using off-site storage, locking cabinets, fireproof safes). If an attacker can gain access to ICS backup media, they can possibly exploit its contents. These exploitations can range from extracting passwords from authentication files to recovering data that can be used to launch different types of cyberattacks.

- Disabling or protecting power buttons from unauthorized access/use.

- Disabling network learning and discovery tools commonly used in traditional enterprise IT software architectures.

Meters

The primary function of any *utility meter* is to measure customer usage for electricity, water, gas, etc. In addition to measuring power, an electrical *smart meter* needs to identify and communicate with the components of the HAN, store customer and usage data, display patterns of consumption, and communicate with the utility's WAN. Figure 4.20 shows the functional block diagram of a typical smart meter.

FIGURE 4.20   Anatomy of a smart meter

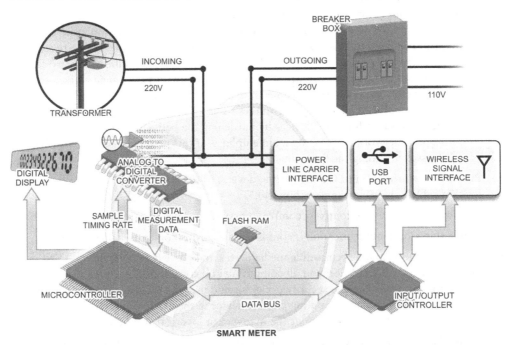

What makes the smart meter *smart* is the presence of an embedded *microcontroller* or *mC* (a specialized microprocessor). This device takes in data about the amount of electric current flowing through the meter's "mains" (contacts) at regular intervals, analyzes the data according to its programming, and stores the data and results in a *Flash random access memory (RAM)* area. It also processes instructions received from the utility and forwards data to the utility from the *home area network (HAN)*.

The current measurements are performed by current sensors that detect the level of current flowing in each conductor passing through the meter. The sensors feed this analog information into *analog-to-digital converter (ADC)* circuits that produce digital representations of each measurement that the micro controller can understand. Figure 4.21 illustrates the operation of a typical A/D converter. 16-bit and 24-bit A/D converter versions are commonly used in digital power meters (the higher the bit count—also referred to as *resolution*—the more accurate the digital representation produced).

FIGURE 4.21 Typical A/D converter operation

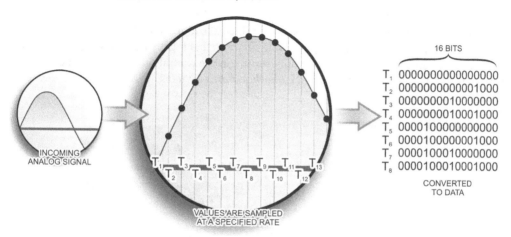

The microcontroller also typically interfaces with a customer display device such as a *liquid crystal display (LCD)* that can show customer usage data or messages.

The other key component of a smart meter is its *Input/Output (I/O) controller*. This unit is responsible for providing physical connectivity compatibility between the other system components and the outside world. In particular, it converts the parallel data that moves between the system's different digital devices into a serial bit stream that is more appropriate for transmission over longer distances. It also receives serial data from the outside and converts it into parallel data that is compatible with digital devices, such as the microcontroller and RAM modules.

The I/O controller also provides hardware protocol control for movement of data into and out of the meter. As illustrated in the figure, this I/O controller provides a serial communications port that supports both a standard USB port, as well as a *Power Line Carrier (PLC)* connection device.

In the case of wireless communications, data moves between the outside world and the I/O controller through a transmitter/receiver unit. Depending on the design of the specific meter, the transmitter/receiver can be designed to work with different communication solutions including RF wireless, power line carrier, and *General Packet Radio System (GPRS)* data communications.

The microcontroller and all its intelligent support devices require electrical power to run. These modules draw their power supply from the power mains, meaning that the meter uses some of the power from the grid. On a single meter this power usage is almost unnoticeable. However, when numerous structures are attached to the grid, it becomes a large amount of energy used just to have a smart system.

Aggregators

A typical utility grid brings together thousands of customers. With such an installed base, it would be economically and technically impractical to have each customer's smart meter communicating directly with the servers at the utility's headquarters. Instead, devices called *data concentrators* are used to group multiple smart meters together and aggregate their data transmissions for delivery to the utility servers in the central office. Each data concentrator creates a structure known as a *neighborhood area network* or *NAN*, as illustrated in Figure 4.22.

FIGURE 4.22 A NAN

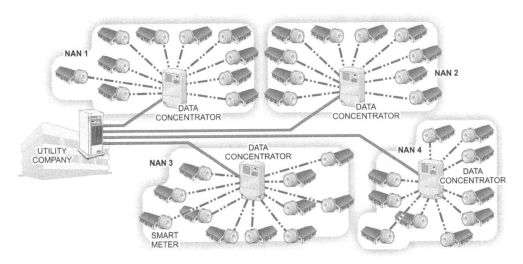

As described earlier, communications in the *customer data acquisition* network is typically performed using wireless technologies—Zigbee or one of the other low-power, IEEE 802.15 wireless piconet protocols for the NAN side of the process, and WiMAX, GSM, GPRS, or telecom networks from the concentrator to the utility servers.

Security Issues

There are many approaches to securing the embedded devices in an OT network environment. However, the general flow for securing these systems is as follows:

1. Physically secure the local sensors and actuators at each location, along with their connections to the network.

2. Secure the field bus and local control network media at each location.

3. Secure the PLCs, RTUs, and IEDs at each location. In many cases, these devices are located in unmanned field stations secured by fences and locked doors.

4. Secure any long-distance communication links between all field sites and the control center. Historically, SCADA protocols haven't tended to have an abundance of built-in security features because they were primarily designed to maximize performance, reliability, robustness, and functionality.

5. Secure the SCADA controllers, servers, and historians in the control center. While these devices are typically deployed in a secured facility, they should be governed by efficient patch management (hardening) policies.

6. As mentioned previously, secure any interconnections between the organization's OT and IT networks. If these two networks must be connected, limit the number of points of connection to a single channel. Use firewalls, routers, and DMZs to control the flow of traffic between the two networks.

For utilities, one of the most worrisome security risks is the *smart meter* located at the demarcation point between the utility and the customer. In a large distribution network, there may be thousands of these devices installed over a wide geographical landscape. Each device represents a potential access point to the utility's consumer data collection network. Each meter is also generally installed in an open location where the general public can gain access to it.

Because these networks represent a high enough target value to make them very interesting, an attacker can exploit their radio frequency AMI transmissions by illegally placing a compatible receiving device anywhere near the smart meter, capturing its signal, and then decrypting its content.

Once the attacker gains access to the meter's communication channel, they can possibly exploit the complete customer data collection network. With access to this network, the attacker could disable service to local utility customers by simply sending one small script out to the network. They could also use this channel to maliciously modify customer data in a positive or negative way.

At the control center or corporate office facilities, physical security typically takes on more of an IT security nature. Major concerns in these environments involve limiting physical access to any information assets in the OT environment.

- Unauthorized physical access to sensitive locations
- Unauthorized physical access to servers, SCADA primary devices, and historians along with the data on them
- Unauthorized physical access to user computers, network devices, and data

As with IT network environments, ICS masters, servers, and historians should be located in secured areas, and devices and mechanisms used to perform authentication for these locations should also be protected. Likewise, any enterprise network connectivity devices on the OT network (endpoints, network switches, gateways, routers, and media) should be located in secured areas, preferably in areas where only authorized personnel can access them.

As you've seen, SCADA systems can be deployed across a local control network in an industrial processing facility or stretched across a large geographical area in a distributed process such as an electrical grid. These systems are vulnerable to attack through disruption of their network communications or falsification of data produced by their field devices.

If the communication network is disrupted, the controllers will not be able to determine the state of the process and will not be able to supply the correct control information to the field controller. This could have serious implications as the process spirals out of control.

Likewise, if the data produced by the sensors and field controllers is falsified, the controller will not be able to take the corrective actions necessary to control the process. The process controller may take erroneous or harmful actions. In addition, even human operators may not be able to take proper corrective actions if they cannot determine the actual condition of the process.

Default Configuration Management

Another major concern with embedded devices is the practice of leaving the device's default configuration settings in place after the installation. Poorly configured devices or systems can provide attackers with easy targets of opportunity in the form of easy access to elevated privileges or known default settings.

As a matter of fact, default settings represent the most common type of configuration vulnerabilities. These vulnerabilities include the following:

- Allowing default accounts and passwords (such as a default router password) to remain active.

- Using default configuration settings (such as leaving TFTP enabled).

- Allowing inadequate software or hardware configuration settings to be used (such as leaving the User Can Modify Setting option enabled).

- Using configuration options that are designed for usability and not for security (such as leaving the AutoRun feature enabled).

- Misconfiguring privilege or permissions settings instead of using least privilege or need-to-know settings.

To remove these vulnerabilities, *configuration settings management (CSM)* policies and their associated processes should be created and implemented to identify poor and insecure configuration settings. This includes developing quality assurance check processes for configuration settings of new devices added to the network and developing policies to prevent unauthorized users from making configuration changes.

In the United States, the *Cybersecurity & Infrastructure and Security Association (CISA)* provides a CSM tool as part of its *Continuous Diagnostics and Mitigation (CDM)* program.

The program provides security practitioners with cybersecurity tools, integration services, and dashboards to help them improve their cybersecurity.

Network Hardening

Network hardening is an active, ongoing network administrative process that includes OS and application hardening for network computing and control devices. This portion of the hardening process involves tightening up and properly configuring network services, protocols, and access control lists.

However, in addition to hardening the software throughout the network, its current configuration must be detailed and evaluated so that a viable plan can be developed to further improve the network's security. This includes evaluating the network's communication media and connectivity devices (switches, routers, hardware firewalls). Typical steps involved in this area of the hardening process include the following:

- Securing the system's servers based on the organization's security policies. If possible, place them in a monitored, centralized server room that has a double-locking door.

- Checking to determine whether there are any network devices whose specifications fail to meet current security goals and therefore represent easy access points to the network.

- Verifying that the network is configured to perform its communication functions and still provide the security levels called for by the organization's security policies. Making certain that devices such as switches, firewalls, and routers are not still set to their default configuration settings.

- Evaluating the cybersecurity plan to make sure that critical devices such as production servers are installed in the correct network segment, security zone, or subnet.

- Establishing and configuring ACLs on network connectivity devices to limit or restrict access to assets as required by the organization's security policies.

- Authentication methods for SSH/HTTPS access.

- Backup configuration of all devices.

- Keeping network devices up to date on all available and current patches.

OT/IT Network Security

As mentioned earlier, IT functions have become an integral part of the OT network to provide critical interfaces and interactions. And of course, this opens up the OT network that was previously secure through obscurity to vulnerabilities associated with IT networks and the Internet. However, the trend to connect the two networks continues to escalate as they become more interdependent on each other.

Unfortunately, most of these OT networks are built on large, flat network topologies as described in Chapter 3. Recall that flat topologies don't implement segmentation to create security zones for areas of the network that have different functions and security requirements. This allows network attacks or disturbances to propagate through the network quickly after the initial penetration occurs.

Flat topologies also make OT networks vulnerable to threats that do not appear on the network map but pose a significant threat when the process control system is networked together. These threats include but are not limited to the following:

- Access from an IT network
- Access from the Internet through the IT network
- PLCs, RTUs, and DCS devices with few or no built-in security features
- Lack of device isolation due to unsegmented networking

Other significant threats to flat networks involve wireless devices that may enter the plant and communicate with the OT network, as well as the ability for USB-based devices to be introduced to ICS-connected hosts. The use of wireless networking technologies must also be highly controlled in OT environments because they enable potential attackers to gain control of process equipment and networking structures without gaining physical access to them. The attacker needs only to gain proximity to the wireless device or network to affect the process.

On the other hand, the presence of a USB port anywhere in the OT network opens a big door for malware of any type to be introduced into the system. Once inside the ICS, the malware can spread rapidly through the nonsegmented or poorly segmented OT network.

If the enterprise network provides a pathway to an Internet connection, there will inevitably be a conversation about using that connection for remote ICS administration and maintenance. From a cost point of view, being able to provide these services remotely from a single source is much more interesting than having highly skilled, and highly paid, network administrators and technicians available at every location an organization might have.

As with pure IT networks, opening remote access channels into an OT network provides a window for unauthorized access, malware, or inappropriate traffic to be introduced to the network and its devices. The difference is that the OT network typically has fewer security tools to prevent or limit the scope of a disturbance or an attack.

For this reason, encrypted protocols, strong authentication mechanisms (token-based, multifactor authentication schemes), and VPNs are strongly recommended for any type of remote access functionality involving the ICS. Any individual given remote access capabilities for the OT network should be required to authenticate both at the enterprise network level and at the network firewall controlling access to the OT network.

When all of these threats come together, the ICS suddenly appears very vulnerable to attack, and even the smallest network disturbance can rapidly spread through the entire OT network, even to remotely located segments and devices.

To compensate for this growing trend in the industrial control industry, the NIST 800-82 r2* Guide to Industrial Control System (ICS) Security identifies three practical considerations for the overall design of the network when corporate and OT networks are combined:

- *Network segmentation and segregation*: Logical and physical network separation
- *Boundary protection*: Security layering, privilege control, and whitelisting
- *The use of firewalls*: Traffic filtering

 * The NIST 800-82 r3 version is in draft form and is scheduled for release in early 2022.

Server Security

Servers require special security considerations and placement within the network. As the previous list illustrates, there may be several different servers operating in an organization's network and delivering a variety of services to its users. In most cases, this involves supplying at least one critical service to multiple users. Therefore, the organization's users are dependent on these servers to perform their work.

As mentioned earlier in this chapter, some of the network's servers, such as database servers, may be tasked with storing large amounts of data. Some or all of that data may be critical or secret information, such as confidential user information, including medical, financial, or personnel records. It may also be used to process and store proprietary organizational information such as trade secrets, patents, inventions, or production information. Network servers with operating systems and applications must be continually maintained with patches and updates to keep them secure.

For these reasons, network servers represent one of the most interesting targets for attackers. While part of the attacker's work involves getting past all the protective equipment in the network, the lucrative part of their operation is accessing the data held on the servers. Therefore, servers require special consideration and placement within the network's security structure.

- Access to a server's shared resources should be limited to users who have both a need and the proper authorization to gain such access. Care should be taken to make sure that unauthorized employees do not gain access to confidential materials.
- Network access to some types of servers should typically be protected by one or more firewalls that limit traffic to the server.
- Use subnets or routers to create secure network segments or zones for different types of servers. For example, a given department, such as the accounting department, may be protected within its own secure subnet and use its own departmental server resources.
- Because servers are frequently used for user authentication, the server's password should be hashed as a preventative measure.

- Periodically audit critical server resources to identify potential problems before they escalate into real problems.

As with stand-alone host security, the next level of server security after securing physical access to the system is to secure its operating system and application software. This involves securely installing, configuring, and maintaining the server operating system and software packages selected for use on the server.

The most important server software component is the operating system. There are five basic steps involved in securing the operating system.

1. Install the server operating system using the manufacturer's installation guidelines.

2. Patch and update the new installation. The operating system developer cannot know the full security requirements for a given organization's servers. In addition, there are new security threats being created every day, so there are security gaps that exist between when the software was created and when it is installed. Applying patches and updates to the new install before it is put into operation should correct any known current vulnerabilities.

3. Configure and harden the new operating system to implement the organization's security policies. Key steps involved in the configuration and hardening of the operating system include the following:

    - Removing or stopping unnecessary services, applications, and protocols.
    - Configuring admin and user authentication systems.
    - Configuring resource controls as required.

4. Install and configure any additional third-party security controls required to address the organization's security policies. This step includes installing and configuring network protection systems including the following:

    - Installing and configuring anti-malware products.
    - Installing and configuring EDR products.
    - Installing host (server)-based IDPS software.
    - Installing and configuring host (server)-based firewalls.
    - Installing or configuring disk encryption software to protect the stored data from attackers that gain physical access to the server.

5. Test the security of the new installation to ensure that it addresses all the organization's security issues. This step involves using vulnerability scanning and penetration detection tools to test the server's security capabilities. This step should be performed annually throughout the lifecycle of the server to ensure that its security capabilities remain acceptable.

Hardening the Server OS

After the operating system and the desired applications have been installed on the server, the next step in securing the server is to take steps to harden the security configuration of the entire server software environment. Hardening involves taking steps to close as many known vulnerabilities as possible while still offering an acceptable usability level to the network's users. These are the steps involved in hardening a server operating system:

1. Map the network topology the server will serve and determine what devices are attached to it. Include a detailed record for each local device on its network along with a list of its operating system version, who should have authorized access to it, expected times of operation, and expected network connections.

2. Compare the level of security provided by the operating system with the needs of the organization. Particularly look for open services running on the different servers to determine whether those services are needed, such as file and print sharing functions, wireless networking services, directory services, and email services. Turn such services off if they are not needed or not being used on the network.

3. Ensure that the network's operating systems are running the most current updates and anti-malware support available.

4. Disable any guest account on any server installed (unless there is a legitimate reason to have that account enabled on a specific server).

Before disabling any default services on a server, verify that the service and any dependencies related to it are not required by different network users.

5. Rename the default administrator account.

6. Remove or disable any unused default or user accounts, along with their existing authentication settings (usernames and passwords).

7. Employ the principle of least privilege access when providing services and access permissions to network users.

8. Remove any unnecessary software packages or utilities from the server, including remote access programs, language compilers and development tools, and any system and network development tools.

9. Remove or disable any network protocols (open TCP/UDP network ports) not required for operation.

Each of these steps requires the server administrator to balance security requirements against users' needs. Ideally, the server would be locked down tight and serve a single function. However, as security increases, functionality decreases.

Logical Server Access Control

The network administrator is also responsible for implementing corporate policy by determining who gains access to the operation of the network's servers, network connectivity devices, and data. In most organizations, this is implemented through the network operating system's administrative tools that control who has access to the network and its resources and what they can do with them.

There are three standard types of network access control strategies available to administrators:

- *Mandatory access control (MAC)*: The system establishes which users or groups may access files, folders, and other resources.

- *Discretionary access control (DAC)*: These are configurations where the user has the discretion to decide who has access to their objects and to what extent.

- *Nondiscretionary, role-based access control (RBAC)*: This is based on job roles each user has within the organization.

MAC strategies assign sensitivity labels to network objects such as files and folders and grants access to the users based on their permission level, as illustrated in Figure 4.23.

FIGURE 4.23 Mandatory access control

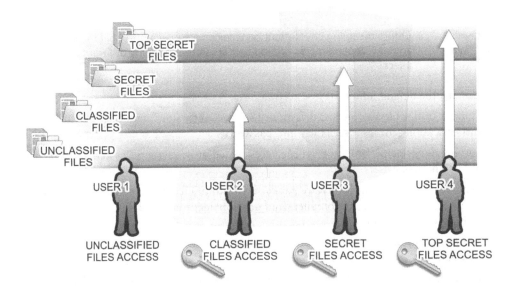

As Figure 4.23 shows, each user's range of access depends on the clearance level they have been given by their administrator. Personnel with a *Top Secret* clearance level have access to all objects that have been assigned a Top Secret label. In addition, they are permitted to access all objects with a lesser label, such as Secret and Classified objects.

Discretionary access control involves giving users the discretion to determine what objects should be restricted or shared. Each object has an owner who is responsible for determining who can gain access to the object. This is how permission is assigned in a peer-to-peer networking environment.

Because each object is subject to a permission level, the owner has the option of making some objects more secure than others. In addition, under DAC the access control strategy can be delivered in an *identity-based* or *user-directed* manner.

RBAC is a strategy designed for centralized control of all network objects and users. The network administrator is given the authority to specify and implement explicit security policies that carry out the designated policies of the organization. Each network user or group is assigned one or more roles, as described in Figure 4.24.

FIGURE 4.24   Role-based access control

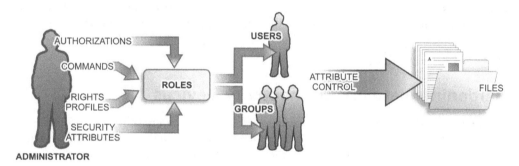

Each role is assigned specific privileges such as *read* or *write* to document files, or *execute*, *full control*, or *no access* to specific objects. The server is responsible for maintaining an *access control list (ACL)* database that tracks each user account, including which group accounts they may be assigned to, as well as what rights and permissions they have to different objects, as shown in the following:

Sample File A

- The individual owner can read, write to, and execute the file.
- Group members can read and write to the file.
- All others can only read the file.

INDIVIDUAL RIGHTS			GROUP MEMBERSHIP			OTHER/NON-MEMBER		
READ	WRITE	EXECUTE	READ	WRITE	EXECUTE	READ	WRITE	EXECUTE
1	1	1	1	1	0	1	0	0

Sample Folder B

- The individual owner can read and write to the folder.

- Group members can only read the folder contents.

INDIVIDUAL RIGHTS			GROUP MEMBERSHIP			OTHER/NON-MEMBER		
READ	WRITE	EXECUTE	READ	WRITE	EXECUTE	READ	WRITE	EXECUTE
1	1	0	1	0	0	0	0	0

- All others are denied any access to the folder.

In each strategy type, the *principle of least privilege access* should be implemented when providing users with access to objects through rights and permissions assignments. Under the least privilege rule, each user is only granted the levels of access required to perform their job role. Applying this principle consistently limits the damage that can be inflicted by a security breech to the initial task, process, or user.

Hardening Network Connectivity Devices

Different *network connectivity devices*, such as *switches* and *routers*, rely on MAC addresses as the basis for building and using internal *content addressable memory (CAM) tables*. The devices use these tables to route messages they receive from one network segment to a location on another network segment based on which hardware port the intended recipient is connected to.

Many connectivity devices build and maintain their CAM tables through a *MAC learning and discovery* process. As they interact with devices connected to their physical ports, they read message headers to acquire the sending and receiving device MAC addresses and record them in the CAM along with their port information.

There are two common types of attacks typically aimed at the MAC layer of a network: *MAC spoofing* and *MAC broadcast flooding*. While MAC addresses were originally intended to be permanent (burned-in) unique identifiers for network adapters, there are software tools available that can be used to change these addresses between the hardware and the operating system.

While being able to manipulate IP-to-MAC address relationships is an important aspect of *virtualization* (such as creating cloud-based environments), it also opens the door for malicious manipulation of MAC addresses in a type of attack referred to as *MAC spoofing*—changing the device's MAC address to change its identity, as illustrated in Figure 4.25. These tools and attacks are described later in this chapter in association with attacks aimed at network connectivity devices, such as network switches.

FIGURE 4.25 MAC spoofing

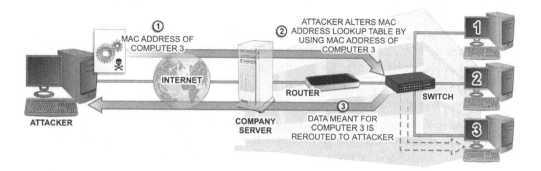

Switches possess monitoring ports that collect information about all their connected ports, including their VLAN ports. This makes them primary targets for attackers who want to gather information. They simply need to identify one of the connected VLAN switches to gain data about all other port connections.

Current switch model interfaces are commonly configured using SSH or HTTPS connections with GUIs. For centralized management, *Terminal Access Controller Access-Control System (TACACS)*, *Remote Access Dial-in User Service (RADIUS)*, or some other *Authentication, Authorization and Accounting (AAA)* tool should be used for secure remote access control. Local administration can be performed using a directly connected console cable to configure these interfaces.

While switches provide an anti-sniffing benefit, they can be exploited through numerous types of layer 2 attacks, such as MAC, ARP, denial-of-service, man-in-the-middle, and spoofing attacks.

Switchport Security

Switchport security is a management feature built into network switches that permits individual physical ports to be configured so that traffic through that port can be limited to a specific MAC address or list of MAC addresses. These addresses can be defined in three different ways:

- *Static secure*: This designation is typically used when the MAC address (or addresses) is always the same. This assumes that the same device is always attached to the port and never changes.

- *Dynamic secure*: This designation is employed when the MAC address (or addresses) changes constantly. Under this configuration the port can be limited so that it can learn only a specific number of devices (MAC addresses) at once.

- *Sticky secure*: This configuration enables the designated port to accept a combination of static and dynamic MAC addresses. The learned addresses are added directly into the switch's running configuration. Therefore, they are discarded if the switch is rebooted.

If the parameters configured for one of these secure port modes is violated, a *switchport security violation* is posted, and the switch responds in one of four ways depending on its response configuration:

- *Protect*: If protect mode response is configured, the port will continue to forward traffic from known MAC addresses but drops traffic from addresses not known before the violation occurred. However, no security notifications are produced.

- *Restrict*: This mode also drops traffic from unknown addresses after a violation occurs. However, syslog messages are logged, and SNMP messages are sent.

- *Shutdown*: When configured for this mode, the switch will shut down the physical port where the violation occurred; no packets will be forwarded through the port. To restart port operations, it will be necessary to disable and re-enable the port.

- *Shutdown VLAN*: Under this configuration, the switch simply disables the specified violating VLAN.

Configuring Switch ACLs

Just as configuring ACLs in servers creates a more secure computing environment, one of the most critical aspects of securing a network is proper configuration of ACLs in network devices. There are basically two major types of configurable ACLs. The first is a list of rights that an object or user has to a specific resource within a network, referred to as a *discretionary access control list (DACL)*.

With this type of ACL, access control is a configurable service (using permissions) that determines what a user can access, change, or view. The other type of configurable network ACL is a list that resides on a firewall or router interface that allows or denies traffic to flow in or out of the network through specific interfaces or ports on the device.

While DACLs allow users or object owners to make decisions about the files or folders they create, an ACL on a router or firewall interface is typically more restrictive. These ACLs are configurable controls that can be used to halt one type of network traffic in a specific direction, while allowing other communications to move through the firewall or router interface. They can be configured to filter or block traffic by closing selected ports, by limiting protocol use, or by denying single or groups of network addresses that can include source or destination addresses.

Determining which ports, protocols, or addresses to allow or deny must be based on the organizational needs of the organization. The network security professional must be aware of the ports and services that should be active in their networks.

Care must always be taken to protect router and firewall ACL configuration files. These devices represent lucrative targets because they are the entry portals of the network. For this reason, direct physical access and Telnet access to an ACL-configured device should always be denied. In addition, all the network's ACL configuration files should be backed up and stored in a secure location along with its data files.

A local host's interface can also be configured to allow or deny specific ports.

Configuring Services and Protocols

Protocols and *services* were initially designed to improve network connectivity and facilitate the sharing of resources between users. By default, many older operating systems were created to have their network services and protocols enabled at installation. This default setting facilitated the end user's need to connect and communicate without much concern for security.

More recently, operating system vendors have designed their newer operating systems so that they install with their services and protocols disabled. Any services or protocols that are needed must be enabled by the network administrator during or after the install. Therefore, the administrator must be able to answer several questions correctly to properly install the operating systems and provide the needed services and security levels:

 This evaluation process may be conducted more efficiently using port scanners or network monitors.

- What protocols and services are currently in use on the network? This might be the most critical question to answer. Administrators should periodically check servers to identify a list of protocols that are bound and active on each network connection.

- What protocols and services are really needed on the network? Like the first question, this question is also critical. Unnecessary protocols running on the network pose a potential security risk.

- What are the dependencies or links established between clients and servers due to these protocols or services? Consider each network protocol. If a connecting protocol is identified, evaluate its source and destination addresses to ensure that a critical protocol that is required within the network is not disabled.

- Are there any enabled protocols or services that have no dependencies and are not required for the network to operate properly? If so, they should be disabled or removed. When fewer services or applications are running on a server, there are fewer interactions and fewer maintenance or log entries, which reduces the network's administrative overhead.

 A network that lacks security consciousness most likely has all types of default services and protocols running along with improperly configured firewalls.

Network Hardening Precautions

There are several potential difficulties with implementing updates in an active enterprise network. While it is important to keep network systems hardened against attack, this does not mean that every product update should be installed directly on the network devices as soon as it's received—quite the contrary. Before any changes are implemented, all critical folders and organizational resources should be backed up.

Because updates may have potential programming glitches or produce unintended/adverse conditions, you would not want to propagate this flaw across the entire network. Likewise, you would not want a critical server service that supports hundreds of clients to stop functioning because you failed to test the update before installing it.

To avoid such potentially destructive or disruptive occurrences, product updates should always be tested on a nonproduction server before being implemented across the organization's network. You might also want to consider installing application updates during the network's least busy times, perhaps at night or over a weekend. Depending on the nature of the update, the network may need to be shut down in segments to complete the change across the entire network without disrupting operations.

For example, for an organization that has a 24-hour network operation, it may be impractical to conduct any type of updates that would disable all protocols. Performing this type of update across the network would mean that there would be no connectivity available to support normal operations. Therefore, the only effective method of implementing such a change in this type of environment may be to make changes one network segment at a time.

Review Questions

The following questions test your knowledge of the material presented in this chapter.

1. Identify the three perimeters of endpoint protection.

2. What is the recommended method for providing physical security for ICS control devices in production environments?

3. What concerns must organizations have about employees bringing their own devices (BYOD) into enterprise and OT network environments?

4. Near field communication systems offer relatively secure authorization options. What concerns should cybersecurity administrators have about using these systems?

5. What is the most important cybersecurity tenet to apply when configuring services and access permission for network users?

6. List the security benefits provided by creating virtual networks within a host.

7. What is the main cybersecurity activity associated with application security?

8. Explain the two items that are included in almost every organization's security policies concerning malware protection on their servers.

9. Explain how malware security policies for OT devices, such as PLCs and SCADA systems, differ from those created in the enterprise network.

10. What is the source of SQL injection attacks?

11. What is the most common method of securing ICS databases, such as data historians?

12. _____ encryption techniques employ two keys to ensure the security of the encrypted data—a public key and a private key. The public key (known to everyone) is used to encrypt the data, and the private or secret key (known only to the specified recipient) is used to decrypt it.

13. Describe the two types of network access control lists that administrators can configure to implement the organization's security policies.

14. _____ is a management feature built into network switches that permits individual physical ports to be configured so that traffic through that port can be limited to a specific MAC address or list of MAC addresses.

15. What requirements should be placed on any account that must have remote access into an ICS network?

16. What precaution should be taken before implementing any patches or updates in an active enterprise network?

Exam Questions

1. Which of the following does not represent one of the three general locations where attackers can gain access to data?

    A. In memory

    B. On a display

    C. On a drive

    D. In transmission

2. From the following list, select the actions that can be used to harden the outer perimeter of most computing and control devices. (Select all that apply.)

    A. Configure passwords.

    B. Disable any unnecessary hardware ports.

    C. Disable all input ports after configuring the device.

    D. Limit bootup/startup options.

    E. Disable any display devices after configuring the system.

3. Select the appropriate options for securing mobile devices from the following list. (Select all that apply.)

    A. Turn off cellular connections when you are within the organization's office or production facilities.

    B. Turn off automatic Wi-Fi connections when you are within the organization's office or production facilities.

    C. Turn on Bluetooth auto-discovery options within the organization's office or production facilities.

    D. Turn off TLS/SSL options when you are within the organization's office or production facilities.

4. From the following options, identify those steps that are typically part of hardening the network's servers. (Select all that apply.)

    A. Implement local login requirements.

    B. Implement additional authentication options.

    C. Disable system auditing and event logging.

    D. Establish firewall settings.

    E. Automatically install security updates and patches.

5. From the following list, identify common security tenets associated with implementing virtual networks. (Select all that apply.)

   A. Isolation

   B. Segmentation

   C. Boundary protection

   D. Data encryption

6. One of the major concerns with the proliferation of embedded devices is poorly configured installations. From the following list, identify steps for hardening these devices against cyber-security threats.

   A. Keep default accounts and passwords active.

   B. Enable TFTP configurations.

   C. Disable configuration options that are designed for usability and not for security.

   D. Implement least privilege and need-to-know configuration settings.

7. Which access control strategy establishes which users or groups may access files, folders, and other network resources?

   A. Mandatory access control (MAC)

   B. Discretionary access control (DAC)

   C. Nondiscretionary, role-based access control (RBAC)

   D. Rule-based access control (RRBAC)

8. What questions must be answered in order to configure secure services and protocol settings for a given network?

   A. What are the default protocols and services running on the network?

   B. Which protocols and services represent the highest cybersecurity risk to the network?

   C. Which protocols and services are really needed on the network?

   D. What protocols and services are currently in use on the network?

9. When configuring a managed switch, what precautions should be taken to harden them against cyberattacks? (Select all that apply.)

   A. They should be configured directly using a standard serial cable.

   B. They should be placed behind a firewall for protection.

   C. They should be configured to require passwords for access to the management console.

   D. They should be configured through a direct console connection or an SSH connection.

10. When configuring switch port security on a managed switch, which secure port response mode will allow the port to continue to forward traffic from known MAC addresses but drop traffic from addresses not known before a violation occurred, with no security notifications produced?

    A. Protect

    B. Restrict

    C. Shutdown

    D. Shutdown VLAN

Chapter 5

Cybersecurity Essentials for ICS

OBJECTIVES

Upon completion of this chapter, you should be able to:

1. **Knowledge of Security Tenets:**
   - CIA
   - Nonrepudiation
   - Least privilege
   - Separation of duties

2. **Knowledge of Availability:**
   - Health and safety
   - Environmental
   - Productivity

3. **Knowledge of Threats:**
   - Nation-states
   - General criminals
   - Inside and outside malicious attackers
   - Hacktivists
   - Inside nonmalicious attackers

4. **Knowledge of Attacks and Incidents:**
   - Man-in-the-middle
   - Spoofing
   - Social engineering
   - Denial of service
   - Denial of view
   - Data manipulating

- Session hijacking
- Foreign software
- Unauthorized access

5. **Knowledge of Cryptographics:**

- Encryption
- Digital signatures
- Certificate management
- PKI
- Public versus private key
- Hashing
- Key management
- Resource constraints

Introduction

In 1982, a 15-year-old high school student named Rich Skrenta wrote the first known computer virus. Originally a joke, the virus was loaded on to a floppy disk and inserted into a friend's Apple II computer. It was attached to a game and designed to launch the 50th time the game was started. It then changed to a blank screen that displayed a poem. This was just the beginning. From there, the virus was placed into the computer's memory, which would then be copied over to uninfected floppy disks whenever they were inserted.

From this seemingly innocent start, the computer *virus* was born. A slightly malicious intent was all that was needed. Although the virus wasn't designed to cause damage, the desire to prank friends and to cause frustration was enough for the author to design the virus so that it would replicate and spread.

Once an issue such as this becomes big enough, designers will start to create solutions to prevent them from happening. It began with creating security devices like read-only disks so that the files written to a disk could not be easily altered. Assuming the packaging was not broken and the disk had not been replaced, it was safe to say that the read-only disk was safe for use.

As the Internet picked up speed and became widely used, the door was opened for viruses to spread and for evil-doers to seek ways to carry out their intentions. It may not have been world domination, but there are many other motivators for people to do what they do. Microsoft puts it this way: "Hackers are often motivated, in part, by their invisibleness. On the Internet, a hacker can 'peek' into a company's private world—its network—and learn a lot while remaining anonymous." Today's more sophisticated hackers are often also motivated by the prospect of a big payday.

Because there are people who want to do harm for many reasons, including money, fame, and destruction, there must be people working to prevent that from happening. In the same way a police force protects citizens, cybersecurity practitioners protect computers, users, employees, and customers from harm.

Basic Security Tenets

In IT/OT network environments, administrators are responsible for implementing the organization's security policies. These policies should be designed to reflect the organization's risk tolerance levels and risk management policies. Typically, these policies are designed with tested *cybersecurity tenets* (principles held as true by members of a profession or group). As such, security practitioners must be aware of these tenets, how they are implemented, and where they are appropriate. The opening sections of this chapter will deal with the most fundamental cybersecurity tenets.

Confidentiality, Integrity, and Availability

One of the most widely recognized tenets associated with the classical model of information security is based on three basic objectives: confidentiality, integrity, and availability (CIA).

- *Confidentiality*: Assurance that data remains secret or private. It is established through sets of rules designed to limit data access to authorized people.

- *Integrity*: Assurance that data is accurate and can be trusted. Data integrity is established through authorization and authentication efforts to make sure that only authorized persons make changes to the data. It is also maintained through mechanisms that ensure that authorized changes can be reversed if correction is needed.

- *Availability*: Assurance that data can reliably be accessed in a timely manner. High data availability is established through hardware and networking designs to ensure that data is available when it is needed. This involves specifying computing resource and network architectures designed to ensure delivery of data to the user as quickly as possible. It also includes supporting architecture that will keep the system in operation in cases of power failure.

Network administrators also typically follow another security tenet known as AAA when implementing organizational policies into their network security structures.

- *Authentication*: Involves making sure that an individual is who they say they are.

- *Authorization*: Applies approval of access to designated information after the individual is authenticated.

- *Accounting*: Creates a tracking list of events using logs or other tracking tools.

In some small to medium-sized organizations the network administrator may also be responsible for generating the company's *security policies*, including physical and logical access controls. As you've seen in all the previous chapters, all security efforts begin at the physical access level. If an unauthorized person can gain physical access to the network servers, media, or connectivity devices, then security can be compromised far more easily. The level of network security is greatly reduced after physical access has been gained.

In larger organizations, specialized administrative roles are typically created to handle different aspects of the network's operation. This may include having separate server and network administrators. The *server admin* is responsible for the design, implementation, and maintenance of the server computers, while the *network administrator* provides the same functions for the network and its media and connectivity devices.

Division of administrative duties may also involve a special *security administrator* who is responsible for performing information security tasks for the servers, hosts, and connectivity devices in the network. In these settings, the separation of administrative duties should be as distinct, defined, and controlled as possible.

Availability in ICS Networks

As has been mentioned several times before, the intent and operation of OT and IT networks are very different. While the main security tenet of an IT network involves providing CIA for data, in an industrial or utility network the main emphasis should shift to consider each CIA impact for each asset or system in the network, with confidentiality being the most important aspect. Basically, the security tenet changes to AIC (availability first and then integrity and confidentiality if possible) to keep the operation running.

Key requirements for industrial process networks include the following:

- *Availability*: Many processes are continuous operations and require that their controllers have high availability, reliability, and maintainability ratings. Availability is typically the highest objective in an industrial control system, along with data integrity. Confidentiality has traditionally been a secondary concern with process control systems. This is completely reversed from the general CIA requirements associated with IT systems.

- *Timeliness*: Process control is a time-sensitive operation that requires quick response times. IT systems generally do not have timeliness constraints. For this reason, front-line intelligent process controllers operate on real-time operating systems.

Therefore, the key requirements for industrial process controllers include *availability*, *timeliness*, *industrial interfacing*, and *physical hardening*.

As mentioned in the previous chapter, bad things happen when data is delayed in an industrial process. Lack of availability in any part of the ICS network can negatively impact the organization in multiple ways:

- *Health and safety*: Because OT networks primarily exist in manufacturing, production, and utility plants where process machinery and humans can occupy the same environment, loss of data due to lack of availability can result in harm to personnel as well as equipment and productivity.

- *Environmental issues*: Many industrial processes involve highly hazardous chemicals and materials that could damage the environment. For example, if a controller in a chemical process does not receive the data required to manage the process in a timely fashion, dangerous or damaging chemicals could be released into the environment.

- *Productivity*: Availability failures due to loss of data result in loss of productivity and profitability. When production machinery is not running, the organization is losing money in the form of productivity and profitability.

In general, availability assurance can be increased through the use of redundant components and systems, elevated access control procedures, and efficient backup policies and procedures. Industrial organizations perform *process hazard analysis (PHA)* to quantify their risks associated with each of the categories listed earlier.

In the United States, these studies are a key requirement of the *Environmental Protection Agency's (EPA's)* risk management program, as well as the Occupational Safety and Health Administration's (OSHA's) process safety management standard. These standards require the PHA studies to cover all toxic, fire, and explosion hazards associated with specific processes, including their potential impacts on personnel, the public, and the environment. PHAs are described in some detail in Chapter 11, "Disaster Recovery and Business Continuity."

Nonrepudiation

Another major tenet in cybersecurity realms is *nonrepudiation*. Generally, in cybersecurity environments this term is used to refer to a service that proves the integrity and origin (authorship) of data. In other words, authentication proves an object (such as a document or graphic) is genuine and that it comes from the person who says they sent it. In cybersecurity environments, this involves using cryptological tools to provide proof of data integrity. Such tools typically include the following:

- *Hashing*: This is a mathematical method used to verify the integrity of the object. A hashing algorithm is applied to the object to generate a unique code to represent the object. The object is then encrypted and sent along with the hashed code. When it is received, the recipient decrypts the message and the hash and compares the two hashes. If they agree, the recipient has a high likelihood that the message is original and has been delivered intact. This is a one-way operation. It is not reversible and always involves a set number of characters.

- *Digital certificates (public key infrastructure)*: Public key certificates are issued to provide information about the identity of an object's owner. They also contain information about the key and the digital signature of the certifying body or certificate authority (CA). If the signature is valid and the certifying body is examined and found to be trustworthy, the key can be used to communicate with a high expectation of security.

- *Digital signatures*: These are mathematical algorithms that are used to authenticate digital messages or documents. In cybersecurity settings, digital signatures are involved in authentication, integrity, and nonrepudiation applications.

- *Trusted third parties (TTPs)*: These include third-party witnesses (on-demand authentication) and digital forensic analysts (after the fact authentication). In cryptography, public key certificates are the only recognized TTPs that create environments where both parties trust the third party.

NOTE   All of these terms are discussed in greater detail in the "Cryptography" section later in this chapter.

Principle of Least Privilege

As referenced several times, the principles of *least privilege* and *need to know* are used by administrators to establish access control levels to different assets. The principle refers to giving each user the least amount of access possible to accomplish their job roles and only to the areas of the network they must have.

In the cybersecurity arena, this principle must first be translated into organizational policy and then into application for people, processes, and technologies. The *International Organization for Standards (ISO) 27002* standard presents recommendations for information security management that include the *least privilege* principle as one of the access control methods to be employed for reducing risk to the network and the organization. Least privilege rights and permissions policies are typically implemented along with separation of duties policies.

Separation of Duties

When it comes to managing critical data or special assignments, one of my personal favorite preventive security measures is a *separation of duties policy*. This type of policy is designed to ensure that no single individual can compromise a system. This may be very useful when dealing with *Secret* and *Top Secret* information for government agencies, or *Confidential* and *Highly Confidential* information in *small-medium business (SMB)* or enterprise organizations.

Separation of duties policies are often implemented in a format known as *two-man control*. As its name implies, two-man control means that two users must review and approve each other's work in order to complete a project. In essence, it takes two people to get the one assigned task done. Although this may not be practical for many tasks, it offers a high level of security for those tasks where it is implemented.

An organization should never have the same employee performing purchasing and receiving activities. If the employee is given authority at both ends of this process, they may be able to conduct transactions and hide them from the organization without the activity being detected.

Other separation of duties policies are designed to prevent individual employees from being involved in different portions of a task to the point they gain enough knowledge or skill to complete the overall task by themselves.

It is also common to separate research and development engineers on projects so that each group handles only small portions of a project. As each group's work is completed, a supervisor usually intervenes to coordinate their work with their counterparts in the other group. This ensures that no single group can replicate the entire project.

Vulnerability and Threat Identification

In every venue, cybersecurity begins with policies and procedures. After the organization's hardware and software assets have been identified, the next step in the cybersecurity policy development process is to accurately identify potential *vulnerabilities* and *threats* those assets are exposed to. These terms are not synonymous:

- A *vulnerability* is any weakness that exposes the network or its devices to a threat.
- A *threat* is the potential to perform actions with the intent to inflict pain, injury, damage, or other hostile action.

After collecting the raw threat information, organize it in terms of levels of concern to the organization. Then put the various threats in context, describing how they would affect the organization and its operations if they occurred. Even seemingly simple actions—such as writing down passwords, failing to secure server rooms, or not properly shutting down computers—create vulnerabilities that the organization must take into account.

In the cybersecurity environment, the *threat identification process* is a preventive measure intended to document vulnerabilities that could produce risk factors that affect the network data's confidentiality, integrity, and availability. While there are many methods used to identify and list risks, the process should be based on information collected through a combination of experience, forecasting, subject-matter expertise, and other available resources. These methods are described in detail in Chapter 8, "ICS Security Governance and Risk Management."

With the exponential, worldwide growth of the Internet over the last two decades, the stereotype of hacker culture has become increasingly ingrained in the global psyche as one of teenage slackers who spend their time attempting to circumvent computer security measures in order to cause harm. However, this is a stereotype that does not provide a cybersecurity professional with a real understanding of the threats associated with different types of hackers.

 Threat actors are people, organizations, or groups that have the ability to create events or incidents that negatively affect the security or safety of another person, organization, or group.

It is important for cybersecurity professionals to have an accurate understanding of different threat actor types and the motivations behind the threats they represent. Figure 5.1 shows the motivational forces behind various types of cyber hacking. The following sections describe these different hacker types and designations, as well as their motivations.

FIGURE 5.1   Attack motivations

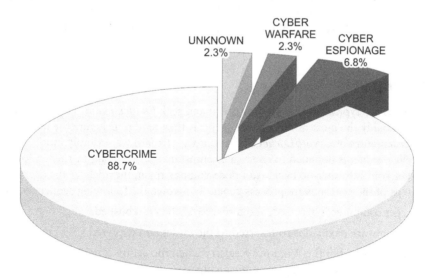

UNKNOWN
2.3%

CYBER
WARFARE
2.3%

CYBER
ESPIONAGE
6.8%

CYBERCRIME
88.7%

Nation-States

A nation-state is defined as a group of people who share the same history, language, or traditions living under one government—in other words, a country or a *sovereign nation*. *Spying* and *espionage* between nations is nothing new; it has been going on since people first began to create borders. However, the development of the interconnected cyber world has opened up a new realm of possibility for the spy landscape.

Cyber espionage is not exactly a new phenomenon, but countries and organizations find themselves scrambling to catch up with the latest tools and techniques. Modern threats are not simply limited to cyber espionage, where the goal is to collect information on enemy states, but outright attacks and even surreptitious destruction of property are all likely to occur with few laws or treaties to prevent them. Cyberattacks such as the Stuxnet virus are excellent examples of the borderless world of the Internet and the ability to cause destruction thousands of miles away with no repercussions to the attacking country.

Cyberterrorists

Cyberterrorists are typically not motivated by money but rather by the furtherance of a *political agenda* or *ideology*. The goal is to cause harm and chaos to the general public. This category of hacker can be quite broad and apply to other kinds of hackers as well.

For instance, a hacker who is motivated by money as well as furthering their agenda can be both a cybercriminal and a cyberterrorist. While these definitions can be overly broad, both kinds of hackers can do serious damage to systems and networks and cost billions of dollars each year.

Cybercriminals

Cybercriminals are typically motivated by greed and seek *financial gain*. This group of hackers is probably the most notable hacker type as they tend to generate the most notice. For instance, creators of *CryptoLocker* (a ransomware trojan) were simply motivated by money. Their product is designed to create a circumstance where you pay them a lot of money to get your information back. And once you pay them, they deliver the decryption key. The steps of the ransomware process generally involve the following sequence of events:

1. The target computer is accessed, and a reverse shell is established.

2. The ransomware payload is transferred to the target and executed.

3. The payload modifies the Windows Registry when the action is performed. This modification will cause the exploit to run on startup.

4. Backup records are deleted.

5. The contents of the file system are encrypted (either with a single encryption or more recently with dual encryptions).

6. The decryption keys are exfiltrated to the attacker's servers.

7. The ransomware notice is sent/displayed to the user with instructions for paying the ransom and gaining access to the decryption tools.

Ransomware such as this is unfortunately common and a pain to recover from. While ransomware/malware researchers have worked diligently to detect flaws in the ransomware codes and provide decryption key tools, if you have incurred a ransomware attack, there are companies that advertise ransomware recovery services.

However, attackers have also increased the complexity of their exploits. Advanced ransomware exploits may involve two-way encryption based on combining RSA and AES encryption algorithms. One algorithm is used to encrypt the target's data, and the other is used to encrypt the decryption key before sending it to the server. It is virtually impossible to decrypt because it uses the same encryption algorithms normally used to protect data.

Cybercriminals are counting on their targets to not have backed up their data, so they must fold to the attacker's demands because of the intrinsic (or financial) value of their data. If you haven't been convinced before this point in the book, backups are extremely important!

A last hope for ransomware recovery involves waiting for the attacker to close up shop and release the keys, or they get caught by government authorities and the keys are released. Keep your data that the ransomware has locked up, as these key releases have actually occurred on multiple occasions.

Script Kiddies

Script kiddies are typically individuals who have very little knowledge of programming, scripting, or cybersecurity in general. They are usually motivated by curiosity or their peers to use information gathered on the Internet (through forums or code repositories) to attack systems, networks, or individual users. Most script kiddies usually don't know the extent of their attack or what it is actually doing to the target system.

Script kiddies are commonly thought of as juveniles who lack the skills required to create well-designed attacks. However, there are many adults who qualify as script kiddies simply due to their lack of knowledge and practice in the ways of hacking. In some ways, they may be considered to be black-hat hackers because their intentions are not good, but actual hackers would refute this and would not want to be included in conversations about them. Most real hackers prefer to go unnoticed and undiscovered. However, script kiddies typically have no knowledge of how to keep their attacks hidden.

A technical report published by the Software Engineering Institute at Carnegie Mellon University (`www.hackmageddon.com/2021/06/08/may-2021-cyberattacks-statistics`) defined script kiddies as follows:

> "The more immature, but unfortunately often just as dangerous, exploiter of security lapses on the Internet. The typical script kiddie uses existing, and frequently well-known and easy-to-find techniques and programs (or scripts) to search for and exploit weaknesses in other computers on the Internet—often randomly and with little regard or perhaps even understanding of the potentially harmful consequences."

Many of the scripts they use, along with software packages and Linux distributions designed for cybersecurity that can be used against systems, can be found online. The script kiddie simply needs to change a few arguments around in the script and fire away.

Some of these tools are freeware applications designed for performing penetration testing on networks. However, due to their easy availability and ease of use, virtually anyone can download these attacks, enter basic parameters, and cause damage or downtime to networks without really knowing what they are doing.

Hacktivists

The term *hacktivism* has been around since the mid-1980s and is generally used to describe an ambiguous idea of cyberterrorism that serves a purpose. Oftentimes, hacktivists feel that their acts and crimes are justified, whether through the outing of classified information or by doing something morally right that would otherwise not have happened.

The hacker group Anonymous, which first appeared in 2003, often refer to themselves as hacktivists in the sense that they are serving the world by righting wrongs and "generally doing good." Anonymous boasts of a decentralized command structure that operates on ideas rather than directives. There is not a defined philosophy or belief system in this group, but it is generally opposed to Internet censorship and seeks to carry out activities that promote their beliefs.

Insider Threats

While major threats to a network may obviously come from the Internet, a significant threat exists inside any network as well. Studies have shown that *insider threats* represent the greatest threat to most networked organizations. Some survey results indicate that insider threats can account for more than 50 percent of malicious network activity ("Insider Threat: The Human Element of Cyberrisk" at www.mckinsey.com).

Network administrators should be vigilant and aware of the significance of these threats. Insider threats are often more damaging than other types of threats simply because they go undetected for longer periods of time and have readily available access to trusted resources. Disgruntled employees can use their access to attack the network by disrupting some portion of the organization's function, or they attempt to gain access to unauthorized resources with malicious intentions.

Insider threats may be malicious or nonmalicious. The motivations of a malicious threat from within your network are many, and disgruntled or dissatisfied workers certainly create certain risks that cannot be ignored. From a cybersecurity perspective, the goal would mostly be to minimize the damage a single internal user could cause. More common, however, are the nonmalicious threats resulting from carelessness or a lack of user education.

Certainly, phishing attacks are the most common insider threat, but accidental corruption or deletion, as well as the insecure handling of data, are major threats as well. Storage media such as USB thumb drives brought from home or other outside networks can often contain malware. The Conficker worm targeted thumb drives and would automatically execute as soon as one was connected to a live USB port.

Laptops, tablets, and even phones brought into a network from outside networks pose the same risks as a USB device. In addition, they pose even more of a threat as a potential unauthorized network device.

Insider threats can be extremely challenging to monitor, as they typically resemble normal activities the user may perform every day. Therefore, they represent an area where network tools are much less able to help. However, these threats should never be overlooked. Policies (such as least privilege and segregation of duties), education (user, administrator, and executive), and an overall strategy are really the keys to dealing with such threats.

Insider attacks can be even harder to detect and deal with when they involve *disgruntled administrators*. Because these individuals have greater access to and control of network assets than normal users, the amount of damage that they can inflict is generally much greater. The standard least privilege and segregation of duties controls are the best tools for mitigating the potential risk associated with these threats.

Even administrative duties should be designed to be shared so that even managers cannot complete critical tasks from beginning to end by themselves. For example, and with the resources available, one member of the administrative team should be tasked with creating new users, while a second administrator is responsible for establishing their permissions (but only after they have been authorized by the other manager).

Events, Incidents, and Attacks

In the normal operation of any network, there are variations that occur, so administrators must constantly monitor their networks for anomalies. Anomalous activities can be segregated into three categories:

- *Cyber events*: These are changes, errors, or interruptions in the network. Events may result from typical computer/network activities such as disk drive failures, network hardware failures, or user errors. However, they can also be activities that provide indications that an incident may be imminent or occurring.

- *Cyber incidents*: These are occurrences that create adverse effects within the network or computing environment that will require actions to mitigate. The term can also be applied to occurrences that violate organizational security policies, procedures, or acceptable use practices.

- *Cyberattacks*: These are attempts to gain unauthorized access to network or computing system services, resources, data, or integrity. This term can also be extended to include any intentional act of attempting to bypass the security services and controls of a network or computing environment.

Threat Vectors

There are many ways for a cyberthreat actor to create incidents and carry out attacks against someone's network. Collectively, these are referred to as *threat vectors* and are tools, techniques, and procedures (TTP) a threat employs to reach a *target*.

The cybersecurity professional must understand how different types of threat vectors are used to research, plan, and carry out a cyberattack on a target. The first step in this process is to understand the cyberattack path. This is followed by understanding how different attack methods, techniques, and tools are used along that path.

The Attack Path

An *attack path* describes the process an attacker takes to research, plan, implement, and execute an attack. While there are various descriptions of the typical cyberattack path, all attacks follow a fundamental six- or seven-step process.

One of the most well-known descriptions of the cyberattack path is the *Cyber Kill Chain*, or Intrusion Kill Chain, described at `https://lockheedmartin.com/en-us/capabilities/cyber/cyber-kill-chain.html`. This process was developed by Lockheed Martin to address multiyear attacks from threats dubbed as *advanced persistent threats (APTs)*. These threats target very specific and very secure systems and have created a demand to address these threats in ways not traditionally managed through cybersecurity best practices.

The *Intrusion Kill Chain*, presented in Figure 5.2, focuses on these seven phases that we discuss throughout this chapter:

- Reconnaissance
- Weaponization
- Delivery
- Exploitation
- Installation
- Command and control (C2)
- Actions on objectives

FIGURE 5.2   Cyber Kill Chain

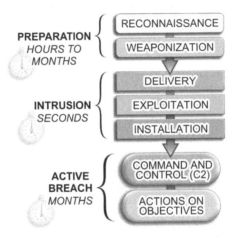

Reconnaissance

In military applications, *reconnaissance*, or recon, is "...observation of a region to locate an enemy or ascertain strategic features" or "preliminary surveying or research." The use of reconnaissance in a hacker's general attack strategy is not really any different.

Reconnaissance is a hacker's first step in familiarizing themself with their target and beginning to find a potential way into the target's critical infrastructure, whether manually or digitally. A hacker will typically spend more time performing reconnaissance on their target and researching the target than actually exploiting vulnerabilities.

This time is well worth the investment, as it can yield extremely useful information about a target's network that can allow a hacker to focus on a particular vulnerability that will be more likely to yield results, disguise their attacks, and limit exposure to potential detection devices on the network.

Social Engineering Exploits

When we think of network vulnerabilities, we don't initially think of human vulnerabilities, but they are the targets of many cybersecurity attacks. *Social engineering* essentially exploits human interactions to circumvent normal security. As traditional security improves and network exploits are increasingly difficult to implement, hackers are turning to physical and psychological human manipulation to achieve their goals.

We tend to laugh off this concept, and often it may seem amazing that a user could be deceived in this way, but these deceptions are becoming more detailed and sophisticated. Some social engineering deceptions are so realistic it is only with extreme scrutiny and proper training that they can be recognized.

For example, *phishing* is a social engineering technique that utilizes an emotional response in an attempt to acquire sensitive information, usually login credentials or credit card data, by masquerading as a trustworthy organization or person. These attacks generally involve emails that direct the user to a bogus website that looks like the real thing, as shown in Figure 5.3.

FIGURE 5.3   Social engineering attacks

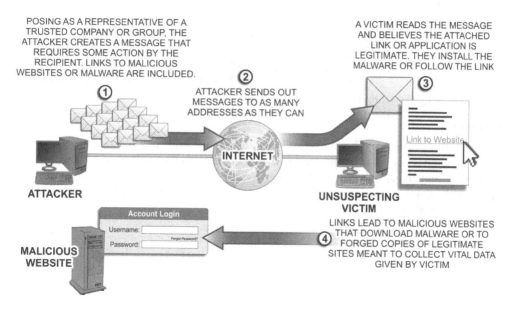

Whether the attacker personally speaks to a victim or sends an email, the goal is the same, which is to extract valuable information from the person that can assist the social engineer in performing additional attacks on the target entity. One of the most intriguing facets of social engineering is that it can be nontechnical in nature. Attacks don't necessarily require keyboards, monitors, or 1s and 0s when it comes to social engineering.

Social engineering relies almost entirely on human interaction and often preys on a human being's innate urge to help a fellow human, conning them into breaking normal security procedures. The ultimate goal in social engineering is to get the victim to eventually do something they normally wouldn't do, such as divulge secret information that wouldn't be known by anyone outside the company, such as passwords, usernames, maintenance schedules, and more. Physical access to restricted areas of a building is often another goal sought by social engineers.

There are many types of social engineering attacks. However, these attacks can be divided into two general categories:

- Those that rely on *physical techniques*
- Those that rely on *psychological techniques*

The following sections of this chapter discuss the various types of social engineering techniques associated with each category.

Physical Social Engineering Techniques

Social engineering involving physical action can potentially yield vast amounts of information by collecting smaller bits of information, such as usernames, passwords, credit card numbers, PINs, etc. There are three keys to successful social engineering:

- Don't get caught!
- Don't be obvious!
- Keep the pretext simple!

Failing any of these requirements could potentially get you into serious trouble. These concepts are described in detail in the Social Engineering Frameworks at `www.social-engineer.org/framework/general-discussion`.

Shoulder Surfing

Shoulder surfing is one of the simplest and most common social engineering attacks that can be employed on a potential victim. During a shoulder surf attack, as shown in Figure 5.4, the attacker will glance over an unsuspecting victim's shoulder in hopes of watching or recording them input some private information, such as name, address, credit card number, Social Security number, etc.

FIGURE 5.4 Shoulder surfing

Shoulder surfing can occur in many different settings, but is usually most effective in a crowded area where the attack can be less obvious than if it were in a more intimate setting. Common opportunities for shoulder surfing include the following acts committed by the victim:

- Fills out information fields on a form or application

- Enters a PIN at an ATM or debit card machine at a store

- Enters username/password credentials in an office or public setting

- Enters a PIN/password/security pattern on a smart phone

- Sitting on an airplane behind or next to someone and viewing spreadsheets, strategy documents, job postings, or presentations

It is also possible for shoulder surfing to be carried out from a distance with the assistance of magnifying devices such as binoculars or well-placed closed-circuit cameras that are concealed without the victim's knowledge. Both of these methods can be used by an attacker to observe a victim as they input potentially sensitive information without as large a threat of being discovered as if they were standing directly behind the victim.

According to a security white paper published by Secure, the European Association for Visual Data Security (`https://visualdatasecurity.eu`), a survey of IT professionals produced the following statistics:

- 85 percent admitted to seeing sensitive information on a screen that they were not authorized to see.

- 82 percent admitted that it was possible for information on their screen to be viewed by unauthorized personnel.

- 82 percent had little to no confidence that users within their organization would protect their screen from being viewed by unauthorized personnel.

It is possible for individuals to try to prevent themselves from falling victim to shoulder surfing. Common techniques for preventing shoulder surfing include the following:

- *Practice situational awareness*: Users need to be aware of their surroundings at all times, but especially when sensitive information is being provided.

- *Obscure any potential attacker's view*: If it is possible for someone to watch you input sensitive information, attempt to obscure their view by covering a PIN pad, installing a special device that obscures content from certain angles, or politely asking them to look away as you type in a password. Use a privacy screen on your laptop so the only way to view the screen is being directly in front of it.

- *Awareness and training*: According to the same survey from Secure, 98 percent of those IT professionals surveyed agreed that "it is important to educate individuals on the overall visual data security threat and how they can prevent a breach. However, only 56% currently had some sort of plan in place to safeguard visual data security."

Awareness and training are the most effective tools in the effort to prevent social engineering attacks.

Eavesdropping

Eavesdropping is the act of secretly listening to a private conversation without the consent of the parties involved, as shown in Figure 5.5. When you were younger, did you ever hide somewhere and try to listen to your parents as they talked about something you weren't supposed to hear? Perhaps they were talking together, or maybe one of them was talking to someone else on the phone. This is a prime example of eavesdropping.

FIGURE 5.5   Eavesdropping

Dumpster Diving

If you've ever heard the old saying "One man's trash is another man's treasure," then that is a good way to think about dumpster diving. In the fields of information technology and ethical hacking, *dumpster diving* is a technique used by a potential attacker to retrieve information that could be used to help them carry out an attack on a target system or computer network.

As shown in Figure 5.6, dumpster diving isn't simply limited to searching through an entity's garbage for obviously helpful pieces of information, such as passwords written down on sticky notes and taken out by janitorial staff. Other information, including phone records, old calendars, or organizational flowcharts, can be used to help a potential attacker social engineer their way into a target's network.

To help prevent dumpster diving from being a concern, it is recommended that companies and organizations implement policies for information disposal where all paper containing sensitive information is shredded in a cross-cut shredder before going on to be recycled.

Straight-line shredders should be avoided since they pose the threat that information can be more easily reconstructed by an attacker and stolen. Storage media such as hard drives should be erased using a high-grade data erasure tool if they are to be used in the future.

FIGURE 5.6   Dumpster diving

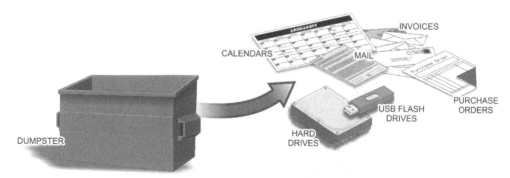

If storage media will not be used again, it either should be physically destroyed using a drive-shredder or can also be degaussed. *Degaussing* is the process of either decreasing or completely eliminating a magnetic field as much as possible. Since data is written to a drive using sequences of electrical charges, degaussing renders the hard drive unreadable and unusable in the future.

Piggybacking and Tailgating

Piggybacking is an act that occurs when a social engineer asks a target to "hold the door" for them and thereby gains access to a restricted area without having to provide credentials to do so. This can be done by simply asking the target and being granted access, or there may be some additional coercion required if the target initially denies the social engineer access and requests to see a credential such as a company badge.

In these cases, the social engineer may claim that they left their badge inside the building when they went on a break or that they left their badge at home when they came to work that morning. The social engineer may also have crafted a fake badge for this purpose and request that a restricted door be held open for them even though the company's policy may be that all employees should swipe their badge to gain entry.

Many employees, out of human nature, will accept a social engineer's request to hold the door open and will be fooled by a fake credential, so they will not ask a fellow employee to swipe their badge to gain legitimate access.

Tailgating, illustrated in Figure 5.7, is similar to piggybacking in that the social engineer's ultimate goal is to gain access to an unauthorized area of a company or organization. Piggybacking is used to describe this act with the consent of the target.

Tailgating is a term used to describe this act occurring *without* the knowledge of the target; the attacker waits for someone to pass through the door and then catches the door and gains entry before the door closes, proceeding with their unauthorized access.

FIGURE 5.7 Tailgating

Diversion

A *diversion* is a tactic intended to distract an individual from monitoring something. Typically, diversions are created so that an attacker can either view sensitive information without being seen or gain entry into a secure area without being questioned. As shown in Figure 5.8, diversions commonly involve a team-based operation, where one attacker creates the diversion and distracts an individual from monitoring a resource or entryway.

FIGURE 5.8 A diversion

However, diversions can also be created by an individual attacker. An example could be some sort of loud noise that gains the attention of a security guard and prompts them to investigate, leaving an entry point open to the attacker.

Psychological Social Engineering

Psychological engineering is a different kind of social engineering, where the mind is the ultimate target. Using psychology and human weaknesses, hackers can craft many different attacks that trick people into believing what they want them to believe and giving up important information that they would not normally give out.

Pretexting

The Merriam-Webster Dictionary defines *pretexting* as "the practice of presenting oneself as someone else in order to obtain private information." Social engineers use elaborate lies to persuade victims to give them desired information or perform a specific act.

For instance, in the 2007 movie *Live Free or Die Hard*, the actor Justin Long breaks into a car and persuades a victim, in this case a representative for OnStar, to start the car without the key using a quickly thought-up lie designed to incite an emotional response from the victim.

Pretexting is used often by real-life private investigators to obtain confidential information that can be used to persuade an employee to give out other personal or private information.

For instance, a company labels their laptops with unique asset tags that can be seen from a few feet away. An employee is taking a break in a local coffee shop and a social engineer takes note of the asset tag of the device, as well as the name on the visible ID tag the employee is wearing.

The social engineer then goes to the company's website to look up the employee's address, which gives them the username for their account as well. Next, they call the company's help-desk line, which is posted on their public website, to ask them to reset the employee's password.

The social engineer tells a very sad story about today being the worst day ever; they can't get into their laptop, and they really, really need help. Since the social engineer has the username and asset tag of the laptop, the help-desk technician resets the password for the social engineer.

The social engineer also notices the company has a preconfigured VPN client available for download by off-site employees. They now log on to the network through the VPN client and gain access to an immense amount of information, all because they knew a few pieces of information acquired by taking advantage of the emotions of a help-desk technician.

Phishing

Phishing is a social engineering tactic that utilizes fraudulent emails in which the attacker sends out emails that appear to be legitimate in an attempt to gather personal information from the recipients. Usually, as shown in Figure 5.9, messages appear to come from well-known and trustworthy websites or companies.

FIGURE 5.9   Phishing examples

Companies and websites that are frequently spoofed include DHL, Microsoft, WhatsApp, LinkedIn, Amazon, FedEx, Roblox, eBay, and PayPal, as well as financial institutions such as Bank of America and Wells Fargo, and email providers such as Yahoo, MSN, and Google. A current listing of the most spoofed companies in phishing attempts can be found at `https://blog.checkpoint.com/2022/01/17/dhl-replaces-microsoft-as-most-imitated-brand-in-phishing-attempts-in-q4-2021`. Like the word *fishing* they are named after, phishing exploits attempt to cast out bait in hopes that individuals will "bite" and fall victim to the bait. This process was illustrated in Figure 5.3 earlier.

Phishing emails have become quite sophisticated over the years, and many recycle previous pieces of phishing emails that were successful. One such occurrence happened in 2014 when a phishing email scam was discovered that spoofed the U.S. Internal Revenue Service.

In this email, the attackers preyed on recipients' eagerness to receive a tax refund. In the body of the email, a link was included to a web page where the recipient would specify payment information for a tax refund, as long as they provided login credentials. Further analysis of this phishing email revealed that the same text on the phishing web page had been used in 2006.

There are a few steps that individuals can use to avoid phishing scams:

- Maintain suspicion of emails asking for sensitive information.

- Never respond to email requests for personal information.

- Never follow a link in an email that is suspected to be a phishing attempt.

- Use web browsers that alert users of known or suspected phishing sites.

- Ask yourself,

  - Is this person known to you?

  - Are you expecting the email?

  - Is the request unusual in nature or with an ask to complete a task immediately or in a short time frame?

- If you answer no to the questions, this is the trigger to scrutinize with a healthy level of skepticism and verify the sender, check the links (if any), and if there are attachments, do not open them, until you can verify they're legitimately from the sender.

Spear-Phishing

Spear-phishing is similar to phishing in that it is a spoofed email fraud attempt. The primary difference, however, is that whereas phishing attacks are sent to a broad range of targets seemingly at random, spear-phishing attacks target a specific organization or individual within that organization to attempt to gain unauthorized access to confidential data. Spear-phishing attacks are more likely to be conducted by attackers who are seeking large financial gain, industry secrets, military information, or specific access to the target.

Similar to regular phishing attacks, spear-phishing messages appear to be sent from a trusted source. One example of a spear-phishing attack is when an attacker discovers a web page from a target organization that contains contact information, either partial or full, for the company.

Using derived details to make the message seem authentic, the attacker will draft an email to a target employee on the contact page that appears to be from an individual who would have reason to request confidential information, such as the company's network administrator. The email will prompt the employee to provide login credentials to a spoofed page that requests the user's username and password and harvests them for the attacker to gain access into the network later.

Alternatively, the email may prompt the user to click a link that will download spyware or other malware without their user's knowledge. This malware may install a backdoor on the user's system that the attacker can use to gain entry to that user's system at a later time. It takes only a single employee to fall for a spear-phishing scam so that the attacker can then masquerade as that duped employee and use additional social engineering techniques to gain further unauthorized access to sensitive information and data.

Whaling

Whaling is another subtype of phishing that targets "high-profile" end users such as corporate executives, politicians, or celebrities. Just like with any phishing attack, the goal of a whaling attack is to trick an individual into divulging personal or corporate information and data through spoofed emails and other social engineering tactics.

Whaling emails and websites can be highly personalized to the target, even to the point of including the target's name, job title, and other legitimately relevant information that has been gleaned from a variety of sources.

The term *whaling* is intended as a play on words due to important people and high-ranking officials in companies often being referred to as a *big fish* or *whale*.

In an enterprise network environment, security administrators can help prevent successful whaling attacks by mandating corporate executives and other high-ranking employees undergo mandatory security awareness training. Sadly, even with advanced security and awareness training, people still fall victim to all types of phishing/spear-phishing/whaling email attacks.

Vishing

Email is not the only method employed by attackers to attempt to fool individuals into providing personal or sensitive information. Attackers will also try to use phones to solicit information from someone. This method of using a phone to conduct a phishing attack is called *vishing (voice-phishing)*. Attackers can also use this method to pretend to be someone else and open new lines of credit if they possess the necessary information to do so.

Individuals can thwart vishing attempts by verifying the phone number they are receiving a suspicious call from. If someone receives a phone call that is supposedly from some organization, such as the Internal Revenue Service, that asks them to call back with a credit card, the person should call that organization's customer service number to verify the request, instead of calling back to the suspicious number.

SMSishing

SMSishing or *smishing* is similar to other phishing-type attacks, except for the fact that it uses cell phone text messages, or SMS messages, to lure in potential targets. Smishing attacks are designed to get an individual to respond to a fraudulent advertisement to gain information from the potential victim later. For example, a smishing attack message will often come from an attacker via email, and the source may be listed as an email address instead of a phone number.

In most cases, smishing attacks are looking for "live" numbers that they can continue to send messages to and, at some point, try to extract information from in some way. The best defense against smishing attacks is to simply not respond to the message and report it to your carrier. If an application is involved, check the application or the website.

Pharming

Pharming is another form of fraud similar to phishing. In a pharming effort, the target may get redirected to a bogus website even though the user has typed in the correct website address. This is most commonly achieved using a DNS cache poisoning attack, shown in Figure 5.10, where the *pharmer* will introduce bogus data into a DNS server resolver cache.

FIGURE 5.10   Pharming

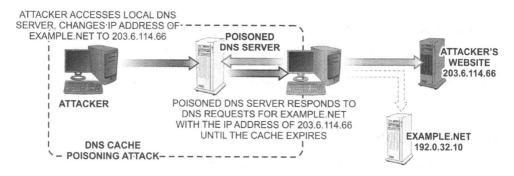

ISPs and major DNS providers will validate DNS responses to make sure they come from an authoritative source. However, many organizations choose to run their own name servers, and if they are not configured properly, they can be poisoned in this manner.

Pharming may also involve the attacker hacking a legitimate website and changing a link to redirect its users to a fraudulent site. This can even involve hacking an *Internet registrar account* where domain name servers can be changed altogether. It is important to use a strong and unique password for your registrar accounts to help prevent this type of attack.

Watering Hole Attacks

Watering hole cyberattacks are exploits that target a group of specified users, such as members of a targeted organization, at some website location they are likely to visit. This is much like a lion laying low near a watering hole where prey animals are likely to come to drink. In these types of attacks, the attacker infects a website or websites that the targeted users are known to frequent. The attack involves setting up the site to download a malicious payload from sites onto a target's computer, giving the attacker access to their network.

Quid Pro Quo

Quid pro quo is a Latin phrase that translates into "something for something." It is commonly referred to in the practice of contract law as an exchange of something that has value for something else of value. In essence, quid pro quo means exchanging one good or service for another.

In ethical hacking, the premise of quid pro quo can be applied to social engineering as well. Basically, the attacker will offer something of value to a social engineering target in hopes that the target will provide something of value in return, such as sensitive information or access to a restricted area.

This technique is often used on disgruntled employees, such as individuals who have been passed over for a promotion or a salary increase. Sometimes, such employees will accept a social engineer's offer in order to harm their employer in retaliation. Disgruntled employees can also be referred to as *inside threats* because they pose a threat to the organization they work for and can cause harm to that organization "from the inside." There have been many instances where cybercriminals use this technique to get employees to launch ransomware within their organizations.

Digital Reconnaissance

Another important component of the attack chain's reconnaissance phase is performing *digital reconnaissance* activities. This typically involves enumerating the network, performing a vulnerability scan, and performing a port scan. These tools and techniques are discussed in Chapter 9, "ICS Security Assessments."

Weaponization

After all the reconnaissance has been done, the attack process migrates into a *weaponization phase*. In this phase, the information collected is applied to creating tools used to mount the attack. In particular, an *exploit* with a backdoor is coupled with a *malicious payload* that can be delivered to a target. This is the second step of the preparation portion of the kill chain, which may take from hours to months to complete.

Lockheed-Martin defines the weaponization phase as "coupling a *Remote Access Trojan (RAT)* with an exploit into a deliverable payload, typically by means of an automated tool called a *weaponizer*." RATs are simply backdoors that grant attackers remote access to a host and can be used to do any number of things.

On the defensive side, Lockheed Martin recommends conducting a full malware analysis to determine what the payload is and how it was built. Also, scan the systems for weaponizers. Examine the malware's creation date to determine how old it is so you can differentiate whether the exploit is older or newer. This can be important in determining the capabilities of the malware.

Delivery

As shown in Figure 5.11, the *delivery phase* occurs by transmitting the payload to the target environment using one or more of various different intrusion methods:

- Email attachments
- Infected flash drives
- Infected websites

- Watering hole—compromised websites
- Social media interactions

This is the first of three steps in the intrusion portion of the kill chain.

JavaScript is often used on websites to load an HTML `<iframe>` containing malicious content. This method can easily send users to places that they would not normally browse.

FIGURE 5.11   Payload deliveries

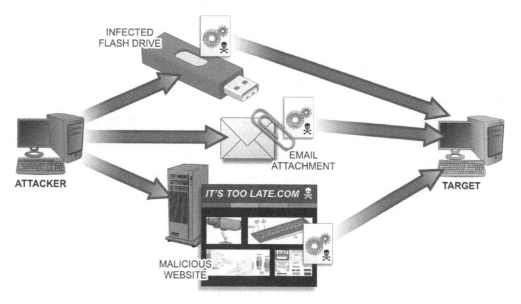

On the defensive side, this step in the chain represents the first opportunity for defenders to stop the intrusion. Ideally, this is the stage where a high percentage of attacks are stopped. The key to defense efforts at this level is to collect and analyze email and web logs for forensic analysis. In particular, you want to analyze the delivery system and determine what its role is in targeting the organization's resources.

Exploitation

Exploitation can be aimed at hardware or software vulnerabilities, but often it is dependent on human vulnerabilities. This includes victim-triggered exploits such as opening email attachments or clicking website links that lead to a malware exploit.

A common *attack vector* for this type of exploitation involves executing malware, such as a weaponized remote access trojan (RAT), through vulnerabilities in the target's operating system or other applications to activate the exploit. Often, these RATs are used to create backdoors into the system to provide control over different tasks ranging from administrative tasks (such as adding users) to shutting down the host, recording keystrokes, and even turning on its webcam.

If you pay close attention to Microsoft updates, you'll notice many of them are security updates for Windows, as well as for Microsoft Office. Because many RATs are embedded into PDFs and Office files, closing vulnerabilities in Office products is of primary importance to Microsoft. Be sure to install those updates!

Other exploits commonly used in this phase include acting on a zero-day exploit and attacker-triggered exploits for server vulnerabilities. A zero-day vulnerability is one that has not yet been discovered by the software manufacturer or the general cybersecurity population. When attackers find these vulnerabilities, they are able to exploit them until the manufacturer produces a security patch for that vulnerability.

On the defensive side of the exploitation link in the kill chain, there are three general avenues to follow:

- Personnel cybersecurity training. This extends to specific cyber training for administrators, management personnel, software and web developers, and employees.

- Penetration testing with regular network vulnerability scanning.

- Endpoint hardening efforts. Endpoint hardening tools and methods are described in detail in Chapter 4, "ICS Module and Element Hardening."

Installation

Now that access has been gained, it becomes necessary to establish a persistent connection to the target. In the example from the previous section, after the RAT has been executed, the next step in the chain is to install a backdoor or implant on the target device so that attackers can maintain access to the compromised system. They may also create points of persistence by adding services to the system to aid in their persistence scheme. This is the final step in the intrusion portion of the kill chain, all of which typically takes only seconds to perform.

RATs can be executed in a number of ways, but the easiest example is creating a RAT that is packaged as an .exe file. Because Windows 7, by default, hides the file extension of known file types, appending .doc on the end of the file can make it appear to be a document file. Running the file actually executes the trojan.

Defensive measures at this stage of the process include installing host-based intrusion detection and prevention technologies to detect and alert/block common software installation paths. It is also necessary to audit endpoint processes to detect abnormal file creations. Endpoint auditing is covered in detail in Chapter 10, "ICS Security Monitoring and Incident Response."

Command and Control

Advanced persistent threat (APT) malware usually requires an attacker to interact with the malware manually, whereas most malware is automated, sending information back to the attacker without requiring the attacker to do anything.

Because of this, APT malware must establish a two-way connection with a *command and control (C2) serv*er to establish what is referred to as a *C2 channel*. This C2 channel gives attackers the ability to directly interact with the compromised host, which can make the threat very dangerous because the attacker can respond to attempts to mitigate the threat.

With the C2 channel in place, the attacker can exfiltrate intellectual property from the target; compromise sensitive data such as confidential emails, company records, and employee information; or infiltrate and infect the entire network.

However, APT operations tend to be much more complicated to execute than other types of cyberattacks. They often begin with more common attacks such as SQL or cross-site (VSS) efforts to establish the initial infiltration into the target. Then trojans with backdoor shells are installed to create the persistent presence between the attacker and the target.

This link in the chain represents the defender's last chance to kill the attack by identifying and blocking the C2 channel. The channel is typically identified through malware analysis methods.

Actions on Objectives

Once the previous steps have been accomplished, attackers can carry out various objectives such as collecting data and sending it back to the C2 server. In many of the attacks that we've talked about, this is one of the main goals of the attackers. The data is anything from credit card information to classified data from companies and governments.

At this point in the chain, the attack has been classified as an incident, and the organization's incident response plan (IRP) must be put into action. The progression of the IRP is as follows:

1. Activate the incident response team (IRT) to identify and validate the nature of the incident.
2. Take steps to contain the incident and limit exposure.
3. Perform a root-cause analysis of the incident to determine the source of the event that caused the incident.
4. Take steps to remediate the incident.
5. Take steps to recover from the incident.
6. Update the IRP with lessons-learned information to prevent similar exploits in the future.

This plan is discussed in detail in Chapter 10.

Attack Methods

The terms *attack method* and *attack mode* are used to describe the manner or technique an attacker may use to assault an asset (network, computing device, program, or data). The following sections cover a number of different attack methods.

Broadcast Storms

When *broadcast traffic* is rebroadcast by every network device, the continuous broadcast or *multicast traffic* can quickly overload switches and routers and overwhelm the network. This type of activity is referred to as a *broadcast storm* or a *network storm*, which is depicted in Figure 5.12.

FIGURE 5.12   Broadcast storm

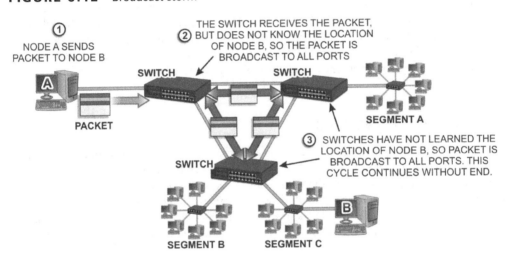

It is important to monitor networks for broadcast storms. However, it is also important to make sure the network is properly configured. If a network node communicates directly with more than one switch, then lookup tables may get confused, causing packets to be flooded between segments. This can represent a major weakness in many networks.

It also important to have hardware that is robust enough to move data quickly and learn routes fast enough to meet the organization's needs. As networks increase to gigabit and faster speeds, it is increasingly important that all network hardware is appropriate for that data rate.

While it may be possible to segment a network in such a way as to minimize the risks of a broadcast storm, the *spanning-tree protocol (STP)* was created to deal with this issue. STP employs the *spanning-tree algorithm (STA)* to understand that a switch may have more than one way to communicate with a network node and manage the optimal pathway while still being able to fall back to a secondary path. Mission-critical networks must make use of STP to minimize broadcast storms.

Layer 2 devices employ a protocol named the spanning tree protocol (STP) to provide loop-free, redundant links for switches in multiple path networks, like the one depicted in Figure 5.13. It accomplishes this by configuring switch ports so they forward or block traffic depending on the type of segment they are connected to.

FIGURE 5.13   Multipath switch connections

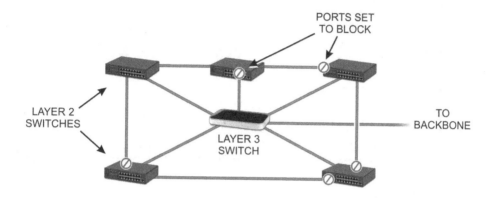

Spoofing

The dictionary defines *spoofing* as "to deceive or hoax." In cybersecurity, spoofing is used to make a device look like another device and can be achieved in many different ways. Many network vulnerabilities focus on obtaining valid credentials in some way. It should be apparent that it isn't terribly difficult for an attacker to fake or spoof a network identity. *Masquerade attacks* may come from stolen credentials, spoofed IP or email addresses, or both. If an attacker can trick a user into giving up their credentials, they can attain the network status of that user. Multifactor authenticating efforts, which involve something you know, something you have, or something you are, can minimize the efficiency of masquerade attacks, but these solutions may not always be practical.

IP Spoofing

IP header manipulation, or *IP spoofing*, is a technique used to change the information contained in the header portion of an IP or TCP network packet in order to conceal one's identity over a network. This operation is also used to perform a myriad of other attacks, such as MITM and DoS attacks.

If we examine the sample IP header provided in Figure 5.14, we can see that the first 12 bytes (top three rows) of data contain various pieces of information about the packet such as length, time to live (TTL), and protocol (IPv4 or IPv6). The next 8 bytes (rows 4 and 5) contain the source and destination IP address information.

FIGURE 5.14   IP header

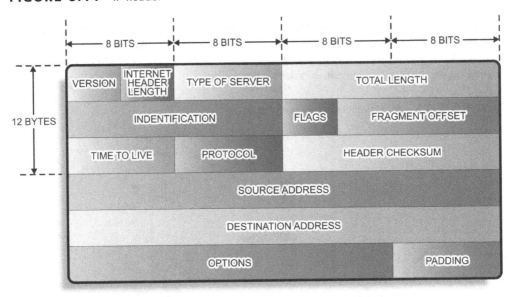

Using one of several tools available on the Internet, an attacker can easily modify these addresses, especially for the "source address" field, to be anything they want. In doing this, the attacker can spoof a network packet's source address and make it appear as if it originated from somewhere entirely different than it actually did. This can be used to conceal their identity during the attack or possibly to gain access to a private internal network from the outside, depending on the network's defenses.

Defending against IP Spoofing

Fortunately, there are a couple of pretty effective methods for defending against IP spoofing:

- Filtering network traffic at the router
- Implementing encryption and authentication

Implementing both *ingress* (incoming traffic) and *egress* (outgoing traffic) filtering on perimeter network routers is the place to begin defending against spoofing attacks. Access control lists should be implemented, as shown in Figure 5.15, so that private IP addresses, including an organization's internal IP address range, are blocked on the downstream interface.

The *downstream interface* is the one that allows traffic to enter a network from the Internet. The Internet is the largest public network in the world, so there is no legitimate reason to allow private and internal traffic to pass through a router's downstream interface, as this is a common way attackers attempt to circumvent firewalls. This is why VPNs were created.

The *upstream interface* of the router allows traffic to go out onto a different subnet or the Internet. That interface should be restricted to only allowing source addresses from within an organization's valid IP range to proceed. This helps prevent spoofed network packets from traveling over the Internet.

FIGURE 5.15   Perimeter network protection

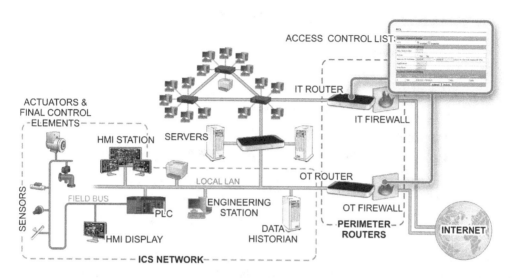

Implementing encryption and authentication also helps to prevent spoofing attacks. These features are included in IPv6, which is designed to eliminate all current spoofing attack threats.

Host-based authentication should also be eliminated within a network. Host-based authentication relies on information (such as MAC addresses and hostnames shown in Figure 5.16) to authenticate to a network. This information is not very secure and can be easily spoofed by an attacker as well. Instead, proper authentication measures should be put in place and implemented over a secure, encrypted connection.

FIGURE 5.16   Secure authentication

MAC Spoofing

MAC spoofing, shown in Figure 5.17, is another common spoofing technique you were introduced to in earlier chapters. Because many security devices and software rely on MAC addresses to control access to network resources, being able to change a MAC address can be quite handy. A good security practitioner will often use this technique to test security devices and other defenses.

FIGURE 5.17 MAC spoofing

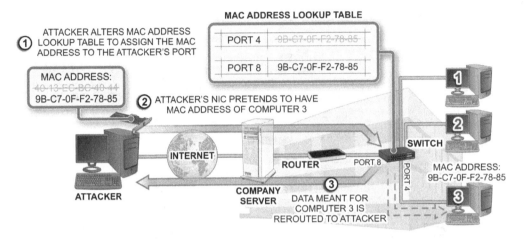

MAC spoofing can be used for many purposes. However, one of the most common scenarios involves using spoofing methods to spoof the MAC address on hardware used to connect to the Internet in a networking environment. ISPs typically use MAC addresses to register their own equipment and allow access to their network.

If a customer purchases a new router/modem device and would like to use it with their existing Internet service provider, they must register the device with the ISP. Instead of registering the new device's MAC address with the ISP, the customer chooses to spoof the MAC address of the old device by using the old device's address in place of the new one. Typically, this violates the EULA between the ISP and the customer and can be considered an illegal act.

ARP Spoofing/Poisoning

To understand *ARP spoofing*, also commonly referred to as *ARP poisoning*, we need to understand why we need ARP and how it works. Address Resolution Protocol (ARP) is used to map IP addresses with MAC addresses. This way, devices are able to communicate through layer 2 devices such as switches. When network traffic reaches a router, it will use the IP address information from the frames to route the packets from one network to another.

For example, envision that there is a simple network with two devices that are separated only by a switch. The first device, which we'll call Smith, has an IP address of 10.0.0.10 and a MAC address of AB:CD:EF:12:34:56. It needs to communicate with a second device, called Jones. We happen to know that Jones's IP address is 10.0.0.20.

Because Ethernet segments only need to communicate using physical MAC addresses, we need to determine what Jones's MAC address is.

Smith will send out a broadcast frame whose destination IP address is set to FF:FF:FF:FF:FF:FF. Keep in mind we already know the source IP address (10.0.0.10), we know the destination IP address (10.0.0.20), and we know the source MAC address (AB:CD:EF:12:34:56).

When the switch receives the broadcast frame, as shown in Figure 5.18, it will send it back out to all other devices connected to the switch. Jones will receive the frame and recognize that the broadcast frame was addressed to it, so it sends back a *reverse ARP (RARP)* frame using the broadcast frame's addresses as the destination addresses.

FIGURE 5.18   ARP

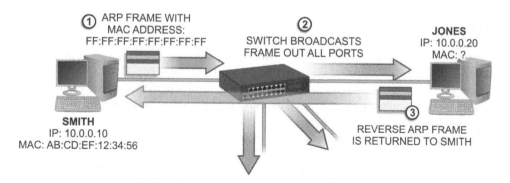

The next thing you may wonder is "what keeps someone who is listening on the network from receiving the broadcast frame and sending back falsified information." The truth is, not a whole lot! One of the more common uses for ARP spoofing is in the case of a man-in-the-middle attack.

DNS Spoofing

In computer networking, the Domain Name System is a hierarchical, meaning multilevel, naming system for computers that can be either centralized or distributed across a network, whether it is a private network or the public Internet. The main responsibility of DNS is to translate domain names, such as `exampledomain.net`, to the actual IP addresses of where those domains are located on a network.

The reason for this is that domain names are easier for human users to remember than IP addresses. Just imagine if you had to memorize and type in 216.58.217.142 every time you wanted to search Google for something on the Internet! The same goes for all of the other favorite websites you visit every day.

If the host computer used to surf the Internet does not know the IP address of a requested domain, it must reach out to the DNS server and ask it for help in finding it, as shown in Figure 5.19. As previously stated, the DNS is made up of multiple levels that are all responsible for different pieces of a domain name.

FIGURE 5.19   DNS process

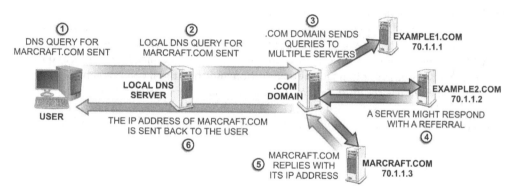

If one of the *DNS name servers (NSs)* does not know all of the requested pieces, it continues to push the request to the next higher-level server in the system. This process continues until the requested domain has been assembled and the IP address found. To speed up this process, a host computer receives an IP address for a requested domain; it will store that information in its local DNS cache for immediate use later when the same domain is requested.

Suppose a DNS server receives false information from an attacker and then caches it for future requests by client systems. This DNS server is now compromised and considered to be poisoned. Because the DNS server is poisoned, it will return an incorrect IP address for a requested domain, which in turn sends traffic to another computer that usually belongs to the attacker.

DNS spoofing can be used by attackers to send spoofed websites to victims, such as phony banking websites or other sites that require personal login credentials to obtain access to sensitive information. These pages are usually very well designed and are difficult to identify.

After the victim inputs their credentials into the login prompts, the network packet is sent back to the attacker who harvests the victim's credentials for later use. Depending on the complexity of the DNS spoof, the page may actually reroute victims to the legitimate website and domain they were originally seeking. Or, it may divert them to some other predetermined domain. In either case, this may simply appear as a "glitch" to the victim.

Although the original DNS service made no provisions for security, it soon became known that it contained multiple exploitable vulnerabilities. To mitigate these vulnerabilities, a suite of *DNS security extensions (DNSSEC)* was developed to protect DNS records. The extensions are based on a process referred to as *zone signing* where the extensions are added to the DNS protocols to provide origin authority, data integrity, and authenticated denial of existence. This makes DNS exploits—such as DNS spoofing—much harder to accomplish.

However, malware can use DNS traffic to create DoS attacks, carry out command-and-control functions, exfiltrate data from the network, and perform DNS tunneling. When segmenting the OT and IT networks from each other, many administrators do not disallow DNS traffic. This enables *DNS tunneling* to be used for sending data into and out of the network using DNS queries and responses aimed at domain names belonging to the attacker. Some estimates indicate that in excess of 90 percent of malware relies on DNS to infiltrate and exploit targets.

While rejecting all DNS traffic for the OT network is the most complete solution for mitigating DNS-related risks, there are some cases where local DNS is needed. In these cases, DNS should be configured to reject DNS requests involving external domains.

On the other hand, DNS data logging efforts can be used to analyze patterns and recognize anomalies in the network. These techniques can be particularly helpful in securing SCADA systems that are notoriously insecure: their firmware is typically insecure, and their communication protocols often lack authentication and encryption components. But all SCADA-connected devices must have an IP address, which permits them to be monitored through the DNS process. Client-facing DNS firewalls/security devices can be used to monitor activity, disrupt attacks, and provide resilience for SCADA-based OT networks.

Denial of Service

Denial-of-service (DoS) attacks are attacks designed to overuse a host, server, or network resource to the point where it functionally ceases to provide its services. A denial-of-service attack is illustrated in Figure 5.20. Depending on the exact nature of the attack the failure may be temporary or indefinite. *Distributed denial-of-service (DDoS) attacks* involve multiple remote systems being used to simultaneously amass the attack on the targeted resource.

FIGURE 5.20   A denial-of-service attack

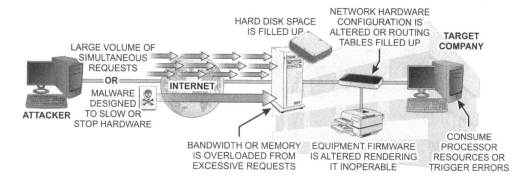

DoS vs. DDoS Attacks

DoS and DDoS attacks are particularly bothersome because they are so easy to perform and there is no way to completely insulate a network from these attacks.

The most common type of DoS attack involves *flooding*, or overloading, a target server or other network resource with an abnormally large number of "garbage" external communication requests, such as traffic generated from the simple ping command. All of those garbage requests will either slow the target's response to the point that it is unusable or prevent the resource from responding to legitimate network traffic resource requests.

The actual resources that are targeted in a DoS attack can be a specific target system, a port on that system, a specific component within a computer network, or the entire network. A DoS attack can also be designed to execute malware that maxes out system resources such as the processor, which will cripple any system in due time. The ultimate goal in a DoS attack is to force a system to not respond to legitimate requests as it did before the attack, whether the service is severely limited or completely denied.

Most DoS attacks are low-cost and difficult to defend against. They are a popular type of attack with script kiddies and technically skilled hackers due to their effectiveness. DoS attacks frequently originate from individuals or organizations that have a grudge against another individual or organization.

A prime example is the hacktivist group Anonymous's alleged DoS attack against Sony in 2011, where the Sony PlayStation Network service was denied for one month. They were hit with another major DoS in 2014 when hactivist groups Lizard Squad and FamedGod took credit for shutting down their PlayStation and Sony Entertainment networks. The attack was initiated by a Network Time Protocol (NTP) amplification that produced network traffic reaching 263.35 Gb/s.

A DoS attack, as shown in Figure 5.21, is comprised of one attacking computer and one Internet connection that are used to flood a server (or other network resource) with garbage packets in an attempt to overload its bandwidth and resources. A DDoS attack, however, uses *many devices* and *multiple Internet connections* to carry out the same process in hopes of achieving the same goal.

FIGURE 5.21 DoS attack

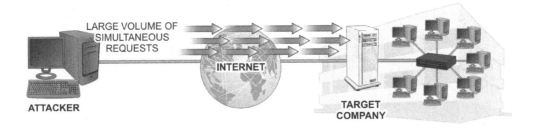

DDoS attacks are often distributed on a global basis utilizing *bots (zombie computers)* to form what is known as a *botnet*. In these attacks, as shown in Figure 5.22, an individual known as a *bot herder* causes this distributed group of computers to be compromised through various means for the purpose of carrying out DDoS attacks. Botnets vary in size and can range from the hundreds to thousands, or even hundreds of thousands of bots, depending on the scope of the attack. As mentioned earlier, these attacks can be rented for a variety of prices on the Internet.

FIGURE 5.22 DDos attack

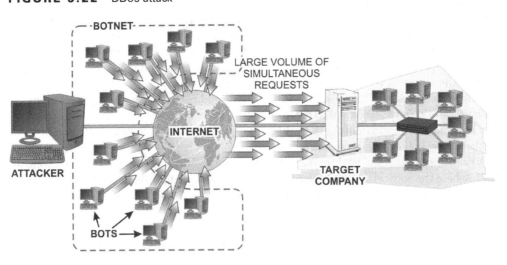

DDoS attacks are much more difficult to defend against than DoS attacks due to the sheer multitude of attacking systems.

A *teardrop attack* is a type of DoS attack where malformed (fragmented) packets are sent to a target system. Older operating systems had bugs in their TCP/IP reassembly mechanisms that caused the fragmented packets to overlap and crash the host. This problem has been solved in any reasonably recent OS version or distribution.

One of the most notable DDoS attacks was carried out against many of the world's most popular websites using the Marai botnet. The Marai bots were designed to seek out and infect thousands of insecurely installed Internet of Things (IoT) devices of different types across the Internet such as smart thermostats, security cameras, and other smart home devices, as well as video game controllers. The Marai software examined these devices looking for default manufacturers' username/password combinations to gain access to them.

Once control had been established on the bot devices, the attacker simply waited to launch the DDoS attack against the desired target—an organization named Dyn, which was the ISP and domain providing DNS services for sites including Twitter, Netflix, GitHub, HBO, Reddit, PayPal, and Airbnb. The attack was a multivector attack involving coordinated traffic from more than 600,000 compromised devices, producing traffic rates of over 1 Terabit/second (Tb/s). The attack continued for seven days.

Larger, more recent DDoS attacks have been aimed at notable high-level organizations including Amazon Web Services (AWS) and Google Cloud Services. The AWS attack in 2020 lasted three days with traffic rates reaching 2.3 Tb/s. The target of the attack was a third-party customer of AWS running a vulnerable connection technique on its servers. Network traffic levels in the Google Cloud attack peaked at 2.5 Tb/s and lasted three days.

Denial of View

Denial-of-view (DOV), also known as *loss-of-view (LOV)* incidents, create situations where operators become blind to the actual state of their processing system, or some component of it. In the case of a DOV attack, the purpose is to cause the operator (or the control program) to take actions that are not appropriate or are potentially destructive. For example, if an attacker introduces a worm into a system to infect the HMI so that operators cannot see the operation of the process, it would become necessary to shut the process down, troubleshoot the loss of view, and restore the control system to operation. In the United States, this has occurred with nuclear power plants, causing them to shut down production until they can be restarted with full control restored.

A similar type of incident known as a *manipulation of view (MOV)* does not hide the state of the process but instead intentionally misrepresents it. Once again, the intent is to cause operators or controllers to take actions that are inappropriate or hazardous. For example, if a temperature sensor on a chemical process is compromised and an inaccurate value is supplied to the SCADA system, the operator (or controller) may respond by attempting to adjust the temperature to a value that is actually unsafe. The effect of these types of activities is to make the operator or controller become the actual attack vector in the control scenario.

Such attacks can also be launched against the control side of the SCADA system. *Denial-of-control (DOC)* and *loss-of-control (LOC)* attacks or incidents prevent operators or controllers to apply corrective actions to critical systems, thereby losing control of the process. These incidents can be created by cyberattacks or through component failures or operator activities.

Ping Flood Attacks

A *ping flood attack* is one of the simplest DoS attacks to perform. It takes advantage of a network protocol called *ICMP*, which is commonly used to test connectivity to a network from a device. *Ping* and *ping6* for IPv6 hosts is available as a command-line tool in many operating systems, and a variety of software products will also offer this capability, often packaged with traceroute features.

In everyday life, you can use the *ping command* to send an *ICMP echo request* to a destination IP address. If you receive a reply from the destination address, you can safely assume you are able to communicate on the network. However, this is a broad assumption and may not always be true.

Ping can be a great way to determine if a host is alive, as well as the quality of the connection between your network and a host. However, ICMP traffic is generally considered low-priority traffic, and thus busy networks may ignore it.

There are some options available with ping, such as adjusting the packet size or sending without waiting for a reply, which can be used to create a *ping flood* that results in a DoS condition. Such a ping flood would certainly consume incoming bandwidth. However, if the network replies to the ICMP requests, then outgoing bandwidth will be consumed as well.

The ping flood attack works by overwhelming the victim with ICMP echo requests. The attacker will send a ping with the flood option enabled, which allows the attacker's network card to not wait for a reply from the victim before sending another echo request. The victim's bandwidth is then flooded with echo requests to which the victim attempts to respond. Ideally, the combination of the incoming and outgoing flooded traffic will disrupt bandwidth and cause network connectivity issues.

Sadly, it is also possible to send malformed ping packets maliciously. Older systems, for example, could not handle a packet larger than 65,535 bytes, and any packet larger than that would crash the computer. Modern routers should examine these packets for size and fragmentation and enforce rules that prevent any problems from a "ping of death."

Because it is possible to flood a network with ping requests, ICMP traffic is often blocked. Most firewall devices can be used to block this traffic completely. While it is typically good practice to allow ICMP traffic on public networks, for a variety of reasons it is critical that the firewall block ICMP traffic for the local network. As a matter of fact, for most networks it may be more desirable to set the firewall to not reply to these requests itself.

A number of tools are available to carry out ping flood attacks. One of these is the Low Orbit Ion Cannon (LOIC), GUI-based tool used to launch very effective ping floods at specified targets. This tool is usually blocked at the host by their antivirus utilities and requires exemptions be put in place to install it.

While LOIC is one of the more popular tools to use, it does come with a cost. The fact that it does nothing to hide the IP address leaves the attacker vulnerable. This is typically not a problem if you are a legitimate pentester but makes it less desirable for other hackers.

Smurf Attacks

A *Smurf attack* is a DDoS attack that floods a network with ICMP packets. This attack builds on the ping flood attack by adding a reflective property. This reflective property is created by using more participants, known as *Smurf amplifiers*, in the attack.

An attacker forges a ping request packet by taking the sender's address (which was originally the attacker's address) and establishing it as the victim's address, as shown in Figure 5.23. Then, the attacker changes the destination address to a broadcast address of the network.

FIGURE 5.23 Smurf amplification

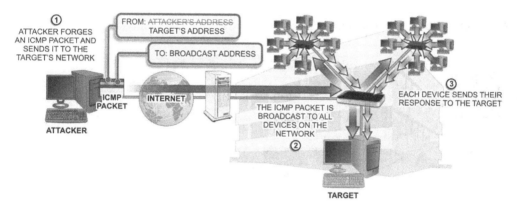

When the attacker sends the ping request, Smurf amplifiers that are on the network and able to respond to the ping request will reply using the victim's IP address as the destination address. Because many devices are responding to the victim, the victim is flooded with traffic and becomes virtually inoperable.

ICMP tunneling can also be used to deliver malicious packets. The best defense here is to configure network devices not to respond to ICMP echo requests. Another option is to simply block all ICMP traffic, as well as inbound broadcast traffic.

UDP Flood Attacks

A *UDP flood attack* is a DoS attack that is similar to a ping flood attack that uses *User Datagram Protocol (UDP) packets*. Because UDP is connectionless and lacks an error-checking ability such as TCP, it lacks the three-way handshake process of TCP.

For this attack, an attacker will send massive amounts of UDP packets to a victim on random ports. Since these packets are sent to specific ports, the victim must check to see if an application is really listening on those ports.

When the victim sees that nothing is listening, it will reply with an ICMP Destination Unreachable packet. In this case, the victim will struggle to send back all the ICMP packets, and anything else trying to connect to the victim will be denied access. Also, the attacker is likely to spoof the IP address being used to send the UDP packets to avoid detection.

A *fraggle attack* is similar in concept and mitigation to a Smurf attack except that it uses UDP packets instead of ICMP.

SYN Flooding

A *SYN flood attack* is a form of a denial-of-service attack where an attacker takes advantage of the TCP handshake that uses SYN and ACK messages to establish a reliable connection between two hosts. Unlike UDP, where packets can be dropped without any sort of error correction, TCP uses a three-way handshake to ensure that messages are being sent properly and reliably, as shown in Figure 5.24.

FIGURE 5.24   SYN flooding

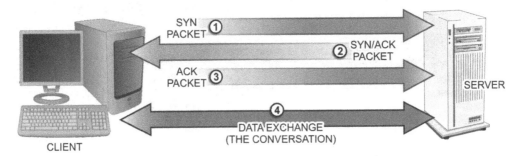

Here's the way a three-way handshake works:

1. A client would like to establish a connection between itself and a server. It sends a SYN message to the server.

2. The server receives the message and sends back a SYN acknowledgment, which is represented as SYN-ACK.

3. The client then responds to the SYN acknowledgment by sending an ACK message to the server.

In a SYN flood attack, the attacker takes advantage of the three-way handshake. The attacker will send numerous SYN messages to the server, dozens if not hundreds of these per second. The server tries to keep up and send SYN-ACK messages back to the attacker, but the attacker never responds with the ACK message. Then, when a legitimate client wants to connect to the server, they are unable to do so because the server is flooded with SYN messages and unable to reply.

Because this could also look like network congestion, the server will usually wait a short time before responding, in hopes the congestion will settle down. A true malicious attack will continue to use up the server's resources, denying its services to other clients. Some servers may malfunction or even crash at this point.

There are effective countermeasures to SYN flooding depending on the operating system involved. One method of dealing with SYN flooding is to use a *calculated sequence number* rather than a *state table*. Unfortunately, this calculation can be quite CPU intensive, so this technique generally involves implementing specialized load balancers or network appliances specifically designed for handling DoS attacks.

Modern firewalls can also deal with SYN flooding to some extent by discarding half-open connections. However, a high-volume SYN flood will generally still manage to have a noticeable impact on network performance.

Data Manipulation Attacks

Not all attacks are designed to steal data; some are designed merely to manipulate data to diminish its integrity. Many cybersecurity experts see *data manipulation* as a larger problem than traditional data theft or physical infrastructure attacks. These types of attacks undermine organizational, customer, and governmental confidence in the data they possess. The end result is the inability to make sound business decisions or make military decisions based on situational awareness data.

For example, the main thrust of the Stuxnet attack was based on data manipulation instead of theft. The attack altered the operational speed data of the Iranian centrifuges so that the operators did not know the true speed of their systems. Therefore, they had no idea that the centrifuges were in danger of destruction.

With the IoT and IIoT markets continuing to grow in every facet of life (including industrial processing and utility operations), the windows of opportunity for data manipulation–based attacks have increased exponentially. This includes items such as sensor networks, residential thermostats, insulin pumps, switching gear, etc.

Because data manipulation attacks are silent, targeted attacks that occur over multiple links in the cyber chain described earlier, it is important that organizations orchestrate their cybersecurity tools to detect, investigate, and mitigate attempts to overwrite data in their networks.

Session Hijacking Attacks

In a TCP session, authentication generally occurs only when the session starts. Often when logging into a website a *session cookie* is given to the user to identify them going forward. If an attacker is able to sniff this connection and obtain the session cookie, they can gain access to that site. This sort of attack is known as *session hijacking*, as shown in Figure 5.25.

FIGURE 5.25   Session hijacking

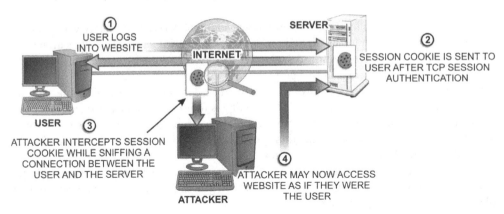

A *clickjacking attack* employs deceptive frame techniques to trick the user into clicking on their content rather than the intended content. This is a popular trick deployed on hacked websites, as it is easy to do and can yield high rewards, as shown in Figure 5.26. The attacker mostly conceals the legitimate frame so the user clicks the attacker's frame. This is often done to social media frames. It is possible for the web page developer to add a little frame-busting code to their web documents, but that can be defeated as well.

FIGURE 5.26   Clickjacking

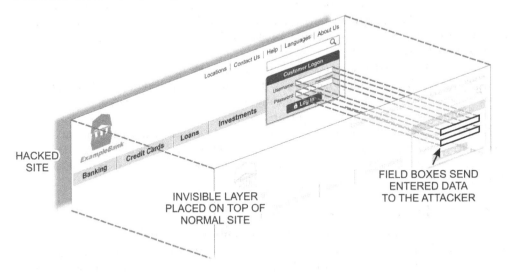

While modern browsers protect against *cross-site scripting (XSS)*, they cannot completely defend against it. This attack, like many others, requires a hacked or otherwise maliciously crafted web page, as shown in Figure 5.27. Educating users about this risk and logging into social media manually rather than from web links can help. Hosted web pages should be periodically scanned for this type of exploit using a utility such as BeEF or Metasploit, described earlier.

FIGURE 5.27   Cross-site scripting

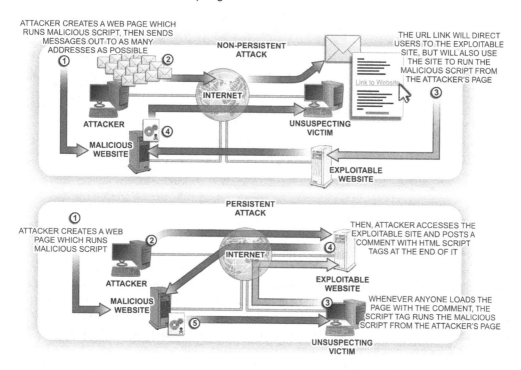

Man-in-the-Middle Attacks

In an MITM attack, the attacker monitors a network and performs different activities depending on the nature of the intended attack. One possibility is that the attacker uses ARP spoofing to intercept traffic that was meant to be sent to a router. When a victim device sends out a broadcast frame, as shown in Figure 5.28, the attacker receives the frame and sends back their own information, causing the victim to think the attacker is the true destination of the information.

When the victim sends the information to its intended destination, the attacker receives it, collects it, and can either forward it to the true destination (which is how it is considered to be a man in the middle) or send back false information.

FIGURE 5.28 Man-in-the-middle attack

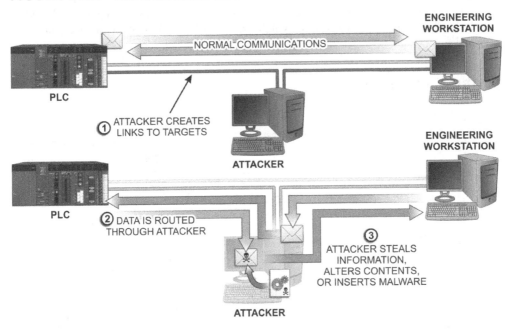

From the ethical hacking perspective, the man-in-the-middle attack can yield a lot of information because of the data that can be collected and redirected in such an attack. For instance, the *Linux Social Engineering Toolkit (SET)* package can be used to make a copy of a website that can aid in the harvesting of credentials of users visiting that site. The SET is an installed tool in Kali Linux and can also be downloaded from https://github.com/trustedsec/social-engineer-toolkit. It is also possible to install the SET tool on Microsoft Windows machines.

If users see what appears to be the website they intended to log into and enter their credentials, the fake website typically redirects them to the real login page. Normally, the user believes they must have entered their credentials incorrectly and eventually logs into the real site.

Meanwhile, the man in the middle has harvested their credentials from the fake website and uses them to then log into the real website and wreak havoc on the user's account. Using HTTPS will provide a secure channel to communicate so the attacker cannot harvest the user's credentials. Although modern browsers alert users if they are about to connect to an HTTP site, users should still be trained in looking for HTTPS instead of HTTP.

Man-in-the-middle (MITM) attacks, or *fire brigade attacks*, are a type of session hijacking that involves intercepting or sniffing and modifying communication between users. You can think of them as a form of network eavesdropping. As such, the attacker is usually on the same network or broadcast domain as the other two parties and will proxy communications between the parties, inserting or altering data in the process. In an SSL connection, the attacker might use ARP spoofing to divert traffic through the attacker rather than the normal network router.

Foreign Software

What's in your software? The idea of hiding malicious content in production software is not new. You should have no problem envisioning a commercial software company supplying tainted security software that includes advanced malware designed to become active at a given point in time. Of course, the software company already has a cure for the malware, ready to go on sale as soon as it overwhelms people, businesses, and government agencies that have installed it.

It should also be no problem envisioning governments and nation-states working with their local software producers to include malware in their commercial products. The malware may lie dormant for an unspecified time waiting for a command from that government to execute an attack.

For example, if one government wanted to make sure it had an advantage over another country in the event that the two nations ever engaged in hostilities, they might insert trojans, backdoors, or other malicious code in commercial SCADA software developed for use in the industrial processing and utility markets. At the onset of any hostilities, the attack embedded in the software could be initiated, removing valuable assets from the other country's chess board. The Stuxnet attack against Iran's nuclear industry in 2010 and the SolarWinds information gathering attack against US federal agencies in 2020 are prime examples of this type of cyber strategy.

For this reason, every country (and its industrial and utility organizations) should view any foreign-produced or foreign-influenced software as a potential national security threat. Strategically, this means that each organization's procurement processes must assess the risks associated with foreign-produced software versus the economics of in-country development of the same type of product.

On a tactical level, it is recommended that all foreign software code be peer reviewed and tested by multiple programmers. In addition, these packages should be scanned with as many different scanning tools as possible to look for dangerous or unnecessary code embedded in the software. Microsoft offers a Security Code Analysis toolkit, while Snyk provides a free source code checker at `https://snyk.io`. Finally, enforce industry standards, such as those in the ISO 15408 *Common Criteria standard* (that can be found at `www.iso.org/standard/50341.html`), when evaluating information security.

Unauthorized Access

Unauthorized access is defined as the act of gaining access to an asset (building, office, machine, server, website, service, folder, or file) using an access method (such as someone else's account or one created by the attacker) that the individual has not been given permission to access. In cybersecurity terms, this is also referred to as *gray-hat* or *black-hat hacking*.

Unauthorized access involves both external and internal network attack methods. External attacks involve individuals who have no legitimate privileges on the network (although they also involve attacks mounted with active or passive collusion of the target network's internal users). The most common types of external access attacks are based on possessing or guessing a valid user's weak, stolen, or lost credentials. However, attacks based on credentials gained through malware attacks are also quite common. Remote access, wireless connections, and modem dial-up attacks represent another common external access attack surface.

On the other hand, unauthorized internal access attacks are mounted by intruders who possess some level of legitimate credentials for accessing the network. These accesses can be made by IT personnel who have not been given permissions to the asset, by non-IT staff members with high levels of permissions within the network, or by legitimate personnel using someone else's stolen credentials.

The following sections of this chapter describe various unauthorized access attack methods.

Password Attacks

Password attacks all fall under the umbrella terms *password cracking, password stuffing,* and *password reuse.* The goal of password cracking is to successfully authenticate through a password prompt without originally knowing the correct password. Password attacks can be performed in a variety of ways using different methods:

- Brute-force attacks
- Rainbow tables
- Password capturing
- Credential stuffing
- Password spraying
- Password reuse

A *brute-force attack* involves using tools, such as John the Ripper, ophcrack, or hydra, to run lists of passwords against a user's login. Such tools are legitimately used in enterprise environments to test employee passwords, but those same tools are often used by attackers to do the same thing.

The password lists are typically generated by various security personnel and contain commonly used passwords, along with different variations. With a brute-force attack, the attacker uses processing power to hash each password on the supplied password list. This can involve considerable time. For this reason, this attack method is best used when short, simple passwords are expected.

However, *rainbow tables* can be used to provide a more elegant and efficient password attack method. These are pregenerated tables that contain millions of passwords that have already been hashed. Because most host systems contain a password file of hashed passwords, they can be compared to the hashed contents supplied by the rainbow table with the hopes of finding a matching password.

Password capturing, or *credential harvesting* as it is sometimes called, is a very straightforward process. An attacker must somehow intercept the password as it is being sent. One common way this can be accomplished is through a man-in-the-middle attack or through phishing.

The most commonly used tool for this attack is the Social Engineering Toolkit software described earlier in this chapter. As shown in Figure 5.29, this package has a variety of different modules that can be used to perform different kinds of attacks. The credential harvesting module is simple to use. It works by cloning a popular website of your choice (or you can provide one for it to use) and then hosting it using Apache.

FIGURE 5.29   The Social Engineering Toolkit

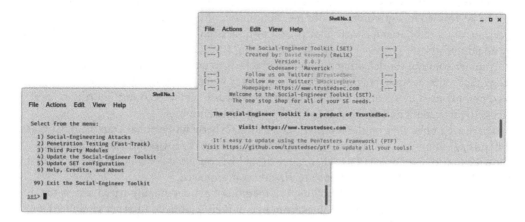

When victims are directed to the IP address of the attacking machine, they will see the cloned website and enter their username and password, which will then show up on the SET terminal. The software will then redirect them to the actual website, making it seem as though they simply entered their password incorrectly. Meanwhile, the attacker now has their username and password and can do with it whatever they want.

To take that attack one step further, the credential harvesting attack can be combined with a DNS poison attack to direct DNS lookups for websites to the attacking machine. This type of attack can be accomplished using a software tool called *Ettercap*.

In this type of combined attack, the victims will be directed to the attacker's website whenever they enter mywebsite.com (or whatever website is used). Without using Ettercap, the attacker would need to devise some method to provide the victim with the IP address of the attacking machine.

Dictionary Attacks

A *dictionary attack* is simply a systematic, brute-force attack using every word in a dictionary as a password. There are many sources of precompiled dictionary files and rainbow tables available on the Internet that provide username/password combinations that can be used to attack a desired target. Some hacking tools such as Kali Linux also provide prepared username/password lists that can be edited and used directly against designated targets.

The largest such list currently available is the *Compilation of Many Breaches (COMB)* database file that contains more than 3.2 billion unique UN/PW credentials. These have been gathered from past account breaches around the world and represent about 70 percent of all the people currently online around the world. Of course, manufacturer default UN/PW combinations are included, and people reuse the same passwords for different accounts. The database also includes the bash scripts used to run the attack, query emails, and manage the data.

This type of attack is simple to eliminate by limiting the number of login attempts that can be performed in a given period of time. In addition, the IP address of any user exceeding a certain number of attempts over that period of time could be banned until they are cleared by an administrator.

Another solution for defeating dictionary attacks is to enforce a strict password methodology that requires something more than a dictionary word for access. This type of attack is commonly used by spammers who guess at passwords of email accounts in order to gain access to an account and then use it for their spam distribution.

There are public sites on the Internet, such as the Cybernews Personal Data Leak Checker (`https://cybernews.com/personal-leak-check`), that provide information about known compromised credentials. These sites should be consulted periodically to ensure that currently used UN/PW combinations are already compromised.

As mentioned earlier, session hijacking is a method of gaining unauthorized access to someone's computer by stealing cookies from one of their legitimate Internet sessions. Those cookies are used to authenticate computers to remote servers and are routinely stored on user computers to provide quick access to web pages.

Attackers can steal these cookies by using a packet sniffer to capture the cookies as they are passed across the network. They can also steal the cookie information from the PC if they can access it by tricking it into believing the code it is receiving is from a trusted location, such as the server. Once the attacker has obtained the cookie information, they can gain access to other privileged information.

The use of multifactor authentication techniques and tools can ensure that even if attackers possess their UN/PW credentials they cannot get into the system. Also, the use of password managers enables strong password credentials to be employed to effectively manage users.

Wireless Attacks

Wireless attacks can be quite different than LAN attacks because of the nature of this method of communication. A user must physically connect a device into a network port to connect to a wired network, so proximity to the network media is very important. With wireless networking, however, that proximity is not as important. Attackers and legitimate users alike can sit in the parking lot in front of a building and connect to the wireless network.

This added variable of distance can be amplified using different creative methods, such as using a *cantenna* (a home-built tin can waveguide antenna), shown in Figure 5.30. This device enables wireless clients to connect to networks much farther away than was ever intended for Wi-Fi communications. From the comfort of their car, attackers can potentially sit and launch attacks from a comfortable distance.

FIGURE 5.30 Cantenna

Just as with LAN security, wireless network security is paramount. The need for encrypted and secure communications is even more important, since eavesdropping and packet capture are much easier with wireless. In addition, taking advantage of vulnerabilities in weak encryption takes only a matter of seconds. The following sections dig deeper into the different ways wireless communications are commonly exploited.

Wardriving

Wardriving is the process of walking or driving around populated areas searching for open or weakly encrypted wireless networks. This is often one of the first activities conducted in the reconnaissance phase of ethical hacking.

Many organizations do not worry too much about wireless networks broadcasting beyond the boundaries of their buildings and campus.

There are numerous tools available to capture wireless network information. These include software such as NetStumbler, inSSIDer, and Kismet, shown in Figure 5.31. Tools such as these are able to capture all sorts of data from wireless networks. In addition, many wardrivers contribute to online databases such as WiGLE that track and log their captured data information, the most troubling of which is the kind of encryption that is used by the various SSIDs in an area.

It is important to keep track of just how far a wireless network can be seen in public. Unfortunately, it can be very difficult to keep networks from bleeding out into public areas. However, depending on how secure the network needs to be and what kind of information it contains, it may be worthwhile to investigate distance-limiting methods of preventing wireless networks from radiating too far.

Wardriving is also perfectly legal. It is the equivalent of writing down house numbers or listening to radio stations. In most situations, the listening devices do not communicate with the networks; they only collect data. It could also be argued that if you don't want your network information to be collected, you probably shouldn't broadcast it!

FIGURE 5.31   Kismet

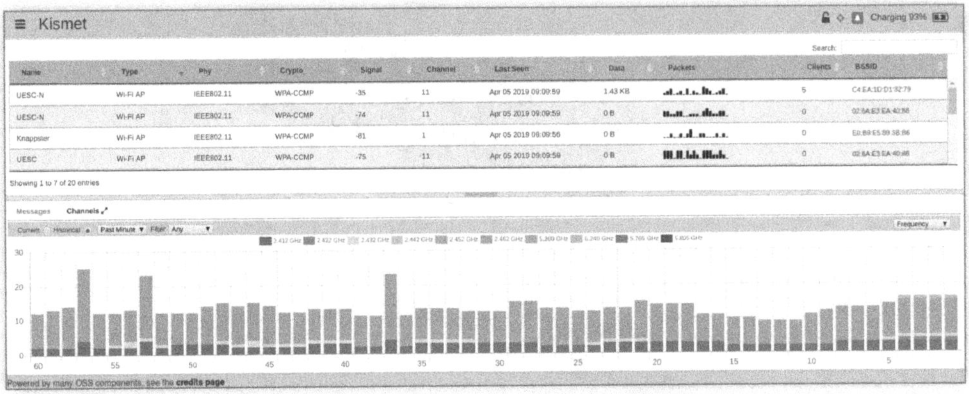

Rogue Access Points

Rogue access points can be a very dangerous vulnerability. However, more often than not, they are not meant to be malicious. Rogue access points tended to be more common when wireless was gaining popularity and wasn't as readily available as it is now.

Employees who can't reach an Ethernet port (or who need multiple Ethernet ports at their location) might be tempted to set up a rogue access point to make their lives easier, without knowing just what security to set up or that it is against company policy to do so.

However, sometimes rogue access points are set up by nefarious characters or penetration testers trying to breach the network. For example, one of these nefarious characters could manage to find their way into an organization's unoccupied conference room and set up a rogue access point on their network. Then, they simply need to sit in the parking lot and snoop on the network, collect info, or spend time trying to break into workstations.

After an attacker is on a network, their possibilities become endless. The users and the network are compromised, and any sort of attack can take place, from DDoSing to exploiting various vulnerabilities.

WPA Key Cracking

To minimize the risk of security compromise on a wireless LAN, the *Institute of Electrical and Electronics Engineers (IEEE)* organization oversees a group of wireless networking specifications under the IEEE-802.xx banner. The IEEE 802.11x (also known as *Wireless Fidelity* or *Wi-Fi*) wireless standards have gained wide acceptance as the preferred wireless networking technology for both business and residential network applications.

There are a number of security issues concerning using them to communicate personal or otherwise sensitive information. Transmissions from wireless network devices cannot simply be confined to the local environment of a residence or business. Although the range of most wireless network devices is typically limited to a few hundred feet, RF signals can easily be intercepted even outside the vicinity of the stated security perimeter. Any unauthorized mobile terminal can accomplish this using an 802.11 receiver.

The most widely used protocols for wireless network security are the *Wi-Fi Protected Access (WPA)* standard, the WPA2 standard (IEEE 802.11i), and the WPA3 standard protocols.

The WPA protocol was designed to improve on earlier Wi-Fi standards that had become vulnerable to cracking activities. It accomplished this by first authenticating network users and then providing more enhanced encryption techniques as a way of ensuring the integrity of the messages passed through it. It is the protocol used with 802.11g and 802.11i networking standards.

The WPA protocol can operate in either WPA-PSK mode (aka Pre-Shared Key or WPA-Personal mode). In the Personal mode, a preshared key or passphrase is used for authentication. The PSK option enables WPA to use *preshared keys* instead of a separate *certificate authority (CA)* computer to provide user authentication. The PSK permits a password to be set on the router and shared with the rest of the users.

WPA2 offers a stronger encryption method where the encryption keys are automatically changed (called *rekeying*) and authenticated between devices after a *specified period of time*, or after a specified number of packets has been transmitted. This method uses a passphrase (also called a *shared secret*) that must be entered in both the wireless access point/router and the WPA clients. This shared secret can technically be between 8 and 63 characters and can include special characters and spaces.

Both WPA and WPA2 employ data encryption using *Temporal Key Integrity Protocol (TKIP)* and IEEE 802.1x *Extensible Authentication Protocol (EAP)* to provide authentication and security for the wireless network. This combination requires users to employ usernames and passwords to access the network. After the user logs in, the *access point (AP)* generates a temporary key that is used to encrypt data transfers between the AP and the client devices.

WPA and WPA2 attacks basically occur in a three-step process: sniffing, parsing, and credential cracking. In the sniffing phase, Wi-Fi transmissions are scanned by a device whose wireless network adapter has been configured for promiscuous mode operations. During the parsing process, the scanned data is processed by a packet analyzer, such as Wireshark, to examine the data in the transmitted packets, looking for connection handshake sequences, in particular looking for packets that contain *PTK authentication* information (using an EAPOL filter). The four-way handshake process is depicted in Figure 5.32 and shows the hand-off of the PTK keys.

Once the keys have been located, you can try to decrypt them, but this takes a lot of time and computing power. Instead, hackers simply employ a cracking tool to run dictionary/brute-force attacks against the keys. The major tools available for doing this in Linux include John the Ripper, Aircrack-ng, or a Pyrit/coWPAtty combination. In Microsoft Windows environments, Aircrack-ng and the Wireless Security Auditor package from Elcomsoft are the leaders but can be quite expensive.

To mitigate these types of activities and protect the information from WPA2 vulnerabilities, it is recommended that additional encryption methods such as HTTPS (SSL or TPS) be employed to add an extra layer of security for transmissions. Users should also use VPNs when working on any public Wi-Fi networks. The VPNs encrypt all data regardless of whether HTTP or HTTPS protocols are being used.

FIGURE 5.32   WPA four-way handshaking

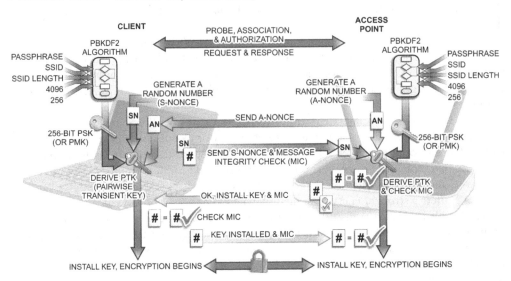

In addition, after all of the wireless clients have been installed and authenticated, set the *Service Set Identifier (SSID)* Broadcast option to Disable so that outsiders do not use SSID to acquire the access point's address and data. Also, change the SSID name from the default value.

If wireless networking technology is being used within a secure area such as a server room, additional *physical hardening* steps should be taken in securing the room. This may include physically hardening the room's architecture, such as electrically isolating the server room's ceiling, floor, and walls to prevent the wireless signals from escaping. This is usually done with some form of Faraday cage or Faraday shield.

The newest WPA version *(WPA3)* employs an advanced connection protocol called *Device Provisioning Protocol (DPP)* that automates the connection process so that it does not rely on shared passwords. Instead, it uses a simultaneous Authentication of Equals (SAE) technique to replace the shared keys used in the PSK mode four-way handshake connection. This enrollment process sends out network enrollment instructions without transmitting a password. These messages can take the form of QR codes or NFC tags to authenticate the device and grant access to the network.

WPA3 encryption differs greatly from that of WPA and WPA2 to render older attack methods such as KRACK and dictionary attacks obsolete. It uses a 256-bit Galois/Counter Mode Protocol (GCMP-256) encryption code that raises the number of calculations needed to generate all of the computation possibilities that would be required to break the code to a number in excess of 1×10^{77}. WPA3 includes a 384-bit Hashed Message Authentication Mode encryption to encrypt the keys when they are being passed between the router and connecting devices.

WPA3 devices work only with other WPA3 devices. Noncompatible
devices will not be able to connect.

802.11 Beacon Flood

Wireless access points periodically broadcast *beacon frames* that let nearby clients know
what networks they are broadcasting. These frames also include the pertinent information
that wireless devices need to know to connect to the AP, such as SSIDs and *beacon intervals*,
as well as *timestamps* that can be used to set local clocks to the network for authentication purposes.

Access points employ a beacon interval that determines the amount of time between
beacons. Increasing the beacon interval decreases the number of beacons sent. Conversely,
decreasing the interval increases the number of beacons sent.

There are a number of tools available that enable hackers to take advantage of the beacon
and its vulnerabilities. One such tool is *MDK3*. As shown in Figure 5.33, this utility allows
for a number of different attacks, including beacon floods and deauthentication attacks, as
well as other DoS attacks.

FIGURE 5.33   MDK3

MDK3 can initiate a beacon flood attack, as shown in Figure 5.34, by broadcasting fake
beacon packets for a network. For instance, the command:

```
mdk wlan1 b -n mynetwork -n -t -c 6 -s 70
```

would cause `mdk3` to start a beacon flood attack (b flag) on `mynetwork`, which is a wireless
N network (n flag) that uses the TKIP security protocol on channel 6 (-c 6) and will send

70 packets per second (-s 70). Once initiated, devices that try to connect to the mynetwork network will not be able to do so until the attack is stopped.

FIGURE 5.34   Beacon flood attack

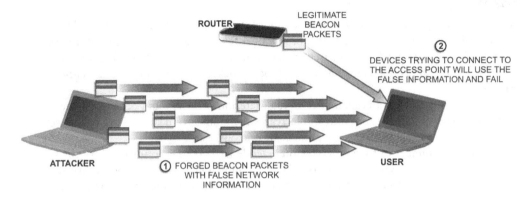

802.11 Deauthenticate Flood

Another type of wireless attack is the deauthentication flood attack, commonly referred to as a *deauth attack*. A deauth attack involves an attacker sending a *deauthentication packet* to an access point that in turn kicks off any devices connected to it. There are a number of different tools out there for performing this attack, such as MDK3, discussed earlier, as well as the more common *aireplay-ng* tool.

Deauth attacks can be useful if you want to prevent clients from connecting to a wireless access point for any reason. For instance, an inexperienced system admin may try to change the encryption to something less secure with the hopes of solving a problem with the access point. On the other hand, they may simply disable the AP.

Cryptographics

Cryptography is simply a term used to describe the concepts and methods for securing information and providing nonrepudiation for data. Many cryptographic techniques involve the use of keys. A key is merely a data string used to encrypt or decrypt information. How the key is used and how large the string is both impact the strength of the encryption.

Encryption keys can be based on a "secret" string that is known only to the software that encrypts and decrypts the data, or may be randomly generated. It could also be a combination of known and random factors. The algorithm that performs this encryption or decryption is known as a *cipher*. A cipher might be a *stream cipher* dealing with one character at a time, or a *block cipher* that deals with multiple blocks of an input string at one time.

If the same key is used for both encryption and decryption, then it is a *symmetric key*. If different keys are used for encryption and decryption, then these are known as *asymmetric keys* even if the keys are based upon one another. Figure 5.35 shows the difference.

FIGURE 5.35   Symmetric vs. asymmetric keys

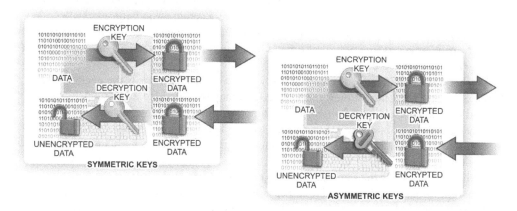

Public-key cryptography uses asymmetric keys incorporating a *public key* and a *private key* (or *secret key*). Public and private keys are different, but the private key may be calculated from the public key. Conversely, the public key is nearly impossible to calculate from the private key.

The strength of this type of cryptography obviously is related to how impossible this calculation is to reverse engineer. The initial authentication process typically involves processing some credential with the private key to produce a digital signature. Subsequent verification is then done by processing the public key against this signature to validate the original credential or message.

Public-key cryptography is used in a number of different encryption protocols and systems, including the following:

- Transport Layer Security and Secure Sockets Layer (TLS and SSL)

- Secure Shell (SSH)

- PGP (Pretty Good Privacy)

- GNU Privacy Guard (GPG)

- Secure/Multipurpose Internet Mail Extensions (S/MIME)

- Digital Signature Standard (DSS)

- RSA encryption algorithm

Symmetric-key cryptography uses the same or easily transformed key for both encryption and decryption. These keys are known as a shared secret between the two sides of the transaction. Symmetric-key encryption is used in *Advanced Encryption Standard (AES)* encryption, *Blowfish*, *RC4*, *3DES*, and many other schemes.

Simple stream ciphers are less secure, so most use 64-bit or better block ciphers. Some schemes will tout their strength by mentioning the block size of their encryption (such as 256-bit encryption). The original plaintext input must be padded too so that it is an even multiple of the block size.

Symmetric-key ciphers are mostly vulnerable to brute-force attacks where the attacker systematically guesses the key based on a known list or a predictive mathematical scheme, so the authentication scheme should try to identify these activities and automatically employ appropriate measures to thwart them. This typically means limiting the number of authentication attempts in a period of time, which can be an inconvenience to users but is a necessary feature nonetheless.

Another component of the strength of a key-based security scheme is the degree of randomness used in key generation. Randomized keys may be generated algorithmically using applications called *pseudorandom key generators*. Randomizers employ some source of *entropy* (or a degree of uncertainty) as a seed for randomization. The degree of entropy can be measured, generally in bits, and is sometimes mentioned in the strength analysis of an encryption scheme.

Ideally the entropy is the same size as the key. The source of this entropy is typically a combination of data readily available to the system, possibly transformed by some multiplier or algebraic equation. For example, a randomizer might combine the milliseconds of time since some time in the past divided by the process ID padded to length.

If the time is somewhat randomly calculated (say randomly chosen between 1,001 and 4,017 seconds ago) and the process ID would be difficult for anyone to predict, you would have an easily generated random key. Some key generation algorithms use wild math to transform keys, but at the heart of entropy is some source of pseudorandom data.

Ultimately, it is desirable to work with asymmetric keys using 256-bit block ciphers where the keys are generated by high-entropy randomizers. Today you are unlikely to see this very often. For large-scale systems, processing such calculations can be processor intensive, and the management of such schemes can be arduous.

Encryption

Encryption is a tool that can be used to ensure that if data is accessed at rest or intercepted in motion by an unauthorized party, it cannot be read. It is rapidly becoming an almost required step in securing any network. Google has led the way in ensuring that every web page will be served and transmitted using secure encryption. Banks and companies that exchange any kind of financial or detailed personal information have used encryption in some form since the early days of the World Wide Web.

Encryption is nothing more than the conversion of electronic data into a form called *ciphertext*. This involves applying a secret code (cipher) to the data to produce a scrambled message that cannot be understood without the knowledge of the cipher that was used to create it. It won't matter how secure the password is if a third party can easily capture it electronically.

Encrypting the information exchange is not enough. We must also make sure that data is never stored without encryption and that the encryption keys are as secure as possible.

On the Internet, data passes through many nodes that you may not control. As such, any credentials passing through external networks in the form of *clear text* may end up in the wrong hands. The occurrence of these types of transmissions has been greatly decreased in IT networking but may still be present in many OT environments. This practice is known as *packet sniffing*, as shown in Figure 5.36. Adding encryption to the credential system is critical in any network security scheme.

FIGURE 5.36   Viewing credentials

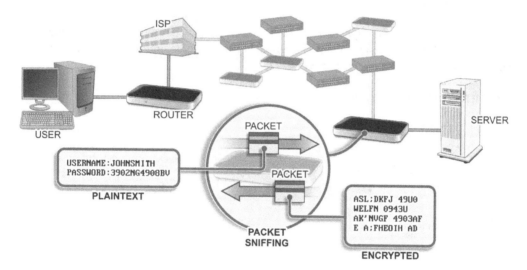

Any password mechanism can employ good security techniques. If the following three conditions exist, then that system can be considered somewhat secure.

- Credentials are never stored anywhere without encryption.

- The encryption keys or secrets are not stored in any nonsecured locations where they can be accessed by unauthorized persons. Key stores must be protected in the same manner as any other sensitive data in storage, transmission, and backup.

- The connection between the client and server is secure and encrypted.

That same system can be made more secure by including more factors and by adding physical factors, such as fingerprint scanning or another biometric authentication system.

If you use a credential-based access system that does not employ good security techniques, then you must understand the risk associated with that activity. If very little is at risk, then simply requiring good passwords might provide enough security.

Digital Certificates

Digital certificates, also known as *public key certificates*, are digital verifications that the sender of an encrypted message is who they claim to be. To obtain a digital certificate you must apply to a *trusted certificate authority (CA)*. The applicant must create a private key and provide a *certificate signing request (CSR)* to the CA.

Depending on the type of certificate involved, the CA will verify your identity in some manner that might be as simple as verifying an email account on that domain but could also involve the verification of public company documents or even a personal interview.

The CA then issues an encrypted digital certificate containing a public key for the applicant, along with their *digital signature* and an expiration date. When the applicant receives the encrypted message, they must use the CA's public key to decrypt the *digital certificate* attached to the message and verify that it was issued by the CA.

Next, the applicant uses the CA's public key and identification to encrypt a reply indicating their trust of this encryption. Finally, the server uses its private key to decrypt the response in order to obtain the symmetric public key that will be used for the data exchange. This process is illustrated in Figure 5.37.

FIGURE 5.37 Digital certificates

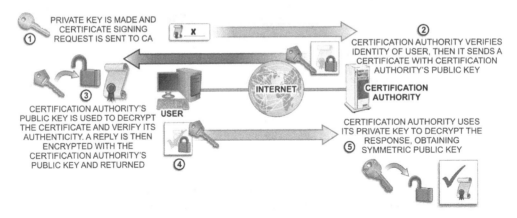

Public Key Infrastructure

Public Key Infrastructure (PKI) supports the distribution of these public keys and certificates to enable trusted connections and secure data exchange based on the information from the CA signer. CAs must obtain their own certificates from a higher-ranking CA. At the top of this hierarchy there must be a *root certificate* or *self-signed certificate* identifying the *root certificate authority*. This is essentially a private key for that organization.

Security issues such as the Heartbleed OpenSSL bug have made it necessary to revoke certificates because the private keys have been compromised on affected servers.

Certificate Management

Software such as web browsers may contain CA keys to facilitate the handling of certificates. However, they should also reference a *certificate revocation list (CRL)* or use the *Online Certificate Status Protocol (OCSP)* to query for revoked certificates. Increasingly, browsers are employing OCSP, but there are still those providers that simply include a CRL with each update of their browser software.

A *certificate chain* is the list of certificates starting with the root certificate followed by each other certificate where the issuer or signer of one certificate is the subject of the next. While a certificate can have only one issuing CA signature, different certificate chains may exist for some certificates because more than one certificate can be created using the same public key.

Secure certificates should be obtained only from known and respected CAs or you risk having the certificates revoked. CAs are increasingly pushing *Extended Validation (EV)* certificates where the identity of the entity is verified much more extensively. EV certificates are no stronger or structurally different than other certificate types, but they imply a greater trust because the site being visited is owned by the certificate holder.

Web browsers typically have some visual indication that the SSL/TLS connection is using an EV certificate. This usually involves displaying information using a green color. EV certificates are typically only used on sites that accept credit cards or other private data (rather than those that handle email or other services).

It is possible to generate and use a self-signed certificate for encryption. This can be useful for testing. However, client software will typically inform the user that this certificate is not trusted.

Key Management

Key management is a critical component of key-based cytological security systems. If the keys involved in the security system are not secured, then the system itself is not secure. Care must be taken to protect the keys throughout their existence, including during generation, distribution, use, and retirement. If the key can be stolen or replicated at any of these points, it becomes a threat to security.

As with all other aspects of cybersecurity, successful key management begins with organizational policies. The organization must establish policies that specify how keys are to be exchanged, stored, used, and retired. The NIST Cybersecurity Framework standards call for such policies to establish and specify rules for providing CIA protection for keys and metadata, along with authenticating the source of these items.

Key Management System (KMS) applications provide integrated management functions for creating, storing, and distributing keys for computing devices and applications. On the server side, these applications are responsible for generating, distributing, and replacing keys throughout the system. On the client side, they are responsible for storing and managing the keys. There are a wide variety of KMS systems available through both open source and proprietary outlets. These applications provide end-to-end protection for keys from generation to retirement and destruction.

The PKI mentioned earlier is a type of key management system that employs digital certificates for authentication and public keys for encryption.

Hashing

As already discussed, in cybersecurity settings *hashing* is a cryptographic technique defined as the application of a mathematical algorithm to a set of data to produce a numeric value that represents the set. The value resulting from the application of the algorithm is known as the *hash value* or *hash*.

Hashing is different than encryption in that the algorithm is designed in such a way as to make the conversion infeasible to deconstruct. It is a one-way conversion.

Hashing is used to provide several security-related functions, including the following:

- Integrity verification for transmitted files or messages

- Password verification

- File identification

- Proof of work

- eSignature security

The classical example of hashing is running an algorithm to generate a hash for a password that can then be regenerated each time the password is used to verify its authenticity. Placing the original hash in a *hash table* enables the creation of a system where the actual password never needs to be seen—only the new hash to compare to the old hash.

A hash table is simply a lookup table that maps keys to values using a *hash function* that converts the keys into hash values. Rather than sequentially searching a table of data looking for a particular value, a hash function can be performed on the lookup key that will return the index to the hash value being searched for. This can save a tremendous amount of time searching for data.

A *distributed hash table (DHT)* is a similar type of function, but the mapping from keys to values is distributed among the different nodes across the network. The node that stores this map can be found by hashing that key.

Resource Constraints

A *resource constraint* is a limit on what a resource can accomplish with the tools that are available to it. The resource can include funding limits, personnel quantity or capability limitations, and device or physical infrastructure capability limits.

As you've seen, DoS attacks are based on constraining a targeted resource and can be conducted in a number of ways:

- Flooding network connectivity devices to disrupt connections and prevent users from accessing them

- Consuming the resources of a targeted computing device (disk space, memory, CPU processing capabilities or bandwidth)

- Manipulating device configuration settings

- Injecting data that a computing or network device cannot process

Review Questions

The following questions test your knowledge of the material presented in this chapter.

1. _____ creates a tracking list of events using logs or other tracking tools.

2. _____ is applying approval of access to designated information after the individual is authenticated.

3. _____ involves making sure that an individual is who they say they are.

4. _____ is an assurance that data remains secret or private. It is established through sets of rules designed to limit data access to authorized people.

5. _____ is an assurance that data is accurate and can be trusted.

6. _____ is an assurance that data can reliably be accessed in a timely manner.

7. What type of cyberattack involves impersonating a user or a system?

8. Describe the objective of performing a DoS attack.

9. How do the basic tenets of enterprise networks differ from those of OT networks?

10. Which phase of a cyberattack is most time-consuming, and at what point in the process does it occur?

11. What security feature can be used to make sure that if data is accessed at rest or intercepted in motion by an unauthorized third party, it cannot be read?

12. Describe the two general categories of social engineering techniques.

13. What cryptographic technique is used to provide integrity verification for transmitted files or messages?

14. Describe three types of password attacks.

15. _____ provides integrated management functions for creating, storing, and distributing keys for computing devices and applications.

Exam Questions

1. This principle refers to giving each user the least amount of access possible to accomplish their job role and only to the areas of the network they must have.
   A. User rights principle
   B. User access principle
   C. Least privilege principle
   D. Access control principle

2. What term is used to refer to a service that proves the integrity and origin (authorship) of data?

   A. Authorization

   B. Authentication

   C. Identification

   D. Nonrepudiation

3. Which threat agent represents the greatest threat to most networked organizations?

   A. Denial of service

   B. Insider threats

   C. Man in the middle

   D. Spammers

4. What is the target of a distributed denial-of-service (DDoS) attack?

   A. A single client is being attacked.

   B. Multiple servers are being attacked.

   C. A single server is being attacked.

   D. Multiple clients are being attacked.

5. Which of the following is associated with occurrences that create adverse effects within the network or computing environment that will require actions to mitigate, or with occurrences that violate organizational security policies, procedures, or acceptable use practices?

   A. Cyber events

   B. Cyber incidents

   C. Cyber occurrences

   D. Cyberattacks

6. What does a SYN attack take advantage of?

   A. The TCP/IP buffer space used during a handshake exchange

   B. The IPX/SPX frame relay used during an initial connection

   C. The UDP header frame used during a handshake exchange

   D. The ICMP echo connection used during connectivity checks

7. What security action involves applying a cipher to data to produce a scrambled message that cannot be understood without the knowledge of the secret code that was used to create it?

   A. Hashing

   B. Encryption

   C. Steganography

   D. Cryptology

8. A close friend wants to know what your job at work is like, so you invite him over to see the operation and test your high-speed Internet connection. The following week, the network administrator tells you that your computer has a virus. What could be the cause?

    A. Unauthorized access

    B. DoS

    C. Social engineering

    D. Spoofing

9. One of the significant features of using digital signatures is that it presents a reliable method to ensure data integrity. Which of the following is used to digitally sign a message?

    A. The sender's public key

    B. The sender's private key

    C. The receiver's private key

    D. The receiver's public key

10. While searching the Web for a specific product, you log into the site using your credentials. The browser appears to be trying to authenticate you but eventually returns you to the login page without an error message. Assuming that you have misentered your credentials, you apply them again, and they are accepted. You were pretty sure your username and password were correct the first time, but they didn't get you into the site. What type of activity might you have been involved in?

    A. Clickjacking

    B. SQL injection

    C. Smurfing

    D. Man in the middle

Chapter

6

Physical Security

OBJECTIVES

Upon completion of this chapter, you should be able to:

1. Define and describe physical security strategies, practices, and devices.

2. Understand the application of the following components of physical security:

   ▪ Access Controls

   ▪ Physical Barriers

   ▪ Biometrics

3. Differentiate between authentication and authorization.

4. Identify typical physical access control devices.

5. Identify strengths and weaknesses of different types of physical security and surveillance systems and devices.

6. Select appropriate camera types when given specific scenarios.

7. Describe basic security terminology as referred to in the NERC CIP 006 standard for Physical Security of Critical Cyber Assets.

Introduction

The overall aim of any security effort is to establish a peace-of-mind condition (a carefree state or free from worries) for an individual, a group, or an organization. This condition is ideally achieved by securing exclusive rights to, access to, and use of *assets* (objects and information). This condition creates value and gives the assets' owner(s) peace of mind.

 In the cybersecurity realm, a carefree state is never actually achieved. New types of cyberattacks are constantly being devised, causing cyber-security specialists and administrators to be constantly on guard against potentially damaging occurrences.

A more structural definition for *security* is the science, technique, and art of establishing a system of exclusion and inclusion of individuals, systems, media, content, and objects. *Exclusion* serves as a major security tool that adds value to an object or information. It also provides increased safety and utilization with physical assets, such as machinery or processing equipment.

Physical security is the science, technique, and art of establishing a system of exclusion and inclusion for *tangible assets*. In practice this involves policies, practices, and steps aimed at combating theft, preventing physical damage, maintaining system integrity and services, and limiting unauthorized disclosure of information.

Similarly, the term *cybersecurity* involves securing physical access to tangible property, electronic systems, and network ports while securing *intangible assets*, including electronic data and access to the system's controls.

In any modern system, security is a function of the synergies of both the physical and cybersecurity domains. Both entities are necessary to support a strong overall security posture and program.

Infrastructure Security

When physical security initiatives are applied to providing security for the basic physical and organizational structures needed for the operation of an enterprise, organization, and society, this is known as *infrastructure security*.

Although we may think of infrastructure security in simple physical terms such as a lockable door, a patrolling security guard, or some other method used to protect our assets, there are several additional components that go into constructing an effective infrastructure security system. Such systems generally involve a combination of several critical security procedures that have been well planned and tested to meet or exceed the operational and organizational security needs.

There are three general layers to designing and implementing a plan to physically secure an infrastructure asset (a property, a building, a physical space, a system, or a device).

- *The outer perimeter*: Securing this space involves controlling who can move (walk, drive, fly) across the physical or logical line that marks this perimeter. Examples of typical physical outer perimeters include property lines or the exterior walls of a building or complex.

- *The inner perimeter*: This perimeter typically involves physical barriers such as walls, doors, and windows, either exterior or interior, depending on the context of the outer perimeter.

- *The interior*: This is the innermost level of security and consists of the interior of the building, office, cubicle, etc., that is surrounded by the inner and outer perimeters.

Cybersecurity also deals with securing logical perimeters. These are covered in later chapters having to do with computing and control systems, networks, and the Internet. The same security concepts developed here will be applied to those topics as they are encountered.

In a comprehensive security plan, control of all three layers is addressed. Security at each layer typically consists of a formulation of specifically selected devices working together to provide an effective physical security system.

At each layer there are two concepts at work: natural access control methods and territorial reinforcement. *Natural access control* involves using natural design elements, such as structures and landscaping to guide people as they enter and exit spaces. On the other hand, *territorial reinforcement* employs structures, systems, and devices to prevent unauthorized entry and create a clear difference between what is public and private.

As illustrated in Figure 6.1, infrastructure security operation and management is based on three basic types of subsystems:

- Access control and monitoring systems

- Intrusion detection and reporting systems

- Video surveillance systems

FIGURE 6.1   Security subsystems

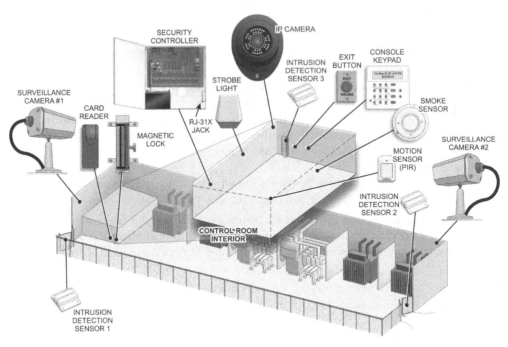

Access Control

From the list presented, you can see that *access control* is the first major component of a physical security system. As a matter of fact, most security experts agree that the first and most basic objective of any infrastructure security system is to deter potential intruders. This is the goal of access control. *You can't damage, destroy, or steal what you can't physically gain access to.*

The basis of designing efficient access control systems involves three terms: *ingress*, *egress*, and *regress*. By definition, *ingress* is the right of an individual to enter a property, while *egress* is the legal right to leave a property. Similarly, *regress* is the term used to describe the legal right to reenter a property.

> On a physical security basis, ingress can be defined as the physical path of an individual to properly enter a property, while egress is the physical path to properly leave a property.

In security terms, a *right* is a *legal privilege* or *permission* granted to someone, or some group, by some recognized source of authority. This source can be a government, a legally recognized governmental agent, or a legally recognized owner of an asset. By extension, a person who has the right to access an asset is said to be *authorized* (by the recognized authority), while anyone who has not been given this right is labeled as unauthorized. When *unauthorized* people attempt to gain access to an asset they do not have rights to access, they become intruders.

Therefore, access control involves being able to control the ingress, egress, and regress to an asset based on *authorization*. In particular, limiting the access of unauthorized personnel to important assets is the most fundamental security step that you can take.

Access control begins at the outer perimeter. Depending on the specific example being studied, this may be the property line of the organization's physical property or the front door of their facilities.

Recall that the goal at the outer perimeter is to control who can walk or cross the perimeter. Control at this point can be as simple as planting hedges at the edge of the property or including appropriate visual signs to warn unauthorized people to stay out, or as complex as a barbed-wire fence with gates and armed guards.

Crime Prevention Through Environmental Design (CPTED) is a set of building and property design principles based on anticipating the thought processes of potential intruders to discourage them from following through.

Access control efforts typically extend into the area between the outer and inner perimeters. These efforts can include natural access control techniques such as strategic placement of employee and guest parking, as well as the use of landscaping features to channel people to selected entrances and exits and inhibit access to other possible entry/exit points. This also extends to clearly marking ingress and egress approaches to facilities and properties.

Inner perimeter control of physical infrastructure involves the use of physical structures such as walls, windows, and doors that can act as *barriers* that impede the ability of an intruder to advance from the outer perimeter to the interior region. Once again, depending on the specific security scenario being discussed, these barriers may be part of the building's external structure that encloses the entire interior environment, or it can be interior structures that control movement into and out of individual work areas.

Interior security is the innermost level of infrastructure security, and it involves monitoring the area inside the inner perimeter. Such monitoring may consist of both human and electronic security systems to observe, track, and detect intruders as well as record evidence of different activities. The mixture of empowered people and electronic devices makes for an effective security tool at the interior security level.

A key component that brings all three levels of security together is a well-designed and documented *security policy* that states how security is implemented at each level. Businesses and organizations develop comprehensive security policies that define who is authorized to access different assets and what they are allowed to do with those assets when they do access them.

For example, allowing employees and visitors to have free access to all the departments inside the organization provides a variety of security risks. You will want to maintain access control to create an environment that reduces the human nature of temptation. If everyone can move freely within the interior of the organization, it is much more difficult to implement safeguards to prevent them from accessing or taking physical or cyber assets.

You also need to maintain access control to prevent accidents. For example, you do not want a sales representative accidentally spilling their coffee on one of your production servers in your engineering department. Instead, develop a cohesive *access control policy* at each level that provides authorized people with appropriate levels of access to selected assets, while inhibiting access to assets by people who are not authorized. Then enforce those policies with the correct types and numbers of access control devices (sensors, barriers, logs, ID badges, or security guards*) as deemed appropriate.

Frequently, badges or smart cards are used to control access. Employees may also be identified by an RFID transponder as they move within proximal range of an RFID sensor. Transponders store access codes and use radio receivers and transmitters.

 *Although access control devices may be cheaper than human guards, guards are able to make valuable judgmental decisions based on the actions of a potential intruder. They offer a symbol of security, can initiate human judgment, and can provide timely intervention during an incident.

These access control techniques, systems, and devices are discussed in detail throughout the remainder of this chapter.

Physical Security Controls

Enforcing access control measures may initially include placing locks on doors that access offices and separating departments or networking sections with similar *physical barriers*. Many companies have a front door or an entranceway that includes a receptionist to control access, as depicted in Figure 6.2. During business hours, the *receptionist* acts as a physical barrier, inquiring about the nature of clients' visits.

In some institutions, the visitor may be required to be accompanied by an *escort* to physically limit their movement through the company. For additional access control, a human guard could be employed to control access to specific restricted interior locations, such as a laboratory, or to an elevator shaft that services a restricted area, such as a basement.

Barriers can be employed to provide security through access control. At night, the physical barrier may simply be a locked door. The door may also be equipped with a sensor and an alarm. The alarm could be a local annunciator such as a siren, or it could be linked directly to an external monitoring system or to the police department.

The primary physical barrier in most security perimeters is the *lockable door* or *gate*, as shown in Figure 6.3. The door provides the physical barrier but in itself will only keep honest people out. The lock, on the other hand, provides the authentication function of the barrier through its key. Having the *key* signifies that the person either possesses or knows the information required to gain access through the door.

FIGURE 6.2   Physical barriers

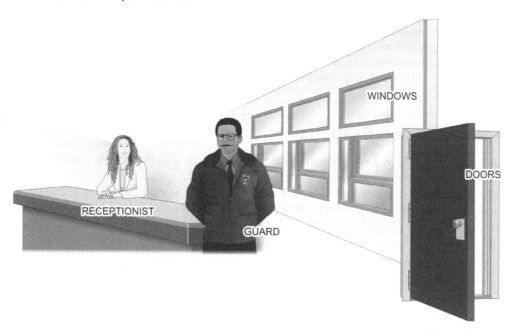

FIGURE 6.3   Access control

 A strict key control policy is required to successfully protect equipment and intellectual property behind locked doors.

There are many different types of locks used with security barriers. Likewise, there are many different types of keys used to disengage the locking mechanism. Depending on the type of lock being used, the key can be either physical or logical.

In most organizations, only select personnel who work in a particular office may possess a key to gain access to their working environment. Maintaining tight key control and using numbered keys that are clearly coded for nonreproduction helps to maintain the locked door as an effective physical barrier.

Authentication Systems

Authentication is the process of determining that someone is who they say they are. Recall that effective access control involves being able to control the ingress, egress, and regress to an asset based on *authorization*. In particular, limiting the access of unauthorized personnel to important assets is the most fundamental security step that you can take. Therefore, authorization is based on authentication. There are multiple factors involved in authentication:

- *Knowledge*: Something that only the designated person should know (something you know)
- *Possession*: Something that only the designated person should have (something you have)
- *Inherence*: Something that only the designated person is (something you are)
- *Location*: Somewhere that only the designated person is (somewhere you are)

Many physical authentication systems are based on *single authentication factors* that depend on possession such as possessing a key device that opens a lock. The key can be a physical or virtual key as needed to open a physical or virtual locking mechanism.

More intelligent and effective authentication methods involve *two-factor authentication*, which is a process that requires two of the factors to grant authorization. This is based on knowledge and possession. Advanced authorization and authentication methods include *multifactor authorize and authentication systems*. In these systems, information must be presented to an authentication device that, in turn, passes it to the security controller's authentication system. There are a number of different authentication devices routinely used in access control systems. The major device types are covered in the following sections of the chapter.

Security and Identification Tools

A growing industry of security products is emerging that is utilizing a variety of affordable technologies. These technologies enable each employee to have some sort of physical device that can provide digital assurance of their identity. These physical tools provide a *hard token* for authentication representing the "something you have" aspect of two-factor authentication.

Figure 6.4 shows these common authentication devices:

- Key fobs or other dedicated wireless devices
- RFID badges and tags
- Smart cards and magnetic swipe cards
- Mobile device applications (cell phone apps, etc.)
- Biometric security devices

FIGURE 6.4   Common security tools

Key fobs that use *near field communication* (NFC)—a short-range wireless connectivity standard that can be used to initiate communication between devices when they are in close proximity to each other—are becoming a popular emergency medical identification solution. After communications have been initiated between the *initiator* and the *target* devices, another wireless technology, such as Bluetooth or Wi-Fi, might be used to take over and perform the data exchange. While these devices show great potential, until standards for this type of medical ID device are sorted out, they will continue to be of limited use.

The main advantage of a key fob is that it can be attached to something the user carries—at least most of the time anyway. Organizations can use this technology to provide one authentication factor that also constrains the user to a given proximity. For example, a staff member that is granted access to a system through such a device may simply have the fob in their pocket and only be required to enter a password on an access panel to authenticate, as long as they are within the fob's active range, as illustrated in Figure 6.5.

FIGURE 6.5   Keyfob operations

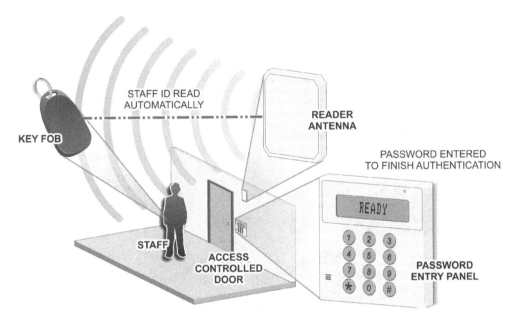

Key fobs and other hardware subscriber identification modules typically contain a microcontroller and an elaborate smart feature set that enables them to offer almost limitless options.

RFID Badges

In a similar manner, *radio frequency identification (RFID)* technology may be deployed as an authentication tool. As shown in Figure 6.6, RFID systems utilize self-powered *RFID tags* that can be used as beacons to track location or authenticate proximity. *Active RFID tags* provide a longer range but are much more expensive and require more power. *Passive RFID tags* are powered by the electromagnetic energy transmitted from the RFID reader and can be quite inexpensive. Lower-frequency RFID tags have a short range but are generally more reliable and less influenced by metal barriers.

Higher-frequency tags have a longer range, but any obstacles will cause more interference. Modern UHF RFID tags seem to work well even when placed on metal surfaces. Passive RFID tags are often used to track inventory items and equipment as well and are replacing barcodes in many applications.

Recall from Chapter 4, "ICS Module and Element Hardening," that NFC is a high-frequency RFID standard that is very appropriate for security applications because it requires close proximity. Proximity is important as this can minimize any unauthorized stealth access attempts. As described in Chapter 4, it is relatively easy to create rogue RFID readers to acquire badge data from a target, as shown in Figure 6.7. Employing NFC technology for the badging system reduces the risk of the data being stolen due to its close proximity requirements.

FIGURE 6.6   RFID systems

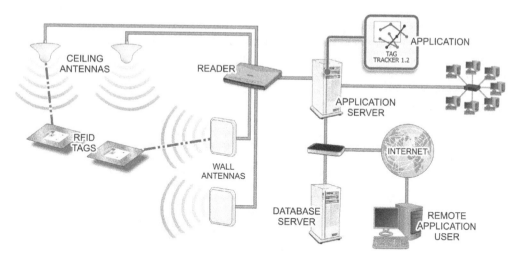

FIGURE 6.7   Rouge ID badge reader

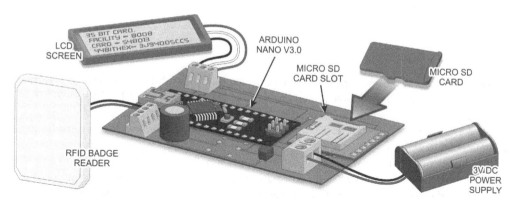

The low-tech method for preventing this type of ID theft involves placing the card or badge in a protective sleeve that will thwart the stealth reader and require the user to remove the card when authenticating. However, this has not always worked as well in practice as hoped for. A more technical approach for preventing unauthorized RFID card access involves using odd frequencies (or multiple frequencies) or using an obscure RFID reader type.

However, it should be apparent that RFID technology is not likely to be secure if it is used as the only authentication factor. On the other hand, it can still be quite useful for identifying a user when they attempt to use any device after a more rigorous authentication has been performed.

Smart Cards

A *smart card* contains an embedded integrated circuit that may be nothing more than a memory chip or a secure microcontroller. It may be able to interface with a reader through direct physical contact, or in the case of a contactless card to communicate through an active RF interface. In some cases, the smart card may employ a combination of ID technologies, as illustrated in Figure 6.8.

FIGURE 6.8   Smart card ID technologies

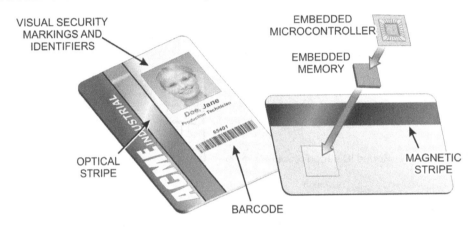

The *International Organization for Standardization (ISO)* and the *International Electrotechnical Commission (IEC)* have issued international standards—*ISO/IEC 7816-4:2020* and *ISO/IEC 1443*—for the standardization of contactless smart cards and smart chips. These devices typically operate at 13.56 MHz and must pass within 4 inches of a reader to communicate with it.

The microcontroller in a smart card can be programmed to perform any number of security functions. Beyond simply *storing* information in the card for authentication purposes, a number of advanced on-card functions are possible, including *encryption* and *PKI authentication* services, as well as random number generating, hashing, and reader validation. In addition, biometric data may be stored on the card and shared with the reader during the authentication process so the reader can compare this data with data it receives from a live biometric scanner, as shown in Figure 6.9.

Many applications will consider a smart card to be any card, key fob, or portable solution including a smart feature set. They are difficult to duplicate and may include additional security features to make duplication more difficult.

Magnetic swipe cards and *barcode cards* are inexpensive ways of providing single-factor physical authentication. It is typically easy to duplicate and, of course, steal these devices. However, the low costs can also allow cards to be generated frequently using short-term credentials that can improve security.

FIGURE 6.9   Storing biometric data on a smart card

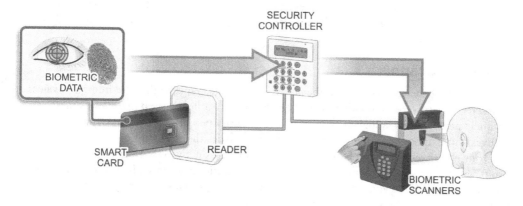

Mobile device (*smart cell phone*) applications can also be configured so that after a more complex authentication process takes place, the application will communicate with an access system to provide one authentication factor. This enables *smart phone applications* to duplicate or replace smart card functionality.

Another way of using mobile phones involves their SMS messaging capabilities. An access panel can recognize a user through a proximity-based methodology (or even through an entered username) and then send that user's mobile phone a temporary access code via SMS, as shown in Figure 6.10. An automated system could even call the user and provide the code using a text-to-speech system. *Pagers* (mobile RF devices that only receive messages) are still popular with physicians because they work even in the most shielded areas of a hospital. These devices can also be integrated into a security solution.

FIGURE 6.10   Using SMS messages for access control

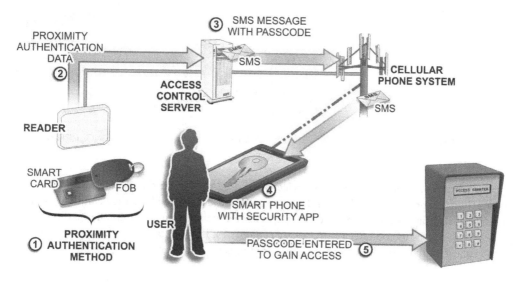

As long as the setup process is secure, using these devices in an authentication role is really no less secure than other convenient proximity solutions. In addition, these kinds of *bring-your-own-device (BYOD)* solutions tend to be popular with many users, as well as very cost-effective.

Biometric Scanners

Biometrics is the term used to describe access control mechanisms that use human physical characteristics to verify individual identities. Biometric authentication involves using uniquely personal physiological characteristics to verify people are who they say they are.

Every human possesses unique physical characteristics that differentiate them from everyone else. Even identical twins have separate and distinctive DNA, voice patterns, fingerprints, eye features, and other characteristics. The qualities most often involved in biometric authentication include voice patterns, fingerprints, palm prints, signatures, facial features, and retinal and iris scans, as shown in Figure 6.11.

FIGURE 6.11 Typical biometric authentication methods

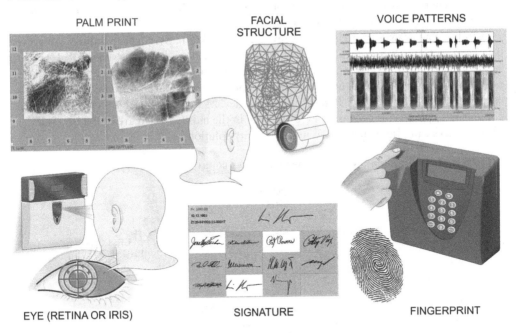

In each case, a biometric scanning device is required to convert the physiological quantity into a digital representation. The results are stored in a database where they can be used in an authentication process. The underlying application will use the truly unique qualities of the data as a basis to compare future access requests to. If the data from a future authentication request matches the key points of the stored version, then access will be granted.

However, not all biometric scanning devices are equally accurate at authenticating users. Table 6.1 shows how different biometric scanning devices rate in terms of their ability to accurately authenticate people.

TABLE 6.1   Biometric Device Comparison

	False Positive Rate	False Negative Rate
Palm print	1.43%	4%
Facial structure	0.1%	0.8–1.6%
Voice patterns	2–5%	5–10%
Eye (retina or iris)	0.1%	1.1–1.4%
Signature	0.49%	7.05%
Fingerprint	2.2%	2.2%

For fingerprints, the US government figures indicate rates of 0.1 percent and 0.4 percent, respectively.

In general, the characteristics of the human eye—iris and retinal scans—tend to make it the most reliable source of authentication. Of the remaining biometric variables in the list, fingerprint readings tend to be more accurate than voice scans. However, fingerprints can be stored on a clear surface and used later. To overcome this possibility, fingerprint vein scanners that convert the vein patterns in the fingertip into digital representations have been developed. On the other hand, illnesses and user stress levels can affect voice patterns.

As the table shows, there are two basic types of authentication failure:

- *Type 1, false rejection or false negative failures*: This is a report that produces an incorrect rejection of the individual, thereby locking them out of a facility or security area that they should have access to.

- *Type 2, false acceptance or false positive failures*: This is a report that incorrectly authenticates the individual, which could lead to providing access to equipment or data that this person should not have access to. Of the two types of authentication failure, this is the most significant in that it could grant access to malicious people.

Because of the potential for false reporting and inaccuracies, a second method of access control may need to be used in conjunction with biometric devices. In areas requiring higher security, a passport, additional fingerprints, or some other type of verification could be used to ensure that the individual was not mistakenly identified.

Remote Access Monitoring and Automated Access Control Systems

Remote monitoring refers to monitoring or measurement of devices from a remote location or control room. In the security realm this involves having external access to the security system through a communication system.

Remote access monitoring systems are used to notify supervisory security personnel when an unauthorized access is attempted. In these systems, the controller monitors the *open/close conditions* of the infrastructure's sensors. When a sensor, such as a magnetic switch or a motion detector, is activated, the system automatically identifies it as an intrusion and notifies specified security personnel of the occurrence.

Various sensors can be used to detect the opened, closed, locked, or unlocked condition of an automated door or gate. They can also be configured to initiate an opened, closed, locked, or unlocked condition at a specified door or gate.

> Because information about the locked/unlocked conditions for a specific movable barrier does not necessarily correlate directly to the open/closed condition of that barrier (the door or gate actually being open and providing access), the information recorded does not differentiate between these conditions. A second or different type of sensor would need to be installed and monitored to perform this differentiation.

Signaling and *reporting* between the sensor and the controller are continuous during the elapsed time between the opening and closing of the barrier. If the barrier is left open for a specified time, that information is also noted and recorded by the system. The condition monitoring system includes an event log, detailing the times and dates of various events. Here are some examples:

- *Locked condition monitoring*: Locked monitoring is a feature that allows the security supervisor to confirm that a door is locked. In addition to monitoring the locked status of a door or gate, the condition monitoring system can also provide details as to how long and during what time periods the door or gate has remained locked.

- *Unlocked condition monitoring*: The condition monitoring system can record and signal each time a specific gate or door is unlocked (granting access) and what type of access was granted. Unlocked monitoring can also identify who was granted access.

- *Time-of-day settings*: Most automated access control systems base decisions about valid or invalid entry requests, also called *transactions*, on preconfigured time-of-day settings. This is normal because any entry request that does not fit the predefined time profile or time schedule of an identified user is subject to suspicion.

Such a situation might occur for a daily delivery that arrives later than normally expected. The user, in this case a recognized delivery agent, has been identified but is seeking entry at an unauthorized time. An authorized human supervisor will need to intervene to accept the delivery.

The *notification* can come in the form of a visual notification on a security control panel, a call via telephone, an instant message, or a text message to a smart phone. The notification can also involve activating strobe lights and high-intensity sirens to call attention to the intrusion attempt. Figure 6.12 shows different options for remotely accessing a typical security system.

FIGURE 6.12   Remote access communication options

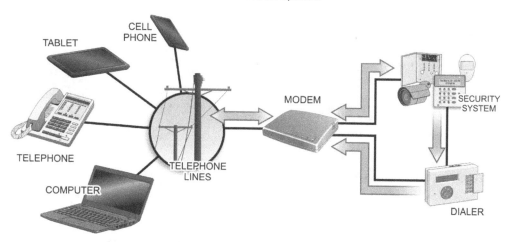

Automated access control capabilities add another dimension to standard security monitoring and reporting functions. Although automated access control is not an integral part of the typical intrusion detection and monitoring system, it adds to the safety and convenience of perimeter access control. Automated access control systems come in two flavors: *remote access control systems* and *remote control access systems*.

Remote access control is a design feature that requires authentication of the identity of a user attempting to access a security zone or computer system from a distant location. Remote access control manages entry to protected areas by authenticating the identity of people entering the area. This can be accomplished by a number of methods including password readers, magnetic key cards, and secret cipher lock codes.

Although the differences are minor, the design considerations for *remote control access* systems are different from those for remote access systems. *Remote control access* is a design feature that works with remote monitoring systems to monitor, control, and supervise doors, gates, and conveyances from a distance. Figure 6.13 shows the typical components involved in a remote access control system.

The remote control function enables the security specialist to initiate communications with a remote site, enter an access code, obtain current conditions, and set system parameters. A *closed circuit television* (CCTV) system may be added to the security system to provide visual recognition functions to the remote control options. Some *remote monitoring and control systems*, such as the one depicted in Figure 6.14, can also be used to obtain status messages concerning any sensor that has detected a value outside of programmed values such as heat, cold, water leakage, loud noises, alarm history, or other custom features.

FIGURE 6.13   Remote control/access operations

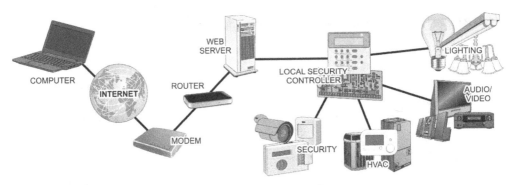

FIGURE 6.14   Remote monitoring systems

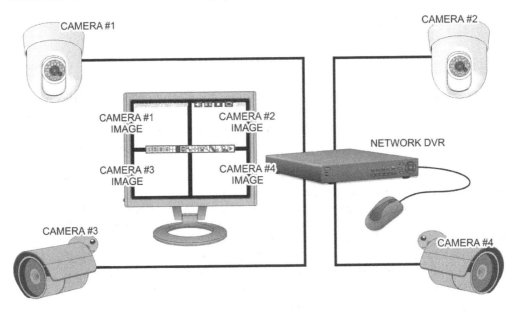

Wireless communications devices are often used to connect the components of an automated access control system together. This type of connectivity is an economical solution that eliminates the need for new wiring between control devices, intercoms, and electrically operated security gates and doors.

Intrusion Detection and Reporting Systems

While preventing unauthorized access is the first line of defense in physical security, layers of additional security measures are crucial to preventing intrusions from escalating into serious events. A closely related second tier of defense is *intrusion detection* that enables potential intruders to be detected and removed before they can cause problems. This level of security involves detection devices (sensors) that are monitored or that can create an alarm.

The components of a basic commercial *security system*, depicted in Figure 6.15, come together to provide a functional *intrusion detection and reporting system*. This system includes an intelligent control panel connected by wires (or radio signals) to sensors at various locations throughout the facility.

FIGURE 6.15   Basic intrusion detection and reporting system

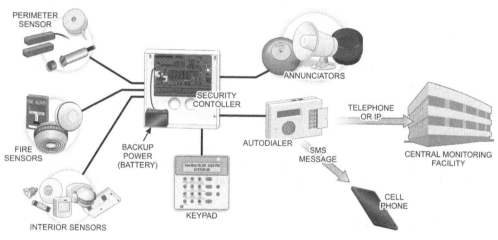

The control panel includes the electronic components and central processor, which monitors and controls the entire system. The processor accepts input information from the various sensors attached to it. In a basic security system, these inputs can be divided into three distinct types: perimeter, interior, and fire.

Perimeter area inputs to the control panel typically include sensors at every perimeter opening including doors, windows, garage doors, and windows and doors to crawl spaces. Additional perimeter protection may include using sound, vibration, and motion detector sensors to guard against entry through broken windows.

Some interior areas may also be protected with various types of sensors, such as motion detectors and interior door sensors. Most security systems also include inputs capable of handling adequate smoke and fire sensors.

When the controller receives an active input signal from one of its input sensors, it evaluates the conditions presented according to its programming (and the type of emergency response required) and, if necessary, sends the appropriate output signals to *annunciators* (sirens or bells). It may also communicate with designated security contacts (security supervisors, monitoring services, or law enforcement/fire agencies) as directed by its programming.

Commercial security systems may use any of several notification methods to notify designated security personnel when an alarm condition is triggered. Some alarm systems use a telephone dialer to alert the remote security contacts that an alarm condition exists. These systems are designed to react when no one is present by placing the call over a standard telephone line or a cell phone. Special digital codes are used to inform the security contacts as to what type of condition has caused the alarm.

It is also possible to have a prepared *text messaging* system such as SMS relayed by a cell phone to the designated security contacts. Another option is *IP-based notification*, which is used to notify the monitoring station via an IP network such as the Internet concerning an alarm condition.

Most security systems typically employ some type of keypad to provide the control interface for supervisors to arm and disarm the system using a programmed access code. The keypad may be designed to provide some level of visual and audible output signals to help monitor the status of the system.

Finally, most security systems include some type of emergency backup power (a backup battery or uninterruptable power supply) to provide emergency DC power to the security system when commercial power outages occur.

The choices for access control and management system components and subsystems are extensive. The following sections will explain the various subsystems typically found in the intrusion detection and reporting portion of a typical infrastructure security system.

Security Controllers

The center of any intelligent security system is the *security controller*. The security controller, shown in Figure 6.16, is typically installed in an enclosure that contains the security controller board, all of the electronic components, wire termination points, backup battery packs, and telephone termination wiring.

A given security controller model is designed to handle a specific number of *programmable zones*. A zone can be a single point of protection, such as a motion detector, or multiple points that have been combined into a single zone. For example, two hallway motion detectors could be connected to form a zone, or a stairway motion detector could be combined with the hallway sensors to form a single zone.

FIGURE 6.16   Typical security system controller

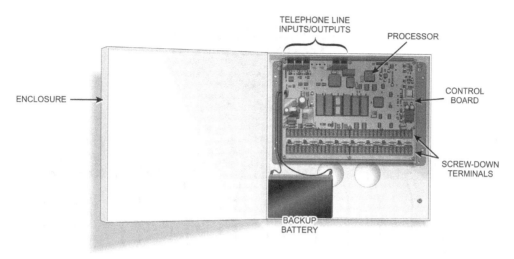

The security controller is the command center and distribution point of the intrusion detection and reporting portions of the security system to which all input and output devices are connected. Each sensor receives power and is managed from the security controller.

The controller must have enough capacity and functionality to connect to and manage all the security devices that will be part of the security system, in addition to providing remote access capability for remote monitoring and control.

The controller's enclosure should be mounted out of plain view and near a 120-volt AC outlet, where a plug-in transformer can supply low-voltage power to the total system.

Physical Security Zones

As mentioned earlier, security controllers possess a fixed number of detection circuits that can be used to create *physical security zones*. For instance, a typical commercial security controller may possess as few as 8 zones or up to 250 zones or more. Typically, one of these inputs is dedicated to the fire detection system. Figure 6.17 shows a typical eight-zone security controller connection scheme.

Suppose that the facility you are installing the security system in has 14 windows, 2 personnel entrance doors, and a roll-up receiving door for the warehouse. Additionally, it has two major hallways to monitor and an integrated fire detection system.

How will you physically install and configure the controller so that it provides full protection for the facility? The answer is to logically group related sensors together to create a security zone. This is accomplished by connecting all of the related sensor switches (all sensors appear as switches to the security controller) together in a serial format, as illustrated in Figure 6.18.

FIGURE 6.17   Security panel zone inputs

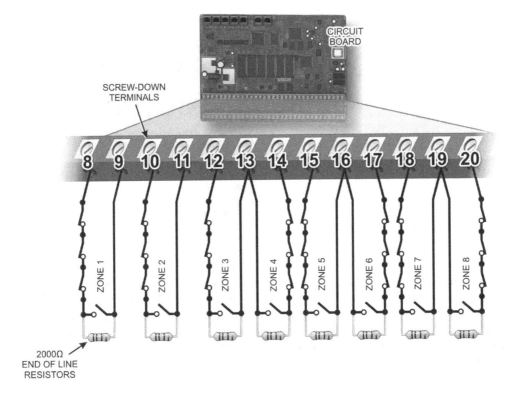

FIGURE 6.18   Creating a physical zone

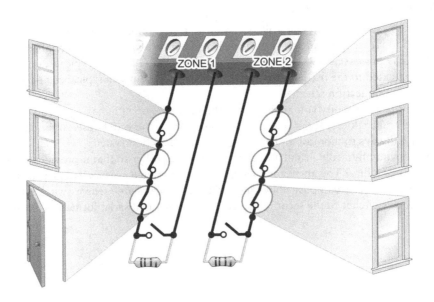

The controller monitors the amount of electrical current flowing between the zone's two connection points (referred to as a *current loop*). The loop requires that a resistor be placed in the loop to regulate the current flow to the correct level for the controller being used (different controller models typically require different resistance levels).

If one of the sensors is activated, its switch moves into an open condition, and current flow through the loop stops. The controller detects the lack of current flow and processes the input according to its configuration programming.

The fact that a certain level of current must be flowing helps to make the loop more difficult to tamper with. If the system used normally open switches that went closed when activated, the system could be circumvented by simply cutting a wire in the loop—no signal would ever be presented to the controller.

For the sample installation presented earlier, it might be logical to wire all of the west side window sensors into one input that can be reported as the *West Side Windows*. Likewise, the two personnel entry doors can be configured together because they will require special settings to allow exit and entry times for setting and disarming the system when leaving or entering the structure. Conversely, the other door may be connected into a different door zone or incorporated into one of the window zones, since it has no timing requirement.

Zoning also enables the system to instantly sound an alarm for intrusion detection in a specific area, while other sensor alerts in a specific zone, such as the main front door, may require a short delay before sounding the alarm. This enables security personnel to arm the system by entering a secret code on a keypad when exiting the facility (*exit delay*).

It also allows them to enter a protected area when arriving at the facility and disarm the system through the entry area keypad within a specified *entry delay* interval (usually 30 to 45 seconds). This feature allows keypads to be installed inside the facility near the exit door to avoid vandalism and tampering with keypads from the outside area.

Interior motion sensors that guard the hallways may be integrated into a window or door zone. However, they are more likely to be configured separately from the exterior sensors so that they can be disabled at night, when people may need to move around but want the perimeter to be protected from outside intruders. Figure 6.19 describes a possible zoning solution for this example.

The use of zoning also enables security personnel to arm only portions of the system, such as the perimeter doors and windows, while *bypassing* interior motion detectors in a specific zone. A *bypass mode* setting is normally accomplished by entering a predetermined numerical code through the keypad. When leaving the facility, all zones including the interior detectors can be armed as required.

A zoned security system layout can also be used by an external monitoring service to indicate which sensor in a designated zone is causing an alarm. If a sensor is reported as just sensor 3, zone 5, this could mean that the event occurred just about anywhere. If the sensor was reported as sensor 3, zone 5 perimeter, this would inform the operator that the violated area is on the outside of the premises.

Zones also provide ease of troubleshooting. For example, if a sensor in zone 3 perimeter is reporting a problem, there is no need to troubleshoot sensors that are located in the interior of the system.

FIGURE 6.19 Zoning concepts

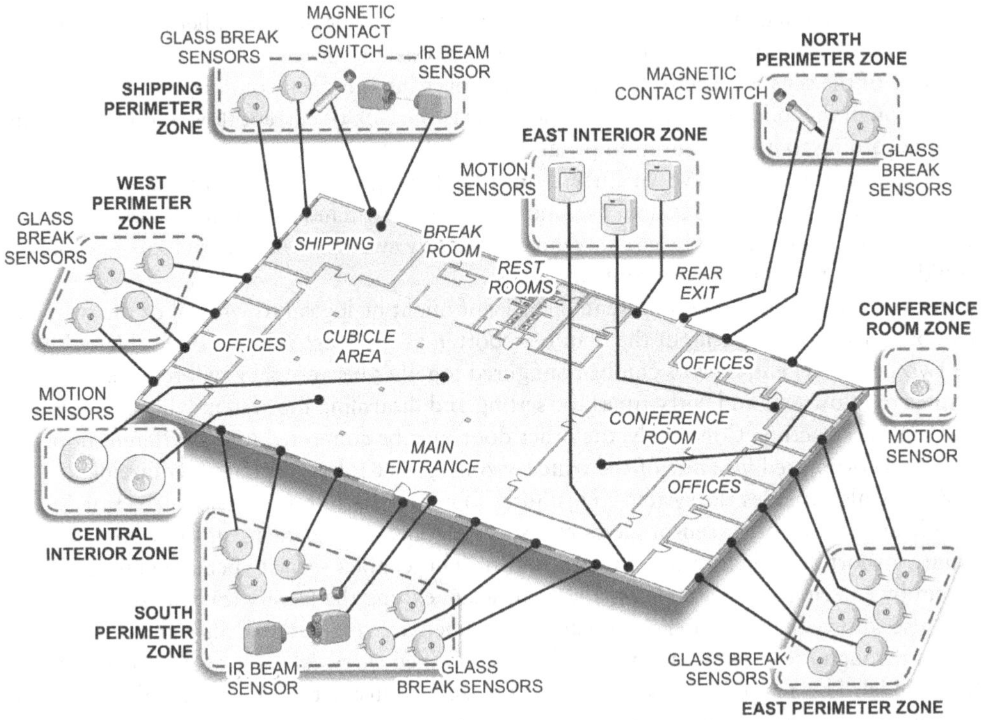

Remote Alarm Messaging

While *strobe lights* and *sirens* call general attention to alarm conditions in a localized environment, it is often necessary to notify specific people (such as a security specialist) or organizations (such as third-party security companies, fire departments, or police services) to respond to different types of alarm conditions.

The most common *remote notification systems* involve the use of a *telephone line* by the security system control panel to automatically call a remote monitoring facility or key personnel when an alarm condition exists. When the security controller receives an active input signal from one of its zones, it activates the telephone dialer unit and causes a digital data message to be transmitted to a predetermined recipient. The message recipient can also use remote access to check on the status of the security system when away from the facility.

Some intrusion detection and reporting systems employ a separate *telephone dialer* like the one depicted in Figure 6.20, or a built-in dialer. However, there are a growing number of systems that possess built-in *cellular communications systems*. Such systems provide additional dependability in that they can function even if the physical telephone lines are damaged.

FIGURE 6.20   Automatic voice/pager dialer console

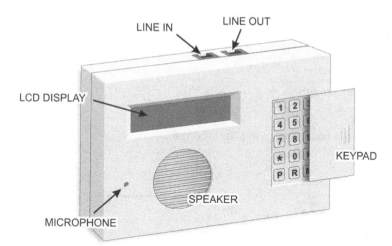

Third-Party Alarm Monitoring Services

Depending on the nature of the organization, the intrusion detection and reporting system may be totally based on employees of the organization. However, in many organizations, the security systems are supported by professional third-party alarm monitoring companies.

These companies provide a 24-hour/7-day-per-week monitoring service for a monthly fee. When they receive an alarm notification, they perform a response action based on their contractual agreement with the subscriber (client) company.

The sequencing of the response typically corresponds to the nature of the alarm notice they receive and when they receive it. They may initially try to contact designated personnel, or they may try to contact law enforcement or fire department agencies when an unanswered alarm condition occurs. They may also dispatch armed or unarmed security personnel from the monitoring company to investigate the alarm.

Video Surveillance Systems

Video surveillance systems are an important element of most commercial security systems. Many organizations include visible cameras in their infrastructure security systems to inhibit unlawful activity and to record events that occur at the perimeter or key interior levels.

Video surveillance systems are based on CCTV systems. The name is derived from the type of system that transmits signals over a "closed circuit" or private transmission circuit rather than over a standard television broadcast system. Figure 6.21 shows the major components of a basic video surveillance system. Common components include the following:

- One or more video cameras
- A time-lapse video recorder
- A switcher (optional)
- A video display monitor

FIGURE 6.21   A basic video surveillance system

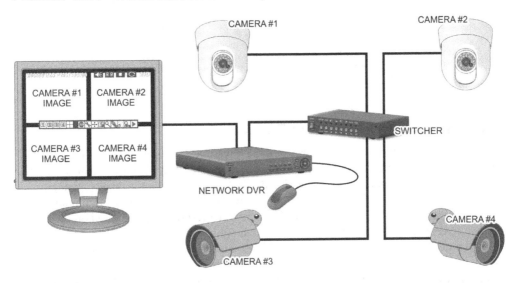

In this basic system, the cameras monitor their fields of vision and pass the information to the video processing equipment. In most cases this equipment consists of a digital video recorder of some type.

In some cases, the flow of video information from the cameras is controlled by *passive infrared (PIR) detectors*. If there is no PIR signature (created by body heat) in the PIR detector's field of view, the video information is not transmitted. However, during event periods of motion detection, the video information flows from the camera to the video recorder. In such events, the cameras can be instructed to speed up the number of frames recorded per second, to provide finer detail.

Some systems are based on *coaxial cable* for component connectivity, while others are *IP-based* and rely on wireless Wi-Fi communications or traditional network cabling.

The digital video processing equipment can provide video output directly to a *video display*, or it can be channeled to a *video switcher*. In some cases, the video processing component may offer its own integrated switcher.

Cameras

Surveillance systems use video cameras that convert a viewed image into standard video transmission formats—*composite video, component video, S-Video,* or *HDMI* signals—for display on a video output device, such as a monitor, a television display, or a personal computing device.

The best surveillance cameras employ *charge-coupled device* (CCD) technology as their *image sensor*. These devices provide high-resolution, low-operating light requirements, less temperature dependence, and high reliability. A typical CCD camera used in video surveillance systems is illustrated in Figure 6.22.

FIGURE 6.22   Video surveillance camera

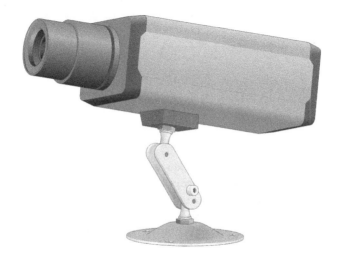

Surveillance cameras are available that use digital or analog interface technologies. *Digital cameras* convert the images they detect directly into digital signals that can easily be transmitted to and manipulated by digital computing devices. *Analog cameras* are based on older analog television signal and resolution standards. Cameras of this type require a separate coaxial cable to connect to a monitor or recording device.

Digital cameras generally offer superior performance over analog cameras. Analog cameras are more susceptible to quality degradation of the information being transmitted.

IP Cameras

IP cameras are actually *digital IP* (Internet Protocol) *devices* that have *IP addresses* that can be connected directly to a network, or to the Internet, rather than directly to a host controller or computer. The advantage of using an IP camera, like the one depicted in Figure 6.23, is that it can be viewed from anywhere in the world where Internet access is available.

FIGURE 6.23 An IP camera

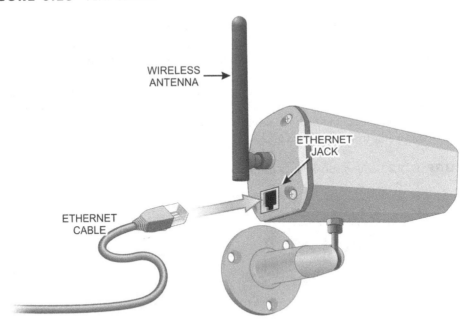

What sets IP systems apart from other video technologies are the abilities to email notification of motion sensing, process simultaneous user logins, and conduct *FTP*, or *secure FTP (sFTP)* if available, upload operations. An additional benefit of these cameras is they can be powered by *Power over Ethernet (PoE)*, where power is provided through the UTP network cable rather than from a dedicated power supply for each camera.

Pan-Tilt-Zoom Cameras

A network IP camera with *pan/tilt/zoom (PTZ)* capabilities, like the one depicted in Figure 6.24, is a stand-alone device that permits users to view live, full-motion video from anywhere. This type of camera is designed for use either on a proprietary computer network or over the Internet using only a standard web browser as its display unit.

Not only is manual PTZ control provided, the ability to remotely direct dozens of positions for each PTZ-capable camera is also possible.

Camera Specifications

The two important specifications that influence the cost of cameras are *light-sensitivity rating* and *resolution*. The camera's resolution specification method depends on whether it is an *analog camera* or a *digital camera*. Resolution for an analog camera is specified as the number of *horizontal lines* it is capable of generating from top to bottom of the display. With digital cameras the resolution is expressed in terms of the X-by-Y (horizontal-to-vertical) dot (*picture elements* or *pixels*) matrix format it produces. Figure 6.25 illustrates the meanings of the different camera resolution specifications.

FIGURE 6.24   PTZ camera

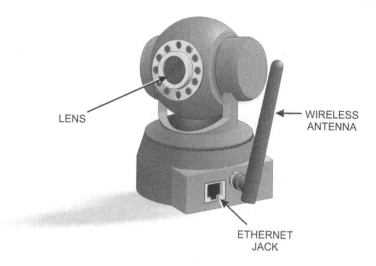

LENS

WIRELESS
ANTENNA

ETHERNET
JACK

FIGURE 6.25   Analog and digital camera resolution

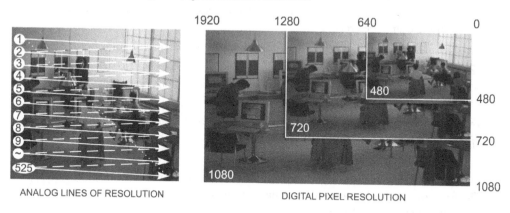

ANALOG LINES OF RESOLUTION

DIGITAL PIXEL RESOLUTION

The amount of light required to obtain a reasonable video camera image is called the *lux rating*. *Lux* is a measure of the amount of light that falls on an object. One lux is approximately the number of lumens falling on one square meter from one candle measured from one meter away. Typical camera ratings range between 0.5 and 1.0 lux.

The *lower* the stated lux rating of the camera, the better the camera is able to differentiate objects at lower light levels. Conversely, the *higher* the number of lines of resolution or the greater the number of pixels for a given surveillance camera, the better it will display the fine details of the view.

Lens Types

Surveillance cameras come in a variety of lens specifications. The lens size determines the camera's *field of view* and zoom capabilities. In general, the larger the lens, the more narrow and zoomed the field of view will be. For example, a fixed lens rated at a 3.6 mm *focal length* is designed to provide a field of view of approximately 72 degrees, while a 6 mm focal length lens should provide a 44 degree field of view. As a general rule, the shorter the focal length of the lens, the wider the field of view.

On the other hand, a lens with a shorter focal length will also produce a view that the camera can obtain. At a distance of 16 ft (5 M) a 3.6 mm fixed lens may only provide a general description of the objects in a parking facility while the same camera with a 12 mm lens would provide sharper details of objects in the field of view (such as faces and license plate numbers) but might cover only a fraction of the facility.

You must also determine what the objective of having surveillance cameras present is—is its purpose to provide a visible deterrant or is it to be used for gathering legal evidence? It is always important to select surveillance cameras with lens specifications that capture the viewing area desired. Common security camera lens types include the following:

- *Varifocal lens*: These are optical assemblies containing several movable elements to permit changing the effective focal length (EFL). Unlike a zoom lens, a varifocal lens requires refocusing with each change. If a surveillance camera has a fixed lens, it can see only one fixed position. If it has a varifocal lens, it can focus at multiple mm settings based on the user's preference.

- *Fixed focal length lens*: These are lenses that are not provided with a means of focusing operation regardless of the distance to the subject.

- *Wide angle lens*: These provide the ability to see a wider image in confined areas than standard lens types.

- *Telephoto lens*: These are the best type of lens for seeing details at long ranges.

- *Fish eye lens*: This type of lens allows you to see an entire room but with some distortion of the image.

- *Pinhole lens*: This lens is used for applications where the camera/lens must be hidden. The front of the lens has a small opening to allow the lens to view an entire room through a small hole in the wall.

Black and White (B&W) vs. Color

There is a common misconception that color CCTV cameras offer a better picture than *B&W CCTV cameras*. The reality is that although color cameras are more enjoyable to view, both types of cameras are fully capable of offering a quality picture. The real question is what type of camera is better suited for a particular situation.

The most important practical difference between color and B&W cameras is that only color cameras can offer a full and accurate clothing and vehicle description. Law enforcement highly relies on the reported color of clothing and suspect vehicle when responding to a call for service, as it greatly increases the likelihood of catching a fleeing suspect.

IR Illumination

Cameras with *infrared illumination* of the image area permit viewing in low-light conditions. This also provides the ability to maintain a degree of secrecy by using illumination that is outside of the visible light spectrum.

An infrared security camera has infrared LED lighting (light from a region of the electromagnetic spectrum that humans cannot see) installed around the outside of the camera lens. This lighting allows the camera to capture a good image in no-light settings. With a small amount of light (a low-light setting), the infrared camera can capture a picture that looks just like daytime. A typical IR camera is shown in Figure 6.26.

FIGURE 6.26   IR camera

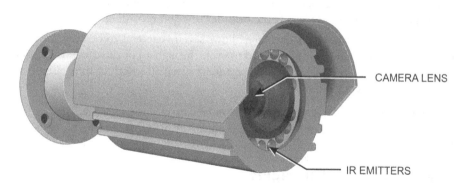

CAMERA LENS

IR EMITTERS

Camera Applications

Surveillance cameras can be mounted outside the facility to provide recognition of someone wanting to enter the security perimeter area, such as a front door or driveway gate. They should be located where no blind spots exist or where it is not practical to use other types of sensors. Cameras can be mounted on any surface area of the facility where coverage is required as long as the area is illuminated sufficiently at all times after dark.

There are certain legal implications involved in using video surveillance cameras. In particular there are privacy concerns that must be taken into account when deploying surveillance cameras. They are not to be used where there is a *reasonable expectation of privacy* by individuals. This obviously does not apply to a person breaking into a facility.

Other applications for cameras include the following categories:

- *Indoor/outdoor*: Indoor cameras are usually less expensive than outdoor types because the outdoor cameras must be housed in weatherproof enclosures. The cabling for outdoor cameras must also be suitable for temperature extremes and seasonal weather conditions.

- *Day/night*: Cameras are available that can switch from color imaging in the daytime to black and white for night operation when the illumination is too low for color. This provides the best trade-off between good color resolution during daytime monitoring and black and white during night hours when the light levels are not sufficient for color imaging.

- *Fixed vs. animated*: Cameras that are mounted in a fixed configuration always show the same areas. They are useful for monitoring areas of importance, such as high-risk areas like parking areas and door entrances. Animated cameras—such as the PZT cameras described earlier—provide the ability to move. They are mounted on a gimbaled assembly where the viewing area can be changed and have support for zooming, pan, and tilt.

- *Recording and external/interior triggers*: Digital video recorders (DVRs) are the preferred type of recording systems rather than older VCRs for surveillance cameras. Cameras can be configured to record only when a trigger is generated to initiate recording.

- Triggers can be internal types where recording is started when the scene changes. External triggers can be programmed to start recording when an alarm condition exists or when a motion detector triggers the recorder to begin recording.

- *Sequencing vs. multiplexing*: Sequencing allows several cameras to be used with a single monitor. A switcher can be programmed to cycle through all of the cameras in a surveillance system or to dwell on each camera for a specified length of time, usually in the range of 1 to 60 seconds.

  Multiplexers route the images from the surveillance system to a specific display device and are capable of recording all the camera images at the same time by tiling them on the monitor.

Camera Deployment Strategies

The purpose of investing in security cameras is to be able to view activity in critical areas or where critical assets are located. In addition to determining what specifications security cameras must possess for a given role, it is equally important to map out a camera *deployment strategy* to maximize the surveillance investment.

To accomplish this, cameras should be positioned to capture important events in all critical security areas. In particular, they should be installed in *passageways* and in locations where their field of vision covers important assets (physical equipment and/or personnel).

Passageways include *chokepoints* in the physical facility where people or other traffic must pass through a portal, such as a gate, doorway, hallway, or access street/road. Cameras in passageways are typically placed there to document entry, exit, and movement through a facility, as illustrated in Figure 6.27.

FIGURE 6.27   Monitoring passageways

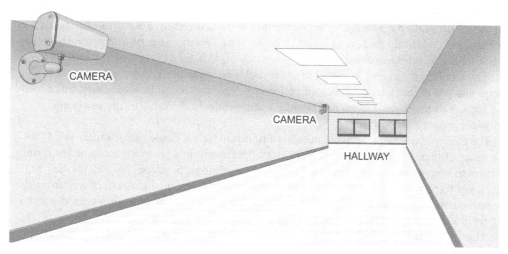

Security cameras are also routinely installed in positions that cover important assets and activities within the facility. This enables management to monitor activities around and associated with those important assets.

Bank lobbies are great examples of both placement strategies; cameras are positioned to record activities around the bank's parking area and exterior, as well as in hallways that lead to the vault and offices, as illustrated in Figure 6.28. In addition, most banks have cameras arranged so they can focus on each teller station to monitor the handling of money and transactions.

FIGURE 6.28   Asset monitoring

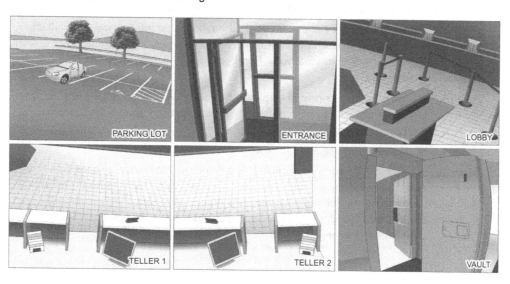

Determining actual camera placement is a matter of first deciding whether the camera is required to provide an *overview* or *detailed view*. An *overview* generally covers a wide field of view such as over a parking lot or warehouse floor. Conversely, a *detailed view* is required for targeting relatively narrow fields of view featuring specific areas of interest, such as the bank teller stations mentioned earlier.

The number of cameras involved in the installation depends on the number of passageways and assets that have been identified for viewing/monitoring. In some cases, this depends on the size of the organization, and in others it depends on the value of the assets and physical geography involved.

For example, a small operation may need to install only a single camera to provide surveillance of their key assets. For medium-sized operations, it is far more common for installations to involve dozens of cameras. In large organizations, hundreds of cameras may be deployed to provide their security and surveillance needs. The goal is to effectively cover the areas and assets identified through risk analysis procedures. These procedures are discussed in detail in Chapter 8, "ICS Security Governance and Risk Management."

After the installation points have been determined, the next step in the deployment strategy is to determine the specifications of the cameras to be used at each installation point. In general, there are four key characteristics to consider:

- *Is a fixed or movable field of view required?* Fixed cameras are typically employed for overview functions. They provide a fixed field of view, so they must be set up to effectively cover the desired passageway or asset. Therefore, they must have the desired focal length and angle to cover these items.

  Remotely controlled PZT cameras are generally used where detailed views are required. However, in some cases, it may be more economical to install several fixed cameras in different locations than to mount a single PZT camera, which requires an attendant to operate effectively.

- *What type of image display is required?* From the previous discussion in this chapter, you should recall that common image display options include the following:

  - *Color*: Color cameras are the default general-purpose cameras in video surveillance applications today. The one application where color cameras lag behind other camera technologies is in low-light situations. In those cases, infrared or thermal cameras are generally advised.

  - *Infrared*: Infrared cameras provide clear black-and-white images in very low-light settings. However, they tend to be significantly more expensive than color cameras.

  - *Thermal*: Thermal cameras tend to be very expensive and produce only silhouettes. However, they also require no light to work.

- *What level of display definition is required?* Is a standard video display acceptable for the view being addressed, or is something with a higher definition required? One of the biggest complaints associated with standard definition systems is their inability to deliver a signal that enables law enforcement and the courts to positively identify criminal suspects after a crime.

- *What type of signal processing and transmission is best suited for the installation?* As described earlier in the chapter, the choices here include analog, digital, and IP cameras. IP cameras continue to gain acceptance over other types of cameras due to their ability to capture and transmit data electronically.

IP cameras provide more robust connectivity options than traditional analog and digital cameras. They can work directly with a host computer without additional hardware. They are also more compatible with wireless networking options than other camera technologies.

Two other important considerations when recording video for security purposes are how much video needs to be stored, and for how long? The answer to these questions enables the organization to determine its *storage capacity* needs.

Security video by its nature requires a substantial amount of *storage space*. As such, there is always a trade-off between storage costs and the risk the organization faces. A single video surveillance camera can consume multiple gigabytes of storage capacity in a single day. With this in mind, the requirement for how long the organization needs to store surveillance video becomes a major decision point. Depending on the nature of the organization and the types of risks they face, the storage requirements may require that several weeks or months of video be stored for each camera they install.

As mentioned earlier, most organizations do not employ a single camera for their surveillance needs; they may employ dozens or hundreds of cameras. To store video data coming from this, many cameras can easily require hundreds of terabytes of data storage.

There are three common video storage types employed to meet such needs:

- *Internal storage*: Storing video information on the internal disk drive (or drives) in the DVR. This solution is practical only for small organizations that use few cameras and only store the video information for a short time.

- *Peripheral storage or direct-attached storage (DAS)*: This technique employs additional disk drive storage devices that are attached directly to the DVR via USB or eSATA connections, as depicted in Figure 6.29. Direct-attached storage does not involve using an IP address to offload the video to the external device.

FIGURE 6.29   DAS video storage

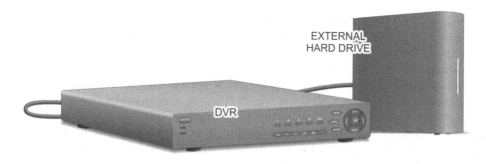

- *Networked storage*: Using networking techniques to store IP-based video on remote computers or video servers. The most common techniques for doing this include network-attached storage (NAS) and storage area network (SAN) technologies, illustrated in Figure 6.30.

FIGURE 6.30   NAS and SAN storage systems

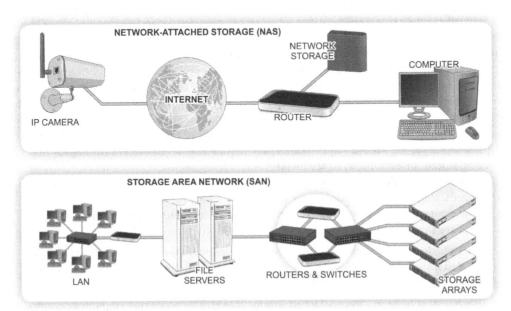

Physical Security for ICS

The first level of protection in an industrial or utility environment must occur at the physical level. As with all other network environments, *physical security* involves taking steps to combat theft, prevent physical damage, maintain system integrity and services, and limit unauthorized disclosure of information.

In industrial and utility settings, the deployment of physical security devices and measures are often subject to a number of different factors including environmental, safety, regulatory, legal, and other requirements that fall outside of the organization's control. These factors must be identified and included in the organization's overall security plan. In many cases, this plan is closely integrated with the organization's overall *plant safety program*.

In addition to securing the equipment against physical access by attackers, the environment for each asset must be compatible with its design. This includes providing reasonable protection from loss, fire, theft, unintentional distribution, or environmental damage.

In addition to securing these assets during normal operation, it is also important to provide physical security controls when they must be transported and/or maintained. This involves creating and implementing specific policies and processes for transporting, handling, storing, performing maintenance procedures, and decommissioning/destruction efforts for all OT/IT network assets.

Industrial Processes/Generating Facilities

One of the primary goals of the physical security plan for industrial settings is to keep personnel out of hazardous situations while still enabling them to do their jobs. Of course, physical access controls must be in place to enforce limited access to the physical components of the production processes and the OT system. In OT settings, these measures are employed to prevent many types of undesirable activities, including the following:

- Theft, damage, destruction, modification, or manipulation of OT devices or systems, including communication media and interfaces

- Visual or photographic observation of critical or sensitive assets, including not taking pictures or creating images of the processes through other means

- The introduction of unauthorized systems or devices into the OT system for the purposes of hardware manipulation, tracking, communication sniffing, or eavesdropping

In addition to providing physical separation for ICS equipment, it is also important that this equipment be clearly identified as ICS equipment through color-coded tagging and labeling.

Sensors and actuators require as much protection as the process controllers and network devices. If an input device can be physically accessed without notice, then it can be manipulated to falsify process system data. The result can be a total loss of control over the process or a subtle generation of harmful effects over some period of time.

Control Center/Company Offices

At the control center or corporate office facilities, physical security typically takes on more of an enterprise security nature. Major concerns in these environments involve limiting physical access to any information assets in the environment.

- Unauthorized physical access to sensitive locations, such as server rooms and security offices

- Unauthorized physical access to servers, SCADA masters, and historians along with the data on them

- Unauthorized physical access to user computers, switches, and routers

Like IT network environments, OT masters, servers, and historians should be located in locked areas, and devices and mechanisms used to perform authentication for these locations should also be protected. Likewise, any network connectivity devices on the OT network (network switches, routers, and media) should be located in secured areas, preferably in areas where only authorized personnel can access them.

Physical Server Access Control

At its most fundamental level, network administrators must have control over their physical server environment to provide a comprehensive security setting. This is accomplished by strictly limiting physical access to the *servers*. This is most commonly accomplished by placing them in protected *server rooms* that have automatic locks on the door and computer chassis.

Depending on the management structure of the network, the server (or network) administrator is generally responsible for determining which personnel can have access to the server room and may require a logbook entry for anyone working inside the server room. The presence of unauthorized individuals in the server room should be reported to the administrator immediately. Violations of any server room security measures should be reported to the appropriate administrator for corrective action.

Reasonable alternatives to a separate or centralized server room include use of a locked cabinet or even a secure rack.

To provide hardware security, companies and utilities often place *physical intrusion detection systems*, such as motion sensors, card readers, cameras, and alarms in server rooms and on their server machines and racks. They also install locks on the doors of the server rooms as well as on each individual server rack. They may also lock each server chassis. Figure 6.31 illustrates typical server security measures.

FIGURE 6.31   Server security points

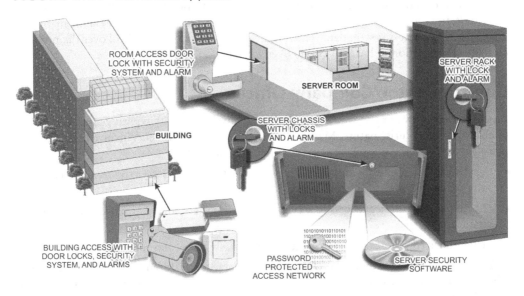

Remote Monitoring

While preventing unauthorized access is the first line of defense in physical security, layers of additional security measures are crucial to preventing security breaches from escalating into serious events. A closely related second tier of defense is *intrusion detection* that enables potential intruders to be detected and removed before they can cause problems. This level of security involves detection devices that are monitored or that can create an alarm.

These intrusion detection devices provide remote monitoring capabilities that can be monitored 24/7/365 by operators in the main office. The images, data, and alarm conditions can also be manipulated by the SCADA system to issue notices to key personnel that may not be in the operations center, such as off-duty security managers, private security response teams, or other first responders.

It is also important to monitor the performance of remote equipment to detect deteriorating conditions and/or security events. The SCADA system should provide supervisory monitoring of specific remotely located security equipment, intelligent process controllers, and networking equipment, as well as the general performance of the power system.

NERC CIP-006-1

In North America, the electrical utility systems are governed by an organization known as the *North American Electrical Reliability Corporation* or *NERC*. One of its major contributions to utility security is the creation and administration of the industry's *Critical Infrastructure Protection (CIP)* standards. These standards are designed to help *Bulk Electrical System (BES)* operators (power generators and suppliers) secure their physical and cyber assets.

The different components of the CIP standard are discussed over several chapters of this book. Of particular interest in this chapter are the requirements specified by *CIP-006-1: Physical Security of Critical BES Cyber Assets*.

This standard requires BES operators to create and implement a strategy with plans and policies to secure their critical cyber assets from unauthorized physical access. While each organization is given latitude in how they meet the requirements, their plans and policies must address the following areas:

- Implement and document acceptable physical access control methods
- Implement and document monitoring and logging of ingress at all points of its physical security perimeters
- Implement and document access log retention strategies
- Implement a physical access control maintenance and testing plan

The plan may use a combination of physical access controls such as smart card key, locks, and perimeter controls. Typical perimeter controls used in BES facilities include fences with locked gates, control rooms or houses, guards, and site access policies. Under this CIP standard, the physical access controls specified in the plan must be active 24 hours per day, 7 days a week.

Monitoring can be used as a complement or alternative to physical access control. Typical monitoring controls employed in BES facilities include physical intrusion detection and control systems (alarm systems to detect motion or entry into a controlled area), video surveillance systems, and human observation plans. As with physical access controls, physical access monitoring controls must be operational 24/7. All unauthorized access attempts shall be reviewed immediately and handled in accordance with the procedures specified in Requirement CIP-008.

Physical entry through any access point of the physical security perimeters must be logged 24/7. The logging system must be capable of uniquely identifying individuals along with their times of access. The plan must also specify the retention policy of the physical access logs. Ordinary logs must be retained for at least 90 days, while reportable incident log retention is specified under CIP-008-6, discussed in Chapter 10, "ICS Security Monitoring and Incident Response," as being three calendar years.

To meet the CIP-006 standard, the plan must include a maintenance and testing program to ensure that the controls are all functioning properly.

Review Questions

The following questions test your knowledge of the material presented in this chapter.

1. _____ is the science, technique, and art of establishing a system of exclusion and inclusion for tangible assets.

2. _____ is a report that incorrectly authenticates the individual, which could lead to providing access to equipment or data that this person should not have.

3. Define lux rating as it applies to surveillance cameras, and describe the typical range of lux ratings for these devices.

4. Using natural design elements, such as structures and landscaping to guide people as they enter and exit spaces, is referred to as _____.

5. What type of security device is used for programming, controlling, and operating access control and management devices?

6. What type of cameras provide the best resolution in low-light conditions?

7. What type of image sensor is used in cameras designed to produce the highest-quality images?

8. _____ systems are used to notify supervisory security personnel when an unauthorized access is attempted.

9. Describe technologies used to report alarm conditions to key personnel or remote monitoring organizations.

10. _____ employs structures, systems, and devices to prevent unauthorized entry and create a clear difference between what is public and private.

11. With _____, the condition monitoring system can record and signal each time a specific gate or door is unlocked (granting access) and what type of access was granted.

12. List locations where perimeter area input sensors are typically placed in an intrusion detection and reporting system.

13. What physical technique is used to create a physical security zone on a security controller?

14. List the four factors involved in an authentication system.

15. Name the two major concerns associated with storing video surveillance information, particularly in larger enterprises.

Exam Questions

1. Securing this space involves controlling who can move (walk, drive, fly) across the physical or logical line that marks a perimeter, such as property lines or the exterior walls of a building or complex.

    A. The interior space

    B. The inner perimeter

    C. The outer perimeter

    D. The primary zone

2. Which of the following is not a subsystem involved in infrastructure security management?

    A. Access control and monitoring systems

    B. Intrusion detection and reporting systems

    C. Video surveillance systems

    D. Corporate cybersecurity policies

3. From the following options, select the entries that represent a physical barrier. (Select all that apply.)

    A. A locked door

    B. A receptionist

    C. An RFID badge reader

    D. A surveillance camera

4. Which surveillance camera type can be viewed from virtually anywhere in the world?

    A. A digital camera

    B. A digital IP camera

    C. An analog camera

    D. A hybrid camera

5. From the following report types, select the options that would produce an incorrect rejection of the individual, thereby locking them out of a facility or security area that they should have access to. (Select all that apply.)

    A. False rejection

    B. False acceptance

    C. False negative failures

    D. False positive failures

6. Being able to control the ingress, egress, and regress to an asset are based on
    _____.

    A. Authentication

    B. Permissions

    C. Inherence

    D. Authorization

7. What type of lens used in surveillance cameras enables operators to view an entire room but with some distortion of the image?

    A. Fisheye lens

    B. Telephoto lens

    C. Fixed focal length lens

    D. Varifocal lens

8. What is the meaning of lux rating as it applies to surveillance cameras?

    A. Rating for the size of the camera lens

    B. Amount of light per square meter required for an acceptable image

    C. Resolution of the camera lens

    D. Specifies the color resolution of a camera

9. Which of the following video storage strategies employ networking techniques to store IP-based video on remote computers or video servers? (Select all that apply.)

    A. Internet area storage (IAS)

    B. Network-attached storage (NAS)

    C. Storage area network (SAN)

    D. Network peripheral storage (NPS)

    E. Direct-attached storage (DAS)

10. Which of the following standards are designed to help bulk electrical system (BES) operators secure their physical and cyber assets in North America?

    A. NERC CIP

    B. ISO/IEC 7816-4:2020

    C. ISO/IEC 1443

    D. NIST 800 R2

Chapter

7

Access Management

OBJECTIVES

Upon completion of this chapter, you will be able to:

1. Demonstrate knowledge of access control models

   - MAC
   - DAC
   - RBAC
   - RB-RBAC
   - ABAC
   - CBAC

2. Demonstrate knowledge of Directory Services

   - Windows
   - Linux

3. Show knowledge of user access management

4. Describe General Access Control Guidance for Cloud Systems

   - IaaS Systems
   - PaaS Systems
   - SaaS Systems

Introduction

In the previous chapter, you were introduced to terminology and practices associated with physical security management. In this chapter, the discussion moves to logical access control models and practices associated with IT and OT networks.

These policies should be designed to reflect the three objectives associated with the classical model of information security: *confidentiality*, *integrity*, and *availability (CIA)*. However, recall from Chapter 5, "Cybersecurity Essentials for ICS," that in an OT environment, an *AIC* approach is typically more important than the traditional CIA efforts used in IT network environments.

The sheriff on any network is the *network administrator*. In network environments, these are the people responsible for implementing the organization's security policies on the network equipment. In larger organizations, specialized administrative roles are typically created to handle different aspects of the network's operation. This may include having separate server and network administrators. The *server admin* or *system administrator (sysadmin)* is responsible for the design, implementation, and maintenance of the organization's security policies and the server computers, while the network administrator provides the same functions for the network and its media and connectivity devices.

The division of administrative duties may also involve a special security administrator who is responsible for performing information security tasks for the servers, hosts, and connectivity devices in the network. In these settings, the separation of administrative duties should be as distinct, defined, and controlled as possible.

One of these administrators is typically responsible for determining who gains access to the operation of the network's servers, network connectivity devices, and data. In most organizations, they implement the organization's policy statements through the network operating system management tools that control "who" has access to the network and its resources and what they can do with them. In Chapter 4, "ICS Module and Element Hardening," you were introduced to three traditional access control models. Those traditional models have been augmented by additional access control models, as described here:

- *Mandatory access control (MAC)*: The system establishes which users or groups may access files, folders, and other resources.

- *Discretionary access control (DAC)*: This includes configurations where the user has the discretion to decide who has access to their objects and to what extent.

- *Nondiscretionary, role-based access control (RBAC)*: This is based on job roles each user has within the organization.

- *Rule-based access control (RB-RBAC)*: Like RBAC, RB-RBAC is first based on job roles but is then further restricted by rule-sets to modify access within the role.

- *Attribute-based access control (ABAC)*: This includes policy-based identity and access control management that operates by combining attributes together to grant or deny access. This concept was introduced in the NIST Cybersecurity Framework and is tied to subject, action, object, and contextual attributes that are combined in if-then-and Boolean statements.

- *Context-based access control (CBAC)*: This is an access control model featured in firewalls to maintain TCP/UDP network traffic for deeper packet payload inspection.

Access Control Models

Access control is basically a strategy for identifying people doing specific jobs, authenticating them through some type of identification system, and then giving them keys only to the assets they need access to and nothing more. In the previous chapter, you were shown how access control is provided in the physical infrastructure environment.

In the IT environment, this begins with providing users with usernames and passwords to get into the computing devices, files, folders, and network connections they need to do their jobs. Then the level of access they are given to each asset must be configured to guarantee that they have the appropriate levels of permissions to resources they need to accomplish their jobs. Does Bob need to be able to create (Full Control) original documents, or is he responsible only for editing them (Write) or simply reviewing them (Read)? To accomplish this, the administrator must determine what levels of permissions are required for each group or individual to perform their duties. This is where access control models come into play.

Mandatory Access Control

Recall from Chapter 4 that *MAC* strategies assign sensitivity labels to network objects and grant access to the users based on their permission level, as illustrated in Figure 7.1. Under this model only the owner (and designated custodians, meaning administrators) are given management of the access controls. This means the end user has no control over any settings that provide any privileges to anyone.

There are actually two versions of the MAC security model—one focused on *data confidentiality* (Bell-LaPadula) and the other on *data integrity* (Biba). The *Bell-LaPadula* version specifies that a user at a specific security level (say top secret) can write at that level but not at lower levels. However, they can read at lower security levels (write up/read down). The *Biba* version permits users with lower security levels to read higher and users with higher security levels can write for lower security levels (read up/write down).

FIGURE 7.1   Mandatory access control

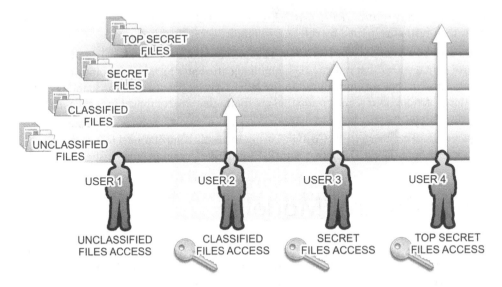

Biba is typically used in business networks where management can write information for employees to read. Bell-LaPadula is more common in government/military networks where clearance levels determine which types of information any user has access to. If you don't have the proper clearance for an asset, you don't need to know about it.

Discretionary Access Control

The *DAC model* is the least restrictive access control model because it provides individual users with complete control over assets they own along with any associated assets. This creates two major weaknesses in the DAC model.

- First, owners are provided with the ability to set a security level for other users that could result in them having higher privileges than they should.

- Second, the permissions that the user has will be extended to other assets through inheritance. This enables users to execute malware without realizing it. Such malware can potentially take advantage of the users' extended privileges to access higher levels of data in the system.

Role-Based Access Control

The *RBAC model* provides access control based on the position the user has within the organization. Each network user or group is assigned one or more roles, as described in Figure 7.2.

Each role is then assigned specific privileges to specific objects.

For the most part, the RBAC model makes it easier for the network administrators to manage multiple users in a medium or large network. However, when users are brought into the network that have special job responsibilities outside of the group, special steps must be taken to provide them with the additional access requirements.

FIGURE 7.2   Role-based access control

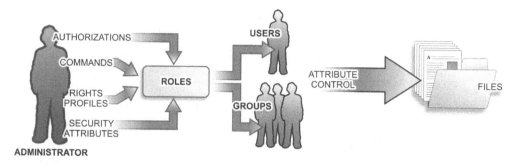

Rule-Based Access Control

Under the *rule-based access control* model, the network administrator defines user roles as in the role-based methodology previously described and then implements rules criteria to those definitions, such as time-of-day restrictions to prevent the user from accessing data outside of work hours.

In each strategy type, the principle of least privilege should be implemented when providing users with access to objects through rights and permissions assignments. Under the least privilege rule, each user is granted only the levels of access required to perform their job roles. Applying this principle consistently limits the damage that can be inflicted by a security breech to the initial task, process, or user.

Attribute-Based Access Control

Compared to the four traditional user-based access control models listed earlier, *attribute-based access control (ABAC)* is considered to be a new-generation AC model based on complex Boolean rule-sets derived from policy statements. This model manipulates three types of components to determine access or denial to a resource.

- *Architecture*: ABAC is applied to apps and data in a three-point architecture: the Policy Enforcement Point (PEP), the Policy Decision Point (PDP), and the Policy Information Point (PIP).

- *Attributes*: Attributes describe the *subject* (user attempting to access the resource), the *action* (the activity is being attempted), the *object* (resource being accessed), and the environment (the context that may involve such things as time, location, IP address, or other control factor).

- *Policies*: These are scenario and technology statements that combine to determine whether access is granted or denied.

When access to a resource is requested, the PEP inspects the request and sends an authorization request to the PDP section. The PDP compares the request to its policy statements and consults the PIP for links to external data and then issues a Permit/Deny decision. Figure 7.3 describes the ABAC process.

FIGURE 7.3   Attribute-based access control

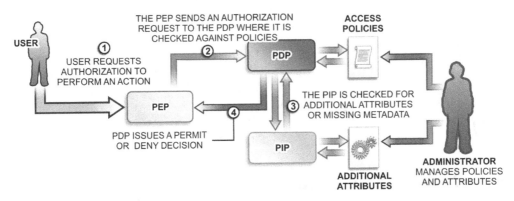

Context-Based Access Control

Context-based access control (CBAC) is an intelligent deep-packet filtering feature used in firewalls to permit specified TCP/UDP traffic to pass through the firewall. It uses stateful inspection information obtained from the Application layer protocol to open ports in the firewall's ACL. This augments the role of the ACL, which provides access control only up to the transport layer.

The CBAC maintains a state table in the firewall's memory. When a device within the trusted network initiates a session, a dynamic entry is placed in the state table, and the traffic is allowed to pass through the firewall and out of the network. The CBAC mechanism opens the temporary hole in the firewall's ACL for the requested session to allow the *reply* to the outbound traffic to pass through into the trusted network. The CBAC only allows traffic from outside the network to enter if it was initiated by devices inside the trusted network.

Key Security Components within Access Controls

Within the AC models described earlier, logical access control is primarily implemented at the server level and is based on four key security components:

- *Passwords*: Passwords are the most basic logical access control mechanism in existence. Password usage and requirements were covered previously in Chapter 4, so we will not revisit them here.

- *Group policies*: These are directory services database objects that administrators use to create group access and restrictions to network assets based on the user's position and job role in the organization. These objects enable administrators to implement these policies across the network from a single management environment.

- *Access control lists (ACLs)*: ACLs are lists that attach permissions to network objects that the system uses to control access to assets (programs, folders, files, printers) as well as what activities can be performed on those assets.

- *User account restrictions*: Account restrictions are the last access control component to be added to the model. These are configurations that administrators apply to user accounts (instead of folders, files, and printers) to limit their activities on a local machine (local accounts) or across the network (domain accounts).

> While the network's servers are the primary location for implementing these tools to create the desired security model, they are not the only components in the network that use these tools. Network connectivity devices such as managed switches, routers, firewalls, and security appliances use passwords, ACLs, and restrictions to control access to organizational assets.

Directory Services

One of the tools that administrators rely on to manage access control across networks are the directory services structures running on network server operating systems. *Directory services* are distributed, customizable information storage structures that provide a single point from which users can search for and locate resources scattered throughout a network.

These structures also provide network administrators with a single point of management for network objects and resources. These resources typically include information about users (names, email addresses, etc.) and systems (hosts, file shares, printers, etc.). They are a necessity for any medium to large enterprise network. As such, an enterprise-level directory service typically provides several critical functions for the network:

- An information store that can be distributed across several geographical locations

- An information store that users can employ to efficiently search through the enterprise for information that may be located throughout the network

- An information store that is accessible from many different operating systems

- An information store that can accept new objects as the network evolves

The most recognizable directory service structure has to be the *Domain Name System (DNS)* that the Internet is based on. Enterprise network-level directory services debuted in the Novel Netware operating system as *Novel Directory Service (NDS)*. This structure has since been purchased from Novell and rebranded as *NetIQ* eDirectory.

The directory services you are likely to encounter in current enterprise networks are based on the *Lightweight Directory Access Protocol (LDAP)*, also known as the *X.500-lite standard*. This protocol provides a vendor-neutral protocol for creation and access control of distributed network directory services using IP networks. A number of different DS software products have been developed on the LDAP protocol. The following sections discuss the directory services used with the Microsoft Windows and Linux network environments.

Active Directory

The central feature of the Microsoft Windows network architecture is the *Active Directory (AD)* structure. Active Directory is a distributed database of user and resource information that describes the makeup of the network (i.e., users and application settings). It is also a method of implementing a distributed authentication process.

Windows remains a domain-dependent operating system. It uses domains as boundaries for administration, security, and replication purposes. Each domain must be represented by at least one domain controller. The domain controller is a server set up to hold the directory database for the network.

This database contains information about user accounts, group accounts, and computer accounts. It tracks the names of all the objects and requests for resources within the domain. You may also find this database referred to as the *Security Accounts Manager* (*SAM*). This feature helps to centralize system and user configurations, as well as data backups on the server in the Windows client network.

The Active Directory structure employs two common Internet standards—LDAP and DNS. The LDAP protocol is used to define how directory information is accessed and exchanged. DNS is the Internet standard for resolving domain names to actual IP addresses. It is also the standard for exchanging directory information with clients and other directories.

Active Directory arranges domains in a hierarchy and establishes trust relationships among all the domains in a tree-like structure, as illustrated in Figure 7.4.

FIGURE 7.4   Basic Active Directory structure

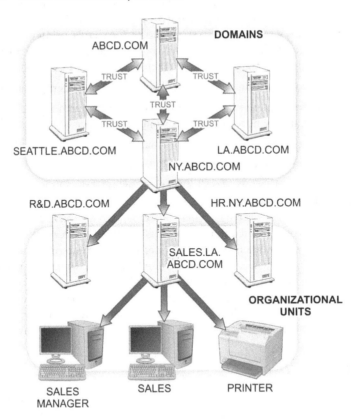

A *tree* is a collection of objects that share the same DNS name. Active Directory can subdivide domains into *organizational units* (sales, administration, etc.) that contain other units, or *leaf objects*, such as printers, users, and so on.

Conversely, Windows can create an organizational structure containing more than one tree. This structure is referred to as a *forest*. Figure 7.5 expands the AD structure to demonstrate these relationships.

The Windows operating system automatically joins all the domains within a tree through two-way trusts. *Trusts* are relationships that enable users to move between domains and perform prescribed types of operations.

If a trust relationship is established between the sales and marketing domains in the example and a similar trust exists between the sales and administration domains, then a trust relationship also exists between the marketing and administration domains. Trusts enable administrators to provide users and groups with different rights to objects.

Rights are permission settings that control a user's (or groups of users') authority to access objects and perform operations (such as reading or writing to a file). Administrative rights provide authority to users down to the organizational unit (OU) level. OUs are containers that hold all the objects within a network domain. These units can be used to provide a hierarchical structure to the domain by holding other OUs.

FIGURE 7.5   Active Directory relationships

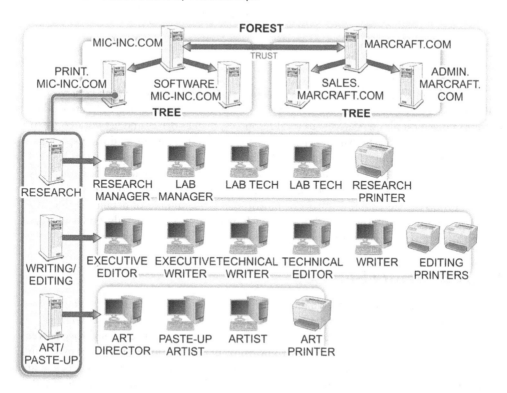

Administrative rights do not cross boundaries established at the domain level, but they can be inherited by other OUs having subordinate positions within the same tree. On the other hand, user rights must be established for individual users or for members of groups.

Using groups allows common rights to be assigned to multiple users with a single administrative action (as opposed to setting up and maintaining rights for each individual in, say, a 150-person accounting staff).

The primary tool for working with the Active Directory is the *Active Directory Users and Computers* console, depicted in Figure 7.6. The organizational units of a domain contain users, groups, and resources. The Active Directory Manager tool is used to add users, groups, and organizational units to the directory.

FIGURE 7.6   Active Directory Users and Computers

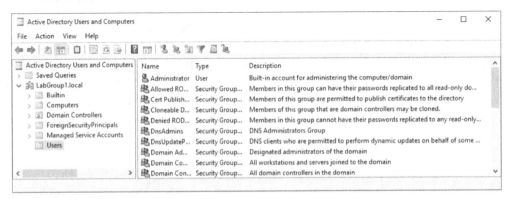

The overall operation of the Windows environments is governed by *system policies*. Basically, policies give administrators control over users. Using system policies, the system administrator can give or limit users' access to local resources, such as drives and network connections.

Administrators can establish policies that force certain users to log in during specified times and lock them out of the system at all other times. System policies also enable the administrator to send updates and configure desktops for network clients. Fundamentally, any item found in the Control Panel can be regulated through system policies.

With group policies, administrators can institute a large number of detailed settings for users throughout an enterprise, without establishing each setting manually. GPOs can be used to apply a large number of changes to machines and users through the AD.

Linux Directory Services

Older Linux distributions supported a directory service structure called *Network Information Services* (NIS). However, newer distributions have shifted to LDAP-based directory services. These include Red Hat's 389 Directory Server, Apache Directory Server, and OpenLDAP, along with a list of lesser known or proprietary directory server platforms.

Like Active Directory, the LDAP-based Linux platforms provide a single directory source for system information lookup and authentication. Storing user information in an LDAP-based directory server makes the network scalable, manageable, and secure.

Unlike Microsoft's AD, directory services are not integral components of the Linux OS structure. Instead, they are added to the structure after it has been installed. However, after installation, Linux-based directory service modules employ GUI-based and menu-driven tools, like the one depicted in Figure 7.7, to define organizational units for the network.

FIGURE 7.7   Linux directory service menu

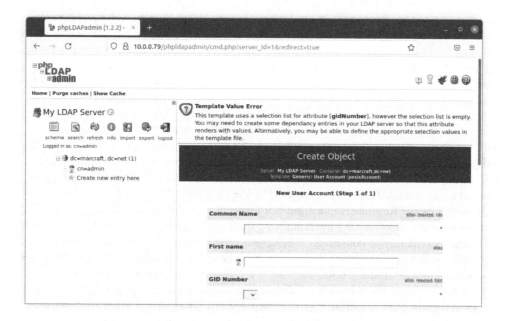

Typically, these directory services servers provide a network-based registry that enables administrators to centrally store user identity and application information, such as the following:

- Application settings
- User profiles
- Group permissions
- Policies
- Access control data

By storing and retrieving this type of information in the directory structure, users and applications become location independent. Users are able to log into any location within the network and have access to the same applications and data they would at a designated location, or any other location within the network.

Application Runtime and Execution Control

Software applications have become increasingly complex, distributed, and interconnected. The move toward cloud computing, containerization, and hybrid architecture solutions has increased the attack surfaces for these applications. As these moves redefine the terms edge and perimeter in our IT/OT network architecture models, the pressure to provide additional security has increased.

Runtime attacks are memory-based attacks that take advantage of the application's code as it executes in runtime memory. Attackers exploit the lack of boundaries between the application's code and data to inject malicious code into the memory structure. These types of attacks have traditionally been extremely hard to detect and defend against.

Most current perimeter security tools, such as firewalls and IPS, are far removed from the applications' runtime environment in memory. These devices have no way of knowing the runtime conditions of applications and therefore, cannot differentiate between real threats and potential threats. Likewise, vulnerability scanners can't keep up with cloud containers that spin up and down rapidly, so they cannot distinguish between vulnerabilities that are exposed to the outside from those protected by the edge protection devices.

However, newer **Runtime Application Self Protection** (**RASP**) tools have been developed to improve application security by monitoring their runtime environment inputs for potential unwanted changes or tampering. When these activities are detected, the RASP-protected application takes action to block them and notify the user or security personnel. Other possible actions include shutting down the app or terminating the session.

Application execution control is a cybersecurity mitigation strategy designed to protect against malicious code executing on computing systems. The strategy begins with identifying approved applications to run on all machines in the environment. Once the apps have been identified, the next step is to create a rule to ensure that only those apps are allowed to run on the machines. Finally, implement encrypted hash rules, publisher certificate rules, and path rules to enforce the application execution controls. Folder, file, and application permissions must be configured to block all unauthorized modifications.

The application control policy should include provisions for logging blocked malicious code execution attempts. These event logs should be configured to provide filenames, date/time stamps, and user names of all blocked attempts. This information can be valuable in identifying the person or organization responsible for the attempt.

These rules should be maintained as part of the organization's change management policy and they should be reviewed and validated at least annually.

User Access Management

There are basically two classes of users in a network—*administrators* and *users*. These classes may also exist at two different levels—in local account databases located on the individual client devices and in network account databases located on network servers. Recall that network account settings typically take precedence over local settings.

In a Microsoft Windows environment, there are several *default user accounts* after installation. These accounts include the following:

- *Administrator*: This is the main administrative management account that has full access to the system and all its management tools.

- *Guest account*: This is a catchall account used to provide access to users who do not have a user account on the computer. This account should be disabled after user accounts have been established.

- *HelpAssistant*: This is a special Windows account used with its Remote Assistance utility to authenticate users connecting through it. This account is enabled whenever a remote assistance invitation is created, and it is automatically disabled when all invitations have expired.

- *SUPPORT_XXXXX*: This is a special Microsoft account used to provide remote support through its Help and Support Service utility.

- *DefaultAccount*: In later versions of Windows 10 and Windows Server 2016, a new system management account, referred to as the Default System Management Account (DSMA) or DefaultAccount, was introduced.

These default user accounts can be renamed but not deleted. The initial Windows Administrator accounts password is set up during the installation process.

As with Microsoft-based network environments, Linux systems employ a "users and groups" structure to control access to local and network resources (files, directories, and peripheral devices). Each person who is enabled to access the Linux system must be given a username. With the exception of the *root superuser*, usernames are created by administrative users as they are required.

Users are added to the Linux system through the useradd command-line tool, while existing user account information can be modified through the usermod command. The passwd command in conjunction with the username created with useradd (*passwd username*) will enable you to establish a password requirement for accessing the system as the new user.

 The root account has unlimited access to the Linux operating system and its configuration parameters and is provided for administrative purposes. For security purposes, you may want to lock the root user account after creating users and groups to prevent others from using the default user account without a username and password.

A given network may employ a single administrator that has comprehensive control over all aspects of the system including servers, network media, and connectivity devices. However, larger networks typically have multiple administrators who have separate, specific network duties, such as server admin, network admin, and security admin. In these situations, it is considered best practice to have only the number of administrator accounts necessary and have those accounts configured with only the rights necessary to perform their functions.

When it comes to network users who can access the services on the computer, security is always balanced against functionality. Some network environments may have a list of authorized users (employees or agents) but still need to accommodate the general public (unauthorized users or customers). In these cases, authentication methods must be set up to accommodate both types of users. Typically this involves establishing different group accounts for the diverse classes of users and then very strictly providing the resources needed by each group.

Establishing User and Group Accounts

Administrators in corporate and industrial networks create user and group accounts for network members that include specific *access rights* and *permissions* to the network and its resources. Network users are allowed or denied access to read, modify, and examine files and folders based upon the access control policy that has been established for them, either as individuals or by their position in different network *groups*.

Authentication may be applied to certain individuals through an inheritance process based on being included in an enabled group. For example, all members of the accounting department may be provided with *inherited access* to accounting programs and files due to their inclusion in the company's *accounting group*.

Administrators use *group accounts* to collectively deal with user accounts that have common needs. Doing so saves time by allowing them to issue user rights and resource access permissions to everyone in the group at once. However, even if a user is granted access to certain resources, the administrator can limit the scope of activities the user can conduct with different files and folders.

Windows Active Directory Default Security Group Accounts

Windows Server versions provide numerous default groups to manage various user types. Windows Server 2019 offers more than 45 default *Active Directory (AD) groups* to work with. A complete list of Active Directory Security Groups for Windows Server versions from 2008 to present can be found at https://docs.microsoft.com/en-us/windows/security/identity-protection/access-control/active-directory-security-groups. Some of the key default group accounts in Windows Server systems include the following:

- *Administrators*: Members of this group have full access to the computer and its tools and can perform all management functions. This group automatically includes the Administrator user account as a member.

- *Guests*: This default group has minimized access to the system, and all members share the same user profile. The Guest user account is automatically a member of this group.

- *Power Users*: Power Users is a special group that has permissions to perform many management tasks on the system but does not have the full administrative privileges of the Administrator account. Power Users can create and manage users and groups. Also, they do not have access to files and folders on NTFS volumes unless they are granted permissions to them through other sources. There are no members in this group when it is created.

- *Backup Operators*: As the name implies, members of this group can back up and restore all files on the computer. Through the backup utility, members of this group have access to the system's entire file system. There are no members in this group when it is created.

- *Network Configuration Operators*: Members of this group can manage different aspects of the system's network configuration. In particular, they can modify TCP/IP properties; enable, disable, and rename connections; and perform `ipconfig` operations. This group is empty when it is created.

- *Users*: This is a catchall group with limited default permissions. Except for the Guest account, all user accounts created on the system, including the administrator account, are made members of this group by default.

- *Remote Desktop Users*: Members of this Windows group have user rights to log on to the system remotely to perform Remote Desktop activities. The group has no members by default.

Windows Domain Accounts

Windows server systems also support *Domain User and Group accounts* when used in a *domain environment*. In a domain environment all the members of the network share a common directory database and are organized into various levels. The domain is identified by a unique name and is administered as a single unit having common rules and procedures.

Domain accounts are created on Windows *domain controllers* through their Active Directory Users and Computers utility and are stored in the *Active Directory database*. When a Windows client device is placed in a domain environment, some group memberships are automatically changed to reflect this.

- *Domain Admins*: This group is added to the local Administrators group so that domain administrators will have administrative control over all the computers in their domain.

- *Domain Users group*: This group is added to the local Users group.

- *Domain Guests group*: This group is added to the local Guests group.

These groups are all a function of the Windows domain controllers and exist only in Windows domain environments. The automatic addition of these groups in domain environments makes it easier for domain administrators to configure access to the local computer's resources. The groups are not permanent additions and can be removed at the administrator's discretion.

Linux Group Accounts

As with other multiuser operating systems, individual Linux users are commonly made members of groups for administrative purposes. Because of the relationships that exist within a group, the file generated by the user becomes the property of the members in the group.

Unlike Windows, the list of default groups that exists after installation varies between different Linux distributions. Some common Linux groups that appear in most distributions include the following:

- *games*: This group provides access to game software.
- *users*: This is the standard, default Linux users group.
- *wheel*: An administrative group that typically provides access to user creation and configuration utilities (su and sudo commands).
- *daemon*: This is a standard, default user/group that has privilege to execute daemon programs (background processes) that run without direction from the user. In the Microsoft realm, this type of program is referred to as a Terminate and Stay Resident program, and most resemble services running in the Windows environment.
- *bin*: This is a standard, default Linux group that historically provided running executable files. The bin reference is based on the binary (executable) file types stored there. The folder contains scripts and commands that can be executed to perform a task. The commands in this directory can be run by every user.
- *mail*: This group has special mail privileges.
- *root*: The root admin group is a standard, default Linux group that has complete administrative control of the system.
- *nobody*: This is the unprivileged group.
- *disk*: This provides access to "block devices" such as disk drives and optical drives.

This list shows only a few of the common groups that may be installed or added to a given Linux installation. The tool for adding groups in Linux is groupadd. Group information is modified through the groupmod command, and users are added to the group through the usermod command.

Group Account Security

When dealing with group accounts, there are a few security-related actions to keep in mind.

- *Remove or disable unused default accounts,* such as the Guest account. Left unattended, these accounts can be used by attackers to exploit them. If default accounts must be retained, change their names as their standard authentication credentials are well known to potential attackers. Also, severely restrict access, along with rights and permissions available, to these accounts.
- *Create user groups* that encompass the functions associated with different types of users who have common needs and then assign rights and permissions to each group according to the functional needs of the group.
- *Create user accounts* and assign them to groups according to their job functions in the organization. Using this approach prevents administrators from having to individually configure each user's account settings. Only create the accounts needed as unused accounts can provide security vulnerabilities if discovered.

- *Set account passwords* to work under the organization's password policy.

- *Install and configure any additional authentication systems*, such as biometric scanning devices or other multifactor authentication applications, selected for use with the network.

Network Authentication Options

At the network level, the *username* and *password* system is still the first line of *authentication options* in use. Even though you may be a member of one or more group accounts, you cannot use one of these accounts to log on to the network. You can only gain access to a system by logging on with a legitimate user account. In a client-server network, the authenticated users list is stored on the server, not at the local computer.

Also, at the network level, the network logon typically overrides any local system logon. Therefore, administrators control who can log on to any portion of the network through password policy statements. They also set the network password policy for how often users must change their passwords, as well as setting length and complexity requirements.

These options, shown in Figure 7.8, enable administrators to make user accounts and passwords more secure. Password policies apply to all users who log on to the system and cannot be configured for individual users.

FIGURE 7.8   Password policies

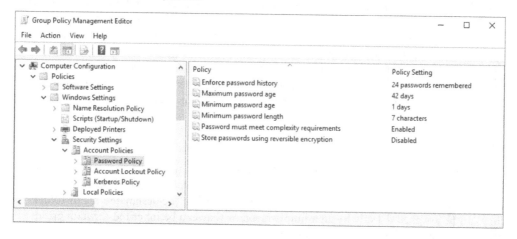

Typically, network administrators can configure the following password-related settings for network users:

- *Enforce password history*: This option is used to specify the number of passwords that will be tracked for each user. When users attempt to change their password, they will not be permitted to reuse any of the passwords being tracked.

- *Maximum password age/minimum password age*: These two settings enable administrators to set passwords so that they expire after the specified number of days and also to prevent users from changing their passwords for some specific number of days. When the password expires, the user is prompted to change it, ensuring that even if a password becomes public, it will be changed within a short period of time to close the security breach.

- *Minimum password length*: This option is used to specify the minimum number of characters that a password may contain. This allows the administrator to force users to employ passwords that are longer and harder to guess. A password of at least eight characters is recommended for secure systems.

- *Passwords must meet complexity requirements*: Administrators can use this option to force users to use more secure, complex passwords that include some combination of lowercase letters, numbers, symbols, and capitalized characters. The administrator sets the level of complexity by establishing password filters at the domain controller level.

Establishing Resource Controls

Server operating systems provide the capability to specify individual *access privileges* for files, folders/directories, and other system resources. The administrator's job is to carefully set access controls so that they permit authorized users to access and use designated system resources and deny unauthorized user access to prevent security breaches.

By applying the principle of *least privilege level* to these configurations (as mentioned earlier), administrators can reduce the opportunities for both malicious and unintended security breaches to occur. For example, denying read access to files and directories helps to protect the confidentiality of information, while denying unnecessary write (modify) access can help maintain the integrity of information.

Limiting the execution privilege of most system-related tools to authorized system administrators can prevent users from making configuration changes that could reduce security. It also can restrict the attacker's ability to use those tools to attack the server or other hosts on the network.

NTFS Permissions

The NTFS file management system used in Windows environments includes security features that enable permission levels to be assigned to files and/or folders on the disk. *NTFS permissions* set parameters for operations that users can perform on the designated file or folder. They can be assigned directly by an administrator, or they can be inherited through group settings, such as the default Everyone group.

NTFS permissions can be configured as *Allow* or *Deny* options. If a user has only Read permissions to a particular folder or file but is assigned to a group that has wider permissions for that folder or file, the individual would gain those additional rights through the group. On the other hand, if the user is assigned the deny option for a given permission level, then they would be denied that permission level even if it were granted by another group that they were part of. In a server environment, the default permission setting for files is No Access.

Standard NTFS folder permissions include the following:

- *Read*: This permission enables the user or group to view the file, folder, or subfolder of a parent folder along with its attributes and permissions.

- *Write*: This permission enables the user or group to add new files or subfolders, change file and folder attributes, add data to an existing file, and change display attributes within a parent folder.

- *Read & Execute*: The Read & Execute permission enables users or groups to make changes to subfolders, display attributes and permissions, and run executable file types.

- *Modify*: The Modify permission enables users to delete the folder and makes it possible for users to perform all the activities associated with the Write and Read & Execute permissions.

- *List Folder Contents*: This permission enables users or groups to view files and subfolders within the folder.

- *Full Control*: The Full Control permission enables the user or group to take ownership of the folder and to change its permissions, as well as perform all of the other activities possible with all the other permissions.

Standard NTFS file permissions include the following:

- *Read*: This permission enables the user or group to view the file along with its attributes and permissions.

- *Write*: This permission enables the user or group to overwrite the file, change its attributes, and view its ownership and attributes.

- *Read & Execute*: The Read & Execute permission enables users or groups to run and execute an application, along with all the options available through the Read permission.

- *Modify*: The Modify permission enables users to modify and delete the file and to perform all the activities associated with the Read, Write, and Read & Execute permissions.

- *Full Control*: The Full Control permission enables the user or group to take ownership of the file and to change its permissions, as well as perform all the other activities possible with all the other permissions.

Linux Permissions

Linux operating systems also employ file and directory permissions to protect them from unauthorized accesses. In Linux (and UNIX) systems, structures other than documents and executables are defined as files. Other system resources such as disk drives, optical drives, modems, input and output devices, and network communications are also accessed as files.

Each file in a Linux system also has an *owning user* and an *owning group* assigned to it, along with access permissions for each owner type. *Permissions* are also established for *unprivileged users*. There are three types of access permissions that can be configured:

- *Read (r)*: When specified, this permission enables the user to read the contents of the file or directory.

- *Write (w)*: When specified for a file, this permission enables the user to modify the file by writing to it. When assigned to a directory, the Write permission allows the user to create or delete files in the directory.
- *Execute (x)*: This permission enables users to execute files and scripts with this permission assigned.

Each permission is established independently for each user category. A typical file permission display (such as that obtained from a list [ls] command) will appear in the following format:

```
drwxrwxrwx user group filesize Jan 01 08:00 filename
```

Each rwx segment of the left column displays the active permission setting for owner user, owner group, and others, respectively. The fact that all three permission types are present in this example would indicate that all three groups have all permissions enabled. When a permission is disabled for a particular user, its space contains a simple dash character:

```
drwxrw-r-- user group filesize Jan 01 08:00 filename
```

In this example, the owning user still has all permissions, but the owning group permissions have been reduced to Read and Write, while other users' permissions have been reduced to simply Read.

When a directory or file is created in a Linux system, it is associated with its creator, who by default becomes its *owner*. Typically, Linux users will assign permissions of -rw-r--r-- to their nonexecutable files. This setting will permit others to read their file, but they will not be able to make changes to it. Similarly, directories are often assigned permissions of -rwxr-xr-x. This enables others to look through the directory and execute without being able to write new files into it or remove existing files from it.

 Linux permission assignments for a file are overshadowed by the permissions assigned to its parent directory. Even though a file may be assigned the permissions -rwxrwxrwx, the user will not be able to access the file unless they have read, write, and execute permissions to the directory above the file.

ICS Access Control

The standard typically used to govern access control in the OT network environment is the ISA-95 Purdue standard first presented in Chapter 1, "Industrial Control Systems." Figure 7.9 revisits the architectural structure described by that standard.* Notice that the enterprise network occupies levels 4 and 5, while the OT network exists at levels 2 and 3.

*This version of the ISA-95 Purdue Reference Architecture subdivides the enterprise level from Chapter 3, "Secure ICS Architecture," into levels 4 and 5. The typical enterprise network functions remain at level 4, while level 5 has been added to provide an enterprise DMZ and some business functions.

FIGURE 7.9   Extended ISA-95 architecture

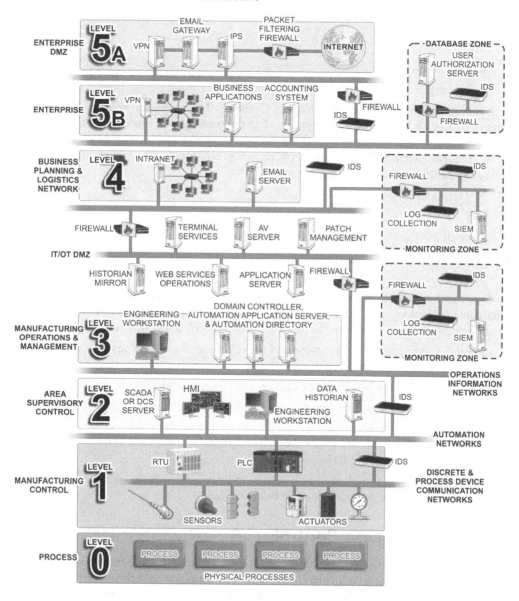

Once again, the two networks are separated by a dual firewall DMZ between levels 3 and 4. One firewall is managed by the IT staff from the enterprise network, while the ICS firewall is managed by the process control network engineers. Notice also that each level employs an *intrusion detection system (IDS)* to monitor each network segment independently from the other segments.

The ISA-95 standard addresses security for ICS interconnected IT/OT networks in four distinct areas:

- Network security

- Access control

- Remote access

- Log management

Network security was covered in detail in Chapter 3. Log management is a major component of Chapter 9, "ICS Security Assessments." In the remainder of this chapter, we will deal with the access control and remote access aspects of implementing the ISA-95 standard.

At each level on the OT side of the network, access control must be maintained for the following components depicted in the figure:

- Workstations

- IDS

- Firewall

- Applications

- Servers

Note that levels 0 and 1 do not require logical access control elements to secure the network environment. However, all other levels do require logical and physical access control solutions. In addition, the following levels require specific access control functions to be in place:

- *Level 2*: Control room workstations and the HMI must have both physical and logical access controls in place.

- *Level 3*: Password policies must be created and enforced at this level.

- *The DMZ*: In this structure, two-factor authentication must be established and required for any OT access.

- *Level 4*: Tools for controlling user access to applications must be in place, and physical user access to servers and IDS equipment must be controlled.

- *Level 5*: A two-factor authentication process must be implemented, and access to the intrusion protection system (IPS) must be controlled.

Remote ICS Access Control

While it is always preferable to have absolutely no pathway from the Internet into the OT, this is becoming continually less probable. Organizations increasingly value their Internet presence and connections. In addition, management wants access to the information from the production floor. Therefore, a pathway is created for outsiders to gain access to the OT network.

As many protections as are practical should be placed in this pathway. In addition to all the safeguards presented in this and previous chapters, there are some very specific security tools that should be allocated to this path:

- A virtual private network (VPN) gateway
- An encrypted VPN tunnel
- A remote access server (RAS)

The Virtual Private Network

The VPN gateway is placed in the DMZ that separates the enterprise network from the Internet at level 5. This device requires remote users to establish an encrypted *VPN tunnel* to the gateway to be authenticated in the network. Using a *virtual private network (VPN)*, remote users can connect to a private network (the organization's enterprise network) over a public network (the Internet) and then authenticate and perform tasks on the private network as if they were connected directly to it, as illustrated in Figure 7.10.

FIGURE 7.10   VPN connections

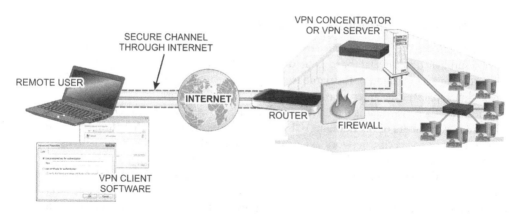

VPNs may be established using a variety of protocols and encryption and can be one of the more complex things a network administrator has to deal with. Many VPNs are simply point-to-point connections over IP or MPLS and do not support layer 2 protocols such as Ethernet. Therefore, most networking is limited to TCP/IP, but newer VPN variants like *Virtual Private LAN Service (VPLS)* or *Layer 2 Tunneling Protocol (L2TP)* can provide Ethernet-based communication.

VPNs may be either *trusted* VPNs or *secure* VPNs. *Trusted VPNs* do not use cryptographic tunneling but rather trust the underlying network to handle security beyond authentication. *Secure VPNs* handle the encryption of the connection.

There are many different types of VPNs available, but the most widely used protocol is the *Point-to-Point Tunneling Protocol (PPTP)*. PPTP does not provide any encryption and uses the simple password authentication taken from the *Point-to-Point Protocol (PPP)*.

L2TP also uses PPP and is unencrypted but can pass another encryption protocol in the tunnel. Often the underlying protocol will be combined with L2TP as with L2TP/IPsec.

Internet Protocol Security (IPSec) is an open standard commonly used in VPNs that actually employs a suite of protocols for encrypting and authenticating IP communications. Protocols in this suite include the following:

- *Authentication Headers (AH)* provides data integrity and origin (IP source) authentication to protect against replay attacks (attacks where a recorded transmission is replayed by an attacker to gain access).

- *Encapsulating Security Payloads (ESP)* offers origin authentication as well as confidentiality through encryption. ESP encrypts and encapsulates the entire TCP/UDP datagram within an ESP header that does not include any port information. This means that ESP won't pass through any device using port address translation.

- *Security Associations (SAs)* offer a number of algorithms and frameworks for authentication and key exchange.

- *Internet Key Exchange (IKE)* is the protocol used to set up a security association in IPSec.

Remote Access Server Authentication

The *VPN gateway* will forward the remote authentication requests to the user database server established in the Database Zone of level 4, Business Planning & Logistics Network. If the remote user is found in the database, they will be forwarded to a RAS located in the DMZ that separates the enterprise network from the OT network.

The RAS is a server that is dedicated to providing network access to *remote users* (users who are not members of the domain ACL). This server is responsible for authenticating these users for access to specific network assets and providing them with logon credentials.

Once again, the user should be required to provide two-factor authentication to be validated in the OT network. If the RAS authentication is successful, the user will be granted access to the areas of the ICS where they are authorized to work. All access at this level should be reviewed by ICS management and follow the least privilege principle. In addition, access should be automatically revocable.

NERC CIP 005

In Chapter 6, "Physical Security," you were introduced to the requirements specified by CIP-006-1, "Physical Security of Critical BES Cyber Assets." CIP-005, "Electronic Security Perimeters," is the electronic companion to that standard. Under this standard, an *Electronic Security Perimeter (ESP)* is the structure that all critical cyber assets reside within and extends to all access points to the perimeter. The BES environment may consist of multiple ESPs.

As with the CIP-006 standard discussed earlier, this standard requires BES operators to create and implement a strategy, plans, and policies to secure their critical cyber assets from unauthorized electronic access. In general, there are two areas of concern addressed in this standard: *dial-up connections* and intelligent electronic access point devices that work with *routable protocols*.

Major strategy, policy, and practices components involved in this standard include the following:

- The organization's wireless network policies
- Acceptable authentication methods and policies
- Identification of trusted and untrusted resources
- Anti-malware policies for remote access devices
- Patch management strategies and policies as they apply to operating systems and applications used to initiate communications with the ESP's electronic access point devices
- Service level agreements (SLAs) with outside vendors that address adherence to the organization's remote access controls

While each organization is given latitude in how they meet the requirements, their plans and policies must address the following areas:

- Implement and document mechanisms for controlling electronic access at all electronic access points to the organization's identified ESP(s). These electronic access controls are designed to reduce risks associated with uncontrolled communications with assets that use routable protocols or dial-up connectivity. These mechanisms must be enacted to restrict electronic access to only inbound and outbound communications to these devices that the organization deems necessary.

NOTE   Some communications that fall under this definition may be exempted from meeting the standard due to their use in time-sensitive protection or control operations.

Technical and procedural mechanisms that can be implemented for controlling electronic access to the ESP include the following:

- Using access control lists to restrict IP addresses, ports, and services
- Implementing data diodes (unidirectional gateways) to control the flow of communications through access points
- Validating all connectivity devices (router, firewall, and switch) configurations
- Installing UTM firewalls to remediate IT network vulnerabilities
- Installing OT protocol-aware firewalls to support operational zones in the enterprise network, as well as to enforce permitted commands between zones and access points
- Installing NIDS systems to inspect inbound and outbound traffic
- Practicing application whitelisting to protect computing assets from harmful applications
- Implement and document processes for monitoring and logging of ingress and egress access at all electronic access points to the ESP. These manual or electronic controls are designed to monitor and log communications at the ESP access points and must be operational 24/7/365.

- Perform cyber vulnerability assessments for the electronic access points to its electronic security perimeter(s). Under CIP-005, the organization must perform these documented vulnerability assessments at least annually.
- Review, update, and maintain all documentation to support compliance with the requirements of the NERC CIP-005 standard.

Access Control for Cloud Systems

In Chapter 3 you were introduced to the use of cloud services in emerging ICS reference architecture models. Like other sections of the IT/OT network, cloud environments require *access control (AC)* measures to establish security for those components of the model. To assist with the development of standardized AC techniques and practices for cloud systems, the NIST organization has developed the Special Publication 800-012, "General Access Control guidance for Cloud Systems." The guidance provided in this document maps to the NIST SP 800-53, Revision 4, "Security and Privacy Control for Federal Information Systems and Organizations," document.

Cloud services provide users with flexible processing power and data storage options that can be accessed over the Internet. The predominant pretext for using these services is to minimize the amount of IT equipment and local support personnel required to support the IT operation of the organization or its subunits. The organization outsources the cost of the environment to the cloud service provider who is responsible for the hardware, software, and networking overhead of the cloud environment. They are also responsible for the overall administration and maintenance of the environment. This frees up the customer to concentrate on their core business objectives.

Figure 7.11 shows the general architecture of a cloud environment. A cloud basically consists of networked hardware systems (servers) providing virtualized computing resources (virtual machines) that are running applications and providing data storage.

There are three common service models for deploying cloud systems:

- *Software as a service (SaaS)*: In this model, the cloud service provider offers customers access and use of software applications they hosted in their clouds. Clients access the cloud applications across the Internet using thin clients or web browsers.
- *Platform as a service (PaaS)*: In a PaaS model, the cloud service provider grants customers limited access to their cloud infrastructure (hardware, operating systems, and virtual machines) to create and deploy their own applications. Clients create their own cloud apps using programming tools and code libraries but have no control over the underlying cloud infrastructure.
- *Infrastructure as a service (IaaS)*: In an IaaS cloud environment, the customer is typically renting the underlying infrastructure from the cloud service. In these cases, the customer is given access to the configuration of the cloud infrastructure as well.

FIGURE 7.11   General structure of a cloud system

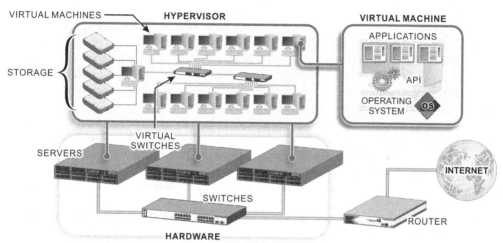

As you might well imagine, given these three service models, access control methods and their application vary between the models. Figure 7.12 depicts the avenues of access to be expected in the three models.

FIGURE 7.12   Cloud access avenues

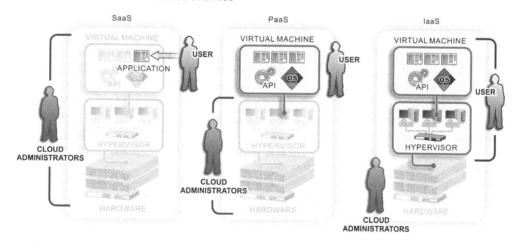

In the SaaS model, the application users must be permitted access on the front end, while software developers and the cloud service provider administrators have access to the backend. In this type of environment, the customer can access the applications to use them, but only really have control over the data produced by them. The cloud service provider retains access and control over most of the infrastructure, including cloud networking, storage, hypervisors, VMs, OSs, any middleware, runtime environments, and the actual applications. They also have access to and some control over the customers' data.

Likewise, in the PaaS model, the software developers have access through the front end, while the cloud administrators retain access to the backend. Like the SaaS model, in the PaaS model the customer has access to and control over their data. However, they also possess access to and control of the applications they create and deploy. The cloud service provider retains access to and control over all the other backend components listed for SaaS clouds.

Finally, in an IaaS model, the customer is provided front-end access to quite a bit of the cloud environment, while the cloud provider retains access to the lower levels of the infrastructure (networking, data storage, hypervisors, and VMs).

In each model there are shared responsibilities between the customer and the cloud service provider to different degrees. The simplest model is the SaaS model where ABAC and RBAC management models are used to apply policies and predefined user roles to manage access rights to user applications and data. The focus here is on users' access to applications. To achieve this, a *security class agreement (SCA)* is typically used to define the access rights of the users.

In the PaaS model, users deploy their own applications on the PaaS supplier's platform. This arrangement requires a more diverse AC strategy that covers three basic elements: subject, object, and operation. *Subjects* include the parties involved such as application users, application developers, and cloud services providers. *Objects* are the components of the cloud environment that require access control such as memory data, application-related data, and other applications within the same host environment. *Operations* describe the type of access rights provided for each subject to the different objects such as read, write, create, and replicate. All of these elements can be constrained by environmental conditions including time, location, security level, etc.

In IaaS cloud models, the SCA is created to establish the access barrier between the customer's data and the IaaS provider's system administrators or other IaaS users. The IaaS administrators are responsible only for access control to the network layers, hypervisor, VMs, and data storage. Because the network is shared between IaaS customers, it is important for the IaaS provider to secure the network and their cloud system. This may involve the use of dedicated VLANs with their ACL whitelists along with IEEE 802.1Q VLAN tagging.

Two other key points of access control in the IaaS cloud are the VMs and the hypervisor. In this model, end users have access to the hypervisor and the VMs and are typically given login, read, write, and create rights. However, access rights provided to other objects through the created VMs and the hypervisor must also be controlled.

Because the IaaS environment may contain VMs created by multiple end users (in a public cloud environment), isolation must be created between VMs to ensure that they do not corrupt each other or provide an attack vector for a malicious user in the IaaS. While the end users may have access to the hypervisor, they should not have *access control* to it unless the cloud environment is a private cloud. If an end user gains access to the hardware resources of the hypervisor, they may be able to escalate their user privileges and hack other user environments running on the hypervisor.

Review Questions

The following questions test your knowledge of the material presented in this chapter.

1. What kind of access control method is needed when users do not have the ability to control access to the files and folders they own?

2. In a large network, which administrative job role would be responsible for performing information security tasks on servers, hosts, and the network's connectivity devices?

3. Which authentication method uses a central authority to determine which users can have access to which objects?

4. What tools do administrators use to create group access and restrictions to network assets based on the user's position and job role in the organization?

5. _____ attach permissions to network objects that the system uses to control access to assets (programs, folders, files, printers) as well as what activities can be performed on that asset.

6. What protocol does IPSec employ to maintain data confidentiality?

7. _____ are configurations that administrators apply to user accounts (instead of folders, files, and printers) to limit their activities on a local machine (local accounts) or across the network (domain accounts).

8. Which protocol does IPSec use to maintain data integrity?

9. _____ are distributed, customizable information storage structures that provide a single point from which users can search for and locate resources scattered throughout a network.

10. A _____ is a collection of objects that share the same DNS name.

11. Which Microsoft database contains information about user accounts, group accounts, and computer accounts, as well as tracking the names of all of the objects and requests for resources within the domain?

12. What directory service do modern Linux distributions employ?

13. What function does an RAS server provide for VPN operations?

14. What are the two classes of users in a network?

15. Which standard, default Linux group has complete administrative control of the system?

Exam Questions

1. Which of the following VPN types handle the encryption portion of the tunnel?

   A. Secure VPNs

   B. Trusted VPNs

   C. Point-to-point VPNs

   D. Hardware VPNs

2. From the following list, identify the security tools that should be allocated to the pathway to the organization's enterprise network and Internet connection. (Select all that apply.)

   A. A VPN tunnel

   B. A honeypot

   C. A VPN gateway

   D. A DMZ

   E. A remote access server (RAS)

3. Select the Standard NTFS folder permission that enables users to delete the folder and makes it possible for users to perform all the activities associated with the Write and Read & Execute permissions.

   A. Execute

   B. Modify

   C. Read & Execute

   D. -rwx

4. From the following list, select the critical functions that an enterprise-level directory service provides for the network. (Select all that apply.)

   A. An information store that can be distributed across several geographical locations

   B. An information store that is accessible from many different operating systems

   C. An information store that administrators use to create group access and restrictions to network assets based on the user's position and job role in the organization

   D. An information store that users can employ to efficiently search through the enterprise for information that may be located throughout the network

   E. An information store that limits users' activities on a local machine (local accounts) or across the network (domain accounts)

5. Remote users need to be authenticated and frequently need their data to be encrypted. Which of the following protocols are used together to meet both needs? (Select two.)

   A. L2TP

   B. DES

   C. IPSec

   D. PPTP

6. Which of the following protocols apply to IPSec? (Select all that apply.)

    A. Authentication Header (AH) for destination IP integrity

    B. Encrypted Security Payload (ESP) for secure authentication

    C. Authentication Header (AH) for IP source authentication

    D. Encapsulating Security Payload (ESP) for confidentiality

7. In which cloud service model are customers given access to the configuration of cloud infrastructure?

    A. Public clouds

    B. SaaS

    C. PaaS

    D. IaaS

8. Which of the following access control methods necessitates security clearance for subjects?

    A. Identity-based access control

    B. Military access control

    C. Role-based access control

    D. Mandatory access control

9. Which of the following access control models is based on complex Boolean rule-sets derived from policy statements?

    A. MAC

    B. RBAC

    C. ABAC

    D. RB-RBAC

10. Which of the following are true statements about discretionary access control methods? (Select all that apply.)

    A. The network administrator or superuser takes ownership of each object.

    B. Each file or object has its own owner.

    C. The network is based on a centralized authority or policy that determines object access.

    D. Object owners have complete power to control access over their files.

Chapter 8

ICS Security Governance and Risk Management

OBJECTIVES

Upon completion of this chapter, you should be able to:

1. Explain the components used to develop Security Policies and Procedures:

   - Exceptions

   - Exemptions

   - Requirements

   - Standards

2. Define and describe the basic components of Risk Management:

   - PHA HAZOP usage

   - Risk acceptance

   - Risk mitigation plan

Introduction

Policies are rules that an organization adheres to. Procedures are the sequence of steps taken to enforce the organizational policies. Guidelines are recommendations provided as reference for proper implementation of policies and procedures. These three elements work together to provide employees with adequate guidance to perform their tasks within the organization.

Although each department in an organization may establish its own policies and procedures to complement organizational goals and objectives, an overall organizational security policy needs to be clearly established for all employees and departments. Management's support of a security policy is the most important component of making the organization successful in securing assets, infrastructure, and data.

Security Policies and Procedure Development

An important part of any organization's corporate policy is its cybersecurity policy. This policy supports the corporate policy by explaining the overall requirements needed to protect an organization's network data and computer systems. Generally, creation of these policies involves stakeholders from several areas of the organization, not limited to the following:

- Corporate management
- Security management
- Network administration
- Human resources department

Together these groups work to produce a suite of documents that will guide the entire organization to ensure the CIA of its data and resources. The result is a collection of policies, procedures, and guidelines that all members of the organization adhere to when accessing the organization's computing and network resources. It also provides members with the tools they need to make good cybersecurity-related choices when using this equipment.

Requirements

The first requirement for delivering an effective cybersecurity policy is that it must be usable. If the resulting document is unclear or presents unrealistic requirements, members will avoid or circumvent them. For example, passwords are a huge nuisance to users. The majority of users can remember only one or two passwords, and if the security policy requires a unique scheme or authentication factor for each login, they might just give up and not participate or devise unsecured methods to get around the requirement.

Therefore, the policy must balance the organization's need for security against the user's willingness to comply with strong password requirements. There will almost always be grumbling, but this balance must be established and enforced, as there will be much more grumbling when user accounts are compromised.

With this in mind, the security policy must also be enforceable and include specific information concerning how failures to comply with the policy will be handled. This section of the policy describes how policy violations are reported and what actions should be taken when they are. This includes what actions will be taken for a given type of infraction, such as verbal warnings, written reprimands, or termination processes.

Policies must also balance security with productivity. If the policies and procedures are so intrusive that productivity is diminished, various levels of management will also be enticed to circumvent the areas they don't appreciate to get more done.

All corporate policies must be top down to be efficient. As with all other components of the corporate policy document, the cybersecurity policy must have a high level of support within the organization. This includes the chief executive officer (CEO) and chief information officer (CIO). If management at any level circumvents published policies, then the rank and file of the organization will see them as something that justifies management's existence and simply put them on the shelf. Management should use all of their policy tools, including their cybersecurity policies, to drive company initiatives and change.

Finally, the organization's cybersecurity policy must address any laws or regulations that establish specific requirements for the confidentiality, integrity, or availability of the data within their networks. Some important examples include the following:

- *The Health Insurance Portability and Accountability Act (HIPAA):* This was designed to do the following:

  - Reduce healthcare fraud and abuse

  - Provide industry standards for healthcare information exchange for electronic billing

  - Require the protection and confidential handling of protected health information

  - Provide the ability to transfer and continue health insurance coverage when a worker loses their job or changes employment

- *Sarbanes Oxley (SARBOX or SOX):* This includes legislative requirements relating to the handling of financial records. While its requirements are similar to those designed for medical records under HIPAA, SOX also details criminal penalties for altering, destroying, or falsifying records to influence a legal investigation. It is essential that organizations be capable of showing their compliance with governmental legislation. For example, a HIPAA violation can cost an organization up to $1,500 per occurrence. Count the number of users in your database and then multiply by that number.

Exceptions and Exemptions

Because no policy can be designed to foresee every possible variation that will appear after the ink dries, it is important that the policy includes methods for addressing variations not covered in the original policy documents. As a matter of fact, the entire corporate policy manual should be considered a living document that changes as needed and is reviewed and updated on a regular, periodic basis.

Because undefined variations do not occur at predictable points in time, it is important that the policy have provisions for addressing exceptions and exemptions.

- Exceptions are defined as someone or something that is not included in a rule, group, or list—or does not behave in an expected way. The exceptions portion of the policy is designed to provide a method for documenting an exception to compliance with established IT and cybersecurity policies, procedures, and guidelines.

- Exemptions are defined as the process of freeing or a state of being free from an obligation or liability imposed on others—in other words, someone or something that is not obligated to follow the cybersecurity policies, procedures, or guidelines stated in the corporate policy.

Exceptions

In most organizations there are situations that occur in normal day-to-day operations where compliance with their policies, procedures, and guidelines cannot be achieved for some reason or another. However, because these occurrences impact ongoing operations, they must be allowed to prevent the operation from incurring significant delays or ceasing to operate. In such cases, an exception must be approved and documented.

This is where a security policy exception process comes into play. The steps of this process should identify the specific places where the issue with compliance occurs so that it can be elevated to the proper level of management to ensure that the risk is recognized and managed effectively. In larger organizations, approvals for policy exceptions must typically be garnered from the CIO or someone designated by that area of management.

The security policy exception process must apply to all IT and cybersecurity policies, standards, and practices, as well as to all organizational users. Any user, IT support staff, or managers responsible for implementing security policies and standards in the network must use the process to request an exception. Typically, an exception request should be required to document the following:

- Why an exception is required, for example, what business requirement exists, what alternatives might exist, and why they are not appropriate

- A description of the specific policy that the exception is being requested for

- The specific device, application, or service for which the exception is being requested

- Assessment of potential risks created by noncompliance if the exception is granted
- Plans for managing or mitigating risks incurred by granting the exception
- Anticipated duration of noncompliance

Exceptions should not have an infinite lifespan. Instead, an exception should be documented and reviewed regularly until the policy can be changed to rectify the exception state. The ongoing review of exceptions provides the organization with a realistic view of its areas of risk instead of indicating that their security plan is complete.

Typically, an exception to the organization's established cybersecurity policies, procedures, or guidelines might be granted to address any of the following situations:

- Where compliance with an existing policy would cause a major adverse financial impact that would not be offset by the reduced risk associated with compliance.
- Where immediate compliance with an existing policy would disrupt critical operations, a temporary exception may be created.

Exemptions

Exemptions are another request/authorize process commonly included in organizational policy documents. Where an exception addresses a temporary condition outside of a policy, exemptions are extended (maybe lifecycle long) exclusions from adherence from one or more of the organization's policies. Exemptions to cybersecurity policies are typically provided for two types of environments:

- Experimental, developmental, or testing environments that do not create risks for the production network.
- Legacy environments that contain older devices or applications that require less secure environments that do not meet compliance to operate. This may extend to otherwise compliant environments that possess legacy devices or applications that production still needs to carry out operations.

Even though these conditions require an exemption from one or more cybersecurity policies, any risks associated with the exemption must be managed. Documentation supporting an exemption request usually includes the following:

- The physical location of the exempt asset (environment, device, or application)
- The person or group that will be responsible for the exempted asset
- How the exempted asset is to be used
- How risks associated with the asset will be mitigated

Standards

There are several international and domestic standards and guidelines available to help organizations create and maintain the cybersecurity portion of their corporate policies and procedures. The following list identifies a few of the most commonly used US National guidelines:

- *NIST SP 800-53 Rev 5, "Security and Privacy Controls for Federal Information Systems and Organizations"*: Published by the National Institute of Standards and Technology, this is a US security standard created to provide a catalog of security and privacy controls for federal information systems and organizations and a process of selecting controls to protect organizational operations, assets, and the nation from a diverse set of threats, including hostile cyberattacks, natural disasters, structural failures, and human errors.

- *NIST Cybersecurity Framework 1.1*: The framework consists of standards, guidelines, and best practices to promote the protection of critical infrastructure. The prioritized, flexible, repeatable, and cost-effective approach of the framework will help owners and operators of critical infrastructure to manage cybersecurity-related risk while protecting business confidentiality, individual privacy, and civil liberties.

- *ISO/IEC 27002*: The ISO/IEC 2700 series of standards are published by the International Organization for Standardization (ISO) and International Electrotechnical Commission (IEC) to provide security standards for information security controls. It provides best practices for implementing and maintaining information security management systems to provide preservation of data CIA.

- *NIST SP 800-82r2, "Guide to Industrial Control Systems (ICS) Security"*: This guide was developed to provide guidance for securing Industrial Control Systems (ICS), including SCADA systems, Distributed Control Systems (DCS), and other PLC control system configurations. This standard provides an overview of ICS topologies, identifies typical threats and vulnerabilities to these systems, and provides recommended security countermeasures to mitigate the associated risks.

- *NERC CIP*: Produced by the North American Electric Reliability Corporation, the Critical Infrastructure Protection (CIP) plan is a group of 9 standards and 45 requirements designed to secure digital assets involved in the operation of bulk electrical generation and distribution systems. In particular, the CIP standards address the security of electronic perimeters, critical cyber assets and personnel, and training to implement and use the plan.

- *Neureg 6847, "Cyber Security Self-Assessment Methods for U.S. Nuclear Power Plants"*: This self-assessment method was developed at the Pacific Northwest National Laboratory (PNNL) to assist nuclear power plant personnel in assessing and managing cybersecurity risks. It is a structured approach for identifying and scrutinizing critical digital assets, systematically evaluating the vulnerabilities of these assets, assessing the consequences to the plant of a successful exploitation of a critical digital asset, estimating cybersecurity risks, and identifying cost-effective protective actions.

- *CIS Critical Security Controls v8 (Originally SANS Top 20)*: Developed by the Center for Internet Security (CIS), these controls are designed to guide organizations in protecting themselves from known attacks. This guidance is embodied in 20 CIS controls that are divided into three categories: Basic, Foundational, and Organizational. CIS provides an ICS-specific guidance document that describes how to apply the CIS Top 20 Controls to ICS environments. These documents are available at www.cisecurity.org.

ICS cybersecurity professionals have several governmental and industry-recognized standards and recommendations they can use to conduct systematic, disciplined, and repeatable security assessments. These basic standards include the following:

- *Committee on National Security Systems Instruction (CNSSI) 1253*: This instruction is designed to provide US government agencies and departments with guidance concerning the Risk Management Framework (RMF) for national security systems. This information is a companion to the NIST SP 800-53 guidelines.

- *International Society of Automation: ISA/IEC-62443 (formerly ISA99) Security Assurance Levels*: These standards are designed to provide coherency and consistency to standards associated with cybersecurity in ICS and related applications. This includes guides such as "Security Risk Assessment for System Design," "Product Security Development Lifecycle," and "Technical Security Requirements for IACS Components."

Along with the basic ICS cybersecurity standards, there are a number of industry-specific guidelines and standards to reference:

- NRC Regulatory Guide 5.71, "Cyber Security Programs for Nuclear Facilities"

- INGAA Control Systems, "Cyber Security Guidelines for the Natural Gas Pipeline Industry"

- NISTIR 7628, "Guidelines for Smart Grid Cyber Security"

The following sections and critical terms are designed to be used to help form the foundation of a sound cybersecurity policy and should be evaluated and agreed upon prior to implementing them.

NIST Cybersecurity Framework

The NIST Cybersecurity Framework was established as a generic set of guidelines that could be applied to every type of network including enterprise, utility, industrial control system, and medical networks. However, because the frameworks were designed to support so many different types of organizations, they are far more broad-based than most networks will require. As such, most organizations will use the parts of the framework that are specific to their networking needs to create their cybersecurity plans.

The five functions identified in the NIST Cybersecurity Framework provide an accepted road map for developing a security policy that aligns their cybersecurity activities with their business requirements, risk tolerances (or risk acceptance), and resources. Together these functions describe specific cybersecurity activities that are common to enterprise networks, as well as to all of the other network types we will cover in the remainder of this course.

While the NIST CSF can be used as a road map for developing a cybersecurity policy, it is not a finished solution for every organization. Typically, the NIST CSF is used to support the organization's IT network and cybersecurity policies, while other standards such as IEC 62443 and other ICS standards are applied to the OT network environment. Every industry and organization has unique types and levels of risk, different risk management priorities, and different network types, tools, and methods. Currently, the NIST CSF is being used by about 50 percent of the organizations in the United States (www.nist.gov/industry-impacts/cybersecurity-framework).

Security experts must use their understanding of these organizational variables and use the framework to create a profile that a unified security policy can be created from. In the complex networks of many organizations, the cybersecurity specialists may create multiple profiles that are aligned with the various components of their organization.

- *Identify (ID)*: Develop the organizational understanding to manage cybersecurity risk to systems, assets, data, and capabilities. Under this initial function, there are five areas that need to be identified at the beginning of the cybersecurity policy development effort:

  - *Asset management*: Identify the data, personnel, devices, systems, and facilities that enable the organization to achieve its business purposes and implement a strategy to manage them in a manner consistent with their relative importance to business objectives and the organization's risk strategy.

  - *Business environment*: Identify the organization's mission, objectives, stakeholders, and activities. Take steps to make sure that they are understood and prioritized properly. This information can then be used to implement cybersecurity roles, responsibilities, and risk management decisions.

  - *Governance*: Identify the policies, procedures, and processes required to manage and monitor the organization's regulatory, legal, risk, environmental, and operational requirements. Take steps to ensure that they are understood and inform the management of their cybersecurity risk.

  - *Risk assessment*: Identify steps that can be taken to ensure that the organization understands the cybersecurity risk to its organizational operations (including its mission, functions, image, or reputation), its organizational assets, and its personnel.

  - *Risk management strategy*: Identify the organization's priorities, constraints, and risk tolerances and establish assumptions that can be used to support operational risk decisions.

  - *Supply chain risk management*: Identify the organization's priorities, constraints, and risk tolerances, and establish assumptions to support risk decisions and develop processes associated with supply chain risk.

- *Protect (PR)*: This function covers five categories that help to develop and implement the appropriate safeguards that will ensure delivery of critical infrastructure services:

  - *Authentication and access control*: Protect critical infrastructure services by properly limiting access to assets and associated facilities to authorized users, processes, or devices, as well as to authorized activities and transactions.

  - *Awareness and training*: Protect critical infrastructure services by ensuring that the organization's personnel and partners are provided cybersecurity awareness education and are adequately trained to perform their information security–related duties and responsibilities consistent with related policies, procedures, and agreements.

  - *Data security*: Implement steps to ensure that information and records (data) are managed consistent with the organization's risk strategy to protect the confidentiality, integrity, and availability of the information.

- *Information protection processes and procedures*: Develop security policies that address purpose, scope, roles, responsibilities, management commitment, and coordination among organizational entities. Also ensure that processes and procedures are maintained and used to manage protection of information systems and assets.

- *Maintenance*: Establish maintenance procedures to ensure that repairs to industrial control and information system components are performed in a manner consistent with the organization's policies and procedures.

- *Protective technology*: Implement activities that ensure technical security solutions are managed to ensure the security and resilience of systems and assets, consistent with related policies, procedures, and agreements.

- *Detect (DE)*: Develop and implement the appropriate activities to identify the occurrence of a cybersecurity event. The Detect function enables timely discovery of cybersecurity events. Examples of outcome categories within this function include Anomalies and Events, Security Continuous Monitoring, and Detection Processes.

  - *Anomalies and events*: Create procedures to ensure that anomalous activity is detected in a timely manner and that the potential impact of events is understood.

  - *Security continuous monitoring*: Implement policies and procedures to ensure that the information system and assets are monitored at discrete intervals to identify cybersecurity events and verify the effectiveness of protective measures.

  - *Detection processes*: Detection processes and procedures are maintained and tested to ensure timely and adequate awareness of anomalous events.

- *Respond (RS)*: Develop and implement the appropriate activities to take action regarding a detected cybersecurity event.

  - *Response planning*: Response processes and procedures are executed and maintained to ensure timely response to detected cybersecurity events.

  - *Communications*: Response activities are coordinated with internal and external stakeholders, as appropriate, to include external support from law enforcement agencies.

  - *Analysis*: Analysis is conducted to ensure adequate response and support recovery activities.

  - *Mitigation*: Activities are performed to prevent expansion of an event, mitigate its effects, and eradicate the incident.

  - *Improvements*: Organizational response activities are improved by incorporating lessons learned from current and previous detection/response activities.

- *Recover (RC)*: Develop and implement the appropriate activities to maintain plans for resilience and to restore any capabilities or services that were impaired due to a cybersecurity event. The Recover function supports timely recovery to normal operations to reduce the impact from a cybersecurity event. Examples of outcome categories within this function include recovery planning, improvements, and communications:

- *Recovery planning*: Recovery processes and procedures are executed and maintained to ensure timely restoration of systems or assets affected by cybersecurity events.
- *Improvements*: Recovery planning and processes are improved by incorporating lessons learned into future activities.
- *Communications*: Restoration activities are coordinated with internal and external parties, such as coordinating centers, Internet service providers, owners of attacking systems, victims, other CSIRTs, and vendors.

NERC CIP

Earlier in this book you were introduced to two of the NERC CIP standards as they applied to specific topics. The CIP standards actually consist of 9 titles and 45 requirements that help organizations (referred to as *responsible entities*) establish their electronic security perimeters (ESPs) and secure the cyber assets they contain. These standards also address personnel, training, security management functions, and disaster recovery. They are designed to be used together to create and maintain a high level of cybersecurity for Bulk Electric System (BES) organizations. The CIP standard titles and functions are as follows:

- CIP-002-5.1a, "Critical Cyber Asset Identification"
- CIP-003-1, "Security Management Controls" (Chapter 9)
- CIP-004-1, "Personnel and Training"
- CIP-005-1, "Electronic Security Perimeters" (Chapters 3, 4, and 7)
- CIP-006-1, "Physical Security of Critical Cyber Assets" (Chapter 6)
- CIP-007-1, "Systems Security Management" (Chapter 8)
- CIP-008-1, "Incident Reporting and Response Planning" (Chapter 10)
- CIP-009-1, "Recovery Plans for Critical Cyber Assets" (Chapter 11)
- CIP-010-3, "Vulnerability Assessments" (Chapter 8)
- CIP-011-2, "Information Protection"
- CIP 013-1, "Cybersecurity Supply Chain Risk Management" (Chapter 11)
- CIP 014-2, "Physical Security" (Chapter 6)
- CIP 012, "Communications between Control Centers"

 A full description of the NERC CIP standards can be viewed at www.nerc .com/pa/Stand/Pages/CIPStandards.aspx.

ICS Security Policies

Like IT networks, OT networks require well-defined security policies to make their operation productive, efficient, and safe. However, in addition to the possible loss of information that directs IT network security policies, OT network policies must take into account potential consequences associated with hazardous processes. When OT networks are disrupted or incapacitated, very bad things can happen to people, facilities, and the environment. Just consider some of the places where OT networks are typically employed:

- Chemical plants
- Assembly lines
- Power generation plants
- Nuclear plants
- Water treatment
- Waste management

Therefore, when an organization undertakes an ICS risk assessment, risk mitigation, and security policy generation plan, they must address the following possible areas of risk:

- Personnel safety
- Equipment safety
- Environmental impact
- Production loss
- Data loss
- Adverse business effects

Tools employed to create policies, and procedures used to manage the additional and unique requirements of ICS risks, are included later in the chapter.

Risk Management

There have already been many references to risk in this book; however, we've never actually defined it before this point. *Risk* is the potential loss of an object of value. According to the NIST glossary (`https://csrc.nist.gov/glossary/term/cybersecurity_risk`), cybersecurity risk is defined as risk related to the loss of CIA of data or information/control systems that reflect potentially adverse impacts to organizational operations. It can also be expressed as an intentional interaction with uncertainty. Risk is also a quantity that can be communicated to the organization's internal and external stakeholders.

Risk management is the process of identifying, assessing, and responding to risk. The NIST Framework describes a four-tier/three-section format that can be used for evaluating organizational risk management. The three sections that describe the organization's position in terms of cybersecurity preparedness are as follows:

- *Risk management process*: The risk management process section deals with whether the organization has formalized risk management practices. It also identifies whether the organization has prioritized its cybersecurity activities with its risk objectives, their threat environment, or their business/mission goals.

- *Integrated risk management programs*: This section identifies organizations based on their awareness of risk associated with their operations, their handling of risk management as an organization, and their processes to distribute cybersecurity information throughout the organization.

- *External participation*: The external participation section deals with the organization's understanding of and interaction with other entities in the larger cybersecurity supply chain they are part of.

These sections can then be used to categorize organizations into four implementation tiers in terms of their cybersecurity preparedness.

- *Tier 1: Partial*: Organizations do not have any organized risk management plan, resulting in ad hoc cybersecurity risk management steps and no processes for coordinating with external organizations.

- *Tier 2: Risk Informed*: Organizations have management-generated cybersecurity practices, which creates an internal level of organizational risk management steps and processes but has no formalized cybersecurity capabilities to interact with outside organizations.

- *Tier 3: Risk Informed and Repeatable*: Organizations have fully approved cybersecurity practices across the organization, which are capable of adjusting to changing threats and technologies. The cybersecurity plan is fully developed and implemented to provide risk-based collaboration with external organizations.

- *Tier 4: Adaptive*: The adaptive organization has a cybersecurity risk management system that can adapt to lessons learned from previous occurrences. Cybersecurity risk management is a shared concern across the organization and evolves through feedback from previous occurrences, information obtained from trusted sources, and continued awareness of activities on their own network. This approach also enables the organization to share their cybersecurity approach with partner organizations to maximize their cyber risk management strategies across the enterprise.

Asset Identification

The first step in developing corporate cybersecurity policies is to identify the network and software assets that are critical to the function of the organization. The next step is to assign a monetary replacement value to each asset and resource identified, as well as the cost of employee downtime created in cases where their equipment fails. This list must include every network component that is critical for normal operations or that is significant for achieving a specific organizational goal.

Another way to develop the asset value list is to annotate which components are most important to the organization by using a scaled rating system, such as the Common Criteria for Informational Security Evaluation (Common Criteria or CC), which establishes evaluation assurance levels (EALs) that can be used to certify equipment reliability or assurance levels of security. The greater the organizational security need, the higher the specific EAL value should be for any given network hardware or software asset.

Using the Common Criteria valuation method will provide a hierarchical picture of which network assets and services require the most attention. For example, a firewall may receive a higher value than a web server and therefore should be valued higher and receive greater security measures.

For most organizations, identifying which assets are critical to the function of an organization is an ongoing but necessary task. However, taking the time to establish actual values for network assets and services will ensure that the assets that are most critical to the organization are properly protected. These assessments are typically handled by the organization's information security (InfoSec) team working with elements of the legal, business, and IT staff.

Risk Assessment

The purpose of a *risk assessment* is to identify steps that can be taken to ensure that the organization understands the cybersecurity risk to its organizational operations (including its mission, functions, image, or reputation), its organizational assets, and its personnel.

This includes understanding both the likelihood and resulting impact of risk events occurring within the different areas of the organization's network. After both variables are fully understood, the organization's management can determine the level of risk that can be tolerated, expressed in terms of risk tolerance or as risk acceptance.

It is impractical to fully remove all risk from any endeavor or any network environment. Therefore, the ultimate goal of all risk assessment activities is to produce guidelines for managing risk in such a way as to minimize threats to a level that is compatible with the organization's priorities, constraints, risk tolerances, and assumptions. With an understanding of their own risk tolerance, organizations can prioritize systems that require attention so that they can optimize their cybersecurity expenditures.

Risk assessments may take several forms, but they are mostly constructed in a matrix format that correlates different identified threats with their projected impact and likelihood levels. Table 8.1 shows an example of a risk assessment matrix. In this particular example, possible threat agents are identified, and existing safeguards are included.

There are multiple steps to this process:

1. Identify and document asset vulnerabilities.

2. Collect threat and vulnerability information from available information sources.

3. Identify and document threats to the organization's assets.

4. Analyze potential impacts.

5. Identify risk responses.

TABLE 8.1 A Sample Risk Assessment Matrix

Threat (What could happen?)	Threat Agent (Who could do it?)	Vulnerability (How is it possible?)	Existing Safeguards (What is in place to prevent it?)	Consequences (What is the worst thing that could happen?)	Impact	Likelihood	Risk
Stored data (e.g., history) program is unintentionally modified or corrupted by unauthorized individual through local access	1. Malicious Insider	1. Disgruntled employee/contractor	1. Personnel screening 2. Access control logs 3. Off-site storage of backups	1. Economic loss 2. Product safety 3. Corp image	Med	Low	Low
Stored data (e.g., history) program is intentionally modified or corrupted by unauthorized individual through remote access	1. Outsider 2. Malicious insider	1. Remote access 2. Disgruntled employee/contractor	1. Corporate firewall/VPN 2. Two-factor authentication 3. Off-site storage of backups	1. Economic loss 2. Product safety 3. Corp image	Med	Med	Med
Malware unintentionally enters the control system through a remotely connected computer	1. Insider	1. Remote access 2. Antivirus protection 3. Training/awareness	1. Antivirus on remote access clients 2. VPN server verification of client antivirus status	1. Economic loss 2. Product safety 3. Personnel injury 4. Environmental 5. Corp image	High	High	High

Threat (What could happen?)	Threat Agent (Who could do it?)	Vulnerability (How is it possible?)	Existing Safeguards (What is in place to prevent it?)	Consequences (What is the worst thing that could happen?)	Impact	Likelihood	Risk
Malware is intentionally installed on control system through a remotely connected computer	1. Outsider 2. Malicious insider	1. Remote access 2. Antivirus protection 3. Disgruntled employee/contractor	1. Antivirus on remote access clients 2. VPN server verification of client antivirus status	1. Economic Loss 2. Product Safety 3. Personal Injury 4. Negative Environmental Impact 5. Tarnish the Corporate Image	High	High	High
Malware enters the system through a laptop connected to the control system network	1. Insider	1. Portable media policy 2. Accessible ports 3. Antivirus protection 4. Training/awareness	1. Antivirus on laptops		High	High	High
Malware enters the system through infected media	1. Insider	1. Portable media policy 2. Accessible ports 3. Antivirus protection 4. Training/awareness	1. Portable media policy		High	Very High	Very High

There are several approved methods for conducting a risk assessment. This discussion includes the most common elements involved in a risk assessment process.

Risk Identification Vulnerability Assessment

After the network's assets have been identified and valued and the potential vulnerabilities and threats have been identified, the next step in developing the cybersecurity plan is to perform risk identification tests on the network to determine how susceptible it is to these threats.

In some cases, the task of performing a vulnerability (or risk) assessment falls to the InfoSec team or to the network administrators and their staff. However, it is also common for enterprises to hire third-party security contractors to determine where there are weaknesses or holes in the network.

Many techniques and software solutions are available to perform vulnerability or risk assessments (penetration testing). The most common penetration testing involves using a highly skilled white-hat hacker to impersonate an attacker and try different methods to attack the network. After notifying upper management and obtaining supervisory approval, the white hat typically performs an array of common techniques for penetration, as shown in Figure 8.1, that include the following:

- *Sniffing*: Using a packet analyzer, the white hat captures data packets as they move across the network, logs them, and then decodes their raw data. They can then analyze the data, in effect spying on the network users.

- *Port scanning*: Using a port scanner package to probe the network servers and devices for open ports that can be exploited. They can also identify services running on a host for potential exploitation.

- *Vulnerability scanning*: Using a network vulnerability scanner package to scan the enterprise for different types of common vulnerabilities such as system misconfigurations and default password usage, as well as to create DoS attacks by generating malformed packets.

- *Psychological (and maybe physical) social engineering attacks*: A majority of all cybersecurity attacks start with phishing or other similar types of SE attacks. These exploits were covered in some detail in Chapter 5, "Cybersecurity Essentials for ICS."

These topics are discussed in detail in the next chapter, Chapter 9, "ICS Security Assessments."

FIGURE 8.1   Typical penetration tests

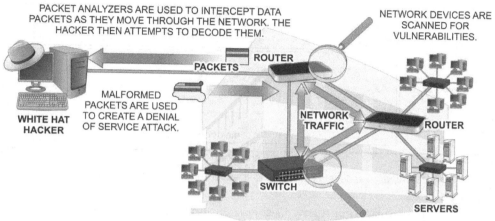

Impact Assessment

Recall that the primary goal when managing security risks is to minimize them to an acceptable level. To accomplish this, the organization must identify which threats pose a real concern to them. This is determined by assessing the impact of each security event actually occurring, though a process known as *impact assessment and analysis*.

Impact assessment and analysis is a purely business function that determines which individual threats pose a danger to the organization so that appropriate proactive measures can be implemented. Using the values established in the asset identification process, a cost can be calculated for occurrences of the different possible incidents noted in the risk identification procedure.

Some security events can be classified as one-time events, or *single loss expectancy (SLE)* events that have a price assigned to them on a one-time basis. For example, if a particular server experiences a DoS attack, the cost can be calculated for that single event.

However, for other potential occurrences, the risk assessment might also involve assessing the probability that an event will occur within a given period of time, such as within one year. If the event is likely to occur again within the year, an *annualized rate of occurrence (ARO)* value must be attached to the event. To correctly assess the financial impact to the organization posed by the occurrence of this particular event, you would have to multiply its SLE value by the ARO value. This produces the *annualized loss expectancy (ALE)* for this event.

Using this approach to the risk assessment process, you might formulate a risk assessment matrix as a *risk assessment scoring document*, similar to the one depicted in Figure 8.2.

FIGURE 8.2 A risk assessment scoring document

		PROBABILITY OF EVENT				
		WILL OCCUR >90%	EXTREME 70%-90%	HIGH 25%-70%	MODERATE 10%-25%	LOW <10%
IMPACT OF LOSS	CATASTROPHIC	8	7	6	5	4
	VERY HIGH	7	6	5	4	3
	NOTICEABLE	6	5	4	3	2
	MINOR	5	4	3	2	1
	NONE	0	0	0	0	0
				RISK POINT VALUE		

ACTION PER RISK POINT VALUE	
6-8	ACTIONS TO REDUCE OR REMOVE THESE RISKS SHOULD BE IMPLEMENTED IMMEDIATELY!
5	ACTIONS TO REDUCE OR REMOVE THESE RISKS SHOULD BE IMPLEMENTED AS SOON AS POSSIBLE.
4-3	ACTIONS TO REDUCE OR REMOVE THESE RISKS SHOULD BE IMPLEMENTED IN THE NEAR FUTURE.
2-1	ACTIONS TO REDUCE OR REMOVE THESE RISKS SHOULD BE IMPLEMENTED WHEN CONVENIENT. THEY WILL ENHANCE THE OVERALL SECURITY.
0	ACTIONS TO REDUCE OR REMOVE THESE RISKS ARE UNNECESSARY, HOWEVER THEY SHOULD STILL BE MONITORED.

After the risk assessment process has been completed, the information gathered is used to create the *risk assessment report*, or reports. Figure 8.3 shows a template for creating an executive summary of the full risk assessment report. This form provides the format and guidelines for the summary report. Simply insert the recommended information in the areas indicated. There are also a variety of full-length risk assessment report templates available on the Internet.

ICS Risk Assessments

Industrial/utility risk assessments include a number of risk analysis tools that are different than those described in the previous discussion for enterprise networks. In particular, a risk assessment for an OT environment must include a process hazard analysis (PHA). A PHA is used to assess the potential hazards in a given industrial process.

In the United States, PHA analyses are mandated by the Occupational Safety and Health Administration (OSHA) and are designed to assist potentially hazardous process operators with determining and ranking the operational risks of their processes. The operators can then implement proper security and mitigation policies to minimize the associated risks to an acceptable level.

The PHA analyzes the impact that production equipment, process control instrumentation, utilities, and human tendencies have on the process. In particular, the PHA is designed to analyze potential consequences that might result from the occurrence of different types of industrial accidents including fires, explosions, and hazardous materials accidents.

FIGURE 8.3   Risk assessment executive summary template

RISK ASSESSMENT EXECUTIVE SUMMARY TEMPLATE

I.   Introduction

- Purpose
- Scope of this risk assessment

Describe the system components, elements, users, locations, and any other details about the system that could be relevant to the assessment.

II.   Risk Assessment Approach

Briefly describe the approach used to conduct the risk assessment, including:

- The participants (all members utilized in performing the risk assessment)
- The technique used to gather information (the use of queries, questionnaires to specific people, online search tools)
- The development and description of risk scale (including matrix diagrams)

III.   System Characterization

Characterize the system, including hardware (servers, routers, switches), software (applications, operating systems, protocols), system interfaces (communication links), data, and users. Provide a connectivity diagram or a system input and output flowchart to help define the scope of this risk assessment effort.

IV.   Threat Statement

Compile and list the potential threats and associated actions that could threaten the applicable system assessed.

V.   Risk Assessment Results

List the observations (vulnerability and associated threat). Each observation must include:

- Observation number and brief description of observation (e.g. Observation 1: User system passwords can be cracked via Brute Force)
- A discussion of the threat and vulnerability pair
- Identification of existing mitigating security controls
- Likelihood discussion and evaluation (High, Medium, or Low likelihood)
- Impact analysis discussion and evaluation (High, Medium, or Low impact)
- Risk rating based on the risk-level matrix (High, Medium, or Low risk level)
- Recommended controls or alternative options for reducing risk (deference, avoidance, etc.)

VI.   Summary

Summarize the findings of the Risk Assessment and necessary measures needed to protect the system.

While there are many methodologies used for developing a PHA, there are typically four major tools that may be used in the development of a PHA:

- *A hazard and operability (HAZOP) study*: This is research and analysis conducted to reveal any hazardous scenarios that exist in a given process. A HAZOP is conducted by a multiparty team to evaluate potential problems in an industrial process to identify risks to humans or equipment. The analysis is based on sets of standard guide words designed to bring these potential problems and their consequences to the surface.

- *A failure mode and effects analysis (FMEA)*: An FMEA is a qualitative analysis tool used to evaluate processes to identify where and how they might fail (failure modes) and assess the relative effects of different failures. The assessment can then be used to identify components of the process that are most likely to fail so the overall system can be innovated.

- *A layer of protection analysis (LOPA)*: An LOPA is a rules-based PHA tool used to create risk assessments and reduction strategies for different industrial processing systems. This procedure takes information discovered through the HAZOP process and suggested screening values and produces a set of safeguards to implement for risk reduction. The numerical risk reduction factor produced by each safeguard implemented can be used along with the organization's unacceptable risk criteria to determine which safeguards to implement.

  These safeguards are implemented in the form of a safety instrument system (SIS). An SIS is an industrial control system designed to monitor critical processes and control them in a way that safety is the main objective. In particular, they are designed and configured to cause the process to enter into a safe state condition whenever an operational problem occurs.

- *A fault tree analysis (FTA)*: An FTA is an analytical system safety and reliability engineering tool used to determine how processes can fail, as well as how best to reduce the risks associated with those processes. The tool is based on creating a digital map (using Boolean logic or digital logic gate drawings) to create a fault tree. The tree identifies causes and event rates for top-level and contributing events associated with "undesirable states" that can occur in the process.

- *Event tree analysis (ETA)*: ETA is a quantitative risk analysis method used to document the progress of specific hazard events. It models the order in which events occur from initiation to consequences.

- *Cause-consequence analysis (CCA)*: CCA is a combination of FTA and ETA methods that produces a graphical representation that combines fault and event trees and can be used to identify the causes and incident outcomes of hazard scenarios.

- *Bow-tie diagrams*: These graphical representations present potential problems (hazards), preventative actions, initiating events, mitigating actions, and consequences in a display that resembles a common bow tie. These diagrams can be used with any of the analysis types listed here.

Risk Mitigation

Risk mitigation (risk reduction) is a systematic approach to reducing the extent of exposure to a risk and/or the likelihood of its occurrence. There are several management plans that come together to produce an effective risk mitigation plan. These include the following:

- Incident response plans (IRPs)
- Business continuity plans (BCPs)
- Disaster recovery plans (DRPs)

These plans must be in place and managed properly to provide a successful cybersecurity risk management plan. These separate plans work together to form the structure of the organization's cybersecurity policies. How the information in the BCP and DRP is employed is discussed in detail in Chapter 11, "Disaster Recovery and Business Continuity."

Incident Response Planning

Knowing what to do before any type of adverse incident occurs allows for a better response during a real crisis. In the case of cyberattacks, they are never expected to occur at a given time, so an *incident response policy (IRP)* should be created so that employees can have greater success in protecting vital assets in the event of an incident. This organizational policy is designed to provide guidelines for who does what, when, and where in cases of a physical disaster, network disaster, or security attack. The IRP is often referred to as the *recipe book* because each anticipated incident has its own recipe for resolution.

The IRP will typically seek to first establish procedures for containing incidents and then to implement procedures to prevent those incidents going forward. The first portion of this process involves the first responders to an incident. For example, the IRP specifies the actions that should be taken by the first responders when an incident occurs. Such specifications may include directing first responders to protect critical server room assets by preventing others from entering the room and notifying the appropriate personnel that an incident is occurring or has occurred.

NERC CIP-008

For electrical utilities, Incident Response Planning and Reporting is governed by the NERC CIP-008 standard. You have already been introduced to other portions of the NERC CIP standards in previous chapters.

Under the NERC CIP-008 standard, an electrical utility's IRP must include a timeline to determine lessons learned and update the plan:

- Conditions for activation of the recovery plan
- Roles and responsibilities of responders
- One or more processes for the backup and storage of information required to recover BES Cyber System functionality
- One or more processes to verify the successful completion of the backup processes and to address any backup failures
- One or more processes to preserve data, per cyber asset capability, for determining the cause of a cybersecurity incident that triggers activation of the recovery plan
- The incident reporting process definition and timeframe

This standard further requires each responsible entity to implement common controls for BES Cyber Systems that identify, classify, and respond to cybersecurity incidents. These controls are required for both high-impact (large control centers) and certain medium-impact (smaller control centers, ultra–high voltage transmission and large substations, and generating facilities) systems. That plan must include the following:

- A requirement to test each recovery plan at least once every 15 months

- A requirement to test a representative sample of information used to recover BES Cyber System functionality at least once every 15 calendar months to ensure it is usable and compatible with current configurations

- For high-impact BES Cyber Systems, a requirement to test each recovery plan at least once every 36 calendar months through an operational exercise of the plan in an environment representative of the production environment

Each responsible entity must also maintain its recovery plans for high-impact BES Cyber Systems and medium-impact BES Cyber Systems at Control Centers not later than 90 calendar days after completion of a recovery plan test or actual recovery, documenting any lessons learned or the absence of any lessons learned, updating the plan, and notifying each person with a defined role in the plan of the updates.

Within 60 calendar days after a change to the roles or responsibilities, responders, or technology that would impact the ability to execute the recovery plan, the plan must be updated, and those with a defined role in the plan must be notified.

Review Questions

The following questions test your knowledge of the material presented in this chapter.

1. _____ are rules that an organization adheres to.

2. _____ are the sequence of steps taken to enforce the organizational policies.

3. What industry was the HIPAA legislation created for, and why is it important for industrial processing organizations?

4. What industry was the Sarbanes-Oxley legislation created for, and why is it important for industrial processing organizations?

5. What security term can be used for the potential loss of an object of value?

6. Describe the purpose of performing a risk assessment.

7. What type of activity is used to identify which threats pose a real concern to the organization?

8. A _____ is used to capture data packets as they move across the network, log them, and then decode their raw data.

9. Which NIST Cyber Security Framework function is intended to help organizations "Develop and implement the appropriate activities to identify the occurrence of a cybersecurity event"?

10. Identify the type of tool that you would use to scan the enterprise for different types of common vulnerabilities, such as system misconfigurations and default password usage.

11. In addition to the possible loss of data confidentiality, integrity, and availability that drives enterprise network security policy, what potential consequences do OT network policies need to address? Identify four out of six areas.

12. What two values are required to correctly assess the financial impact posed by the occurrence of a particular event?

13. A _____ is conducted by a multiparty team to evaluate potential problems in an industrial process to identify risks to humans or equipment. The analysis is based on sets of standard guide words designed to bring these potential problems and their consequences to the surface.

14. Define the terms *risk* and *risk management*.

15. Define the terms *risk assessment* and *risk tolerance*.

Exam Questions

1. Identify the stakeholders typically involved in the creation of the organization's cybersecurity policy. (Select all that apply.)

   A. Corporate management

   B. Security management

   C. The change management team

   D. Network administration

   E. Corporate legal counsel

2. What documentation must be generated to support an exemption request from the cybersecurity policy? (Select all that apply.)

   A. The management group contact for the exempt asset

   B. The physical location of the exempt asset

   C. The network segment address of the exempt asset

   D. How risks associated with the asset will be mitigated

   E. How the exempt asset is segregated from the network

3. Identify the correct order of execution when using the NIST Cyber Security Framework to develop a cybersecurity policy.

   A. Identify, detect, protect, respond, recover

   B. Identify, protect, detect, recover, respond

   C. Detect, identify, protect, recover, respond

   D. Identify, protect, detect, respond, recover

4. From the following list, identify the standard that provides standards, guidelines, and best practices to promote the protection of critical infrastructure for the electrical generation and distribution environment.

   A. NERC CIP

   B. NISTSP 800-53, "Security and Privacy Controls for Federal Information Systems and Organizations"

   C. NIST Special Publication 800-18, Revision 1

   D. ISO/IEC 27002:2013, "Information technology – Security techniques – Code of practice for information security management"

5. Identify a common penetration tool employed in pentesting a network. (Select all that apply.)

   A. Vulnerability scanners

   B. Baseline monitors

   C. Keyloggers

   D. Port scanning tools

   E. Sniffing tools

6. Identify the major components of the risk mitigation strategy. (Select all that apply.)

   A. IRP

   B. BCP

   C. DRP

   D. SIS

   E. PHA

7. Identify the first two steps in developing the corporate cybersecurity policy.

   A. Identify the organization's risk tolerance levels

   B. Identify critical network and software assets

   C. Assign monetary replacement values to each critical asset

   D. Conduct third-party tests to identify network vulnerabilities

   E. Conduct an impact assessment to determine the organization's risk levels

8. From the following list, identify the major tools involved in the development of a PHA. (Select all that apply.)

   A. A layer of protection analysis (LOPA)

   B. A safety instrumented system analysis (SISA)

   C. A failure mode and effects analysis (FMEA)

   D. An annualized rate of occurrence analysis (AROA)

   E. An impact assessment analysis (IAA)

9. _____ is a qualitative risk assessment process used to assess the potential hazards in a given industrial process.

   A. A HAZOP analysis

   B. A failure mode and effects analysis

   C. A process hazard analysis

   D. A layer of protection analysis

10. Which part of an organization's overall security/cybersecurity plan is designed to provide guidelines for who, what, where, and when a physical disaster, network disaster, or security attack occurs?

    A. The risk mitigation plan

    B. The incident response plan

    C. The business continuity plan

    D. The disaster recovery plan

Chapter

9

ICS Security Assessments

OBJECTIVES

Upon completion of this chapter, you should be able to:

1. Demonstrate knowledge of Security Assessment

2. Describe concepts and practices associated with ICS Device Testing:

   - Communication robustness

   - Fuzzing

   - Risk

   - Criticality

   - Vulnerability

   - Attack surface analysis

   - Supply chain

3. Apply standard practices associated with Penetration Testing and Exploitation

4. Describe the use of industry standard Security Tesing Tools:

   - Packet sniffer

   - Port scanner

   - Vulnerability scanner

Introduction

In the previous chapter, you were introduced to the cybersecurity policy generation process, as well as the risk management process. Recall that after the organization's network assets have been identified and valued, and the potential vulnerabilities and threats against it have been identified, the next step in developing the cybersecurity plan is to perform a risk assessment.

> The risk assessment is a key component of the organization's risk management strategy. It identifies steps that can be taken to ensure that the organization understands the cybersecurity risk to its organizational operations (including its mission, functions, image, or reputation), its organizational assets, and its personnel.

After the threats have been identified and the risks have been quantified, the next step in the process is to conduct actual vulnerability tests on the network to determine how susceptible it is to these threats. This is accomplished through a process known as a *security assessment*.

In this chapter, you will be introduced to common terminology, tools, techniques, and processes associated with planning and conducting a security assessment. This includes an introduction to penetration testing, or *pentesting*, the network (and possibly its administrative and support personnel) for risk identification purposes.

Security Assessments

In both IT and OT network environments a security assessment involves performing a sequence of exercises designed to locate vulnerabilities within the organization's network and computing environment. These organizations then use the results obtained from the assessment to help them evaluate their security postures. This is where the potential threats and vulnerabilities identified early in the risk assessment are verified.

As you will see later in this chapter, there are many references and guidelines available for conducting a security assessment. However, all of these methodologies are generally performed in a four-phase process.

1. The *Discovery phase* (identification) identifies systems and processes in use within the enterprise or OT network.

    a. Examine the organization's cybersecurity practices. Gather information about its cybersecurity policies, procedures, and practices. Also, gather information about resources that can play a role in the cybersecurity of critical digital assets, such as computers and network devices.

    b. Identify assets to be assessed. Perform an initial consequence analysis for each identified critical asset to determine the potential consequences to the organization if it were to be compromised.

2. The *Vulnerability Scan phase* (assessment) follows the Discovery phase and uses automated tools to search for security issues within the network.

    a. Conduct tabletop reviews and validation testing of the identified digital assets. This should include physical inspections as well as electronic testing (scanning identified critical assets).

3. The *Vulnerability Assessment phase* (mitigation) builds on the Discovery and Vulnerability Scan phases to identify vulnerabilities and verify the level of exposure the organization faces from the vulnerabilities that get uncovered. The outcomes of the assessment generate context that can be used to help management understand the magnitude of risks within their network.

    a. Conduct assessments of susceptibility. Use results from the tabletop reviews and validation testing to assess the susceptibility to cyber exploitation of each critical asset. The product of this stage is an estimate of the overall susceptibility level for each critical digital asset (CDA).

    b. Conduct risk assessment activities. Reassess the initial consequence analyses and use these results in conjunction with the results of susceptibility assessments to estimate the risks of cyber exploitation for each asset.

    c. Conduct risk management activities. These activities include the identification and characterization of potential new countermeasures that could be implemented to enhance cybersecurity.

    d. Compare the benefits of these countermeasures with the costs to implement and operate these countermeasures.

    e. Identify cost-effective risk management options and prepare recommendations for management.

4. The *Reporting phase* (prevention) enables the organization to view its cybersecurity posture holistically from the perspective of potential attackers. The organization can use the report's recommendations to implement tools and processes to reduce their risk exposure based on the assessed threats and vulnerabilities. Typically, a security assessment report will contain the following topics:

    a. An executive summary

    b. A project scope description

    c. An assessment methodology description

    d. InfoSec strengths

    e. Network vulnerabilities

- Open TCP ports
- Open UDP ports

    f. Network remediation recommendations

Within these four phases, the security assessment should be careful to investigate facets of the seven foundational requirements for *Industrial Automation and Controls Systems (IACS)* security defined in the ISA/IEC-62443-3-X series of functional security assessments, listed here:

- Access control
- Use control
- System integrity
- Data confidentiality
- Restricted data flow
- Timely response to event
- Network resource availability

ICS Device Testing

In the IT network environment, there is a wealth of information available for securing different network devices. Enterprise network administrators and security administrators are typically well aware of the strengths and potential weaknesses of computing and connectivity devices within their networks. However, this has not been proven to be the case in ICS network environments. OT network devices have historically been assumed to be secure through obscurity and lack of outside attack vectors associated with enterprise networks and the Internet.

Data communication has become an important component of most ICS systems. With the trend toward migrating to Ethernet-based networking for its communication infrastructure, the OT network has become increasingly vulnerable to cybersecurity threats.

Vulnerability

Currently, there are many vulnerability challenges facing ICS and SCADA-based networks attached to the organization's IT network. The most prevalent challenges include the following:

- Obsolete or out-of-date ICS technologies that continue to operate
- Nonsecure interfaces

- Nonexistent or insufficient monitoring
- Nonexistent or out-of-date software patching
- Lack of virus protection tools for OT systems
- Nonsecure network connectivity
- Software overflow vulnerabilities
- Remote access vulnerabilities due to lack of access controls
- Lack of equipment and software vendor security participation
- Other hardware/software vulnerabilities from third-party suppliers

Two facets are involved in locating and correcting (or compensating for) these vulnerabilities:

- The ICS supply chain (hardware and software vendor security assurances and support)
  - Vulnerability notifications from vendors and other appropriate sources should be monitored and assessed for all systems and applications associated with both the enterprise and OT network environments.
- The organization's security assessments based on ICS device testing and network penetration testing
  - Vulnerability assessment must be performed on all new IT and OT devices and systems (or ones undergoing significant change) before putting them online. Such activities are typically conducted in a sandbox environment, as doing so in an operational production network could impact availability and productivity.
  - Periodic vulnerability assessments must also be performed on OT networks and devices so that appropriate measures can be taken to address the risk associated with identified vulnerabilities.

Supply Chain

To compensate for the increased threat vectors and attack surfaces appearing in the OT network environment, OT device manufacturers have escalated their vulnerability testing procedures to include such activities as the following:

- Port scanning tests
- Network flooding activities
- Vulnerability scanning
- Protocol fuzzing

These tests are conducted by the manufacturers to review and ensure the device's ability to maintain operational performance and *security assurance levels* (*SALs*) in the face of common cyberattack methods. However, the ICS world is full of obscure and sometimes obsolete technology that does not provide any reliable SALs.

The *ISA99* committee has produced a series of documents, described in Figure 9.1, to address the different aspects of cybersecurity for the ICS. Of particular interest for those conducting security assessments are the two items located in the bottom group of documents. These documents focus on the technical security requirements for individual components in the OT network: hardware, software, and informational pieces of the system.

FIGURE 9.1   ISA/IEC-62443 document series

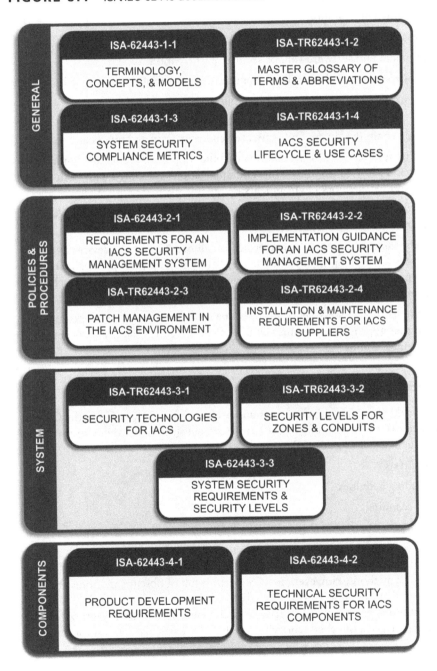

Part of the *ISA/IEC-62443* initiative is to provide a conformance certification program for ICS device manufacturers to follow when developing their products. The *ISASecure* (www .isasecure.org) program has been developed to provide the industry with a certifiable conformity assessment scheme for ICS devices and systems. It certifies commercial off-the-shelf (COTS) ICS products and systems, addressing how to secure the ICS supply chain. Currently, there are two COTS certifications available through this program.

- Embedded Device Security Assurance (ISASecure-EDSA), certifying IACS products to the IEC 62443-4-2 standard

- System Security Assurance (ISASecure-SSA), certifying IACS systems to the IEC 62443-3-3 standard

There is also a third certification, Secure Development Lifecycle Assurance (SDLA), that certifies IACS development organizations to the IEC 62443-4-1 standard. This certification is designed to provide assurances that a supplier organization has institutionalized cybersecurity into their product development practices.

Because there is a lack of vulnerability research in the OT environment to provide better tools for scanning OT devices and networks, the ISASecure program includes a process for recognizing test tools to ensure the tools meet the functional requirements necessary and sufficient to execute all required product tests and that test results will be consistent among the recognized tools.

While these programs are coming online, the OT side of the network does not yet possess a robust system for increasing the security of their devices and systems. In the enterprise network environment, there are many tools available to scan networks for vulnerabilities, and product vendors actively pursue and correct vulnerabilities that are discovered and reported. Patching in the enterprise network is a customary, accepted, and continuous activity.

This is not the case in the ICS world. One source estimates that there are an average of more than 1,800 undiscovered vulnerabilities in each OT computer. In addition, between 15 and 25 percent of patches issued for OT operating systems are incorrect and adversely affect the end user by resulting in crashes, hangs, data disruptions, and increased security issues.

Device Testing Risks

As noted earlier, many organizations resist the push for upgrading to new OT devices because doing so could create a disturbance in their operational flow. Therefore, device testing becomes an important component of the ICS security assessment. However, the risk associated with OT device testing in the field also includes the real possibility of process downtime (or outages) associated with using scanning tools and techniques on ICS or SCADA devices. As mentioned earlier, such tasks are typically performed in a digital-twin or sandbox environment before introducing them to the operational environment.

Device Criticality

The term *criticality* refers to the quality, state, or degree of being of the highest importance. Criticality assessment and analysis processes should be performed on each OT network device to determine the consequences of its failure or lack of function. When an organization undertakes an ICS security assessment, risk mitigation, and security policy generation plan, they must address the following possible areas of risk:

- Personnel safety

- Equipment safety

- Environmental impact

- Production loss

- Data loss

- Adverse business effects

These concerns are addressed in the *Hazard and Operability* (HAZOP) study described in Chapter 8, "ICS Security Governance and Risk Management." In particular, the *Failure Modes, Effects and Criticality Analysis (FMECA)* portion of the study analyzes the process's devices to identify how they might fail and assesses their relative impacts on the organization. As the title implies, there are three general areas involved in the FMECA:

- *Failure modes* involve classifying ways (modes) in which devices or systems might fail. This portion of the analysis identifies the specific manner or manners in which a component's function can fail.

- *Effects analysis* refers to classifying the consequences of those failures. This portion of the analysis identifies how seriously each mode affects the organization and produces a severity (S) rating for each. It also produces an occurrence (O) rating for each mode that estimates the probability of failures occurring.

- *Criticality analysis* involves prioritizing the order in which potential failures should be addressed based on severity and occurrence (S x O) calculations.

The resulting *criticality assessment* can be used to identify which components in the system are most likely to fail. This in turn enables the organization to take actions to mitigate likely failure events and their frequencies. This may involve substituting components with higher reliability ratings, adding redundant components to compensate for potential failure, or reducing the stress level at which critical devices operate. Depending on the severity of the vulnerability, the organization may want to implement additional monitoring activities for devices and systems that produce high *criticality rankings*.

The FMEA/FMECA is basically a mathematically driven process that arrives at a risk priority number (RPN) calculation based on the product of the severity, occurrence, and detection (S x O x D) ratings. There are many FMEA and FMECA tools available to help organizations calculate their ICS risks.

Attack Surface Analysis

The term *attack surface* is used to define all the different points in a device or system through which an attacker could gain access or extract data. An *attack surface analysis* process is designed to specify what aspects of a device or system represent vulnerabilities, so that the organization understands the risks associated with that particular device or system. The organization can then determine the amount of effort and types of resources it is willing to commit to minimizing those risks.

The process begins with identifying all the *attack vectors* (paths, channels, or means) that can be used to access the target. This includes noting physical access paths, remote access paths, and interfaces with outside systems (particularly paths that interface with the Internet), as illustrated in Figure 9.2. The relative security of protocols associated with each channel is also considered in the analysis.

FIGURE 9.2 Attack surfaces

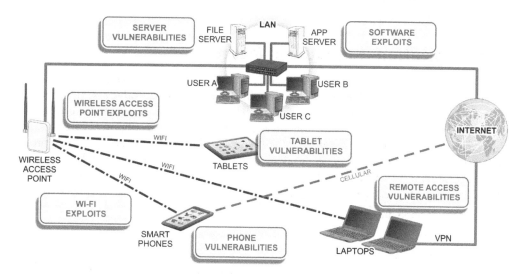

The analysis process also involves identifying all of the protective measures defending each path—connectivity and control devices, authentication and authorization tools, as well as data activity logging systems and data encoding systems.

Next, the various roles and privileges (access rights) given to different types of users must be factored into the analysis. In particular, highly privileged users (such as administrators and security personnel) and unauthorized and anonymous (guest account) users must be evaluated.

> Microsoft offers a threat modeling card game called Elevation of Privilege (EoP) that provides an interesting exercise to help IT and information security personnel understand and be familiar with attack surfaces (www.microsoft.com/en-us/download/details.aspx?id=20303).

Finally, each attack vector should be grouped into risk types (external or internal facing), purposes, implementations, and technologies. Then count the number of attack vectors associated with each group so you can examine cases from each and concentrate assessment activities on those designated as high-risk areas. Such analysis processes are typically performed internally by red team members such as network security personnel and *penetration testers* (*pentesters*).

Mathematical formulas are available that security analysts use to calculate the ability of a device or system to be attacked.

Attack surface analysis can be used to identify the following:

- Facets of the network that the organization needs to review or test for security vulnerabilities
- High-risk areas of the network that require defense-in-depth protection strategies
- When the device or network's attack surface has changed and a new threat assessment is needed

Communication Robustness Testing

Robustness testing refers to testing to determine a device's ability to handle errors and failures. It is common for embedded devices to remain in the field for several years, and they may need to survive multiple technology changes over their lifetime. A device is considered to be robust if it can continue to function after an event such as a loss of power occurs.

Communication robustness testing (CRT) for embedded devices is based on sending protocol messages to the device and then checking its communication status. If the device fails to continue providing system control and reporting functions, then a vulnerability is indicated. Three types of messages are generally tested:

- Correctly formed messages
- Erroneous messages
- Malformed messages

The device should be expected to adequately maintain essential services, such as the operation of the process control/safety loop, command capabilities, and process alarms.

Fuzzing

Fuzzing is an automated, black-box data-injection technique where malformed data is injected into software structures to detect software structure, configuration, and implementation faults. As such, fuzzing is commonly used to expose vulnerabilities (attack vectors or *fuzz vectors*) in software that can be exploited by an attacker. It is typically one portion of the communication robustness testing procedure. Typical fuzz vector categories include the following:

- SQL injection
- Cross-site scripting (XSS)
- LDAP injection
- XML injection
- Buffer overflows (BFO)
- Format string errors
- Integer overflows

The fuzzing process begins with establishing a communication channel into the target device. Then a software tool referred to as a *fuzzer* is used to inject the malformed data into the target's software structure, looking to create any of the conditions listed earlier. These tests are designed to create conditions ranging from instability to complete failure, which can be detected through simple observation. If the device fails or behaves erratically, a vulnerability condition is indicated, and a risk mitigation plan must be created for the device.

Protocol fuzzing involves introducing faults (malformed messages) into a protocol to test the robustness of the target device. The malformed message is simply a protocol message with incorrect syntax. There are several different protocols such as SIP, SCADA, IPv6, Wi-Fi, Bluetooth, ARP, DHCP, and Modbus that can be tested through fuzzing efforts.

Protocol fuzzing requires knowledge of the protocol's header/packet format and tools for creating/manipulating the header and message. Figure 9.3 depicts a typical TCP/IP header. By injecting various values into different fields, particularly undefined values reserved for future use, packets can be sent to the target that will attempt to process it.

FIGURE 9.3   TCP/IP header

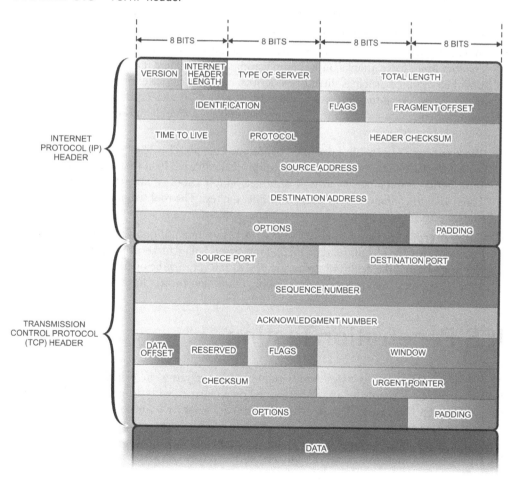

When the target device receives an unexpected value, such as fields with incorrect lengths (particularly zero lengths or payloads that are too short or long), it becomes confused and may react in a number of different ways, including going into infinite program loops, buffer overflow conditions, or simply crashing. *State-based fuzzing* involves manipulating the order of messages instead of the contents of the messages.

The failure conditions listed earlier are typical software-related conditions recognized by every software programmer. Programmers can easily create messages to initiate them. There are, however, several commercial and open-source fuzzing packages available for pentesters to use:

- *W3af* (`https://docs.w3af.org`): W3af is a flexible framework for building vulnerability discovery/exploit tools. This framework enables the user to integrate other tools (plugins) into the package for exploitation or monitoring purposes. This utility is available in Kali Linux as well as Windows.

- *Wapiti* (`https://wapiti-scanner.github.io`): Wapiti is designed to audit the security of web applications by looking for scripts and forms where it can inject data. After it creates a list of potential vulnerabilities, it injects payloads into the scripts (fuzzes) to determine whether it is truly vulnerable.

- *Wfuzz* (`https://github.com/xmendez/wfuzz`): The Wfuzz fuzzer is designed to conduct brute-force attacks on web applications. In particular, it can be used to locate unlinked resources, such as directories, scripts, etc., that can be exploited. In addition, it can be used for different types of injection attacks (SQL, XSS, LDAP, etc.) and fuzzing/brute-forcing user/password parameters. Wfuzz is available in Kali Linux and as a Windows-based utility.

- *Peach* (`https://github.com/MozillaSecurity/peach`): The Peach fuzzer is designed to run with different test definitions (called Peach Pits) that contain specific information about a particular type of target. Simply choose a target type, use a web-based GUI to configure parameters, and start the test. The tool will automatically generate a prioritized report of each issue it encounters.

- *Sulley* (`https://github.com/OpenRCE/sulley`): In addition to the data generation functions provided by all fuzzers, the Python-based Sulley fuzzer framework monitors the network and the health of the target device and returns the operation to a "good state." In general, Sulley requires less coding than other fuzzers to set up and use.

ICS Penetration Testing

The other facet of a security assessment's vulnerability analysis is the *penetration test*, or *pentest*. A pentest is simply an attack performed on a network with the goal of finding security weaknesses. This essentially involves trying to hack your own (or your customer's) systems. Pentesting exists as a way for organizations to use resources (external or internal) to attempt to break into their network or system and possibly attack it for the purpose of gaining information about their network's vulnerabilities so they can assess their level of risk.

Penetration testing not only looks for vulnerabilities but also searches a database of *exploits* (computer programs designed to take advantage of particular vulnerabilities). These exploits might be used to deliver a payload to the target system that will grant the hacker access to that system.

Penetration testing is a thriving business for outside security firms. This service can be a valuable tool for helping organizations to discover vulnerabilities in their networks. However, there are many open-source penetration testing tools available for use by individuals or organizations. Certain Linux distributions include not only penetration testing utilities but also *vulnerability emulators* that can be deployed as targets for these tests.

The Pentest Process

Several standard frameworks and methodologies exist for conducting penetration testing. These are some of the most noteworthy pentest frameworks:

- The Open-Source Testing Methodology Manual (OSTMM, `www.isecom.org/research.html#content5-9d`)

- The Penetration Testing Execution Standard (PTES, `www.pentest-standard.org`)

- The NIST SP 800-115 (`https://csrc.nist.gov/publications/detail/sp/800-115/final`)

- The Information System Security Assessment Framework (ISSAF, `www.oissg.org/issaf`)

- The Open Web Application Security Project Testing Guide (OWASP, `http://owasp.org/www-project-web-security-testing-guide`)

- The Lockheed-Martin Cyber Kill Chain (`www.lockheedmartin.com/en-us/capabilities/cyber/cyber-kill-chain.html`)

Each of these pentesting methods presents its own approach to the flow of the pentest process. However, there are three general sections of the pentest process that are common to them all:

- *Negotiating*: Defining and agreeing on the scope of the test
  - Negotiate who will be involved.
  - Commit to the rules of engagement to be employed.

- *Pentesting*: Conducting the attacks
  - Assess the risk.
  - Undertake discovery.
  - Develop a test plan.
  - Conduct the technical security tests.

- *Documenting*: Generating reports and documentation
  - Analyze the test results.
  - Publish and deliver the test results.

Pentest Negotiations

The skills a pentester uses to research and attack a network are no different than those used by a *black-hat hacker* to gain access to an organization's network. The main difference, however, is that legitimate pentesters are *white-hat hackers* who do not use their skills to steal valuable and sensitive information or to vandalize an organization's property. Instead, they will generate and provide a report to the organization, known as a *brief*. This brief will highlight areas of weakness found in the organization's security policies and practices during the test, including such items as how the hacker was able to gain access through their network's perimeter defenses.

In situations where companies hire an outside pentest organization or company to conduct the test, the two entities will work together to determine who will play what role in the test. There are usually three groups:

- A *red team* that conducts the attack

- A *blue team* that typically comprises the victims (i.e., network administrators)

- A *white team* that oversees the test

Initially, it might be easy to think that the pentest company would just come in and perform a full set of attacks to make sure that the network is 100 percent tested for vulnerabilities. However, this is usually not the case. Before the testing begins, the pentester and the customer must negotiate and establish exactly what the parameters of the test will be.

For example, many pentest companies believe that because a hacker doesn't have limitations on what can or cannot be attacked, neither should the pentesters. This idea is very true and can be uncomfortable for some companies, which is why so much time can be spent defining what is open to attack.

It will be important for the company to also set a reasonable window for attacks to take place. In this case, the company knows that if they get hacked outside that window, it is not the pentesters but an actual nefarious attack.

Key items to define during this portion of the process include the following:

- *What is to be accomplished?* Maybe the company has problems with phishing attacks and users innocently giving out passwords. In such cases, the goal would be to decrease the number of successful phishing attempts.

- *What systems (human or otherwise) are open to attack and for how long?* For instance, if I am conducting a phishing attack, the pentester would not necessarily be interested in attacking something that is out of the scope of the goal. Keep in mind, depending on how the company operates, this can be a very gray area and oftentimes one of the biggest areas the white team administrators will work to define.

- *Who on the blue team will know about the attack?* Let's say you are conducting social engineering with the goal of infiltrating the company in order to gain access to a server closet. What happens when you walk down a hall, looking very suspicious, and someone calls you out? What if they ask for identification and you failed to acquire a visitor's badge from the front desk? Maybe they will just escort you out of the building. However, if this were to happen at night when the building was closed, there could be a very different result, one where you may end up in handcuffs. This would be a great time to have the point of contact for the company on speed dial, or a letter from the chief information security officer (CISO) or chief security officer (CSO). In other words, it is important that someone in the company knows what's going on, yet they remain out of the test itself. This way, if something goes awry, you can quickly get to that person and explain what's going on.

- *Legalities*: There are many laws involved in ethical and unethical hacking. Companies need to be aware of what they are getting into, and pentest companies also need to know what is and isn't illegal at the local, state, and federal levels. A company needs to be sure that the pentesters sign all the necessary confidentiality and nondisclosure agreements that are by required federal laws.

Pentest Types

After the details of the pentest have been negotiated and agreed to, the next phase involves performing the different attacks that have been agreed to. Basically, pentests can be conducted under three types of circumstances:

- *Black box*: A black-box penetration test is a method of penetration testing in which the ethical hacker has no prior knowledge of the system or network infrastructure being attacked and is not given any of these crucial details by the client company either.

- *White box*: White-box penetration testing refers to a pentesting method where the ethical hacker has full and complete knowledge of the system or network infrastructure being attacked.

- *Gray box*: An ethical hacker conducting a gray-box penetration test will have partial knowledge of the target system or infrastructure they are attempting to attack.

Consider for a minute what you are able to see around you when you are blindfolded. You are only able to see darkness and a black color. You cannot see anything about the world around you. No physical details are available to you, and you have to rely on your other senses to find your way around. A black-box penetration test is similar to this.

The ultimate goal for a *black-box penetration test* is to attempt to simulate an attack on a client's infrastructure by an external entity because, unless the attacker is an inside threat, external entities should not have access to the intimate details of a company's network infrastructure and defenses, as shown in Figure 9.4.

FIGURE 9.4   Black-box testing

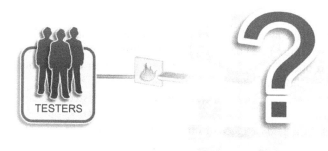

Black-box tests generally start with reconnaissance of various means to collect as much information as possible on the company itself. Oftentimes user credentials can be generated based on the email addresses of employees, and calling the company's help desk to reset an employee's password can easily grant access to the network. Then, a penetration tester would attempt one of a couple of scenarios.

The first scenario would involve spending more time on premises than may be comfortable by going to the company and sitting in the lobby and connecting an Ethernet cable to an unsecured port. Or an even more daring professional may go so far as to plant a battery-powered *Raspberry Pi* loaded with penetration software in a workroom or conference room where Ethernet ports are usually abundant.

Once on the network, the device phones home, and access to the network is granted. With a set of user credentials recently acquired through social engineering, the pentester then starts to dig further into the network.

As shown in Figure 9.5, *white-box pentesting*, also referred to as *glass-box testing*, is basically the exact opposite of a black-box penetration test. The ultimate goal of a white-box penetration test is to simulate a malicious *insider threat* from someone who has intimate knowledge of the client's critical network infrastructure and the credentials to access it.

FIGURE 9.5   White-box testing

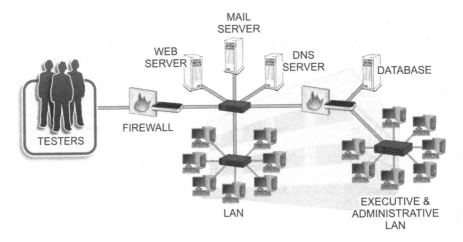

Gray-box pentesting combines the methodologies used in both black- and white-box penetration testing, as shown in Figure 9.6. For example, a gray-box pentester may be given information about the different operating systems that comprise the target network but may not be given credentials to access those systems.

Another possible gray-box pentest combination could be that the pentester is given specific information about perimeter network defenses on the client's network, but information about interior network defense mechanisms is not provided.

FIGURE 9.6   Gray-box pentesting

Conducting the Attack

After the pentest parameters have been negotiated and agreed to, the attack process follows the phases of the attack kill chain described in Chapter 5, "Cybersecurity Essentials for ICS."

1. *Reconnaissance*: In this stage, activities are conducted to find exploitable vulnerabilities in the target's network structure and configurations. This can include scanning for network hardware and software attack surfaces, as well as using physical and logical social engineering methods to identify possible attack vectors.

2. *Weaponization*: After the attack vectors and surfaces have been identified, it is time to evaluate the likelihood of successful penetration and exploitation of the vulnerabilities discovered. This information permits the pen tester to design an attack strategy and assemble tools that can be used to exploit those vulnerabilities that present a high likelihood of success.

3. *Delivery*: This portion of the intrusion phase may be immediate or carried out over a period of time. After the network has been penetrated, the next question is what to do now that you've reached the inside. Do you immediately activate a payload, or do you look around inside for additional opportunities? In a pentesting situation, this answer is usually specified in the contract agreement.

4. *Installation and exploitation*: At this point in a pentest, it is normally time to install the exploits and execute the attack strategy. This can involve installing back doors to provide the pentester with command-and-control functions in the network or a computing device. Malware of different types can be installed including Trojans, bots, or ransomware.

5. *Action on objectives*: This phase of the attack involves exploring the options created by exploiting the vulnerabilities identified earlier. The black-hat hacker can sit on the network and extract such data as company secrets, credit card information, patient medical data, etc. This typically involves spoofing attacks of different types, keyloggers, session hijacking, etc. The attacker can also use their access to degrade, disrupt, deny, or destroy

their target's assets. This option usually involves viruses, denial-of-service (DoS)/distributed denial-of-service (DDoS) attacks, man-in-the-middle (MitM) attacks, broadcast storms, etc.

Pentest Documentation

For pentesters, *documentation* is extremely important and can make or break a test, as well as keep you out of serious trouble. For example, if you are hired by an organization to pentest their network, it is important to have something tangible to give them along with your findings and recommendations regarding their network.

 Regardless of whether the report is for a government entity or private company, the results and findings (as well the technical aspects of the report) should be kept secured and out of the hands of those who don't need access to it.

Even if you are an inside pentester, you will need to generate clear and accurate documentation that can educate management and advise technical personnel responsible for organizational security. There's an old saying that says, "If you didn't document it, it didn't happen." This is an unfortunately true statement because so much of what cybersecurity professionals produce is technical writing and reports for the consumption of the customer.

Report writing may not be the most exciting thing in the world, but it is essential and should be treated with the highest respect, as the information contained in the report is typically very sensitive, if not classified.

The report should be aimed at administrative-level executive staff and IT personnel. Copies of the report and who receives them should be documented as well. The master copy should be stored in a very secure place where other valuable information is stored.

For the pentester, documenting everything done and discussed is vital. Whether it's through screenshots, data dumps, packet captures, or anything like that, the more documentation you have to support your claim, the stronger your argument will be.

Along with collecting data, pentesters need to be sure to take carefully written notes so that any findings can be duplicated by the IT staff of the company. Also, clearly written notes will help the report writers go back and remember exactly what happened so that the report is clear and concise.

Reporting to the Customer

A *pentest report* should be created for the customer. The report itself should be formatted so that it is easy to read, contains page numbers, and includes any other feature of a professional report or whitepaper. While these reports aren't published (and should *never* be published), it is important to maintain professionalism throughout the report and refrain from using any sort of slang terminology that may hinder the understanding of the readers. There are several key parts involved in creating a professional pentest report:

- *Executive summary*: The target audience for the executive summary should be the executive staff of the company. This section is meant to be relatively nontechnical, so that the executives understand what is going on and why changes need to be made. Keep in mind that, for the most part, executives see numbers and dollar signs, so they will want to know about risk and why they should invest money in security.

- *Scope of work*: The scope of work will contain any information supplied by the company as well as how the assessment was carried out. It will also detail exactly what was targeted and what was off limits to the pentesters. It might be a good idea to include the rules of engagement that were established before the test so that the executives and IT staff understand how and why you were able to target the systems in the report.

- *Project objectives*: This section may seem redundant, but keep in mind that some of the executives who are involved in this report may be seeing this for the first time, so reiterating your objectives in this section is important so that everyone is on the same page. Keep in mind that many people are not "tech savvy" and may not understand why they're involved in the report. However, the report will ideally help them see the risk analysis and dollar signs involved and understand that security is everyone's concern.

- *Assumptions*: Because the client may provide you with technical information prior to the start of the test, it is acceptable for some assumptions to be made so that the audience understands your thought process and how you came to certain conclusions.

- *Timeline*: The timeline can be considered part of the rules of engagement and defines the start and end dates for the testing window. It will also give the IT staff an idea of when to expect incidences to occur, and if something happens outside that window, it is definitely not the pentesters.

- *Summary of findings*: A summary of findings is a very helpful tool for many of the customer's executives. A good summary should include the following:

  - Statistics

  - Impact

  - Risk evaluation

- *Detailed findings*: The target audience for the detailed findings section should be the top-level IT staff of the company. Information in the following sections will include any elements that enhance the understanding of the findings, including diagrams and graphs.

- *Vulnerabilities*: This section should list the following information for each vulnerability:

  - Vulnerability (can be a name or short description)

  - Threat level

  - Impact

  - Risk

  - Analysis with detailed information

  - Recommendation for how to mitigate the vulnerability

- *Solutions and recommendations*: This section summarizes the detailed findings as well as the impact and risk of the overall list of vulnerabilities. This information would be used to quantify the impact of a vulnerability if something were to happen and information is compromised.

- *Closing remarks*: The closing remarks section is where the authors add any final thoughts and suggestions and summarize the overall test.

Security Testing Tools

In the previous chapter you were introduced to three activities that are commonly performed in the Vulnerability Scan and Assessment phases of a security assessment (or risk identification). Recall that they included the following:

- *Packet sniffing*: Using a packet analyzer, the white hat captures data packets as they move across the network, logs them, and then decodes their raw data. They can then analyze the data, in effect spying on the network users.

- *Port scanning*: Using a port scanner tool, the pentester probes the network servers and devices for open ports that can be exploited. They can also identify services running on a host for potential exploitation.

- *Vulnerability scanning*: Using a *network vulnerability scanner* package, the pentester scans the organization's networks for different types of common vulnerabilities such as system misconfigurations and default password usage, as well as generating malformed packets to create DoS attacks.

These and other network testing tools enable the white hat to more easily audit the network to understand its resources, evaluate its risks, assess its vulnerabilities, and create a plan for mitigating (or exploiting) these risks and vulnerabilities.

Packet Sniffers

A *packet sniffer* (also known as a *packet analyzer* or a *protocol analyzer*) is a software monitoring tool that is used to scan network traffic that passes through it. A computing device running these tools is typically inserted into the network so that network traffic flows through it, allowing packets to be captured in real time, as shown in Figure 9.7. As the network traffic passes through the analyzer, the analyzer "sniffs" the packets looking for promiscuous activity or just logs what's going on.

Packet/protocol analyzers require two network interfaces so they can examine the network activity as it flows through them. Because they do not require tremendous CPU resources, an older laptop that can support two Ethernet interfaces can be ideal. Performance monitoring products can run on older hardware as well and can be a great way to use unwanted aging computer hardware.

FIGURE 9.7   A packet analyzer tool

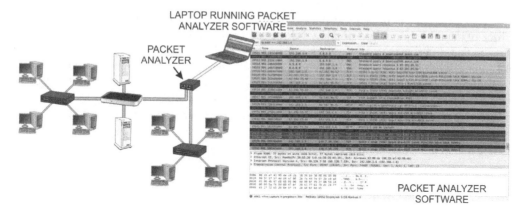

Network Enumeration/Port Scanning

No matter what situation you run into, the first thing a good security practitioner (or hacker) does is *enumerate* the network. This means to map the network to determine what is on it so you know what hosts can be found.

You can discover all sorts of information by performing this operation, including that there may be devices on your network that shouldn't be there. For instance, let's say you're a network security engineer for a hospital and you're doing a routine scan of the network. Thanks to the mapping and enumeration software, you discover that there is a Raspberry Pi connected to your network, as shown in Figure 9.8, that definitely should not be there.

FIGURE 9.8   Network enumeration

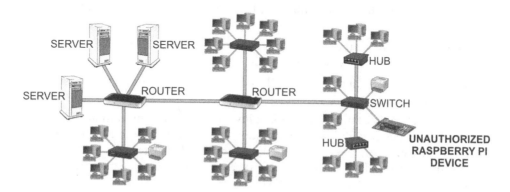

Because you know how the network is set up and that the layer 3 switches possess specific DHCP ranges, you can pinpoint which switch the device is connected to. You are quickly able to disable the port on the switch. In this case, knowing exactly what is on the network alerted you to a serious security issue.

There are a number of ways to enumerate a network and various tools to do so. *Nmap* is one of the most common examples of these tools and can be used to scan networks of all sizes to find different types of network information, such as what operating system each host is running, what ports could potentially be open, or what hosts are on a particular network.

Figure 9.9 shows output generated by the Nmap tool used to map networks and collect information. In this case, the command nmap 10.0.0.0/24 -O was used to produce the results of a network scan that also attempts to reveal the operating system of a device.

FIGURE 9.9   Nmap output

```
Nmap scan report for 10.0.0.13
Host is up (0.018s latency).
Not shown: 995 closed ports
PORT      STATE SERVICE
3689/tcp  open  rendezvous
5000/tcp  open  upnp
7000/tcp  open  afs3-fileserver
7100/tcp  open  font-service
62078/tcp open  iphone-sync
MAC Address:            (Apple)
Device type: general purpose|media device|phone
Running: Apple Mac OS X 10.7.X|10.9.X|10.8.X, Apple iOS 4.X|5.X|6.X
OS CPE: cpe:/o:apple:mac_os_x:10.7 cpe:/o:apple:mac_os_x:10.9 cpe:/o:apple:mac_os_x:10.8 cpe:/o:apple:ip
hone_os:4 cpe:/a:apple:apple_tv:4 cpe:/o:apple:iphone_os:5 cpe:/o:apple:iphone_os:6
OS details: Apple Mac OS X 10.7.0 (Lion) - 10.10 (Yosemite) or iOS 4.1 - 8.1.2 (Darwin 10.0.0 - 14.0.0)
Network Distance: 1 hop
```

As you can see, this scan found a device on the network running OS X or iOS with several ports open. From an attacker's perspective, if you were able to install Nmap on a device and place it on the network, you would have an excellent view into the network.

The following are other notable network enumeration tools:

- *NBTscan*: A CLI-based information enumeration utility that retrieves user lists, device lists, share lists, name lists, group/member lists, and password information from a targeted network.

- *DumpSec*: A GUI-based tool that provides lists of permissions and audit settings from the target file system, along with user, group, and replication data.

- *Legion*: A GUI-based utility that scans IP address ranges for shared resources such as files, directories, printers, etc.

- *Netcat*: A CLI-based computer network utility that performs enumeration and port scanning activities. In addition to enumeration tasks, Netcat can use TCP or UDP protocols to connect to a port on a target host. Listen to a designated port for inbound connections, transfer files across the network, and execute scripts on the target. A similar tool called *Ncat* is housed in the NMAP suite of utilities. While not a derivative of Netcat, Ncat is similar in use.

Port Scanning

Port scanners are software tools designed to probe computing devices for open logical ports and their associated services. Figure 9.10 depicts one of the tools attackers use to locate and exploit vulnerabilities on a targeted device such as a server or endpoint.

FIGURE 9.10   Port scanning

The port scanner sends service requests out across a network connection to a targeted host. The requests are sent to a range of well-known port values to identify network services running on the target. A form of port scanning referred to as *portsweeping* is used to scan network environments for devices responding to a specific port, such as a computer responding to port 530 (*Remote Procedure Call, RPC*).

For network administrators, a port scan should be viewed as a possible first step in an attack sequence. In the example just presented, if the hacker locates such a port, they can begin to prepare an attack using that port to exploit potential vulnerabilities associated with it. In cases where a port scan is combined with a vulnerability scan, the administrator should consider a follow-on attack as being imminent.

Vulnerability Scanning

A *network vulnerability* scanner package is used to scan the enterprise for different types of common vulnerabilities (such as system misconfigurations and default password usage), as illustrated in Figure 9.11. Some are also able to create Denial of Service (DoS) attacks by generating malformed packets.

FIGURE 9.11   Vulnerability scan

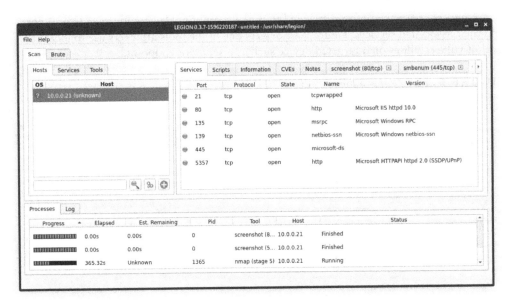

These tools are used by cybersecurity professionals and hackers alike to identify vulnerabilities or gain unauthorized access. They are particularly valuable in identifying the following types of vulnerabilities:

- Active hosts on a network (including those that may be hiding on the network)

- Active ports and services that are vulnerable

- Vulnerabilities associated with operating system server applications

All vulnerability scanners are database-driven tools designed to search computers for known vulnerabilities that have been identified and added to the database. As such, they are only as good as their last update. For this reason, it is imperative that all vulnerability scanners be updated just before using them.

While using vulnerability scanners is time- and resource-consuming, doing so is an important part of ongoing security, as it allows vulnerabilities that are found to be addressed as soon as possible, ideally before they are discovered and exploited.

There are a number of free and commercial products as well as a growing service industry ready to provide these monitoring services. Free products are a great place to start, as they are generally easy to set up and don't require a lot of resources. The following are just a few products to consider:

- Nagios (www.nagios.org) is probably the most well-known network monitoring tool that still has a free version, but it has grown to offer a full-featured commercial enterprise version as well. A fork of this project, Icinga, is an open-source alternative that is more full-featured than the free version of Nagios. Both products have plenty of monitoring, reporting, and notification options that are best suited to uptime monitoring but can monitor performance as well.

- SolarWinds (`www.solarwinds.com/network-performance-monitor`) offers an incredibly powerful commercial network performance monitoring product (NPM) that is part of their Orion platform. While this product is somewhat expensive, it is immensely powerful and can monitor uptime, performance, traffic flow, and utilization, and it can offer a plethora of reporting, graphing, and notification options.

- Microsoft Network Monitor (`https://docs.microsoft.com/en-us/ troubleshoot/windows-server/networking/network-monitor-3`) is a packet analyzer that can help you view your traffic flows and troubleshoot network problems. As you might expect, this product does a wonderful job interacting with proprietary Microsoft protocols, but most common public protocols are supported as well.

- Wireshark (`wireshark.org`) is a mature open-source and cross-platform network protocol analyzer. It is probably the most well-known protocol analyzer, and it supports just about every protocol and runs on nearly any platform.

- Wireshark, shown in Figure 9.12, is a valuable tool for capturing and subsequently analyzing traffic to discover and troubleshoot network issues. It works by taking advantage of a function of network adapters called *promiscuous mode*. This mode enables the network adapter to listen to traffic going through a wire (or over radio waves in the case of a wireless network adapter). The analyzer software then collects all the packets of data and organizes them into a graphically useful system where the user can sift through the information.

FIGURE 9.12   Wireshark

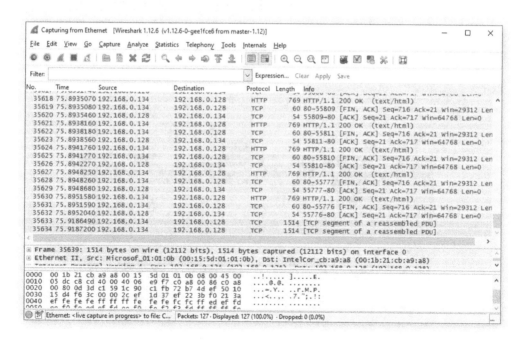

It can be used to learn more about the protocols used on a given network. This tool is easy to employ but requires experience and practice to accurately analyze the results it produces.

- Snort (`snort.org`) is an open-source, cross-platform intrusion detection system that provides real-time traffic analysis, packet logging, and protocol analysis as well as active detection for worms, port scans, and vulnerability exploit attempts. This is useful in monitoring the network in real time. It is well suited to identifying probes and attacks but can act as a network sniffer as well. Snort, shown in Figure 9.13, is an excellent product for networks that feature public services.

FIGURE 9.13   Snort

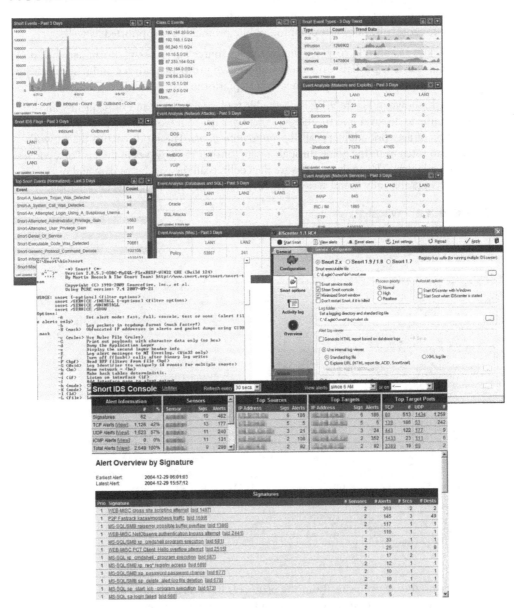

- Nmap, shown in Figure 9.14, is an open-source and cross-platform network mapper utility used for network discovery operations, security auditing operations, and for creating network inventories. It is also used to perform network monitoring functions and to track upgrade scheduling. This is an excellent product for examining and profiling your network as well as discovering ports and versions.

FIGURE 9.14   Nmap utility

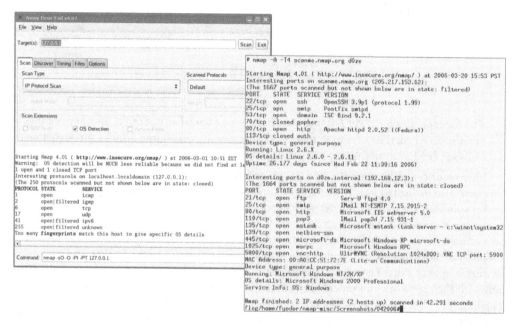

- Nikto (`https://cirt.net/nikto2`) is an open-source web server scanner that can identify issues on a web server. This tool can perform comprehensive tests against a web server, checking for more than 6,700 security threats. Nikto comes preinstalled in the Vulnerability Analysis category of Kali Linux distributions, or it can be sourced from the GitHub site (`https://github.com/sullo/nikto`).

- OpenVAS (`openvas.org`) is an open-source vulnerability scanner for Linux and Windows that is a fork of the last free version of the now commercial Nessus. Built as a full vulnerability management solution, this tool uses SCAP and can perform a number of network vulnerability tests (NVTs) and look for common vulnerabilities and exposures (CVE). This product has a bit of a learning curve, but it is a well-respected and powerful tool worth consideration.

- Metasploit (`metasploit.com`) is one of the most popular open-source penetration testing frameworks available. It is available for both Windows and Linux environments. It is commonly used to identify and validate network vulnerabilities, including simulating attacks that prey on human vulnerabilities, as shown in Figure 9.15. Metasploit can also be used to prioritize responses to network vulnerabilities discovered.

FIGURE 9.15 Metasploit operation

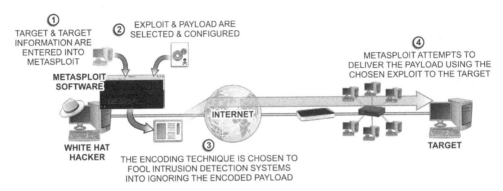

- The *Browser Exploitation Framework (BeEF)* (beefproject.com) is another notable open-source penetration testing tool, but it focuses on web-borne attacks through a web browser. BeEF is available for macOS, Windows, and Linux.

Other security products worth evaluating include Nessus, Core Impact, and Nexpose. There are also dedicated hardware solutions such as Netscout from nGenius that offer serious solutions for monitoring network services and performance. Every network should have some sort of monitoring enabled at all times, and every network administrator should have access to a dependable packet-sniffing tool as well.

Software tools such as the products mentioned are very useful to the hacker and the network engineer alike. The network engineer might use them to discover various problems with their network equipment. To a hacker, though, the information can be far more revealing. They use the tools to begin to form a picture of what the network looks like and what systems are using which protocols, and they may even find some unencrypted data containing compromising information.

Review Questions

The following questions test your knowledge of the material presented in this chapter.

1. A _____ involves performing a sequence of exercises designed to locate vulnerabilities within the organization's network and computing environment.

2. What type of embedded device testing is based on sending protocol messages to the device and then checking its communication status?

3. What type of embedded device testing injects malformed data into software structures to detect software structure, configuration, and implementation faults?

4. Which processes should be performed on each OT network device to determine the consequences of its failure or lack of function?

5. Describe the first step of the attack surface analysis process.

6. What cybersecurity process is designed to specify which aspects of a device or system represent vulnerabilities so that the organization understands the risks associated with that particular device or system?

7. Identify cybersecurity assurances that production organizations should look for from their supply chain when ordering OT devices.

8. _____ exists as a way for organizations to use resources (external or internal) to attempt to break into their network or system and possibly attack it for the purpose of gaining information that will tell the network owner how to fix the insecurities of their network.

9. What term describes the tools used to deliver payloads to target systems that display specific vulnerabilities?

10. What type of tool would a white-hat hacker employ to capture data packets as the packets move across the network and then log the packets and decode their raw data so that they can then analyze the data to spy on the network users?

11. Which class of security tool would the hacker use to probe the network's servers and devices for open ports and identify services running on a host for potential exploitation?

12. What type of software package would the hacker use to scan the organization's networks for different types of common vulnerabilities, such as system misconfigurations and default password usage?

13. _____ are software tools designed to probe computing devices for open logical ports and their associated services. Attackers use these tools to locate and exploit vulnerabilities on a targeted device, such as a server or endpoint.

14. Which type of software tool is used to discover both authorized and unauthorized devices on the network?

15. You have been hired to break into the ACME Co. enterprise network. The organization has given you no inside information about their network. What type of pentesting have you been engaged to carry out?

Exam Questions

1. Which portion of the security assessment employs automated tools to search for security issues within the network?

    A. The Discovery phase

    B. The Vulnerability Scan

    C. The Vulnerability Assessment

    D. The Exploitation Phase

2. Which type of security testing tools can be used to identify active ports and services that are vulnerable?

    A. Packet analyzers

    B. Network mappers

    C. Vulnerability scanners

    D. Network enumeration tools

3. What are the general areas involved in the Failure Modes, Effects, and Criticality Analysis (FMECA) portion of the HAZOP? (Select all that apply.)

    A. Failure modes

    B. Adverse business effects

    C. Effects analysis

    D. Criticality analysis

4. Which device tests are commonly performed by ICS device manufacturers on their devices to ensure the device's ability to maintain operational performance and security assurance levels (SALs) in the face of common cyberattack methods?

    A. Port scanning tests

    B. Packet scanning tests

    C. Protocol fuzzing

    D. MTBF testing

5. Which of the following pentest teams is responsible for conducting the attacks on the organization's network?

    A. The red team

    B. The blue team

    C. The white team

    D. The gold team

6. What category of pentesting is employed to simulate a malicious insider threat that would have intimate knowledge of the client's critical network infrastructure and the credentials to access it?

   A. White-box testing

   B. Gray-box testing

   C. Black-box testing

   D. Clear-box testing

7. From the list, identify those items that are members of the seven foundational requirements for industrial automation and controls systems (IACS) security. (Select all that apply.)

   A. Access control

   B. Unrestricted data flow

   C. Use control

   D. Network resource availability

   E. Data encryption

8. Identify the tools you would employ to discover that there are unauthorized devices connected to your network.

   A. Network enumeration tools

   B. Port scanners

   C. Vulnerability scanners

   D. Network monitoring tools

9. Which of the following activities would be performed in the initial reconnaissance phase of a black-box pentest?

   A. Design an attack plan specific to the ACME Co. network.

   B. Conduct psychological social engineering attempts to gain information about the ACME Co. network.

   C. Install command-and-control software to monitor the ACME Co. network for vulnerabilities.

   D. Scan the ACME Co. network for attack surfaces.

10. What should a security administrator assume if they detect external port scanning activities as well as signs of vulnerability scans occurring?

   A. That their pentesters are conducting vulnerability tests on the network

   B. That their intrusion detection system needs to be reconfigured to eliminate false positive notifications

   C. That their intrusion prevention system needs to be reconfigured to eliminate false negative notifications

   D. That a follow-on attack is probably imminent

Chapter

10

ICS Security Monitoring and Incident Response

OBJECTIVES

Upon completion of this chapter, you should be able to:

1. Demonstrate the knowledge of Change Management:
   - Baselines
   - Equipment connections
   - Configuration auditing

2. Knowledge of Distribution and Installation of Patches

3. Knowledge of Software Reloads and Firmware Management

4. Knowledge of event, network, and security monitoring:
   - Event monitoring
   - Network monitoring
   - Security monitoring

5. Knowledge of logging:
   - Event logging
   - Network logging
   - Security logging
   - Knowledge of archiving logs

6. Knowledge of incident recognition and triage:
   - Log analysis/event correlation
   - Anomalous behavior
   - Intrusion detection
   - Egress monitoring
   - IPS

7. Knowledge of incident response:

- Recording/reporting
- Forensic log analysis
- Containment
- Incident response team
- Root cause analysis
- Eradication/quarantine

8. Knowledge of incident remediation/recovery

Introduction

An organization's cybersecurity policy should contain several interdependent plans working together to address the following areas:

- Configuration management
- Patch management
- Patch testing
- Organization/local data backup/retrieval
- Incident response
- Disaster recovery

After the cybersecurity policy plan has been fully developed and implemented, it is important to periodically assess all of the components of the plan; review any change in system status, functionality, design, etc.; and ensure that the plan continues to reflect the correct information about the organization's security posture. This documentation and its accuracy are critical for maintaining the organization's cybersecurity levels.

The policy should specify operational practices and implementation standards to perform the following activities:

- Test and document the initial implementation of the plan by establishing baselines of connectivity, device configuration, system operation, and performance for the network and its components.
- Monitor physical and operational parameters of the system for connectivity, device configuration, network operation, and performance changes.
- Monitor the system for the occurrence of incidents and events.
- Manage necessary changes to the system in an orderly and controlled manner.
- Execute the organization's incident response plan each time an incident occurs in the network to respond to and recover from network incidents.

This chapter addresses how the *configuration management*, *patch management*, and *incident response* portions of the cybersecurity policy are used to maintain the cybersecurity levels established by the organization's cybersecurity plan after it has been implemented. The other components are addressed in Chapter 11, "Disaster Recovery and Business Continuity."

ICS Lifecycle Challenges

The first step in developing an effective cybersecurity policy for ICS operations is to recognize the *lifecycle challenges* associated with OT devices and how they are different from typical devices employed in an IT environment. Industrial control devices such as PLCs, RTUs, and DCSs are typically installed in applications where they are expected to operate for a period ranging up to 20 or 30 years or longer. Their function is to control processes that make the organization's widgets. As long as the widgets are being made, the company is producing their product and making money to pay the bills. It is generally a serious thing to consider doing anything that will stop or slow down the production of widgets. Over the lifecycle of these devices, process modifications, business integrations, and major production plant overhauls present security implications for them.

Recall from Chapter 4, "ICS Module and Element Hardening," that ICS devices don't have provisions for many of the security features commonly used with IT devices. They don't use anti-malware products, and they may not possess any authentication and authorization safeguards. They have historically been insecure by design. Therefore, ICS devices present an elevated security risk throughout their active lifecycle and require individualized attention concerning change management and patch management efforts. They also require ongoing monitoring and auditing to guard them against exploitation.

Change Management

Too often the new cybersecurity plan is designed and implemented and then left to stand as it was originally implemented. However, network architecture changes occur because organizations and their processes change. In addition, the threats aligned against the network are constantly changing and being innovated. Yesterday's plan is exactly that—outdated.

To stay abreast of these changing threats, all facets of the cybersecurity plan should be reviewed and, if appropriate, updated on a regular, documented schedule. In most IT organizations, this interval is typically one year. In many OT environments, the timeframe is much longer.

 The policies and procedures related to the change management plan should be disseminated, reviewed, and updated on a periodic basis.

The key to effectively controlling these conditions is having an effective *change management policy* that controls who can make changes and establishes processes for accurately documenting them. Together these two elements ensure that changes to the network, computing and control devices, software, and configurations are made in an orderly and controlled manner. Some items to automatically address in a change management policy include procedures to cover when there are changes in the following:

- Information system ownership
- System architecture
- System status
- Additions/deletions of system interconnections
- System scope
- Certification and accreditation status

While these items should automatically trigger change management processes, the policy should be designed to provide a structured review process for handling *requests for change (RFCs)* submitted from the field. The review process is typically a function of a *configuration review board* made up of key individuals from the organization (ideally representatives from IT, cybersecurity, process engineering, operations, and management) to be established.

This board is responsible for monitoring, prioritizing, authorizing, and controlling changes to the organization's processes and networks. It must evaluate the value and potential risks associated with making any requested change. Particularly in an ICS environment, the board must determine the likelihood of disruptions (and their resulting effects) that making a given change will cause to the organization's productivity.

Establishing a Security Baseline

To manage change there must be a reference point to evaluate changes against. This point is referred to as a *baseline*. After the potential impact of all the identified risks have been established, the next step for the organization is to create a *security baseline* that defines the level of risk they are comfortable with—their *risk tolerance level*. In an enterprise IT network environment, this baseline defines the minimum security requirements necessary to protect the confidentiality, integrity, and availability (CIA) of the organization's IT systems, along with the data processed, stored, and transmitted by those systems.

In some contexts, the term *baseline* is used to refer to a particular version of something that is considered to be a trusted version—such as a network configuration. After the security baseline has been defined, any changes introduced to the network are compared to this baseline version, and the new version can be evaluated and identified as the new trusted version—or baseline. This is referred to as a "change and promote" context.

In the enterprise environment, the security baseline includes defining the organization's best configuration parameters and setting policy so that the system does not vary from that state. When variances are discovered, the policy specifies what actions are taken to return the device or system to the standard configuration. There are tools available to automate this activity for administrators in the enterprise environment.

Recall, though, that in an OT network, availability is typically the more desirable commodity than confidentiality, and therefore, different actions are mandated when an unauthorized configuration change is discovered. While the baseline configuration is established in the security baseline, when changes in production occur and a configuration change is detected, the configuration is typically not automatically forced back to the standard state.

In the North American Electric Reliability Corporation (NERC) Critical Infrastructure Protection (CIP) context, the term *baseline* refers to a standard of configuration (or ideal configuration).

This is because common OT devices, such as PLCs, RTUs, and IEDs, are not designed to handle abrupt changes, such as automated reversions to known good states. Instead, the variances are left in place until the change management team investigates the unapproved change to determine the effects of returning the device or system to its previous configuration. Human intervention is typically required to respond to variances from the standard ICS configuration baseline.

In some OT environments, organizations may be required by external regulators, such as the NERC CIP standards that pertain to electrical power generation and distribution throughout North America, to develop, document, and implement a baseline configuration for its network that includes operating systems (or firmware where no independent operation system exists), commercial or open-source software applications, custom software installed, and any security patches applied, as well as any logical network accessible ports.

The NERC CIP specification for power generation and distribution operators in North America contains roughly 200 performance-based requirements and subrequirements for protecting cyber assets. Two of the major components of these requirements involve mandatory baseline configuration and monitoring of security patches, ports and services, and software versions.

This typically includes developing and documenting policies specifying that all changes that deviate from the existing baseline configuration must be authorized and documented. Before implementing such a change from the existing baseline, any cybersecurity controls that could be impacted by the proposed change must be determined. After the change has been implemented, steps must be taken to verify and document that the cybersecurity controls are not adversely affected.

When changes are approved, the desired pathway to implementation requires that the change be modeled in a test environment that reflects the organization and operation of the production environment. This enables the team to monitor the change and take steps to minimize any adverse effects and ensures that the required cybersecurity controls are not diminished.

After the change has been implemented, the baseline configuration document should be updated to reflect the change within a specified amount of time, such as within 30 days of the change. Likewise, a timeline should be established for monitoring the new baseline for unauthorized changes, such as every 30 days.

Unauthorized configuration changes can signal the occurrence or impending occurrence of cyberattacks.

Change Management Documentation

One of the major components of the change management policy is the *documentation and tracking specifications* for approved changes. *Documentation* is the recording or record keeping of significant changes in equipment, software, plans, or actual events (such as security violations). Having good documentation procedures is one of the keys to effective ongoing change management. The change management policy should address the following documentation by assigning responsibility for creating and maintaining these items to specific personnel or groups:

- *A current, functional software code library for all the ICS components*—This library should contain the latest stable software versions deployed for each ICS component (PLCs, data historians, engineer's stations, switches, routers, and firewalls).

- *An archive library of ICS software*—This library should contain at least one previous software revision for each ICS component in the ICS. This code library should be maintained in a separate and secure location.

The NERC CIP v5 reliability standard covers software monitoring requirements that refer to OS and firmware, intentionally installed software, custom software, and security patches.

- *A current hardware inventory of all ICS control and network devices*—This inventory should be cross-referenced to the software code library.

- *A current network architecture schematic*—This map should show the physical paths and locations of all wiring, junction boxes, and data communications connections. Documentation should be maintained to annotate where each piece of network equipment belongs and who should have access to that equipment. This is particularly true for critical servers, routers, switches, IDSs, and firewalls.

- *Equipment change history*—A history of equipment upgrades can prove to be extremely important in production environments. When any new equipment arrives, it should be inventoried, physically tagged, tested, and fully documented.

The change management policy should specify what controls are used to prevent unauthorized access or changes to operational code. Access to all the configuration documentation listed should be controlled to prevent public or casual access. Update capabilities should be limited to authorized staff.

Archives of the software library, hardware inventory, current configuration, and schematics should be maintained in a physical location separate from the production system copies. This is typically specified in the disaster recovery plan, discussed in the next chapter.

Configuration Change Management

Any changes from the baseline introduce the opportunity for misconfigurations, misuse, interruptions, and dysfunction that can reduce the productivity and profitability of the organization. Therefore, changes must be controlled and implemented in an orderly manner that minimizes these opportunities. This is typically accomplished by implementing and enforcing the *configuration change management* portions of the organization's overall change management policy.

Configuration change management is a process of tracking all the individual configurable objects in the network. Tracking these objects is essential to maintaining reliable and secure operation of the process and its network. As mentioned earlier, configuration changes to network devices can be tracked and managed manually or automatically. There are software tools available to aid administrators in this task, which may become complex as their networks expand and change.

New administrators who inherit an organizational network may inherit a nightmare to unscramble, unless the previous administration had created and maintained a well-designed, documented system architecture.

Managing Equipment Connections

As indicated earlier, a critical part of the organization's change management process is its *systems architecture* documentation. Most network administrators develop and document a network diagram or systems architecture that depicts their network's design, topology, flow of information, and procedures. However, network architecture changes occur because organizations and their processes change.

Therefore, any changes in network equipment, connectivity, or procedures must be documented to keep the system's architecture current. This includes implementing documented processes that address specified requirements related to managing ports and services for network devices, such as the following:

- Implementing documented processes to monitor, identify, and protect network computing and connectivity devices against the use of unnecessary physical ports, such as those used for network connectivity, console commands, or removable media, as described in Chapter 4.

- Implementing documented processes to ensure that only logical ports that are currently needed for the systems architecture to work as designed are enabled.

The systems architecture documentation should be tightly controlled within the organization's IT/OT departments. It is important to carefully restrict access to this information to maintain security levels. Care must be taken not to allow administrative passwords and other network information to be given to junior administrators without proper training. Usually, only limited access is authorized and personnel with supporting job roles are provided access on a need-to-know basis.

Configuration Auditing

Configuration auditing is an ongoing process that compares detected changes in an environment to approved *requests for changes (RFCs)*. Configuration settings for computing devices, software, and connectivity devices are compared to the organization's policies and industry-recognized best practices.

Monitoring is an ongoing process used to ensure processes are working as intended. It is an effective detective control within a process. *Auditing*, on the other hand, is a preplanned method to examine objects or determine whether problems exist within an area being monitored.

For example, in an OT network someone or something has to be in place to *audit* (examine and analyze) the configuration information being produced by the network's monitoring system(s). This responsibility typically falls to the network or security administrator(s). An important part of most administrators' job and the overall network security plan is auditing.

Auditing network configuration objects often involves using manual techniques, automated tools, or both to gather specified configuration data, review it, and analyze it for compliance with the current best standards. This activity must be conducted on a regular basis to ensure that no network devices fall out of policy or best-practices compliance.

The organization's *configuration auditing policy* is typically a subset of their change management policy, which is a subset of the overall security policy. These policies usually specify a standard, such as the baseline configuration established earlier, that the network device configurations must adhere to. It also specifies how and under what circumstances updates to the OT, IT, and network devices' operating systems and configurations are to be deployed. Finally, the plan specifies how often the configurations are to be audited for continued compliance.

Nearly all servers and endpoints, as well as wired and wireless network connectivity devices, possess monitoring/auditing tools that can be used to evaluate the performance of their software and the hardware platforms that support them. Administrators use these tools to verify that the controls they have implemented are working on a routine basis and that identified risks are being addressed. In turn, auditors use the results of monitoring efforts to identify risks, reduce audit duration or frequency, and/or focus more audit efforts in other areas.

In the enterprise network environment, there are a number of widely used *network security monitoring (NSM)* packages available. These packages provide automated configuration auditing by collecting and analyzing network device configuration files. They can be configured to produce detailed security issue reports with recommendations, network configuration reports, and other scripted network information reports. These tools are typically designed to work with configuration files obtained from firewalls, routers, and managed switches from various manufacturers, as well as with most major OS platforms.

 While NSM packages are readily available for use in IT networks, they are not widely implemented in OT networks, although some notable packages, such as Forescout, Dragos, and Checkpoint, have made their way into ICS/SCADA networks.

Controlling Patch Distribution and Installation for Systems

In IT networks, an important part of hardening local computing and controller devices against attacks is to secure their operating systems and applications. This involves updating vulnerable code segments of the OS and its applications as they become known. OS hardening occurs through the application of new programming in the form of service packs, patches, and updates.

OT network administrators are hesitant about patching computing and control devices in their networks for almost any reason, including their age, their proprietary functions, or their perceived obsolescence. Some older OT control devices are simply not patched because patches are no longer available for them. It is recommended that a *patch review team* (once again made up of IT, cybersecurity, process engineering, production operations, and senior management personnel) be used to analyze and determine whether a patch should be applied to the OT.

In a production environment, the priority and concerns of the different parties in the patch review team are not the same—even in a cybersecurity setting. When an exploit has been identified and a patch is created, all these parties must work together to determine the following:

- How vulnerable is their ICS to this threat, and what are the potential impacts of the threat covered by the patching operation? From this the board can determine what the urgency is to deploy the patch.

- What are the expected effects on production due to the unscheduled downtime required to conduct the patch activities? Would no action be an acceptable action, or would an effective workaround provide better or more immediate temporary protection than a patch deployment?

All patch review team parties must bring their department's issues and concerns to the discussion to determine whether and when to patch the ICS. For those patches that the team deems applicable, a plan for mitigating the vulnerabilities addressed by each security patch must be created along with a timeframe to complete the mitigation steps.

Timeframes vary depending on the severity of the vulnerability the patch is designed to mitigate. If the threat is imminent and significant, the patch application may be deemed as ASAP. However, if the threat is less severe but still rises to the level where it is deemed necessary, the application of the patch may be scheduled for a time when the device receives maintenance or when the plant has a scheduled outage.

If the mitigation plan cannot be implemented within the specified timeframe, an extension of the timeframe must be approved by an appropriate member of senior management or a specified delegate from the team.

Patch Decision Trees

Some organizations employ *patch decision trees* to make decisions about if and when patches are applied to their OT devices. The tree is a collection of dependent nodes that move the decision to patch from issuance of the patch to application of the patch. The application of the decision tree to the patching process is intended to provide an automated process that would reduce the time and burden associated with individually evaluating each patch created for the devices in the OT.

The root of the tree is anchored in the risk reduction factor associated with applying a patch to a given OT device. The first factor in the tree, depicted in Figure 10.1, is the *exposure factor*. Depending on the nature of the exposure—Indirect, Direct, or Small—the tree branches out from central trunk nodes that represent security posture impact, safety impact, and technical impact decision points.

An *indirect exposure* factor indicates that the cyber asset has no direct access to any security zone, which has a lower trust level, but other assets in the zone may be accessible from other lower-trust security zones. This is the case for most OT assets. Devices with a *small exposure* factor are those devices that are in highly isolated and controlled security zones. They have no connections to or from any security zones with lower trust levels. *Direct exposure* devices are those devices that are directly accessible from zones that have lower trust levels than the asset's zone.

The device's exposure factor is initially applied to the organization's security posture to determine its impact. Depending on whether the impact is trivial, minor, or major, a decision can be made (defer applying the patch), or the process branches to address any safety posture issues. If the safety impact on security is major and the impact on safety is either direct or indirect, the decision could be made to implement the patch as soon as possible.

If the impact on the security posture is minor, then the safety impact would be directed toward either a process impact decision if there is no safety impact or a technical impact evaluation if the safety impact is indirect or direct. If there is no safety impact and nonessential degraded process impact, then the technical impact assessment would produce the options to schedule the patch or apply the patch as soon as possible, depending on the determination of low, medium, or high technical impact evaluation.

Depending on the initial exposure factor designation, the branching of the patch decision tree may take on different branching patterns.

FIGURE 10.1 A patch decision tree

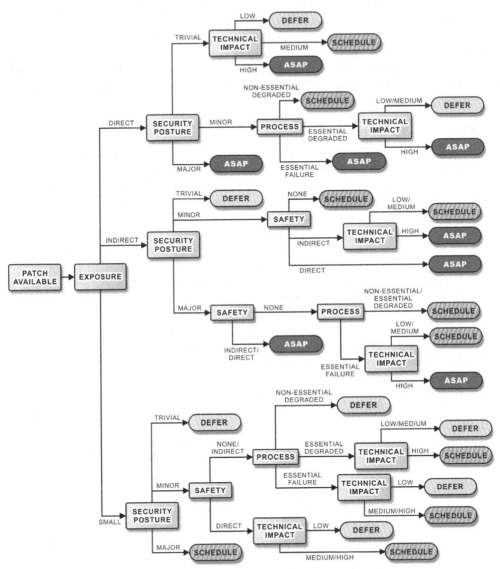

There are two key sources of information that apply to the decision points on the tree—*ICS-Patch* and *CVSS*. ICS-Patch is a document available at https://dale-peterson .com/wp-content/uploads/2020/10/ICS-Patch-0_1.pdf. This document addresses risk matrices and vulnerability management. The stakeholder-specific Common Vulnerability Scoring System (CVSS) tool is a system for prioritizing actions during vulnerability management operations. It is available through GitHub at https://github.com/ CERTCC/SSVC.

An *ICS asset inventory and detection management tool* is key when implementing patch decision trees. These tools provide the ability to identify missing patches on OT cyber assets. They are used to maintain an aggregation of hardware and software data for the devices operating in the organization's OT network. A well-prepared tool will track hardware specifications, IP addresses, OS versions, patch revisions, user accounts, and patch status of all the devices. It will also include known vulnerabilities, attack vectors, and CVSS scores assigned to each device.

Patch Testing

In both IT and OT network environments, patches often have unintended consequences associated with their deployment. For example, consider an enterprise network with thousands of computers being patched with software that causes unexpected or erratic operations after it has been installed. The network administrators might have to spend hours of time to roll back the installation across so many machines. In addition, the users may lose hours of productivity due to the loss of functionality across all of those machines.

Because of the requirement for very high uptime in OT networks, problems associated with patching are even more serious. For example, some industrial sectors require their ICS to be up 99.999 percent of the time (also referred to as five nines uptime) or greater. When you apply this requirement to a calendar year, you find that the ICS can be down for any reason for only 5.5 minutes or less. With this in mind, it is easy to see why OT devices are often left unpatched.

For such ICS environments, patching must be scheduled to fit within their uptime requirements. Bringing a previously functioning process system to a stop until the effects of a botched patching effort are tracked down and corrected can be very costly in a production environment. If other processes happen to be dependent on the affected process, the problem compounds exponentially. Still other OT environments may involve patching hundreds of devices located at multiple sites. The scope of this undertaking makes patch scheduling even more important in these organizations.

Because both network environments are susceptible to problems associated with patching, *patch testing* before deployment into the live network is particularly important. This testing is typically performed using a *test bed* or *sandbox* network running the same type of hardware being used in the live network so that it closely simulates the operational environment. This configuration is usually dedicated specifically for testing purposes.

The actual testing should be designed to verify that the patch fixes the problem or removes the vulnerability identified by the supplier. It should also verify that the patch does not cause conflicts with existing hardware and applications on the network. In addition, the testing should include removing the patch from the system after it has been installed.

This portion of the test should verify that the patch can be removed without adversely affecting the operation of the device or the network. Removing a patch can be somewhat problematic, and the patch test must prepare installers with procedures and options for recovering critical system functions.

Finally, documentation should be created for each patch test. First, a checklist and procedure should be created to guide the patching activities in the field to ensure both initial accuracy and repeatability of the patching process. A record of the patch, the test, and any configuration changes should be documented and kept on file as part of the configuration management documentation.

In critical OT environments, outside regulation has led to requirements that include establishing documented procedures that address security patch management so that it is performed in a manner that identifies, assesses, and corrects deficiencies in the process. This includes processes for tracking, evaluating, and installing applicable cybersecurity patches for networker assets in an orderly, timely fashion—say within 30 calendar days after evaluation.

The NERC CIP-007-6 standard is designed to ensure that new cyber assets, or significant changes to existing cyber assets, do not adversely affect existing cybersecurity controls. This portion of the NERC CIP calls for BES organizations to provide a patch management process for tracking, evaluating, and installing cybersecurity patches for their applicable cyber assets, including operating systems, applications, database platforms, and third-party software/firmware. The tracking portion of the standard requires identifying the sources of the patch releases that apply to their patchable devices. Potential patches must be evaluated within 35 calendar days from the last evaluation from that source.

Software Reloads and Firmware Management

In an OT network, *embedded devices* do not operate from software platforms; instead, they are *firmware-driven devices*. In many cases management of this firmware is not viewed as part of the overall security policy. Instead, it is treated as an operations function with little concern for it as a security risk. Recall that SCADA and OT systems were originally designed for reliability and safety—not security.

There is ever-increasing evidence that attackers target industrial firmware in their attacks. In addition to the many breaches and vulnerabilities associated with social engineering efforts and lack of software patching, many breaches and vulnerability discoveries are being traced back to firmware problems.

A 2021 Microsoft report states that more than 80 percent of enterprises have experienced at least one firmware attack over the previous two-year period. In addition, the NIST *National Vulnerability Database (NVD)* showed a five-time increase in these types of attacks over a four-year period. The most notable firmware attacks include the *Thunderclap* and *ThunderSpy* attacks, which exploited Thunderbolt controllers via hardware access through the Intel Thunderbolt Port. In these attacks, the attacker connected an external Thunderbolt controller and a writable memory chip combination to the Thunderbolt port and could then read kernel-level memory even if the machine was powered off.

Firmware dumping is another form of extracting and potentially exploiting vulnerabilities and data in the firmware devices of endpoints, controllers, networking devices, and servers. In this process, a reader device is provided access to the flash memory device where the firmware is stored. This can be accomplished by connecting the pins of the reader device to the appropriate physical pins of the integrated circuit using jumper wires or Saleae probes. Next, the reader's application executes a series of operations to detect the memory structure of the target device and copy its contents to the attacker's memory device—this is referred to as a *hex memory dump*. From this point, the only thing left to do is use software packages designed to unpack the binary files and scan them for useful information, such as passwords, private keys, backdoors, sensitive URLs, and config files that are stored in firmware.

Conversely, the attacker could also use a similar read/write device to modify the firmware of an OT device to establish an advanced persistent threat against the target's network.

As such, ICS organizations are becoming increasingly aware of the growing importance of firmware security. As a result, they are specifically including firmware management in their change management policies and auditing practices.

While security patching is the key to addressing many software vulnerabilities in the enterprise network environment, this is a constant, cyclic process conducted over the IT product's lifecycle. However, SCADA/ICS environments just can't be shut down and started up with the frequency associated with the enterprise patching process.

In addition, automated *firmware management solutions* for OT devices are not widely available. For this reason, most ICS patching operations remain a manual endeavor. However, for critical ICS environments, external requirements (such as the NERC CIP standards) include firmware management as part of the overall documented configuration management process.

The responsible entity shall ensure that new cyber assets and significant changes to existing cyber assets within the electronic security perimeter do not adversely affect existing cybersecurity controls. For the purposes of Standard CIP-007-6, a significant change shall, at a minimum, include implementation of security patches, cumulative service packs, vendor releases, and version upgrades of operating systems, applications, database platforms, or other third-party software or firmware.

Monitoring

As mentioned earlier, network monitoring and auditing are critical pieces of any organization's network management/security operation. Monitoring involves using a system or tool to constantly watch device and network objects, looking for specific types of activities or events. In general, there are three common types of activities that should be examined in any network:

- *Event monitoring* tracks specific types of occurrences called for by the monitoring system's configuration settings. When a specified type of activity occurs, the monitoring system notes the occurrence and commits it to a log for later inspection. The monitor may also be configured to create and send an announcement to specified recipients.

- *Network monitoring* examines network traffic and activities called for by the monitoring system's configuration settings. Network monitoring responsibilities can be distributed across several different types of devices, such as intrusion detection systems that monitor the network for threatening activities from outside the network; network connectivity devices, such as managed switches, routers, firewalls, and utility devices that monitor network traffic; and servers that monitor computing device activities.

- *Security monitoring* tracks occurrences of specific types of activities that have been defined as security events. These events typically include such items as login/authentication failures, attempted access of critical system files, etc.

Event Monitoring

Event monitoring is the practice of tracking an activity and watching for certain occurrences (events) to appear. When a designated event appears in the flow of the activity, event information is stored in a log, and a notification may be issued to inform designated personnel of the occurrence. Endpoint devices, servers, and network devices all possess capabilities to monitor their operations for different types of events.

In Microsoft Windows environments, the primary event monitoring tool is the built-in Event Monitor application. The tool is configured through the use of filters that define the Category, Description, and Type attributed to the event that is to be monitored and logged. Event types that can be monitored include Errors, Warning Information, Success Audits, and Failure Audits. The information returned from the monitoring tasks is stored in the operating system's *Windows Event Log*. Windows products include three types of event logs by default—Application, Security, and System logs.

Linux operating systems include 12 critical event log files that server administrators need to monitor to keep track of the important events occurring on their devices. These are the Linux log files associated with the server, kernel, services, and applications running on their devices. These log files can generally be classified into four different categories: Application logs, Event logs, Service logs, and System logs. Monitoring these logs enables administrators and infosec personnel to anticipate impending issues before they occur.

The following are the key Linux logs to monitor:

- /var/log/messages—Generic system activity logs that track nonkernel boot errors and application-related service errors from system startup.

- /var/log/syslog—Debian-based generic system activity logs that track nonkernel boot errors and application-related service errors from system startup.

- /var/log/auth.log—Debian- and Ubuntu-based authentication and authorization events. Failed login attempts, brute-force attacks, etc.

- /var/log/secure—RedHat- and CentOS-based authentication and authorization events. Failed login attempts, brute-force attacks, etc. Also tracks SSH logins and errors.

- /var/log/boot.log—System initialization script bootup messages. Issues associated with improper shutdowns, unplanned reboots, and boot failures.

- /var/log/dmesg—Kernel buffer messages concerning device status and hardware errors.

- /var/log/kern.log—Critical kernel information.

- /var/log/faillog—Listing of failed logon attempts. Key to identifying attempted security breach activities.

- /var/log/cron—Information about cron job operations.

- /var/log/yum.log—New package installation information associated with using YUM to install.

- /var/log/mail.log—Mail server logs for email relate services running on the mail server—sent and received mail, possible spamming attempts, origins of incoming emails.

- /var/log/httpd—Apache server logs related to httpd errors.

- /var/log/mysqld.log—MySQL logs.

There are many open-source tools available to centralize the monitoring and analysis of these logs to take the burden off administrators. One widely used commercial package for managing server logs is Nagios Log Server. These applications enable administrators to view, sort, configure, and analyze logs obtained from different sources across a network.

Network Monitoring

It is common for both IT and OT networks to employ a number of different network monitoring tools including firewalls, IDS/IPS systems, OS logs, commercial monitoring tools, custom monitoring tools, and advanced log management systems, as well as *Security Information Event Management (SIEM)* tools. In addition, there are a number of NSM packages that are used to provide automated management of these monitoring systems. The following components are required to provide an effective proactive management and monitoring program:

- *Monitoring software*—Various hardware and software operations are selected for tracking during the configuration of the monitoring software. The resulting event information can be stored in a log file.

- *Alarm/warning systems*—Immediate warnings either in the form of an alert to the management console or a page to the administrator can be issued if and when the network or one of its devices shows signs of an intrusion or a failure.

- *Remote management features*—Administrators can log into their endpoints, servers, and network devices to check on their conditions from a remote location. Diagnostic logs can be reviewed remotely, and a failed server system can be powered on, powered off, or even rebooted to get it back up and running without waiting for a technician to arrive.

Using these critical network management components, administrators can proactively monitor and manage their networks to optimize their availability. By providing system administrators with advance warnings before failures occur, network monitoring software helps them recognize and deal with problems before they become catastrophic and cost the organization lost productivity and profits.

Network administrators typically configure their monitoring/auditing tools to evaluate specific network objects or events and then track those results in an audit log for later evaluation. On the other hand, some firewalls, *intrusion detection systems (IDSs)*, and NSM software can be configured to provide immediate alerts or notifications to administrators when unusual patterns or events are recognized.

The OT side of the organization's network model does not typically have to deal with items that cause difficulty for IT-based NSM operations. These include encrypted networks, widespread use of NAT, devices moving between network segments, extreme network traffic levels, and privacy concerns. Common tools applied to this function include the following:

- *Security Onion*—An open-source Linux distribution designed for threat hunting, enterprise-wide security monitoring, and log management. It is commonly used in NIDS, HIDS, and SOC analysis and static analysis. (See www.securityonionsolutions.com.)

- *FlowBAT*—A basic network analysis tool that provides network visibility, security monitoring, incident response, and low storage overhead. (See www.flowbat.com.)

- *NetFlow*—A Cisco network protocol developed to collect IP traffic information and monitor network traffic flow. When matched with a NetFlow management application, it can translate granular data into user-friendly graphs and reports to identify network utilization. (See www.solarwinds.com/netflow-traffic-analyzer.)

- *Pcap*—An API packet capture utility designed for capturing network traffic. It is commonly used for anomaly analysis, including ARP spoofing, abnormal DNS traffic originating in the ICS, or identifying malformed Modbus packets. The Pcap utility is available through many outlets on the Internet and has been integrated into many other security tools designed for specific uses.

- *Zeek IDS* (formerly Bro IDS)—An open-source network security monitoring IDS tool. It provides comprehensive network traffic analysis. It offers transaction data and extracted content data in the form of logs summarizing protocols and files moving across the network. In the OT network, it can parse DNP3 and Modbus protocols. (See www.zeek.org.)

- *Snort IDS*—An open-source intrusion prevention system (IIPS) that employs a rules-based approach to defining acceptable/malicious network activities. It employs those rule-sets to locate and identify packets that do not obey and generate alerts for users to review. It can also be configured to stop those packets as well. Snort also works with DNP3 and Modbus preprocessors, as well as specific SCADA packages. (See www.snort.org.)

- *Suricata IDS*—An open-source threat detection engine. Suricata combines IDS, IPS, NSM, and Pcap processing functions into a product designed to identify, stop, and assess cyberattacks. Suricata offers a DNP3 parser and ET SCADA rules. (See https://suricata.io.)

- *Syslog*—An industry-standard message logging utility that listens to the network on a well-known or registered port for protocol requests that indicate log messages and stores them in a syslog server. This tool is commonly used for system management and security auditing purposes. It is also used with a wide array of devices, including network, server, and endpoint devices. (See www.kiwisyslog.com.)

Security Monitoring

In critical OT environments, the organization may be required to implement one or more documented processes that address the specified requirements for *security event monitoring*. Compliance with these requirements involves logging security events and generating alerts for those events that the organization has determined necessitate an alert.

> At a minimum, alerts should be generated for all detected malicious code events as well as any detected failure event (such as failed login attempts).

These security event monitoring processes may include requirements for regularly reviewing logged security event samples or summaries at given intervals (for example, intervals no greater than 15 calendar days) to identify cybersecurity incidents. They may also include requirements for retaining security event logs for some stated amount of time (such as at least 90 consecutive calendar days).

At the implementation level, security monitoring involves using devices and tools to monitor and report on network or device security issues. In the documentation for its latest SP800-137, "Information Security Continuous Monitoring (ISCM) for Federal Information Systems and Organizations," the NIST organization defines continuous security monitoring as including the following:

- Vulnerability monitoring
- Application monitoring
- Threat monitoring

Together these monitoring activities provide OT security administrators with situational awareness of their systems, users, and activities, as well as possible attacks being conducted against their networks. There are generally two categories of tools associated with these activities:

- *Proactive tools*—These are tools, such as IDSs and SIEMs, which are aware of network devices and their security states. These tools help ICS security administrators to monitor the system for a number of different types of issues, such as misconfigured devices, incorrect software versions, device firmware defects, hardware failures, unexpected internal and external IP addresses, and unexpected protocols on the network. They can then use the resulting information to correct their device configurations, work with their vendors to fix software and firmware problems, and also harden their networks.

- *Detective tools*—These are tools that provide context-aware threat monitoring, analysis, and alerting capabilities. These are continuous NSM tools that collect log data from network devices and applications, analyze the network traffic, and supply administrators with real-time reports of threats and advanced problems. OT security administrators can use these tools to combat advanced problems, such as zero-day malware, command-and-control traffic, and data exfiltration activities.

Logging and Auditing

The work product of all monitoring activities is information produced in response to the occurrence of specific events or activities. For this data to be useful, it must be retained until it can be analyzed—either manually or automatically. Network administrators configure monitoring/auditing tools to record specific network activities or *events* and then track their results in an *audit log* for evaluation. *Logging* is the process of recording and storing specific events and transactions for analysis (auditing) purposes. Almost all computing and network devices in use today produce logs in some format or another.

Although audit logs typically provide several pieces of information, organizations primarily use audit logs to evaluate their networks for vulnerabilities. Therefore, it is an important part of every administrator's job, and the overall network security plan is auditing logs. Routine log auditing is essential for identifying security incidents, policy violations, fraudulent activities, and operational problems. It is also the key to forensic analysis that is performed after an incident occurs. An audit trail may be able to provide evidence of attackers and intruders, both from within the local network as well as from outside of the network.

In some cases, the auditing operation involves nothing more than sifting through logs to find errors or other issues, which can be a more than daunting task for network administrators. However, a fundamental problem with auditing logs in enterprise and OT network environments is the sheer amount of log data generated within the network. This often results in logs that are monitored only on a part-time or irregular basis.

The organization must balance a limited amount of auditing resources with the continually occurring supply of log data. Software tools that summarize or even graph this log data are tremendous productivity tools for administrators.

To mitigate the stress put on the network security teams by monitoring and auditing operations, a number of *security, orchestration, automation, and response (SOAR)* tools have come into the IT/OT security market. These are software tools that enable organizations to automate and standardize their security operations and incident response activities.

These security tools collect security data to identify, analyze, and address threats and vulnerabilities from different attack vectors. They are designed to work with other security tools in the network to retrieve and analyze security information generated from the network. The infosec team builds workflow instructions sets, called *playbooks*, into the SOAR to automate many of their security operations and thereby reduce repetitive tasks.

This class of security tools relies on artificial intelligence and machine learning to automate and fine-tune the organization's routine security tasks. Leading examples of SOAR tools available include Splunk Phantom, IBM Resilient, DFLabs IncMan, Insightconnect, RespondX, Exabeam, ServiceNow, and SIRP.

Event Logging

Event logging refers to recording system events performed by the operating systems of network equipment, servers, clients, and intelligent network connectivity devices. OS logs typically record a variety of different types of system information. A considerable amount of this data is related to management and compliance functions.

When discussing operating systems, the term *auditing* is used to describe a security function of the OS that enables the user and operating system activities performed on a computer to be logged (monitored and tracked). This information can then be used to identify or analyze potentially undesirable activities, such as unauthorized intrusion efforts. Event logging is set up at the local computer level, while auditing is established at the server level.

OS logs are routinely used to obtain additional information from particular devices after suspicious activities have been identified by a network security device/system. There are two common types of OS audit records to consider for these activities:

- **Native audit records**—Event records generated by most modern multiuser operating systems. Because these records are already being generated by the operating system, they are always available, but they may not contain the desired events or be in a readily usable form.

- **Detection-specific audit records**—Records generated to provide specific information about desired actions or events. These actions or events can be based on operating system activities, application events, or security events.

The auditing systems available with most operating systems consist of two major components: an *audit policy* (or *audit rules*), which defines the types of events that will be monitored and added to the system's *security logs*, and *audit entries* (or *audit records*), which consist of the individual entries added to the security log when an audited event occurs. The system administrator implements the audit policy.

Event log management is one of the most important facets of monitoring an IT/OT network. At the OS level, a simple utility such as *Windows Event Viewer* or the *Linux Security Auditing Framework* provides the first-line tool for event-monitoring activities.

Windows Auditing Tools

In a Microsoft Windows environment, audit entries are maintained in the *security log file*. Figure 10.2 shows a typical security log displayed in the Windows Event Viewer utility. For auditing to be an effective security tool, the security log should be reviewed and archived regularly.

In Windows, auditing is configured through the Local Security Policy option located under the Administrative Tools menu, as shown in Figure 10.3.

FIGURE 10.2   Viewing security audit logs

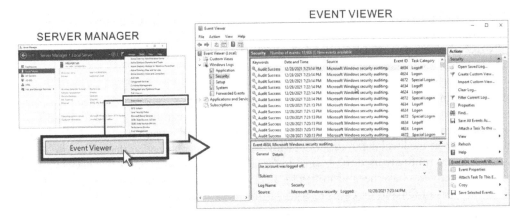

FIGURE 10.3   Configuring auditing in Windows

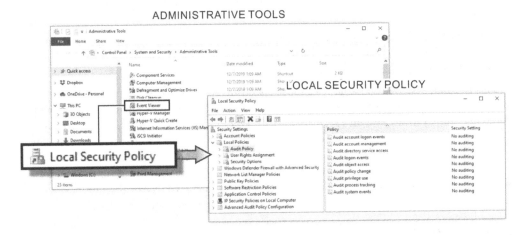

Selecting a policy to be configured in the right-hand pane will produce the Local Security Setting window, depicted in Figure 10.4. Place checkmarks beside the option or options that should be tracked and audited: Success, Failure, or both.

In Windows, auditing must be configured both as a general system policy setting and on each object (file, folder, and printer) that requires auditing. With this in mind, when you are configuring an audit policy, you must consider what effect the policy will have on the system and its performance. If you were to set up auditing on every file, folder, and printer in a system, the auditing process would place so much extra work on the system that the system could literally slow to a halt.

FIGURE 10.4   Establishing a local security policy setting

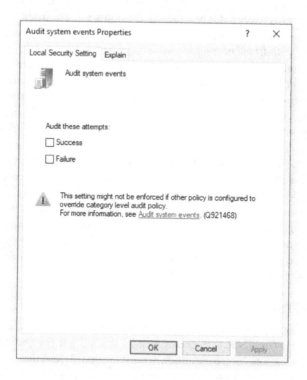

Linux Auditing

Linux systems also feature security auditing capabilities for tracking specified security events. Figure 10.5 provides a generic representation of a Linux security auditing framework. As with other auditing systems, the Linux modules map computer processes to user IDs so that administrators can trace exploits to exactly the user who owns the process and is performing potentially malicious activities in the system.

FIGURE 10.5   Linux auditing system

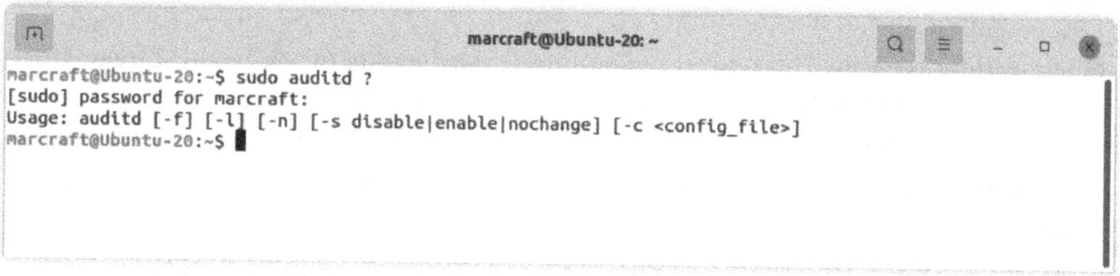

```
marcraft@Ubuntu-20:~$ sudo auditd ?
[sudo] password for marcraft:
Usage: auditd [-f] [-l] [-n] [-s disable|enable|nochange] [-c <config_file>]
marcraft@Ubuntu-20:~$
```

At the heart of the system is the *audit daemon* that works with the Linux kernel's audit module to record relevant events and write them to a log file on the disk. Audit rules are configured in a file that is executed when the system boots up. The audit controller utility employs the parameters in these rules to determine which system events are tracked and how they are written to the *audit event log file*.

When an application encounters a situation that triggers a preconfigured audit event, a message is presented to the kernel's audit interface and passed to the audit controller. Under the direction of the audit controller, the audit daemon writes the event away to the audit event log.

Linux auditing systems also include a report generation tool that the administrator can use to generate custom security reports. It may also include a search utility to provide quick/specific examination of log entries for specific events.

As with Windows Group Policy configurations, you must consider the level of auditing you want the Linux audit system to perform on the host and its operational consequences.

There is a very good auditing tool available for Linux and MAC systems called *Lynis*. This tool can be downloaded from GitHub and installed on a Linux platform. After Lynis is installed and configured, it can scan the system and provide reports, warnings, and suggestions for mitigating system vulnerabilities. Other notable auditing tools include Qualio, AuditBoard, Hyperproof, Onspring, Audit Prodigy, Audits Management Software, HighBond, Standard Fusion, and Benchmark ESG.

Network Logging

Logs from network devices such as managed switches, routers, firewalls, and wireless access points—as well as logs from NSM programs located throughout the network—can contain security-related information. Network administrators primarily use these types of logs for management and auditing, while security administrators are more interested in security logs from different sources to maintain the organization's cybersecurity goals.

Security Logging

Security logs are used to track security-related activities or events specified through the device's audit policy configuration. While security logs are configured primarily to store computer security information, there are a number of other logs, such as operating system and application logs, that also typically contain some security-related information along with a variety of other event documentation.

Audit entries are maintained in the security log, which can be viewed by the administrator. For auditing to be an effective security tool, the security log should be reviewed and archived regularly.

Organizations typically run several types of host-based and network-based software tools that generate security log data. The most common software types that do this include but are not limited to the following (each of the items log more than what is stated):

- *Anti-malware software*—These tools typically record all instances of detected malware encounters.
- *IDS/IPS systems*—These devices or tools typically log anomalous or threatening activities occurring in the network.

- *Authentication servers*—These devices log authentication attempts and include information about the origin, date/time, and username of the attempts along with success or failure indications.

- *Remote Access/VPN software*—These tools typically log successful and failed logon attempts.

- *Web proxies*—These devices typically log all URLs accessed through them.

- *Vulnerability scanners*—These tools typically log security items such as patch installations and vulnerability status of the different hosts in the network. This may include known vulnerabilities and missing software update data.

These are the logs that security administrators are typically most interested in. In all cases, there are many options as to what should be audited. For example, success or failure of logon attempts may provide a clue to pending attack activities and should provide information that would lead to modification of the organization's password policy or the need for continued user education. Auditing results that indicate an attacker has attempted to identify and use passwords, attempted to break through access control lists, or attempted to unscramble encrypted data may all lead to the conclusion that someone is attempting to penetrate the network.

The result of an audit may show that a user account is being used at irregular hours. This audit may indicate that the user's logon account has been compromised. Objects such as restricted folders may be audited for access attempts and improper user access permissions. Usually, individual printers are not audited, although they could be audited for short periods of time.

Auditing user *logon attempts* is probably one of the most important ways to identify whether a user's password has been compromised. Network administrators should be aware of the normal work schedule of assigned employees. If an employee works only days or is on a scheduled vacation, their account should not be active at night or when they are gone.

Auditing *user privileges* is a useful technique for identifying whether a local host has picked up a virus that escalates the user's privileges. *Privilege escalation* refers to users who are able to execute a program with embedded code that gives them administrative privileges after logging onto the server.

Network firewalls can be configured to audit whether internal organizational users are accessing inappropriate websites. These same firewalls can be configured to identify files, folders, and services that are being accessed by users from the Internet. Results of these audits are placed in audit logs that provide an *audit trail*. Users who fail to meet company policies can be counseled and, in some instances, terminated.

Logging Considerations

Auditing is an important security feature that must be carefully planned. Audits can be planned to scan for inappropriate activity from within the organization's network (an internal audit) or from external activity attempting to penetrate the network. However, prior to configuring an audit system, considerable thought should be taken to determine which objects and events should be audited and when. Turning on several auditing tools will tax most networks, resulting in poor performance.

For example, logging all objects and events occurring in a network is impractical, particularly in an OT network, as this would significantly impact its performance. Doing so would cause the network to come to a screeching halt or at least significantly slow down. Therefore, judicial use of logging/auditing tools has always been the standard approach to network- and device-level auditing.

Of course, auditing requires additional resources, including time and personnel, to review the audit data. When considering auditing events, time must be allocated to evaluate the audit reports, logs, or alert notifications. The only way to ensure that the system's logs are providing an effective security measure is to require network administrators to review the logs on a regular basis. Creating too many audit logs can lead to the possibility of not reviewing or identifying the critical events that could be related to a security concern or violation. Therefore, care must be taken to be very selective when deciding what needs to be audited and who should receive the audit logs and alerts.

Another important consideration associated with event logging is managing the size, location, and overwrite policy for each log. For example, the Windows operating system is configured by default to overwrite logs when they reach a certain size.

SIEM Systems

Many *security information and event management (SIEM)* systems are adding *artificial intelligence (AI)* and *machine learning* functions to track human and machine activity in near real time. These functions include *user behavior analysis (UBA)* tools that are useful in identifying patterns of behavior in both users and machines across the network. UBA tools build activity profiles for the network's users and devices. The SIEM uses these profiles to compare current activities to past patterns of human and machine activities and classify them as normal or abnormal.

Because every network environment in different, SIEM systems require initial configuration and ongoing "tuning." The configuration effort involves creating customized rules for event correlations from different network sources that will trigger alerts. These rules focus on activities such as the following:

- User authentication efforts (reported by auditing systems in endpoint devices and servers)
- Attacks detected (reported by intrusion detection systems)
- Infections detected (reported by antivirus and anti-malware packages)

Typically, these rules rely on threshold levels established for the number of times certain events occur. For example, the rule may be configured to generate an alert if any host in the network records three failed login attempts within one minute.

The AI components are used to tune the SIEM's operation and build the profiles of normal user and device activities from ongoing activities from the various devices across the network. When the SIEM is first installed, network administrators are typically quite busy responding to all the false positive indicators the system reports. However, as the AI components "learn" the normal activity of the network's users and devices, the operation becomes more automated and streamlined.

Because the UBA tools learn what is classified as normal activity, SIEMs become very good tools for detecting insider threats and may be one of the best tools for detecting such threats when they involve disgruntled administrators.

Figure 10.6 depicts the structure of a fully integrated IT/OT network configuration. Examine the figure and take note of the number and variety of devices generating event information across the network (as indicated by the star next to each device). In particular, consider the number of devices that would reasonably be expected to generate security-related logs. In this network, it would be unreasonable to expect that an administrator could physically check each of the logs these devices generate on a daily basis, much less correlate the data from each device for meaningful analysis.

FIGURE 10.6   IT/OT network logging

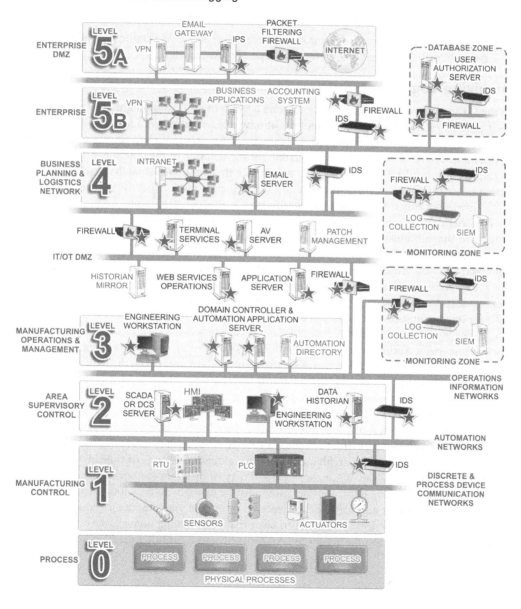

When monitoring this many devices across an ICS/enterprise network, the amount of data collected will far exceed the ability of an administrator to manage, so clearly some type of centralized log management system is required. This function is typically filled by some type of SIEM system. There are three general varieties of SIEMs that may be employed.

- A *security information event management (SIEM)* system—This designation includes data inspection tools that collect logs generated by other network devices and compile them in a centralized network location. These tools also typically provide interpretation and analysis functions to automatically aid administrators in auditing their networks.

- A *security event management (SEM)* system—This term is normally applied to SIEM tools that provide real-time event analysis and notification.

- *Security information management (SIM)* systems—This SEIM version typically refers to systems created to provide long-term storage of network logs.

Archiving Logs

In the OT environment there are many reasons why an organization might need to *archive* their production logs for extended amounts of time (e.g., years or decades). For instance, process control records of components manufactured for use in nuclear reactor or aerospace applications might be required to be available for the lifecycle of the component. For example, audit results for processes used to produce the component may be required if legal action related to its production becomes necessary. Such storage requirements might extend to the storage of other data including security log data.

The organization's auditing policies should specify the requirements and guidelines for log storage so that administrators can properly manage the storage of the logs and ensure that they are retained for the required period of time. For example, members of NERC CIP power generation and distribution are audited on a regular basis and must show evidence that they are in compliance with all the CIP categories. There are more than 50 evidence retention requirements in the existing NERC guidelines. A portion of the NERC CIP 006-3 standard calls for documentation related to physical access control in the form of access control logs. These logs must be maintained for a full calendar year unless directed by the NERC Compliance Enforcement Authority to retain them longer as part of an ongoing investigation.

If the storage requirement is long (more than simply days or weeks), the logs will need to be archived. This may require the administrator to determine whether the log's file format is likely to remain usable over the indicated time period.

For example, some devices produce security logs in proprietary formats that may not remain valid over a period of years. In such cases, the administrator may decide to archive the files in their original format, in a standard format, or in both formats.

The other consideration in archiving log files for extended periods of time involves choosing the storage media to use. While there are a variety of different storage media options available for archiving log data, consideration must be taken as to how long that media (and its supporting hardware and software) is expected to remain viable over the required retention period. If any of the formats appear to be at risk of becoming unavailable or inaccessible, administrators must take action to transfer their logs to another media type.

Typical archival media options include tape, CDs/DVDs, storage area network (SAN) systems, log servers, and specialized storage appliances.

As with other backup types, administrators are responsible for ensuring that the log storage media is stored securely. This includes implementing physical and logical access control strategies and devices to prevent unauthorized access to the media. It also involves providing proper environmental controls to ensure the media is not damaged. Often this involves storing copies of the log archive media in an off-site facility or in a cloud storage environment.

Finally, administrators are also responsible for ensuring that like other data backups, archived logs are properly destroyed when their required data retention period has ended.

Incident Management

Incident management is a process designed to restore operations to "normal" levels as quickly as possible after an incident in order to minimize negative impacts on the organization's production and profitability. In the preceding portions of this chapter, you have been dealing with monitoring, logging, and auditing "events." However, events are not technically the objects you are concerned with in cybersecurity settings. Part of the reason for this confusion is terminology. Just as monitoring and auditing are often used interchangeably, the terms *event* and *incident* are also commonly interchanged.

An *event* is commonly defined as "any change, error, or interruption within a network environment." In their SP 800-61r2 document, "Computer Security Incident Handling Guide," the NIST organization defines events as "any observable occurrence in a network environment." This definition covers such items as system crashes, disk errors, and forgotten access credentials. These are occurrences that are routinely handled in the normal course of operation.

An *incident*, on the other hand, is defined by NIST as "a violation (or imminent threat of violation) of security policies, acceptable use policies, or standard security practices." Under this definition, incidents are occurrences that require security personnel to manage.

NIST 800-61r2 advises that in order to establish an efficient incident response capability, the organization should take the following actions:

1. Create an incident response policy and plan.
2. Develop procedures for performing incident handling and reporting.
3. Set guidelines for communicating with outside parties regarding incidents.
4. Select a response team structure and staffing model.
5. Establish relationships and lines of communication between the incident response team and other groups, both internal (e.g., legal department) and external (e.g., law enforcement agencies).
6. Determine what services the incident response team should provide.
7. Staff and train the incident response team.

While analyzing security logs, administrators may uncover incidents that require some type of response to resolve. This includes such things as the discovery of malware on the network, occurrence of DoS/DDoS attacks, evidence of unauthorized changes to software, firmware or hardware configurations, and reports of individual or institutional identity theft. When this occurs, they must invoke the organization's cybersecurity plan and begin executing its incident response plan (IRP), as described in Chapter 8, "ICS Security Governance and Risk Management."

Recall that the IRP is designed to identify potential emergency and disastrous activities that would trigger the need to engage the BCP and DRP. It is designed to be proactive first—in monitoring activities to spot potential troubles. However, it must also be responsive in that it is designed to be activated in situations where the organization's edge protection and personnel training efforts have failed.

This plan generally addresses information security, forensics, and cybersecurity functions that are used to identify sources, vectors, and targets of attacks or exploits against the organization's systems. The outcome of the plan's steps should set the path for implementing the correct course of action moving forward.

The Incident Response Lifecycle

In the remaining sections of this chapter, you will examine the phases of the incident response process to see how these actions are implemented. Just as no one knows when an earthquake will occur, no one knows when an attacker will launch a cyberattack on their network. By having a well-documented IRP in place, organizations should have greater success in protecting their vital network resources. The NIST SP 800-61-r2, "Computer Security Incident Handling Guide," views the process of incident response in terms of a four-phase lifecycle, as described in Figure 10.7. The full SP 800-61r2 document is available at `https://nvlpubs.nist.gov/nistpubs/SpecialPublications/NIST.SP.800-61r2.pfd`.

FIGURE 10.7 Incident response phases

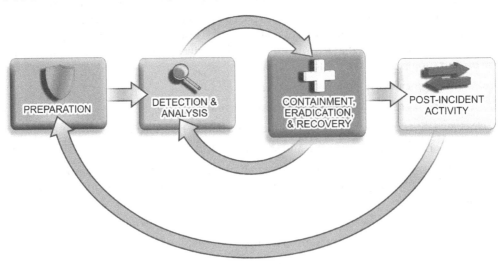

The National Institute of Standards and Technology (NIST) developed a Computer Security Incident Handling Guide (SP 800-61 Rev2), which provides guidance to security personnel in developing an incident response procedure.

Preparation

This initial (*preparation*) phase of the *incident management plan* deals with creating and training a *computer security incident response team (CSIRT)* and putting preventive controls in place to limit the number of incidents that occur based on the results of the organization's risk assessments. This involves four major activities:

1. Creating and publishing the policies, procedures, processes, and guidelines to handle incidents in a format similar to that described in the previous table. To be effective, the IRP must include a process for personnel to identify, classify, and respond to cybersecurity incidents. This includes providing guidelines for personnel to use in determining whether the incident is a reportable cybersecurity incident.

2. Creating the CSIRT along with a process for activating the team. This includes identifying appropriate people and assigning them roles and responsibilities to perform in the incident response process described in the IRP. The IRP typically includes requirements for how and in what timeframe to notify the CSIRT of a reportable incident. In critical ICS environments, these requirements may involve reporting to an external agency, such as the NERC's E-ISAC center in a given timeframe (such as within 24 hours).

3. Develop a communication plan for all stakeholders. This includes identifying the interactions and communications that need to be performed. For example, the plan should establish criteria for when to report incidents and to whom, as well as how information is to be exchanged when an incident report is received.

4. Train all personnel to understand the IRP and their role in it. Define how tasks are to be performed, how different processes in the plan relate, and how actions are coordinated—no matter who is performing the work.

5. Ensure that any equipment that may be required to respond appropriately to any of the incident types is available.

During this phase, the organization should be conducting the following recommended practices for securing their networks, computing devices, and software assets:

- Conducting risk assessments
- Hardening and monitoring all host devices in the network
- Hardening the networks' outer perimeters
- Establishing and maintaining their malware prevention activities
- Conducting cybersecurity awareness training for all users

Creation of the Incident Response Team

The key to making the organization's IRP work efficiently is its computer security incident response team. This team is a group (or organization) that receives reports of suspected security incidents, conducts analyses of those reports, and responds to incidents to return operations to normal levels. According to NIST, the incident response team should be available for anyone in the organization who discovers or suspects that an incident involving the organization has occurred.

In most ICS organizations, the CSIRT is composed of a cross section of stakeholders, such as those described in Figure 10.8. Depending on the size and nature of the organization, the CSIRT may be an established group of stakeholders or a group generated on an ad hoc basis when a security event or incident is reported.

FIGURE 10.8   CSIRT members

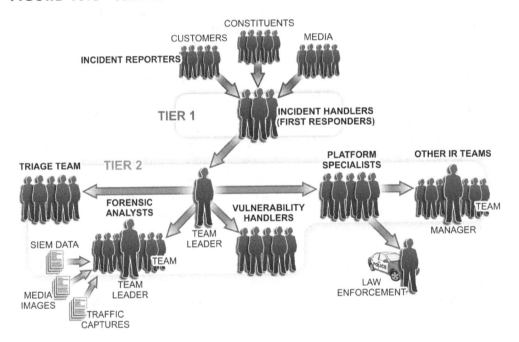

For a given IRP, the roles and responsibilities of each CSIRT member should be clearly identified and assigned to specific people. In any particular organization, the CSIRT may specify personnel for any of the following team roles:

- CSIRT team leader
- Incident handlers
- IR triage manager

- IR forensic analysts
- IR platform specialists
- Vulnerability handlers

Important considerations for including specific people on the CSIRT include their availability and skill sets. The ability to quickly assemble and deploy the CSIRT when an incident is escalated is a key requirement for all members. The CSIRT must be able to come online, thens target and respond effectively to incidents to minimize their impact on the organization's operation and productivity. If the members of the team cannot be counted on to respond quickly when needed, alternative personnel should be appointed.

Likewise, the members of the team must have the necessary skill sets and tools that will enable the team to track down the root cause of the incident and neutralize it. They should also have the ability to identify the perpetrators for possible prosecution.

 Larger organizations may develop incident response teams that are trained to respond to any type of emergency, including security violations, terrorist threats, natural disasters, and computer attacks.

Detection and Analysis

The foremost function of the detection and analysis phase is to identify and verify that a reported incident has occurred and that it is an actual incident. Incident reports can come from anywhere in the organization—users, administrators at different levels, monitoring tools, or even outside organizations.

When an individual detects an unusual event or incident occurring on the network, they must be trained to follow the organization's security policy that requires them to take appropriate action as part of an incident response. The individual's role in the response to an observed incident normally includes items such as contacting a designated member of the incident response team, documenting what activities were going on when the incident occurred, and keeping the attacked computer on.*

 *Unless otherwise instructed by a security administrator, users should never turn their computing devices off during an attack.

After a potential incident has been reported, it must be validated. As mentioned earlier, the IRP should specify what constitutes an incident, who to report it to, and how. So, this first step in the recognition phase is to report the suspected incident to the *incident handler* specified in the plan. At this point, the incident handler takes over ownership of the report.

Their next step is to gather information about the details of the incident report. Regardless of the source of the report, whether from an individual that makes a call or an IDS signal that reports an incident, the incident handler must investigate the incident for accuracy. The primary purpose of this initial investigation is to determine the severity of the incident and decide whether it needs to be escalated to the incident response team.

For example, if an unusual event is reported by one of the network's intrusion detection systems, the incident handler must determine whether the report is accurate or a false positive. This typically involves evaluating the IDS logs and clinical situation. If the IDS is configured correctly and functioning properly, the incident handler reports the incident to the network security administrator who, in turn, activates the CSIRT to carry out the IRP processes.

 The initial incident handler is also responsible for establishing a chain of custody for handling the incident information that could become evidence. The chain of custody should clearly specify the "who, what, where, when, and possibly why" in case the evidence becomes a legal requirement.

Automated Intrusion Detection Tools

As with physical security efforts, preventing unauthorized access is the first line of security at the local computing and control device level. However, it is just as important at this level to be able to detect the occurrence of an intrusion and notify the proper authorities of its nature.

Computer-based intrusion detection systems (IDSs) can be implemented in two ways, as a *network-based IDS (NBIDS)* or as a *host-based IDS (HBIDS)*. In both cases, the system is designed primarily to monitor the system (local computer or network environment), log key events and policy violations, and report them as directed.

While an HBIDS is similar to a firewall in that it monitors inbound traffic, it is different in that it also monitors the outbound traffic leaving the device. All IDS devices are based on one of two strategies:

- *Signature analysis*—Incoming and outgoing traffic is compared with a database of stored specific code patterns that have been identified as malicious threats.

- *Anomaly analysis*—Incoming and outgoing traffic is compared to an established baseline of normal traffic for the system. The baseline is "learned" (generated) by applying mathematical algorithms to data the system obtains from the traffic flow.

Signature-based IDS/IPS products generally work by looking for specific patterns in content, known as *signatures*. If a "known bad" pattern is detected, then the appropriate actions can be taken to protect the host. However, because of the dynamic nature of programming languages, scripting in web pages can be used to evade such protective systems.

The *signature-based IDS* database is typically generated and distributed by its manufacturer in response to observed malicious signatures. Thus, the malicious code is already in existence before a signature can been identified and added to the database to be acted on. The time delay between the release of the malicious code and the issuing of its signature presents its own security issue.

Anomaly-based IDS/IPS systems apply statistical analysis techniques to the data stream to determine whether it is "normal" or "anomalous" at any given time. There are two common methods of implementing statistical anomaly detection:

- *Profile-based anomaly detection systems*—These systems use mathematical algorithms to monitor normal data traffic and develop a "profile" of rules that describe what normal traffic for that system looks like. The profile developed reflects evaluations of users' past behaviors and is configured to signal when deviations from these behaviors reach a certain level (or threshold).

  - *Rule-based anomaly detection*—This detection method analyzes audit records to generate rules based on past usage patterns to generate the "rules" set. The system then monitors the traffic looking for patterns that don't match the rules.

  - *Penetration detection*—These systems generate rules based on known penetration occurrences, system weaknesses, or behavior patterns. For this reason, they are normally specific to a given host system. They also typically include rules generated by security experts who are current with security activities.

- *Threshold-based anomaly detection systems*—These IDS systems are designed to track the number of occurrences of specific events over time and generate an intrusion warning if the number of events exceeds a predetermined number.

Most commonly available IDS systems are designed for use on local host systems. However, there are similar systems available for network-wide implementation. Ultimately the most effective IDS/IDPS defense is a combination of the two types of systems working together in what are referred to as *distributed IDS systems.*

In all IDS types the administrator is notified when a potential attack is detected.

Figure 10.9 shows a sample of a distributed IDS implementation. In this network architecture example, each local host attached to the network has its own IDS module installed. There is also an IDS management module installed in a network server that coordinates the flow of information to and from the individual local IDS modules.

The local IDS modules pass local audit information to the IDS manager, which filters the incoming information to build a signature database. The database can be built on detected anomalies, on known patterns of misuse, or on both types of data. When an action matches one of the signatures stored in the database, the IDS will generate an intrusion alarm under the direction of its configuration manager.

When implementing a distributed IDS system, there are two major performance factors to consider: security and efficiency.

FIGURE 10.9 Distributed IDS

FIGURE 10.9 Distributed IDS

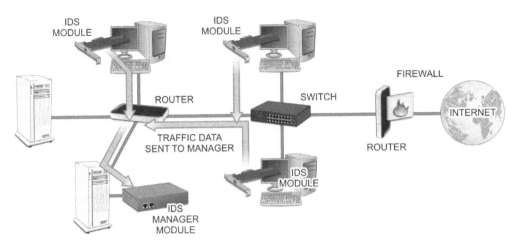

Intrusion Detection and Prevention Systems

Some systems referred to as *intrusion detection and prevention systems (IPSs)* provide an additional level of activities aimed at preventing the detected threat from succeeding. These systems are classified as reactive IDS systems, while simple IDSs are referred to as passive IDS systems. As their definitions imply, the two types of IDS systems operate in different areas of the computer/network environment.

In the case of IPS systems, like the one depicted in Figure 10.10, the management module forwards the attack signal to a separate countermeasure module that conducts appropriate response activities based on the nature of the detected intrusion signature.

FIGURE 10.10 IPS systems

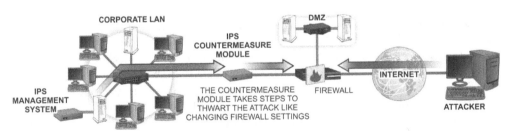

Egress Monitoring

Most cybersecurity efforts are typically aimed at fortifying the perimeter of the network and monitoring inbound traffic (*ingress monitoring*). It is just as important to monitor and filter outbound or *egress traffic*. By doing so, network administrators can restrict the services that internal network hosts can access and limit one attack vector that can be used to bring malware into the network.

Egress monitoring is instituted at the cybersecurity policy level in both the security and acceptable use policy areas. As with all other cybersecurity policies, these policies are used to develop egress rules for proxy servers, firewalls, and other SIM tools to limit the outward flow of network traffic from trusted networks to less trusted networks. These rules are configured to block packets that don't meet the security specifications established by the *egress filtering rules*. These rules are configured to block specific types of traffic in the outward traffic flow.

- *Unsecured data transmissions*—These are communications involving intellectual property or copyrighted materials.

- *Unauthorized communications*—These are communications involving servers or endpoint devices on the organization's network that do not have authorization to send data out of the network.

- *Unsanctioned requests to external sites*—These are transmissions involving known malicious Internet destinations such as botnet command-and-control centers, hostile ISPs, and hijacked address spaces.

- *Outbound malware activities (software residing on compromised systems or unauthorized users that exploit network resources to spread attacks or malware)*—This includes using bots in DDoS attacks or spreading spam.

In *advanced persistent threat (APT)* cases, attackers invade one or more of the network's devices and cover their *command-and-control* activities for prolonged periods of time, exfiltrating data to an undesired location. Egress monitoring may be the only indication that security activities are going on.

Not all outbound traffic is suspect. Therefore, egress policies must be created in a way that still provides outbound services as needed. This involves analyzing network usage to determine which users and applications legitimately require services located on external servers or across the Internet. Then management must decide which of those services should be allowed to receive outbound data. As part of the same process, management should define any types of content to be blocked or permitted for the organization as a whole, as well as noting specific types of content for certain user groups or departments.

This resulting permitted services list typically features network assets that support the organization's web functions (HTTP and HTTPS, SMTP, POP/IMAP, and NTP services), as well as domain names and IP addresses of approved external connections.

Incident Response

If the *incident handler* concludes that a true attack has occurred and an incident is declared, the next step may be to determine how to restore critical network resources and data to operational levels. The CSIRT team must be alerted, and the initial incident information is transferred from the incident handler to the team. The CSIRT must take over the execution of the remainder of the IRP. This includes but is not limited to the following:

- Conducting detailed analysis of the information (log analysis) provided by the designated incident handler

- Taking steps to contain the incident and limit the organization's exposure

- Performing root-cause analysis activities to identify the source of the event that caused the incident

- Remediating the incident by determining whether to eradicate or quarantine the root cause of the incident (provided the root cause is some form of malware)

- Implementing specific steps to recover from the effects of the incident

- If necessary, updating the IRP with information gathered from the incident response report created at the conclusion of the IR process

Forensic Log Analysis

Digital forensics is the science of investigating and recovering information from digital devices. This definition actually involves different subsets of digital forensics:

- **Computer forensics**—The science of employing data recovery techniques to identify, preserve, recover, and analyze digital information from a digital computing device

- **Network forensics**—The monitoring and analysis of network traffic for anomalous traffic types and for intrusion detection purposes

- **Forensic data analysis**—The examination of data structures to discover patterns of activity

While it may be necessary to perform forensic data analysis during a given incident response, most of the OT CSIRT efforts are involved in computer and network forensic activities. Most specifically, they are involved in performing forensic log analysis. And while there is an evolving science for forensic log analysis, IR analysts typically spend their time searching logs looking for two elements: event correlation and signs of intrusion.

In some OT environments, these elements may be difficult to find as such data may be unavailable or insufficient to be useful. This is because in many ICS networks, there is often no real-time monitoring occurring. Many legacy OT devices have poor or no logging capabilities. In addition, in these environments what logging capabilities do exist are often not configured properly or regularly monitored. Together these factors can lead to incidents being missed altogether.

Analysis/Event Correlation

Much of the analysis work done in the analysis portion of the plan involves collecting system and network logs and correlation event data from them.

Some of the key items the incident analyst is looking for include all types of *anomalous behavior*. For instance, the analyst typically examines the logs for signs of cybersecurity incidents that include *detected successful login attempts, detected failed access attempts*, and *failed login attempts*, as well as occurrences of *detected malicious code*.

For example, unusual numbers of successful or failed logon attempts may point to an attacker attempting to penetrate the network. When uncovered, such auditing results are typically viewed as attackers attempting to identify and use passwords, attempting to break through access control lists, or attempting to unscramble encrypted data. As such, this information should lead the organization to modify its password policy or specify additional user education. Similarly, if analysis of the logs shows that a particular user's account is being used at irregular hours, this might indicate that the user's logon account has already been compromised.

Auditing user logon attempts is probably one of the most important ways to identify whether users' passwords have been compromised.

IR analysts may filter the log files to aggregate specific types of events together in a single report or to discover matching patterns of events that show specific repeated activities. For example, recall that IDSs, firewalls, managed switches, routers, and network appliances provide logs and alert notifications of unusual or unaccepted network packets or unusual network traffic. Incident responders might analyze these logs looking for a number of different types of anomalies:

- Unauthorized connections to third-party business networks
- Unexpected internal connections to the Internet or known malicious domains/IP addresses
- Evidence of ICS-specific protocol attacks (Modbus, DNP3, Profinet, EtherNet/IP)
- Signs of remote access exploitation—login attempts using default accounts or credentials
- Unusual server and connectivity device log entries, such as devices going offline or behaving strangely
- Alerts or error messages from anti-malware tools, intrusion detection systems, or other security devices/systems
- Occurrences of high CPU or network bandwidth usage
- Undocumented software or firmware changes from the baseline

Containment, Eradication, and Recovery

The next step in the incident response process is *containment*. After the incident has been investigated and confirmed as legitimate, it is time to activate the CSIRT and obtain the initial information gathered from the incident handler.

When there is an identified incident, the first step in containing it should be to notify all appropriate stakeholders that might be affected by the incident. Getting the stakeholders involved is a key step in stopping the spread of many types of attacks.

Next, the CSIRT must work with the stakeholders to create a consensus on actions that should be taken to prevent attacks from getting further into the organization or spreading to additional areas of the network. It can be very unproductive and costly to have stakeholders from different facets of the organization implementing their own efforts to contain the incident.

To accomplish this, the technical members of the team must bring their resources into the process to implement the containment actions. Additionally, the public relations management members of the team should begin controlling communications with the public concerning the incident.

At this point, the team should also be aware that the actions they take might involve information that could become evidence. Therefore, they must take actions related to obtaining and preserving potential evidence. It is important to make sure they do not blindly destroy evidence to achieve a quick or short-term containment level. This typically involves creating and documenting backups of all activities before each new step forward is performed.

Eradication/Quarantine

Containing the incident removes the urgency from the situation and provides time for developing and implementing a tailored remediation course of action. Is the incident related to a denial of service, an intrusion, or a malware infection? The reason this is important is because the different types of incidents are typically remediated differently. If an intrusion is identified, the first step taken should be to limit the intruder's ability to send traffic into or out of the network.

For example, take steps to fortify the network's boundary protection by updating the firewalls at the edges of the network to make sure they block IP addresses used by known threats. Also, search for and deny outbound connections so that servers and critical infrastructure devices do not have the ability to communicate directly with the Internet.

On the other hand, if the incident is based on a malware infection, you must find and mitigate the malware responsible for the attack. You must also delete or disable the process/protocol used to launch the attack as well as remove the service/application that created the vulnerability.

If the root cause has been identified as malware, a decision must be made whether to *clean*, *quarantine*, or *eradicate* it. In many cases, if the wrong option is selected, there are unexpected results. For example, choosing the Delete (Eradicate) All Infected Files option on an antivirus program could adversely impact the normal features and functionality of the operating system or application.

Before conducting any eradication activities, the most current backups should be located to ensure that if any unforeseen consequences arise from the deletion, the system can be restored so other alternatives can be considered. Vulnerability tests should be run on the network to determine whether any new vulnerabilities may have been introduced into the environment by the removal.

Choosing the *Clean* option for an incident related to a worm or a Trojan would do nothing to remediate the incident because the root cause is the file and therefore cannot be cleaned. This option removes the infection from the file but does not actually delete the file itself. This is helpful only where a legitimate file has been infected with nonlegitimate code.

Choosing the *Quarantine* option would move the file to a reserved area controlled by the antivirus program. The file is not removed permanently, nor is it repaired—it is simply isolated. This is often a fairly safe option since it preserves the file in cases where removing it would impact the operation of the system.

Recovery

In the *recovery* portion of the containment, eradication, recovery phase of the IRP process, actions are taken to validate that all systems and services affected by the incident are fully restored to a normal operational condition. After the CSIRT has concluded that the incident has been completely remediated, they must restore the confidence of the stakeholders in the system.

To accomplish this, system personnel must test the operation of the system (or systems) that was affected by the incident to ensure that it is fully functional. In addition, involve the system management stakeholders in observing the restored system and have them declare that it is fully operational.

In critical OT environments, organizations may be required to have procedures in place to protect data that would be useful in the investigation of an incident that requires execution of their IRP. Always take steps to maintain positive control of any evidence and log everything in an appropriate chain of custody form to maintain its integrity.

As mentioned earlier, while remediation steps such as removing infected assets/files and returning the process to a normal operational state is the primary goal of all incident response plans, it is important to be aware that activities leading to this goal, such as deleting files, powering down a system to replace a hard drive, or restoring the system to a previous version, might destroy forensic evidence that could be used to determine root cause.

In many cases, capturing forensic information prior to restoring the system is the only way to determine what happened after the fact. The forensic collection process is also typically the basis for any legal actions that might be taken related to an attack.

At the top of the forensic collection process to-do list is actually a don't-do item—do not turn off computing devices during an attack or before information about the incident can be obtained and recorded. Before powering off affected devices, it is important to collect images of any volatile data from system RAM and the hard drive, if possible. After these images have been created, it is safe to disconnect the affected devices from the network and shut them down.

The final step is to restore the affected devices to their fully operational states. This typically involves restoring them from backup copies or baseline snapshots.

Post-Incident Activities

The NIST guidelines identify the *lessons learned* and improvement steps of the *post-incident activities* as the most important part of the incident response lifecycle. These steps help the organization to evolve in anticipation of new threats and improved technologies. All the parties involved in a major incident should be involved in a lessons-learned meeting following the conclusion of the response effort to determine what occurred, what was done, what could have been done that wasn't, and how well the response plan worked.

Root-Cause Analysis

After containment actions have been implemented, the CSIRT must turn its attention to locating the root cause of the incident. This is accomplished through *root-cause analysis (RCA)*. RCA is a problem-solving method that is used to separate causal factors from root causes. A causal factor is any condition that will provide an improved condition if removed but does not prevent the recurrence of the incident. A *root cause* is the condition or item that does prevent the incident from recurring after it has been removed or neutralized.

All of the collected incident data should be brought together and analyzed thoroughly. The analysis of the incident's characteristics may show a systemic security problem that needs to be addressed, or it may point out singular vulnerabilities that must be mitigated. In either case, the analysis can be used to update the IRP and suggest any additional controls that need to be put in place to strengthen the organization's cybersecurity posture.

Recording/Reporting

All the procedures listed in the previous sections, including actions taken during the response, must be documented. If warranted, help from federal authorities, such as CISA or NERC, may be requested for a more in-depth analysis. At the very least, lessons learned should be shared and company security policies adjusted to prevent similar follow-up attacks.

Recall that the initial incident handler is responsible for establishing a *chain of custody* for handling the incident information that may become evidence. This includes creating a chain of custody document. The chain of custody document should clearly specify the "who, what, where, when, and possibly why" in case the evidence becomes a legal requirement.

At the completion of the IRP process, an incident report should be produced and distributed to all stakeholders affected. This report should include the root-cause analysis findings, the remediation actions taken, and recovery activities implemented. The purpose of the report is to educate the management team about what is/was required to make the network more secure.

The *Cybersecurity & Infrastructure Security Agency (CISA)* has produced guidelines for government agencies specifying how federal, state, local, and tribal government organizations submit incident notifications to the *National Cybersecurity and Communications*

Integration Center (NCCIC) and *United States Computer Emergency Readiness Team (US_CERT).*

The guidelines require that organizations report information security incidents where the CIA of information systems have been compromised within one hour of the incident being validated by a member of their CSIRT team, its Security Operations Center (SOC), or its IT department. The report must include information from three categories:

- Impact and Severity Categories

- Attack Vectors

- Incident Attributes

Impact and Severity Categories

The NCCIS collects incident impact and severity information to analyze incident attributes for a National Cyber Incident Scoring System (NCISS). The collected information is also used to calculate a severity score developed by the NCISS. Severity score categories range from Baseline (White or Blue Levels) to Low (Green level) to Medium (Yellow level) to High (Orange level) to Severe (Red level) to Emergency (Black level). The impact and severity category data required by the NCISS includes the following:

- *Functional impact*—This is a measure of the impact to business functionality or ability to provide services. Severity levels assigned include No Impact, Minimal Non-Critical, Minimal Critical, Significant Non-Critical, Denial of Non-Critical Services, Significant Critical Services, and Denial of Critical Services Loss of Control.

- *Information impact*—This entry describes the type of information lost, compromised, or corrupted. Impact reporting options include No Impact, Suspected But Not Identified, Privacy Data Breach, Proprietary Information Breach to Destruction of Non-Critical Systems, Critical Systems Data Breach, Core Credential Compromise, and Destruction of Critical System.

- *Recoverability*—This entry is used to identify the scope of resources needed to recover from the incident. Options include Regular, Supplemented, Extended, and Non-Recoverable.

Attack Vectors

The SP800-61r2 guidelines also require that attack vectors associated with cyber incidents be identified, tracked, and reported. The document describes terms and relationships between those terms used to create a uniform reporting system. It lists the following attack vector definitions:

- *Unknown*—Cause is unidentified but may be identified in a follow-up report.

- *Attrition*—A brute-force attack used to compromise, degrade, or destroy systems. This can be a DoS/DDoS attack or attack against an authentication mechanism.

- *Web*—An attack initiated from a website or web application.

- *Email/Phishing*—An attack executed via email or attachment.

- *External Removable Media*—An attack launched from a removable media source.
- *Impersonation/Spoofing*—An attack involving the replacement of legitimate content/services.
- *Improper Usage*—Any incident resulting from the violation of organizational policies by an authorized user.
- *Loss or Theft*—The loss or theft of organizational computing devices or media.
- *Other*—Any attack that does not fit in another listed category.

Incident Attributes

The attributes associated with the reported incident are also tracked by the NCISS. They define their attribute categories as follows:

- *Location of observed activity*—This category describes where the observed activity was detected. Standard attribute definitions include Business DMZ, Business Network, Business Network Management, Critical System DMZ, Critical System Management, Critical Systems, Safety Systems, and Unknown.
- *Actor Characterization*—This category is used to describe the types of actors involved in the incident.
- *Cross-Sector Dependency*—This entry is a weighting factor determined by a cross-sector analysis conducted by the Department of Homeland Security (DHS) Office of Critical Infrastructure Analysis (OCIA).
- *Potential Impact*—This entry is an estimate of the overall national impact resulting from the affected entity.

The complete copy of the guidelines and their definitions can be obtained from www.
cisa.gov/uscert/sites/default/files/publications/Federal_Incident_
Notification_Guidelines.pdf.

NERC CIP 008-6

In the electrical generating and distribution market, NERC CIP 008-6, "Cybersecurity Incident Response Plan Specifications," provides guidance for BES operators to generate incident handling procedures for cybersecurity incidents.

These guidelines include establishing roles and responsibilities for cybersecurity incident response teams and individuals. It also specifies requirements for incident handling procedures as described in the four-phase model presented earlier in this chapter. As with the other CIP standards, the CIP 008 standard specifies the conditions and timing for conducting IRP tests (every 15 calendar months) and reporting requirements.

Review Questions

The following questions test your knowledge of the material presented in this chapter.

1. What is the reference point established to define the level of risk an organization is comfortable with (their risk tolerance level)?

2. _____ is an ongoing process that compares detected changes in an environment to approved requests for changes (RFCs).

3. In an ICS network environment, who is responsible for analyzing and determining whether a specific patch should be applied and when?

4. According to NERC CIP-007, what is the overriding requirement when implementing security patches, cumulative service packs, vendor releases, and version upgrades of operating systems, applications, database platforms, or other third-party software or firmware?

5. _____ involves using a system or tool to constantly watch device and network objects, looking for specific types of activities or events.

6. _____ is the process of recording and storing specific events and transactions for analysis (auditing) purposes. Almost all computing and network devices in use today produce logs in some format or another.

7. When storing log information for extended periods of time, what two considerations must be taken before implementing an archival logging policy?

8. Describe items normally included in an individual's role as part of the incident response plan.

9. Which type of intrusion detection system is designed to apply statistical analysis techniques to the data stream to determine whether it is "normal" or "anomalous" at any given time?

10. Which type of intrusion detection system is designed to track the number of occurrences of specific events over time and generate an intrusion warning if the number of events exceeds a predetermined number?

11. Why would an organization be interested in establishing egress monitoring to block unsecured data transmissions out of the network?

12. What is the first step in the incident response process after an incident has been confirmed as legitimate?

13. _____ is a problem-solving method that is used to separate causal factors from root causes.

14. Why is it important to determine whether an incident is related to an intrusion or malware?

15. Identify the portion of the IRP process where actions are taken to validate that all systems and services affected by the incident are fully restored to a normal operational condition.

Exam Questions

1. Which of the following should the change management policy documentation address by assigning responsibility for creating and maintaining? (Select all that apply.)

    A. A code library for all the ICS components

    B. A current hardware inventory of all ICS control and network devices

    C. Patch management

    D. Software/firmware reloads

    E. An up-to-date equipment change history

2. What is the first factor located at the root of a patch decision tree?

    A. Security posture impact

    B. Safety impact

    C. Technical impact

    D. Exposure factor

3. From the following list, identify reasons why ICS software and firmware management strategies differ from those encountered in a typical enterprise IT network. (Select all that apply.)

    A. ICS control devices do not have firmware update capabilities.

    B. Automated firmware management solutions for ICS devices are not widely available.

    C. Industrial production facilities should not be stopped for updating, as this creates lost productivity and profitability for the organization.

    D. SCADA/ICS environments can't just be shut down and started up with the frequency associated with the enterprise patching process.

    E. Management of firmware is not viewed as part of the overall security policy. Instead, it is treated as an operations function with little concern for it as a security risk.

4. From the following list, identify monitoring activities that the NIST organization defines as part of continuous security monitoring. (Select all that apply.)

    A. Vulnerability monitoring

    B. Risk monitoring

    C. Application monitoring

    D. Asset monitoring

    E. Proactive monitoring

5. Which type of network security information event management system is installed to provide long-term storage of network logs?

    A. A security information event management (SIEM) system

    B. A security event management (SEM) system

    C. A security information management (SIM) system

    D. A network security event management (NSEM) system

6. Which part of the incident response plan applies to verifying that a reported incident occurred and that it is an actual incident?

    A. The Reporting portion of the incident recognition phase

    B. The Identification portion of the incident recognition phase

    C. The Validation portion of the incident recognition phase

    D. The Validation portion of the incident triage phase

7. From the following list, select the activities the CSIRT team must perform in the incident response. (Select all that apply.)

    A. Performing a root-cause analysis to identify the source of the event.

    B. Taking all steps necessary to contain the incident and limit the organization's exposure

    C. Eradicating the root cause of the incident after it has been identified

    D. Creating plans for retaliating against the intruder or attacker

    E. Updating the IRP plan

8. Where are most of the ICS CSIRT team's efforts focused when an incident occurs?

    A. Searching logs for event correlation and signs of intrusion

    B. Examining data structures to discover patterns of activity

    C. Monitoring and analyzing network traffic for anomalous traffic

    D. Performing data recovery operations to identify, preserve, recover, and analyze digital information obtained from computing devices

9. From the following list, identify roles commonly assigned to CSIRT personnel. (Select all that apply.)

    A. Team leader

    B. First responder

    C. Forensic analyst

    D. Platform specialist

    E. IR administrator

10. After the organization has completely remediated a cyber incident, what step must be taken to finalize the incident response action?

    A. Present evidence to the proper legal entity for follow-up and possible prosecution

    B. Restore the confidence of the stakeholders in the system

    C. File CSIRT reports and look for lessons learned that can be implemented to prevent the same incident from occurring again

    D. Remove and replace affected devices across the network

Chapter

11

Disaster Recovery and Business Continuity

OBJECTIVES

Upon completion of this chapter, you should be able to:

1. Demonstrate knowledge of Disaster Recovery and Business Continuity

   - Describe key components of a Business Continuity Plan

   - Describe key components of a Disaster Recovery Plan

   - Define alternate site options for Business Continuity Plans

2. Describe Common System Backup and Restore options, advantages and disadvantages

   - Be aware of the different backup and restore options available for securing the organization's important data

   - Describe how cloud storage integrates with organizational disaster recovery plans

Introduction

A disaster can be defined as an event that creates disruptions in the operation of the organization's processes that adversely affect its productivity and profitability and require recovery efforts to correct. Organizations must be able to continue operations despite all types of small emergencies and large disasters to ensure the health and continuation of the organization.

Modern enterprises are so dependent on their communications infrastructure that "the network" is one of the most important components of any organization's continuity plan. Lost data translates into system downtime, wasted production, customer dissatisfaction, and a reduction in company earnings.

Although preventive measures are always the preferred tool to use against possible disasters, they cannot guarantee that system recovery will never be necessary. Therefore, a disaster recovery process should be designed to restore all or part of the organization's network in the event of a critical failure caused by accident, theft, intentional sabotage, or a naturally occurring disaster.

As mentioned in Chapter 8, "ICS Security Governance and Risk Management," organizations rely on three interrelated types of plans to contend with these possibilities: the *incident response plan (IRP)*, the *business continuity plan (BCP)*, and the *disaster recovery plan (DRP)*. These plans typically share overlapping functions, but they are different. The BCP is designed to anticipate and offer guidance for key components, objectives, and processes for continued operations during an interruption of the organization's business flow. As such, it is not triggered into action so much as it is referenced when an interruption or disaster occurs. The DRP is typically activated when a loss of operations or data has occurred. The IRP is triggered when an incident or potential incident has been detected or reported. Knowing what each plan is designed to do, how it is related to the other two plans, and when to trigger each one are key to effectively securing the operations and functions of the organization.

The IRP was introduced in Chapter 8 and covered in detail in Chapter 10, "ICS Security Monitoring and Incident Response." In this chapter, the focus will shift to address the purposes and functions of the business continuity plan and the disaster recovery plan.

Business Continuity Plans

A business continuity plan is a document designed to describe the organization's preparation, growth plans, and future planning in case either type of damaging event occurs.

The BCP is designed to be the overriding plan that guides the design and implementation of the other plans. As such, it will have linkage to both the incident response and disaster recovery plans.

The top of the BCP attempts to identify the critical business functions and must provide processes and procedures for responding to and recovering from business interruptions due to occurrences pointed out by the organization's risk analysis and business impact assessment and analysis to provide for the most cost-effective continuance of their operations. The BCP is applied to every internal business unit throughout the organization, as well as its outside vendors. As you may be able to imagine, plans created at this level of the organization are developed by executive teams.

Another function of the BCP is to attempt to identify all the possible disaster scenarios that could hamper or stop the organization's various business functions. This typically includes items such as potential natural disasters, loss of utilities (such as electrical power or network resources), or manmade interruptions (such as hacker or terrorist activities).

Along with the DRP, a solid BCP includes a risk analysis, a business impact analysis, plan maintenance, training, and integration processes, as well as validation of the plan. These items are usually created by the organization's enterprise resource planning (ERP) or information security (infosec) teams. For a BCP to be successful, it is critical that it has the endorsement of upper management.

System Redundancy

Redundancy is the practice of devoting additional hardware to maintain system and network resources. By adding additional devices, components that represent single points of failure can be removed from operation. A point of failure is any element in the network that if it fails, a critical process shuts down. An example of a *point of failure* would be if the only data historian in the OT network were to fail. In this case, the organization would be unable to record production data until the data historian function was restored.

System redundancy is the process of creating parallel systems in the operation to provide alternative pathways for continuing the organization's operation. Creating this type of redundancy typically involves providing secure recovery through alternate sites, installing high-availability fault-tolerant network resources, and implementing data backup systems and methods to provide a redundant source of data.

Alternate Sites

Creating and maintaining alternative sites for redundancy purposes runs at the top end of the BCP redundancy options. Establishing an alternate site enables the organization to temporarily continue operations during a major disaster and throughout the recovery period. After the disaster is over, the organization may be able to return operations to their main site. As operations are being reestablished at the primary site, start with the least critical process. It may be necessary to temporarily work out of two sites until the primary site is completely restored.

Alternate sites are facilities that can be used in cases of disaster:

- Hot sites
- Warm sites
- Cold sites
- Cloud sites

The main purpose of each of these different facility types is to provide for the recovery of secure data and continued functional operations of the organization. *Secure recovery* is of paramount importance in organizations that deal with confidential or secret data. Especially in a disaster, it is critical to be able to continue secure operations at an alternate site without compromising data integrity or confidentiality. Secure recovery and continued operations should be the primary goal when planning for a disaster that might affect the network.

Hot sites offer nearly all the resources to continue operations in the event of a disaster. These sites may be a scaled-down version of the primary site. In some instances, the hot site possesses minimal staffing and functions simultaneously, offering backup as well as fault tolerance.

Databases created at the parent location can be either simultaneously backed up at the hot site or backed up within hours. If not staffed, a hot site can typically be placed into operations within minutes of personnel arriving at the alternate site. These sites typically include current data backups and all the equipment necessary to function immediately in case there is a disaster at the primary site. Computers, cables, network peripherals, electricity, climate control, and connectivity are all immediately functional at a hot site.

Testing a hot site during a disaster drill is much easier when all equipment is readily available. However, because this is extremely costly, most organizations either create a scaled-down version of a hot site, called a *warm site*, or employ a *cold site* instead.

Unlike a hot site, a *warm site* may be equipped with antiquated equipment and most likely would be unmanned until a true disaster occurs. A warm site may also store backup data in a secure vault or safe but would require longer time to get critical operations functioning again after a disaster strikes.

A *cold site* typically provides only the most limited functions until additional resources are added. Critical phone calls and portable laptops will initiate operations at this alternate site. This type of off-site facility will not be very functional in a real emergency but may provide extra storage space and house backup data in a secured room or vault. Regardless of the type of alternate site you establish, you should periodically test that site for continued functionality.

At a cold site, the equipment is typically limited to the basic facility functions, including flooring, walls, electricity, lighting, and air conditioning. Networked computers are usually not installed in a cold site. However, some organizations may opt to make equipment available in their cold site that is not operational. The determining factor is the investment cost versus expected return on the nonproductive equipment package.

Logically, cold sites are the most difficult to test since they lack most of the equipment needed for daily operations. Just possessing a cold site without testing it provides a false sense of security. When a real disaster strikes, a cold site may be inadequate to meet recovery needs.

Cloud-based disaster recovery sites enable the organization to safely migrate their data operating systems and software tools to the cloud to take advantage of cost savings over the other site types. The operation of cloud-based services can expand or contract on the *cloud service provider's (CSP's)* virtual servers as needed. Because the data is always available over the Internet, designated members of the organization always have access to it—at a single location from anywhere and at any time. By taking advantage of high network bandwidth and sustainable scalability of services, the cloud ensures the efficiency and reliability of the recovery process.

Private cloud services are increasingly popular and so they are more commonly supported by in-house IT staff. *Public cloud services* generally require little local support, but software-as-a-service offerings may require that certain firewall rules be enabled for optimal use. A *hybrid cloud service* is one that offers a combination of both public and private cloud environments and can be so seamless that the user might forget that their data is not exclusively stored locally.

High Availability/Fault Tolerance Systems

For a production facility to be successful, it must be able to produce products. Lost minutes usually mean lost revenue; therefore, great effort is placed on the organization's ability to maintain high availability in its OT environment. Fault tolerance is one method that can be used to ensure this high availability.

Within small organizations, one server may be dedicated to providing an array composed of several physical disk drives to provide fault tolerance. This type of implementation of data availability is called a *redundant array of independent disks (RAID)*. If one of the physical drives has a failure, it can be replaced, and data can be regenerated from the other disks within the RAID array.

While there are several types of RAID, some of them are not designed to provide fault tolerance. Instead, they are used to increase available space or volumes to store larger quantities of data. However, RAID 1 and RAID 5 solutions do provide fault tolerance. *RAID 1* provides a mirror image of a primary disk, usually used to protect the operating system from failure. RAID 1 can be used with a single controller and two physical disks, known as a *mirror*, or two controllers and two physical disks, known as *disk duplexing*, which is a safer method than disk mirroring. Figure 11.1 illustrates the operation of a mirrored array used in a RAID 1 application.

FIGURE 11.1 RAID 1

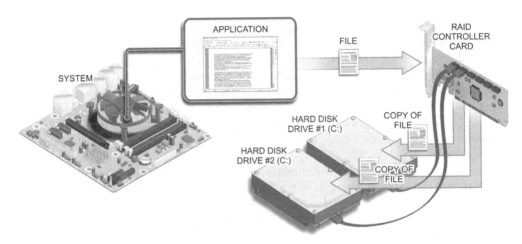

RAID 5 requires a minimum of three physical disks, with similar partition sizes to implement. A mathematical parity element generates the fault tolerance between the disks like a simple algebraic equation: A + B + C = D. If any partition element fails, it can be regenerated. For example, if A fails in the previous equation, A can be regenerated because A = D − (B + C). Figure 11.2 shows the operation of a RAID 5 array.

FIGURE 11.2 RAID 5

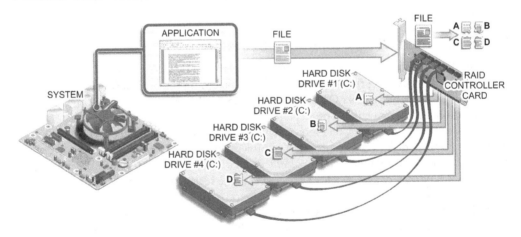

RAID has generally been a fairly effective method of maintaining data for most operating systems and is a technical solution that supports high availability. However, if the RAID array copies malicious code to corrupt other disks, it becomes ineffective, and data may still be lost. Because of this potential threat, backups are still necessary.

Another method to increase the availability of networking services is the clustering of servers. *Clustering* involves grouping or networking several servers to perform the same client services, as shown in Figure 11.3. In this way, if one of the servers fails, the others continue to perform the required services.

FIGURE 11.3   Server clustering/load balancing

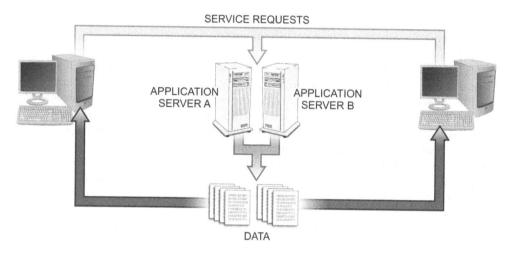

For some operating systems, clustering may also be used to balance traffic load, boost fault tolerance, and require that all systems process client service requests. Care should be taken not to rely only on clustering, though. Even though clustering of servers offers high availability while functioning, such grouping of servers becomes a single point of failure target when only one external control or storage device is used. Backups are still highly recommended.

Local Virtualized Storage

By their very nature, enterprise networks tend to generate large amounts of data. In some cases, much of this data may need to be stored for an extended period of time. Depending on the organization's data handling policies, that data may at least initially be stored on local computers. However, in an enterprise network it is more likely that the data is stored remotely on a database server somewhere in the network.

Individual servers commonly virtualize data storage through RAID strategies as described earlier. However, when the network's storage needs expand to multiple servers, network-based virtualization techniques are typically employed to create a unified storage solution that can be managed seamlessly. This is accomplished through *storage virtualization*.

The ultimate goal for storage virtualization is the creation of a single storage pool capable of being managed across various platform types and widely dispersed geographic locations. Two basic technologies provide these storage services:

- *Network-attached storage (NAS)*: A virtualized storage system that provides both storage and a file system structure

- *Storage area networks (SANs)*: A storage system that appears as a single disc in disk and volume management tools

These virtualized storage solutions help administrators properly manage large individual storage pools.

Although many SAN implementations consist of heterogeneous collections of storage servers and disk arrays, virtualization creates a logical view of these disks quite distinct from their physical architecture. This provides a storage administrator with a consolidated resource map of all disks connected to a server, which appears as a single server resource. The individual physical disk drives are basically decoupled from their normal operations and reconfigured into a "logical" and consolidated storage image.

Virtual network storage solutions are currently implemented in two ways: through the use of a dedicated hardware *appliance-based virtualization* or through *switch-based virtualization*. Both technologies perform the same services, but they accomplish them in different ways.

Appliance devices are closed storage management systems that are placed between the user network and the storage network, as illustrated in Figure 11.4.

FIGURE 11.4 Appliance-based virtualization

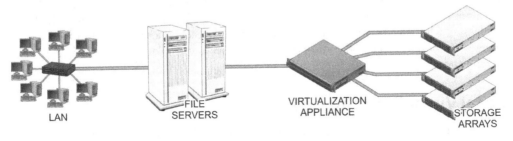

LAN   FILE SERVERS   VIRTUALIZATION APPLIANCE   STORAGE ARRAYS

As shown in Figure 11.5, switch-based storage virtualization is implemented through the managed switches used to connect the SAN devices together, as described for other VLAN implementations earlier in this chapter. These devices also sit between the user and storage networks but may employ different techniques to provide storage management functions.

FIGURE 11.5   Switch-based storage virtualization

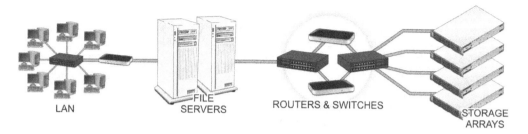

LAN   FILE SERVERS   ROUTERS & SWITCHES   STORAGE ARRAYS

Cloud Storage

Because disaster recovery plans rely on performing data backup and restore through replication to ensure that the organization's data will be available to help them get back to business as usual as quickly as possible, *cloud storage* has become an import facet in the disaster recovery processes of many organizations because of its flexibility, cost-effectiveness, reliability, and scalability.

When designing a cloud storage–based disaster recovery plan, the main concern is, does the solution provide an efficient backup and recovery plan that guaranties high data reliability at a reasonable cost prior to the occurrence of a disaster? There are several models already in use to address these concerns.

The first option is a *single-cloud environment* that can be implemented in a private, public, or hybrid cloud environment. The disaster recovery plan's developers must evaluate the cost, best facilities location, optimal amount of data that will need to be stored, and method of storage and replication to be used. However, data security associated with a centralized storage solution places the data in a single storage point at high risk if any failure occurs at the cloud service provider.

Other models include *multiple-cloud environments* that are geographically distributed so that there is a very low probability of all the cloud storage sites in use being affected at once. Figure 11.6 depicts the architecture of a typical cloud storage solution in a private cloud model. It consists of a server where application data is stored. That server is remotely connected to a set of backup servers distributed over different areas. Each backup server is connected to two additional backup servers: the local backup server and the remote backup server. To provide minimal demand on the network and accelerate the backup and restore operations, an incremental backup methodology is used to progressively update the data. Most CSPs provide this type of data backup and recovery model so their customers who experience widespread outages due to disasters can recover rapidly.

While cloud computing provides cost-effective storage options to the organization, sharing the organization's data with a third-party vendor introduces a reduction in data control security. Because the CSP owns the environment, the organization is somewhat dependent on the reliability of their environment to guarantee the integrity and privacy of the organization's data.

FIGURE 11.6 The architecture of a typical cloud storage solution in a private cloud model

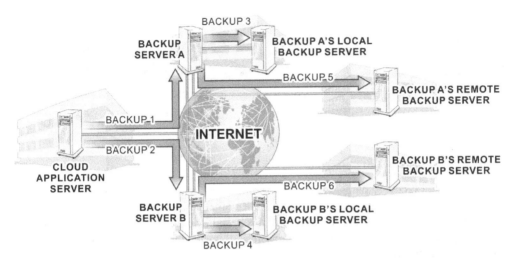

 The one drawback of using cloud-based or other Internet-related applications is that the user is dependent on the CSP's security capabilities. In the case of public utilities, this has traditionally been a major point of concern. On the other hand, several very powerful cloud providers, such as Amazon S3, Google, GFS, and Apache, have come online that have massive security appliances operating to ensure their SLAs meet client needs. Because customers have more options for cloud computing, they build excessive resources and controls into their security configurations.

Even the most advanced CSPs have experienced widespread outages and discontinued public services for different reasons. This possibility of data availability and reliability disruptions must be taken into account in the BCP. To protect the organization from these types of occurrences, it may be necessary to specify employing cloud services from multiple vendors using multiple cloud service centers.

System Backup and Restoration

One of the key elements of the BCP is to establish a *data backup and recovery policy* to be implemented in the event of a disaster. It is typically the responsibility of the network and/ or server administrators to implement those policies in a backup and recovery plan that will assure that the network's operation (and that of the organization) can recover in the case of a disaster.

Without backed-up data, there can be no contingency plan for an efficient recovery (or possibly any recovery at all). Backup utilities enable the organization to create extended copies of files, groups of files, or entire disk drives for use in the event that a server's disk drive crashes or its contents become corrupt.

Typically, only administrators or specially designated members of Backup Operators groups are given appropriate permissions to back up and restore all data on the server, regardless of their permissions level. However, any user can back up any local files that they have at least the Read permission for. Likewise, they can restore anything they have at least the Write permission for. Users generally have these permissions for their own files, so they can perform backups and restores of their data as necessary.

Administrative responsibilities associated with implementing the backup recovery portion of the business recovery plan include the following:

- *Establishing types of backups to be performed*: This includes configuring the backup utilities to conduct normal, differential, incremental, copy, or daily backup options.

- *Defining how to back up*: This includes configuring options for verifying the backup and enabling compression (if it's supported by the backup device). Verifying the backup involves comparing the stored data version with the data that was designated to be backed up (to make certain that all information was copied properly during the backup).

- *Specifying whether to replace the existing data on the backup media or append the new data to the end of the media.*

- *Establishing backup labeling so that different backup copies that exist on the backup media can easily be identified and differentiated from each other*: Normally this involves labeling backups with the date and time they were performed.

- *Determining when to back up*: This selection involves scheduling when different types of backups occur so that they have the least negative impact on the network's operation, such as late at night or on weekends when fewer users are likely to be using the network's resources.

Backup Options

Most backup utilities available on the market today allow backups to be performed in a variety of ways. Typically, backup operations fall into the following categories:

- Full or total backup
- Partial backup
- Other backup methods

In a full/total backup process, shown in Figure 11.7, the entire contents of the subject disk are backed up. This includes all the files on the disk, including each directory, subdirectory, and the contents of each. This backup method requires scheduling the most time each day to perform the backup, but also allows restoring the system in the case of a failure in the shortest time. Only the most recent backup copy is required to restore the system.

FIGURE 11.7 Full or total backup

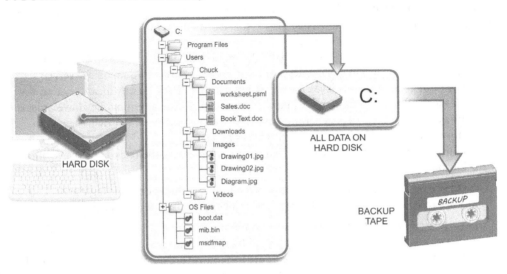

Partial backups are often used instead of regular full backups to conserve space on the backup storage device. There are typically three partial backup techniques used to store data: incremental backups, differential backups, and selective backups.

- *Incremental backup*: In an incremental backup operation, shown in Figure 11.8, the system backs up those files that have been created or changed since the last backup. Restoring the system from an incremental backup requires the use of the last full backup and each incremental backup taken since the full backup was performed. This method of backup requires the least time to back up the system but the most time to restore it.

FIGURE 11.8 Incremental backup

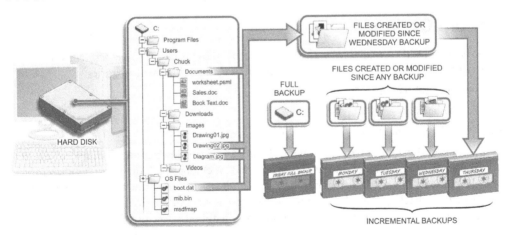

- *Differential* or *modified-only backup*: Specifying a differential backup causes the backup utility to examine each file to determine whether it has changed since the last full backup was performed. If not, it is bypassed. If the file has been altered, however, it will be backed up. This option is a valuable time-saving feature in a periodic backup strategy. To restore the system, you need a copy of the last full backup and the last differential backup. Figure 11.9 shows a differential or modified-only backup.

FIGURE 11.9   Differential or modified-only backup

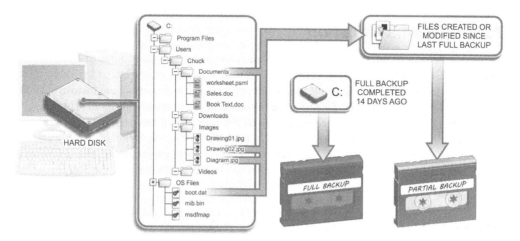

- *Selective* or *copy backup*: To conduct a selective backup, the operator moves through the tree structure of the disk marking, or tagging, directories and files to be backed up. After all the desired directories/files have been marked, they are backed up in a single operation. This form of backup is very labor intensive and may inadvertently miss saving important data. Figure 11.10 shows a selective backup.

FIGURE 11.10   Selective or copy backup

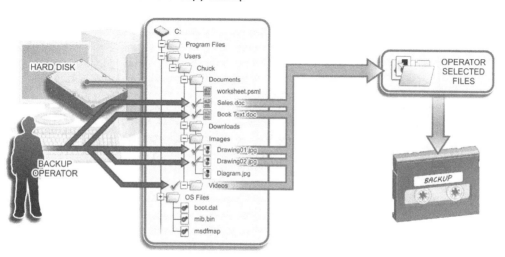

Backups are critical to business continuity plans because quick data restoration is typically of paramount importance after an incident or a disaster occurs. In such cases, differential backup has the fastest restore time. However, if accurate and complete data is critical to the business success, then full backups offer the most complete restoration.

Regardless of which backup method is designated in the BCP, it will not be effective unless it is endorsed by upper management and properly implemented and tested. The designated method must be rehearsed with key personnel, and employees must be trained to implement the backup procedures as specified in well-established policies and procedures.

Backup Media Rotation

After it has been confirmed that the backup plan has the necessary attributes to ensure system recovery, the timeframe for maintaining historical copies of the backup must be determined. The *backup media rotation* scheme employed will determine the historical timeframe within which you will be able to retrieve data. There are numerous media rotation methods that can be employed, each having its own timeframe of recovery.

The Grandfather-Father-Son method, illustrated in Figure 11.11, is the most common methodology employed today. This method uses three different groupings of backup media: the Grandfather for monthly backups, the Father for weekly backups, and the Son for daily backups.

FIGURE 11.11   The Grandfather-Father-Son method

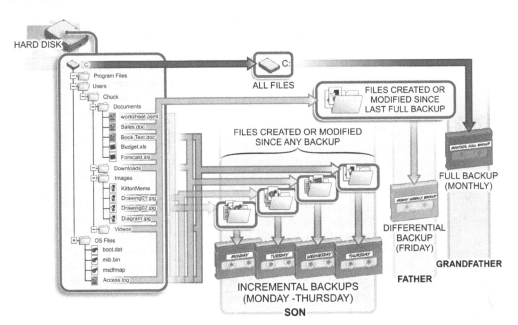

The Son uses four tapes, one for every weekday, normally covering Monday through Thursday, typically applying the incremental backup method. The Father's weekly backup, normally performed on Friday, uses one tape, applying the differential method of backup. After this, you reuse the corresponding Son tapes for the following daily backups. At month's end, you will use one tape to run the Grandfather backup. This backup would be a full backup of the system. Depending on the organization's needs, you may store these backups to support an ongoing historical backup library or reuse the tape for future backups.

Securing Backup Media

Another important network security issue is the care and protection of backup media. Because the backup media contains all the company's valuable proprietary data, if someone gains access to the media, they could retrieve the company's privileged information and misuse it. Backup media should be stored in a room that has a locking door, and there should also be a sign-in/out sheet or access control device for tracking people entering and exiting the room. Backup data should also be stored in an encrypted format so that even if it is stolen or accessed by unauthorized personnel, it will remain secure.

Remember that it is possible for others to access the data from a stolen backup and restore it on another system where they have administrator privileges. Make sure backup copies are stored securely.

Off-Site Storage

Because backup media contains the organization's proprietary information, it must be kept in a secure location and under secure conditions. Ideally, there should be at least two sets of backup media kept, one on-site and the other off-site. For this reason, many organizations store copies of their backups in off-site storage facilities. In case there is a disaster or theft at the original workplace, off-site storage provides a proactive method to protect critical resources.

For both the on-site and off-site locations, hardened fireproof safes are the most secure containers for backup media. For security purposes, only a limited number of people should know where the backups are stored and have access to the safes' keys or combinations.

Other BCP Considerations

There are several outside variables that are not under the direct control of the organization that the BCP must take into consideration to minimize the effects of events and disasters that negatively impact the organization. Two key variables include utilities and supply chains. The organization has to depend on these outside systems to continue in order to maintain their business processes. In the event of a disaster, alternative sources must be available or be able to be brought online to replace them.

Utility Considerations

Certain utilities, such as electrical power and Internet provision, are critical to the operation of the production processes, as well as the enterprise and OT networks. Therefore, policies, procedures, and guidelines must be included in the BCP to specify how the organization plans to deal with the loss of these services during a disaster. These policies and procedures must address items such as the following:

- Where to place protective equipment such as backup generators or uninterruptible power supplies (UPSs) in case the electrical utility is unable to deliver

- If necessary, knowing where there are alternative Internet connectivity/communication methods available to the organization in the event of a disaster

In addition to electrical and data/communication utilities, the proximity of water and waste material should be considered in a business continuity plan. Water needs to be available for personnel consumption and in cases of Class A fires. However, these facets of the BCP are not generally related to the recovery or operation of the enterprise or OT network environments.

Supply Chain Considerations

The *supply chain* is the system that moves a product or service from its raw components to a finished product ready for delivery to a customer. This is the very nature of what manufacturing organizations and utilities do. However, the complete chain of organizations involved directly or peripherally with the production process may include many independent organizations.

For this reason, any organization's BCP must include risk analysis and mitigation plans for the other members of the chain.

Supply Chain Risk Management (NIST 800-161)

The NIST Special Publication (SP) 800-161, "Supply Chain Risk Management Practices for Federal Information Systems and Organizations," was produced to guide organizations in their efforts to identify, assess, and mitigate their IT/OT supply chain risks. These chains can be complex and diverse, involving "geographically diverse" routes, as well as multiple layers of organizations. For these reasons, purchasers of network-related goods and services have reduced abilities to assess the security of the goods and services they are purchasing to use in their OT networks.

In such a long supply chain, it is entirely possible for attackers to build in, or attach, unwanted or malicious functionality to the product. For example, with access to an uncontrolled link in the supply chain, a nation-state actor could inject malicious code into the programming of products used to control sensitive processes. After the product has been installed in a working process, the attacker could then exploit the code to steal information, degrade production, or cause the process to fail completely.

The SolarWinds attack in 2020 was just such an attack. It involved a software supply chain attack by an outside state actor that exploited updates to their Orion network monitoring utility. The attack affected more than 250 Fortune 500 companies and delivered trojans in the Orion updates SolarWinds supplied to its customers. The trojans established backdoors that enabled third-party servers to have remote access to the customer's emails, files, and other data.

Disaster Recovery

Disaster recovery is the process of restoring production systems to normal operational levels after a disaster occurs. This process is different from the incident response process described in the previous chapter, as it deals with restoring the organization's processes to normal operation after the occurrence of a critical failure due to accident, theft, intentional sabotage, or natural disaster. The most important elements in successful disaster recovery operations are the following:

- Proper planning
- Documentation
- System redundancies
- Effective backup policies and procedures

Disasters can be classified into four main categories based on their nature:

- *Climate disasters*: Floods, fires, landslides, storms, contamination, and other hazards
- *Deliberate disruption*: Arson, legal disputes, terrorism, and sabotage
- *Loss of utilities and services*: Electrical power failures, network outages, service breakdowns
- *Equipment or system failures*: Cooling failures, Internet failure, and equipment failure

The organization's disaster recovery process should be designed to restore all or part of their critical systems in the event of a critical failure caused by events in any of these categories.

A reliable DRP is an important component of the organization's BCP. By planning for the worst possible data security scenario, the organization and its employees will be prepared to recover from any network failure or system disaster that might occur. The most important elements for successfully recovering from a disaster include planning, system redundancy, security, and scheduled backup.

The plan is generally created by senior management based on significant input from their IT and infosec teams. One of the main areas of emphasis in the plan typically deals with technology assets and redundancy operations to be triggered whenever a loss of infrastructure or data is likely to happen or has already, happened. This point is typically identified by the incident response team.

The plan should include procedures that describe how power is to be restored in the event of an electrical failure and how to recover lost or corrupted data using the backup systems and methodologies specified in the business continuity plan. It may also contain documentation for spinning up alternative site and cloud restore options to begin the recovery process.

The plan itself is the first and foremost factor in preparing for a successful disaster recovery. It should include a complete inventory of all the components that make up each network segment in the system, as well as all components that make up each server and workstation. This includes all associated software that will need to be restored.

This inventory should be prioritized; it should list which systems are most critical to the organization's operation to indicate that they must be restored first. These priorities are most easily identified by considering how valuable the data is on each system.

The DRP must contain all the necessary elements for an expeditious restoration of the system with no data loss. This includes reliable methods by which each department can continue to function productively during those periods when the network is down, along with a means to successfully synchronize and integrate newly generated data when the infrastructure is restored.

This is reinforced in the NIST Cyber Security Framework. The guidelines in that document point out that an organization's recovery processes and procedures should be maintained and tested to ensure timely restoration of systems or assets affected by cyber security events. This basically involves the following:

1. Creating the disaster recovery plan

2. Testing and evaluating the plan

3. Updating the plan

4. Implementing the plan

5. Conducting ongoing periodic testing, evaluation, and updating of the plan

 A printed copy of the disaster recovery plan is the most important part of the plan. Remember that if you plan for the worst event that can happen and you are prepared for it, you can easily recover from almost any failure the organization may experience.   .

Planning

Preparing for disaster recovery is a critical element in managing and administering the organization's data communications channels. Lost data means system downtime and lost production and therefore lost money. The best tool to preclude having to recover your system, of course, is proper prevention. In the event of that inevitable failure, you must have a sufficient DRP with the necessary elements for expeditious restoration with no lost data. Recall that the DRP was introduced in Chapter 8 as a key component of the risk mitigation plan, along with the IRP and the BCP.

To be effective, the DRP must include a process for personnel to identify, classify, and respond to disasters. Like the IRP, creating the DRP involves five major objectives:

- Creating and publishing the policies, procedures, processes, and guidelines to respond to the occurrence of a disaster:

  - Identify and prioritize the criticality of the organization's operations. Determine which operations are most critical to the survival of the organization and in what order they should be restored after a disaster has occurred.

  - Identify resources that will be required to restore each operation.

  - Create procedures for declaring a disaster situation, including identifying the circumstances that constitute a disaster.

  - Express expected timeframes for recovery from disaster occurrences. *Recovery time objectives (RTOs)* express an allotted time for recovery of a processing operation or resource after a disaster.

  - Create processes for recovering data that has been lost or corrupted.

NOTE   Be aware that organizations may create different BCPs and DRPs for different locations. Likewise, a given BCP or DRP may contain different directions based on the nature of the disaster being addressed.

- Creating a *disaster response team* along with a process for activating the team. This includes the following:

  - Identify appropriate people and assign them roles and responsibilities to perform in the disaster response process described in the DRP.

  - Identify personnel who are responsible for implementing/overseeing each facet of the plan. While larger organizations may develop and train a disaster recovery team, smaller organizations may designate a single person to be trained as the disaster recovery manager. In either case, there must be an individual who is empowered to make short-term decisions immediately after a disaster.

- Developing a communication plan for all stakeholders and employees. This includes the following:

  - Identify the interactions and communications that need to be performed when a state of disaster is declared. For example, the plan should establish criteria for when to report and to whom, as well as how information is to be exchanged during and after a disaster.

  - Create escalation procedures.

- Training all personnel to understand the DRP and their roles in it. Define how tasks are to be performed, how different processes in the plan relate, and how actions are coordinated—no matter who is performing the work. Depending on the nature of the disaster, this may include evacuation procedures.

- Finally, ensuring that any equipment that may be required to respond appropriately to any of the disaster types is available. This includes clearly identifying all resources required to restore normal operations as identified and prioritized in step 1. The DRP should include a complete inventory of the organization's network's components along with any associated software that must be restored after a disaster. This inventory listing should have a priority structure, indicating which systems are most critical to the company's operation and need to be restored first. It should also include methods for each department to function while networks and processes are down, and a means to successfully synchronize data after the infrastructure has been restored.

Disaster recovery measures should be well planned and rehearsed so that in the event of a disaster, such as flood, earthquake, major fire, or even theft, procedures are in place to be able to continue operations.

Documenting the Disaster Recovery Plan

The DRP is critical, but it will quickly become obsolete if it is not updated on a regular basis. As with the IRP, changes to the DRP must be documented as it provides *lessons learned* to avoid catastrophe and can be used to improve security policies and procedures. The plan should include requirements set by the organization's security policies for how and when it will be updated, as well as how it will be stored and preserved. There must also be processes that ensure that all stakeholders are aware of the plan and able to implement it when necessary.

The DRP should include provisions for recovery after various types of data loss and system failures. These situations can include natural disasters (flood, fire, etc.), electrical-related failures (power outage, etc.), or system data loss (viruses, sabotage, hacking, etc.).

The DRP documentation should be duplicated in hard copy and available not only on site but also stored with the off-site system backups. As the plan is updated, all copies must also be revised. The disaster recovery plan should at least include the following supporting documentation:

- Printed copies of the official DRP for proper distribution to all involved parties of the disaster recovery team
- Complete listing of what comprises the DRP documentation package
- Listing of the names and contact information for all individuals who are members of the disaster recovery team
- Hardware and software listings associated with all endpoint and network connectivity devices, along with copies of any applicable information manuals
- Copies of critical software and hardware drivers stored on removable hard drives or other media that can be stored safely and securely away from the facility in encrypted and password-protected formats

- Location and contact data of primary and off-site backup data packages
- Baseline metrics, both the latest and necessary historical data

 Archives of the software library, hardware inventory, current configuration, and schematics should be maintained in a physical location separate from the production system copies.

The Disaster Response/Recovery Team

Depending on the nature of the disaster event, select individuals who are part of the disaster recovery team may be earmarked to continue critical operations while other employees are excused or evacuated.

As pointed out earlier, larger organizations may develop and train extensive, multifaceted disaster recovery teams. The makeup of the team varies from one organization to another; however, every disaster recovery team should have a designated leader. Even in smaller organizations, one person should be trained as the disaster recovery manager and be able to make short-term decisions immediately after a disaster.

Members of the disaster recovery team must be trained to document events, changes, and revisions associated with disaster response and recovery efforts. Although taking care to effectively document these activities during emergencies and especially during a disaster may be difficult, it is critical for disaster recovery efforts to be effective.

Testing the DRP

As with any organization-wide installation, upgrade, or troubleshooting operation, testing a DRP within the company's actual working environment can be difficult. A *disaster recovery drill* should be a yearly scheduled event. The difficulties involved with implementing a DRP are not fully understood without experience. Exercising the DRP will reinforce the importance of performing timely and consistent backups so that data recoveries are always possible.

Various strategies can be developed to test the DRP without shutting down the network. To become familiar with the critical elements, members of the disaster recovery team should study the plan and dry-run portions of it throughout the year. By doing so, they will reveal, consider, and correct various weaknesses in the plan, and new features might be added as required. Although even the most thoughtful plans can have weaknesses, a consistently rehearsed and edited plan will serve to minimize them.

When testing the DRP, the disaster recovery team must make sure it functions properly and that all personnel are aware of their individual roles. Areas of the plan deserving review include the following:

- Ensuring that the documentation is usable and that any necessary components can be located easily.

- Testing the notification procedures so that there is always a reliable means to contact personnel when the network or one of its key components goes down. For example, if the company's ecommerce site is down, those supervisors will need to be informed.
  - Ensure that current phone numbers for these people are on hand, for all times of the day and night.
  - Verify that the telephone numbers for all equipment vendors and manufacturers are available and correct.
  - Check all support contracts and ensure that phone numbers are available for any that are still in effect.
- Verifying that the location and identity of all spare components or servers listed in the plan are correct.

Backup media and techniques should be tested at least once a month, or as often as once a week for more critical network segments. The administrator should perform a full restore test at least once a quarter. This restore testing should be performed by restoring the data to a different folder than its original location to ensure that the backup contains all the necessary data without being contaminated by pre-existing files.

Large enterprises often conduct periodic testing of full disaster recovery plans. To maintain business continuity while testing the recovery plan, they often bring a commercial hot-site facility online as a systems backup. This facility has a complete backup of the organization's online data and can provide business continuity during the time that the main site is down for testing. This arrangement provides a real-time testing environment for their IT staff in the knowledge and execution of the DRP.

After the DRP test has been completed, the results might indicate that more planning or troubleshooting is required. For example, if data was accidentally restored to an email server that should have been restored to the file server, the DRP must be examined carefully to determine what went wrong. Then it will need to be edited and tested again to ensure that the problem has been eliminated.

Updating the Plan

As critical as it might be, any DRP will quickly become obsolete if it is not updated periodically. The plan should contain detailed procedures for how and when it will be updated, stored, and preserved. Additionally, DRP documentation should be duplicated in hard copy and immediately available on site. Copies should also be stored with all off-site system data backups. These copies must also be continually revised as the plan is updated.

Implementing the DRP

In the event of an actual disaster, the steps outlined in the DRP should be followed in sequential order to ensure that the network will be restored to full operation and that the actual cause of the failure is found.

1. Take steps to discover what caused the network or one of its components to go down.
2. Determine how to perform the necessary repair.

3. Identify any failed components.

4. Match failed components to existing good components.

5. Implement the recovery and restoration process in accordance with the DRP.

The DRP should provide enough documentation and test results to permit the full restoration of the organization's IT/OT operations and data. After it has been implemented, the network should be returned to normal operation.

NERC CIP-009-6

The *NERC CIP-009-6* standard, "Recovery Plans for Critical Cyber Assets," provides BES organizations with directions for creating, implementing, and testing business continuity and disaster recovery plans for their critical cyber assets. This portion of the CIP standards contains three major areas:

- *Recovery plan specifications*: BES organizations are directed to develop and review one or more recovery plans for their critical cyber assets as identified under the CIP-002 standard:

  - Specify events or activities that would trigger the activation of the recovery plan.

  - Define the roles and responsibilities of the members of the CIRT team that will be called into action when the plan is activated.

  - The plan must also contain policies for storing and testing backup media to ensure that it is available for use to recover BES Cyber System functionality. Under the CIP-009 standard, this practice must be conducted at least annually.

  - The BES organization must create, implement, and test policies for the backup and storage of all data required to return the cyber assets to operation after an incident. This may also include maintaining spare components or copies of software related to the critical cyber assets.

  - The organization must conduct activities to simulate actual incidents that would activate the recovery plan. These exercises can be paper-based in nature or fully operational. Under the CIP-009 standard, these exercises must be conducted at least annually.

- *Recovery plan implementation and testing*: This should include the following:

  - *Testing*: The plan must include evidence that the recovery plan is working. This information can be in the form of a report based on recovery from an actual incident or through a tabletop exercise or an operational exercise. This evidence must be updated in the plan at least every 15 calendar months.

  - *Functionality*: The plan must include evidence that verifies that representative samples from a BES Cyber System recovery are usable and compatible with current configurations.

  - *Operational testing*: Each of the organization's recovery plans must be tested through an operational exercise at least once every 36 months.

- *Lessons learned, including recovery plan review, updates, and communications*: This includes the following:

  - *Timeframe*: A recovery plan review and update is required within 90 calendar days after the completion of a recovery plan test or an actual recovery operation.

  - *Notification*: The plan must notify each person or group that has a defined role in the recovery plan as to all updates to the plan based on lessons learned.

Review Questions

The following questions test your knowledge of the material presented in this chapter.

1. A _____ is a document designed to describe the organization's preparation, growth plans, and future planning in case either type of damaging event occurs.

2. What is the purpose of the disaster recovery plan (DRP)?

3. Why would partial backups be performed instead of regular backups?

4. Describe the operation of a Grandfather-Father-Son backup media rotation scheme.

5. List the key items that should be covered in the communication plan portion of the DRP document.

6. What two items should be covered in the organization's business continuation policy concerning third-party members of the production supply chain?

7. What is the major concern with testing the DRP?

8. _____ is the practice of devoting extra hardware to maintain network resources.

9. Describe the reasons why an organization would absorb the additional expense of creating and maintaining an alternative site for redundancy purposes.

10. A _____ is any element in the network that if it fails, a critical process shuts down.

11. Describe the type of equipment found in a typical warm site location.

12. What type of virtualized storage system provides both storage and a file system structure?

13. Identify two basic steps that should be taken to secure backup media.

14. What is the most serious drawback of using a cloud-based storage system for data storage?

15. _____ express an allotted time for recovery of a processing operation or resource after a disaster.

Exam Questions

1. What is the disaster recovery process designed to accomplish?

   A. To describe the organization's preparation, growth plans, and future planning in case either type of damaging event occurs

   B. To create and publish policies, procedures, processes, and guidelines for responding to the occurrence of a disaster

   C. To identify and prioritize the criticality of the organization's operations and determine which operations are most critical to the survival of the organization and in what order they should be restored after a disaster has occurred

   D. To restore all or part of the organization's network in the event of a critical failure caused by accident, theft, intentional sabotage, or a naturally occurring disaster

2. In general, how often should disaster recovery drills be conducted?

   A. Monthly

   B. Yearly

   C. Semi-annually

   D. Biannually

3. What other documents are typically bundled with the DRP? (Select all that apply.)

   A. Contact information for all individuals on the disaster recovery team

   B. Copies of the BCP and IRP documents

   C. Copies of critical software and hardware drivers

   D. EMS contact information

   E. Executive staff contact information

4. Which virtualized storage system provides data storage structure that appears as a single disc?

   A. RAID 1

   B. NAS

   C. SAN

   D. VLAN

5. How often should backup media and techniques be tested?

   A. Monthly

   B. Yearly

   C. Semi-annually

   D. Biannually

6. Under the NERC CIP-009-6 standard, how often should a full restore test be performed from the backup media/system?

   A. Weekly

   B. Monthly

   C. Quarterly

   D. Annually

7. Which RAID versions provide fault tolerance capabilities for the network server? (Select all that apply.)

   A. RAID 0

   B. RAID 1

   C. RAID 3

   D. RAID 5

   E. RAID 10

8. How many different storage media copies are involved in a Grandfather-Father-Son backup media rotation scheme?

   A. 3

   B. 4

   C. 6

   D. 8

9. Which type of alternate site can typically be up and running within minutes of personnel arriving?

   A. A cold site

   B. A mirror site

   C. A RAID site

   D. A hot site

10. What is the main purpose associated with each of the different alternate site facility options considered in the BCP?

    A. To provide data storage for backup and restore operation in the event of a disaster

    B. To provide offline services for the organization in the event of a disaster

    C. To provide alternative communication methods in the event of a disaster

    D. To provide fully functional replacements for facilities and operations disabled in the event of a disaster

    E. To provide for recovery of secure data and continued functional operations of the organization in the event of a disaster

Appendix A

GICSP Objective Map

The Global Industrial Cyber Security Professional (GICSP) Exam is a vendor-neutral Industrial Control System Security certification designed to bridge IT cybersecurity with industrial control networking environments. The objectives of the exam are aimed at assessing the candidate to ensure that they possess a minimum level of knowledge to function successfully in an operating technology/industrial control system (OT/ICS), engineering, cybersecurity job role. The certification meets the requirements of the US Department of Defense (DoD) 8570.0.1 Information Assurance Workforce Improvement program. It is also approved for the DoD's CND-A, CND-IS, and IAT Level II workforce categories.

The exam is administered and delivered by the Global Information Assurance Certification (GIAC) certification arm of the SANS Institute, an organization that specializes in information and cybersecurity training.

The GICSP is a single exam comprised of 115 questions. There is a time limit of three hours to complete the exam, and a minimum score of 71 percent is required for passage. The exams are delivered by proctored Pearson VUE testing centers and must be scheduled in advance. Scheduling can be performed using the instructions found at:

`www.giac.org/information/schedule_proctored_exam.pdf`

This certification is valid for four years and must be renewed before that point to remain valid. The topics covered in the GICSP exam are listed in the next section.

The ICS410: ICS/SCADA Security Essentials course, provided by SANS, supports the GICSP exam and provides a foundational set of standardized skills and knowledge for industrial cybersecurity professionals. The course is designed to ensure that the workforce involved in supporting and defending industrial control systems is trained to keep the operational environment safe, secure, and resilient in the face of current and emerging cyber threats.

ICS410.1 ICS: Global Industrial Cybersecurity Professional (GICSP) Objectives

Overview

- Overview of ICS
  - Processes & Roles

- Industries
- Learning from Peers
- Purdue Levels 0 and 1
  - Controllers and Field Devices
  - Programming Controllers
  - Programming a PLC
- Purdue Levels 2 and 3
  - HMIs, Historians, Alarm Servers
  - Specialized Applications and Master Servers
  - Control Rooms and Plants
  - SCADA
  - Programming an HMI
- IT & ICS Differences
  - ICS Life Cycle Challenges
- Physical and Cyber Security

ICS410.2 Architecture and Field Devices

Field Devices and Controllers
- ICS Attack Surface
  - Threat Actors and Reasons for Attack
  - Attack Surface and Inputs
  - Vulnerabilities
  - Threat/Attack Models
  - Information Leakage
  - Identifying External Attack Surfaces
- Secure ICS Network Architectures
  - ICS410 Reference Model
  - Larger ICS Sites
  - Remote Access
  - Regional SCADA
  - Architecting a Secure ICS Site
- Purdue Level 0 and 1
  - Purdue Level 0 and 1 Attacks
  - Control Things Platform

- Passwords in EEPROM Dumps
- Purdue Level 0 and 1 Technologies
- Fieldbus Protocol Families
- Exploring Fieldbus Protocols
- Purdue Level 0 and 1 Defenses
- Safety Instrumented Systems (SIS)

ICS410.3: Communications and Protocols

Supervisory Systems
- Ethernet and TCP/IP
  - Ethernet Concepts
  - TCP/IP Concepts
  - Network Capture Analysis
  - ICS Protocols over TCP/IP
  - Wireshark and ICS Protocols
  - Attacks on Networks
  - Enumerating Modbus TCP
- Enforcement Zone Devices
  - Firewalls and NextGen Firewalls
  - Modern Data Diodes
  - NIDS/NIPS and Netflow
  - USB Scanning and Honeypots
- Understanding Basic Cryptography
  - Crypto Keys
  - Encryption, Hashing, and Signatures
  - Manual Cryptography
- Wireless Technologies
  - Satellite and Cellular
  - Mesh Networks and Microwave
  - Bluetooth and Wi-Fi

- Wireless Attacks and Defenses
    - 3 Eternal Risks of Wireless
    - Sniffing, DoS, Masquerading, Rogue AP

ICS410.4: Supervisory Systems

Workstations and Servers

- Supervisory Servers
    - Supervisory Attacks
    - Historians and Databases
    - Bypassing Auth with SQL Injection
- User Interfaces
    - HMI and UI Attacks
    - Web-based Attacks
    - Password Defenses
    - Password Fuzzing
- Defending Microsoft Windows
    - Windows Services
    - Windows Security Policies and GPOs
    - Host Firewalls
    - Baselining with PowerShell
- Patching ICS Systems
    - Patch Decision Tree
    - Vendors, CERTS, and Security Bulletins

ICS410.5: Security Governance

ICS Security Governance

- Defending Unix and Linux
    - Differences with Windows
    - Daemons, SystemV, and SystemD
    - Lynis and Bastille
    - Hardening Linux

- Endpoint Protection and SIEMS
  - Application Runtime and Execution Control
  - Configuration Integrity and Containers
  - Logs in Windows and Linux
  - Windows Event Logs
- Building an ICS Cyber Security Program
  - Starting the Process
  - Frameworks: ISA/IEC 62443, ISO/IEC 27001, NIST CSF
  - Using the NIST CSF
- Creating ICS Cyber Security Policy
  - Policies, Standards, Guidance, and Procedures
  - Culture and Enforcement
  - Examples and Sources
  - ICS Security Policy Review
- Measuring Cyber Security Risk
  - Risk Approaches and Calculations
  - DR and BC Planning
- Incident Response
  - Six Step Process

Appendix B

Glossary

800-82-r2, "Guide to Industrial Control System (ICS) Security"   International guidelines for implementing cybersecurity in Industrial Control Systems.

800-61-r2, "Computer Security Incident Handling Guide"   A NIST Special Publication designed to guide organizations in the process of incident response using a four-phase life-cycle approach.

800-115, "Technical Guide to Information Security Testing and Assessment"   A NIST Special Publication designed to assist organizations in planning and conducting penetration tests, analyzing findings, and developing mitigation strategies.

800-137, "Information Security Continuous Monitoring (ISCM) for Federal Information Systems and Organizations"   A NIST Special Publication designed to guide organizations in their efforts to conduct continuous security monitoring operations.

800-161, "Supply Chain Risk Management Practices for Federal Information Systems and Organizations"   A NIST Special Publication designed to guide organizations in their efforts to identify, assess, and mitigate their IT/OT supply chain risks.

A

AAA protocol   Authentication, authorization, and accounting that uses different link layer protocols such as PPP and authenticates using PAP or CHAP.

acceptable use policy (AUP)   A documented policy that defines employee roles and limitations when using their organization's computer and network equipment.

access control   Security precautions that ensure resources are granted only to those users who are entitled to them.

access control list   A list that controls access to a network segment via whitelisting or blacklisting.

Active Directory   A directory service provided by Microsoft that handles domain management, which includes authentication, authorization, certificate management, and more.

active RFID tags   Self-powered tags that provide a longer range but are much more expensive. Active Radio Frequency Identifier tags transfer identifying information by way of electromagnetic fields.

actuator   A device, such as an electric motor starter or pneumatic or solenoid-activated valve, that is responsible for controlling a mechanical system.

Adaptive Frequency Hopping Spread Spectrum (AFHSS)   A secure RF transmission method that rapidly changes its carrier frequency over a large bandwidth according to a pattern known only to the transmitter and receiver. The Bluetooth specification implements this transmission method in the license-free 2.4GHz range to provide security and avoid crowded frequency ranges, by hopping between previously divided subfrequencies.

Address Resolution Protocol (ARP) spoofing attack   An attack where the attacker sends fake ARP messages to associate their MAC address with the IP address of another user. Once the association has been established, messages directed to that address will be diverted to the attacker. The attacker can then use information obtained from the intercepted messages to mount other types of attacks, such as DoS or man-in-the-middle attacks.

Advanced Encryption Standard (AES)   A block-level encryption algorithm that uses symmetric keys. Announced by NIST in 2001, it has been adopted by the US government and supersedes DES.

Advanced Metering Infrastructure (AMI)   The corresponding infrastructure for the new digital power monitoring meters that provide a communication path between the utility's central office and a HAN of smart energy devices at the customer's end.

advanced persistent threats   Threats that target very specific and very secure systems over a continuous period of time.

adware   Unwanted, unsolicited advertising, usually displayed in web browsers.

algorithm   As related to computer security, an algorithm is arithmetic code, known as a *cipher*, that is applied to data to alter its contents (encryption algorithms) so that unauthorized people cannot read it. Common encryption algorithms used in digital processing include Triple DES, AES, RSA, Blowfish, and Twofish.

annunciator   An alarm system device that signals the operating condition of the system by sound, light, or other indication.

anomaly analysis   An analysis system that applies statistical analysis techniques to the data stream in order to determine whether it is "normal" or "anomalous" at any given time.

anonymous proxy   A proxy server that provides client anonymity by concealing their original IP address.

antispyware   Programs that defend against spyware by detecting and then removing them and/or blocking them in the first place.

antivirus   Programs that defend against computer viruses by detecting and then removing them and/or blocking them in the first place.

application-level encryption   A method of applying encryption within the application to protect data (at rest, in motion, in use). Other levels at which encryption is normally applied include at the folder, file, and disk levels.

application service provider (ASP)   The ancestor of modern-day cloud computing. An enterprise that provides application-based services to paying customers across a network.

application servers   Servers configured to provide a specific role in the organization's business activities, provided for the organization's internal users.

application zone   A delegated zone defined by the usage of applications within an intranet environment. The zone is created by use of firewalls, routers, and switches.

asymmetric keys   A two-key system used in encryption algorithms, where one key is used for encryption and another key is used for decryption. These key types are also referred to as public keys and private keys.

asymmetrical (out-of-band) virtualization   The virtualization device is installed outside the actual data path between the network and the storage system.

attack surface   The sum of the different opportunities for being attacked.

attenuation   A measure of how much signal loss occurs as the information moves across a transport medium such as a fiber-optic cable.

audit entries   Items added to the security log when an audited event occurs.

audit policy   A policy that defines the types of events that will be monitored and added to the system's security logs. The internal guidelines and standards to review and govern an organization.

audit trail   A record of a user's computer usage.

auditing   A form of accounting that is a preplanned monitoring method to evaluate or determine if problems exist within a specific area.

authentication   The process of determining that someone is who they say they are.

authentication, authorization, and accounting (AAA)   A method with which network administrators can keep information secure.

Authentication Header (AH)   A protocol used by IPSec to prevent packet changes in transport. This provides integrity and authentication.

authentication server (AS)   A server whose function is to provide network users with authentication.

authentication system   A network system used to provide authentication.

authoritative   A server that provides definitive answers to DNS queries rather than from a cache or by requesting that information from another name server.

authorization   The resources that a user has permission to access and what actions they can perform.

automated access control   A design feature that requires authentication of the identity of a user attempting to access a security zone or computer system from a distant location.

automated provisioning   A method similar to rule-based access control, where a rule is the basic element. The rule defines what operations can be performed.

B

backup media   The media where data backups are stored, such as magnetic tape or DVD-Rs.

backup policy   A policy that defines what to back up, when to back up, and where to store the backups. Also includes who has authorization over the backups and how they are made.

barriers   Impediments that deter the ability of an intruder to advance from the outer perimeter to the interior region. Also referred to as bollards.

bastion host   A specific computer designed to be located in the DMZ and may be a firewall, a router, a server, or a group of computers that are not protected behind another firewall, but that have direct access to the Internet.

beacon frames   Beacon frames are managed frames in the 802.11 wireless LANs that let nearby clients know what networks they are broadcasting.

beacon interval   The beacon frame interval is the specified amount of time between beacon frames being broadcast.

biometrics   Access control mechanisms that use human physical characteristics to verify individual identities. The use of the unique physical features of a person, fingerprints, voiceprints, and/or retinal scans to provide identification and authentication.

BitLocker   A native utility on some Windows OSs that provides full disk-level encryption.

black-hat hacker   An individual who possesses extensive cybersecurity skills and uses them for the purpose of breeching or bypassing network security structures for malicious or criminal purposes.

blacklisting   A means of only denying access to users matching given criteria, based on users, software, systems.

block cipher   A cipher that applies an algorithm to a block of data, rather than a single bit at a time.

Blowfish   A block-level encryption algorithm that uses symmetric key encryption.

blue team   The team that is typically the target during a penetration test.

Bluetooth   A wireless networking specification for personal area networks (PANs) that meshes together personal devices including cell phones, digital cameras, PCs, notebooks, and printers.

bot herder   The unauthorized person in control of a botnet.

botnet   A large collection of zombies, or bots, controlled by a bot herder.

bots (zombie computers)   PCs, IoT devices, or other smart programmable devices controlled by an unauthorized person.

bring-your-own-device (BYOD)   Authorizing the use of an employee's own device, instead of providing one, for business-related activities.

broadcast storm   The rebroadcasting of broadcast traffic by every network device, eventually causing traffic delivery failure. This can quickly overload switches and routers and overwhelm a network.

broadcast traffic   The sending of messages to all possible destinations on a network.

Browser Exploitation Framework (BeEF)   A notable open-source penetration testing tool that focuses on web-borne attacks through a web browser.

brute-force attack   This is where the attacker employs an application to systematically guess the key or password based on a known list or a predictive mathematical scheme. This can involve hundreds or thousands of attempts.

buffer overflow   An anomaly where a program overruns the buffer boundary, thus resulting in erratic behavior, memory access errors, and/or system crashes. The system is effectively disabled to the point where the user cannot use it.

buffer overflow attack   An attack designed to cause a computing system to have a buffer overflow condition.

Building Automation and Control Network (BACnet)   A protocol that was developed by the American Society of Heating, Refrigerating, and Air Conditioning Engineers for networking building automation equipment together.

business continuity plan   A document describing the organization's preparation, growth plans, and future planning in case damaging events occur.

business-to-business (B2B)   Network channels that organizations use to conduct secure transactions with other trusted organizations.

bypass mode   A mode available for many alarm systems designed to let someone through the alarm area without triggering the alarm. Turning off or disabling a sensor, a device, or an entire zone without affecting the rest of the system.

C

C2 channel   A C2 channel (command and control) gives attackers the ability to interact directly with the compromised host, which can make the threat very dangerous because the attacker can respond to attempts that would mitigate the threat.

cache poisoning   When an attacker establishes a rogue DNS server and then uses that server to feed false information back to the primary DNS server, thus poisoning the primary DNS server's cached resources.

caching servers   Using cached web pages, a proxy server will serve already-accessed web pages placed in its cache to requesting clients without requiring outside access to the Internet.

caching web proxies   Local servers that cache (store) web resources for quicker access.

certificate chain   The list of certificates starting with the root certificate, followed by each subsequent certificate where the issuer or signer of one certificate is the subject of the next.

Challenge-Handshake Authentication Protocol (CHAP)   An authentication method using a three-way handshake (syn, syn-ack, ack) to identify remote clients. CHAP is used to authenticate a user or network—Challenge, Response, Success, or Failure—it protects against replay attacks.

chokepoints   A place where people or other traffic must pass through a portal, such as a gate, doorway, hallway, or access street/road that may lead to a single point of failure.

chroot   A Linux-based command that adjusts the root directory location of a currently running process. May also be used for creating and managing multiple virtualized copies of an operating system.

cipher   In cryptography, a cipher is the algorithm used to encrypt data.

cipher locks   Locks that operate by unlocking magnetic door locks when the correct programmed code is entered by the user on the cipher lock keypad.

ciphertext   The text of any data after it has been encoded by a cryptographic key.

Cisco Discovery Protocol (CDP)   The CDP protocol enables Cisco devices to communicate with other Cisco devices to exchange information. Attackers can use this protocol to gather information about the switches and other network devices running CDP on the network.

cleartext   Stored or transmitted data that has not been encrypted.

clickjacking attack   An attack that employs deceptive frame techniques to trick the user into clicking on their content rather than the intended content.

client-server model   A network model based on a centralized, controlling server device that provides services for some number of client devices attached to the network.

cloud-based services   Hosted services with special client application software that extends the users' desktop or mobile file and data storage to an Internet service.

cloud computing   Utilizing remote, networked servers for resources. These resources may include data storage, data processing, and others, thus reducing the hardware needs of a local machine.

Common Platform Enumeration (CPE)   A standardized method of describing and identifying operating system, hardware devices, and application classes on a network.

Common Vulnerabilities and Exposures (CVE)   A system for referencing publicly known vulnerabilities. Maintained by MITRE Corporation and backed by the US Department of Homeland Security.

Common Vulnerability Scoring System (CVSS)   A system for scoring vulnerabilities from CVE, making it easier to understand the associated risks.

completely automated public Turing test to tell computers and humans apart (CAPT-CHA)   A form input request for a word, phrase, group of random characters and numbers, or a simple request to perform a simple test that cannot be automated easily.

complexity   As it relates to passwords, complexity is the combination of the length, width, and depth of an input.

Conficker   A worm targeting thumb drives that would automatically execute as soon as it was connected to a live USB port.

confidentiality, integrity, and availability (CIA)   The classic model of information security.

connectivity devices   Devices used to create network connections, including hubs, switches, and routers.

contingency planning   Planning for disasters/emergencies before they happen.

control mode   The technique the controller employs to correct the difference between the measure PV and the designated SP.

controller   The controller is a hardware device or software program responsible for taking the input information, comparing that information to a predetermined condition or a reference, making decisions about what action should be taken, and finally sending corrective error signals to the final element, which adjusts the manipulated variable.

cookies   Small files that web servers send to web browsers when their pages are accessed. The purpose of sending cookies is to allow information to be retained between sessions of a web page or web-based application being accessed.

cracking   Utilizing software that would guess at passwords in loops until access is granted.

CRAM-MD5   A challenge response authentication mechanism that supports an email authentication system that transfers passwords in a hashed form.

credential harvesting   Any method used to collect users' authentication information.

cross-site scripting (XSS)   An attack method that allows the injection of client-side script into a web page that may be used by other, unsuspecting users.

crypt   The original encryption utility included with older versions of UNIX.

cryptography   The procedures, processes, and techniques used to convert data into secret code.

CryptoLocker   A ransomware trojan.

cryptology   The study of cryptography.

current loop   The amount of electrical current flowing between a zone's two connection points.

Cyber Kill Chain®   A process that was developed by Lockheed Martin to address attacks from threats through a series of steps that trace the stages of cybersecurity attacks: Reconnaissance, Weaponization, Delivery, Exploitation, Installation, Command and Control, and Actions on Objective.

cyber warfare   A virtual conflict that involves politically motivated attacks on an adversary's IT or ICS networks.

cybercriminals   Individuals who are typically motivated by greed and seek financial gain. This group of attackers is probably the most notable hacker type, as they tend to generate the most notice.

cybersecurity   The securing of the physical access to property, systems, and equipment ports while securing intangible assets including electronic, optical, and informational access to the system's data and controls.

cybersecurity policy   A company policy that explains the overall requirements needed to protect an organization's network data and computer systems.

cyberterrorists   Individuals who are typically not motivated by money, but rather by furtherance of a political agenda or ideology. The goal is to cause harm and chaos to the general public. Also known as hacktivists.

D

daemon   A standard, default user/group that has privilege to execute programs (background processes) that run without direction from the user.

data concentrators   Data collection devices that are used to group multiple smart meters together and aggregate their data transmissions for delivery to the utility servers in the central office. These devices are the core of data and energy management in AMI operations.

data diodes   A device that creates a one-way connection between networks or network segments that possess differing security level classifications.

Data Encryption Standard (DES)   A symmetric key algorithm used for the encryption of data.

Data Execution Prevention (DEP)   A sandboxing scheme that isolates a given program to a specific memory region to protect the rest of the system from potential attack.

data historian   A software component responsible for recoding and retrieving data obtained from the PLC.

data in motion   The process of data that is being transmitted through a wired or wireless network.

data in use   Data that is in the process of being created, updated, retrieved, or deleted.

deadband   A band of inactivity above and below the set point of IPC. Also known as a neutral zone or dead zone.

deauthentication flood attack   A cyberattack that involves an attacker sending a deauthentication packet to an access point, which in turn removes any previously authenticated devices connected to it.

decryption   The process of converting previously encrypted data back to its original form. The process of using the relevant key to unlock the scrambled cipher text into plain text so that it might be understood.

decryption key   The key used to decrypt a secret code.

dedicated control system   A stand-alone type of process control system that employs a single controller to monitor and control a single process or a set of closely integrated processes.

deep packet inspection (DPI)   The process of examining the actual data in a TCP/IP packet searching for signs of viruses, spam, and other defined threats to determine whether the packet should be forwarded.

defense in depth   A defense strategy that includes a number of different overlapping security mechanisms, which potentially minimizes the effects of a single mechanism being overcome by an attacker.

demarcation point   The point at which a publicly switched line ends and connects with the beginning of a customer's network.

demilitarized zone (DMZ)   The DMZ is a separate perimeter network that isolates the secure intranet from the outside world yet enables public access to outward-facing dedicated resources.

denial of service (DoS)   Attacks designed to overuse a host, server, or network resource to the point where it functionally ceases to provide its services.

derivative control   A control scheme that applies a rate control factor to the percentage of change in the difference measurement.

Dynamic Host Configuration Protocol (DHCP)   An automated addressing protocol that uses a range of IP addresses that can be dynamically leased to the requesting external devices for a preconfigured length of time.

DHCP server   A server that uses the network protocol to distribute network parameters such as IP addresses. See Dynamic Host Configuration Protocol.

DHCP snooping   A security technology built into an operating system to filter and block ingress (incoming) DHCP server messages that are deemed unacceptable.

dictionary attack   A systematic, brute-force attack using every word in a dictionary as a password for a given username.

digital certificates   Digital verifications that the sender of an encrypted message is who they claim to be.

digital video recorders (DVRs)   The preferred type of recording systems (rather than VCRs) for surveillance cameras. DVR technology for CCTV permits images to be transferred to disk, lessening the negative impact of poor quality video storage media.

direct-attached storage   A technique that employs additional disk drive storage devices that are attached directly to the DVR via USB or eSATA connections.

directory harvest attacks (DHAs)   A process whereby a spammer simply guesses email addresses at a domain and then connects to the email server of that domain. Any addresses that are not rejected are considered valid.

directory traversal   As it relates to an attack, directory traversal exploits software or web applications to access files that should not be accessible. This is done by traversing to a higher-level folder or directory.

disaster recovery plan (DRP)   The plan itself is the first and foremost factor in preparing for a successful disaster recovery. It should include a complete inventory of all the components that make up each network segment in the system, as well as all components that make up each server and workstation. This includes all associated software that will need to be restored.

discretionary access control (DAC)   Configurations where the user has the discretion to decide who has access to their objects and to what extent.

discretionary access control list (DACL)   A list of rights that an object or user has to a specific resource within a network.

disk-level encryption   A process that involves using technology to encrypt an entire disk structure. This technique offers value in that it protects everything on the disk from unauthorized access, including the operating system files and structure (while at rest or while in motion).

distorting proxy   A proxy server that hides or modifies your IP address and related information.

distributed control system (DCS)   An intelligent control system that processes many control loops using multiple autonomous controllers throughout the process without the coordination of a supervisory controller. However, DCS may operate in conjunction with remote monitoring and supervision systems. When processes become too complex for a single controller, or its components are geographically separated, it becomes necessary to distribute the control function over multiple controllers to form a DCS.

distributed denial-of-service (DDoS) attacks   A process that involves multiple remote systems being used simultaneously to perform a mass DoS attack on the targeted resource.

Distributed Network Protocol (DNP3)   A suite of industrial communication protocols that was developed to provide networking between central SCADA masters and different types of remotes (controllers such as IEDs, PLCs, and RTUs) in electrical grid systems.

Distributed Reflection and Amplification Denial of Service (DRDoS)   A cyberattack where the attacker uses a relatively small botnet in a distributed attack on reflection servers that redirect the queries they receive, making it appear as though the reflection server is the actual source.

diversion   A tactic intended to distract an individual from monitoring something. Typically, diversions are created so that an attacker can either view sensitive information without being seen or gain entry into a secure area without being questioned.

domain   A computer environment where all the members of the network share a common directory database and are organized into various levels. The domain is identified by a unique name and is administered as a single unit having common rules and procedures.

domain controller   A centralized server that controls the objects, rules, and procedures of a domain.

Domain Name System (DNS) servers   Servers that contain DNS databases (`*.dns` files) that are used to resolve computer names to IP addresses. These servers also contain mappings between fully qualified domain names (`www.marcraft.com`) and the IP addresses they represent.

double encapsulation VLAN hopping attack   A cyberattack that results in two headers being added (double tagged) to the original frame. One of the tags represents the target's VLAN ID, while the other is the VLAN ID of the attacker's switch. When the packet hits the attacker's switch, the first tag is stripped out, but the second tag remains with the packet. The packet is then forwarded to the target's switch, which reads the tag and forwards the packet to the target host.

dual-firewall DMZ   A network configuration where firewalls are positioned on each side of the DMZ to filter traffic moving between the intranet and the DMZ as well as between the DMZ and the Internet. These firewalls are used to route public traffic to the DMZ and internal network traffic to the intranet.

due care policy   A policy that requires all levels of management to take steps to ensure that specific security protection is provided throughout the organization. Such actions reduce the probability of damage to equipment or injury to personnel and visitors.

dumpster diving   The process of searching through an entity's garbage for helpful pieces of information. Information can be, but is not limited to, phone records, old calendars, organizational flow charts, and notebooks. This act is part of the reconnaissance phase of the CyberKill Chain.

dynamic ARP inspection (DAI)   A configuration feature that is designed to thwart MITM attacks. DAI uses the DHCP snooping database to check and validate ARP requests to prevent ARP spoofing attacks.

Dynamic Trunking Protocol (DTP) request   An attacker sends a request to a network switch that would configure the attacker's port as a trunk connection.

dynamic variable   A physical parameter that can change spontaneously from external influences or internal influences.

E

eavesdropping   The act of secretly listening to a private conversation without the consent of the parties involved, often for applicable information.

eCryptfs   A built-in package that the major Linux operating systems possess, which provides file system–level encryption services. This level of encryption enables the encryption service to be applied at the individual file or directory without significant disk management overhead.

egress   The action of leaving a place, whether physically or logically.

Encapsulating Security Payloads (ESP)   The ESP protocol offers integrity, confidentiality, and authentication as well as encryption within the IPSec protocol suite. ESP encrypts and encapsulates the entire TCP/UDP datagram within an ESP header that does not include any port information.

Encrypting File System (EFS)   The Microsoft Windows file- and folder-level encryption service.

encryption   Encrypting data involves taking the data (plaintext) and processing it with a key code (cipher) that defines how the original version of the data has been manipulated (ciphertext).

encryption key   The key or algorithm used to convert plaintext to ciphertext, and vice versa.

entropy   A measure of randomness, or a lack of predictability and order, leading to a degree of uncertainty.

entry delay   A delay that a security zone can be configured with that gives those entering the premises time to access an internal security panel to deactivate an alarm before it activates.

enumerate   Establishing a map of any network, or determining what devices and hosts can be found.

error signals   Corrective signals sent to a final element, which adjusts the manipulated variable.

ethical hacking   Any hacking technique that is used to test or evaluate a system and its resources, with the consent of the data and network owners, for the purposes of assessing any weaknesses. Because there is no commonly accepted ethic, ethical hacking actually resolves to legal hacking, where the owner of the asset being pentested has given legal (contractual) authority to the tester to conduct their prescribed tests.

ethics   Determining what actions are right or wrong in particular circumstances based on moral principles.

Ettercap   A free and open-source software tool used to perform a number of network and security analyses.

EV certificate   Extended Validation (EV) certificates require verification of an individual by a certificate authority. These are typically used on sites that are using SLL/TLS.

exclusion   A method, device, or system security professionals use to forbid, prohibit, or remove access to excluded assets.

eXecute Disable (XD) bit   A feature built into microprocessor hardware to protect certain areas of memory that contain specific blocks of instruction code, such as the kernel.

exFAT   Microsoft's extended File Allocation Table file system for flash memory devices.

exit delay   A time delay on the activation of a security system to give an individual time to leave the premises without triggering the alarm.

exploits   Software programs or tools designed to take advantage of particular vulnerabilities or flaws in a computer system.

export-grade encryption   An encryption method created to be good enough yet still allow the NSA to decrypt communication outside the United States. The NSA lifted this export requirement in the late 1990s, but those cipher suites have remained in both client and server libraries.

ext#   The ext# series of Extended File Systems are the primary files management systems designed for the Linux kernel. ext2 is also widely used in SD cards and other flash-based storage devices.

extranet   An intranet structure that grants limited access to authorized outside users, such as corporate business partners. In other words, a partially private, partially public network structure.

F

F2FS   Samsung's Flash-Friendly File System (version 2) is an open-source Linux file system for flash storage devices.

fail-safe   A method that responds to certain types of failures in a way that will cause minimum harm to personnel or devices. Also known as fail-secure.

fail-secure   A method that responds to certain types of failures in a way that will cause minimum harm to personnel or devices. Also known as fail-safe.

fail-soft   A mode that will terminate any nonessential processing when a hardware or software failure occurs.

Failure Mode and Effects Analysis (FMEA)   A qualitative analysis tool used to evaluate processes to identify where and how they might fail (failure modes) and assess the relative effects of different failures. The assessment can then be used to identify components of the process that are most likely to fail so the overall system can be innovated.

false negative   A report that produces an incorrect rejection of the individual, thereby locking them out of a facility or security area that they should have access to. In terms of logging or forensic analysis, a false negative result is one that incorrectly indicates that a particular condition or attribute is missing when it is not.

false positive   A report that incorrectly authenticates the individual, which could lead to providing access to equipment or data that this person should not have access to. In terms of logging or forensic analysis, a false positive result is one that incorrectly indicates that a particular condition or attribute is present when it is actually not. Of the two types of authentication failure, this is the most significant in that it could grant access to malicious people.

fault tree analysis (FTA)   An analytical system safety, and reliability, engineering tool used to determine how processes can fail, as well as how best to reduce the risks associated with those processes.

feedback   A pathway from the output of the process that feeds back to the controller, which then applies appropriate corrective action to the process input.

field bus network   Collectively this is what the process input and output lines of a PLC are called.

field devices   Industrial controllers that are designed to be deployed in close proximity to the process being controlled.

field of view   The extent a given surveillance camera can see. Also known as field of vision.

file- and folder-level encryption   Encryption applied to individual files and folders. File- and folder-level encryption tools enable users to encrypt files stored on their drives using keys only the designated user (or an authorized recovery agent) can decode. This prevents theft of data by those who do not have the password or a decoding tool. This technology is used to protect data when it is at rest (being stored).

FileVault   The disk level–based data encryption service included with the Apple OS X operating systems.

fire brigade   A man-in-the-middle attack hijacks a session by intercepting or sniffing and modifying communication between users.

firewall   A device that usually consists of some combination of hardware and software used to protect a private network from unauthorized access by way of an untrusted network, like the Internet.

firewall rules   The rules a firewall uses to determine what communication will be filtered.

firmware   Firmware is permanent software that has been programmed into read-only memory.

fisheye lens   An ultra-wide-angle lens that forgoes straight line perspective for the purpose of viewing a larger area. Images from a fisheye lens are often distorted near the edges.

fixed focal length lens   Lenses whose focal length is fixed and cannot be adjusted like common zoom lenses.

flat network   A type of network that is one network segment where all devices can communicate with each other without the use of connectivity devices (routers and switches).

fraggle attack   A denial-of-service attack, much like a smurf attack, where the attacker sends spoofed UDP packets to a broadcast address in a network.

G

gain   A multiplier function to the percentage of difference in proportional control systems.

gateway device   A gateway device is often a router, but could also be a switch, a modem, an access point, or even a Voice over Internet Protocol (VoIP) adapter.

GEOM-Based Disk Encryption (GBDE)   A block device–layer disk-level encryption system.

glass breakage detection   A sensor that detects breaking glass; they come in two types. The vibration type is mounted on the glass or on a nearby wall. Acoustical or sound discriminators sense the sound of breaking glass.

gray-box testing   A combination of white box and black box, a gray-box pentester may be given partial information about the network before testing begins.

gray-hat hacker   A computer hacker whose moral compass falls somewhere between altruistic and malicious in nature. The manner in which they operate is often without the appropriate permissions; however, they may offer the findings to the vendor affected.

grayware   Software applications that may not have malware assigned to them yet still contain undesirable functions.

H

hacker   An individual who uses their skills in computers to gain unauthorized access to data and resources.

hardening   The process of making any device (hardware and software) more secure. Often involves many steps and procedures, while taking into account acceptable usability.

hardware firewall device   A device specifically and solely designed to operate as a firewall.

hardware ports   An interface between various computer and networking devices.

hardware token   A physical device that can provide authentication. Also known as a security token.

hash table   A lookup table that maps keys to values using a hash function that converts the keys into hash values. Also known as a hash map.

Hazard and Operability (HAZOP) study   Research and analysis conducted to reveal any hazardous scenarios that exist in a given process.

Hierarchical File System   Proprietary Apple file system developed as the primary file system for their Macintosh line of computers using macOS. It is also used in Apple's line of iPod music devices.

historian   A database management system that stores historical data in the form of control points, referred to as tags.

home area network (HAN)   A specialized LAN made up of automated electrical device controllers, usually within or in close proximity to a home.

honey pot   A decoy server, network device, or network segment designed to attract attackers away from the real network. This is accomplished by providing attackers with relatively easy access to decoy systems on the network and hiding truly critical systems.

host-based authentication   A form of authentication that relies on information (such as MAC addresses and hostnames) to authenticate to a network, as opposed to the user's credentials.

Human Machine Interface (HMI)   An interface that enables human operators to observe the operating parameters of the different processes and take charge of the processes to change parameters or make corrections.

hypervisor   A virtual operating platform (similar to a virtual operating system) that hosts other guest operating systems.

I

Icinga   An open-source network monitoring application.

ICMP   The Internet Control Message Protocol is commonly used to test connectivity to a network from a device.

identity proofing   The process in which a particular individual is associated and verified with an existing identity.

identity theft   The act of obtaining, by subterfuge, a person's various pieces of identification, usually for financial gain.

IDS/IDPS   Intrusion detections systems or intrusion detection and prevention systems are systems designed to primarily monitor the system (local computer or network environment), log key events and policy violations, and report them as directed. IDPS is a system designed to monitor the technical environment (computers or networks), log key events and policy violations, report them, and prevent them as directed. Types include *anomaly-based IDS/IDPS*, which are intrusion detection systems that use anomaly analysis to detect and prevent unauthorized access to a network. A distributed IDS system is an IDS system where local hosts attached to a network have their own IDS modules installed. Additionally, there is an IDS management module installed on a network server that coordinates the flow of information to and from the individual local IDS modules. *Host-based IDS (HBIDS)* is an intrusion detection system that is installed on and protects a single system. *Signature-based IDS/IDPS* is a system that works by looking for specific patterns in content, known as signatures. If a known bad pattern is detected, then appropriate actions are taken to protect the host.

IEC/ISA 62443   A group of International Society for Automation standards that define procedures for implementing security in an industrial automation and control systems setting. The standard exists in the form of four categories that relate to general security concept metrics, system owner policies and procedures, security system design (using a zone and conduit method to implement security), and system security products or components.

impact assessment and analysis   A business function that determines which individual threats pose a danger to the organization so that appropriate proactive measures can be implemented.

in-band   A virtualization scheme that positions the appliance in a direct path between the storage servers and the disk farm. This configuration eliminates the need to install appliance-related software on each server, as required by an out-of-band configuration.

incident response policy (IRP)   An organizational policy designed to provide guidelines for who does what, when, and where in cases of a physical disaster, network disaster, or security attack.

industrial process controllers (IPCs)   Control devices that produce output conditions based on the current states of their inputs according to their internal configuration or programming. These devices may be stand-alone or networked together, they may also be analog or digital in nature. Examples include PLCs, RTUs, IEDs, analog controllers, etc.

industrial/utility risk assessments   Risk assessments for industrial and utility processes that include a number of risk analysis tools that are different from those for use in enterprise networks. In particular, a risk assessment for an OT environment must include a process hazard analysis or PHA.

infrastructure security   The physical security initiatives applied to providing security for the basic physical and organizational structures needed for the operation of an enterprise, organization, or society.

ingress   The right of an individual to enter a property.

inner perimeter   A perimeter that typically involves physical barriers such as walls, doors, and windows—either exterior or interior depending on the context of the outer perimeter.

input device   A device that is used to introduce information into electronic devices.

input transducers   Devices that gather information about a given system that needs to be controlled.

input/output (I/O) controller   A device or system that connects inputs and outputs to a central control device, such as a microprocessor or CPU. The part of a smart meter responsible for providing physical connectivity compatibility between the meter's other system components and the outside world.

insider threat   A type of threat that exists inside the network, sometimes as an employee.

intangible property security   The process of securing property that is not physical in nature, such as electronic data, patents, and trademarks.

integral control   A control strategy that applies calculus-based algorithms to the measured variable/set point difference to reset the proportional action of the controller.

intelligent electronic device (IED)   A device that provides a direct interface for monitoring and controlling the different sensors and actuators in the process and can communicate directly with the supervisory controller, a local RTU, or other IEDs.

intelligent sensors   Sensors that package the sensing device with an A/D circuit and an embedded microprocessor so that they can communicate directly with the controller, a master controller, or other types of control systems.

Inter-Control Center Communications Protocol (ICCP)   A protocol used by utilities throughout the world for real-time data communication between SCADA master servers, between utility control centers, and between utilities across wide area networks.

interior security   The innermost level of infrastructure security; involves monitoring the area inside the inner perimeter.

Internet Assigned Numbers Authority (IANA)   The organization that oversees the allocation of IP addresses and root zone management of DNS.

Internet Engineering Task Force (IETF)   The main standards body of Internet protocols operates as a large open international community of network designers, operators, vendors, and researchers concerned with the evolution of Internet architecture and the smooth operation of the Internet.

Internet gateways   Routers that are used to connect networks to always-on, broadband Internet connections.

Internet Key Exchange (IKE)   The protocol used to set up a security association in IPSec.

Internet of Things (IoT)   The network comprised of everyday physical objects that has network connectivity and can communicate with other objects to collect and exchange data.

Internet Protocol Security (IPSec)   An open standard commonly used in VPNs that actually employs a suite of protocols for encrypting and authenticating IP communications.

interoperability   The ability for devices made by one company to interface with the related devices of another company.

intranet   A local or restricted network within the realm of a single organization.

intruders   Unauthorized people who gain access to an asset that they do not have rights to access.

iOS   Apple's mobile operating system designed to support Apple's line of iPhones and iPads. While iOS shares many structures with macOS, it is not compatible with macOS applications.

IP address spoofing   The process of using a forged source IP address to create IP packets for the purpose of concealing an identity.

IP blocking   A form of security that blocks a specific IP, or range of IPs, from establishing a connection.

IP cameras   Digital Internet Protocol (IP) devices that have IP addresses that can be connected directly to a network or to the Internet, rather than directly to a host controller or computer.

IP header manipulation   A technique used to change the information contained in the header portion of an IP or TCP network packet in order to conceal one's identity over a network.

IPSec   A protocol suite to establish secure communications. IPSec employs AH and ESP to authenticate and encrypt each IP packet.

IPv4   Internet addresses that exist in the numeric format of XXX.YYY.ZZZ.AAA. Each address consists of four 8-bit fields separated by dots (.).

IPv6   A newer IP addressing protocol developed to cope with the shortage of available IPv4 addresses. Under IPv6, the IP address has been extended to 128 bits and has a hexadecimal format, separated by colons (:).

ISO 15408   The Common Criteria for Information Technology Security Evaluation international standard.

ISO 2700xx   A group of ISO information security management system standards designed to provide management the ability to keep assets secure.

isolation   Physical or logical segmentation used to isolate or separate parts of a network.

J

jamming   An intentionally transmitted stream of arbitrary noise on the same frequency that a device or network operates on.

JFFS2   The Android default Journal Flash File System (version 2). This FS version replaced the YAFFS2 (Yet Another Flash File System) as the default Android flash file system used in earlier kernel versions.

K

Kerberos   A network authentication protocol that involves a trusted third-party ticket-granting server (TGS) to authenticate client/server interaction.

kernel files   The fundamental logic files of the operating system responsible for interpreting commands obtained from software programs for the central processing unit.

keyfob   A wireless keychain device that can be used to lock, unlock, and alarm a device.

keypad   Input devices that are typically equipped with a set of numerical push buttons. Keypads are used to program, control, and operate various access controls and management devices.

keys   As it relates to cryptography, cryptographic keys are data strings used to encrypt or decrypt information. Encryption keys can be based on a secret string that is only known to the software that encrypts and decrypts the data or may be randomly generated. It could also be a combination of known and random factors.

KillerBee   Framework for exploiting ZigBee and other 802.15.4 networks. KillerBee offers sniffing, packet decoding and manipulation, as well as injection techniques.

L

ladder logic diagram   A type of electrical diagram commonly used to define switch and relay contacts of most control functions.

latency   The delay of an input system to the desired output.

layer 7 attacks   A type of DDoS attack that focuses on the application layer and generally targets specific areas of a website in hopes of exhausting resources.

Layer of Protection Analysis (LOPA)   LOPA is a rules-based PHA tool used to create risk assessments and reduction strategies for different industrial processing systems. This procedure takes information discovered through the HAZOP process and suggested screening values and then produces a set of safeguards to implement for risk reduction.

least privilege   A function where each user is granted only the level of access required to perform their job role

Lightweight Directory Access Protocol (LDAP)   An application protocol used for queries and modifying items in directory service providers. LDAP offers a single login system that can lead to access to many services.

local firewall   A software firewall that is installed, configured, and implemented on a network host.

locked condition monitoring   A feature that allows the security supervisor to confirm that a door is locked. In addition to monitoring the locked status of a door or gate, the condition monitoring system can provide details as to how long and during what time periods the door or gate has remained locked.

lockout policy settings   Policies that enable administrators to enact password policies that prevent attackers from repeatedly trying to access the system via brute-force attacks.

logic bombs   Computer code that, much like other malware, is attached to a legitimate program. The code sits idle until a specific logical event is concluded, after which a harmful effect may occur.

logjam attack   A security vulnerability that targets the Diffie-Hellman key exchange, convincing the connection to use DHE Export ciphers.

lux rating   A measure of the amount of light that falls on an object. One lux is approximately the amount of light falling on one square meter from one candle measured from one meter away.

M

MAC address   Media Access Control (MAC) addresses are unique identifiers for every device attached to a network. These addresses are typically assigned to the devices by their manufacturers and stored in their firmware.

MAC address filtering   A filtering technique that requires the manual entering of static MAC addresses into the content-addressable memory (CAM) table or requires specifying the maximum number of devices allowed on a port.

MAC address table   An onboard memory structure where managed switches collect MAC address information to keep track of the devices attached to them. As they interact with those devices, the switches record their MAC information in their MAC address tables.

MAC duplicating attacks   A cyberattack where the attacker updates their own MAC address with the target's MAC address. This causes the switch to forward traffic to both locations. Also known as a MAC cloning attack.

MAC flooding   A technique used to compromise the security of network switches. An attacker connected to a switch port floods the switch interface with a large number of fake MAC addresses, causing the switch to broadcast the frames.

MAC learning and discovery   The process by which connectivity devices interact with other devices connected to their physical ports and read message headers to acquire the sending and receiving devices' MAC addresses. This information is recorded in the CAM along with their port information.

MAC spoofing   A technique used to change the factory-assigned MAC address of a device on a network.

malicious proxy servers   Proxy servers that are used for various purposes including malware delivery, ad injection, and simple information gathering. While these proxy servers may not pass on your IP address, they will know your IP address and could use this information for other purposes.

malware   A term describing any number of intrusive software programs, designed to be malicious in nature.

man-in-the-middle (MITM) attacks   A cyberattack involving an attacker that creates links to two or more victims in order to intercept messages moving between them.

managed switches   Devices that have programmable management functions built into them that enable administrators to configure them for a specific network environment.

mandatory access control (MAC)   A type of access control that utilizes the operating system to establish which users or groups may access files, folders, and other resources.

manipulated variable   The variable that an ICS is controlling such as temperature, pressure, level, etc.

man-machine interface (MMI)   The interactive portion of the interface providing human operators with onscreen tools to adjust or override control instructions.

masquerade attack   An attack that involves an attacker assuming the identity of another system.

MDK3   A penetration testing tool used to exploit common 802.11 protocol weaknesses.

meaningful use   Using certified EHR technology in ways that can be measured significantly in both quality and quantity.

mesh network   A decentralized topology where each node relays data for the network.

metadata   Information that describes or defines data. The term is used to describe all data that might be considered secondary to the purpose of the record. Typically, metadata is thought of as automatically generated, often embedded, data that is created by the information system to supplement or even validate the record.

Metasploit   A penetration testing framework used to identify and validate network vulnerabilities, including simulating attacks that prey on human vulnerabilities. It is one of the most popular open-source penetration testing frameworks available.

microcontroller   A small computer located on a single integrated circuit.

Modbus TCP/IP   The Modbus RTU protocol with a TCP interface.

Modbus   The de facto standard communication protocol for interconnecting intelligent industrial control devices. Modbus is a serial communication protocol that was developed specifically to provide networking capabilities for industrial control applications.

motion detectors   A device that detects moving objects, often integrated in an infrastructure security system.

multifactor authentication (MFA)   A method of access control that requires at least two of the following: knowledge, possession, and inherence.

MultiSpeak   A specification that is a key industry-wide standard for enterprise application interoperability.

N

Nagios   One of the most well-known network monitoring tools that helps to ensure systems, applications, and processes.

nation-state   A geographic area that contains a group of people who share the same history, language, or traditions living under one government.

National Institute of Standards and Technology (NIST)   The federal technology agency responsible for development of the Cyber Security Frameworks, Medical Device Security, and Guide to Industrial Control System (ICS) Security guides.

natural access control   A process using natural design elements, such as structures and landscaping, to guide people as they enter and exit spaces.

need-to-know policy   A process that limits the employee's knowledge of the entire network system. It is similar to a separation of duties policy.

neighborhood area network (NAN)   Often used for a smart meter network, NANs can provide network connectivity to a small WLAN group.

Network Address Translation (NAT)   The translation of an IP address used in one network to an IP address known within another network.

network analyzer   Tools used by penetration testers to listen to network traffic, looking for items such as passwords and usernames sent across the network in a plain-text mode, or sensitive information such as credit card or other financial information. Also referred to as a packet sniffer.

network-attached storage (NAS)   A virtualized storage system that provides both storage and a file system structure within a network.

network connectivity devices   Devices that have connectivity purposes, such as routers, hubs, switches, and bridges.

network firewall   A firewall that performs security on an entire network by granting or rejecting access to specific traffic flows between trusted and untrusted networks.

network hardening   All processes and techniques involved in securing a network.

network monitoring tools   Any tool that can be used to ensure that servers or other devices are up and running appropriately.

network packet   A unit of data that is routed on a network.

network segmentation   The process of separating or splitting a network into one or more subnetworks, resulting in each being its own network segment.

network topologies   Layer 1 physical (or logical) connection strategies that fall into four basic configurations: star, bus, ring, and mesh.

network virtualization   The process of creating a software-based administrative entity, utilizing hardware and software network resources, along with network functionality.

network vulnerability scanner   Used to scan a network for different types of common vulnerabilities, such as system misconfigurations and default password usage.

Nikto   An open-source web server scanner that can identify issues on a web server.

NIST 800-82 r2, "Guide to Industrial Control System (ICS) Security"   A document that provides guidelines for implementing cybersecurity for industrial control systems.

nmap   A popular security scanner tool that enumerates networks.

No eXecution (NX) bit   Technology used in CPUs to separate areas of memory into regions for distinct uses. For example, a section of memory can be set aside exclusively for storing processor instruction code, while another section can be marked only for storage of data.

NTFS permissions   New Technology File System Permissions are those that can set parameters for operations, which users can perform on a designated file or folder.

O

OAuth   An authentication protocol that allows applications to act on behalf of a user without sharing passwords.

On/Off control   A control scheme based solely on the relationship between the measured variable and the reference variable. The output condition can assume only two conditions—completely on or completely off. This type of control is provided by on/off devices such as relays and electrical switches.

open loop control   A process that does not observe feedback output to adjust the process it is controlling. As such, the controller has no mechanism for adjusting the input level to control the value of the process variable at the designated level in these systems.

Open Platform Communications (OPC)   A series of standards and specifications for industrial clients/servers, designed to facilitate the exchange of data between industrial control applications and intelligent control devices.

open systems interconnection (OSI) model   The primary networking model that defines and characterizes the communication functions in a network environment.

Open Vulnerability and Assessment Language (OVAL)   A security community standard for communicating security information such as configuration, vulnerabilities, patch levels, and more. OVAL is essentially a group of XML schemas that describe a language to provide the details needed to assess a network resource for security vulnerabilities.

open/close conditions   The state, or condition, of an alarm sensor indicated as open being off and closed being tripped.

OpenVAS   The Open Vulnerability Assessment System is an open-source framework of several services and tools that provide vulnerability scanning and management.

outer perimeter   The first line of defense in a given area or boundary, which can be physical or logical in nature.

out-of-band   The virtualization device is installed outside the actual data path between the network and the storage system. A communication method that occurs outside of a specific telecommunications band. A different way to send multichannel messaging or signaling.

overlay networks   A situation where a network is built on top of another physical or underlay network.

owner   The rightful possessor of an asset.

owning group   Linux permission term that refers to a group of users that collectively have access to data.

owning user   Linux permission term that refers to an individual who has control of and access to data.

P

packet analyzer   A computer program used to analyze network traffic. Also known as a packet sniffer.

packet filtering   The process of passing or blocking network packets based on their source/destination addresses, logical ports, or protocols.

packet filtering firewall   Firewalls configured with packet filtering rules to allow or deny client access based upon factors such as their source address, destination address, or port number.

packet sniffing attacks   A cyberattack in which attackers use packet sniffers to listen to network traffic looking for items, such as passwords and usernames, sent across the network in a plaintext mode, or sensitive information such as credit card or other financial information.

pairing process   The process of connecting two Bluetooth devices together.

panning   The process of traversing a camera left and right, tilting, inclining, or declining a camera up and down.

passive controls   Controls that are in place but are not adjusted based upon any action.

passive infrared (PIR) detector   A detector that uses a lens mechanism in the sensor housing to detect any change in infrared energy across the horizontal sectors covered by the sensor. This type of detector is insensitive to stationary objects but reacts to rapid changes that occur laterally across the field of view.

passive RFID tags   Tags that are powered by the electromagnetic energy transmitted from the RFID reader and allow for authentication.

passphrase   A sequence of works of text used to control access, much like a password, but generally longer in the number of characters.

password   A secret word or random string used as an authentication tool.

password attacks   Any password attempt that successfully authenticates through a password prompt without originally knowing the correct password.

Password Authentication Protocol (PAP)   An authentication protocol used with PPP that utilizes passwords.

password capturing   A technique used to view and save (capture) a password as it is transferred for authentication.

password cracking   The process of attempting to recover passwords from stored data or data in transit, for the purpose of later use.

password encryption   The process of taking a standard password and applying an algorithm to it in such a way as to make it meaningless to sniffers, crackers, or other eavesdroppers.

password management policy   Policies put into place to manage the passwords of users in a networked environment.

password manager   Software applications that store and organize a user's passwords.

password-authenticated key agreement (PAKE)   An interactive method for two or more entities to establish cryptographic keys based upon one entity's knowledge of a password.

patches   General improvements to a given operating system or application that has been released for distribution. Many patches and updates are purely cosmetic and convenient add-on features, while others are critical security upgrades designed to respond to a particular virus, discovered threat, or weakness.

PathPing   A utility, found on many Windows systems, that combines the `ping` and `traceroute` command-line tools.

penetration test   The process of testing a network with the goal of finding security weaknesses.

permissions   Defined privileges and authorization on specific data and assets.

persistent cookie   A cookie that will remain on the computer hard drive until the specified expiration date is reached. Also known as a permanent cookie.

personal area network (PAN)   A type of network that combines personal devices such as PDAs, cell phones, digital cameras, PCs, notebooks, and printers.

pharming   A type of malicious activity that redirects an unsuspecting user to a forged website in hopes obtaining personal information.

phishing   A social engineering technique that attempts to acquire sensitive information, usually login credentials or credit card data, by masquerading as a trustworthy organization.

These attacks generally involve emails that direct the user to a bogus website that looks legitimate.

photoelectric sensor   An optical control that detects a visible or invisible beam of light and responds to a change in the received light intensity. Photoelectric beam devices use this feature by aiming a narrow beam of light through an area of interest, such as a parking lot gate. When the light beam is interrupted, the photoelectric device sounds an alarm, or in the case of a garage door safety system, stops or reverses the automatic garage door's lifter motor.

physical intrusion detection system   Any system whose purpose is to detect and signal intrusions, including motion sensors, card readers, cameras, and alarms.

physical security   Any process or device that is concerned with protecting physical boundaries and property.

piconet   A small Bluetooth network composed of up to eight devices.

PII   Personally identifiable information (PII) is any information that has the ability to identify an individual. Examples of PII include first and last name, home address, Social Security number, date of birth, fingerprints, and other information that may distinguish one individual from another.

piggybacking   The act that occurs when a social engineer asks a target to "hold the door" for them and therefore can gain access to a restricted area without having to provide credentials to do so.

ping   A network utility used to evaluate the ability to reach another IP host. The ping utility will send Internet Control Message Protocol (ICMP) request packets to the target host and wait for a response, measuring the trip time and any packet loss.

ping flood attack   A simple DoS attack where an attacker overwhelms a victim with ICMP Echo Request (ping) packets.

pinhole lens   A lens that's a very small hole, possibly made by a pin, that forces the light into parallel lines to create a clear image.

point-of-sale (POS) terminals   Intelligent and networked terminals used for the time and place where a retail transaction takes place.

policies   The rules and procedures adopted by an individual or business.

port scan   The process of probing or scanning a server, client, or host for open ports.

port scanner   A software application that performs the probing of a network device for open ports.

port-based VLAN   A range of ports on an Ethernet switch that are defined as a network segment.

PoSeidon Portable Operating System Interface (POSIX)   A set of interoperability standards developed to standardize variations of UNIX and UNIX-like operating systems. POSIX-compliant systems (UNIX, Linux, and Apple macOS systems) support some type of ACL for managing traditional UNIX file access permissions.

power line carrier (PLC)   Communications that use the power wires as the transportation media between the host utility, its substations, and the smart meters.

Power over Ethernet (PoE)   This is the process of drawing power through the UTP network cable, rather than from a dedicated power supply. This is used for intelligent devices, like VoIP phones.

Presentation zone   The Presentation zone in a zoned security model is the zone that separates the Application zone from the outermost security layer (typically the Internet) and is where the organization's user network segments are housed. The Presentation zone is also used to house public interfaces, such as web servers delivering public information, as well as the organization's transfer security tools and structures.

Pretty Good Privacy (PGP)   A widely used UNIX encryption tool. This tool does both private and public key encryption/decryption and offers a very strong method to secure data.

pretexting   A form of social engineering that is the practice of presenting oneself as someone else in order to obtain private information.

promiscuous mode   A mode used to listen to traffic going through a medium. It is the opposite of nonpromiscuous mode.

Privacy Rule   A rule intended to limit the circumstances in which an individual's protected health information may be used or disclosed.

Private Encrypted File System (PEFS)   A stacked cryptographic file system for UNIX.

private key   In cryptography, is an encryption/decryption key known only to the specified recipient.

Private VLAN (PVLAN) attacks   A cyberattack that involves an attacker sending packets into a PVLAN that contain a destination IP address of a targeted computer and a MAC address of the PVLAN router. The switch sees the destination MAC address and forwards the packet to the router's switch port (a promiscuous port type that can communicate with any port). The router in turn directs the packet to the targeted host.

privilege escalation   The act of exploiting a vulnerability that enables an unauthenticated user to gain elevated administrative access.

privilege management   Through the privilege management policy, an administrator is provided with guidelines as to how the organization's privileges should be implemented. Access control privileges can be role-based (RBAC), discretionary (DAC), or mandatory (MAC).

procedures   An established way of performing an action, often used to enforce policies.

process hazard analysis (PHA)   Used to assess the potential hazards in a given industrial process. In the United States, PHA analyses are mandated by the Occupational Safety and Health Administration (OSHA) and are designed to assist potentially hazardous process operators with determining and ranking the operational risks of their process.

process variable (PV)   A dynamic variable that is controlled within a process.

profile-based anomaly detection systems   Systems that use mathematical algorithms to monitor normal data traffic and develop a profile of rules that describe what normal traffic for that system looks like. The profile developed reflects evaluations of users' past behaviors and is configured to signal when deviations from these behaviors reach a certain level (or threshold).

programmable logic controller (PLC)   Programmable logic controllers (PLCs) are intelligent digital computing devices that are designed specifically to perform industrial control functions such as opening and closing valves, switches, and relays to control processes.

programmable zones   A zone that can be programmed to encompass a single point of protection, such as a motion detector, or multiple points can be combined into a single zone.

promiscuous port   A port configured to be able to communicate with any other port, usually in a VLAN instance.

proportional control   A control scheme that provides a more refined control method where the output is analog in nature so that it can vary from a minimum value to a maximum value. The level of output provided by the controller is based on the proportional difference between the PV and the set point.

proportional plus integral (PI) controller   A control scheme that combines proportional and applies them to the difference between the setpoint value and the measured process variable value. Each control mode can be tuned to add just the desired level of each mode to the output.

proportional plus integral plus derivative (PID)   A controller that processes three different parameters that represent the present error, the accumulation of past errors, and a prediction of future errors.

protocols   A set of rules that governs how communications are conducted across a network. For devices to communicate with each other on the network, they must all use the same network protocols.

proxy filtering firewalls   Servers configured to filter out unwanted packets. During this filtering process, each packet is disassembled, evaluated, and reassembled, making this type of connection significantly slower than other firewall types.

proxy server   A server that acts as a barrier, as it allows clients to make indirect network connections that are routed through a proxy.

psychological social engineering   A process by which attackers use psychology and human weaknesses to craft many different attacks that trick people into believing what they want them to believe and giving up important information that they would not normally give up.

public key   A cryptographic key that can be obtained and used to allow to anyone to encrypt messages intended for a particular user.

public key certificates   Digital verifications that the sender of an encrypted message is who they claim to be.

public key encryption (PKE)   An encryption technique that employs two keys to ensure the security of the encrypted data—a public key and a private key. The public key (known to everyone) is used to encrypt the data, and the private or secret key (known only to the specified recipient) is used to decrypt it.

public key infrastructure (PKI)   An infrastructure that supports the distribution of public keys and certificates to enable trusted connections and secure data exchange based on the information from the CA.

public switched telephone network (PSTN)   A system that uses physical cabling to interconnect and transmit voice grade signals between a sender and a receiver. Also referred to as the Plain Old Telephone Server (POTS).

Q

quality of service (QoS)   Allows for the prioritization and differential treatment of network traffic based on special rules or policies. A common use for QoS is to ensure that a VoIP phone system will always have enough bandwidth for phone service, regardless of how busy the network is.

quid pro quo   A Latin phrase, which translates into "something for something."

R

race condition attack   A race condition exists when an attacker exploits the timing of consecutive events in a multiuser/multitasking environment to insert malicious code into the system between the events.

radio frequency identification (RFID)   RFID systems utilize self-powered RFID tags that can be used as beacons to track location or authenticate proximity.

rainbow tables   Pregenerated tables that contain millions of hashed passwords to compare for the purpose of cracking passwords on user accounts.

reconnaissance   A hacker's first step to familiarizing themselves with their target and beginning to find a potential way into the target's critical infrastructure, whether manually or digitally. A hacker will typically spend more time performing reconnaissance on their target and researching them than actually exploiting vulnerabilities.

red team   As it relates to penetration testing, this is an independent group that challenges or tests a network of a specified organization.

reflection servers   Used in DDoS attacks, forged echo requests are sent out and the echo replies are aimed toward the victim.

regress   As it relates to security, the term is used to describe the legal right to reenter a property.

relay   An electromechanical switching device used to control the operation of electrical circuits.

remote access control   A design feature that requires authentication of the identity of a user attempting to access a security zone or computer system from a distant location.

remote access monitoring   Systems that are used to notify supervisory security personnel when an event or incident has occurred.

remote access trojan (RAT)   A malware program that provides a backdoor to a system and can grant administrative control from a remote location.

Remote Authentication Dial In User Service (RADIUS)   A network protocol that provides centralized AAA protocol (authentication, authorization, and accounting).

remote monitoring   Monitoring or the measurement of devices from a remote location or control room.

remote notification systems   When an alarm condition exists, this set of systems will coordinate and inform the appropriate parties.

remote telemetry unit (RTU)   Small intelligent control units deployed at selective locations within a process, or set of processes, to gather data from different sensors and deliver commands to control relay outputs.

repeater   A network hardware device that extends the range and reach of a network.

replay attack   A network attack where a recorded transmission is replayed or delayed by an attacker to gain access.

rerouting attack   A network attack that attempts to redirect (reroute) traffic from its valid destination to a false one.

reverse proxy server   A server that handles public requests for web resources and then forwards them to one or more of the servers.

right   A legal privilege or permission granted to someone, or some group, by some recognized source of authority.

risk   The potential for the loss of an object of value. It can also be expressed as an intentional interaction with uncertainty. Risk can also be calculated as a quantity that can be communicated to the organization's internal and external stakeholders.

risk assessment   A systematic process that includes understanding both the likelihood and resulting impact of risk events occurring within the different areas of the organization's network.

risk mitigation   Taking the necessary steps to reduce the extent of exposure to a risk and/ or the likelihood of its occurrence.

risk tolerance level   The level of risk that an individual or business has deemed tolerable.

role-based access control (RBAC)   An access control method that uses job roles to differentiate permissions and privileges.

rootkits   A type of software designed to gain administrative control of a computer system while remaining undetected. Rootkits can occur in hardware or software by going after the BIOS, boot loader, OS kernel, and sometimes applications or libraries.

router flood attacks   Routers are vulnerable to flood attacks designed to consume all, or a significant part, of their resources, thereby rendering them nonfunctional.

routers   Network connectivity devices that, unlike switches, can forward information across different network segments. This gives routers the ability to join different networks together through a process known as routing.

routing   The process of selecting the best path for transmitting data over a network or between networks.

routing protocol   A set of rules used by routers to determine appropriate paths in which data should be transmitted.

routing table   A database used by routers to store and update routing information.

RS-232 asynchronous serial communication standard   A standard for serial communication transmission of data.

rule   In networking, to move packets through the device, a rule must be explicitly created on the device to forward (or map) the desired protocol port to a private IP address and port in the local area network.

rule-sets   Rules that are normally based on data source and destination information, data type, or data content. They are used to control what types of information can move between security zones.

rule-based access control (RBAC)   An access control model based on rules assigned to an account based on the role of the account holder within the organization. A rule is the basic element of a role. The rule defines what operations the role can perform. Also known as automated provisioning.

rule-based anomaly detection   A detection method that analyzes audit records to generate rules based on past usage patterns. The system then monitors the traffic looking for patterns that do not match the rules created.

S

safety instrumented system (SIS)   An industrial control system designed to monitor critical processes and control them in a way that safety is the main objective.

sanitize   Making data on an HDD unrecoverable, either by overwriting the data multiple times and/or by physically destroying the drive so that it cannot be reassembled.

satellite communications   Many companies employ very small aperture terminal (VSAT) satellite communications between their headquarters and their field sites to carry supervisory control data. These systems are self-contained and do not involve third-party technologies such as the public telephone system.

script   A list of commands able to be executed without user interaction.

script kiddies   Individuals who use previously made scripts or programs developed by others to attack a system.

Secure Remote Password (SRP)   A protocol that is an augmented form of PAKE, designed to work around existing patents.

Secure Shell (SSH)   An encrypted network protocol for secure client-server connections. Designed to replace insecure shell protocols such as Telnet, SSH employs public-key cryptographic authentication.

Secure Sockets Layer (SSL)   A protocol for managing both authentication and communication between clients and servers, using both a public key and a private key. SSL uses the sockets method to exchange data between client and server programs, usually as a website and a browser.

security   The science, technique, and art of establishing a system of exclusion and inclusion of individuals, systems, media, content, and objects.

security associations (SAs)   The establishment of shared attributes between two network devices to support a secure connection.

security baseline   A security control that defines the minimum security requirements necessary to protect the confidentiality, integrity, and availability (CIA) of the organization's information systems, along with the data processed, stored, and transmitted by those systems.

Security Content Automation Protocol (SCAP)   A method of using various open standards for evaluating vulnerabilities and measuring the potential impact of those vulnerabilities.

security patches   Updates issued for the specific purpose of correcting an observed weakness to prevent exploitation of a vulnerability.

security policy   Documentation stating how security should be implemented at each level. Businesses and organizations develop comprehensive security policies that define who is authorized to access different assets and what they are allowed to do with those assets when they do access them.

security topology   The defined arrangement of all hardware devices on a given network, with security requirements and needs taken into consideration.

security zones   A network segment created to provide specific levels of security for specific network assets (resources and data) based on their security vulnerability or criticality. The idea is to place more valuable or critical network assets into segments or security structures that offer more protection.

segregation   In a network, a physical or logical separation. Often used to separate individuals, data, and other assets.

sensor   These devices convert the value of a measured physical quantity such as temperature, fluid flow rate, or pressure into a corresponding signal (pressure, electrical, differential pressure, etc.) that can be understood by a control system.

service pack   Major operating system updates and/or collections of many individual Windows updates.

session cookie   A cookie stored in temporary memory that is erased when the web browser is closed.

session replay attack   An attack that involves the attacker stealing a user's session ID and then gaining access to do anything an authorized user would be able to do on a given website.

set point (sp)   The set point may be a fixed reference, such as a simple liquid-level sensor mounted on a post, or it can be an adjustable reference, like a common thermostat where the user can set a desired temperature to be maintained.

seven-level network security model   A layered, seven-level network security model from the SANS Institute that is linked to the seven-layer OSI model.

shoulder surfing   An attack where someone glances over an unsuspecting victim's shoulder, in hopes of watching and/or recording them input some private information.

side channel attack   An attack on virtual machines, where one virtual machine obtains private key information from another virtual machine running on that same physical server.

signature analysis   A process where incoming and outgoing traffic is compared with a database of stored specific code patterns (signatures) that have been identified as malicious threats.

single authentication   Authentication that requires the possession of only one form of verification. This represents the lowest level of security available.

single firewall DMZ   A network DMZ that has a lone firewall associated with it.

single loss expectancy (SLE)   Security events that are classified as one-time events. These events have a price assigned to them on a one-time basis.

smart card   A card device that often resembles magnetic stripe cards. They typically contain information about their owners, such as their passwords, personal identification numbers (PINs), network keys, digital certificates, and other PII that can be used in the authentication process.

smart meters   An intelligent electronic device that records utility consumption and can communicate the information for monitoring and billing.

smart phone applications   Applications that run specifically on mobile devices, such as tablets and phones.

smishing   Smishing, short for SMS phishing, is an attack that tricks users into visiting a website to download malware onto a smart phone or tablet via an SMS message.

smurf amplifiers   Infected network computing devices that are used to reflect ping requests from an attacker toward a designated target, thereby building an ICMP flood attack against the target.

smurf attack   A DDoS attack that floods a victim with ICMP reply packets. This attack builds on the ping flood attack by adding a reflective property. This reflective property is created by using more participants, known as smurf amplifiers, in the attack.

Snort   An open-source, cross-platform intrusion detection system that provides real-time traffic analysis, packet logging, and protocol analysis, as well as active detection for worms, port scans, and vulnerability exploit attempts.

social engineering   A nontechnical method using physical or psychological manipulation to exploit human interactions, in hopes of circumventing normal security.

socket   One endpoint of a two-way communication. A socket is bound to a port number.

soft targets   Devices that are vulnerable to disruption because they have few or no built-in security features and few options for adding security features. If they can be accessed directly or virtually, they can easily be manipulated.

Social Engineering Toolkit (SET)   A Linux software package used in penetration testing that can be used to perform advanced attacks against a target.

software as a service (SAAS)   Software licensed and delivered on a subscription basis. The software is hosted outside the business and is accessed in a network via a thin client.

software exploitation   Cyberattacks designed to take advantage of vulnerabilities or weaknesses in software products, operating systems, and applications.

software firewall   Firewalls that are installed on a host computer, much like any other application.

software-defined networking (SDN)   An approach to computer networking that analyzes the connection between any two nodes and can filter that connection based upon a defined policy.

SolarWinds   A software product that offers an incredibly powerful commercial network performance–monitoring product. It can monitor uptime, performance, traffic flow, and utilization and offer a plethora of reporting, graphing, and notification options.

spanning tree attack   If packets are circulated just between the layer 2 switches in this type of topology, their Time-To-Live (TTL) settings never get decremented, and they never die—instead continuing to loop through the redundant links. This creates a broadcast storm that floods the network with traffic.

Spanning Tree Protocol (STP)   A protocol that provides loop-free, redundant links for switches in multiple path networks. It accomplishes this by configuring switch ports so they forward or block traffic depending on the type of segment they are connected to.

spear phishing   An attack that targets a specific organization or individual within that organization to attempt to gain unauthorized access to confidential data.

spoof   Any form of forging a false identity, thereby gaining access to assets.

spoofing attack   Attacks that are based on changing a device's MAC or IP address to change its apparent identity.

spyware   A software program that monitors the system's operation and collects information such as usernames, passwords, credit card numbers, and other PII.

SQL injection   An attack to manipulate SQL input field boxes on web pages. Valid SQL commands are entered through the field boxes, which causes the SQL database to reveal information other than what the input was created for.

SSH tunneling   A process that creates a secure connection between a remote host and a local device or computer, through which unencrypted traffic can be transferred through an encrypted channel.

stateful packet filtering firewalls   Firewalls that collect network connection information and maintain dynamic state tables that are used for subsequent connections, enabling ports to be opened and closed when defined against packet filtering rules.

stateless packet filtering firewalls   Firewalls that act more as an ACL. They do not keep track of the state of a connection between two computers; however, they compare packets against filtering rules.

storage area network (SAN)   A network-based storage system that appears to the host machine as locally attached.

stream cipher   A symmetric key cipher that converts plaintext characters one at a time.

Stuxnet   A virus that targeted the programmable logic controllers that guided the operation of the Iranian nuclear program's centrifuges.

subnet   A segregated network that is ultimately part of a larger network.

super cookies   A security exploit that aims to gather information from or influence the program execution of a system by measuring or exploiting indirect effects of the system or its hardware. Third-party cookies that are harder to remove than other types of cookies. Many of these do not use the traditional cookie storage methodology, but rather use a local browser HTML5 database storage or even Adobe Flash data storage.

Supervisory Control and Data Acquisition (SCADA)   A type of distributed control system architecture that provides two distinct functions—data acquisition (input) and supervisory control functions (output). Used to monitor and provide high-level control of machines and processes.

supervisory control device   A device used to centrally manage a set of remote local control devices.

supervisory password   Used to establish a password that can be employed to access the CMOS setup utility.

switch port stealing   A technique used to alter the direction of switch traffic, causing a switch to send traffic intended for another recipient to an attacker.

switch-based virtualization   A network virtualization process implemented through managed switches used to connect the SAN devices together. These devices also sit between the user and storage networks but may employ different techniques to provide storage management functions.

switchers   Devices used with multiple camera surveillance systems. They allow several cameras to be used with a single monitor.

symmetric key   A cryptographic algorithm will use the same key to perform both encryption and decryption.

SYN flood   A form of denial-of-service attack, where an attacker takes advantage of the TCP handshake that uses SYN and ACK messages to establish a reliable connection between two hosts.

T

tagged packet   A packet that has a VLAN ID inserted into the packet header to identify which VLAN the packet belongs to.

tailgating   Similar to piggybacking, the social engineer's ultimate goal is to gain access to an unauthorized area of a company or organization. This method involves sneaking in behind an unsuspecting party, thus gaining access without their explicit knowledge.

tangible property security   Classically known as physical security, which consists of protecting physical boundaries and property.

teardrop attack   A type of DoS attack where fragmented packets are sent to a target system. Older operating systems had bugs in their TCP/IP reassembly mechanisms that caused the fragmented packets to overlap and crash the host.

telemetry   The automated, wireless transmission of measured data for the purpose of remote monitoring.

Telnet   An application client-server protocol that can establish a TCP connection between a computer (or device) to any remote Telnet server to allow for text-based communications.

territorial reinforcement   A physical security method that employs structures, systems, and devices to prevent unauthorized entry and creates a clear difference between what is public and private.

threat   The potential to perform actions, with the intent to inflict pain, injury, damage, or other hostile action.

threat agent   An individual, group, piece of software, or a hardware device that has the knowledge, power, and intent to establish an attack. Also referred to as a threat actor.

threat identification process   A preventive measure intended to document vulnerabilities that could produce risk factors that affect network data confidentiality, integrity, and availability.

threat vector   The method an attacker may employ to get to a desired target.

threshold-based anomaly detection systems   IDS systems designed to track the number of occurrences of specific events over time and then generate an intrusion warning if the number of events exceeds a predetermined number.

Top Secret   Usually, the highest level of a three-tiered security clearance.

topology   A physical and/or logical definition of a network connection structure.

tracking cookies   Nonmalicious text files placed on a host computer, designed to track a user's web browsing habits.

transparent proxy   A proxy server that communicates on behalf of a host machine, without modifying requests, as opposed to most proxy services. A transparent proxy is typically not something the user is even aware they are using.

Transport Layer Security (TLS)   A successor to the SSL protocol, TLS is a protocol used to ensure privacy by encrypting communications between applications.

trojans   Malware that appears to be legitimate applications so that users will be tricked into using them, and although they function and work properly, they have malicious code that initiates when the application is launched.

trunk   A communication link designated to handle and combine multiple traffic signals, often to other network devices, for the purpose of consolidating physical port usage.

Trusted Platform Module (TPM)   A built-in microchip on many computer motherboard designs that is used to store cryptographic information, such as the encryption key (also known as startup key).

Trusted VPNs   VPNs that do not use cryptographic tunneling, but rather trust the underlying network to handle security beyond authentication.

TrustedGrub   A Linux module that is capable of detecting and supporting TPM functionality in Linux systems. It is a downloadable extension of the Grub bootloader, which has been modified for this purpose.

tunneling   A process that allows remote users to securely connect to internal resources after establishing an Internet connection. This is accomplished by securing the data in motion using data transfer encryption.

two-factor authentication   A process that requires two differing factors to grant authorization, based on what you know, what you have, or what you are.

two-person control   A practice that requires that two users must review and approve each other's work in order to complete a project. Although this may not be practical for many tasks, it offers a high level of security for those tasks where it is implemented.

U

UDP flood attack   A DoS attack that is similar to a ping flood attack, that uses User Datagram Protocol packets.

unauthorized access   An individual gains access to a service, application, network, or device without owning proper credentials.

unidirectional security gateways   Used to create a one-way connection between networks, or network segments, that possess differing security classifications.

unified threat management (UTM) devices   Security appliances that feature gateway, antivirus, firewall, and intrusion prevention and detection services within a single product.

Universal Plug and Play (UPnP)   A zero-configuration network architecture that brings a certain amount of compatibility between different brands and types of network hardware. While primarily intended to help the unskilled home networker, UPnP is supported by some nonconsumer hardware manufacturers as well.

UNIX   The UNIX line of operating systems provide a modular, multitasking, multiuser OS environment originally developed to run on mainframe and mini-computers. Proprietary versions of the UNIX OS include several BSD (Berkley Software Distribution) variations, along with Apple's macOS and iOS operating systems and Google's Android OS.

UNIX file system   This is the first file structure designed for the original UNIX operating system and is still in use with UNIX and its derivatives. The structure of this file system standard presents a unified tree structure beginning at a main director known as the root (/).

unlocked condition monitoring   The condition monitoring system can record and signal each time a specific gate or door is unlocked (granting access), indicating and recording which type of access was granted.

untagged packet   A packet that does not have a VLAN ID inserted into the packet header.

update   A service pack, or patch, that improves the reliability, security, or attractiveness of an operating system. The most reliable source of operating system updates is the OS manufacturer. Some updates may make the OS more convenient, but may not necessarily be more secure.

V

varifocal lens   An optical assembly containing several movable elements, to permit changing of the effective focal length (EFL) of a surveillance camera. Unlike a zoom lens, a variable focal lens requires refocusing with each change. If it has a varifocal lens, it can focus at multiple millimeter settings based on the user's preference.

video surveillance systems   An important element of most commercial security systems. The system employs cameras for prevention and recovery.

virtual access control lists (VACLs)   Access lists that filter traffic entering the VLANs, as well as filter traffic moving between members of the VLANs.

virtual LAN (VLAN)   Software configured network that is segregated at the data link layer.

virtual private network (VPN)   Remote users can connect to a private network over a public network, such as the Internet, and then authenticate and perform tasks on the private network as if they were connected directly. It enables users to communicate with another device across a public network as if it were a private network, ensuring security.

viruses   Malware programs designed to replicate and spread within a local computer environment. This most often happens when users download programs from the Internet or open email attachments.

vishing (voice-phishing)   The use of phones to conduct a phishing attack.

VLAN hopping attacks   These attacks, also known as switch spoofing attacks, involve an attacker sending a dynamic trunking protocol (DTP) request to a switch to configure the attacker's port as a trunk connection. Once configured, this connection routes all traffic in the VLANs to the attacker.

VLAN Trunking Protocol attacks   These attacks target Cisco's layer-2 VLAN Trunking Protocol (VTP). This protocol provides automated ISL/802.1Q trunk configuration between switches across an entire network so they can share packets. The automated nature of VTP provides access to all of the network's VLAN by default. It can be used to add or remove a VLAN from the network. This makes switches with the trunk ports vulnerable to attack.

vulnerability   Any weakness that may allow an attacker access to network assets.

vulnerability assessment   The process of identifying and prioritizing known vulnerabilities in a network or system.

vulnerability emulators   Training simulators for penetration testing.

vulnerability scanners   Database-driven tools designed to search computers for known vulnerabilities that have been identified and added to the database. They are designed to assess computer systems, networks, and applications.

W

weaponization phase   A phase in which the information collected is applied to creating tools used to mount an attack.

web proxy   A computer or server that functions on behalf of a host, or network of hosts, that are accessing the Web.

web server   Servers employed by enterprises to host web pages that advertise their organization on the Internet. These are front-end servers that deal directly with the Internet.

whaling A form of personalized phishing that targets high-profile end users, such as corporate executives, politicians, or celebrities. Just like with any phishing attack, the goal of a whaling attack is to trick an individual into divulging personal or corporate information and data through spoofed emails and other social engineering tactics.

white box A penetration test with the goal of simulating a malicious insider threat that would have intimate knowledge of the client's critical network infrastructure and credentials to access it, rather than breaking its functionality.

white hat hackers Hackers that use their expertise in compromising and infiltrating computer networks and security systems for good, ethical, and, most importantly, legal purposes.

white team The group that oversees and has knowledge of the penetration test. Sometimes referred to as the blue team.

whitelisting The process of permitting only the users that match some criteria or authentication to have access.

whitelists Registries of users that are trusted to have specific privileges, services, or access to an asset.

WiGLE An online database that users use and contribute to, to track and log wireless network information.

WiMAX Worldwide Interoperability for Microwave Access; a broadband wireless access standard designed to provide Internet access across large geographic areas, such as cities, counties, and in some cases countries.

wireless access point (WAP) A network connectivity device that allows wireless clients to connect to a wired network.

wireless networks Any network that is connected not using a traditional cabling scheme. It connects computer nodes together using high-frequency radio waves. The IEEE organization oversees a group of wireless networking specifications under the IEEE-802.xx banner.

Wireshark An open-source and cross-platform network protocol analyzer. This is one of the most well-known protocol analyzers, and it supports nearly every protocol.

worms Malware programs that are circulated through a network connection. Worms search for vulnerabilities to exploit in an application, and once the worm has taken advantage of the vulnerability, it seeks to replicate to another computer on the network. Sometimes referred to as a network virus.

Z

zero-day attack An attack that exploits a zero-day vulnerability.

zero-day vulnerability A vulnerability unknown to the product vendor, and therefore no patch is available to mitigate the effects.

Z-Force   A packet interception and injection tool, used to compromise and exploit Z-Wave AES encryption.

Zigbee   A standard that is a wireless, mesh-networked PAN protocol that provides for a 10-meter communication range with data transfer rates at 250Kbps. The Zigbee standard has been embraced by the smart home automation and industrial controls communities, as well as several areas of the smart grid consortium.

ZigBee Alliance   An open, nonprofit association working to develop new ZigBee standards.

zombies   Infected computers that can be placed under the remote control of a malicious user. Zombies can be used to create denial-of-service attacks that flood targeted networks. Computers are often infected and become zombies by way of viruses, worms, and trojans.

zoning   The separation of the network into subnetworks, each of which becomes a segment. Also known as network segmentation.

Z-Wave   A wireless communication standard created to support communication between devices in the home automation market. It was designed for simple monitoring and control as well as interdevice wireless communication.

Appendix C

Standards and References

There are several international and domestic standards and guidelines available to help organizations create and maintain the cybersecurity portion of their corporate policies and procedures. One of the driving forces in the ongoing development of cybersecurity initiatives in the United States is the National Institute of Standards and Technology (NIST).

These frameworks were developed to assist governmental and business organizations in the design and development of systems and techniques to provide security for their critical infrastructure. These guidelines were key references in the development of this *Practical Industrial Cybersecurity* book.

The following list identifies a few of the most commonly used guidelines:

- *NIST SP 800-53, Security and Privacy Controls for Federal Information Systems and Organizations*—Published by the National Institute of Standards and Technology, this is a US security standard created to provide a catalog of security and privacy controls for federal information systems and organizations and a process of selecting controls to protect organizational operations, assets, and the nation from a diverse set of threats, including hostile cyberattacks, natural disasters, structural failures, and human errors. See `https://nvd.nist.gov/800-53`.

- *NIST Cybersecurity Framework (CSF)*—The CSF consists of standards, guidelines, and best practices to promote the protection of critical infrastructure. The prioritized, flexible, repeatable, and cost-effective approach of the framework will help owners and operators of critical infrastructure to manage cybersecurity-related risk while protecting business confidentiality, individual privacy, and civil liberties. See `www.nist.gov/cyberframework/framework`.

- *NIST SP 800-82r2, Guide to Industrial Control Systems (ICS) Security*—This guide was developed to provide guidance for securing industrial control systems (ICS), including SCADA systems, distributed control systems (DCS), and other PLC control system configurations. This standard provides an overview of ICS topologies, identifies typical threats to and vulnerabilities of these systems, and provides recommended security countermeasures to mitigate the associated risks. See `https://csrc.nist.gov/publications/detail/sp/800-82/rev-2/final`.

- *NIST SP 800-61-r2, Computer Security Incident Handling Guide*—A NIST Special Publication designed to guide organizations in the process of incident response using a four-phase lifecycle approach. See `https://csrc.nist.gov/publications/detail/sp/800-61/rev-2/final`.

- *NIST 800-115, Technical Guide to Information Security Testing and Assessment*— A NIST Special Publication designed to assist organizations in planning and conducting penetration tests, analyzing findings, and developing mitigation strategies. See `https://csrc.nist.gov/publications/detail/sp/800-115/final`.

- *NIST 800-137, Information Security Continuous Monitoring (ISCM) for Federal Information Systems and Organizations*—A NIST Special Publication designed to guide organizations in their efforts to conduct continuous security monitoring operations. See `https://csrc.nist.gov/publications/detail/sp/800-137/final`.

- *NIST 800–161, Supply Chain Risk Management Practices for Federal Information Systems and Organizations*—A NIST Special Publication designed to guide organizations in their efforts to identify, assess, and mitigate their IT/OT supply chain risks. See `https://csrc.nist.gov/publications/detail/sp/800-161/final`.

- *NERC CIP*—Produced by the North American Electric Reliability Corporation, the Critical Infrastructure Protection (CIP) plan is a group of 9 standards and 45 requirements designed to secure digital assets involved in the operation of bulk electrical generation and distribution systems. In particular, the CIP standards address the security of electronic perimeters, critical cyber assets and personnel, and training to implement and use the plan. See `www.nerc.com/pa/Stand/Pages/CIPStandards.aspx`.

- *Nureg 6847, Cybersecurity Self-Assessment Methods for U.S. Nuclear Power Plants*— This self-assessment method was developed to assist nuclear power plant personnel in assessing and managing cybersecurity risks. It is a structured approach for identifying and scrutinizing critical digital assets, systematically evaluating the vulnerabilities of these assets, assessing the consequences to the plant of a successful exploitation of a critical digital asset, estimating cybersecurity risks, and identifying cost-effective protective actions. See `www.cisa.gov/uscert/sites/default/files/c3vp/ framework_guidance/nuclear-framework-implementation-guide-2015-508 .pdf`.

ICS cybersecurity professionals have several governmental and industry-recognized standards and recommendations they can use to conduct systematic, disciplined, and repeatable security assessments. These basic standards include the following:

- *Committee on National Security Systems Instruction (CNSSI) 1253r5*—This document describes minimum standards for Security Categorization and Control Selection for National Security Systems. See `www.dcsa.mil/portals/91/documents/ctp/nao/ CNSSI_No1253.pdf`.

- *International Society of Automation, ISA/IEC-62443 (formerly ISA99) Security Assurance Levels*—This series of standards provides a flexible framework to address and mitigate current and future security vulnerabilities in industrial automation and control systems (IACSs). See `www.isa.org/intech-home/ 2018/september-october/departments/new-standard-specifies- security-capabilities-for-c`.

Along with the basic ICS cybersecurity standards, there are a number of industry-specific guidelines and standards to reference:

- *NRC Regulatory Guide 5.71, Cyber Security Programs for Nuclear Facilities*—These guidelines provide direction for cybersecurity programs for nuclear facilities. The guidelines are directed toward protecting digital computing and communications systems and networks from cyberattacks. See `www.nrc.gov/docs/ML0903/ML090340159.pdf`.

- *INGAA Control Systems Cyber Security Guidelines for the Natural Gas Pipeline Industry*—These documents are designed to protect computing systems and SCADA systems associated with gas pipeline systems from cyberattack. See `www.ingaa.org/Pipelines101/Security/26504.aspx`.

- *NISTIR 7628, Guidelines for Smart Grid Cyber Security*—This three-volume report provides guidelines for protecting smart grid devices from cyberattack. The guidelines are tailored to address particular combinations of characteristics, risks, and vulnerabilities associated with smart grid operations.

Reference Links

The following reference list provides links to sites that can provide additional information about ICS-related specifications and regulations:

- `www.nist.gov/publications/guide-industrial-control-systems-ics-security`
  This is the NIST Guide to Industrial Control Systems (ICS) Security.

- `www.nerc.com/comm`
  Check this site for reliability and security guidelines produced by the Operating, Planning, and Critical Infrastructure Protection Committees.

- `www.nrc.gov/docs/ML0037/ML003706139.pdf`
  This document provides recommendations for electromagnetic operating envelopes for safety-related I&C systems in nuclear power plants.

- `www.isa.org/standards-and-publications/isa-standards/isa-standards-committees/isa99`
  The International Society of Automation (ISA) is the developer of the ISA-95 (Purdue) and ISA-99 standards for cybersecurity in industrial automation and control systems.

- `www.nrc.gov/docs/ML0903/ML090340159.pdf`
  This document provides guidelines and recommendations for protecting computing devices, communication systems, and networks associated with nuclear facilities from cyberattacks.

- `https://nvd.nist.gov/vuln/detail/CVE-2017-13017`

  This link takes you to an entry on the NIST National Vulnerability Database where you can find analysis of different vulnerabilities that have been reported to the organization.

- `https://csrc.nist.gov/publications/detail/sp/800-123/final`

  This site contains a NIST guide to general server security. It provides organizations with an understanding of fundamental activities involved in securing and maintaining security for servers.

- `www.iad.gov/iad/library/ia-guidance/security-configuration/index.cfm`

  This NSA site provides configuration guidance for a wide variety of software packages following the best security practices.

- `www.cisa.gov/uscert/sites/default/files/documents/Guidelines%20for%20Application%20Whitelisting%20in%20Industrial%20Control%20Systems_S508C.pdf`

  This DHS site is an appendix to their "Seven Steps to Defend Industrial Control Systems" document. It features procedures for Application Whitelisting (AWL), a procedure that can be used to detect and prevent attempted execution of uploaded malware.

- `www.dhs.gov/sites/default/files/publications/Strategic_Principles_for_Securing_the_Internet_of_Things-2016-1115-FINAL_v2-dg11.pdf`

  This publication from the US Department of Homeland Security provides strategic Principles for Securing the Internet of Things (IoT).

- `www.isa.org/standards-and-publications/isa-standards/isa-standards-committees/isa95`

  ISA95, "Enterprise-Control System Integration," is the ISA-95 committee site that lists all the standards and supporting materials associated with the ISA-95 (Purdue) reference model.

The following list provides links to different sites associated with penetration testing standards and methods:

- The Open-Source Testing Methodology Manual (OSTMM—`www.isecom.org/research.html#content5-9d`)
- The Penetration Testing Execution Standard (PTES—`www.pentest-standard.org`)
- The NIST SP 800-115 (`http://csrc.nist.gov/publications/detail/sp/800-115/final`)
- The Information System Security Assessment Framework (ISSAF—`www.oissg.org/issaf`)
- The Open Web Application Security Project Testing Guide (OWASP—`owasp.org/www-project-web-security-testing-guide`)
- The Lockheed-Martin Cyber Kill Chain (`www.lockheedmartin.com/en-us/capabilities/cyber/cyber-kill-chain.html`)

Appendix D

Review and Exam Question Answers

The following are the answers to the questions presented in the reviews and exams for each chapter.

Chapter 1: Industrial Control Systems

Review Question Answers

1. To cause the PV to remain at some specific, predetermined value referred to as the set point (sp). The set point may be a fixed reference, such as a simple liquid level sensor mounted on a post, or it can be an adjustable reference like a common thermostat where the user can set a desired temperature to be maintained. For more information, see the section "Basic Process Control Systems."

2. Remote Telemetry Units (RTUs). For more information, see the section "Remote Telemetry Units."

3. Controller. For more information, see the section "Basic Process Control Systems."

4. Programmable logic controller or PLC. PLCs are intelligent digital computing devices that are designed specifically to perform industrial control functions. For more information, see the section "Programmable Logic Controllers."

5. Unlike IT computers, industrial process controllers are not designed to store data and process it later. Instead, they produce output conditions based on the current states of their inputs according to their internal configuration or programming. For more information, see the section "Industrial Process Controllers."

6. A distributed control system (DCS). When processes become too complex for a single controller, or its components are geographically separated, it becomes necessary to distribute the control function over multiple controllers to form a DCS. For more information, see the section "Distributed Control Systems."

7. A supervisory control and data acquisition (SCADA) system is a type of distributed control system that provides two distinct functions: data acquisition (input) and supervisory control functions (output). For more information, see the section "Supervisory Control and Data Acquisition Systems."

8. Telemetry. For more information, see the section "Remote Telemetry Units."

9. The SCADA software provides the supervisory role for all the PLCs operating in the process. It also provides the human machine interface (HMI) that enables human operators to observe the operating parameters of the different processes and take charge of the processes to change parameters or make corrections. For more information, see the section "Supervisory Control and Data Acquisition Systems."

10. Safety instrument systems (SIS). For more information, see the section "Safety Instrument Systems."

11. The ICS package and the SIS package. Safety instrument systems (SIS) are basically automated process control systems specifically designed to monitor and control conditions in and around the process that have been defined as unsafe or potentially unsafe. The SIS is typically created as an integral part of the overall ICS package (but not the same components). The SIS must be able to successfully perform its functions when the process control system fails. Together these two systems are referred to as the integrated control and safety system (ICSS). For more information, see the section "Safety Instrument Systems."

12. Emergency shutdown systems (EMS). For more information, see the section "Emergency Shutdown Systems."

13. The recorded vibration patterns generated can be compared to previous points in time to determine the rate of machine wear. Devices called accelerometers are attached to rotating machines to monitor these vibration patterns over time. The recorded patterns can be compared at preset intervals to determine the rate of machine wear. For more information, see the section "Vibration Monitoring."

14. Leak detectors. For more information, see the section "Industrial Leak Detection."

15. Assure the safe startup, operation, and shutdown of burners in a process control system. For more information, see the section "Burner Management Systems."

Exam Question Answers

1. **A, B, C.** Availability, timeliness, industrial interfacing. Process control is a time-sensitive operation that requires quick response times. IT systems generally do not have timeliness constraints. For this reason, frontline intelligent process controllers operate on real-time operating systems. Industrial controllers typically provide few if any user-friendly interface features, such as keyboards, pointing devices, or LCD displays. Instead, they provide industrial-style input and output ports for connecting sensors and actuators. For more information, see the section "Industrial Process Controllers."

2. **B, D.** Remote telemetry units, programmable logic controllers. For more information, see the section "Field Devices."

3. **A, B, E, F.** Power supply unit (PSU) modules, central processing unit (CPU) modules, output modules, communication modules. For more information, see the section "Programmable Logic Controllers."

4. **A.** Distributed control system (DCS). When processes become too complex for a single controller, or its components are geographically separated, it becomes necessary to distribute the control function over multiple controllers to form a DCS. For more information, see the section "Distributed Control Systems."

5. **D.** Physically the SCADA system is an industrial software application running on some type of computer platform. Part of that software application is a database management system that stores historical data that it can use to generate tracking and trending data for graphical display or auditing purposes. For more information, see the section "Supervisory Control and Data Acquisition Systems."

6. **C.** Fail secure. Fail secure is a device or system designed so that the process being controlled will assume its most secure condition in the event of a power or component failure. For more information, see the section "SIS Equipment."

7. **B.** In an ICS network, the PLCs, RTUs, and IEDs are connected to the various input sensors and output actuators through a field bus network. The field bus also connects to a separate human machine interface console to display the activities of the process and its various sensors. For more information, see the section "Field Buses."

8. **D.** A USD is a shutdown of an individual process or utility system to prevent equipment from operating in an unsafe manner (outside of process limits). At this level, the safety control system shuts down the local process where the safety condition has been detected. However, it will not affect the operation of other processes running in the plant. For more information, see the section "SIS Equipment."

9. **B.** Level 1. Levels 0, 1, and 2 apply to the ICS functions of the organization provided by the SCADA or DCS systems, while Level 4 maps in the business functions of the organization that track to the enterprise network's operation. Level 3 functions provide the information exchange interface between the ICS and enterprise networks. For more information, see the section "Purdue (ISA 95)."

10. **C.** Level 2 is where the standard prescribes DSC or SCADA systems to reside. For more information, see the section "Purdue (ISA 95)."

Chapter 2: ICS Architecture

Review Question Answers

1. Because asynchronous communication methods such as the RS-485 protocol are very efficient in transferring data in real time. For more information, see the section "Ethernet Connectivity."

2. There are basically three general types of communication media used to move data between networked devices. These media types include copper wire (twisted copper cabling and coaxial cabling), light waves (fiber-optic cabling and infrared light), and wireless radio frequency (RF) signals (Wi-Fi, WiMAX, Bluetooth, Zigbee, Z-Wave). For more information, see the section "Network Transmission Media."

3. High-speed and long-distance signaling capabilities. For more information, see the section "External Network Communications."

4. Digital control. Before intelligent controllers were introduced into process control, the relay was the most widely used electronic final element. They were also used to create very sophisticated digital control systems. It was common for multiple relays to be interconnected in different configurations to provide digital control of complicated processes. For more information, see the section "Relay Logic."

5. For modern PLCs, the programming software is located and runs on the engineer's station, which is typically some type of personal computer. When the program is needed, it can be transferred to the PLC via field bus link, to the network connection, or directly from the PC. For more information, see the section "Programming the PLC."

6. The most widely used industrial sensor in process control environments is the electromechanical switch. Electrical switches are devices used to enable or interrupt current flow within a circuit. For more information, see the section "Industrial Switches."

7. Process units are groups of operations within a production system that could be defined and separated from the other unit processes of the system. For more information, see the section "Process Units."

8. Modbus. For more information, see the section "Modbus."

9. The major consideration when using the Modbus TCP protocol is the different Modbus protocol variants. Because the different Modbus protocol variants are not interchangeable, Modbus TCP devices must be used with this format. For more information, see the section "Modbus TCP."

10. Because EtherNet/IP is built on the TCP/IP stack, it is relatively easy to integrate ICS devices with enterprise servers and the Internet. For more information, see the section "EtherNet/IP Protocol."

11. The Distributed Network Protocol (DNP3) is actually a suite of industrial communication protocols that was developed to provide networking between central SCADA masters and different types of remotes (controllers such as IEDs, PLCs, and RTUs) in electrical grid systems. For more information, see the section "DNP3."

12. The Open Platform Connectivity (OPC) protocol standard is a widely accepted industrial client-server specification designed to facilitate the exchange of data between industrial control applications and intelligent control devices. It was originally designed to bring Microsoft/Windows products into the industrial control world. For more information, see the section "OPC."

13. The Domain Name System (DNS) service works with the hierarchical DNS naming system that converts readable domain names into numerical IP addresses used to locate computing devices attached to the network. For more information, see the section "TCP/IP."

14. The Dynamic Host Configuration Protocol (DHCP) is used to automatically assign users IP addresses from a rotating pool of available addresses. For more information, see the section "TCP/IP."

15. There are several reasons organizations choose TCP/IP-Ethernet strategies for their ICS networks; many have designated their existing IT staff to implement and maintain both their IT and ICS networks. TCP/IP-Ethernet networking on the enterprise side has provided a wealth of inexpensive, off-the-shelf hardware and software tools. TCP/IP-Ethernet is widely known, so there is a larger pool of technicians and administrators who are already familiar with it; organizations want their IT and ICS networks to work together for improved productivity and profits. For more information, see the section "Ethernet Connectivity."

Exam Question Answers

1. **D.** When the Start button in the ladder diagram is activated, the warning light illuminates, motor 1 turns on, and motor 2 turns off. For more information, see the section "Relay Logic."

2. **B.** Normally closed. A switch that is designated as normally closed (NC) will have its contacts made when the switch activator is in its unactivated position and current can flow through the switch. When the actuator is moved into the active state, the contacts are moved away from each other, and the circuit is opened. No current will flow through the switch in this state. For more information, see the section "Passive/Active State Configuration."

3. **D.** Sinking inputs are used in connection schemes where the inputs of the PLC accept conventional current flow from a sensing device. For more information, see the section "Input Sinking and Sourcing Configurations."

4. **B.** Relay outputs. While the voltages and currents used with solid-state outputs is limited (typically =/< 24Vdc and 0.5Adc), the capabilities of relay outputs can be much higher (240Vac/Vdc) and can control much higher current loads. For more information, see the section "The Output Section."

5. **B, C, D.** There are three common methods of programming PLCs: using graphical software tools that create ladder diagrams (LDs), software tools that build function charts (FCs) that can be converted into PLC code, and programming tools that can be used to build strategies directly from the PLC's instruction set (IS). For more information, see the section "Programming the PLC."

6. **C.** The problem that ICS networks have with Ethernet technology is that data delivery times can vary and are not deterministic (predictable) due to the underlying design of the Ethernet standard. An Ethernet packet can be delayed for several basic reasons. For more information, see the section "Ethernet Connectivity."

7. **B.** Data historian server. For more information, see the section "PLC Implementations."

8. **C.** There is no ProfiNet RT option; it is actually Profinet CBA for IO applications. ProfiNet, also known as Process Field Net, is a real-time, Ethernet-based industrial networking protocol suite that incorporates three protocol levels to provide very high-speed data transfers required for efficient control of some industrial processes, a basic TCP/IP protocol component (ProfiNet CBA for production plants); a relatively quick real-time (RT) protocol (ProfiNet CBA for IO applications); and a very high-speed Isochronous Real Time (IRT) transfer protocol (ProfiNet IO). For more information, see the section "ProfiNet/ProfiBus."

9.   **D.** The heart of the PLC is its microprocessor. Like all other digital computing devices, it obtains instructions and data from its supporting memory areas and performs arithmetic and logic functions based on the program instructions it receives. 1. It scans the status of each input terminal in sequence, 2. Processes the input status according to its programming, and 3. Passes the results to specified output terminals. For more information, see the section "Field Device Architecture."

10. **A.** Modbus is a serial communication protocol that was developed specifically to provide networking capabilities for industrial control applications. Because it was designed specifically for these applications, Modbus was optimized to provide quick, low-overhead communications that do not include a great deal of data security features. For more information, see the section "Modbus."

Chapter 3: Secure ICS Architecture

Review Question Answers

1.   Network firewall. One of the first lines of defense for interboundary communications is the network firewall. For more information, see the section "Boundary Protection."

2.   Defense-in-depth strategy. For more information, see the section "Boundary Protection."

3.   Firewall rules. A good firewall will provide packet filtering using defined rules to reject or accept both incoming and outgoing packets. This can be more challenging to configure, but effective firewall rules are really critical to security on most networks. For more information, see the section "Firewalls."

4.   Network segmentation is also referred to as zoning, and the individual layers of the security plan are referred to as security zones. A security zone is a network segment created to provide specific levels of security for specific network assets (resources and data) based on their security vulnerability or criticality. The idea is to place more valuable or critical network assets into segments or security structures that offer more protection. For more information, see the section "Security Zoning Models."

5.   Network segregation. For more information, see the section "Network Segregation."

6.   Databases and file servers. In this model, zoning is reduced to a two-level arrangement featuring an Application zone and a Presentation zone. The Data and Application zones are combined into a single level in this model. As such, the databases and file servers share a similar security level. For more information, see the section "Security Zoning Models."

7.   Any device that sends an ARP broadcast looking for a valid network IP address (an address that is assigned to an active server or device) will receive a reply. If an attacker gains access to the network, they could see every asset in the network, including servers, users, and devices. With the right skill set and enough time, they can exploit all of these devices. If a worm, such

as the famous Stuxnet virus, penetrates the outer perimeter security, then there is nothing to stop it from spreading to the entire network. Also, there is very little protection from any malicious activities that originate within the network. For more information, see the section "Flat Network Topologies."

8. A gateway must be provided in the intermediary zone (or zones) to provide them with secure access. A prime example of this is when an organization has employees, such as sales personnel, who need to access interior levels of data from remote locations. In these situations, a gateway device such as a reverse proxy or terminal server is placed in the intermediate zone to provide access to these users, along with virus and malware scanning tools. For more information, see the section "Controlling Intersegment DATA Movement."

9. This ICS/IT model was developed for the International Society of Automation (ISA) by the Industry-Purdue University consortium and was designed as a reference for interfacing enterprise and ICS systems. It has become the international standard for interconnecting enterprise and ICS networks. For more information, see the section "ICS Reference Architecture."

10. Managed switches. Switches can also be used to create logically secured virtual local area networks (VLANs). A VLAN is a security topology that restricts visibility of network traffic by limiting the movement of network packets so that they only pass between designated ports. For more information, see the section "Network Switches."

11. The security benefit of using tunneling to transmit private data between security zones is that the connectivity devices that separate the zones are unaware that the communication is part of a private network. By encapsulating the private data and protocol information within a public transmission packet, the private data is hidden to the system. Anyone scanning the tunneled transmission across the network would not be aware of the message contents. For more information, see the section "Tunneling."

12. In very high security applications, network devices called unidirectional security gateways or data diodes are used to create a one-way connection between networks or network segments that possess differing security classifications. For more information, see the section "Security Zoning Models."

13. In the ICS/IT network environment, the DMZ is not positioned between the outer security level of the corporate network and the uncontrolled Internet. Instead, it is placed between the more secure ICS network and the less trusted enterprise network. Another DMZ should be created between the corporate network and the Internet. For more information, see the section "ICS Security Zoning."

14. The idea of using wireless sensors, controllers, and actuators to eliminate long cable runs between ICS devices in the process control network has been discussed and pursued for many years. For more information, see the section "Wireless Networking."

15. A Zigbee/Ethernet gateway. In communications and digital networking, a gateway is defined as a device that interfaces a network with another network that employs a different protocol. For more information, see the section "Wireless Gateway/Routers."

Exam Question Answers

1. **D.** A VLAN is a security topology that restricts visibility of network traffic by limiting the movement of network packets so that they pass only between designated ports. For more information, see the section "Network Switches."

2. **C.** Stateful packet filtering firewalls do keep track of the connection state between entities. For more information, see the section "Firewalls."

3. **A.** A multihomed DMZ. For more information, see the section "Using DMZs."

4. **C.** The zone depicted between Level 4 and Level 3 is where the DMZ is placed to separate the business planning and logistics portion of the network from the manufacturing operations and management portion. The DMZ places a firewall at each end of the zone programmed with different rule-sets to provide the desired security functions for each interface. For more information, see the section "ICS Reference Architecture."

5. **B, C.** The technologies typically used to create the partitions between the zones include devices such as switched VLANs, firewalls, or routers. For more information, see the section "Security Zoning Models."

6. **B.** A proxy is a barrier that prevents outsiders from entering a local area network and prevents insiders from directly connecting to outside resources. Instead, it allows clients to make indirect network connections that are routed through it. For more information, see the section "Proxies."

7. **B.** Access to the DMZ is controlled by one or more firewalls. For more information, see the section "Using DMZs."

8. **A, C, D.** Wireless network technology has some well-known challenges that make them less interesting as ICS components. These drawbacks include decreased security, robustness, delays, reliability, and safety. Even so, the push to overcome these challenges and produce wireless ICS technologies continues. For more information, see the section "Wireless Networking."

9. **A, C.** One of the major drawbacks of using wireless technologies in ICS networks is their vulnerability to electrical interference and the potential consequences if their data is interfered with. Another potential problem associated with wireless sensor networks is the need for local power supply or a battery. Adding local AC power connections in each sensor location can be quite costly. If battery power is required, the task of tracking and changing out the batteries can become a maintenance issue. For more information, see the section "Wireless Sensors."

10. **B.** The Zigbee (IEEE 802.15.4) standard is a wireless, mesh-networked PAN protocol that provides for a 10-meter communication range with data transfer rates at 250kbps. The Zigbee standard has been embraced by the smart home automation and industrial controls communities, as well as several areas of the smart grid consortium. For more information, see the section "Wireless Communication Protocols."

Chapter 4: ICS Modules and Element Hardening

Review Question Answers

1. You can think of protecting individual IT or ICS devices in terms of three layers of security:

    1. The outer perimeter is the space around the outside of the physical device and its housing.

    2. The inner perimeter should be viewed as the device's operating system and application programs.

    3. The interior of the device consists of the intangible data assets—the information created, obtained, and stored electronically in the device.

    For more information, see the section "User Workstation Hardening."

2. Autonomous or semi-autonomous ICS control devices, such as PLCs or stand-alone micro-controllers, can normally be placed in secure, lockable enclosures where access is limited to only those people possessing the key. For more information, see the section "User Workstation Hardening."

3. Just as joining the ICS network to the enterprise network opens new avenues for outsiders to exploit the previously more secure ICS, bringing BYOD devices into the network opens even more vulnerabilities. Network administrators and security personnel must determine whether such a BYOD environment creates security gaps for their networks. For more information, see the section "Mobile Device Protection."

4. While not trivial, these systems are vulnerable to being exploited by those who possess some specialized hardware and a few skills. By getting close to a user with an RFID badge, a hacker can read the target's badge information using their own reader. Once they have captured the badge data, they can make their own badge to circumvent access controls. This could occur while the user is in the cafeteria, at a local coffee shop, or even through a small IoT device hidden in the office or production facility. For more information, see the section "Near Field Communications."

5. The principle of least privilege access. This principle should be implemented when providing users with access to objects through rights and permissions assignments. Under the least privilege rule, each user is only granted the levels of access required to perform their job role. Applying this principle consistently limits the damage that can be inflicted by a security breech to the initial task, process, or user. For more information, see the section "Logical Server Access Control."

6. Isolation, segmentation, firewalling, and least privilege usage configuration: Virtual networks are by default isolated from each other. And, because communications within the virtual network never leave the virtual environment, there is no need for network segmentation to be configured and maintained with the physical network or firewall. For more information, see the section "Virtualization."

7. Applying software updates and patches. Security patches are updates issued for the specific purpose of correcting an observed weakness to prevent exploitation of the vulnerability. For more information, see the section "Applying Software Updates and Patches."

8. In almost every environment, organizational policy will call for all servers to have a real-time scanning antivirus application installed, along with a real-time antispyware program. In particular, these applications are required if the server is a file server or has nonadministrative users who have remote access capabilities. For more information, see the section "Implementation."

9. Antivirus and other anti-malware programs have traditionally been inappropriate for use with OT computing and control devices. These types of scanning applications are performance hogs when they are running. Due to the real-time computing requirements of ICS controllers, the presence of these types of security applications would introduce communication and computing delays that would be unacceptable and potentially dangerous to equipment and personnel. However, growing numbers of organizations are opting to run anti-malware applications in their OT environments, under strictly controlled implementation and management. For more information, see the section "Implementation."

10. Poorly written programming code for public-facing forms, such as login forms. For more information, see the section "SQL Injection."

11. As with servers in enterprise networks, the most important question concerning database security is, where should the database be located in the network? The most common method of securing the data historian is to place it in a secure network structure, such as a DMZ, between the enterprise and ICS networks. For more information, see the section "Database Hardening."

12. Public key encryption (PKE). This technique employs two keys to ensure the security of the encrypted data: a public key and a private key. For more information, see the section "File System Security."

13. The first is a list of rights that an object or user has to a specific resource within a network, referred to as a discretionary access control list (DACL). With this type of ACL, access control is a configurable service (using permissions) that determines what a user can access, change, or view. The other type of configurable network ACL is a list that resides on a firewall or router interface that allows or denies traffic to flow in or out of the network through specific interfaces or ports on the device. For more information, see the section "Configuring Switch ACLs."

14. Switch port security. This is a management feature built into network switches that permits individual physical ports to be configured so that traffic through that port can be limited to a specific MAC address or list of MAC addresses. For more information, see the section "Switch Port Security."

15. Any individual given remote access capabilities for the ICS should be required to authenticate both at the enterprise network level and at the network firewall controlling access to the ICS network. For more information, see the section "ICS/IT Network Security."

16. There are several potential difficulties with implementing updates in an active enterprise network. Before any changes are implemented, all critical folders and organizational resources should be backed up. To avoid potentially destructive or disruptive occurrences, product updates should always be tested on a nonproduction server before being implemented across the organization's network. You might also want to consider installing application updates during the network's least busy times—perhaps at night or over a weekend. For more information, see the section "Network Hardening Precautions."

Exam Question Answers

1. **B.** For both computing and intelligent control devices, there are three general locations where attackers can gain access to these items. First, while they're in memory, second while they're in storage devices such as hard drives and flash drives, and third, when they're being transferred from one place to another. For more information, see the section "User Workstation Hardening."

2. **A, B, D.** A. These options include setting user passwords to control access to the system and supervisory passwords to control access to the CMOS setup utility. B. By disabling these ports, users and administrators can help to ensure that unauthorized users cannot use the ports to gain unauthorized access to the system, transfer information out of the system, or download malware programs into the system. D. Most BIOS provide boot device enabling, disabling, and sequencing functions that should be used to control the circumstances of how the computer can be booted up for operation. For more information, see the sections "BIOS Security Subsystems"; "BIOS Port Enabling Functions"; and BIOS Boot Device Sequence Controls."

3. **B.** All mobile users should exercise caution when using their mobile devices in the workplace. Bluetooth autodiscovery should be turned off unless you are pairing with a device and need this capability. Look for other security options on your Bluetooth devices as well. Avoid the use of public hotspots. If you do use public hotspots, be aware of the potential mischief, use TLS/SSL connections, and only enter credentials into secured systems. Turn off automatic connection (re-connection) to Wi-Fi access points. Cellular networks are less likely to be compromised, so use cellular when high security is needed. All wireless technologies are more secure if encryption is implemented from end to end. For more information, see the section "Securing Mobile Devices."

4. **A, B, D.** These steps include implementing local login requirements, implementing additional authentication options, using local administrative tools, and providing remote access protection (establishing firewall settings). For more information, see the section "Common Operating System Security Tools."

5. **A, B.** Creating virtual networks within a host provides several security features. One is *isolation*. Unless the host is configured for interconnection between its external physical network and its internal virtual network, virtual networks are by default isolated from the physical network. Communications within the virtual network never leave the virtual environment. Another is *segmentation*. Unless the host is configured otherwise, communications within the virtual network don't leave the virtual environment, so there is no need for network segmentation to be configured and maintained with the physical network or firewall. There is also *firewalling*. Installing a host-based firewall on a VM configured to be the head of the virtual network provides protection between the virtual network and the host's physical

network connection, *least privilege usage configuration.* For more information, see the section "Virtualization."

6.   **C, D.** This makes antivirus and other anti-malware programs inappropriate for use with ICS computing and control devices. These types of scanning applications are performance hogs when they are running. Due to the real-time computing requirements of ICS controllers, the presence of these types of security applications would introduce communication and computing delays that would be unacceptable and potentially dangerous to equipment and personnel. For more information, see the section "Implementation."

7.   **A.** Under mandatory access control (MAC), the system establishes which users or groups may access files, folders, and other resources. For more information, see the section "Logical Server Access Control."

8.   **C, D.** Any services or protocols that are needed must be enabled by the network administrator during or after the install. Therefore, the administrator must be able to answer several questions correctly to properly install the operating systems and provide the needed services and security levels:

   1.   What protocols and services are currently in use on the network?

   2.   What protocols and services are really needed on the network?

   3.   What are the dependencies or links established between clients and servers due to these protocols or services?

   Consider each network protocol. If a connecting protocol is identified, evaluate its source and destination addresses to ensure that a critical protocol that is required within the network is not disabled. For more information, see the section "Configuring Services and Protocols."

9.   **B, C, D.** Because switch interfaces are commonly configured using Telnet or HTTP, they should also be placed behind a firewall for protection. In addition, passwords should be required, and SSH, or a directly connected console, should be employed when configuring these interfaces. For more information, see the section "Hardening Network Connectivity Device."

10.   **A.** Protect. If protect mode response is configured, the port will continue to forward traffic from known MAC addresses but drops traffic from addresses not known before the violation occurred. However, no security notifications are produced. For more information, see the section "Switch Port Security."

Chapter 5: Cybersecurity Essentials for ICS

Review Question Answers

1.   **Accounting** creates a tracking list of events using logs or other tracking tools. For more information, see the section "Confidentiality, Integrity, and Availability."

2. **Authorization** is applying approval of access to designated information after the individual is authenticated. For more information, see the section "Confidentiality, Integrity, and Availability."

3. **Authentication** involves making sure that an individual is who they say they are. For more information, see the section "Confidentiality, Integrity, and Availability."

4. **Confidentiality** refers to the assurance that data remains secret or private. It is established through sets of rules designed to limit data access to authorized people. For more information, see the section "Confidentiality, Integrity, and Availability."

5. **Integrity** refers to the assurance that data is accurate and can be trusted. For more information, see the section "Confidentiality, Integrity, and Availability."

6. **Availability** refers to the assurance that data can reliably be accessed in a timely manner. For more information, see the section "Confidentiality, Integrity, and Availability."

7. Spoofing. The dictionary defines spoofing as "to deceive or hoax." In cybersecurity, spoofing is used to make a device look like another device and can be achieved in many different ways. For more information, see the section "Spoofing."

8. It creates conditions that result in the inability to use a targeted system. For more information, see the section "DoS vs. DDoS Attacks."

9. While the main security tenet of an enterprise network involves providing CIA for data, in an industrial or utility network the main emphasis should shift to consider each CIA impact for each asset or system in the network. Basically, the security tenet changes to AIC (availability first and then integrity and confidentiality if possible) to keep the operation running. For more information, see the section "Availability in ICS Networks."

10. Reconnaissance. Reconnaissance is a hacker's first step in familiarizing themselves with their target and beginning to find a potential way into the target's critical infrastructure, whether manually or digitally. A hacker will typically spend more time performing reconnaissance on their target and researching them than actually exploiting vulnerabilities. For more information, see the section "Reconnaissance."

11. Encryption. Encryption is nothing more than the conversion of electronic data into a form called ciphertext. This involves applying a secret code (cipher) to the data to produce a scrambled message that cannot be understood without the knowledge of the cipher that was used to create it. For more information, see the section "Encryption."

12. Physical and psychological activities. For more information, see the section "Social Engineering Exploits."

13. Hashing. Hashing is used to provide several security-related functions, including integrity verification for transmitted files or messages, password verification, file identification, proof of work, and eSignature security. For more information, see the section "Hashing."

14. Brute-force attacks, rainbow tables, and password capturing. A brute-force attack runs lists of passwords against a user's login. Rainbow tables are pre-generated tables that contain millions of passwords that have already been hashed. Because most host systems contain a

password file of hashed passwords, they can be compared to the hashed contents supplied by the rainbow table with the hopes of finding a matching password. Password capturing, or credential harvesting, is where an attacker intercepts the password as it's being sent. One common way this can be accomplished is through a man-in-the-middle attack. For more information, see the section "Password Attacks."

15. Key management. Key Management System (KMS) applications provide integrated management functions for creating, storing, and distributing keys for computing devices and applications. For more information, see the section "Key Management."

Exam Question Answers

1. **C.** Least privilege principle. The principles of least privilege and need-to-know are used by administrators to establish access control levels to different assets. The principle refers to giving each user the least amount of access possible to accomplish their job roles and only to the areas of the network they must have. For more information, see the section "Principle of Least Privilege."

2. **D.** Nonrepudiation. Generally, in cybersecurity environments this term is used to refer to a service that proves the integrity and origin (authorship) of data. In other words, authentication that proves an object (such as a document or graphic) is genuine and that it comes from the person who says they sent it. For more information, see the section "Nonrepudiation."

3. **B.** Insider threats. Studies have shown that insider threats represent the greatest threat to most networked organizations. Some survey results indicate that insider threats can account for more than 20 percent of malicious network activity. For more information, see the section "Insider Threats."

4. **C.** A single server is being attacked. Distributed denial-of-service (DDoS) attacks involve multiple remote systems being used to simultaneously amass the attack on the targeted resource. For more information, see the section "Denial of Service."

5. **B.** Cyber incidents are occurrences that create adverse effects within the network or computing environment that will require actions to mitigate. The term can also be applied to occurrences that violate organizational security policies, procedures, or acceptable use practices. For more information, see the section "Events, Incidents, and Attacks."

6. **A.** The TCP/IP buffer space used during a handshake exchange. A SYN flood attack is a form of denial-of-service attack where an attacker takes advantage of the TCP handshake that uses SYN and ACK messages to establish a reliable connection between two hosts. For more information, see the section "SYN Flooding."

7. **B.** Encryption is nothing more than the conversion of electronic data into a form called ciphertext. This involves applying a secret code (cipher) to the data to produce a scrambled message that cannot be understood without the knowledge of the cipher that was used to create it. It won't matter how secure the password is if a third party can easily capture it electronically. For more information, see the section "Encryption."

8. **C. Social engineering.** Social engineering essentially exploits human interactions to circumvent normal security. As traditional security improves and network exploits are increasingly difficult to implement, hackers are turning to physical and psychological human manipulation to achieve their goals. For more information, see the section "Social Engineering Exploits."

9. **B.** A sender's private key is used to create a unique digital signature. Note that this is not true for PKI implementations, where the creator of the message uses the receiver's public key to encrypt a message. For more information, see the section "Cryptographics."

10. **D.** A man-in-the-middle attack. If you see what appears to be the website you intend to log into and enter your credentials, a fake website typically redirects them to the real login page. Normally, the user believes they must have entered their credentials incorrectly and eventually logs into the real site. The person in the middle of the attempted login has just obtained your credentials. For more information, see the section "Man-in-the-Middle Attacks."

Chapter 6: Physical Security

Review Question Answers

1. Physical security. In practice this involves policies, practices, and steps aimed at combating theft, preventing physical damage, maintaining system integrity and services, and limiting unauthorized disclosure of information. For more information, see the section "Introduction."

2. False acceptance or false positive failures. For more information, see the section "Biometric Scanners."

3. The amount of light required to obtain a reasonable video camera image is called the lux rating. Lux is a measure of the amount of light that falls on an object. One lux is approximately the amount of light falling on one square meter from one candle measured from one meter away. Typical camera ratings range between 0.5 and 1.0 lux. For more information, see the section "Camera Specifications."

4. Natural access control. Natural access control involves using natural design elements, such as structures and landscaping, to guide people as they enter and exit spaces. For more information, see the section "Infrastructure Security."

5. Keypads. Most intrusion detection and reporting systems employ a keypad device for programming, controlling, and operating various access control and management devices. For more information, see the section "Intrusion Detection and Reporting Systems."

6. An infrared (IR) camera. An infrared security camera has infrared LED lighting (light from a different region of the electromagnetic spectrum than we are normally used to seeing) installed around the outside of the camera lens. This lighting allows the camera to capture a good image in no light at all. With a little bit of light (called low light) the infrared camera

can capture a picture that looks just like daytime. For more information, see the section "Camera Deployment Strategies."

7. CCD. The best surveillance cameras employ charged coupled device (CCD) technology. They have high resolution, low operating light requirements, less temperature dependence, and high reliability. For more information, see the section "Cameras."

8. Remote access monitoring systems are used to notify supervisory security personnel when an unauthorized access is attempted. For more information, see the section "Remote Access Monitoring and Automated Access Control Systems."

9. Telephone lines or cellular communication systems. The most common remote notification systems involve the use of a telephone line by the intrusion detection and reporting system's control panel to automatically call a remote monitoring facility or key personnel when an alarm condition exists. However, there are a growing number of systems that possess built-in cellular communications systems. Such systems provide additional dependability in that they can function even if the physical telephone lines are damaged. For more information, see the section "Remote Alarm Messaging."

10. Territorial reinforcement. Territorial reinforcement employs structures, systems, and devices to prevent unauthorized entry and create a clear difference between what is public and private. For more information, see the section "Infrastructure Security."

11. Unlocked condition monitoring. For more information, see the section "Access Control Systems."

12. Doors and windows. Perimeter area inputs to the control panel typically include sensors at every perimeter opening including doors, windows, garage doors and windows, and doors to crawl spaces. Additional perimeter protection may include using sound, vibration, and motion detector sensors to guard against entry through broken windows. For more information, see the section "Intrusion Detection and Reporting Systems."

13. Logically group related sensors together to create a security zone. This is accomplished by connecting all of the related sensor switches (all sensors appear as switches to the security controller) together in a serial format that connects to a specific set of contacts on the controller's panel. For more information, see the section "Physical Security Zones."

14. There are multiple factors involved in authentication. *Knowledge* is something that only the designated person should know (something you know). *Possession* is something that only the designated person should have (something you have). *Inherence* is something that only the designated person is (something you are). *Location* is somewhere that only the designated person is (somewhere you are). For more information, see the section "Authentication Systems."

15. Two of the most important considerations when recording video for security purposes is, how much video needs to be stored, and for how long? The answers to these questions enable the organization to determine its storage capacity needs. For more information, see the section "Camera Deployment Strategies."

Exam Question Answers

1. C. The outer perimeter. For more information, see the section "Infrastructure Security."

2. D. Corporate cybersecurity policies. For more information, see the section "Infrastructure Security."

3. A, B. A locked door and a receptionist. For more information, see the section "Physical Security Controls."

4. B. A digital IP camera. For more information, see the section "IP Cameras."

5. A, C. False rejection and false negative failures. For more information, see the section "Biometric Scanners."

6. D. Authentication. For more information, see the section "Authentication Systems."

7. A. Fish-eye lens. For more information, see the section "Lens Types."

8. B. Amount of light required for an acceptable image. For more information, see the section "Camera Specifications."

9. B, C. Network-attached storage (NAS) and storage area network (SAN). *Networked Storage* is using networking techniques to store IP-based video on remote computers or video servers. For more information, see the section "Camera Deployment Strategies."

10. A. NERC CIP. For more information, see the section "NERC CIP 006-1."

Chapter 7: Access Management

Review Question Answers

1. Mandatory access control. For more information, see the section "Mandatory Access Control."

2. The security admin. The division of administrative duties may involve a special security administrator who is responsible for performing information security tasks for the servers, hosts, and connectivity devices in the network. In these settings the separation of administrative duties should be as distinct, defined, and controlled as possible. For more information, see the section "Introduction."

3. RBAC. The role-based access control model is a strategy designed for the centralized control of all network objects and users. It provides access control based on the position the user has within the organization. The network administrator is given the authority to specify and implement explicit security policies that carry out the designated policies of the organization. Each network user or group is assigned one or more roles. For more information, see the section "Role-Based Access Control."

4. Group policies. These are directory services database objects that administrators use to create group access and restrictions to network assets based on the user's position and job role in the organization. These objects enable administrators to implement these policies across the network from a single management environment. For more information, see the section "Access Control Models."

5. Access control lists (ACLs) attach permissions to network objects that the system uses to control access to assets (programs, folders, files, printers) as well as what activities can be performed on that asset. For more information, see the section "Access Control Models."

6. Encapsulating security payloads ESPs offer origin authentication as well as encryption. ESP encrypts and encapsulates the entire TCP/UDP datagram within an ESP header that does not include any port information. For more information, see the section "The Virtual Private Network."

7. User account restrictions are the last access control component to be added to the model. These are configurations that administrators apply to user accounts (instead of folders, files, and printers) to limit their activities on a local machine (local accounts) or across the network (domain accounts). For more information, see the section "Access Control Models."

8. Authentication Header (AH) provides data integrity and origin authentication to protect against replay attacks (attacks where a recorded transmission is replayed by an attacker to gain access). For more information, see the section "The Virtual Private Network."

9. Directory services are distributed, customizable information storage structures that provide a single point from which users can search for and locate resources scattered throughout a network. For more information, see the section "Directory Services."

10. A tree is a collection of objects that share the same DNS name. Active Directory can subdivide domains into organizational units (sales, administration, etc.) that contain other units, or leaf objects, such as printers and users. For more information, see the section "Active Directory."

11. This database contains information about user accounts, group accounts, and computer accounts. It tracks the names of all of the objects and requests for resources within the domain. You may also find this database referred to as the security accounts manager (SAM). For more information, see the section "Active Directory."

12. Newer distributions have shifted to LDAP-based directory services. Like Active Directory, the LDAP-based Linux platforms provide a single directory source for system information lookup and authentication. Storing user information in an LDAP-based directory server makes the network scalable, manageable, and secure. For more information, see the section "Linux Directory Services."

13. The RAS is a server that is dedicated to providing network access to remote users (users that are not members of the domain ACL). This server is responsible for authenticating these users for access to specific network assets and providing them with logon credentials. For more information, see the section "Remote Access Server Authentication."

14. Administrators and Users. These are basically the two classes of users in a network. For more information, see the section "User Access Management."

15. Root. The root admin group is a standard, default Linux group that has complete administrative control of the system. For more information, see the section "Linux Group Accounts."

Exam Question Answers

1. A. Secure VPNs. Trusted VPNs do not use cryptographic tunneling but rather trust the underlying network to handle security beyond authentication. Secure VPNs handle the encryption of the connection. For more information, see the section "The Virtual Private Network."

2. A, C, E. There are some very specific security tools that should be allocated to this path: a virtual private network (VPN) gateway, an encrypted VPN tunnel, and a remote access server (RAS). For more information, see the section "Remote ICS Access Control."

3. B. Modify. The Modify permission enables users to delete the folder and makes it possible for users to perform all the activities associated with the Write and Read & Execute permissions. For more information, see the section "NTFS Permissions."

4. A, B, D. An information store that can be distributed across several geographical locations. An information store that is accessible from many different operating systems. An information store that users can employ to efficiently search through the enterprise for information that may be located throughout the network. For more information, see the section "Directory Services."

5. A, D. L2TP and PPTP. For more information, see the section "The Virtual Private Network."

6. C, D. IPSec uses Authentication Header (AH) for IP source authentication and Encapsulated Security Payload (ESP) for confidentiality. For more information, see the section "The Virtual Private Network."

7. D. IaaS. In infrastructure-as-a-service cloud environments, the customer is typically renting the underlying infrastructure from the cloud service. In these cases, the customer is given access to the configuration of the cloud infrastructure as well. For more information, see the section "Access Control for Cloud Systems."

8. D. Mandatory access control necessitates security clearance for users. The capability of a user to access an object is dependent on sensitivity labels, which verify the user's clearance level. For more information, see the section "Mandatory Access Control."

9. C. Attribute-based access control (ABAC) is considered to be a new generation AC model based on complex Boolean rule-sets derived from policy statements. This model manipulates three types of components to determine access or denial to a resource: *architecture*, *attributes*, and *policies*. For more information, see the section "Attribute-Based Access Control."

10. B, D. With DAC each file or object has an owner who has complete control over that file or object. For more information, see the section "Discretionary Access Control."

Chapter 8: ICS Security Governance and Risk Management

Review Question Answers

1. Policies are rules that an organization adheres to. For more information, see the section "Introduction."

2. Procedures are the sequence of steps taken to enforce the organizational policies. For more information, see the section "Introduction."

3. The medical industry dealing with the security and confidentiality of healthcare records. It is essential that organizations be capable of showing their compliance with governmental legislation. For example, a HIPAA violation can cost an organization up to $1.5 million per occurrence. For more information, see the section "Requirements."

4. The financial industry dealing with the security and confidentiality of customer financial records. It is essential that organizations be capable of showing their compliance with governmental legislation. For more information, see the section "Requirements."

5. Risk. Risk is defined as the potential loss of an object of value. It can also be expressed as an intentional interaction with uncertainty. Risk is also a quantity that can be communicated to the organization's internal and external stakeholders. For more information, see the section "Risk Management."

6. The purpose of a risk assessment is to "Identify steps that can be taken to ensure that the organization understands the cyber security risk to its organizational operations (including its mission, functions, image, or reputation), its organizational assets and its personnel." For more information, see the section "Risk Assessment."

7. An impact assessment. The organization must identify which threats pose a real concern to them. This is determined by assessing the impact of each security event actually occurring, though a process known as impact assessment and analysis. For more information, see the section "Impact Assessment."

8. A packet analyzer is a software tool that captures data packets as they move across the network, logs them, and then decodes their raw data. It can then analyze the data, in effect spying on the network users. For more information, see the section "Risk Identification Vulnerability Assessment."

9. The Detect (DE) function. Develop and implement the appropriate activities to identify the occurrence of a cybersecurity event. The Detect function enables timely discovery of cybersecurity events. Examples of outcome categories within this function include anomalies and events, security continuous monitoring, and detection processes. For more information, see the section "NIST Cybersecurity Frameworks."

10. A network vulnerability scanner package to scan the enterprise for different types of common vulnerabilities such as system misconfigurations and default password usage, as well as to create DoS attacks by generating malformed packets. For more information, see the section "Risk Identification Vulnerability Assessment."

11. Personnel safety, equipment safety, environmental impact, production loss, data loss, and adverse business effects. For more information, see the section "Device Criticality."

12. It is assigned single loss expectancy (SLE) price and its annualized rate of occurrence (ARO) value. To correctly assess the financial impact to the organization posed by the occurrence of this particular event, you would have to multiply its SLE value by the ARO value. For more information, see the section "Impact Assessment."

13. A HAZOP is conducted by a multiparty team to evaluate potential problems in an industrial process to identify risks to humans or equipment. The analysis is based on sets of standard guide words designed to bring these potential problems and their consequences to the surface. For more information, see the section "ICS Risk Assessments."

14. Risk is defined as the potential loss of an object of value. It can also be expressed as an intentional interaction with uncertainty. Risk is also a quantity that can be communicated to the organization's internal and external stakeholders. Risk management is the process of identifying, assessing, and responding to risk. For more information, see the section "Risk Management."

15. The purpose of a risk assessment is to "Identify steps that can be taken to ensure that the organization understands the cyber security risk to its organizational operations (including its mission, functions, image, or reputation), its organizational assets and its personnel." This includes understanding both the likelihood and resulting impact of risk events occurring within the different areas of the organization's network. After both of these quantities are understood, the organization's management can determine the level of risk that can be tolerated, expressed in terms of risk tolerance. For more information, see the section "Risk Assessment."

Exam Question Answers

1. **A, B, D.** Generally, creation of these policies involves stakeholders from several areas of the organization: corporate management, security management, and network administration. For more information, see the section "Security Policies and Procedures Development."

2. **B, D.** Documentation supporting an exemption request usually includes the physical location of the exempt asset (environment, device, or application), the person or group that will be responsible for the exempted asset, how the exempted asset is to be used, and how risks associated with the asset will be mitigated. For more information, see the section "Exemptions."

3. **D.** How risks associated with the asset will be mitigated. For more information, see the section "Exemptions."

4. **A.** NERC CIP is a group of 9 standards and 45 requirements designed to secure digital assets involved in the operation of bulk electrical generation and distribution systems. In particular, the CIP standards address the security of electronic perimeters, critical cyber assets and personnel, as well as training to implement and use the plan. For more information, see the section "Standards."

5. **A, D, E.** Vulnerability scanners, port scanning tools, and sniffing tools. For more information, see the section "Risk Identification Vulnerability Assessment."

6. **A, B, C.** Risk mitigation (risk reduction) is a systematic approach to reducing the extent of exposure to a risk and/or the likelihood of its occurrence. There are several management plans that come together to produce an effective risk mitigation plan: business continuity plans, disaster recovery plans, and incident response plans. For more information, see the section "Risk Mitigation."

7. **B, C.** Identify critical network and software assets and assign monetary replacement values to each critical asset. For more information, see the section "Asset Identification."

8. **A, C.** A layer of protection analysis (LOPA) and a failure mode and effects analysis (FMEA). For more information, see the section "ICS Risk Assessments."

9. **C.** A risk assessment for an ICS environment must include a process hazard analysis (PHA). A PHA is used to assess the potential hazards in a given industrial process. For more information, see the section "ICS Risk Assessments."

10. **B.** The incident response plan should be created so that employees can have greater success in protecting vital assets in the event of an incident. This organizational policy is designed to provide guidelines for who, what, when, and where a physical disaster, network disaster, or security attack occurs. For more information, see the section "Incident Response Planning."

Chapter 9: ICS Security Assessments

Review Question Answers

1. Security assessment. A security assessment involves performing a sequence of exercises designed to locate vulnerabilities within the organization's network and computing environment. For more information, see the section "Security Assessments."

2. Communication robustness testing (CRT). For more information, see the section "Communication Robustness Testing."

3. Fuzzing is an automated, black-box data-injection technique where malformed data is injected into software structures to detect software structure, configuration, and implementation faults. As such, fuzzing is commonly used to expose vulnerabilities (attack vectors or fuzz vectors) in software that can be exploited by an attacker. For more information, see the section "Fuzzing."

4. Criticality assessment and analysis processes should be performed on each OT network device to determine the consequences of its failure or lack of function. For more information, see the section "Device Criticality."

5. Reconnaissance. The process begins with identifying all of the attack vectors (paths, channels, or means) that can be used to access the target. This includes noting physical access paths, remote access paths, and interfaces with outside systems (particularly paths that interface with the Internet). The relative security of protocols associated with each channel is also considered in the analysis. For more information, see the section "Attack Surface Analysis."

6. An attack surface analysis process is designed to specify what aspects of a device or system represent vulnerabilities so that the organization understands the risks associated with that particular device or system. For more information, see the section "Attack Surface Analysis."

7. The ISASecure certifications are designed to provide assurances that their supplier organizations have institutionalized cybersecurity into their product development practices. For more information, see the section "Supply Chain."

8. Penetration testing. Pentesting exists as a way for organizations to use outside resources (or internal resources) to attempt to break into a network or system and possibly attack it for the purpose of providing information to the network owner on how to fix the insecurities of their network. For more information, see the section "ICS Penetration Testing."

9. Exploits, which are computer programs designed to take advantage of particular vulnerabilities. These exploits might be used to deliver a payload to the target system that will grant the hacker access to that system. For more information, see the section "ICS Penetration Testing."

10. Packet sniffer. Using a packet analyzer, the white hat captures data packets as they move across the network, logs them, and then decodes their raw data. They can then analyze the data, in effect spying on the network users. For more information, see the section "Security Testing Tools."

11. Port scanning. Using a port scanner tool to probe the network servers and devices for open ports that can be exploited. They can also identify services running on a host for potential exploitation. For more information, see the section "Security Testing Tools."

12. A vulnerability scanner. Vulnerability scanning is using a network vulnerability scanner package to scan the organization's networks for different types of common vulnerabilities such as system misconfigurations and default password usage, as well as generating malformed packets to create DoS attacks. For more information, see the section "Security Testing Tools."

13. Port scanners are software tools designed to probe computing devices for open logical ports and their associated services. Attackers use these tools to locate and exploit vulnerabilities on a targeted device such as a server or endpoint. For more information, see the section "Port Scanning."

14. A network mapper. For more information, see the section "Vulnerability Scanning."

15. Black-box pentesting. The ultimate goal for a black-box penetration test is to attempt to simulate an attack on a client's infrastructure by an external entity because, unless the attacker is an inside threat, external entities should not have access to the intimate details of a company's network infrastructure and defenses. For more information, see the section "Pentest Types."

Exam Question Answers

1. B. A Vulnerability Scan phase that follows the Discovery phase and uses automated tools to search for security issues within the network. For more information, see the section "Security Assessments."

2. C. For more information, see the section "Vulnerability Scanning."

3. A, C, D. Failure modes involve classifying ways (modes) in which devices or systems might fail, effects analysis refers to classifying the consequences of those failures, and criticality analysis involves prioritizing the order in which potential failures should be addressed based on severity and occurrence (S x O) calculations. For more information, see the section "Device Criticality."

4. A, C. ICS device manufacturers have escalated their vulnerability testing procedures to include such activities as: port scanning tests, network flooding activities, vulnerability scanning, and protocol fuzzing. For more information, see the section "Supply Chain."

5. A. There are usually three groups: a red team that conducts the attack, a blue team that are typically the victims (i.e., network administrators), and a white team that oversee the test. For more information, see the section "Pentest Negotiations."

6. A. White-box pen testing, also referred to as glass-box testing, is basically the exact opposite of a black-box penetration test. The ultimate goal of a white-box penetration test is to simulate a malicious insider threat that would have intimate knowledge of the client's critical network infrastructure and credentials to access it. For more information, see the section "Pentest Types."

7. A, C, D. For more information, see the section "Security Assessments."

8. A. You can discover all sorts of information by performing network enumeration operations, including discovering that there may be devices on your network that shouldn't be there. For more information, see the section "Network Enumeration/Port Scanning."

9. B, D. Reconnaissance. In this stage activities are conducted to find exploitable vulnerabilities in the target's network structure and configurations. This can include scanning for network hardware and software attack surfaces, as well as using physical and logical social engineering methods to identify possible attack vectors. For more information, see the section "Conducting the Attack."

10. D. In cases where a port scan is combined with a vulnerability scan, the administrator should consider a follow-on attack as being imminent. For more information, see the section "Port Scanning."

Chapter 10: ICS Security Monitoring and Incident Response

Review Question Answers

1. The security baseline. After the potential impact of all the identified risks have been established, the next step for the organization is to create a security baseline that defines the level of risk they are comfortable with—their risk tolerance level. For more information, see the section "Establishing a Security Baseline."

2. Configuration auditing is an ongoing process that compares detected changes in an environment to approved requests for changes. For more information, see the section "Configuration Auditing."

3. It is recommended that a patch review team (once again made up of IT, cybersecurity, process engineering, production operations, and senior management personnel) be used to analyze and determine whether a patch should be applied to the ICS. For more information, see the section "Controlling Patch Distribution and Installation for Systems."

4. The responsible entity shall ensure that new cyber assets and significant changes to existing cyber assets within the Electronic Security Perimeter do not adversely affect existing cybersecurity controls. For purposes of Standard CIP-007, a significant change shall, at a minimum, include implementation of security patches, cumulative service packs, vendor releases, and version upgrades of operating systems, applications, database platforms, or other third-party software or firmware. For more information, see the section "Software Reloads and Firmware Management."

5. Monitoring involves using a system or tool to constantly watch device and network objects looking for specific types of activities or events. For more information, see the section "Monitoring."

6. Logging is the process of recording and storing specific events and transactions for analysis (auditing) purposes. Almost all computing and network devices in use today produce logs in some format or another. For more information, see the section "Logging and Auditing."

7. Is the log's file format likely to remain usable over the indicated time period and what storage media should be used? If the storage requirement is long (more than simply days or weeks), the logs will need to be archived. This may require the administrator to determine whether the log's file format is likely to remain usable over the indicated time period. The other consideration in archiving log files for extended periods of time involves choosing the storage media to use. While there are a variety of different storage media options available for archiving log data, consideration must be taken as to how long that media (and its supporting hardware and software) is expected to remain viable over the required retention period. If any of the formats appear to be at risk of becoming unavailable or inaccessible, administrators must take action to transfer their logs to another media type. For more information, see the section "Archiving Logs."

8. Contacting a designated member of the incident response team, documenting what activities were going on when the incident occurred, and keeping the attacked computer on. When an individual detects an unusual event or incident occurring on the network, they must be trained to follow the organization's security policy that requires them to take appropriate action as part of an incident response. The individual's role in the response to an observed incident normally includes items such as contacting a designated member of the incident response team, documenting what activities were going on when the incident occurred, and keeping the attacked computer on. For more information, see the section "Detection and Analysis."

9. Anomaly-based IDS/IPS systems apply statistical analysis techniques to the data stream to determine whether it is "normal" or "anomalous" at any given time. For more information, see the section "Automated Intrusion Detection Tools."

10. Threshold-based anomaly detection systems. These IDS systems are designed to track the number of occurrences of specific events over time and generate an intrusion warning if the number of events exceeds a predetermined number. For more information, see the section "Automated Intrusion Detection Tools."

11. To block unsecured data transmissions such as communications involving intellectual property or copyrighted materials. For more information, see the section "Egress Monitoring."

12. Notify stakeholders. When there is an identified incident, the first step in containing it should be to notify all appropriate stakeholders who might be affected by the incident. Getting the stakeholders involved is a key step in stopping the spread of many types of attacks. For more information, see the section "Containment, Eradication, and Recovery."

13. Root-cause analysis (RCA). RCA is a problem-solving method that is used to separate causal factors from root causes. For more information, see the section "Root-Cause Analysis."

14. Because the two types of incidents are typically remediated differently. If an intrusion is identified, the first step taken should be to limit the intruder's ability to send traffic into the network. On the other hand, if the incident is based on a malware infection, you must find and mitigate the malware responsible for the attack. You must also delete or disable the process/protocol used to launch the attack as well as remove the service/application that created the vulnerability. For more information, see the section "Eradication/Quarantine."

15. Recovery phase. The final portion of the IRP is the recovery phase. In this part of the IRP process actions are taken to validate that all systems and services affected by the incident are fully restored to a normal operational condition. After the CSIRT has concluded that the incident has been completely remediated, they must restore the confidence of the stakeholders in the system. For more information, see the section "Recovery."

Exam Question Answers

1. A, B, E. The change management policy should address the following documentation by assigning responsibility for creating and maintaining these items to specific personnel or groups: a current, functional software code library for all the ICS components; an archive

library of ICS software; a current hardware inventory of all ICS control and network devices; a current network architecture schematic; an equipment change history. For more information, see the section "Change Management Documentation."

2. **D.** The root of the tree is anchored in the risk reduction factor associated with applying a patch to a given OT device. The first factor in the tree is the exposure factor. Depending on the nature of the exposure—Indirect, Direct, or Small—the tree branches out from central trunk nodes that represent security posture impact, safety impact, and technical impact decision points. For more information, see the section "Patch Decision Trees."

3. **B, D, E.** While security patching is the key to addressing many software vulnerabilities in the IT network environment, this is a constant, cyclic process conducted over the IT product's lifecycle. However, SCADA/ICS environments just can't be shut down and started up with the frequency associated with the enterprise patching process. In addition, automated firmware management solutions for OT devices are not widely available. For more information, see the section "Software Reloads and Firmware Management."

4. **A, C.** In its latest SP800-137, "Information Security Continuous Monitoring (ISCM) for Federal Information Systems and Organizations," the NIST organization defines continuous security monitoring as including vulnerability monitoring, application monitoring, and threat monitoring. For more information, see the section "Security Monitoring."

5. **C.** Security Information Management (SIM) systems. This SEIM version typically refers to systems created to provide long-term storage of network logs. For more information, see the section "SIEM systems."

6. **B.** The foremost function of the detection and analysis phase is to identify and verify that a reported incident has occurred and that it is an actual incident. Incident reports can come from anywhere in the organization such as users, administrators at different levels, monitoring tools, or even outside organizations. For more information, see the section "Detection and Analysis."

7. **A, B, E.** The CSIRT must take over the execution of the remainder of the IRP. This includes but is not limited to conducting a detailed analysis of the information (log analysis) provided by the designated incident handler; taking steps to contain the incident and limit the organization's exposure; performing root-cause analysis activities to identify the source of the event that caused the incident; remediating the incident by determining whether to eradicate or quarantine the root cause of the incident (provided the root cause is some form of malware); implementing specific steps to recover from the effects of the incident; and if necessary, updating the IRP with information gathered from the incident response report created at the conclusion of the IR process. For more information, see the section "Incident Response."

8. **A.** While it may be necessary to perform forensic data analysis during a given incident response, most of the ICS CSIRT efforts are involved in computer and network forensic activities. Most specifically, they are involved in performing forensic log analysis. And while there is an evolving science for forensic log analysis, IR analysts typically spend their time searching logs looking for two elements: event correlation and signs of intrusion. For more information, see the section "Forensic Log Analysis."

9. **A, C, D.** For a given IRP, the roles and responsibilities of each CSIRT member should be clearly identified and assigned to specific persons. In any particular organization, the CSIRT may specify personnel for any of the following team roles: CSIRT team leader, incident handlers, IR triage manager, IR forensic analysts, IR platform specialists, and vulnerability handlers. For more information, see the section "Creating the Incident Response Team."

10. **B.** After the CSIRT has concluded that the incident has been completely remediated, they must restore the confidence of the stakeholders in the system. For more information, see the section "Recovery."

Chapter 11: Disaster Recovery and Business Continuity

Review Question Answers

1. A business continuity plan (BCP) is a document designed to describe the organization's preparation, growth plans, and future planning in case either type of damaging event occurs. For more information, see the section "Business Continuity Plans."

2. The DRP deals with restoring the organization's processes to normal operation after the occurrence of a critical failure due to accidents, theft, intentional sabotage, or natural disasters. For more information, see the section "Disaster Recovery."

3. Partial backups are often used instead of regular full backups to conserve space on the backup storage device. For more information, see the section "Backup Options."

4. The Grandfather-Father-Son method uses three different groupings of backup tapes: the Grandfather for monthly backups, the Father for weekly backups, and the Son for daily backups. For more information, see the section "Backup Media Rotation."

5. Identify the interactions and communications that need to be performed when a state of disaster is declared. For example, the plan should establish criteria for when to report and to whom, as well as how information is to be exchanged during and after a disaster, as well as escalation procedures. For more information, see the section "Planning."

6. Any organization's BCP must include risk analysis and mitigation plans for the other members of the chain. For more information, see the section "Supply Chain Considerations."

7. When testing the DRP, the disaster recovery team must make sure it functions properly and that all personnel are aware of their individual roles. For more information, see the section "Testing the DRP."

8. Redundancy is the practice of devoting extra hardware to maintain system and network resources. For more information, see the section "System Redundancy."

9. Establishing an alternate site enables the organization to temporarily continue operations during a major disaster and throughout the recovery period. For more information, see the section "Alternate Sites."

10. A point of failure is any element in the network that if it fails, a critical process shuts down. For more information, see the section "System Redundancy."

11. Unlike a hot site, a warm site may be equipped with antiquated equipment and most likely would be unmanned until a true disaster occurs. A warm site may also store backup data in a secure vault or safe but would require more time to get critical operations functioning again after a disaster strikes. For more information, see the section "Alternate Sites."

12. Network-attached storage (NAS) is a virtualized storage system that provides both storage and a file system structure. For more information, see the section "Local Virtualized Storage."

13. Backup media should be stored in a room that has a locking door. There should also be a sign-in/out sheet or access control device for tracking people entering and exiting the room. Backup data should also be stored in an encrypted format so that even if it is stolen or accessed by unauthorized personnel, it will remain secure. For more information, see the section "Securing Backup Media."

14. The one drawback of using cloud-based or other Internet-related applications is that the user is dependent on the cloud service provider's security capabilities. In the case of public utilities, this has traditionally been a major point of concern. For more information, see the section "Cloud Storage."

15. Recovery time objectives (RTOs) express an allotted time for recovery of a processing operation or resource after a disaster. For more information, see the section "Planning."

Exam Question Answers

1. **D.** Although preventive measures are always the preferred tool to use against possible disasters, they cannot guarantee that system recovery will never be necessary. Therefore, a disaster recovery process should be designed to restore all or part of the organization's network in the event of a critical failure caused by accident, theft, intentional sabotage, or a naturally occurring disaster. For more information, see the section "Introduction."

2. **B.** A disaster recovery drill should be a yearly scheduled event. The difficulties involved with implementing a DRP are not fully understood without experience. Exercising the disaster recovery system will reinforce the importance of performing timely and consistent backups so that data recoveries are always possible. For more information, see the section "Testing the DRP."

3. **A, C.** The following supporting documentation is usually bundled with a DRP: contact information for all individuals on the disaster recovery team and copies of critical software and hardware drivers. For more information, see the section "Documenting the Disaster Recovery Plan."

4. **C.** Storage area networks (SANs). A SAN provides a storage system that appears as a single disc in disk and volume management tools. For more information, see the section "Local Virtualized Storage."

5. **A.** Backup media and techniques should be tested at least once a month or as often as once a week for more critical network segments. For more information, see the section "Testing the DRP."

6. **D.** Under the CIP-009-6 standard, the organization must conduct activities to simulate actual incidents that would activate the recovery plan. These exercises can be paper-based in nature or fully operational and must be conducted at least annually. For more information, see the section "NERC CIP-009-6."

7. **B,D.** RAID 1 and RAID 5 solutions do provide fault tolerance. For more information, see the section "High Availability/Fault Tolerance Systems."

8. **C.** The Son uses four media, one for every weekday normally covering Monday through Thursday, typically applying the incremental backup method. The Father's weekly backup, normally performed on Friday, uses one medium, applying the differential method of backup. After this, the corresponding Son media is reused for the following daily backups. At month's end, one piece of storage media is used to run the Grandfather backup. This backup would be a full backup of the system. For more information, see the section "Backup Media Rotation."

9. **D.** If not staffed, a hot site can typically be placed into operation within minutes of personnel arriving at the alternate site. For more information, see the section "Alternate Sites."

10. **E.** The main purpose associated with each of the different alternate site facility options considered in the BCP is to provide for recovery of secure data and continued functional operations of the organization in the event of a disaster. For more information, see the section "Alternative Sites."

Index

D

H

I

O